professional
beauty therapy

HAIRDRESSING AND BEAUTY INDUSTRY AUTHORITY SERIES – RELATED TITLES

HAIRDRESSING

Mahogany Hairdressing: Steps to Cutting, Colouring and Finishing Hair *Martin Gannon and Richard Thompson*
Mahogany Hairdressing: Advanced Looks *Richard Thompson and Martin Gannon*
Essensuals, Next Generation Toni & Guy: Step by Step
Professional Men's Hairdressing *Guy Kemer and Jacki Wadeson*
The Art of Dressing Long Hair *Guy Kemer and Jacki Wadeson*
Patrick Cameron: Dressing Long Hair *Patrick Cameron and Jacki Wadeson*
Patrick Cameron: Dressing Long Hair Book 2 *Patrick Cameron*
Bridal Hair *Pat Dixon and Jacki Wadeson*
Trevor Sorbie: Visions in Hair *Kris Sorbie and Jacki Wadeson*
The Total Look: The Style Guide for Hair and Make-up Professionals *Ian Mistlin*
Art of Hair Colouring *David Adams and Jacki Wadeson*
Begin Hairdressing: The Official Guide to Level 1 *Martin Green*
Hairdressing – The Foundations: The Official Guide to Level 2 *Leo Palladino* (contribution Jane Farr)
Professional Hairdressing: The Official Guide to Level 3 4e *Martin Green, Lesley Kimber and Leo Palladino*
Men's Hairdressing: Traditional and Modern Barbering 2e *Maurice Lister*
African-Caribbean Hairdressing 2e *Sandra Gittens*
Salon Management *Martin Green*
eXtensions: The Official Guide to Hair Extensions *Theresa Bullock*

BEAUTY THERAPY

Beauty Therapy – The Foundations: The Official Guide to Level 2 *Lorraine Nordmann*
Beauty Basics – The Official Guide to Level 1 *Lorraine Nordmann*
Professional Beauty Therapy: The Official Guide to Level 3 *Lorraine Nordmann, Lorraine Williamson, Jo Crowder and Pamela Linforth*
Aromatherapy for the Beauty Therapist *Valerie Ann Worwood*
Indian Head Massage *Muriel Burnham-Airey and Adele O'Keefe*
The Official Guide to Body Massage *Adele O'Keefe*
An Holistic Guide to Anatomy and Physiology *Tina Parsons*
The Encyclopedia of Nails *Jacqui Jefford and Anne Swain*
Nail Artistry *Jacqui Jefford, Sue Marsh and Anne Swain*
The Complete Nail Technician *Marian Newman*
The World of Skin Care: A Scientific Companion *Dr John Gray*
Safety in the Salon *Elaine Almond*
An Holistic Guide to Reflexology *Tina Parsons*
Nutrition: A Practical Approach *Suzanne Le Quesne*
An Holistic Guide to Massage *Tina Parsons*

professional
beauty therapy

THE OFFICIAL GUIDE TO LEVEL 3 SECOND EDITION

LORRAINE NORDMANN

HABIA

THOMSON
™

Australia • Canada • Mexico • Singapore • Spain • United Kingdom • United States

Professional Beauty Therapy: The Official Guide to Level 3, Second Edition

Copyright © Thomson Learning 2005

The Thomson logo is a registered trademark used herein under licence.

For more information, contact Thomson Learning, High Holborn House, 50–51 Bedford Row, London, WC1R 4LR or visit us on the World Wide Web at: http://www.thomsonlearning.co.uk

British Library Cataloguing-in-Publication Data
A catalogue record for this book is available from the British Library

ISBN 1-86152-943-0

First edition published 2001 by Thomson Learning
Reprinted 2002 by Thomson Learning
Second edition published 2005 by Thomson Learning

Typeset by Meridian Colour Repro Ltd, Pangbourne-on-Thames, Berkshire RG8 7HY
Text design by Design Deluxe
Illustrations on pp. 79–82, 86, 89, 92, 94–5, 97–105, 109–22, 124, 126–45, 147–50, 170–3, 176–8, 260, 263, 281, 288, 355–61, 426, 583 by Oxford Designers and Illustrators

Printed in Italy by Canale

contents

BEAUTY THERAPY UNITS 167

about the authors

Lorraine Nordmann has over twenty years' of experience in the beauty therapy industry – an industry she has seen grow significantly in status, technology and specialisms during her roles as lecturer, assessor and external verifier for City & Guilds. She aims to ensure that this high profile of the beauty therapy industry is maintained. Lorraine is also the author of the HABIA official guides, *Beauty Basics* and *Beauty Therapy – the foundations*, covering the latest industry standards at NVQ/SQV levels 1 and 2.

Lorraine Williamson is a fully qualified beauty therapist and lecturer who has been actively involved in the beauty industry for many years. An experienced salon owner, therapist and lecturer, Lorraine has also judged nail competitions at national level. She was a full-time lecturer at Bury College where she also developed a thriving sports therapy department. Lorraine now combines teaching part-time with bringing up two young sons.

Pamela Limforth is the Director of Human Resources at Ellisons. A fully qualified beauty therapist, electrologist, lecturer, assessor and member of the CIPD, she has made her career in the beauty therapy industry. She has a unique blend of experience both as a lecturer and within the industry, and is well known in her chosen field. She is the driving force behind implementing the Investors in People standard at Ellisons and is a champion of training and developing people to achieve their full potential.

Jo Crowder has been an international freelance make-up artist and hairstylist since 1990. Her work has appeared extensively on TV, films and theatre, and graced the pages of magazines, national newspapers and books. She is also currently course co-ordinator and lecturer for the make-up artistry courses at Liverpool Community College.

acknowledgements

The authors and publishers would like to thank the following for their help with providing images for the book:

Elaine Almond

Dr. M. H. Beck

Heather Brown at Blanchard Schaefer Advertising & Public Relations

Angela Barbagelata at Carlton Professional

Chubb Fire Ltd

Cosmopro Inc:
T: 001 386 239 8260 –
E: cosmopro@cosmopro.com –
W: www.cosmopro.com

Gerard McCarthy at Dalesauna Ltd

Dianne Burkhill at Depilex

Designer Nails UK Ltd.

Dream Workwear

Emma Kenny and Pam Linforth at Ellisons (www.ellisons.co.uk)

Chapter 13: Nails and Nail Art by Gina Wallace, Principal International Educator
for Essential Nail Products, Ltd., http://www.ginawallace.com, UK Headquarters: 01440-820999.

Finders Health International (www.findershealth.com)

Floataway (www.floatway.com)

Dr John Gray

Sarah Daniel at Helionova and Smart Buy

HMSO

HSE

Trevor Cash at Mad Beauty

Peter Hyun at Mehron, Inc.

Adele O'Keefe

Sally Smith at Original Additions Ltd.

Pevonia UK:

Pevonia UK – T: 01449 727000 –
E: info@pevoniauk.com –
W: www.pevonia.co.uk

Hugh Rushton

SAKS: Covent Garden

Smith and Nephew, Hull

Adam Birtwistle at Sorisa

Spirit Health Club, Holliday Inn Hotel, Lodge Lane, Newton-le-Willows for allowing us to reproduce their safety check sheets in Chapter 16. Contact:
spirit.haydock@Ichotelsgroup.com

United Beauty Products Ltd.

Mark Lord at UV-Power UK

Valerie Ann Worwood

The students at Liverpool Community College

Incognito, Birkenhead

Gail Burke and Ostensia Gordon-Wallace

Jane Rutherford

Cath Isherwood

Pam Young

Ian Littlewood

Elizabeth and Norman Whiteside

Lee@graduate-centre.com

Janine Rigby: beauty therapist

Nicola Hulbert: beauty therapist , New Woman, Westhoughton

Vicky Kennedy: salon owner, New Woman, Westhoughton

Jonathon Knott and staff at Spirit Health Club, Holiday Inn Hotel, Lodge Lane, Newton-Le-Willows

Adrian.palmer@Philips.com

Trish Smith Sunquest Tanning Systems Ltd

foreword

As I write the foreword for this second edition of *Professional Beauty Therapy*, written by the remarkable Lorraine Nordmann, the first thing I notice is how the industry has grown in status. The introduction of pioneering technology and the recognition of specialist areas are now providing a much greater choice for career development since the publication of the outstanding first edition.

Talking of status, the success of this book comes down to the creative and expert skills of the contributors of Lorraine Williamson, Pamela Linforth and Jo Crowder, who pour their tremendous knowledge into the vast pool of expertise so magically created by Lorraine.

Lorraine Williamson, an experienced salon owner, therapist, lecturer and skilled nail practitioner, contributes an abundance of professional knowledge and expertise to these learning units. This is combined with Jo Crowder's contribution to the make-up units through her extensive experience and expert knowledge of the industry and Pamela Linforth's commitment to education and influence in initiatives such as developing people.

Professional Beauty Therapy, second edition is the most comprehensive text to cover the new beauty therapy standards at Level 3 produced by HABIA. Thanks again to Lorraine for her commitment and dedication, and to Jo, Lorraine and Pamela for their invaluable contributions.

Alan Goldsbro
Chief Executive Officer
HABIA

introduction

AN INTRODUCTION TO NVQS

National Vocational Qualifications (NVQs) are nationally recognised qualifications and have a common structure and design. They follow a similar format for all occupational and vocational sectors. The award of an NVQ/SVQ demonstrates that the person has the competence (having sufficient skill and knowledge) to perform job roles/tasks effectively in their occupational area. An NVQ at Level 3 involves the application of knowledge in a wide range of varied work activities, most of which are complex and non-routine and require the candidate to use their initiative and make independent decisions. Supervision and guidance for others may be required.

Each NVQ/SVQ is structured the same way, and is made up of a number of units and elements.

The **unit** relates to a specific task or skill area of work. It is the smallest part of an award, which can be accredited separately. The **element/s** describes in detail the skill and knowledge components of the unit.

An example from NVQ Level 3 Beauty Therapy is shown below:

The title of the unit is - **Unit BT 31 Provide self tanning treatments**

The elements for the unit detail the practical skills and underpinning knowledge essential to provide self tanning treatments.

The elements which detail the unit components include:

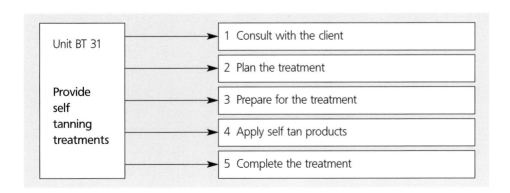

UNITS AND ELEMENTS

For each unit, when all competence requirements have been achieved, a unit of certification may be awarded, such as **Unit BT31 Provide self tanning treatments**.

Each NVQ is made up of a specific number of units required for the occupational area. Some of the units are termed **mandatory** (compulsory) some are **optional** (not all compulsory).

Mandatory units must be competently achieved to gain the NVQ/SVQ award.

Optional units are selected for study by the candidate in addition to the mandatory units to attain the qualification.

The NVQ/SVQ will state the mandatory, compulsory units to achieve the qualification plus the number of optional units which must be completed in order to achieve the full NVQ/SVQ award.

The Beauty Therapy NVQ/SVQ employment routes in Beauty Therapy at Level 3 employment are shown opposite.

Each qualification structure shows the compulsory mandatory units and optional units to be achieved.

BEAUTY THERAPY NVQ/SVQ – LEVEL 3

Candidates will need to achieve the core mandatory units, plus the mandatory units from one of the five routes, and the specified number of optional units for that route.

Core Mandatory Units (all units must be achieved)

G1   Ensure your own actions reduce risks to health and safety

G6   Promote additional products or services to clients

G11 Contribute to the financial effectiveness of the business

Routes

Beauty Therapy General (mandatory units)	Beauty Therapy Massage (mandatory units)	Beauty Therapy Make-up (mandatory units)
BT16 Epilate the hair follicle using diathermy, galvanic and blend techniques BT17 Provide head and body massage treatments BT18 Improve body condition using electro-therapy BT19 Improve face and skin condition using electro-therapy	BT17 Provide head and body massage treatments BT20 Provide Indian head massage treatment BT21 Provide massage using pre-blended aromatherapy oils	BT26 Enhance appearance using cosmetic camouflage BT27 Design and create images for fashion and photographic make-up
Plus one optional unit (see following page)	*Plus* one optional unit (see following page)	*Plus* three optional units (see following page)

Spa Therapy (mandatory units)	Nails Services (mandatory units)
BT17 Provide head and body massage treatments BT28 Set up, monitor and shut down water, temperature and spa facilities BT29 Provide specialist spa treatments	BT22 Enhance the appearance of natural nails using artificial nail systems BT23 Maintain, repair and enhance artificial nail structures BT24 Plan, design and provide nail art services to clients
Plus two optional units	*Plus* two optional units

Choice of optional units for each training route have been identified

Optional Units (the relevant number of units must be achieved)	Beauty Therapy General	Nail Services	Beauty Therapy Make-up	Spa Therapy	Beauty Therapy Massage
BT16 Epilate the hair follicle using diathermy, galvanic and blend techniques			✓	✓	✓
BT17 Provide head and body massage treatments			✓		
BT18 Improve body condition using electro-therapy			✓	✓	✓
BT19 Improve face and skin condition using electro-therapy			✓	✓	✓
BT20 Provide Indian head massage treatment	✓		✓	✓	
BT21 Provide massage using pre-blended aromatherapy oils	✓		✓	✓	
BT22 Enhance the appearance of natural nails using artificial nail systems	✓		✓		✓
BT23 Maintain, repair and enhance artificial nail structures	✓		✓		✓
BT24 Plan, design and provide nail art services to clients	✓		✓		✓
BT25 Design and create images incorporating nail art techniques	✓	✓	✓		✓
BT26 Enhance appearance using cosmetic camouflage	✓				✓
BT27 Design and create images for fashion and photographic make-up	✓	✓			✓
BT28 Set up, monitor and shut down water, temperature and spa facilities	✓		✓		✓
BT29 Provide specialist spa treatments	✓		✓		✓
BT30 Provide UV tanning treatments	✓	✓	✓	✓	✓
BT31 Provide self tanning treatments	✓	✓	✓	✓	✓
BT32 Prepare to change performers' appearance (skill set)	✓		✓		✓
BT33 Assist with the continuity of performers' appearance (skill set)	✓		✓		✓
BT34 Apply make up to change the performers' appearance (skill set)	✓		✓		✓
BT35 Apply special effects (skill set)	✓		✓		✓
BT36 Improve the appearance of the skin using micro-dermabrasion	✓		✓	✓	✓
G12 Check how successful your business idea will be (SFEDI)	✓	✓	✓	✓	✓
G13 Check what law and other regulations will affect your business (SFEDI)	✓	✓	✓	✓	✓

Note: Where units are achieved as mandatory units in one of the five routes, these do not count as optional units as well.

As you can see, there is a choice of five employment routes to achieve NVQ/SVQ Beauty Therapy level 3:

1 Beauty therapy general

2 Nail services

3 Beauty therapy make-up

4 Spa therapy

5 Beauty therapy massage

Whichever route you choose, you must achieve the mandatory units plus the required number of optional units from the selection of units provided.

The **core mandatory units** are fundamental, essential units to be achieved whichever route is chosen.

	G1 Ensure your own actions reduce risks to health and safety
Core mandatory units	**G6** Promote additional products or services to clients
	G11 Contribute to the financial effectiveness of the business

PERFORMANCE CRITERIA

The performance criteria lists the necessary actions that you must achieve to complete the task competently (demonstrating adequate practical skill and experience to the assessor).

The **performance criteria** requirements for BT31 Provide self tanning treatments Element1: Consult with the client are:

a. using **consultation techniques** in a polite and friendly manner to determine the client's treatment plan

b. discussing and agreeing the service and outcomes that are acceptable to your client and meet their needs

c. maintaining the client's modesty and privacy at all times

d. establishing, agreeing and recording the client's skin type and colouring

e. recognising contra-indications and taking the **necessary action**

f. advising the client on other suitable tanning treatments where there are indications of skin sensitivity

g. checking the client's understanding according to guidelines on safe tanning.

RANGE

Range statements are often identified for each element. The assessment range relates to the different conditions in which a skill must be demonstrated competently for the element.

For example the range assessment requirements for Unit BT31 Element 1, Consultation techniques are shown below:

Range: Your performance must cover the following situations

1   Consultation techniques
    a. questioning
    b. visual
    c. reference to client records

It is not sufficient only to be able to practically perform the task, you must understand why you are doing it, and be able to transfer your competence to a variety of situations. This is referred to as your knowledge and understanding.

Further assessment of your **knowledge and understanding** of the skill, the knowledge specification, may be assessed through theoretical tasks such as written tests, assignments and oral questioning.

The **knowledge and understanding** requirements that you are required to know for **Unit BT31 Client consultation** are listed below:

- how to use effective communication and consultation techniques
- the reasons why it is important to encourage clients with contra-indications to seek medical advice
- the importance of, and reasons for, not naming specific contra-indications when encouraging clients to seek medical advice
- why it is important to maintain clients' modesty and privacy.

What often occurs is that the same knowledge and understanding may be necessary for similar units. This can be seen, for example, in the knowledge and understanding for **Organisational and legal requirements**. This duplication is necessary because some units may be studied and accredited as an individual skill/unit.

Where evidence has been achieved this is cross-referenced (directed), in the portfolio (a file that holds your assessment evidence) to where the evidence can be found.

To achieve unit competence, all performance criteria, range and knowledge and understanding requirements must have been met and evidence presented as necessary. Evidence is usually provided in your assessment book and portfolio.

Where there is evidence of previous experience and achievement this may be presented to the assessor for consideration for accreditation. This is called accreditation of prior learning (APL).

Professional Beauty Therapy follows the Beauty Therapy NVQ/SVQ Level 3 syllabus and covers both the practical and theoretical requirements for both the mandatory and optional units.

about the book

The book relates to the NVQ/SVQ Level 3 qualification structure, and has been divided into four parts:

1 Core units
2 Anatomy and physiology
3 Client treatments
4 Beauty therapy units

CORE UNITS

The core units relate to the three core mandatory units required for each of the five Beauty Therapy NVQ/SVQ Level 3 training route options.

The core unit chapters cover:

G1 Ensure your own actions reduce risks to health and safety

G6 Promote additional products or services to clients

G11 Contribute to the financial effectiveness of the business

ANATOMY AND PHYSIOLOGY

Certain units have an anatomy and physiology knowledge requirement. This chapter provides the essential knowledge, and also contains a useful reference chart that states the specific anatomy and physiology requirements to be studied for each unit. In addition, anatomy and physiology is discussed within the general beauty therapy units to aid understanding.

CLIENT TREATMENTS

This chapter details how to carry out an effective consultation with the client. A thorough consultation, analysis or diagnosis is vital to enable the therapist to make an accurate assessment of the client's needs.

BEAUTY THERAPY UNITS

These chapters discuss the Beauty Therapy NVQ/SVQ technical practical skills and underpinning knowledge for both the mandatory and optional units for each of the five training routes.

FEATURES WITHIN CHAPTERS

Within each chapter appears common features, an explanation for each is provided below:

Learning objectives
Learning objectives introduce chapters and list those elements that make up the unit and must be achieved in order to be accredited with the NVQ unit. When you feel confident and competent with the skills/knowledge requirements you are ready to be assessed.

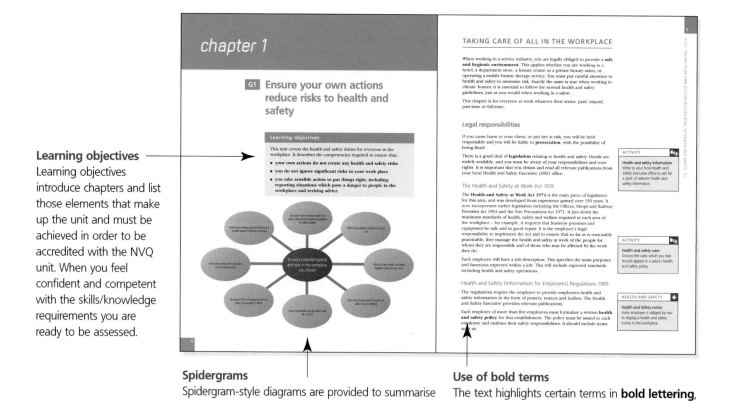

Spidergrams
Spidergram-style diagrams are provided to summarise the skills/knowledge requirement for each element. These provide a useful checklist for you to refer to.

Use of bold terms
The text highlights certain terms in **bold lettering**, this information is often an important technical term which is explained and that you must become familiar with to gain knowledge competence for the unit.

TIP boxes

The authors experience is shared through tip boxes which provide positive suggestions to improve your knowledge and skills for each unit.

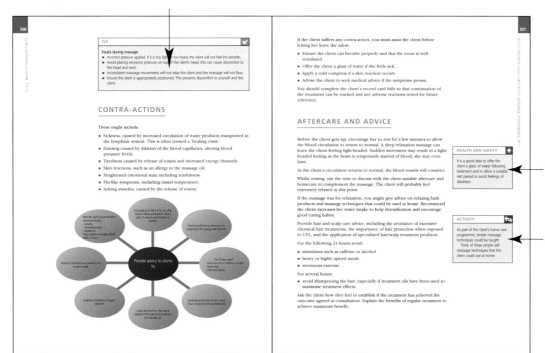

Health and safety boxes

In addition to the core chapter, G1 Ensure your own actions reduce risks to health and safety, health and safety boxes are provided in each chapter. They serve to draw your attention to related health and safety information for each technical skill.

Activity boxes

Where relevant, useful learning activities are provided within the chapter to assist learning and understanding.

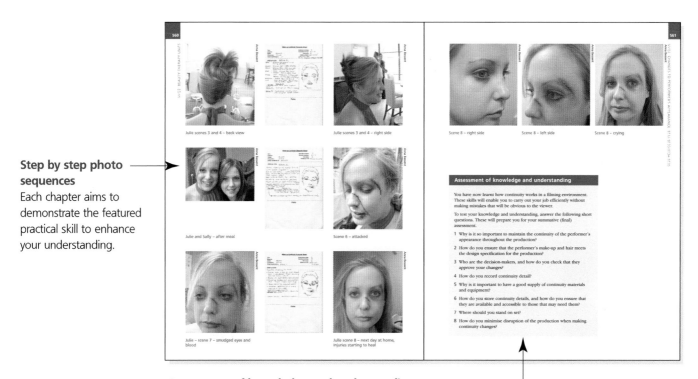

Step by step photo sequences

Each chapter aims to demonstrate the featured practical skill to enhance your understanding.

Assessment of knowledge and understanding

Review questions are provided at the end of each chapter to assess knowledge and understanding. These questions relate to the specific essential knowledge and understanding requirements for the unit you have just read. You can use the questions to prepare for oral and written assessments. Seek guidance from your supervisor/assessor if there are any areas that you are unsure of. Remember also to check the anatomy and physiology chapter, referring to the chart, to include revision in the related anatomy and physiology requirement as applicable.

glossary

Acid mantle the combination of sweat and sebum on the skin's surface, which creates an acid film. The acid mantle is protective and discourages the growth of bacteria and fungi

Acrylic sculptured nails the use of powder and liquid to make a strong acrylic from which to form artificial nail structures

Aftercare advice recommended advice given to the client following treatment to continue the benefits of the treatment

Airbrush used in the application of nail art airbrushing technique and soft tan application. The brush is attached to a compressor by a hose and is held in the hand. In the airbrush, air is mixed with paint before being forced out under pressure to create a coloured spray

Allergen a substance that the skin is sensitive to and which causes an allergic reaction

Alternating current (AC) an interrupted electrical current which reverses the direction of flow of electrons

Anagen the active growth stage of the hair growth cycle

Anion a negative ion, an atom that has gained more electrons than protons

Anode a positive electrode or pole of a constant electrical current

Aromatherapy massage the use of essential oils combined with massage to bring about a feeling of well-being

Assessment (client) techniques used to assess the needs of the client to ascertain the treatment objectives, including questioning and natural observation

Audiosonic a hand-held electrical massage treatment applied to the face or body. The equipment produces sound waves, which vibrate through the skin's cells and tissues. The treatment is used for its physiological benefits on the skin and muscle tissues

Ayur-veda (art of life) a sacred Hindu text written around 1800BC. In Ayurveda life consists of body, mind and spirit – each person is different. By restoring balance and harmony of the body, mind and spirit, the health of the individual improves

Base note a measure of the evaporation rate of essential oils – base notes have the slowest evaporation rate of all essential oils and are absorbed slowly into the skin

Blend epilation the combined use of both high frequency and direct current to destroy the hair; both currents retain their individual effects in the hair follicle

Blood nutritive liquid circulating through the blood vessels; it transports essential nutrients to the cells, removes waste

products and transports other important substances such as oxygen and hormones

Body language communication using the body rather than speech

Body mass index (BMI) a formula that uses weight and height to calculate an individual's body fat

Body wrapping a body treatment where the body is wrapped in bandages, plastic sheets or thermal blankets to achieve different therapeutic effects

Camera film it is good practice for the make-up artist to know what sort of camera film is involved in film production or at a photographic shoot when planning their make-up application

Camouflage make-up cosmetic make-up products used for remedial work to disguise blemishes or scars to the face or body

Catagen a brief, transitional stage in the cycle of hair growth – anagen, catagen and telogen – in which the hair moves up the hair follicle

Cathode a negative electrode or pole of constant electrical current

Cation a positive ion; an atom that has lost an electron and has more protons than electrons

Cell the smallest and simplest unit capable of life

Cellulite terminology used to describe fatty tissue that causes the overlying skin to appear dimpled

Chakras non-physical energy centres, located about an inch away from the physical body, which cannot be seen. In ancient Eastern belief the body is said to have seven major chakra centres each with a function, all of which work together in balance with each other

Circulatory system transports material around the body

Cold therapy spa treatments that use temperatures lower than the body temperature to improve circulation, e.g. cold water showers

Compressor a piece of equipment used to compress air; the air pressure is then regulated by the attachment of a regulator. Used in the application of nail art airbrushing and self tan application

Conductor a substance that conducts electricity and heat. Good conductors include metals and solutions which have conducting properties such as acids and alkalis

Consultation assessment of the client's needs using different techniques, including questioning and natural observation

Consumer Protection (Distance Selling) Regulations 2000 these regulations are derived from a European Directive and cover the supply of goods/services made between

614

Glossary

For easy reference definitions are provided for key words or technical terms.

Record cards

Client treatment record cards are featured in each of the general beauty therapy units. They illustrate the information that you need to gain from the client and assess at consultation in order to establish client suitability and the treatment aim. It also provides guidance on information that should be provided following treatment, including aftercare advice and the promotion of additional products and services.

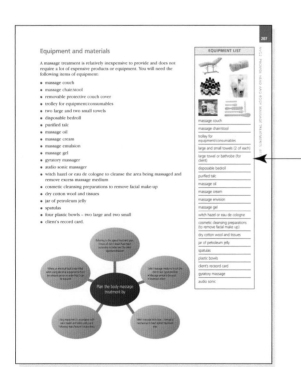

Equipment lists

To assist you preparing for each practical treatment an essential equipment list is provided, supported with images of treatment tools, materials and products required.

professional
beauty therapy

core units

chapter 1

G1 Ensure your own actions reduce risks to health and safety

Learning objectives

This unit covers the health and safety duties for everyone in the workplace. It describes the competencies required to ensure that:

- **your own actions do not create any health and safety risks**
- **you do not ignore significant risks in your work place**
- **you take sensible action to put things right, including: reporting situations which pose a danger to people in the workplace and seeking advice**

Be aware of the workplace health and safety policy and your legal responsibility in its implementation

Ensure your working practice minimises the possible spread of infection or disease

Follow the workplace policies for your job role

Know the workplace fire evacuation practice and procedure

To avoid potential hazards and risks in the workplace you should

Follow the latest health and safety legislation related to your work

Be aware of first aid arrangements in the event of an accident or illness

Report immediately any risk which could be a hazard

Know who is responsible for health and safety in your workplace

TAKING CARE OF ALL IN THE WORKPLACE

When working in a service industry, you are legally obliged to provide a **safe and hygienic environment**. This applies whether you are working in a hotel, a department store, a leisure centre or a private beauty salon, or operating a mobile beauty therapy service. You must pay careful attention to health and safety to minimise risk. Exactly the same is true when working in clients' homes: it is essential to follow the normal health and safety guidelines, just as you would when working in a salon.

This chapter is for everyone at work whatever their status: paid, unpaid, part-time or full-time.

Legal responsibilities

If you cause harm to your client, or put her at risk, you will be held responsible and you will be liable to **prosecution**, with the possibility of being fined.

There is a good deal of **legislation** relating to health and safety. Details are widely available, and you must be aware of your responsibilities and your rights. It is important that you obtain and read all relevant publications from your local Health and Safety Executive (HSE) office.

The Health and Safety at Work Act 1974

The **Health and Safety at Work Act 1974** is the main piece of legislation for this area, and was developed from experience gained over 150 years. It now incorporates earlier legislation including the Offices, Shops and Railway Premises Act 1963 and the Fire Precautions Act 1971. It lays down the minimum standards of health, safety and welfare required in each area of the workplace – for example, it requires that business premises and equipment be safe and in good repair. It is the employer's legal responsibility to implement the Act and to ensure that so far as is reasonably practicable, they manage the health and safety at work of the people for whom they are responsible and of those who may be affected by the work they do.

Each employee will have a job description. This specifies the main purposes and functions expected within a job. This will include expected standards including health and safety operations.

Health and Safety (Information for Employees) Regulations 1989

The regulations require the employer to provide employees with health and safety information in the form of posters, notices and leaflets. The Health and Safety Executive provides relevant publications.

Each employer of more than five employees must formulate a written **health and safety policy** for that establishment. The policy must be issued to each employee and outlines their safety responsibilities. It should include items such as:

ACTIVITY

Health and safety information
Write to your local Health and Safety Executive office to ask for a pack of relevant health and safety information.

ACTIVITY

Health and safety rules
Discuss the rules which you feel should appear in a salon's health and safety policy.

HEALTH AND SAFETY

The Health and Safety Information for Employees Regulations 1989: Health and safety notice
Every employer is obliged by law to display a health and safety notice in the workplace.

- details of the storage of chemical substances
- details of the stock cupboard or dispensary
- details and records of the checks made by a qualified electrician on specialist electrical equipment
- names and addresses of the keyholders
- escape routes and emergency evacuation procedures.

Regular health and safety checks should be made to ensure that safety is being satisfactorily maintained.

Employees must co-operate with their employer to provide a safe and healthy workplace. As soon as they observe any **hazard**, this must be reported to the designated authority so that the problem can be put right. Hazards include:

- obstructions to corridors, stairways and fire exits
- spillages and breakages.

Obstructions   An obstruction is anything that blocks the traffic route in the salon work environment. In an emergency such as a fire an obstruction could delay people leaving the building, cause injury, or prevent the emergency services entering the premises.

Accidents can damage stock, resulting in breakage of containers and spillage of contents. Breakage of glass can cause cuts; spillages may cause somebody to slip and fall. Any breakages or spillages should therefore be dealt with immediately and in the correct way.

You must determine whether the spillage is a potential hazard to health, and what action is necessary. To whom should you report it? What equipment is required to remove the spillage? How should the materials be disposed of?

HEALTH AND SAFETY

Breakages and spillages
When dealing with hazardous breakages and spillages, the hands should always be protected with gloves. To avoid injury to others, broken glass should be put in a secure container prior to disposing of it in a waste bin.

ACTIVITY

Avoiding accidents
Discuss potential causes of accidents in the workplace. How could these accidents be prevented?

Accidents

Accidents in the workplace usually occur through negligence by employees or unsafe working conditions.

Any accidents occurring in the workplace must be recorded on a **report form**, and entered into an **accident book**. The report form requires more details than the accident book – you must note down:

- the date and time of accident
- the name of the person or people involved
- the accident details
- the injuries sustained
- the action taken
- what happened to the person immediately afterwards (e.g. went home or to hospital)
- name and address of the person providing treatment should be entered into the accident book.

Always consider your COSHH data and check to see how the product should be handled and disposed of.

Reporting of Injuries, Diseases and Dangerous Occurrences Regulations (RIDDOR) 1995

RIDDOR requires the employer to notify the local enforcement officer, in writing, in cases where employees or trainees suffer personal injury at work resulting in absence from work for three consecutive days. When this occurrence results in death, major injury or more than 24 hours in hospital, it must be reported by telephone first, and followed by a written report on HSE Form F2508, within 10 days of it happening. In all cases where personal injury occurs, an entry must be made in the workplace accident book. It is a legal requirement to keep an accident book. Where visitors to the work premises are injured this must be reported also. This information assists the HSE in investigation of serious accidents. Certain work-related industrial diseases such as asthma are also reportable, but statements must be supported by the employee's GP. Dangerous occurrences where there is no personal injury should also be reported, e.g. significant workplace structural damage.

In 1992 European Union (EU) directives updated the legislation on health and safety management. Current legislation (at the time of writing) is outlined below.

The Management of Health and Safety at Work Regulations 1999

These require employers to make formal arrangements for maintaining and improving safe working conditions and practices. This includes training for employees and the monitoring of risk in the workplace on an ongoing basis, known as **risk assessment**.

This requires:

- identification of potential hazards
- an assessment of the potential risks associated with the hazard
- identifying who is at risk from the hazard
- identifying how risk is to be minimised or eliminated
- training staff to identify and control risks
- reviewing the risk assessment process regularly.

Where there are five or more people employed this also includes a requirement to:

- introduce a health surveillance system, if the risk assessment identifies a need
- the risk assessment details must be recorded.

The Personal Protective Equipment (PPE) at Work Regulations 1992

The **Personal Protective Equipment (PPE) at Work Regulations 1992** require managers to identify through a **risk assessment** those activities or processes which require special protective clothing or equipment to be

---

ACTIVITY

Risk assessment
Carry out your own risk assessment. List the potentially hazardous substances handled in beauty therapy. What protective clothing should be available?

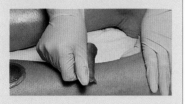
worn. This clothing and equipment must then be made available, in adequate supplies. Employees must wear the protective clothing and use the protective equipment provided, and make employers aware of any shortage so that supplies can be maintained.

Potentially hazardous substances include:

- aerosols
- disinfectants
- water treatment chemicals used in the spa pools
- artificial nail glues/adhesives
- dust created from treatments such as a nail extension service.

The Workplace (Health, Safety and Welfare) Regulations 1992

The **Workplace (Health, Safety and Welfare) Regulations 1992** require all at work to maintain a safe, healthy and secure working environment. The regulations include legal requirements in relation to the following aspects of the working environment:

- maintenance of the workplace and equipment
- ventilation to ensure the air is changed regularly
- working temperature
- lighting
- cleanliness and handling of waste materials
- safe salon layout
- falls and falling objects
- windows, doors, gates and walls
- safe floor and traffic routes
- escalators and moving walkways
- sanitary conveniences
- washing facilities
- drinking water
- facilities for changing clothing
- facilities for staff to rest and eat meals
- fire-fighting equipment and fire exits.

TIP ✔

The salon temperature should be a minimum of 16°C within one hour of employees arriving for work. The salon should be well ventilated, or carbon dioxide levels will increase, which can cause nausea. Many substances used in the salon can become hazardous without adequate ventilation.

If the working environment is too warm, this can cause heat stress, a condition recognised by the HSE.

Lighting should be adequate to ensure that treatments can be carried out safely and competently, with the minimum risk of accident.

Manual Handling Operations Regulations 1992

These regulations apply in all occupations where manual lifting occurs. The employer is required to carry out a risk assessment of all activities undertaken which involve manual lifting.

The risk assessment should provide evidence that the following have been considered:

● risk of injury
● the manual movement involved in performing the activity
● the physical constraint the load incurs
● the environmental constraints imposed by the workplace
● workers' individual capabilities
● action taken in order to minimise potential risks.

Manual lifting and handling Always take care of yourself when moving goods around the salon. Do not struggle or be impatient: get someone else to help. When **lifting**, lift from the knees, not the back. When **carrying**, balance weights evenly in both hands and carry the heaviest part nearest to your body.

left Lifting a box
centre Carrying several boxes
right Carrying equal weights in both hands

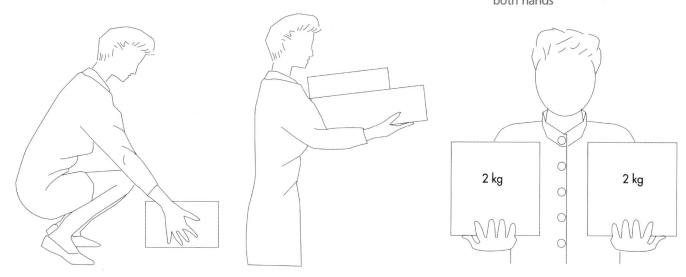

Provision and Use of Work Equipment Regulations (PUWER) 1998

These regulations lay down the important health and safety controls on the provision and use of work equipment. They state the duties for employers and for users, including the self-employed. They affect both old and new equipment. They identify the requirements in selecting suitable equipment and in maintaining it. They also discuss the information provided by equipment manufacturers, and instruction and training in the safe use of equipment. Specific regulations address the dangers and potential risks of injury that could occur during operation of the equipment.

Health and Safety (Display Screen Equipment) Regulations 1992

These regulations cover the use of visual display units and computer screens. They specify acceptable levels of radiation emissions from the screen, and identify correct posture, seating position, permitted working heights and rest periods.

ACTIVITY

COSHH assessments
Carry out a COSHH assessment on selected treatment products used in the salon. Consider manicures, nail extensions, waxing, and facial and eye treatments.

Control of Substances Hazardous to Health (COSHH) Regulations 1998 (recently consolidated in 2002)

These regulations were designed to make employers consider the substances used in their workplace and assess the possible risks to health. Many substances that seem quite harmless can prove to be hazardous if used or stored incorrectly.

Employers are responsible for assessing the risks from hazardous substances and controlling exposure to them to prevent ill health. Any hazardous substances identified must be formally recorded in writing, and given a hazard risk rating. Safety precaution procedures should then be implemented and training given to employees to ensure that the procedures are understood and will be followed correctly.

Hazardous substances are usually identified through the use of known symbols, examples of which are shown on the right. Any substance in the workplace that is hazardous to health must be identified on the packaging and stored and handled correctly.

Hazardous substances may enter the body via:

- the eyes
- the skin
- the nose (**inhalation**)
- the mouth (**ingestion**).

Each beauty product supplier is legally required to make available guidelines on how materials should be used and stored; these will be supplied on request.

HIGHLY FLAMMABLE TOXIC
HARMFUL CORROSIVE
EXPLOSIVE OXIDIZING

ACTIVITY

Identifying hazards
Make a list of potential electrical hazards in the workplace.

HEALTH AND SAFETY

COSHH assessment
All hazardous substances must be identified when completing the risk assessment. This includes cleaning agents such as a wax equipment cleaner.
  Where possible high-risk products should be replaced with lower risk products.
  COSHH assessment should be reviewed on a regular basis, and updated to include any new products.

HEALTH AND SAFETY FOR HAIRDRESSERS

COSHH RISK ASSESSMENT

HABIA

Staff Member Responsible: Date: Review Dates:

Hazard	What is the risk?	Who is at risk?	Degree of risk High/Med/Low	Action to be taken to reduce/control risk
Aerosols (list aerosols used in your salon)	These can contain flammable gases and irritant chemicals. There is a risk of fire, explosion and intoxication.	Everyone in the salon, but in particular the user of the aerosol and the client.	Low	Look for aerosols with non-flammable gases if possible. Do not expose to temperatures above 50 C. Do not pierce or burn containers. Do not inhale.
Nail polish remover (list products used in your salon)	Irritant to the skin and eyes. Moderately toxic if swallowed or inhaled.	Beauty therapists, juniors, trainees and clients.	Medium	Store in a cool place. Reseal after use. Do not use on damaged or sensitive skin. Avoid breathing in. Never place in an unlabelled container.

HSIP 2a

A COSHH assessment

Electricity at Work Regulations 1989

The Electricity at Work Regulations 1989 cover the installation, maintenance and use of electrical equipment and systems in the workplace.

These regulations state that every piece of electrical equipment in the workplace should be tested every 12 months by a qualified electrician.

In addition to annual testing, a trained member of staff should regularly check all electrical equipment for safety. This is recommended every three months. Records must be kept of the check including;

- electrician's name/contact details
- itemised list of electrical equipment complete with serial number for identification purposes
- date of purchase/disposal
- date of inspection.

You can compile your own safety checklist for your workplace. Report to your supervisor if you see any of these potential hazards:

- exposed wires in flexes
- cracked plugs or broken sockets
- worn cables
- overloaded sockets.

Although it is the responsibility of the employer to ensure all equipment is safe to use, it is also the responsibility of the employee to always check that equipment is safe before use, and to never use it if it is faulty.

Any pieces of equipment that appear faulty must be immediately checked and repaired before use. They should also be labelled to ensure that they are not used by accident.

First aid

Employers must have appropriate and adequate first aid arrangements in the event of an accident or illness occurring.

All employees should be informed of the first-aid procedures including:

- where to locate the first-aid box
- who is responsible for the maintenance of the first-aid box
- which staff member to inform in the event of an accident or illness occurring
- the staff member to inform in the event of an accident or emergency.

The **Health and Safety (First Aid) Regulations 1981** state that workplaces must have first-aid provision. An adequately stocked first-aid box should be available. This should contain a minimum level of first aid equipment:

Contents of the first-aid box

No. of employees	1–5	6–10	11–50
First-aid guidance notes	1	1	1
Individual sterile adhesive dressings	20	20	40
Sterile eye pads	1	2	4
Sterile triangular bandages	1	2	4
Safety pins	6	6	12
Medium size sterile unmediated dressings	3	6	8
Large size sterile unmediated dressings	1	2	4
Extra-large size sterile unmediated dressings	1	2	4

Inspection and registration of premises

The Local Authority Environmental Health Department enforces the Health and Safety at Work Act, and an **environmental health officer** visits and inspects local business premises.

If the inspector identifies any area of danger, it is the responsibility of the employer to remove this danger within a designated period of time. The

---

HEALTH AND SAFETY

First aid

- This should only be given by a qualified first-aider.
- A first aid certificate is only valid for three years and after this period, it must be renewed. This may mean additional first aid training.
- Know what action you can take *within your responsibility* in the event of an accident occurring.
- An accident book should be available to record details of any accident that has occurred.

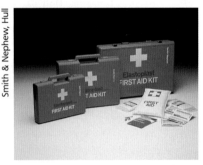

Smith & Nephew, Hull

A first-aid kit

inspector issues an **improvement notice**. Failure to comply with the notice will lead to prosecution. The inspector also has the authority to *close* a business until he or she is satisfied that all danger to employees and public has been removed. Such closure involves the issuing of a **prohibition notice**.

Certain treatments carried out in beauty therapy, such as ear piercing and electrical hair epilation techniques, pose additional risk as they may produce blood and body tissue fluid. Inspection of the premises is necessary before such services can be offered to the public. The inspector will visit and observe that the guidelines listed in the **Local Government (Miscellaneous Provisions) Act 1982** relating to this area are being complied with. When the inspector is satisfied, a **certificate of registration** will be awarded.

Disposal of waste

Waste should be disposed of in an enclosed waste bin fitted with a polythene bin liner, durable enough to resist tearing. The bin should be regularly sanitised with disinfectant in a well-ventilated area: wear protective gloves while doing this. Hazardous waste must be disposed of following the COSHH procedures and training by the employer.

Contaminated waste, should be disposed of as recommended by your local authority. Items which have been used in the skin, such as needles, should be safely discarded in a disposable **sharps container**. Again, contact your local authority to check on disposal arrangements.

Fire

The **Fire Precautions Act 1971** states that all staff must be aware of and trained in fire and emergency evacuation procedures for their workplace. The **emergency exit route** will be the easiest route by which staff and clients can leave the building safely.

Fire drill notices should be visible to show the emergency exit route.

A **fire certificate** is a compulsory requirement of the Act if there are more than 20 employees, or more than 10 employees are on different floors at any one time.

The Fire Precautions (Workplace) Regulations 1997

This requires that every employer must carry out a risk assessment for the premises, under the **Management of Health and Safety Regulations 1999**.

- Any obstacles that may hinder fire evacuation should be identified as a hazard and dealt with.
- Suitable fire detection equipment should be in place, such as a **smoke alarm** to forewarn you of a fire.
- A method to warn of a fire should be in place, this may be an automatic alarm or a trained employee shouting to raise the alarm and evacuate the building. A fire alarm system should be tested weekly to ensure it is in full operational condition.
- All escape routes should be clearly marked and free from obstacles. Emergency lighting which will provide illumination and directions to the fire exit may be used in work environments such as the spa.

ACTIVITY

Fire drill
Each workplace should have a fire drill regularly. This enables staff to practice so that they know what to do in the event of a real fire. What is the fire drill procedure for *your* workplace?

HEALTH AND SAFETY

Fire!
If there is a fire, never use a lift. A fire quickly becomes out of control. You do not have very long to act!

HEALTH AND SAFETY

Fire exits
Fire exit doors must be clearly marked and remain unlocked during working hours, and be free from obstruction.

- Firefighting equipment should be available and maintained, to be used only by those trained in its use.
- All employees should be trained in fire evacuation practice and procedures and be absolutely clear as to their role in the event of a fire.
- Fire evacuation procedure should be reviewed regularly to account for changes to the staffing or premises. A fire drill should be carried out *at least* once a year to monitor evacuation procedures.

Firefighting equipment

Firefighting equipment must be available, located in a specified area. The equipment includes fire extinguishers, blankets, sand buckets, and water hoses. Firefighting equipment should be used only when the cause of the fire has been identified – using the *wrong* extinguisher could make the fire worse. Never use firefighting equipment unless you are trained in its use.

Fire extinguishers

Fire extinguishers are available to tackle different types of fire. These should be located in a set place known to all employees. It is important that these are checked and maintained as required.

Cause of fire and choice of fire extinguisher

Cause	Extinguisher	Label colour
Electrical fire	Carbon dioxide (CO_2) extinguisher	Black
Solid material fire (paper, wood, etc.)	Water extinguisher	Red
Flammable liquids	Foam extinguisher	Cream/yellow
Vaporising liquids	BCF extinguisher	Green
	Dry-powder extinguisher	Blue

Note: green and blue labelled extinguishers can be used with all types of fire, apart from flammable metal fires.

Fire blankets are used to smother a small, localised fire or if a person's clothing is on fire. **Sand** is used to soak up liquids if these are the source of the fire, and to smother the fire. **Water hoses** are used to extinguish large fires caused by paper materials and the like – buckets of water may be used to extinguish a small fire. *Turn off the electricity first!*

Never put yourself at risk – fires can spread quickly. Leave the building at once if in danger, and raise the alarm by telephoning the emergency services on the emergency telephone number, **999**.

Other emergencies

Other possible emergencies that could occur relate to fumes and flooding. Learn where the water and gas stopcocks are located. In the event of a gas leak or a flood, the stopcocks should be switched off and the appropriate emergency service contacted.

TIP

Fire extinguishers
Label colours and symbols indicate the use of particular fire extinguishers. Make sure you know the meaning of each of the colours and symbols.

HEALTH AND SAFETY

Using fire extinguishers
The vapours emitted when using vaporising liquid (BCE) extinguishers 'starve' a fire of oxygen. They are therefore dangerous when used in confined spaces, as people need oxygen too! The use of this extinguisher is to be discontinued.

ACTIVITY

Causes of fires
Can you think of several potential causes of fire in the salon? How could each of these be prevented?

Chubb Fire Ltd

Firefighting equipment

Chubb Fire Ltd

Firefighting blanket

Fire extinguisher symbols

In the event of a bomb alert staff must be trained in the appropriate emergency procedures. This will involve recognition of a suspect package, how to deal with a bomb threat, evacuation of staff and clients and contacting the emergency services. Your local Crime Prevention Officer will advise on bomb security.

Insurance

Public liability insurance protects employers and employees against the consequences of death or injury to a third party while on the premises. It is a requirement by law that employers have liability insurance.

Professional indemnity insurance extends the public liability insurance to cover named employees against claims. This is an important consideration when performing high-risk treatments such as electrical epilation.

Product and **Treatment Liability Insurance** is usually included with your public liability insurance, but you should check this with the insurance company.

Second, every employer must have **employer's liability insurance**. This provides financial compensation to an employee should she be injured as a result of an accident in the workplace. It is a requirement by law.

PERSONAL HEALTH, HYGIENE AND APPEARANCE

Your appearance enables the client to make an initial judgement about both you and the salon, so make sure that you create the correct impression! Employees in the workplace should always reflect the desired image of the profession that they work in.

Dream Workwear

Dream Workwear

Professional appearance

Assistant therapist

The assistant therapist qualified to pre-foundation level will be required to wear a clean protective overall as they will be preparing the working area for client treatments, and they may be involved in preparing clients also.

Beauty therapist

Due to the nature of many of the services offered, the beauty therapist must wear protective, hygienic clothing. The cotton overall is ideal; air can circulate, allowing perspiration to evaporate and discouraging body odour. The use of a colour such as white immediately shows the client that you are clean. A cotton overall may comprise a dress, a jumpsuit or a tunic top, with coordinating trousers.

Overalls should be laundered regularly, and a fresh, clean overall worn each day.

Receptionist

If a receptionist is employed solely to carry out reception duties, she may wear a different salon dress, complementary to those worn by the practising therapists. As she will not be as active, it may be appropriate for her to wear a smart jacket or cardigan. If on the other hand she is also carrying out services at some times, the standard salon overall must be worn.

General rules for employees

Make-up

Wear an attractive make-up, and use the correct skin-care cosmetics to suit your skin type. A healthy complexion will be a positive advertisement for your work.

HEALTH AND SAFETY

Aprons and The Personal Protective Equipment (PPE) at Work Regulations 1992
For certain treatments, such as waxing, it is necessary to wear a protective apron over the overall. Assistant therapists may wear an apron whilst preparing and cleaning the working area, to protect the overall and keep it clean.

> **ACTIVITY**
>
> **Personal appearance**
> 1 Collect pictures from various suppliers of overalls. Select those that you feel would be most practical for an assistant therapist and for a Level 2 beauty therapist. Briefly describe *why* you feel these are the most suitable.
> 2 Design various hairstyles, or collect pictures from magazines, to show how the hair could be smartly worn by a therapist with medium-length to long hair.

Jewellery

Keep jewellery to a minimum, such as a wedding ring, a watch, and small earrings.

Nails

Nails should be short, neatly manicured, and free of nail polish unless the employee's main duties involve nail treatments or reception duties. Flesh-coloured tights may be worn to protect the legs.

Shoes

Wear flat, well-fitting, comfortable shoes that enclose the feet and which complement the overall. Remember that you will be on your feet for most of the day!

Ethics

Beauty therapy has a **code of ethics**. Although not a legal requirement, this code may be used in criminal proceedings as evidence of improper practice.

Diet, exercise and sleep

A beauty therapist requires stamina and energy. To achieve this you need to eat a healthy, well-balanced diet, take regular exercise, and have adequate sleep.

Posture

Posture is the way you hold yourself when standing, sitting and walking. *Correct* posture enables you to work longer without becoming tired; it prevents muscle fatigue and stiff joints; and it improves your appearance.

Good standing posture

If you are standing with good posture, this will describe you:

- head up, centrally balanced
- shoulders slightly back, and relaxed
- chest up and out

> **ACTIVITY**
>
> **Building stamina**
> Ask your tutor for guidelines before beginning this activity.
> 1 Write down all the foods and drinks that you most enjoy. Are they healthy? If you are unsure, ask your tutor.
> 2 How much exercise do you take weekly?
> 3 How much sleep do you regularly have each night?
> 4 Do you think you could improve your health and fitness levels?

> **ACTIVITY**
>
> **Code of ethics**
> As a professional beauty therapist it is important that you adhere to a code of ethical practice. You may wish to join a professional organisation, which will issue you with a copy of its agreed standards.

- abdomen flat
- hips level
- fingertips level
- bottom in
- knees level
- feet slightly apart, and weight evenly distributed.

ACTIVITY

The importance of posture
1 Which treatments will be performed sitting, and which standing?
2 In what way do you feel your treatments would be affected if you were *not* sitting or standing correctly?

Good sitting posture

Sit on a suitable chair or stool with a good back support:

- sit with the lower back pressed against the chair back
- keep the chest up and the shoulders back
- distribute the body weight evenly along the thighs
- keep the feet together, and flat on the floor
- do not slouch, or sit on the edge of your seat.

Personal hygiene

It is vital that you have a high standard of personal **hygiene**. You are going to be working in close proximity with people.

Bodily cleanliness is achieved through daily showering or bathing. This removes stale sweat, dirt and bacteria which cause body odour. An anti-perspirant or deodorant may be applied to the underarm area to reduce perspiration and thus the smell of sweat.

Clean underwear should be worn each day.

ACTIVITY

Hand hygiene
What further occasions can you think of when it will be necessary to wash your hands when treating a client?

Hands

Your hands and everything you touch are covered with germs. Although most are harmless, some can cause ill health or disease. Wash your hands regularly, especially after you have been to the toilet and before eating food. You must also wash your hands before and after treating each client, and during treatment if necessary. Washing the hands before treating a client minimises the risk of cross-infection, and presents to the client a hygienic, professional, caring image.

HEALTH AND SAFETY

Soap and towels
Wash your hands with liquid soap from a sealed dispenser. Don't refill disposable soap dispensers when empty: if you do they will become a breeding ground for bacteria.
   Disposable paper towels or warm-air hand dryers should be used to dry the hands.

HEALTH AND SAFETY

Protecting yourself
You will be wise to have the relevant inoculations, including those against tetanus and hepatitis, to protect yourself against ill health and even death.

Feet

Keep your feet fresh and healthy by washing them daily and then drying them thoroughly. Deodorising foot powder may then be applied.

Teeth

Avoid bad breath by brushing your teeth at least twice daily and flossing the teeth frequently. Use breath fresheners and mouthwashes as required to freshen your breath. Visit the dentist regularly, to maintain healthy teeth and gums.

Hair

Your hair should be clean and tidy. Have your hair cut regularly, and shampoo and condition your hair as often as needed.

If your hair is long, wear it off the face, and taken to the crown of the head. Medium-length hair should be clipped back, away from the face, to prevent it falling forwards.

Hygiene in the workplace

Infections

Effective hygiene is necessary in the salon to prevent *cross-infection* and *secondary infection*. These can occur through poor practice, such as the use of implements that are not sterile. Infection can be recognised by the skin being red and inflamed, or pus being present.

Cross-infection occurs because some micro-organisms are contagious – they may be transferred through personal contact or by contact with an infected instrument that has not been sterilised. **Secondary infection** can occur as a result of injury to the client during the treatment, or if the client already has an open cut, if bacteria penetrate the skin and cause infection. **Sterilisation** and **sanitisation** procedures (below) are used to minimise or destroy the harmful micro-organisms which could cause infection – bacteria, viruses and fungi.

Infectious diseases that are contagious **contra-indicate** beauty treatment: they require medical attention. People with certain other skin disorders, even though these are not contagious, should likewise not be treated by the beauty therapist, as treatment might lead to secondary infection.

Sterilisation and sanitisation

Sterilisation is the total destruction of all living micro-organisms. **Sanitisation** is the destruction of some, but not all, micro-organisms. Sterilisation and sanitisation techniques practised in the beauty salon involve

An ultra-violet light cabinet

An dry-heat sterilising cabinet

Glass bead steriliser

the use of *physical* agents, such as radiation and heat; and *chemical* agents, such as antiseptics, disinfectants and vapour fumigants.

Radiation A quartz mercury-vapour lamp can be used as the source for **ultraviolet light**, which destroys micro-organisms. The object to be sanitised must be turned regularly so that the UV light reaches all surfaces. (UV light has limited effectiveness, and cannot be relied upon for sterilisation.)

The UV lamp must be contained within a closed cabinet. This cabinet is an ideal place for storing sterilised objects.

Heat Dry and moist heat may both be used in sterilisation. One method is to use a dry **hot-air oven**. This is similar to a small oven, and heats to 150–180°C. It is seldom used in the salon.

More practical is a **glass-bead steriliser**. This is a small electrically-heated unit which contains glass beads: these transfer heat to objects placed in contact with them. This method of sterilisation is suitable for small tools such as tweezers and scissors.

Water is boiled in an **autoclave** (similar to a pressure cooker): because of the increased pressure, the water reaches a temperature of 121–134°C. Autoclaving is the most effective method for sterilising objects in the salon.

HEALTH AND SAFETY

Using an autoclave

- Not all objects can safely be placed in the autoclave. Before using this method, check whether the items you wish to sterilise can withstand this heating process.
- To avoid damaging the autoclave, always use distilled deionised water.
- To avoid rusting, metal objects placed in the sterilising unit must be of good-quality stainless steel.

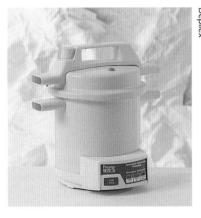

An autoclave

Sterilisation tray with liquid

Gases Gases used in sterilising include **ethylene oxide** and **formaldehyde**. These chemicals are hazardous to handle, however, and are therefore unpopular.

Disinfectants and antiseptics If an object *cannot* be sterilised, it should be placed in a chemical **disinfectant** solution such as **quaternary ammonium compounds (quats)** or **glutaraldehyde**. A disinfectant destroys most micro-organisms, but not all. **Hypochlorite** is a disinfectant: bleach is an example of a hypochlorite. It is particularly corrosive and therefore unsuitable for use with metals. Use on hard surfaces, such as work surfaces, and non-corrosive materials such as plastic tools. Always use as directed by the manufacturer.

An **antiseptic** prevents the multiplication of micro-organisms. It has a limited action, and does not kill all micro-organisms. Because it is milder than a disinfectant, it can be used directly on the skin.

All sterilisation techniques must be carried out safely and effectively:

1 Select the appropriate method of sterilisation for the object. *Always* follow the manufacturer's guidelines on the use of the sterilising unit or agent.

2 Clean the object in clean water and detergent to remove dirt and grease. (Dirt left on the object may prevent effective sterilisation.)

3 Dry it thoroughly with a clean, disposable paper towel.

4 Sterilise the object, allowing sufficient time for the process to be completed.

5 Place tools that have been sterilised in a clean, covered container.

Keep several sets of the tools you use regularly, so that you can carry out effective sterilisation.

General salon hygiene rules

- *Health and safety* Follow the health and safety policies for the workplace.
- *Personal hygiene* Maintain a high standard of personal hygiene. Wash your hands with a detergent containing **chlorhexidine**, which is widely used for skin cleansing.
- *Cuts on the hands* Always cover any cuts on your hands.
- *Cross-infection* Take great care to avoid cross-infection in the salon. *Never* treat a client who has a contagious skin disease or disorder, or any other contra-indication.
- *Use hygienic tools* Never use an implement unless it has been effectively sterilised or sanitised, as appropriate.
- *Disposable products* Wherever possible, use disposable products.
- *Working surfaces* Clean all working surfaces (such as trolleys and couches) with a chlorine preparation, diluted to the manufacturer's instructions. Cover all working surfaces with clean, disposable paper tissue.
- *Gowns and towels* Clean gowns and towels must be provided for each client.
- *Laundry* Dirty laundry should be placed in a covered container.
- *Waste* Put waste in a suitable container lined with a disposable waste bag. A yellow **'sharps' container** should be available for waste contaminated with blood or tissue fluid, such as needles used in electrical hair epilation techniques.
- *Hazardous waste* Must be disposed of following the COSHH procedures and training by the employer.

HEALTH AND SAFETY

Using disinfectant
Disinfectant solutions should be changed as recommended by the manufacturer to ensure their effectiveness.

After removing the object from the disinfectant, rinse it in clean water to remove traces of the solution. (These might otherwise cause an allergic reaction on the client's skin.)

TIP

Before sterilisation, surgical spirit may be used to clean small objects.

HEALTH AND SAFETY

Damaged equipment
Any equipment in poor repair must be repaired or disposed of. Such equipment may be dangerous and may harbour germs.

HEALTH AND SAFETY

Cuts on the hands
Open, uncovered cuts provide an easy entry for harmful bacteria, and may lead to infection. Always cover cuts.

HEALTH AND SAFETY

Using chemical agents
Always protect your hands with gloves before immersing them in chemical cleaning agents, to minimise the risk of an allergic reaction.

- *Eating and drinking* Never eat or drink in the treatment area of the salon. It is unprofessional and harmful chemicals may be ingested.
- *Smoking* Never smoke in the treatment area of the salon or other prohibited areas.
- Never carry out treatments in the workplace under the influence of drugs or alcohol. Your competence will be affected putting both yourself, clients and possibly colleagues at risk.

<table>
<tr><td>HEALTH AND SAFETY </td></tr>
</table>

Skin problems
If you are unable to identify a skin condition with confidence, so that you are uncertain whether or not you should treat the client, *don't*! Tactfully refer her to her physician before proceeding with the planned treatment.

SKIN DISEASES AND DISORDERS

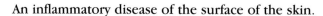

The beauty therapist must be able to distinguish a healthy skin from one suffering from any skin disease or disorder. Certain skin disorders and diseases **contra-indicate** a beauty treatment: the treatment would expose the therapist and other clients to the risk of cross-infection. It is therefore vital that you are familiar with the skin diseases and disorders with which you may come into contact in the workplace.

Bacterial infections

Bacteria are minute single-celled organisms of varied shapes. Large numbers of bacteria inhabit the surface of the skin and are harmless (**non-pathogenic**); indeed some play an important positive role in the health of the skin. Others, however, are harmful (**pathogenic**) and can cause skin diseases.

Impetigo

An inflammatory disease of the surface of the skin.

Infectious? Yes.

Appearance: Initially the skin appears red and is itchy. Small thin-walled blisters appear; these burst and form into crusts.

Site: The commonly affected areas are the nose, the mouth and the ears, but impetigo can occur on the scalp or the limbs.

Treatment: Medical – usually an antibiotic or an antibacterial ointment is prescribed.

Conjunctivitis or pink eye

Inflammation of the mucous membrane that covers the eye and lines the eyelids.

Infectious? Yes.

Appearance: The skin of the inner conjunctiva of the eye becomes inflamed, the eye becomes very red and sore, and pus may exude from the area.

Site: The eyes, either one or both, may be infected.

Treatment: Medical – usually an antibiotic lotion is prescribed.

Hordeola or styes

Infection of the sebaceous glands of eyelash hair follicles.

Infectious? Yes.

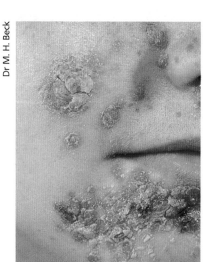

Dr M. H. Beck

Impetigo

Appearance: Small lumps containing pus.

Site: The inner rim of the eyelid.

Treatment: Medical – usually an antibiotic is prescribed.

Furuncles or boils

Red, painful lumps, extending deeply into the skin.

Infectious? Yes.

Appearance: A localised red lump occurs around a hair follicle; it then develops a core of pus. Scarring of the skin often remains after the boil has healed.

Site: The back of the neck, the ankles and the wrists.

Treatment: Medical.

Carbuncles

Infection of numerous hair follicles.

Infectious? Yes.

Appearance: A hard, round abscess, larger than a boil, which oozes pus from several points upon its surface. Scarring often occurs after the carbuncle has healed.

Site: The back of the neck.

Treatment: Medical – usually involving incision, drainage of the pus, and a course of antibiotics.

Paronychia

Infection of the tissue surrounding the nail.

Infectious? Yes.

Appearance: Swelling, redness and pus in the cuticle and in the area of the nail wall.

Site: The cuticle and the skin surrounding the nail.

Treatment: Medical.

Viral infections

Viruses are minute entities, too small to see even under an ordinary microscope. They are considered to be **parasites**, as they require living tissue in order to survive. Viruses invade healthy body cells and multiply within the cell: in due course the cell walls break down, liberating new viral particles to attack further cells, and thus the infection spreads.

Herpes simplex

This is a recurring skin condition, appearing at times when the skin's resistance is lowered through ill health or stress. It may also be

Dr A. L. Wright

> **HEALTH AND SAFETY**
>
> **Boils**
> Boils occurring on the upper lip or in the nose should be referred immediately to a physician. Boils can be dangerous when near to the eyes or brain.

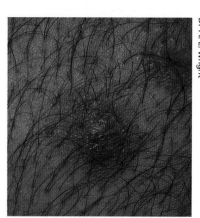

Boil

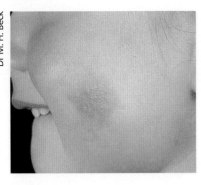

Dr A. L. Wright

Herpes simplex

caused by exposure of the skin to extremes of temperature or to ultraviolet light.

Infectious? Yes.

Appearance: Inflammation of the skin occurs in localised areas. As well as being red, the skin becomes itchy and small vesicles appear. These are followed by a crust, which may crack and weep tissue fluid.

Site: The mucous membranes of the nose or lips; herpes can also occur on the skin generally.

Treatment: There is no specific treatment. A proprietary brand of anti-inflammatory antiseptic drying cream is usually prescribed.

Herpes zoster or shingles

In this painful disease, the virus attacks the sensory nerve endings. The virus is thought to lie dormant in the body and be triggered when the body's defences are at a low ebb.

Infectious? Yes.

Appearance: Redness of the skin occurs along the line of the affected nerves. Blisters develop and form crusts, leaving purplish-pink pigmentation.

Site: Commonly the chest and the abdomen.

Treatment: Medical – usually including antibiotics. Any lasting pigmentation may be camouflaged with cosmetics.

ACTIVITY ⟷

Avoiding cross-infection

1 List the different ways in which infection can be transferred in the salon.
2 How can you avoid cross-infection in the workplace?

Verrucae or warts

Small epidermal skin growths. Warts may be raised or flat, depending upon their position. There are several types of wart: plane, common, and plantar.

Infectious? Yes.

Appearance: Warts vary in size, shape, texture and colour. Usually they have a rough surface and are raised. If the wart occurs on the sole of the foot it grows inwards, due to the pressure of body weight.

Site:
- plane wart: the fingers, either surface of the hand, or the knees
- common wart: the face or hands
- plantar wart: the sole of the foot.

Treatment: Medical – using acids, solid carbon dioxide, or electrocautery.

Veruccae – plantar warts

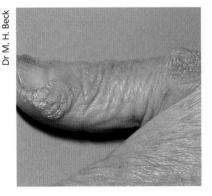

Dr M. H. Beck

A wart

Infestations

Scabies or itch mites

A condition in which an animal parasite burrows beneath the skin and invades the hair follicles.

Infectious? Yes.

Appearance: At the onset, minute papules and wavy greyish lines appear, where dirt has entered the burrows. Secondary bacterial infection may occur as a result of scratching.

NVQ2 ENSURE YOUR OWN ACTIONS REDUCE RISKS TO HEALTH AND SAFETY G1
Dr M. H. Beck

Site: Usually seen in warm areas of loose skin, such as the webs of the fingers, and the creases of the elbows.

Treatment: Medical – an anti-scabetic lotion.

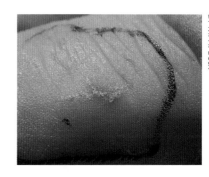

Scabies burrow

Pediculosis capitis or head lice

A condition in which small parasites infest scalp hair.

Infectious? Yes.

Appearance: The lice cling to the hair of the scalp. Eggs are laid, attached to the hair close to the skin. The lice bite the skin to draw nourishment from the blood; this creates irritation and itching of the skin, which may lead to secondary bacterial infection.

Site: The hair of the scalp.

Treatment: Medical – an appropriate lotion.

Pediculosis pubis

A condition in which small parasites infest body hair.

Infectious? Yes.

Appearance: The lice cling to the hair of the body. Eggs are laid, attached to the hair close to the skin. The lice bite the skin to draw nourishment from the blood; this creates irritation and itching of the skin, which may lead to secondary bacterial infection.

Site: Pubic hair, eyebrows and eyelashes.

Treatment: Medical – an appropriate lotion.

Pediculosis corporis

A condition in which small parasites live and feed on body skin.

Infectious? Yes.

Appearance: The lice cling to the hair of the body. Eggs are laid, attached to the hair close to the skin. The lice bite the skin to draw nourishment from the blood; this creates irritation and itching of the skin, which may lead to secondary bacterial infection. Where body lice bite the skin, small red marks can be seen.

Site: Body hair.

Treatment: Medical – an appropriate lotion.

Fungal diseases

Fungi are microscopic plants. They are parasites, dependent upon a host for their existence. Fungal diseases of the skin feed off the waste products of the skin. Some fungi are found on the skin's surface; others attack the deeper tissues. Reproduction of fungi is by means of simple cell division or by the production of spores.

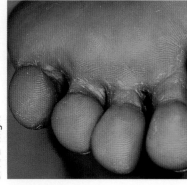

Tinea pedis

Tinea pedis or athlete's foot

A common fungal foot infection.

Infectious? Yes.

Appearance: Small blisters form, which later burst. The skin in the area can then become dry, giving a scaly appearance.

Site: The webs of skin between the toes.

Treatment: Thorough cleansing of the area. Medical application of fungicides.

Tinea corporis or body ringworm

A fungal infection of the skin.

Infectious? Yes.

Appearance: Small scaly red patches, which spread outwards and then heal from the centre, leaving a ring.

Site: The trunk of the body, the limbs and the face.

Treatment: Medical – using a fungicidal cream, griseofluvin.

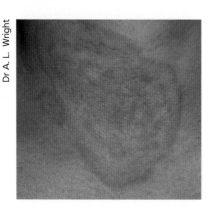

Tinea corporis

Tinea unguium

Ringworm infection of the fingernails.

Infectious? Yes.

Appearance: The nail plate is yellowish-grey. Eventually the nail plate becomes brittle and separates from the nail bed.

Site: The nail plates of the fingers.

Treatment: Medical application of fungicides.

Sebaceous gland disorders

Milia

Keratinisation of the skin over the hair follicle occurs, causing sebum to accumulate in the hair follicle. This condition usually accompanies dry skin.

Infectious? No.

Appearance: Small, hard, pearly-white cysts.

Site: The upper face or close to the eyes.

Treatment: The milium may be removed by the beauty therapist or by a physician, depending on the location. A sterile needle is used to pierce the skin of the overlying cuticle and thereby free the milium.

Comedones or blackheads

Excess sebum and keratinised cells block the mouth of the hair follicle.

Infectious? No.

Site: The face (the chin, nose and forehead), the upper back and chest.

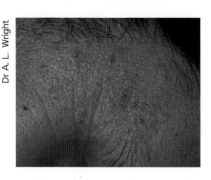

Comedones or blackheads

Treatment: The area should be cleansed, and an electrical vapour treatment or other pre-heating treatment should be given to relax the mouth of the hair follicle; a sterile comedo extractor should then be used to remove the blockage. A regular cleansing treatment should be recommended by the beauty therapist to limit the production of comedones.

Seborrhoea

Excessive secretion of sebum from the sebaceous gland. This usually occurs during puberty, as a result of hormonal changes in the body.

Infectious? No.

Appearance: The follicle openings enlarge and excessive sebum is secreted. The skin appears coarse and greasy; comedones, pustules and papules are present.

Site: The face and scalp. Seborrhoea may also affect the back and the chest.

Treatment: The area should be cleansed to remove excess grease. Medical treatment may be required – this would use locally applied creams.

Steatomas, sebaceous cysts or wens

Localised pockets or sacs of sebum, which form in hair follicles or under the sebaceous glands in the skin. The sebum becomes blocked, the sebaceous gland becomes distended, and a lump forms.

Infectious? No.

Appearance: Semi-globular in shape, either raised or flat, and hard or soft. The cysts are the same colour as the skin, or red if secondary bacterial infection occurs. A comedo can often be seen at the original mouth of the hair follicle.

Site: If the cyst appears on the upper eyelid, it is known as a **chalazion** or **meibomian cyst**.

Treatment: Medical – often a physician will remove the cyst under local anaesthetic.

Acne vulgaris

Hormone imbalance in the body at puberty influences the activity of the sebaceous gland, causing an increased production of sebum. The sebum may be retained within the sebaceous ducts, causing congestion and bacterial infection of the surrounding tissues.

Infectious? No.

Appearance: Inflammation of the skin, accompanied by comedones, pustules and papules.

Site: Commonly on the face, on the nose, the chin and the forehead. Acne may also occur on the chest and back.

Treatment: Medical – oral antibiotics may be prescribed, as well as medicated creams. With medical approval, regular salon treatments may be given to cleanse the skin deeply, and also to stimulate the blood circulation.

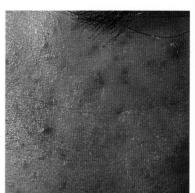

Dr M. H. Beck

Acne vulgaris

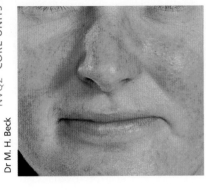

Dr M. H. Beck

Acne rosacea

Acne rosacea

Excessive sebum secretion combined with a chronic inflammatory condition, caused by dilation of the blood capillaries.

Infectious? No.

Appearance: The skin becomes coarse, the pores enlarge, and the cheek and nose area become inflamed, sometimes swelling and producing a butterfly pattern. Blood circulation slows in the dilated capillaries, creating a purplish appearance.

Treatment: Medical – usually including antibiotics.

Pigmentation disorders

Pigmentation of the skin varies, according to the person's genetic characteristics. In general the darker the skin, the more pigment is present, but some abnormal changes in skin pigmentation can occur.

- **hyperpigmentation** – increased pigment production;
- **hypopigmentation** – loss of pigmentation in the skin.

Ephelides or freckles

Multiple small pigmented areas of the skin. Exposure to ultra-violet light (as in sunlight) stimulates the production of melanin, intensifying their appearance.

Infectious? No.

Appearance: Small, flat, pigmented areas, darker than the surrounding skin.

Site: Commonly the nose and cheeks of fair-skinned people. Freckles may also occur on the shoulders, arms, hands and back.

Treatment: Freckles may be concealed with cosmetics if required. A sun block should be recommended, to prevent them intensifying in colour.

Lentigines

Pigmented areas of skin, slightly larger than freckles, which do not darken on exposure to ultra-violet.

Infectious? No.

Appearance: Brown, slightly raised, pigmented patches of skin.

Site: The face and hands.

Treatment: Application of cosmetic concealing products.

Chloasmata or liver spots

Increased skin pigmentation in specific areas, stimulated by a skin irritant such as ultraviolet. The condition often occurs during pregnancy, and usually disappears soon after the birth of the baby. It may also occur as a result of taking oral contraceptive pills. The female hormone oestrogen is thought to stimulate melanin production.

Infectious? No.

TIP		✔

Hypopigmentation may result from certain skin injuries, disorders or diseases.

Appearance: Flat, smooth, irregularly shaped, pigmented areas of skin, varying in colour from light tan to dark brown. Chloasmata are larger than ephelides, and of variable size.

Site: The back of the hands, the forearms, the upper part of the chest, the temples and the forehead.

Treatment: A barrier cream or a total sun block will reduce the risk of the chloasmata increasing in size or number, and thereby becoming more apparent.

Dermatosis Papulosa Nigra

Often called flesh moles, this is characterised by multiple benign, small brown to black hyperpigmented papules, common among black skinned people.

Infectious? No.

Appearance: Raised pigmented markings resembling moles.

Site: Usually seen on the cheeks and forehead, although they may appear on the neck, upper chest and back.

Treatment: Medical – by drug therapy or surgery.

Vitiligo or leucoderma

Patches of completely white skin which have lost their pigment, or which were never pigmented.

Infectious? No.

Appearance: Well defined patches of white skin, lacking pigment.

Site: The face, the neck, the hands, the lower abdomen, and the thighs. If vitiligo occurs over the eyebrows, the hairs in the area will lose their pigment also.

Treatment: Camouflage cosmetic concealer can be applied to give even skin colour; or skin-staining preparations can be used in the de-pigmented areas. Care must be taken when the skin is exposed to ultra-violet light, as the skin will not have the same protection in the areas lacking pigment.

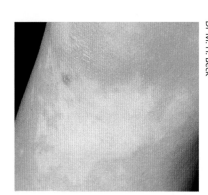

Dr. M. H. Beck

Vitiligo

Albinism

The skin is unable to produce the melanin pigment, and the skin, hair and eyes lack colour.

Infectious? No.

Appearance: The skin is usually very pale pink and the hair is white. The eyes also are pink, and extremely sensitive to light.

Site: The entire skin.

Treatment: There is no effective treatment. Maximum skin protection is necessary when the client is exposed to ultraviolet light, and sunglasses should be worn to protect the eyes.

Vascular naevi

There are two types of naevus of concern to beauty therapists: vascular and cellular. **Vascular naevi** are skin conditions in which small or large areas of skin pigmentation are caused by the permanent dilation of blood capillaries.

TIP	

If there is a vascular skin disorder, avoid overstimulating the skin or the problem will become *more* noticeable and the treatment may even cause further damage.

Erythema An area of skin in which blood capillaries have dilated, due either to injury or inflammation.

Infectious? No.

Appearance: The skin appears red.

Site: Erythema may affect one area (locally) or all of the skin (generally).

Treatment: The cause of the inflammation should be identified. In the case of a skin allergy, the client must not be brought into contact with the irritant again. If the cause is unknown, refer the client to their physician.

Dilated capillaries Capillaries near the surface of the skin that are permanently dilated.

Infectious? No.

Appearance: Small red visible blood capillaries.

Site: Areas where the skin is neglected, dry or fine, such as the cheek area.

Treatment: Dilated capillaries can be concealed using a green corrective camouflage cosmetic, or removed by a qualified electrologist using diathermy.

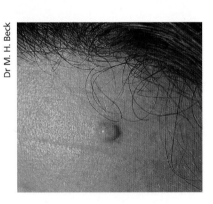

Dr M. H. Beck

Spider naevus

Spider naevi or stellate haemangiomas Dilated blood vessels, with smaller dilated capillaries radiating from them.

Infectious? No.

Appearance: Small red capillaries, radiating like a spider's legs from a central point.

Site: Commonly the cheek area, but may occur on the upper body, the arms and the neck. Spider naevi are usually caused by an injury to the skin.

Treatment: Spider naevi can be concealed using a camouflage cosmetic, or treated by a qualified electrologist with diathermy.

Dr M. H. Beck

Benign pigmental naevus

Naevi vasculosis or strawberry marks Red or purplish raised marks which appear on the skin at birth.

Infectious? No.

Appearance: Red or purplish lobed mark, of any size.

Site: Any area of the skin.

Treatment: About 60 per cent disappear by the age of 6 years. Treatment is not usually necessary; concealing cosmetics can be applied if desired.

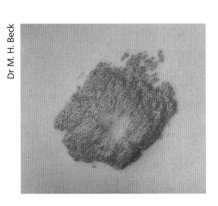

Dr M. H. Beck

Strawberry naevus

Capillary naevi or port-wine stains Large areas of dilated capillaries, which contrast noticeably with the surrounding areas.

Infectious? No.

Appearance: The naevus has a smooth, flat surface.

Site: Some 75 per cent occur on the head; they are probably formed at the foetal stage. Naevi may also be found on the neck and face.

Treatment: Camouflage cosmetic creams can be applied to disguise the area.

Cellular naevi or moles

Cellular naevi are skin conditions in which changes in the cells of the skin result in skin malformations.

Malignant melanomas or malignant moles
Rapidly-growing skin cancers, usually occurring in adults.

Infectious? No.

Appearance: Each melanoma commences as a bluish-black mole, which enlarges rapidly, darkening in colour and developing a halo of pigmentation around it. It later becomes raised, bleeds, and ulcerates. Secondary growths will develop in internal organs, if the melanoma is not treated.

Site: Usually the lower abdomen, legs or feet.

Treatment: Medical – *always* recommend that a client has any mole checked if it is changing in size, structure or colour, or if it becomes itchy or bleeds.

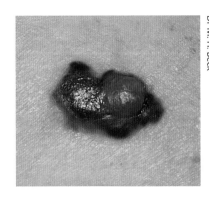

Malignant melanoma

HEALTH AND SAFETY

Moles
If moles change in shape or size, if they bleed or form crusts, seek medical attention.

Junction naevi
Localised collections of naevoid cells that arise from the mass production locally of pigment-forming cells (melanocytes).

Infectious? No.

Appearance: In childhood junction naevi appear as smooth or slightly raised pigmented marks. They vary in colour from brown to black.

Site: Any area.

Treatment: None.

Dermal naevi
Localised collections of naevoid cells.

Infectious? No.

Appearance: About 1cm wide, dermal naevi appear smooth and dome-shaped. Their colour ranges from skin tone to dark brown. Frequently one or more hairs may grow from the naevus.

Site: Usually the face.

Treatment: None.

Hairy naevi
Moles exhibiting coarse hairs from their surface.

Infectious? No.

Appearance: Slightly raised moles, varying in size from 3cm to much larger areas. Colour ranges from fawn to dark brown.

Site: Anywhere on the skin.

Treatment: Hairy naevi may be surgically removed where possible, and this is often done for cosmetic reasons. Hair growing from a mole should be cut, not plucked: if plucked, the hairs will become coarser and the growth of further hairs may be stimulated.

Dr M. H. Beck

Psoriasis

Skin disorders involving abnormal growth

Psoriasis

Patches of itchy, red, flaky skin, the cause of which is unknown.

Infectious? No. Secondary infection with bacteria can occur if the skin becomes broken and dirt enters the skin.

Appearance: Red patches of skin appear, covered in waxy, silvery scales. Bleeding will occur if the area is scratched and scales are removed.

Site: The elbows, the knees, the lower back and the scalp.

Treatment: There is no known treatment. Medication including steroid creams can bring relief to the symptoms.

Seborrheic or senile warts

Raised, pigmented, benign tumours occurring in middle age.

Infectious? No.

Appearance: Slightly raised, brown or black, rough patches of skin. Such warts can be confused with pigmented moles.

Site: The trunk, the scalp, and the temples.

Treatment: Medical – the warts can be cauterised by a physician.

Verrucae filliformis or skin tags

These verrucas appear as threads projecting from the skin.

Infectious? No.

Appearance: Skin-coloured threads of skin 3–6mm long.

Site: Mainly seen on the neck and the eyelids, but may occur in other areas such as under the arms.

Treatment: Medical – cauterisation with diathermy, either by a physician or by a qualified electrologist.

Xanthomas

Small yellow growths appearing upon the surface of the skin.

Infectious? No.

Appearance: A yellow, flat or raised area of skin.

Site: The eyelids.

Treatment: Medical – the growth is thought to be connected with certain medical diseases, such as diabetes or high or low blood pressure; sometimes a low-fat diet can correct the condition.

Keloids

Keloids occur following skin injury and are overgrown abnormal scar tissue which spreads, characterised by excess deposits of collagen. To avoid skin discolouration the keloid must be protected from UV exposure.

Infectious? No.

Appearance: The skin tends to be red, raised and ridged.

HEALTH AND SAFETY ✚

Skin tags
Skin tags often occur under the arms. In case they are present, take care when carrying out a wax depilation treatment in this area: do not apply wax over tags.

Dr John Gray

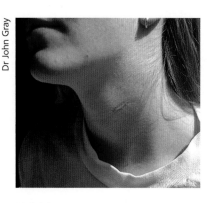

Keloid scar.

Site: Located over the site of a wound or other lesion.

Treatment: Medical by drug therapy or surgery.

Malignant tumours

Squamous cell carcinomas or prickle-cell cancers

Malignant growths originating in the epidermis.

Infectious: No.

Appearance: When fully formed, the carcinoma appears as a raised area of skin.

Site: Anywhere on the skin.

Treatment: Medical – by radiation.

Basal-cell carcinomas or rodent ulcers

Slow-growing malignant tumours, occurring in middle age.

Infectious? No.

Appearance: A small, shiny, waxy nodule with a depressed centre. The disease extends, with more nodules appearing on the border of the original ulcer.

Site: Usually the face.

Treatment: Medical.

Skin allergies

The skin can protect itself to some degree from damage or invasion. **Mast cells** detect damage to the skin; if damage occurs, the mast cells burst, releasing the chemical **histamine** into the tissues. Histamine causes the blood capillaries to dilate, giving the reddening we call 'erythema'. The increased blood flow transports materials in the blood which tend to limit the damage and begin repair.

If the skin is sensitive to and becomes inflamed on contact with a particular substance, this substance is called an **allergen**. Allergens may be animal, chemical or vegetable substances, and they may be inhaled, eaten, or absorbed following contact with the skin. An **allergic skin reaction** appears as irritation, itching and discomfort, with reddening and swelling (as with nettle rash). If the allergen is removed, the allergic reaction subsides.

Each individual has different tolerances to the various substances we encounter in daily life. What causes an allergic reaction in one individual may be perfectly harmless to another.

Here are just a few examples of allergens known to cause allergic skin reactions in some people:

- metal objects containing nickel
- sticking plaster
- rubber
- lipstick containing eosin dye
- nail polish containing formaldehyde resin

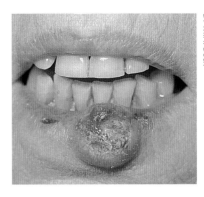

Squamous cell carcinoma

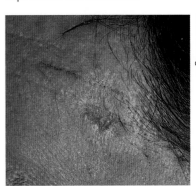

A basal-cell carcinoma

HEALTH AND SAFETY

Record any known allergies
When completing the client record card, always ask whether your client has any known allergies.

HEALTH AND SAFETY

Hypoallergenic products
The use of hypoallergenic products minimises the risk of skin contact with likely irritants.

Allergies
You may suddenly become allergic to a substance that has previously been perfectly harmless. Equally, you may over time *cease* to be allergic to something.

- hair and eyelash dyes
- lanolin, the skin moisturising agent
- detergents that dry the skin
- foods – well-known examples are peanuts, cow's milk, lobster, shellfish, and strawberries
- plants such as tulips and chrysanthemums.

HEALTH AND SAFETY

Infection following allergy
Following an allergic skin reaction in which the skin's surface has become itchy and broken, scratching may cause the skin to become infected with bacteria.

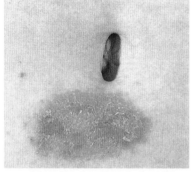

Allergic contact dermatitis (to the nickel in a stud on jeans)

Dermatitis

An inflammatory skin disorder in which the skin becomes red, itchy and swollen. There are two types of dermatitis. In *primary dermatitis* the skin is irritated by the action of a substance upon the skin, and this leads to skin inflammation. In *allergic contact dermatitis* the problem is caused by intolerance of the skin to a particular substance or group of substances. On exposure to the substance the skin quickly becomes irritated and an allergic reaction occurs.

Infectious? No.

Appearance: Reddening and swelling of the skin, with the possible appearance of blisters.

Site: If the skin reacts to a skin irritant outside the body, the reaction is localised. Repeated contact with the allergen will lead to a general hypersensitivity. If the irritant gains entry to the body it will be transported in the bloodstream and may cause a general allergic skin reaction.

Treatment: Barrier cream can be used to help avoid contact with the irritants. When an allergic dermatitis reaction occurs, however, the only 'cure' is the absolute avoidance of the substance. Steroid creams such as hydrocortisone are usually prescribed, to sooth the damaged skin and reduce the irritation.

Eczema

Inflammation of the skin caused by contact, internally or externally, with an irritant.

Infectious? No.

Appearance: Reddening of the skin, with swelling and blisters. The blisters leak tissue fluid which later hardens, forming scabs.

Site: The face, the neck and the skin, particularly at the inner creases of the elbows and behind the knees.

Treatment: Refer the client to their physician. Eczema may disappear if the source of irritation is identified and removed. Steroid cream may be prescribed by the physician, and special diets may help.

Dr A. L. Wright

Dr M. H. Beck

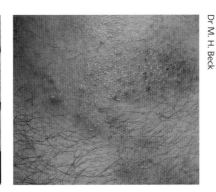

Eczema

Dr M. H. Beck

Urticaria (nettle rash) or hives

A minor skin disorder caused by contact with an allergen, either internally (food or drugs) or externally (for example, insect bites).

Infectious? No.

Appearance: Erythema with raised, round whitish skin weals. In some cases the lesions can cause intense burning or itching, a condition known as **pruritis**. Pruritis is a *symptom* of a disease (such as diabetes), not a disease itself.

Site: At the point of contact.

Treatment: Antihistamines may be prescribed to reduce the itching. The visible skin reaction usually disappears quickly, leaving no trace. Complete avoidance of the allergen 'cures' the problem.

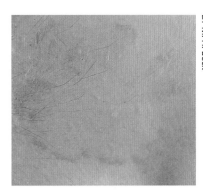

Urticaria

Assessment of knowledge and understanding

You have now learnt about the health and safety responsibilities for everyone in the workplace. This will enable you to ensure your own actions reduce risks to health and safety.

To test your level of knowledge and understanding, answer the following short questions. These will prepare you for your summative (final) assessment.

Action to avoid health and safety risks

1 What are your main legal responsibilities under the Health and Safety at Work Act 1974?

2 What is the purpose of a salon health and safety policy? What sort of information does it include?

3 What is the importance of personal presentation in maintaining health and safety in the salon?

4 Why is your personal conduct important to maintain the health and safety of yourself and colleagues and clients?

5 Why must regular health and safety checks be carried out in the workplace?

6 How often should electrical equipment be safety tested? Who carries out this procedure?

7 When completing a client's record card you recognise that treatment is contra-indicated as the client has impetigo, an infectious skin disorder. What action do you take and why?

8 Effective sterilisation methods prevent cross-infection and secondary infection. What do you understand by these terms?
- sterilisation
- cross-infection
- secondary infection.

9 How should a large box be lifted from floor level to be placed on the work surface?

Dealing with significant risks in your workplace

1 What hazards may exist in the beauty therapy workplace?

2 Why must you always be aware of potential hazards?

3 Why should obstructions that prevent access always be removed immediately?

4 What do you understand by the term 'risk assessment'?

5 Whilst checking the faradic electrical leads for safety before treatment application, you notice that the wires in the lead are exposed. What action should you take?

6 If you were unable to deal with a risk because it was outside of your responsibility, what action would you take?

7 What does the abbreviation COSHH stand for? Why is it important to follow the suppliers' and manufacturers' instructions for the safe use of materials and products?

8 A high-frequency glass electrode is accidentally broken. How should this be disposed of?

9 What do you understand by the legislation RIDDOR 1985?

Taking the right action in the event of danger

1 What is the procedure for dealing with an accident in the workplace?

2 What is a fire drill? What is the fire evacuation procedure in your salon? How often should this be carried out?

3 In the event of a real fire, after having safely evacuated the building, how would you contact the appropriate emergency service?

4 In reception, you discover a smoking bin, in which the fire has been caused by an unextinguished cigarette. How should this fire be extinguished?

5 What action should be taken in the event of a bomb alert?

6 The air conditioning system in the salon has broken. Who should be contacted to deal with this? And what would be the potential risk of inadequate ventilation?

chapter 2

Promote additional products or services to clients

G6

Learning objectives

This chapter discusses ways to promote products and services to clients. It describes the competencies to enable you to:

- **identify additional products or services that are available**

- **inform clients about additional products or services**

- **gain client commitment to using additional products and services**

Clients need to be regularly informed about what products and services the business is promoting. Often this will improve the experience of the client's salon visit.

Staff knowledge of products and services is vital to ensure personal effectiveness and to create a positive impression. If you have got it right the client will maintain their loyalty to you and this enables the business to grow.

THE IMPORTANCE OF SALES

Retail sales are of considerable importance to the beauty salon: they are a simple way of greatly increasing the income without too much extra time and effort. Beauty therapy treatments are time-consuming and labour-intensive; selling a product in addition to providing the treatment will greatly increase the profitability.

For example: a facial treatment might take 1 hour and cost the client £20. You might then sell the client moisturiser costing £20, of which £10 might be clear profit. Supposing that you sold eight products each day, each yielding £10 profit, that would be a profit of £80 per day, or £400 per week, or £1600 each month – and thus, £19,200 profit over the whole year: a significant sum.

SELLING PRODUCTS

When selling a client products, first find out about her needs. Consider the following:

- Is she allergic to any particular substance, contact with which should be avoided?
- Has she a skin disorder or nail disease which might contra-indicate use of a particular product? Contra-indication to products must always be noted and explained to the client.
- Is she planning to use the product over cuts and abrasions, or over areas with warts and moles? If so, is this safe?
- How much is she used to spending on products? Ask about what she is presently using: this will give you an idea of the types of product she has experience of using, and the sort of prices she is used to paying.

Ellisons

A lipstick display

A nail polish display

Ellisons

TIP ✔

Encourage your client to try the testers out. Make-up can look very different on the face compared with its appearance on the palette.

Bearing in mind her needs, you can now guide her to the most suitable product. This is where your expertise and your product knowledge are so important: you can describe fully and accurately the features, functions and benefits of the products you stock.

The products themselves must be presented to the client in such a way that they seem both attractive and desirable: the presentation should encourage her to purchase them. The packaging and the product should be clean and in good condition, and **testers** should be available wherever possible so that the client can try the product on herself before purchasing it.

The final choice of product is with the client, of course, but often she will ask for a recommendation, for example if she cannot decide between two possibilities. It is in these circumstances that your ability to answer technical questions fully, from a complete knowledge of the product, will help in closing the sale. Speaking with confidence and authority on the one product that will particularly suit her requirements may well persuade her to buy it.

If the client does not know what an **allergic reaction** is – or how to recognise it – it is important that you describe it to her (red, itchy, flaking and even swollen skin). If she experiences this sort of contra-action she should immediately stop applying the product she suspects is producing it.

Keeping knowledgeable about products and services available which may meet client needs.
Take part in staff training.

Seeking support as necessary. If unable to deal with a request for advice refer the client to a relevant person promptly.

Identify additional products or services available to the client by

Keeping the client informed about the products and services being promoted to improve the client experience

Promoting products and services using:
• Promotional material, e.g. a flier
• Salon literature
• Promotional launch, e.g. a social event
• Complimentary samples
• Web site

HEALTH AND SAFETY

Patch tests

If the client has not tried a product before, or if there is doubt as to how her skin will react, a skin patch test must be carried out.

1 Select either the inner elbow or the area behind the ear.
2 Make sure the skin is clean.
3 Apply a little of the product, using a spatula.
4 Leave the area alone for 24 hours.
5 If there is no reaction after 24 hours, the client is not allergic to the product: she can go ahead and use it.

     If there has been any itching, soreness, erythema, or swelling in the area where the product has been applied, the client is allergic to it and should not use it.

TECHNIQUES IN SELLING

Preparation

The first rule of selling is: *know your products*. This applies to all retail products and to all salon services.

Staff training

It is important that everybody is knowledgeable and able to advise the clients on their questions. This includes the receptionist, who is often the first and last person the client comes into contact with. In conversation, especially during quieter periods, they have the opportunities to discuss products and services informally.

Often product companies provide training either at the salon or at another venue. This is a great opportunity to update your knowledge and skills, which you will be able to share enthusiastically with your clientele.

Sometimes certificates to prove training are issued and these should be professionally displayed.

If not all staff can participate it is important that new information is passed onto them to make them effective in their job. Team meetings are a good opportunity to discuss salon policy and new products and promotions.

Information must be supplied for clients to read, and **displays** must be set up. Be aware of your **competitors** and their current advertising displays and campaigns.

Promoting products and services

When promoting products and services it is good to use the following:

- Eye-catching promotional material (usually provided by the product supplier). Display it in the window to encourage new clients!
- Updated salon literature discussing benefits and costs.
- A promotional launch event, where clients can enjoy a social event and perhaps book services or buy products at discounted prices.
- Promotional packages may be presented.
- Samples may be given following a service.
- If you have a web site you may wish to promote products and services on your home page.

Know your products

Product usage must be discussed with clients, as necessary, and advice given on which product will best suit each of them. The only way to be able to do this is to memorise the complete range: all your products, including which skin types or treatment conditions each is for, what the active ingredients are, when and how each should be used, and its cost. Any questions asked must be answered with authority and confidence. Clients expect the staff in the beauty salon to be professionals, able to provide expert advice.

If the client requests advice on products for which you are not responsible, you can suggest an alternative or refer her to another source.

TIP

Use the products on yourself. It is always good to be able to speak from experience.

ACTIVITY

Learning the product range
Learn about and memorise the product range sold in the training establishment you attend.

ACTIVITY

Increasing product knowledge
With colleagues, discuss and note down the features, functions and benefits of a range of cosmetic products sold in your training establishment.

Information to read

The **information** available to clients can start from the window display. Use the **window stickers** if supplied with product ranges, and include stickers that advertise the salon's treatments. Few salons use windows for product displays, but you could consider doing so.

Posters are supplied with good-quality product ranges, and most suppliers provide **information leaflets** for clients. Use the posters and **display cards** in the reception area; clients can then help themselves, and read about the products. This will generate questions – and sales.

Product and retail displays

Two types of display can be used in the beauty salon. In the first, the display is there simply to be looked at, and seen as part of the decor. It should be attractive and artistically arranged, and can use dummy containers. It is not meant to be touched or sold from, so it can be behind glass or in a window display.

In the second, on the other hand, products are there to be sold. In this case products must be attractive but also accessible. The display should include testers so that clients can freely smell and touch. Each product must be clearly priced, and small signs placed beside the products or on the edge of the shelves to describe the selling points of each product.

This sort of active display must always be in the part of the salon where most people will see and walk past it – the area of 'highest traffic'. A large proportion of cosmetic and perfume sales are **impulse buys**. It is no accident that perfumery departments are beside the main entrances to department stores, or right beside access points such as escalators.

ACTIVITY

Collecting information
Collect information leaflets from local salons and beauty product or perfume counters in department stores. Is this literature attractive? Will the presentation encourage sales?

Write to wholesalers and product companies for information about the display packs they supply with their products.

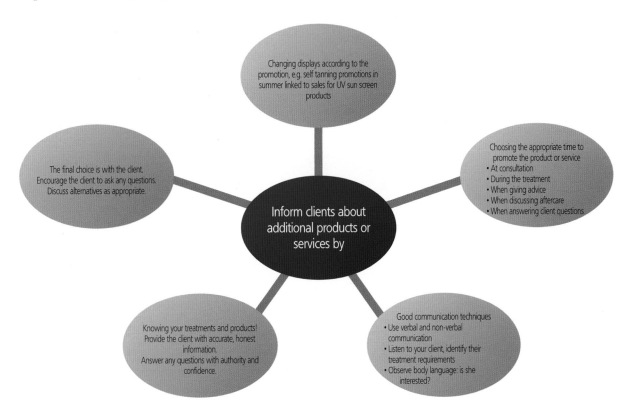

Product displays must always feature in the beauty treatment area. As the beauty therapist uses the products, she can discuss and recommend them for the client. If displays are there to see and to take from, the sale can be closed even before the client returns to reception. Although in theory clients can of course change their minds between the treatment area and actually paying, in practice once they have the product in their hands they will go on to buy it.

Displays

Ellisons

A cosmetic range

Most small salons will design and create their own displays using the counter **display packs** provided by the product companies. Some will have a professional **window dresser** to regularly change the window displays for the best effect.

Displays should be well stocked, with smart undamaged packaging. Eye-level displays are best and should ideally be accessible. Change the display regularly according to the promotion, e.g. UV skin protection products in summer.

Displays must be checked and cleaned regularly – in busy salons this will usually mean daily. A window display will need to be dusted, straightened, and looked at from outside to make sure that it looks its best. The display from which products are being sold will also need to be dusted, perhaps wiped over (if testers have dripped), and straightened up. Testers need to be checked to make sure they are not sticky and spilt, and that no one has left dirty fingerprints on them.

Ellisons

Retail packs of nail polish

Gain client commitment to using additional products or services by

- Monitoring client satisfaction with use of the product or service
- Observing client body language
  – If she is interested, she will appear relaxed and attentive
  – If not, she may not agree and appear uninterested in what you are saying
- If a client appears interested, provide recommendations to enable her to make her decision
- Immediately provide the client with goods, advising on their use, or book the client for their treatment service
- Never pressure a client into a sale
- If a sale is achieved be positive about the client's good decision
- Never provide information on a product or service outside your authority. Seek guidance as applicable from the relevant person
- Ensuring the client understands any specific treatment requirements – regularity of use etc. to gain maximum treatment benefit

The range of products

It is not enough to stock just a few items and expect clients to fit in with the range you carry: different ranges must be available for each skin type, and a number of products – such as eye gel or throat cream – that will suit all skin types. Make-up and nail enamels should be attractive to all ages and types of customer. Sales must not be lost because of a lack of product range.

A retail make-up brush display

CUSTOMERS' RIGHTS

When selling and providing products and services, you need to be aware of the legislation which affects the customer's legal rights.

Legal requirements

The salon has a legal obligation to implement legislation designed to protect client's and their rights.

Health and safety

Following the consultation, you may feel that the client is unsuitable for treatment. Tactfully explain to the client why this is and ask her to seek permission from her GP before the treatment is given. The expectations of some clients may be unrealistic. If this is the case, tactfully explain why and aim to agree to a realistic treatment programme.

Remember your legal duty under the **Health and Safety at Work Act 1974** to take reasonable care to avoid harm to yourself and others. Never use equipment for which you do not have the professional expertise. As well as the obvious potential hazards, you would not have the expertise to adapt the treatment to suit the client's treatment needs, and you would not be able to provide the relevant treatment advice in order to obtain the optimum treatment results.

Data Protection Act 1998

Through communication with your client it is necessary to ask the client a series of questions before the treatment plan can be finalised.

Client details are recorded on the client record card; this information is confidential and should be stored in a secure area. The client should always understand the reason behind the questions asked of them.

Confidential information on staff or clients should only be made available to persons to whom consent has been given.

The United Kingdom has specific legislation on equality that outlaws discrimination, protecting employees and also covers the provision of goods and services.

Equal opportunities

The **Race Relations Act 1976** makes it unlawful to discriminate on the grounds of colour, race, nationality, ethnic or national origin.

The **Disability Discrimination Act (DDA) 1995** makes it unlawful to discriminate on the grounds of disability.

Under the DDA from 1996 as a provider of goods, facilities and services your workplace has the duty to ensure that clients are not discriminated against on the grounds of disability. Because of disability it is unlawful without justification to:

- Provide a service to a lesser standard
- Provide a service on worse terms
- Fail to make reasonable adjustments to the way services are provided.

From 2004 this will include failure to make reasonable adjustments to the physical features of service premises, in order to overcome physical barriers to access.

Service can be denied to a disabled person if the denial is justified and if any other client would be treated in the same way.

Your employer has a responsibility under the DDA to ensure that you receive adequate training to prevent discrimination practice, and as such is responsible for your actions. They must also make reasonable adjustments to the premises to facilitate access for disabled persons.

Equal opportunity policy

The Equal Opportunity Commission (EOC) states it is best practice for the workplace to have a written **Equal opportunities policy**. This will include a statement of the commitment to equal opportunities by the employer and the details of structure for implementing the policy.

All employees should know this policy and it should be monitored regularly to review effectiveness.

CONSUMER PROTECTION LEGISLATION

There are certain regulations and legislation that affect the way products and services can be delivered to clients. You need to be aware of the following Acts, which affect the customers legal rights.

Prices Act 1974

The price of products has to be displayed in order to prevent the buyer being misled.

Trades Description Acts 1968 and 1972

These Acts prohibit the use of false descriptions of goods and services.

The retailer must not:

- Supply misleading information
- Describe products falsely
- Make false statements.

In addition the retailer must not:

- Make false comparisons between past and present prices
- Offer products at what is said to be a 'reduced' price, unless they have been previously been on sale at the full price quoted for 28 days minimum
- Make misleading price comparisons.

When retailing the information supplied, both in written and verbal form, it must always be accurate. Products must be clearly labelled.

Resale Prices Acts 1964 and 1976

The manufacturer can supply a recommended price (MRRP), but the seller is not obliged to sell at the recommended price.

Sales and Supply of Goods Act 1994

This Act has replaced the Supply of Goods Act 1982, to include service standards requirements.

Goods must be as described, of merchantable quality and fit for their intended purpose. The Act also covers the conditions under which customers can return goods.

Consumer Protection Act 1987

This Act implements the European Community (EC) directive, ensuring that the consumer is protected against services and products, used or sold, which are unsafe. Dissatisfied clients may contact a number of organisations dealing with consumer protection for legal advice. If proven at fault the business will face legal action.

Consumer Safety Act 1978

This Act aims to reduce risk to consumers from potentially dangerous products.

Consumer Protection (Distance Selling) Regulations 2000

These regulations are derived from a European Directive and cover the supply of goods/services made between suppliers acting in a commercial capacity and consumers. They are concerned with purchases made by telephone, fax, Internet, digital television, and mail order, including catalogue shopping. Consumers must receive:

- Clear information on goods or services, including delivery arrangements and payment, suppliers details and consumers' cancellation rights which should be made available in writing.
- The consumer also has a seven working day cool-off period during which they may cancel their purchase.

TIP

Create your own selling opportunity

- If the client is having a skin rejuvenating treatment you could recommend a course of facial micro-current treatments and appropriate skin care.
- If the client is going away on holiday tell her about the special 'holiday treatment package promotion', self-tanning treatments.
- If the client is having an eyelash tint, tell her how simple an eyelash perming treatment is and the difference it can make!

PROMOTIONS

Informing clients about additional products or services

Choose the most appropriate time to inform the client about additional products and services. If the client is receiving a treatment this may be at the consultation, when you are getting to know the client, during the treatment when you have the opportunity to share advice, or when discussing aftercare. Here you will be able to reinforce the importance of further products and services to enhance the treatment benefits gained. This may be further use of products or service that the client has used before or something that is new to the client.

Communication

Communication, both verbal and non-verbal, with your client is important.

Listen to your client; this will help you to identify her treatment requirements and personality.

Observe her body language: is she interested in what you are telling her?

If the client is interested, she will agree with you and her body language will be relaxed yet attentive.

If she is not interested she will probably not agree, and appear inattentive. If this happens go back to the beginning and suggest alternatives and try to regain her interest, but avoid pressurising the client.

If a sale is achieved, be positive. Smile! This will help to make her feel she has made a good decision.

Promotions

Promotions are an ideal opportunity to increase awareness of your business and its products with new and existing clients. If the promotion aims to attract further clients this may also be achieved if you market it effectively.

Is the promotion for existing clients – *internal promotion* – or to attract new clients – *external promotion*?

Whatever the aim, thoughtful planning is required to ensure its success.

The aim of the promotion should be identified and clearly understood by all staff members. A team meeting is important to discuss the aim and to gather views on how best this will be achieved.

A list of tasks to be completed should be drawn up, with dates set for their completion and names of staff who should complete each task.

Reasons for promotion include:

- It helps to motivate the staff.
- It help business profit in quieter periods such as following Christmas.
- Launch of a new product/s or piece of equipment.
- To generate and maintain client interest.
- To increase the client base.
- Incentives for clients, such as financial discounts on services booked following the promotion.

Preparation

Ensure:

- That you set your budget and work within it.
- That the venue chosen for the promotion is suitable: consider the number of attendees and the facilities and resources required – are they available and adequate? Check especially that parking is adequate.
- If additional resources are required in terms of specialist lighting and audio, has somebody booked them?
- If providing refreshments, decide what would be most suitable. Are external caterers required? Some venues will require that you use their catering facilities.
- That you prepare promotional material, including flyers, advertisements using the preferable media e.g. newspaper, radio etc. Use your client database to inform clients and invite them to the promotion.
- All staff are confident to answer questions if asked about the promotion.

Evaluation

Following the promotion, reflect on its success – did it achieve its aim and if not, why not? Discuss this with the team and analyse strengths and weaknesses. This will help with planning and implementation of future promotions.

Advertising

When advertising you should be clear about what it is you want to promote. Marketing material must be well designed. It is a good idea to have a logo which will become recognisable and which clients will associate with good quality service.

A salon web site can be used to inform people about your salon 24 hours a day, as millions of people in the UK are Internet users. An Internet consultant would be able to advise you on your requirements. This is an ideal opportunity to promote special offers. If you do not wish to have a web site you can still list your salon on local directory web sites.

Public Relations

Public relations (PR) can effectively market your business. PR can be organised by yourself or larger organisations employ a PR consultant. Examples include the local press, magazines, journals, radio and television.

Local press

The local press is important for marketing purposes. They may have a regular feature which may help you to promote the business. Offer a free treatment for a journalist for them to evaluate and report on. You may wish to work with them on offering a special prize for a competition feature, e.g. bride of the year, slimmer of the year, where the winner would receive complimentary beauty therapy services and your business would be promoted.

Local radio

Local radio which advertises is another useful method to promote the business.

Local television

Make local television aware of anything unique that they might wish to feature.

Once you have established good links with the media your professional expertise will often be sought, which is good promotion.

A group demonstration

Demonstrating to an audience needs particularly careful planning if the demonstration is to achieve the maximum benefit. Everything required must be in place: the products, the means to apply them, and all the relevant literature to be given out to the audience or clients.

What type of demonstration is required? Will you be working on one client, to demonstrate and sell a product, or demonstrating to a group? Is a range of products to be demonstrated, or just one item?

The presentation should include an introduction to the demonstrator and the product, the demonstration itself, and a conclusion with thanks to the audience and model. Written **promotional material** can be placed on the seats before the audience arrives, or handed out at an appropriate point during the demonstration; **samples** can be handed around the audience for them to try.

The demonstration itself must be clear, simple and not too long. The audience *must* be able to see what is being done and hear the commentary. Maximise the impact of the demonstration by giving the audience the opportunity to buy the product immediately.

If this is not possible – because the demonstration is in another room, away from the products, or at another venue, such as at a woman's club meeting – ensure that members of the audience leave with a **voucher** to exchange for the product. This should offer some incentive, such as a **discount**, to encourage potential buyers to make the effort to come to the salon and buy. Never sell the features and benefits to potential customers, creating the desire for the product, without also giving them the chance to buy it.

Questions must be accurate and detailed. You are the expert: show your knowledge. Do not ask the client what sort of skin she has – she is not the expert, and will probably give the wrong answer. Instead, ask more detailed questions, such as 'Does your skin feel tight?' (which may indicate dryness), or 'Do you have spots in a particular area?' (which may indicate an oily patch).

Listening is a skill. Always listen carefully to the answers your customer gives: do not talk over her answer or interrupt. Only when she has finished should you give a considered, informed reply. You may need to ask another question, or you may be able straightaway to direct her to the best product for her needs.

TIP	
An effective demonstration will always create sales. Have the product ready to sell, or give out vouchers to encourage clients to visit the business.	

TIP	
Always pay careful attention to your client and her responses. Remember: *question, listen, answer*:	

- *Question* your client as to her needs.
- *Listen* to the answer.
- *Answer* with the relevant information.

Targets

The setting of financial targets for the business and for individuals is important to enable analysis of overall performance. The salon owner must have an overall idea of productivity against the targets set. Targets may vary for different employees depending upon experience, length of service and workload.

Productivity

Levels of performance will take into account expected treatment and retail sales. Treatments are normally costed on the products used, including consumables such as cotton wool and tissues – and should include other hidden costs such as laundering of towels. There will also be a mark-up to include your overheads and profit.

Your sales volume productivity can be increased through:

- Incentives
- Promotions
- Personal targets.

Poor levels of performance and productivity may indicate a need for additional training. Also, it may be that you do n ot have staff qualified to offer a popular service: this is a skills gap. Through staff training, increased productivity and salon profit can be achieved.

Certain companies provide rewards for employees who develop ideas for increased productivity. Commission is a method of rewarding individuals who achieve and exceed the personal targets set.

Gaining client feedback

As a service industry, feedback from clients is important when measuring levels of service. It enables you to evaluate the following marketing methods, salon image and service.

Client feedback can be gathered in a variety of ways, both formally and informally.

Client questionnaires can be used at random to evaluate performance, for example following a promotion. The results should be analysed and appropriate action taken to improve areas of weakness, build on strengths and investigate potential areas of development.

Simply asking the client if she has enjoyed or been satisfied with the treatment received is another method of service evaluation.

You could also hold a client focus group to gather their opinions and offer an incentive, for example a treatment voucher as a thank you for their time.

A single client demonstration

When demonstrating to a client, for example a make-up application, have a mirror in front of her so that you can explain as you go along and the client can watch. She can then see the benefit of the product and learn how to use it at the same time. This is a simple but effective way to sell products.

Assessment of knowledge and understanding

You have now learnt about methods to promote sales of products and services to clients. This will enable you to promote additional products and services to clients, thus increasing salon income.

To test your level of knowledge and understanding, answer the following short questions. These will prepare you for your summative (final) assessment.

Identify additional products or services that are available

1 Why are retail sales important to the beauty salon?

2 Why is it important that you have a good knowledge of the products and services available in your salon?

3 How can you ensure that you are up-to-date with the beauty products and service you have on offer? Why is this important?

4 What are the opportunities that occur where you can promote a product or service? Think of examples from your experience.

Inform clients about additional products or services

1 Communication is important when selling. Why is it important to observe the client's body language?

2 In what ways can you promote the products and services available in your salon?

3 If the client required advice about a product or service on which you were not qualified to advise, what action would you take?

4 How must displays of retail stock be kept? Why is this important?

5 Clients have 'consumer rights'. Why is it important to give accurate information about products or services?

6 Name three pieces of legislation/regulations relating to the way products or services are delivered to clients to protect their legal rights.

Gain client commitment to using additional products and services

1 Why must the client's needs be ascertained before selling her products or services?

2 What are the benefits to the client of using additional products at home, as advised by the therapist?

3 Why is it important to offer a range of products and services?

4 How do you think speaking with confidence and authority on a product or service will influence the client?

5 Staff training is important to ensure that everybody is knowledgeable and able to advise clients on their questions. What other benefit does this have to the clients, employees and salon?

6 What are the benefits of sales targets set for employees to the individual and the organisation?

chapter 3

G11 Contribute to the financial effectiveness of the business

Learning objectives

This unit describes how to contribute to the financial effectiveness of the business by following procedures for the use of resources – human, stock, tools and equipment – and time and meeting your own personal targets. It describes the competencies to enable you to:

- **contribute to the effective use and monitoring of resources**
- **meet productivity and development targets**

When providing beauty therapy services it is important to use the skills you have learnt in the following core mandatory units:

Unit G1 Ensuring your own actions reduce risks to health and safety

Unit G6 Promote additional products or services to clients

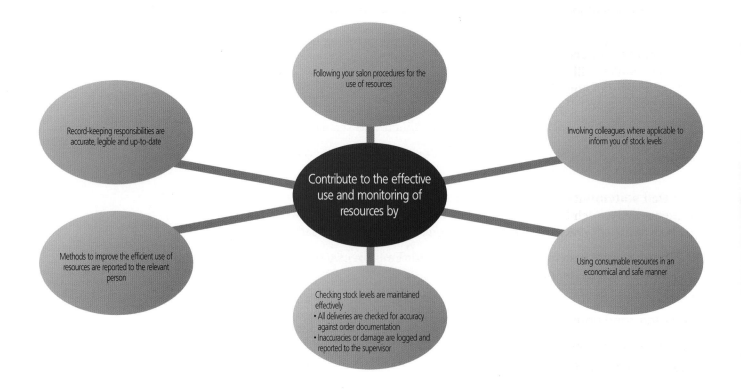

Following your salon procedures for the use of resources

Involving colleagues where applicable to inform you of stock levels

Record-keeping responsibilities are accurate, legible and up-to-date

Contribute to the effective use and monitoring of resources by

Methods to improve the efficient use of resources are reported to the relevant person

Using consumable resources in an economical and safe manner

Checking stock levels are maintained effectively
• All deliveries are checked for accuracy against order documentation
• Inaccuracies or damage are logged and reported to the supervisor

CONTRIBUTE TO THE EFFECTIVE USE AND MONITORING OF RESOURCES

Resources and how effectively and efficiently they are used contribute to the financial effectiveness of the business. Procedures should be followed according to your salon's requirements.

Resources contributing to the financial effectiveness of the business include:

- Human resources
- Stock
- Tools and equipment
- Time.

HUMAN RESOURCES

Human resources (HR) are the people employed in the business. HR is the term used to refer to their qualifications, talents and abilities. HR are the most important asset in the business, which profits from services and retail sales. At induction new staff are familiarised with their job. It is important that each member of staff has a written **job description**; this should detail their specific role, duties and responsibilities.

They will also have personal productivity and development targets, for which their performance will be reviewed at regular intervals.

This ensures that each member of staff knows what is expected of them and that they work within their limitations, involving others when their expertise is required.

There should be a **grievance** and **disciplinary** procedure, provided to each employee, which will emphasise the importance of staff discipline. This is vital in the case of complaints, poor performance, staffing issues and misconduct.

Working conditions

A **written statement of the terms of employment** or **contract of employment** (which includes all terms and conditions listed below) should be given to an employee within two months of them starting work.

The statement or contract includes the employer's and employee's name, when employment commenced, and when the period of continuous employment began.

Terms and conditions should be listed including:

- Scale or rate of pay
- Payment interval, i.e. weekly, monthly

TIP

Payment
- A statutory national minimum wage was introduced on 1 April 1999. For further information, obtain the Department of Trade and Industry (DTI) national minimum wage guide.
- As part of an employee's contract of employment, bonuses and commission are identified if applicable.
- A detailed written pay statement should be provided before or when an employee is paid. This should identify any deductions and what they are for.
- Sick pay may be provided by the employer identified in the employment contract, or if this has not been agreed, an employee may be entitled to statutory sick pay (SSP). For more information on SSP see the Inland Revenue National Insurance Contributions (IRNIC) Statutory Sick Pay leaflet.

- Hours of work
- Holidays, including bank holidays, and how holiday pay is calculated
- Place of work
- Job title and roles and responsibilities
- Information should also be provided on eligibility for sickness pay, pension schemes etc.

TIP

Working time directives taken from the Working Time Directive Legislation 1998
- Working hours must be limited to an average of no more than 48 hours per week. An employee can agree to work more but it must be in writing.
- Employee's are entitled to one uninterrupted rest day in every seven.
- A working day should be no longer than 13 hours, although this will depend upon the agreed break between each shift.
- Night workers are entitled to a break of 11 consecutive hours in each 24-hour period.
- If working more than 6 hours per day, employees are entitled to a minimum 20 minute break.
- After three months employment employees are entitled to four weeks' paid holiday a year. Holiday pay is pro rata for part-time employees.

Staff training

Investment in staff training is important. Ineffective staff training will affect the quality of services, productivity and financial performance. If staff carry out treatments in which they are inexperienced, the results will not be as effective, resulting in client dissatisfaction and potential loss of clientele.

Product knowledge, both technical and retail, is important – poor product knowledge will hinder effective sales and lose client confidence.

Good working relationships between colleagues are essential. Every member of staff, or the *team*, plays a different role, each ensuring the success of the business. Poor working relationships create an unpleasant environment for

---

Job description – Beauty Therapist

Location:	Based at salon as advised
Main purpose of job:	To ensure customer care is provided at all times To maintain a good standard of technical and client care, ensuring that up-to-date methods and techniques are used following the salon training practices and procedures
Responsible to:	Salon manager
Requirements:	To maintain the company's standards in respect of beauty services
	To ensure that all clients receive service of the best possible quality
	To advise clients on services and treatments
	To advise clients on products and after-care
	To achieve designated performance targets
	To participate in self-development or to assist with the development of others
	To maintain company policy in respect of: • personal standards of health/hygiene • personal standards of appearance/conduct • operating safely whilst at work • public promotion • corporate image as laid out in employee handbook
	To carry out client consultation in accordance with company policy
	To maintain company security practices and procedures
	To assist your manager in the provision of salon resources
	To undertake additional tasks and duties required by your manager from time to time

---

both staff and clients. Good communication systems are important, especially when staff responsibilities are shared.

Communication systems

Information may be written or orally communicated.

Oral information may be provided via the telephone or given to a client at consultation or during the treatment service. If you are in a position of responsibility, oral information may be used to deal with a complaint, when liaising with external bodies or during communication with staff on occasions such as discussing a grievance, appraisal and training. Oral information is important when advice is required quickly which will improve both performance and productivity.

When communicating orally, consider:

- The tone of your voice and body language; gestures if face-to-face.
- The setting in which the information is given.
- How clearly and concisely the information is given.

Staff communication can be improved through regular individual and group **staff meetings**. These enable the supervisor of the salon to update the staff on new initiatives, as well as providing an opportunity to share ideas for system and individual performance improvements, and to raise and discuss any concerns.

Meetings may be **informal** – not planned, or **formal** – planned with a purpose, usually for decision-making and action. Successful formal meetings should have:

- An identified purpose.
- An agenda, indicating all topics for discussion forwarded to those participating (this should be circulated in advance of the meeting).
- A suitable venue – it may be necessary to arrange the seating to encourage participation, and if delivering a presentation to ensure all can see and hear clearly.
- A person allocated to lead the meeting, called the **chairperson**.
- A person allocated to take the minutes of the meeting, which are later circulated to those who attended and those who were unable to attend. Minutes can be distributed by traditional methods, such as paper copies, or electronically by e-mail.

Working relationships

Professional relationships with colleagues should be maintained at all times. Good working relationships will improve productivity towards individual and business targets.

General codes of conduct

Be polite and courteous with colleagues at all times:

- Never talk down to colleagues.
- Never lose your temper with a colleague in front of a client.
- Never ridicule a colleague in front of a client or other colleagues.
- If there are any personal issues between yourself and a colleague, do not show these in front of a client. Settle grievances (reasons for complaint) as soon as possible, or job satisfaction and productivity can be affected.

Grievances

It is important to understand the salon's staffing structure. If you feel you are being treated unfairly, you can report the incident to the appropriate supervisor. All staff should understand the grievance and appeals procedure.

EMPLOYMENT LEGISLATION

Working Time Directive 1998

The Working Time Directive (WTD) aims to ensure that employees are protected against adverse conditions with regard to their health and safety, caused by working excessively long hours, with inadequate rest or disrupted work patterns.

The working time directive provides for:

- a maximum 48-hour working week
- a minimum daily rest period of 11 hours
- a rest break where the working day is longer than 6 hours
- a minimum rest period of 1 day per week
- night work on average must not exceed 8 hours.

EQUAL OPPORTUNITIES

Discrimination on grounds of sex, race, disability, marital status or union membership is against the law.

Sex Discrimination Acts 1975 and 1985 and the Equal Pay Act 1970

These pieces of legislation were implemented to prevent discrimination or less favourable treatment of a man or woman on the basis of gender. The Acts cover pay and conditions as well as promotion of equal opportunities.

Race Relations Act 1976

Implemented to prevent discrimination on the basis of colour, race, ethnic or national origins. The Commission for Racial Equality has produced a code of conduct to eradicate racial discrimination practice.

Disability Discrimination Act 1995

Implemented to prevent disabled persons being discriminated against during both recruitment and employment.

Employers have a responsibility to remove physical barriers and to adjust working conditions to prevent discrimination on the basis of having a disability.

Trade Union and Labour Relations (Consolidation) Act 1992

To prevent trade union members being treated less favourably than non-members, or visa versa. If penalised the employee can complain to an employment tribunal.

INFORMATION SYSTEMS

Information systems ensure the smooth running of the business and provide data for the supervisor and external agents as legally required; for example to Customs and Excise and the Inland Revenue at the end of the financial year.

Information systems can be manual or computerised. If using a manual system you will need an index of filing to access information quickly. Computerised systems allow you to input and access information in relation to:

- Client information, personal details, records of treatments, retail sales, etc.
- Management information, data on staff and salon performance.
- Current stock levels and ordering systems.
- Daily till reports.

STOCK

Stock is the total amount of consumables for use on clients within salon services plus retail products for client purchase.

Information systems should be in place for stock maintenance, which should be accurate, up to date and legible. Responsibilities should be identified as to who:

- orders stock
- maintains stocking records and levels
- receives incoming stock, checking deliveries for quality and discrepancy
- unpacks stock and locates it in the correct storage/display area.

Salon ordering systems

Stock can be ordered from different places and in different ways.

The wholesalers

These are cash and carry outlets which sell wholesale products to businesses. Some companies offer mail-order facilities.

Representatives from companies

Some companies have sales representatives who will regularly visit the business and with whom you can place purchase orders. The order is returned to the company to be processed and despatched. Representatives are useful as they can advise you of new product ranges and promotions that you may wish to take part in, to help in increasing financial productivity.

Ordering stock

When you make an order, the supplier will normally open a credit account for you and provide information on how to order and pay. Cash and carry wholesalers do not normally have minimum orders, but mail order companies usually charge postage on small orders. It is important to consider which is the most cost-effective way to order.

Principles of stock control

Stock levels can only be maintained if accurate records are kept of how much stock the business has. The records will identify stock used, and what requires to be reordered. Maintaining accurate records avoids having to count all stock. Importantly, it also avoids you running out of stock, especially of popular items, and avoids over-ordering products.

A good stock-keeping checklist:

- **Anticipate needs** Stock must be ordered regularly, *before* it runs out. Orders should be placed as stock becomes low so new stock will be arriving as the existing stock is being used or sold. There may be short-term influences on needs such as seasonal factors, for example there may be an increased demand for cosmetic UV-screening preparations in summer.

- **Check incoming stock** What has been ordered should be checked when it arrives against a delivery note. This lists all the items that have been despatched and any that are to follow, such as items that are out of stock. Never assume that the order received will be correct. Inaccuracies must be reported to the supplier immediately, before countersigning the order and confirming the delivery. Any damaged goods must be dealt with and either returned to the sender or replaced, according to the policy of the supplier. Never return anything without the relevant paperwork or without confirmation from the supplier.

Inform your supervisor of any discrepancies as applicable.

> **TIP**
>
> **Stock orders**
> Some companies require a large minimum set-up order. This means that your money will be tied up in stock. It is important that you are confident that it will sell and will match your client market.
>   Capital should not be tied up unnecessarily and unproductively.

> **TIP**
>
> **Supplier reliability**
> It is important that your supplier is reliable. An efficient business cannot afford to be uncertain as to delivery schedules, which if late may mean certain stock items have been exhausted, affecting retail and service sales!

> **TIP** ✔
>
> **Returning goods**
> Goods may have to be returned to the supplier:
> - If they were damaged
> - If they were not what was ordered
> - If they had have been incorrectly ordered.
>
> Goods returned to the supplier should be logged using either a manual or electronic system.

- **Rotate the stock** Stock must be stored and used in rotation, so that new items go to the back of the shelf and older items are used first. This is often referred to as FIFO – first in first out.
- **Keep accurate and up-to-date records** Stock levels may be recorded manually or electronically. Whichever method is used records must be accurate and updated regularly as per the business policy, usually weekly.

Manual and computerised stock-control systems

The two main types of stock control systems used to collect and collate stock information are *point of sale systems* and *stock-check systems*, which can be manual or computerised.

Point-of-sale systems

Point-of-sale systems collect information concerning sales at the time the sale is made. The person making the sale has to complete a form, such as a sales bill, which includes stock information.

A typical sales bill

BEAUTY WORKS

CASH SALE INVOICE

Date and
Tax Point:

Invoice No: 32622

Quantity	Description	Price £	p	
1	Moisturiser (sensitive) – 20g	6	50	
1	Toner (oily) – 200ml	5	60	
1	Nail varnish – tropical red	4	50	

The Beauty Garden
Mytown
The Midlands
Tel: 456789

Goods   16.60
VAT   2.82
Invoice Total   £19.42

Computers can read price tickets coded by means of barcodes printed on the packaging. As the products are sold, the code numbers are read by the computer via a scanning barcode reader, which recognises the product and automatically updates its records. This system is essential for large businesses with a high rate of stock turnover.

Stock-check systems

Stock-check systems allow the stock-keeper to refer quickly to the quantity of stock available. If you have a record of how many stock items you started with and what is left, you will know immediately how many you have sold.

With a regular stock check you can set a reorder level: whenever the quantity of goods falls to a predetermined level, it is time to reorder this product.

A simple stock-check system is the stock record card. With a regular stock check you can set a reorder level. Whenever the quantity of goods falls to a predetermined level, it is time to reorder this product. Alternatively, stock information is fed into the computer, which analyses the sales details, recalculates stock levels and calculates when to reorder, and other details as required. This provides automated stock control information and printouts for use when performing manual stock-taking checks.

The stock-taking record needs to show:

- a description of the product and its size
- how much is in stock
- what has been sold and used
- what has come in
- the minimum and maximum holding levels
- the point at which the product is to be reordered.

ISBN 0-333-68902-X

A bar code

Manual stock recording system

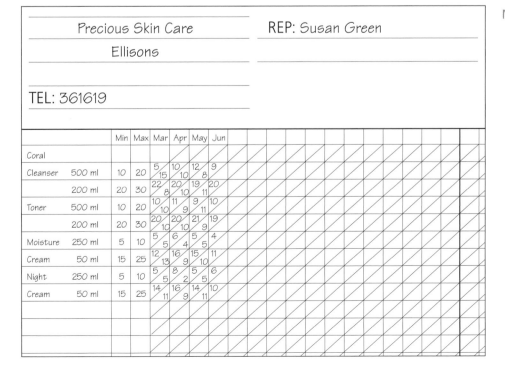

Precious Skin Care
Ellisons

REP: Susan Green

TEL: 361619

		Min	Max	Mar	Apr	May	Jun
Coral							
Cleanser	500 ml	10	20	5 / 15	10 / 10	12 / 8	9
	200 ml	20	30	22 / 8	20 / 10	19 / 11	20
Toner	500 ml	10	20	10 / 10	11 / 9	9 / 11	10
	200 ml	20	30	20 / 10	20 / 10	21 / 9	19
Moisture	250 ml	5	10	5 / 5	6 / 4	5 / 5	4
Cream	50 ml	15	25	12 / 13	16 / 9	15 / 10	11
Night	250 ml	5	10	5 / 5	8 / 2	5 / 5	6
Cream	50 ml	15	25	14 / 11	16 / 9	14 / 11	10

HEALTH AND SAFETY

Stock deterioration
Stock that is deteriorating may change in consistency, look discoloured, and the smell may change or become unpleasant. Bacterial or fungal growth may even be seen on the product surface.

HEALTH AND SAFETY

An employer must have **employers liability insurance** to provide cover for injury or disease an employee may get as a result of their work. The latest certificate must be displayed.

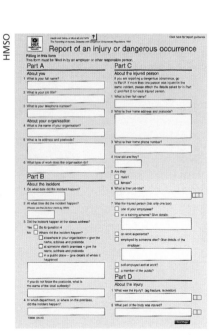

Stock rotation

When new stock arrives it must go to the back of the shelf and existing stock should be brought forward.

Many products have a shelf-life or best before date. This is because many products contain the minimum amount of preservatives in their formulation.

Products that have exceeded their shelf-life should be disposed of.

Moving and storing stock

Stock should be taken to the appropriate storage area following checking. This maybe into storage, into the retail area, or into the treatment area for use within the service.

Always take care of yourself when moving goods around the salon. Do not struggle, get assistance as necessary.

The **Health and Safety at Work Act 1974** relates to all workplace health and safety. Both employers and employees have a duty to work in as safe and healthy a way as possible. Employees have a responsibility not to endanger their own health and safety, but the employer must ensure that rules are laid down for safe working practices. They must:

- train staff in safe working practices
- provide safe systems for the handling, transit and storage of all materials.

The legislation to ensure safe working practice when handling resources is the **Manual Handling Regulations 1992**.

Manual handling in the workplace can be described as the transporting or supporting of loads by hands or by bodily force. The employer is required to carry out a risk assessment of all activities undertaken which involve manual lifting.

The risk assessment should provide evidence that the following have been considered:

- risk of injury
- the manual movement involved in performing the activity
- the physical constraint that the load incurs
- the environmental constraints imposed by the workplace
- worker's individual capabilities
- action taken in order to minimise potential risks.

HEALTH AND SAFETY

Manual handling injuries account for 25 per cent of injuries reported to enforcing authorities each year.
In the case of employees suffering a personal injury at work which results in:
- major injury
- more than 24 hours in hospital
- an incapacity to work for more than three calendar days
this must be reported under the Reporting of Injuries, Diseases and Dangerous Occurences Regulations 1995 (RIDDOR).

Safe practice advice when lifting includes: stand in front of the object with feet shoulder width apart, assess the weight of the load, only lift if it is safe to do so.

Take a firm grasp of the object. Lift from the knees, not the back. Avoid twisting the body this may lead to injury (see p.9).

When carrying, balance weights evenly in both hands and carry the heaviest part nearest to your body (see p.9).

Stock must be easily accessible and products need to be found easily. Place the labels of stock towards the front.

Remember the oldest stock should be issued first – FIFO. Therefore, place new stock at the back of the shelves.

Certain substances may require special storage and handling requirements. Legislation relating to the storage and handling of resources is located in the **Control of Substances Hazardous to Health Regulations (COSHH) 1998**. All cosmetic products come under the strict legislation of the **Cosmetics Products (Safety) Regulations 1989**. Written by the Cosmetic, Toiletry and Perfumery Association (CTPA), with the co-operation of the Hairdressing and Beauty suppliers Association (HBSA).

Security

Security concerns should be taken into consideration to prevent loss of stock through theft.

- The retail area should be designed to be in full view of staff, with a sercurity camera placed for additional security.
- Retail and product resources should be kept in a secure area, accessed only by those with authority to do so.
- Open display areas should be stocked with replica 'dummy' products and minimal sample products.

Dealing with theft

If you suspect a client of stealing and you have reasonable evidence, you have the right to make a citizen's arrest under the Police and Criminal Evidence Act 1984. You must know your employer's policy on theft and apprehending a thief.

Below is additional legislation relevant to beauty therapy salons relating to technical services and retail resources.

CONSUMER PROTECTION LEGISLATION

You must be aware of current legal requirements relating to the sale and retail of goods. These are identified in Chapter 2, p.45.

Consumer Protection Act 1987

This Act follows European Community (EC) directives to protect the customer from unsafe, defective services and products that do not reach safety standards. It also covers misleading price indications about goods or services available from a business.

TOOLS AND EQUIPMENT

All physical resources should be provided in sufficient quantity and of a suitable standard to comply with all relevant health and safety requirements and legislation. All tools and equipment should be cleaned after every use, then sterilised or disinfected in an appropriate way.

Adequate staff training should be given to ensure staff use equipment in the most efficient, safe manner. When purchasing equipment it is important to consider the following:

- Is there a client demand for it?
- Is it possible to lease the equipment? (This is useful when the equipment is very expensive.)
- Is it durable? In the event of it breaking, what back-up support is provided?

If equipment appears faulty in any way staff should report it to the supervisor immediately.

Adequate records should also be kept to show when equipment has been electrically checked and serviced, usually every 12 months in compliance with the **Electricity at Work Regulations Act 1989** (EAW Regulations), by a qualified electrician. An electrical testing record should be kept for each piece of equipment.

TIME

Time management is important. When booking clients for a service it is essential that sufficient time is allocated to the service. In a salon, therefore, the receptionist's role is important ensuring that clients are booked correctly for their treatment.

It is also important to carry out treatments in the allocated time and not to overrun, to avoid keeping future clients waiting for their treatment.

When booking time for a treatment, there may be preparation time to consider. Also, some specialist treatments may require longer following manufacturer's instructions.

The table below is a list of commercial times allocated to different Level 3 services.

TIP

In the case of overrunning, seek and follow the supervisor's advice on the most effective remedial action. If the client cannot wait, the solution may be to offer an alternative therapist or an alternative treatment time. If the client is able to wait, make the wait as enjoyable as possible, for example, offer refreshments or magazines. Another therapist may be able to prepare the client for you.

Service (excluding consultation and preparation)	Max time (mins)
1 All facial treatments	60
2 Nail extensions	120
3 Partial body massage	30
4 Full body massage without head	60
5 Full body massage including head	75
6 Aromatherapy body massage	60
7 Aromatherapy face and body massage	75
8 Indian head massage	45

Note: Standard service times have not been specified for the following treatments:

9 Camouflage treatment

10 Make-up design

11 Maintain and camouflage of nail structures

12 Nail art services

13 Nail art design

14 Epilation

15 Body treatments

16 Spa treatments

This is because service times will vary dramatically according to client needs, treatment requirements and service delivery.

Ensure that you regularly check scheduled appointments and plan ahead where you can see any potential problem – put a strategy in place to rectify it. This may involve asking others to help you.

Working under pressure

Sometimes you will be extremely busy and may be feeling tired and irritable. This is not your client's or colleague's problem, however! Remain cheerful, courteous and helpful. You should also use your initiative in helping others, for example preparing a colleague's work area when you are free and they are busy.

You must be able to cope with the unexpected:

- clients arriving late for appointments;
- client's treatments overrunning the allocated treatment times;
- double bookings, with two clients requiring treatment at the same time;
- the arrival of unscheduled clients;
- changes to the bookings.

With effective teamwork such situations can usually be overcome.

HEALTH AND SAFETY +

Relevant health and safety considerations should also be considered. If the client requires a skin test or consultation before the service is received, this should be discussed when the client makes the appointment. Income will be lost and the client will be disappointed if, when they arrive for the service they find they are unable to have it because of poor reception management.

TIP

- In quieter periods observe colleagues who have more advanced qualifications and experience.
- Practice your skills! The more you practise the more skilled and efficient you will become.

HEALTH AND SAFETY +

The Health and Safety (First-aid) Regulations 1981 require employers to provide adequate facilities, resources and staff to enable first aid to be given to employees if they are injured or become ill at work.

Further guidance can be found in HSE document, the Approved Code of Practice and Guidance: First Aid at Work. The Health and Safety Regulations 1981 LT4.

Avoiding client dissatisfaction

Some dissatisfied clients will voice their displeasure; others will remain silent and simply not return to the salon. The situation can often be prevented through good customer care and effective communication.

- Always ensure that a client has a thorough consultation before any new service. This should be carried out by a colleague with appropriate technical expertise.
- Regularly check client satisfaction. If there is any concern, notify the supervisor of this immediately.
- Inform the client of any disruption to service – do not leave her wondering what the problem maybe. Politely inform her of the situation.
- Inconvenience caused by disruption to service can usually be compensated in some way. It is important to resolve problems and keep clients satisfied.

Customer care is vital: clients provide the salon's income and the staff wages. The success of the business depends upon client satisfaction.

Complaints procedure

Unfortunately problems in which the client cannot be appeased do sometimes arise. A **complaints procedure** is a formal standardised approach adopted by the business to hand any complaints.

Time should be spent on staff training. This time may be used to update staff on new treatment techniques or salon policy.

Although this is a time when direct income is not incurred, it has long-term benefits.

Planning the most efficient use of HR is essential, and a rota is required to ensure there are always sufficient, experienced staff available.

Careful rotating is important to allow for holidays, sickness, maternity leave and time off during the week. Certain periods of the year are busier than others, e.g. Christmas and during special promotions. It may be necessary to recruit staff during these periods to maintain an efficient service and avoid loss of clients and revenue.

You may have other responsibilities such as stock control. Ensure that you manage your time effectively to ensure that all your responsibilities are fulfilled.

Utilities

Utilities include power and water. It is important that these are used in the most economic way to contribute to the profitability of the business.

PRODUCTIVITY AND DEVELOPMENT TARGETS

In order to develop personally and to improve your skills professionally, it is important to have personal targets against which you can measure your achievement.

If these are confidential, salon policy regarding confidentiality should be observed.

Targets should follow the **SMART** principle:

- **Specific** – clearly defines
- **Measurable** – quantifiable in some way
- **Agreed** – between both parties
- **Realistic** – achievable
- **Timed** – for the duration of a fixed period.

To an employer it is important that you are consistent. You must always perform your skills to the highest standard, and present and promote a positive image of the industry and the business in which you are employed and which you represent.

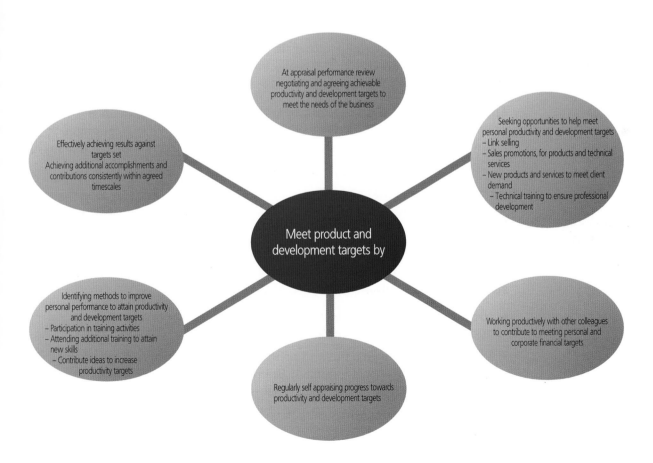

Productivity

Productivity and development targets are set for the business, for individuals and the team as a whole. These review quality, efficiency and results.

Personal targets will include:

- what training activities will take place and by what date or time;
- productivity targets, e.g. with regard to technical and retail sales;
- what tasks need to be performed;
- what standards are expected to be reached;
- when a review of progress towards the agreed targets set is to take place.

TIP

- Certain companies provide rewards for employees who develop ideas for increased productivity.
- Commission is a method of rewarding individuals who achieve and exceed targets.
- When making recommendations, clearly show the benefits of implementing your suggestions.

Appraisal

Appraisal or progress reviews are an important method of communication, where one member of staff looks at the way another member of staff is performing in their job role. It is usual for an employee to receive an appraisal from their supervisor.

Appraisals provide an opportunity to review individuals' performance against targets set. Each member of the team will have their own strengths and weaknesses and it is important to utilise their strengths and action plan to improve weaknesses with appropriate personal goals.

Performance appraisal will look at:

- Results achieved against agreed targets set.
- Additional accomplishments and contributions.

This may seem daunting, but it is an important and useful process. You can also use it to your advantage:

- Identify with your supervisor the tasks you see that need to be accomplished, and how these will be met.
- Identify training needs, this will provide you with a greater range of skills and expertise. This will ultimately improve your opportunities for promotion, giving you increased responsibilities.
- Identify obstructions which are affecting your progress.
- Identify and amend any changes to your role.

- Identify what additional responsibilities you would like.
- Identify and focus on your achievements to date against targets set.
- Update your action plan, which will help you achieve your targets.

If personal targets are not being met it is important to identify the problem. Following this new performance targets should be put in place to resolve any difficulties.

At the next appraisal the agreed objectives and targets set for the previous period will be reviewed.

Being positive about negative feedback

Your appraisal may not always be a positive experience. It is important to be positive about improvements and any recommendations to improve your performance, and to work towards achieving these.

Not meeting targets may ultimately result in disciplinary procedure which can lead to dismissal.

Your achievement of the productivity targets set leads to the financial effectiveness of the business.

> **TIP**
>
> Internal promotion may require an employee to put in extra work, take on more responsibility or come up with new ideas.

Assessment of knowledge and understanding

You have now learnt about the about the business resources available and how they can be effectively utilised to meet the financial targets of the business.

To test your level of knowledge and understanding, answer the following short questions. These will prepare you for your summative (final) assessment.

Salon procedures and requirements

1 What is the function and what are the benefits of an induction process?

2 What should be included in a job description?

3 Why is it necessary to have a job description?

4 Identify four different relevant workplace health and safety regulations and give examples of how they are implemented and monitored in the workplace.

5 How often should electrical equipment be safety tested? Who carries out this procedure?

6 What action should be taken in the event of the malfunction of a piece of electrical equipment?

7 How should a large box be lifted from floor level to be placed on the work surface?

8 State four different legal requirements regarding the sale of retail goods.

9 What security measure can be taken to prevent theft of stock?

Resource use, monitoring and recording

1 Why should stock obstructions that prevent access always be removed immediately?

2 What does the abbreviation COSHH stand for? Why is it important to follow the supplier's and manufacturer's instructions for the safe storage of materials and products?

3 When unpacking an order of new stock you find that a glass container has broken. How should this be disposed of?

4 How and where can you order stock?

5 What are the main points of good stock-keeping?

6 Why must accurate stock records be kept?

7 When should goods be returned?

8 What could happen if goods were not stored correctly?

9 How should flammable liquids be stored?

Communication

1 Why is it important to communicate effectively?

2 Why is it important to maintain positive relationships with your colleagues?

3 a. What is the benefit of involving others to rectify a problem, e.g. a client arriving without an appointment she thinks she has already made. What action would you take in this situation?
   b. What benefit does it have for you and the business to efficiently rectify problems such as the above?

4 List examples of effective teamwork.

5 Feedback on your job role performance may not always be positive and may identify areas for improvement.
   a. Why is it important to respond positively to such feedback?
   b. How may this information improve your performance in the future?

6 If you had a grievance, how and to whom would you report this?

7 Review a service that has lost popularity, consider the reasons and draw up an action plan of how you can renew interest in the treatment to increase business. Discuss your ideas with your supervisor.

Work and time management

1 Why is it important to work to a commercial treatment time when delivering treatment services?

2 How would you organise the effective promotion of a micro-dermabrasion treatment which is to be introduced to ensure maximum financial productivity?

List all the different methods of promotion and how these will be effectively planned for. What considerations will you need to take into account with regard to staff training including, reception staff?

Productivity and development targets

1 What is the purpose of an appraisal or performance review?

2 Why is it important to meet your productivity and development targets?

3 What opportunities can be used in the salon to achieve your productivity and development targets? Give three examples.

4 What action would you take if you found your individual targets to be unachievable?

anatomy
and
physiology

chapter 4

Anatomy and physiology

This chapter has been written to cover the knowledge of anatomy and physiology required for students studying for an NVQ/SVQ accredited course in Beauty Therapy at Level 3. It covers the following topics:

- the cells and tissues
- the skin
- the hair
- the nails
- the skeletal system
- the nervous system
- the urinary system
- the digestive system
- the respiratory system
- the endocrine system
- the reproductive system
- the muscular system
- the heart and circulatory system
- the lymphatic system
- the brain
- the olfactory system
- the limbic system.

Anatomy and physiology knowledge and understanding is located in this chapter, but it can also be found within each of the chapters where essential anatomy and physiology are identified (see on p.76).

As a beauty therapist it is important that you have a good understanding of anatomy and physiology, as many of your treatments aim to improve the particular functioning of systems of the body. For example, a body massage will improve blood and lymph circulation locally, as you massage the skin's surface, and increase cellular renewal as you improve nutrition to the living cells and remove dead skin cells. The result is a healthier-looking skin.

ANATOMY AND PHYSIOLOGY KNOWLEDGE REQUIREMENTS

It is necessary for you to know and understand anatomy and physiology as relevant to each beauty therapy unit. This may be assessed through oral questioning, or a written test or assignment. To guide you in your studies, the **essential** anatomy and physiology you need to know and understand for each unit has been identified with a ✓ symbol in the table on the next page.

The beauty therapy units with an essential anatomy and physiology knowledge requirement are:

BT16 Epilate the hair follicle using diathermy, galvanic and blend techniques

BT17 Provide head and body massage treatments

BT18 Improve body condition using electro-therapy

BT19 Improve face and skin condition using electro-therapy

BT20 Provide Indian head massage treatment

BT21 Provide body massage using pre-blended aromatherapy oils

BT22 Enhance the appearance of natural nails using artificial nail structures

BT23 Maintain, repair and enhance artificial nail structures

BT24 Plan, design and provide nail art services to clients

BT26 Enhance appearance using cosmetic camouflage

BT28 Set up, monitor and shut down water, temperature and spa facilities

BT29 Provide specialist spa treatments

BT30 Provide UV tanning treatments

BT31 Provide self tanning treatments

BT36 Improve the appearance of the skin using micro-dermabrasion

Anatomy and Physiology ✓ essential knowledge for unit

UNIT	BT16	BT17	BT18	BT19	BT20	BT21	BT22	BT23	BT24	BT26	BT28	BT29	BT30	BT31	BT36
Structure and function of cells and tissues	✓	✓	✓	✓	✓	✓	✓	✓	✓		✓	✓	✓	✓	✓
Skin structure and function	✓	✓	✓	✓	✓	✓	✓	✓	✓	✓	✓	✓	✓	✓	✓
Factors affecting skin condition	✓	✓	✓	✓	✓	✓	✓	✓	✓	✓	✓	✓	✓	✓	✓
Structure and type of hair	✓														
Hair growth cycle	✓														
Nail structure and function							✓	✓	✓						
Nail growth							✓	✓	✓						
Muscle groups in parts of the body, position, structure and function		✓	✓	✓	✓	✓		✓	✓						
Muscle tone		✓				✓	✓	✓	✓						
Bones in parts of the body, position, structure and function		✓	✓	✓											
Structure and function of the heart			✓	✓	✓	✓	✓	✓							
Principles of the blood circulatory system	✓	✓	✓	✓	✓	✓					✓	✓			✓
Principles of the lymph system	✓	✓	✓	✓	✓	✓					✓	✓			✓
Composition and function of blood and lymph	✓	✓	✓	✓	✓	✓			✓		✓	✓			✓
Blood flow and pulse rate	✓	✓	✓	✓	✓	✓					✓	✓			✓
Central nervous system and autonomic system		✓	✓	✓	✓	✓					✓	✓			✓
Endocrine system	✓	✓													
Respiratory system		✓									✓	✓			
Olfactory system		✓													
Digestive system		✓													
Excretory system		✓													
Reproductive system		✓													

BASIC STRUCTURES

The human body consists of many trillions of microscopic **cells**. Each cell contains a chemical substance called **protoplasm**, which contains various specialised structures whose activities are essential to our health. If cells are unable to function properly, a disorder results.

Surrounding the cell is the **cell membrane**: this forms a boundary between the cell contents and their environment. The membrane has a porous surface which permits food to enter and waste materials to leave.

In the centre of the cell is the **nucleus**, which contains the **chromosomes**. On these are the **genes** we have inherited from our parents. The genes are ultimately responsible for cell reproduction and cell functioning.

The liquid within the cell membrane and surrounding the nucleus is called **cytoplasm**. Scattered throughout this are other small bodies, the **organelles**; each has a specific function within the cell.

CELLS OF THE BODY

Cells in the body tend to specialise in carrying out particular functions. Groups of cells which share function, shape, size or structure are called **tissues**. Tissues, in turn, may be grouped to form the larger functional and structural units we know as **organs**.

TIP

The skin accounts for one-eighth of the body's total weight. It measures approximately 1.5m² in total, depending on body size. It is thinnest on the eyelids (0.05 mm), and thickest on the soles of the feet (approximately 5 mm).

Types of tissue and general function

Name of tissue	Examples	General functions
Epithelial	Epidermis	Forms surfaces and linings for protection
Connective	Bone, cartilage, areolar	A structural tissue that supports, surrounds and connects different parts of the body
Muscular	Voluntary or skeletal, involuntary	Contracts and produces movement
Nervous	Neurones	Forms a communication system between different parts of the body

The skin

The human skin is an organ – the largest of the body. It provides a tough, flexible covering, with many different important functions.

FUNCTIONS OF THE SKIN

Protection

The skin protects the body from potentially harmful substances and conditions.

- The outer surface is **bactericidal**, helping to prevent the multiplication of harmful micro-organisms. It also prevents the absorption of many substances (unless the surface is broken), because of the construction of the cells on its outer surface which form a chemical and physical barrier.
- The skin cushions the underlying structures from physical injury.
- The skin provides a **waterproof coating**. Its natural oil, **sebum**, prevents the skin from losing vital water, and thus prevents skin dehydration.
- The skin contains a pigment called **melanin**. This absorbs harmful rays of ultraviolet light.

HEALTH AND SAFETY

Skin protection
Although the skin is structured to avoid penetration of harmful substances by absorption, certain chemicals can be absorbed through the skin. Always protect the skin when using potentially harmful substances.

Heat regulation

Body **temperature** is controlled in part by heat loss through the skin and by sweating.

Excretion

Small amounts of certain **waste products**, such as water and salt, are removed from the body by excretion through the surface of the skin.

Warning

The skin affords a warning system against outside invasion. **Redness** and **irritation** of the skin indicate that the skin is intolerant to something, either external or internal.

Sensitivity

The skin allows the feelings of **touch**, **pressure**, **pain**, **heat** and **cold**, and allows us to recognise objects by their feel and shape.

Nutrition

The skin provides storage for **fat**, which provides an energy reserve. It is also responsible for producing a significant proportion of our **vitamin D**, which is created by a chemical action when sunlight is in contact with the skin.

Moisture control

The skin controls the movement of moisture from within the deeper layers of the skin.

THE STRUCTURE OF THE SKIN

If we looked within the skin, using a microscope, we would be able to see two distinct layers: the **epidermis** and the **dermis**. Between these layers is a specialised layer which acts like a 'glue', sticking the two layers together: this is the **basement membrane**. If the epidermis and dermis become separated, body fluids fill the space, creating a **blister**.

Situated below the epidermis and dermis is a further layer, the **subcutaneous layer** or **fat layer**. The fat layer consists of cells containing fatty deposits, called adipose cells. The thickness of the subcutaneous layer varies according to the body area, and is, for example, very thin around the eyes.

The fatty layer has a protective function and:

- acts as an insulator to conserve body heat
- cushions muscles and bones below from injury
- acts as an energy source as excess fat is stored.

Skin

THE EPIDERMIS

The epidermis is located directly above the dermis. It is composed of five layers, with the surface layer forming the outer skin – what we can see and touch. The main function of the epidermis is to protect the deeper living structures from invasion and harm from the external environment.

Nourishment of the epidermis, essential for growth, is received from a liquid called the **interstitial fluid**.

Each layer of the epidermis can be recognised by its shape and by the function of its cells. The main type of cell found in the epidermis is the **keratinocyte**, which produces the protein **keratin**. It is keratin that makes the skin tough and that reduces the passage of substances into or out of the body.

Over a period of about four weeks, cells move from the bottom layer of the epidermis to the top layer, the skin's surface, changing in shape and structure as they progress. The process of cellular change takes place in stages.

TIP

The epidermis is the most significant layer of the skin with regard to the external application of skin-care cosmetics and make-up.

TIP

Every five days we shed a complete surface layer. About 80 per cent of household dust is composed of dead skin cells.

- *The cell is formed* – by division of an earlier cell.
- *The cell matures* – it changes structure and moves upwards and outwards.
- *The cell dies* – it moves upwards and becomes an empty shell, which is eventually shed.

The layers of the epidermis

The layers of the epidermis

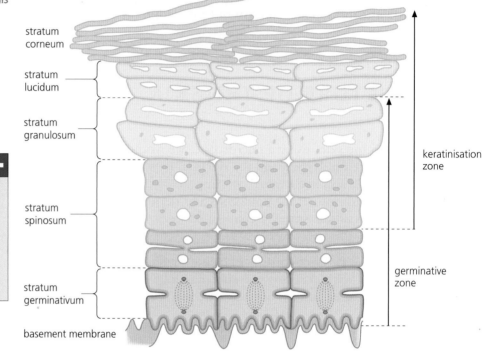

The germinative zone

In the **germinative zone** the cells of the epidermis are living cells.

Stratum germinativum

The **stratum germinativum**, or **basal layer**, is the lowermost layer of the epidermis. It is formed from a single layer of column-shaped cells joined to the basement membrane. These cells divide continuously and produce new epidermal cells (keratinocytes). This process of cell division is known as mitosis.

Stratum spinosum

The **stratum spinosum**, or **prickle-cell layer**, is formed from two to six rows of elongated cells; these have a surface of spiky spines which connect to surrounding cells. Each cell has a large nucleus and is filled with fluid.

Langerhan cells and melanocyte cells

Two other important cells are found in the germinative zone of the epidermis.

Langerhan cells **Langerhan cells** absorb and remove foreign bodies that enter the skin. They then move from the epidermis to the dermis below, and finally enter the lymph system (the body's waste-transport system).

Melanocytes **Melanocytes** are the cells that produce the skin pigment **melanin**, which contributes to our skin colour. About one in every ten germinative cells is a melanocyte. Melanocytes are stimulated to produce melanin by ultra-violet rays, and their main function is to protect the other epidermal cells in this way from the harmful effects of ultra-violet.

The quantity and distribution of melanocytes differs according to race. In a white Caucasian person the melanin tends to be destroyed when it reaches the granular layer (see below). With stimulation from artificial or natural ultra-violet light, however, melanin will also be present in the upper epidermis.

In contrast a black skin has melanin present in larger quantities throughout *all* the epidermal layers, a level of protection that has evolved to deal with bright ultra-violet light. This increased protection allows less ultra-violet to penetrate the dermis below, reducing the possibility of premature ageing from exposure to ultra-violet light. The more even quality and distribution of melanin also means that people with dark skins are less at risk of developing skin cancer.

Another pigment, **carotene**, which is yellowish, also occurs in epidermal cells. Its contribution to skin colour lessens in importance as the amount of melanin in the skin increases.

Skin colour also increases when the skin becomes warm. This is because the **blood capillaries** at the surface dilate, bringing blood nearer to the surface so that heat can be lost.

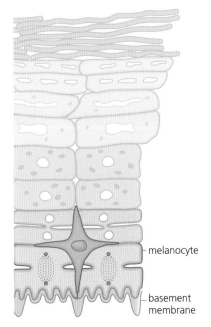

melanocyte

basement membrane

A melanocyte

TIP ✔

Many skin-care products and cosmetics, including lipsticks and mascaras, now contain *sunscreens*. This is because research has shown that ultra-violet exposure is the principal cause of skin ageing.

HEALTH AND SAFETY ✚

Potential dangers and risks of over-exposure to UV radiation
vitiligo: Lack of skin pigment is called *vitiligo* or *leucoderma*. It can occur with any skin colour, but is more obvious on a dark skin. Avoid exposing such skin to ultra-violet light as it does not have the melanin protection
sunburn: If the skin becomes red on exposure to sunlight, this indicates that the skin has been over-exposed to ultra-violet. It will often blister and shed itself
keratitis: inflammation of the cornea (the transparent front to the eye)
conjunctivitis: inflammation of the conjunctiva (the thin skin covering the cornea and eyelids)
cataracts: changes to the lens of the eye, making it opaque
skin cancer: this is more common in fair-skinned people and those who have suffered episodes of sunburn during childhood. It can take many years to develop
skin ageing: changes to connective tissues in the dermis make skin less elastic, showing more wrinkles and folds. The epidermis becomes thicker and more leathery
allergic reactions: exposure to sunlight may induce allergic reactions including **prickly heat** – a prickly, burning sensation accompanied by a rash, and **polymorphic light eruption** which can produce itchy, red blisters.

Stratum granulosum

The **stratum granulosum**, or **granular layer**, is composed of one, two or three layers of cells which have become much flatter. The nucleus of the cell has begun to break up, creating what appear to be granules within the cell cytoplasm. These are known as **keratohyaline granules** and later form keratin. At this stage the cells form a new, combined layer.

The keratinisation zone

The **keratinisation zone**, or **cornified zone**, is where the cells begin to die and where finally they will be shed from the skin. The cells at this stage become progressively flatter, and the cell cytoplasm is replaced with the hard protein keratin.

Stratum lucidum

The **stratum lucidum**, **clear layer** or **lucid layer**, is only seen in non-hairy areas of the skin such as the palms of the hands and the soles of the feet. The cells here lack a nucleus and are filled with a clear substance called **eledin**.

Stratum corneum

The **stratum corneum**, or **cornified layer**, is formed from several layers of flattened, scale-like overlapping cells, composed mainly of keratin. These help to reflect ultra-violet light from the skin's surface; black skin, which evolved to withstand strong ultra-violet, has a thicker stratum corneum than does Caucasian skin.

It takes about three weeks for the epidermal cells to reach the stratum corneum from the stratum germinativum. The cells are then shed, a process called **desquamation**.

THE DERMIS

The dermis

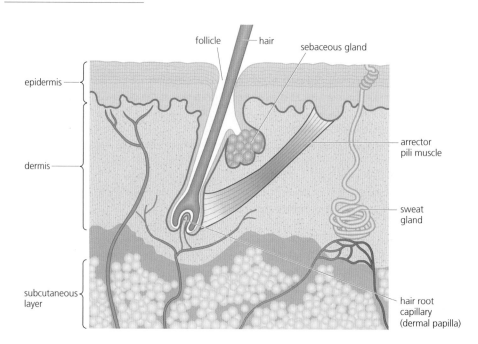

HEALTH AND SAFETY

Calluses
Constant friction causes the skin to thicken as a form of protection, developing calluses.

TIP ✔

The skin will become much thicker in response to friction. A client with a manual occupation may therefore develop hard skin (calluses) on her hands. The skin condition can be treated with an *emollient* preparation, which will moisturise and soften the dry skin.

The dermis is responsible for the elasticity of the skin. It also contains the skin appendages – nerves, blood vessels, glands and hair follicles.

The dermis is the inner portion of the skin, situated underneath the epidermis and composed of dense **connective tissue**. It is much thicker than the epidermis.

The reticular layer

The dermis contains a network of protein fibres called the **reticular layer**. These fibres allow the skin to expand, to contract, and to perform intricate, supple movements.

This network is composed of two sorts of protein fibre, yellow **elastin** fibres and white **collagen** fibres: elastin fibres give the skin its elasticity, and collagen fibres give it its strength. The fibres are produced by specialised cells called **fibroblasts**, and are held in a gel called the **ground substance**.

While this network is strong, the skin will appear youthful and firm. As the fibres harden and fragment, however, the network begins to collapse, losing its elasticity. The skin then begins to show visible signs of ageing.

A major cause of damage to this network is unprotected exposure of the skin to ultraviolet light and to weather. Sometimes, too, the skin loses its elasticity because of a sudden increase in body weight, for example at puberty or pregnancy. This results in the appearance of **stretch marks**, streaks of thin skin which is a different colour from the surrounding skin: on a white skin they appear as thin reddish streaks; on a black skin they appear slightly lighter than the surrounding skin. The lost elasticity cannot be restored.

Mature skin

The change in appearance of women's skin during ageing is closely related to the altered production of the hormones oestrogen, progesterone and androgen at the menopause.

Mature skin has the following characteristics:

- The skin becomes dry, as the sebaceous and sudoriferous glands become less active.
- The skin loses its elasticity as the elastin fibres harden, and wrinkles appear due to the cross-linking and hardening of collagen fibres.
- The epidermis grows more slowly and the skin appears thinner, becoming almost transparent in some areas such as around the eyes, where small veins and capillaries show through the skin.
- Broken capillaries appear, especially on the cheek area and around the nose.
- The facial contours become slack as muscle tone is reduced.
- The underlying bone structure becomes more obvious, as the fatty layer and the supportive tissue beneath the skin grow thinner.
- Blood circulation becomes poor, which interferes with skin nutrition, and the skin may appear sallow.

HEALTH AND SAFETY

Sunbathing
When sunbathing, always protect the skin with an appropriate protective sun-care product, and always use an emollient after-sun preparation to minimise the cumulative effects of premature ageing.

HEALTH AND SAFETY

UV light and ageing
The ageing process is accelerated when the skin is regularly exposed to ultraviolet light.

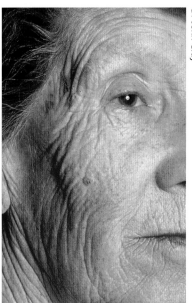

Dr John Gray

Aged skin

ACTIVITY

The ageing process
Cut out photographs from magazines or newspapers showing men and women of different cultures and various ages.
1 Can you identify the visible characteristics of ageing?
2 Does ageing occur at the same rate in men and women and in different cultures?
3 Discuss your findings with your tutor.

TIP

Mild acids, such as the natural fruit acids used in face creams and known as AHA's, allow the removal of surface cells by dissolving the compounds holding them together. A stronger AHA called glycollic acid is used in some anti-ageing preparations. These are designed to remove the dull outer layer of cells and reveal fresher skin beneath but continuous use can make the skin sore.

Stronger acids have a shrinking or drying effect on the skin. The very strong AHA, salicylic acid, is included in some preparations used to destroy warts.

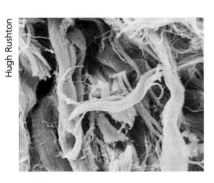

Collagen and elastin fibres

- Due to the decrease in metabolic rate, waste products are not removed so quickly, and this leads to puffiness of the skin.
- Patches of irregular pigmentation appear on the surface of the skin, such as lentigines and chloasmata.

The skin may also exhibit the following skin conditions, although these are not truly *characteristic* of an ageing skin:

- Dermal naevi may be enlarged.
- Sebhorrheic warts may appear on the epidermal layer of the skin.
- Verruca filiformis warts may increase in number.
- Hair growth on the upper lip or chin, or both, may become darker or coarser, due to hormonal imbalance in the body.
- Dark circles and puffiness may occur under the eyes.

Nerve endings

TIP

Sensory nerve endings are most numerous in sensitive parts of the skin, such as the fingertips and the lips.

The dermis contains different types of sensory **nerve endings**, which register touch, pressure, pain and temperature. These send messages to the **central nervous system** and the **brain**, informing us about the outside world and what is happening on the skin's surface. The appearance of each of these nerve endings is quite varied.

The papillary layer

Near the surface of the dermis are tiny projections called **papillae**; these contain both nerve endings and blood capillaries. This part of the dermis is known as the **papillary layer**, and it also supplies the upper epidermis with its nutrition.

Growth and repair

The body's blood system of arteries and veins continually brings blood to the capillary networks in the skin and takes it away again. The blood carries the nutrients and oxygen essential for the skin's health, maintenance and growth, and takes away waste products.

HEALTH AND SAFETY

Scars
When the surface has been broken, the skin at the site of the injury is replaced but may leave a scar. This initially appears red, due to the increased blood supply to the area, required while the skin heals. When healed, the redness will fade.

Defence

Within the dermis are the structures responsible for protecting the skin from harmful foreign bodies and irritants.

One set of cells, the **mast cells**, burst when stimulated during inflammation or allergic reactions, and release **histamine**. This causes the blood vessels nearby to enlarge, thereby bringing more blood to the site of the irritation.

In the blood, and also in the lymph and the connective tissue, are another group of cells: the **macrophages**. These destroy micro-organisms and engulf dead cells and other unwanted particles.

Waste products

Lymph vessels in the skin carry a fluid (**lymph**) containing waste products such as used blood cells. The waste products are eliminated, and usable protein is recycled for further use by the body.

Control of functioning

Hormones are chemical messengers transported in the blood. They control the activity of many organs in the body, including the cells and glands in the skin. These include **melanosomes**, which produce skin pigment, and the **sweat glands** and **sebaceous glands**.

Hormone imbalance at different times of our life may disturb the normal functioning of these cells and structures, causing various **skin disorders**.

Skin appendages

Within the dermis are structures called **skin appendages**. These include:

- sweat glands
- hair follicles, which produce hair
- sebaceous glands
- nails.

TIP

Appropriate external massage movements can be used to increase the blood supply within the dermis, bringing extra nutrients and oxygen to the skin and to the underlying muscle. At the same time, the lymphatic circulation is increased, improving the removal of waste products that may have accumulated.

ACTIVITY

The emotions
Emotions can affect blood supply to the skin: blood vessels in the dermis may enlarge or constrict. Think of different emotions, and how these might affect the appearance of the skin.

Sweat glands

Sweat glands or **sudoriferous glands** are composed of **epithelial tissue**, which extends from the epidermis into the dermis. These glands are found all over the body, but are particularly abundant on the palms of the hands and the soles of the feet. Their function is to regulate body temperature through the evaporation of sweat from the surface of the skin. Fluid loss and control of body temperature are important to prevent the body overheating, especially in hot, humid climates. For this reason, perhaps, sweat glands are larger and more abundant in black skins than white skins.

> **HEALTH AND SAFETY** ✚
>
> Moisture balance
> Excessive sweating, which can occur through exposure to high temperatures or during illness, can lead to *skin dehydration* – insufficient water content. Fluid intake must be increased to rebalance the body fluids.

> **TIP** ✔
>
> Pores allow the absorption of some facial cosmetics into the skin. Many facial treatments are therefore aimed at cleansing the pores, some with a particularly deep cleansing action, as with *cosmetic cleansers* and *facial masks*.
>
> The pores may become enlarged, because of congestion caused by dirt, dead skin cells and cosmetics. The application of an *astringent* skin-care preparation creates a tightening effect upon the skin's surface, slightly reducing the size of the pores.

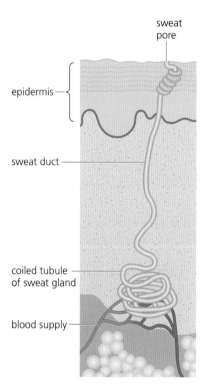

epidermis

sweat pore

sweat duct

coiled tubule of sweat gland

blood supply

An eccrine sweat gland

There are two types of sweat glands: *eccrine glands* and *apocrine glands.* **Eccrine glands** are simple sweat-producing glands, found over most of the body, appearing as tiny tubes (**ducts**). The eccrine glands are responsive to heat. These are straight in the epidermis, and coiled in the dermis. The duct opens directly onto the surface of the skin through an opening called a **pore**.

Eccrine glands continuously secrete small amounts of sweat, even when we appear not to be perspiring. In this way they maintain the body temperature at a constant 36.8°C.

Apocrine glands are found in the armpit, the nipples, and the groin area. This kind of gland is larger than the eccrine gland, and is attached to a hair follicle. Apocrine glands are controlled by hormones, becoming active at puberty. They also increase in activity when we are excited, nervous or stressed. The fluid they secrete is thicker than that from the eccrine glands, and may contain urea, fats, sugars and small amounts of protein. Also present are traces of aromatic molecules called **pheromones** which are thought to cause sexual attraction between individuals.

An unpleasant smell – **body odour** – develops when apocrine sweat is broken down by skin bacteria. Good habits of personal hygiene will prevent this.

> **ACTIVITY** ↔
>
> Preventing body odour
> Produce a checklist which should be followed daily to reduce the possibility of body odour.

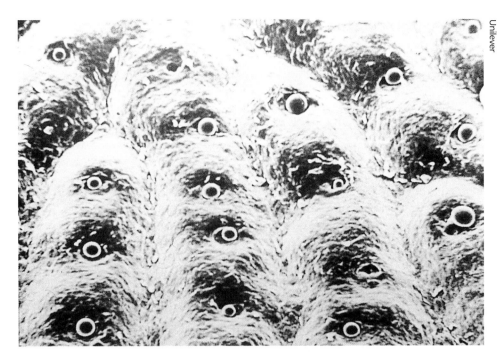

Unilever

Sweat pores

Cosmetic perspiration control To extend hygiene protection during the day, apply either a deodorant or an anti-perspirant. **Anti-perspirants** reduce the amount of sweat that reaches the skin's surface: they have an astringent action which closes the pores. **Deodorants** contain an active antiseptic ingredient which reduces the skin's bacterial activity, thereby reducing the risk of odour from stale sweat.

HEALTH AND SAFETY

Anti-perspirants
The active ingredient in most anti-perspirant products is *aluminium chlorhydrate*. This is known to cause contact dermatitis in some people, especially if the skin has been damaged by recent removal of unwanted hair. Bear this in mind if you are performing an underarm depilatory wax treatment.

THE HAIR

The structure and function of hair and the surrounding tissues

A hair is a long, slender structure which grows out of, and is part of, the skin. Each hair is made up of dead skin cells, which contain the protein called keratin.

Hairs cover the whole body, except for the palms of the hands, the soles of the feet, the lips, and parts of the sex organs.

Hair has many functions:

- *scalp hair* insulates the head against cold, protects it from the sun, and cushions it against bumps;
- *eyebrows* cushion the browbone from bumps, and prevent sweat from running into the eyes;
- *eyelashes* help to prevent foreign particles entering the eyes;
- *nostril hair* traps dust particles inhaled with the air;
- *ear hair* helps to protect the ear canal;
- *body hair* helps to provide an insulating cover (though this function is almost obsolete in humans), has a valuable sensory function, and is linked with the secretion of sebum onto the surface of the skin.

Hair also plays a role in social communication.

The structure of hair

Most hairs are made up of three layers of different types of epithelial cells: the *medulla*, the *cortex*, and the *cuticle*.

The **medulla** is the central core of the hair. The cells of the medulla contain soft keratin, and sometimes some pigment granules. There is usually no medulla in thinner hairs.

The **cortex** is the thickest layer of the hair, and is made up of several layers of closely-packed elongated cells. These contain pigment granules and hard keratin.

The **cuticle** is the protective outer layer of the hair, and is composed of thin, unpigmented flat cells. These contain hard keratin, and overlap from the base to the tip of the hair.

It is the **pigment** in the cortex that gives hair its colour. When this pigment is no longer made, the hair appears white. As the proportion of white hairs rises, the hair seems to go 'grey': in fact, however, each individual hair is either coloured as before, or white.

The parts of the hair

Each hair is recognised by three parts: the *root*, the *bulb*, and the *shaft*:

- the **root** is the part of the hair that is in the follicle
- the **bulb** is the enlarged base of the root
- the **shaft** is the part of the hair that can be seen above the skin's surface.

The structure of skin

Each hair grows out of a tube-like indentation in the epidermis, the **hair follicle**. The walls of the follicle are a continuation of the epidermal layer of the skin.

The **arrector pili muscle** is attached at an angle to the base of the follicle. Cold, aggression or fright stimulates this muscle to contract, pulling the follicle and the hair upright.

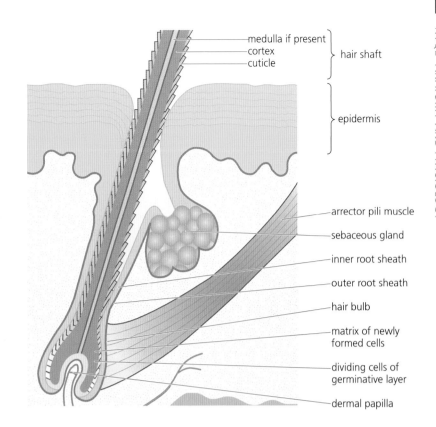

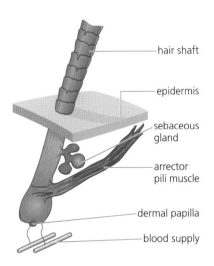

A cross-section of the hair follicle and hair

The **sebaceous gland** is attached to the upper part of the follicle; from it, a duct enters directly into the hair follicle. The gland produces an oily substance, **sebum**, which is secreted into the follicle. Sebum waterproofs, lubricates and softens the hair, and the surface of the skin; it also protects the skin against bacterial and fungal infections. The contraction of the arrector pili muscle aids the secretion of sebum.

There are two types of **sudoriferous** (sweat) **glands**: the *eccrine* and the *apocrine* glands. The **eccrine glands** are simple sweat-producing glands, distributed over most of the body's surface and responsive to heat. The **apocrine glands** are larger and deeper.

Associated with the hairs in the groin and underarm, their ducts open directly into the hair follicles near to the surface of the skin. These glands, which are under hormonal control, become active at puberty. They also become more active in response to stress. Apocrine glands produce sweat which decays with a characteristic smell.

The **dermal papilla**, a connective tissue sheath, is surrounded by a hair bulb. It has an excellent blood supply, necessary for the growth of the hair. It is not itself part of the follicle, but a separate tiny organ which serves the follicle.

The **bulb** is the expanded base of the hair root. A gap at the base leads to a cavity inside, which houses the papilla. The bulb contains in its lower part the dividing cells that create the hair. The hair continues to develop as it passes through the regions of the upper bulb and the root.

The **matrix** is the name given to the lower part of the bulb, which comprises actively dividing cells from which the hair is formed.

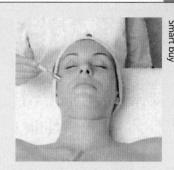

Smart buy

TIP ✔

Associated beauty therapy treatments
Epilation using diathermy or galvanism involves destroying matrix cells of the hair root. Heat can be used to destroy the cells.
Diathermic epilation causes the contents of the cells to coagulate due to the heat produced at the end of the epilation needle. This is similar to egg white coagulating as you cook it.
Galvanic epilation induces an alkali, sodium hydroxide, to form around the needle situated at the hair root which, given a little time, affects the proteins of cells and destroys them. The same alkali is also responsible for the removal of sebum in desincrustation and loosening of cells in galvanic treatments promoting skin peeling.

Desincrustation

TIP ✔

When hairs break off due to incorrect waxing technique, they will break at the level at which they are locked into the follicle by the cells of the inner root sheath.

The hair follicle The hair follicle extends into the dermis, and is made up of three sheaths: the *inner epithelial root sheath*, the *outer epithelial root sheath*, and the surrounding *connective-tissue sheath*.

The **inner epithelial root sheath** grows from the bottom of the follicle at the papilla; both the hair and the inner root sheath grow upwards together. The inner surface of this sheath is covered with cuticle cells, in the same way as the outer surface of the hair: these cells lock together, anchoring the hair firmly in place. The inner root sheath ceases to grow when level with the sebaceous gland.

The **outer epithelial root sheath** forms the follicle wall. This does not grow up with the hair, but is stationary. It is a continuation of the growing layer of the epidermis of the skin.

The **connective-tissue sheath** surrounds both the follicle and the sebaceous gland, providing both a sensory supply and a blood supply. The connective-tissue sheath includes, and is a continuation of, the papilla.

The *shape* of the hairs is determined by the shape of the hair follicle – an angled or bent follicle will produce an oval or flat hair, whereas a straight follicle will produce a round hair. Flat hairs are curly, oval hairs are wavy, and round hairs are straight. As a general rule, during waxing curly hairs break off more easily than straight hairs.

TIP ✔

An angled follicle may cause the hair to be broken off at the angle during waxing, instead of being completely pulled out with its root. If this happens, broken hairs will appear at the skin's surface within a few days. This will affect treatment application technique for electrical needle epilation.

The nerve supply The number, size and type of nerve endings associated with hair follicles is related to the size and type of follicle. The follicles of vellus hairs (see below) have the fewest nerve endings; those of terminal hairs have the most.

The nerve endings surrounding hair follicles respond mainly to rapid movements when the hair is moved. Nerve endings that respond to touch can also be found around the surface openings of some hair follicles, as well as just below the epidermis.

The three types of hair

There are three main types of hair: *lanugo*, *vellus* and *terminal*.

Lanugo hairs are found on foetuses. They are fine and soft, do not have a medulla, and are often unpigmented. They grow from around the third to the fifth month of pregnancy, and are shed to be replaced by the secondary vellus hairs around the seventh to the eighth month of pregnancy. Lanugo hairs on the scalp, eyebrows and eyelashes are replaced by terminal hairs.

Vellus hairs are fine, downy and soft, and are found on the face and body. They are often unpigmented, rarely longer than 20mm, and do not have a medulla or a well-formed bulb. The base of these hairs is very close to the skin's surface. If stimulated, the shallow follicle of a vellus hair can grow downwards and become a follicle that produces terminal hairs.

Terminal hairs are longer and coarser than vellus hairs, and most are pigmented. They vary greatly in shape, in diameter and length, and in colour and texture. The follicles from which they grow are set deeply in the dermis and have well-defined bulbs.

Hair growth

All hair has a cyclical pattern of growth, which can be divided into three phases: *anagen*, *catagen* and *telogen*.

Anagen **Anagen** is the actively growing stage of the hair – the follicle has re-formed; the hair bulb is developing, surrounding the life-giving dermal papilla; and a new hair forms, growing from the matrix in the bulb.

Catagen **Catagen** is the stage when the hair separates from the papilla. Over a few days it is carried by the movement of the inner root sheath, up the follicle to the base of the sebaceous gland. Here it stays until it either falls out or is pushed out by a new hair growing up behind it.

This stage can be very rapid, with a new hair growing straight away; or slower, with the papilla and the follicle below the sebaceous gland degenerating and entering a resting stage, telogen.

Telogen **Telogen** is a resting stage. Many hair follicles do not undergo this stage, but start to produce a new hair immediately. During resting phases, hairs may still be loosely inserted in the shallow follicles.

TIP
Some areas of the body – for example, the bikini line and underarm areas – often have terminal hairs with very deep follicles. When these hairs are removed, the resulting tissue damage may cause minor bleeding from the entrance of the follicle. Removal of these deep-seated hairs is obviously more uncomfortable than the removal of shallower hairs.

TIP
A hair pulled out at the *anagen* stage will be surrounded by the inner and outer root sheaths and have a properly formed bulb.

TIP
A hair pulled out at the *catagen* or *telogen* stage can be recognised by the brush-like appearance of the root.

The hair growth cycle

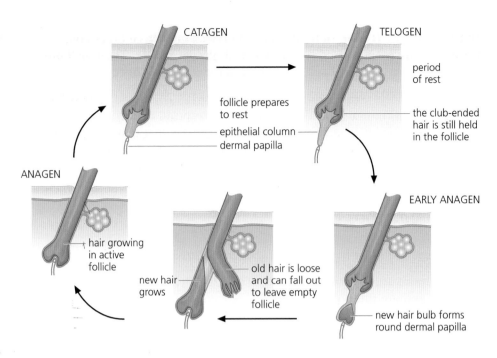

CATAGEN

follicle prepares
to rest
epithelial column
dermal papilla

TELOGEN

period
of rest

the club-ended
hair is still held
in the follicle

ANAGEN

hair growing
in active
follicle

new hair
grows

old hair is loose
and can fall out
to leave empty
follicle

EARLY ANAGEN

new hair bulb forms
round dermal papilla

TIP

Because of the cyclical nature of hair growth, the follicles are always at different stages of their growth cycle. When the hair is removed, therefore, the hair will not all grow back at the same time. For this reason, waxing can appear to reduce the quantity of hair growth. This is not so; given time, all the hair would regrow. Waxing is classed as a temporary means of hair removal.

Speed of growth

The anagen, catagen and telogen stages last for different lengths of time in different hair types and in different parts of the body:

- *scalp hair* grows for 2–7 years, and has a resting stage of 3–4 months
- *eyebrow* hair grows for 1–2 months, and has a resting stage of 3–4 months
- *eyelashes* grow for 3–6 weeks, and have a resting stage of 3–4 months.

After a waxing treatment, body hair will take approximately 6–8 weeks to return.

Because hair growth cycles are not all in synchronisation, we always have hair present at any given time. On the scalp, at any one time for example, 85 per cent of hairs may be in the anagen phase. This is why hair growth after waxing starts within a few days: what is seen is the appearance of hairs that were already developing in the follicle at the time of waxing.

Types of hair growth

Hirsutism **Hirsutism** is a term used to describe a pattern of hair growth that is abnormal for that person's sex, such as when a woman's hair growth follows a man's hair-growth pattern.

TIP

Vellus hairs grow slowly and take 2–3 months to return after waxing. They can remain dormant in the follicle for 6–8 months before shedding.

Hypertrichosis **Hypertrichosis** is an abnormal growth of excess hair. It is usually due to abnormal conditions brought about by disease or injury.

Superfluous hair **Superfluous hair** (excess hair) is perfectly normal at certain periods in a woman's life, such as during puberty or pregnancy. Terminal hairs formed at these times usually disappear once the normal hormonal balance has returned. Those newly formed during the menopause are often permanent unless treated with a permanent method of hair removal, such as electrical depilation.

Factors affecting the growth rate and quantity of hair

Hair does not always grow uniformly:

- *Time of day* Hair grows faster at night than during the day.
- *Weather* Hairs grow faster in warm weather than in cold.
- *Pregnancy* In women, hairs grow faster between the ages of 16 and 24, and (frequently) during mid-pregnancy.
- *Age* The rate of hair growth slows down with age. In women, however, facial hair growth continues to increase in old age, while trunk and limb hair increases into middle age and then decreases.
- *Colour* Hairs of different colour grow at different speeds – for example, coarse black hair grows more quickly than fine blonde hair.
- *Part of the body* Hair in different areas of the body grows at different rates, as do different types and thicknesses of hair. The weekly growth rate varies from approximately 1.5mm (fine hair) to 2.8mm (coarse hair), when actively growing.
- *Heredity* Members of a family may have heritable growth patterns, such as excess hair that starts to grow at puberty and increases until the age of 20–25.
- *Health and diet* Health and diet are crucial in the rate of hair growth.
- *Stress* Emotional stress can cause a temporary hormonal imbalance within the body, which may lead to a temporary growth of excess hair.
- *Medical conditions* A sudden unexplained increase of body hair growth may indicate a more serious medical problem, such as malfunction of the ovaries; or result from the taking of certain drugs, such as corticosteroids.

The quantity as well as the type of hair present may vary with race:

- *People of Latin extraction* tend to possess heavier body, facial and scalp hair, which is relatively coarse and straight.
- *People of Eastern extraction* tend to possess very little or no body and facial hair growth, and usually their scalp hair growth is relatively coarse and straight.
- *People of Northern European and Caucasian extraction* tend to have light to medium body and facial hair growth, with their scalp hair growth being wavy, loosely curled, or straight.
- *People of African-Caribbean extraction* tend to have little body and facial hair growth, but usually their scalp hair growth is relatively coarse and tightly curled.

HEALTH AND SAFETY

African-Caribbean clients
The body hair of African-Caribbean clients is prone to breaking during waxing, and to ingrowing after waxing. Skin damage can result in the loss of pigmentation (hypopigmentation).

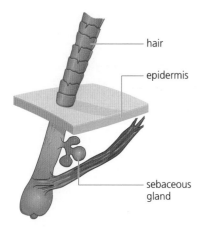

A sebaceous gland

Sebaceous glands

The **sebaceous gland** appears as a minute sac-like organ. Usually it is associated with the hair follicle with which it forms the **pilosebaceous unit**, but the two can appear independently.

Sebaceous glands are found all over the body, except on the palms of the hands and the soles of the feet. They are particularly numerous on the scalp, the forehead, and in the back and chest region. The cells of the glands decompose, producing the skin's natural oil, **sebum**. This empties directly into the hair follicle.

The activity of the sebaceous gland increases at puberty when stimulated by the male hormone, **androgen**. In adults activity of the sebaceous gland gradually decreases again. Men secrete slightly more sebum than women; and on black skin the sebaceous glands are larger and more numerous than on white skin.

Sebum is composed of fatty acids and waxes. These have **bactericidal** and **fungicidal** properties, and so discourage the multiplication of micro-organisms on the surface of the skin. Sebum also reduces the evaporation of moisture from the skin, and so prevents the skin from drying out.

> **TIP** ✔
>
> Cosmetic moisturisers mimic sebum in providing an oily covering for the skin's surface to reduce moisture.

> **HEALTH AND SAFETY** ➕
>
> **The lips**
> Sebaceous glands are not present on the surface of the lips. For this reason the lips should be protected with a lip emollient preparation, to prevent them from becoming dry and chapped.

> **HEALTH AND SAFETY** ➕
>
> **Using alkaline products**
> Because the skin has an acid pH, if alkaline products are used on it the acid mantle will be disturbed. It will take several hours for this protective film to be restored: during this time, the skin will be irritated and sensitive.

Acid mantle Sweat and sebum combine on the skin's surface, creating an acid film. This is known as the **acid mantle**, and discourages the growth of bacteria and fungi.

Acidity and alkalinity are measured by a number called the pH. An *acidic solution* has a pH of 0–7; a *neutral solution* has a pH of 7; and an *alkaline solution* has a pH of 7–14. The acid mantle of the skin has a pH of 5.5–5.6.

THE NAILS

The nail

The structure and function of the nail

Nails grow from the ends of the fingers and toes and serve as a form of protection. They also help when picking up small objects. Dark streaks caused by pigmentation are common on the nail plate of black skinned clients. These tend to increase with age.

The nail plate

The **nail plate** is composed of compact translucent layers of keratinised epidermal cells: it is this that makes up the main body of the nail. The layers of cells are packed very closely together, with fat but very little moisture.

The nail gradually grows forward over the nail bed, until finally it becomes the free edge. The underside of the nail plate is grooved by longitudinal ridges and furrows, which help to keep it in place.

In normal health the plate curves in two directions:

- transversely – from side to side across the nail
- longitudinally – from the base of the nail to the free edge.

There are no blood vessels or nerves in the nail plate: this is why the nails, like hair, can be cut without pain or bleeding. The pink colour of the nail plate derives from the blood vessels that pass beneath it.

Function: To protect the living nail bed of the fingers and toes.

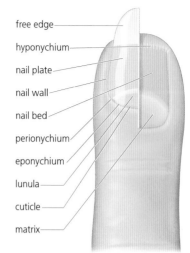

The structure of the nail

The free edge

The **free edge** is the part of the nail that extends beyond the fingertip; this is the part that is filed.

Function: To protect the fingertip and the hyponychium (see below).

The matrix

The **matrix**, sometimes called the **nail root**, is the growing area of the nail. It is formed by the division of cells in this area, which is part of the germinating layer of the epidermis. It lies under the eponychium (see below), at the base of the nail, nearest to the body. The process of keratinisation takes place in the epidermal cells of the matrix, forming the hardened tissue of the nail plate.

Function: To produce new nail cells.

The nail bed

The **nail bed** is the portion of skin upon which the nail plate rests. It has a pattern of grooves and furrows corresponding to those found on the underside of the nail plate; these interlock, keeping the nail in place, but separate at the end of the nail to form the free edge. The nail bed is liberally supplied with blood vessels, which provide the nourishment necessary for continued growth; and sensory nerves, for protection.

Function: To supply nourishment and protection.

The nail mantle

The **nail mantle** is the layer of epidermis at the base of the nail, before the cuticle.

Function: To protect the matrix from physical damage.

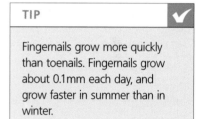

TIP

Fingernails grow more quickly than toenails. Fingernails grow about 0.1mm each day, and grow faster in summer than in winter.

The lunula

The **lunula** is located at the base of the nail, lying over the matrix. It is white, relative to the rest of the nail, and there are two theories to account for this:

- newly formed nail plates may be more opaque than mature nail plates
- the lunula may indicate the extent of the underlying matrix – the matrix is thicker than the epidermis of the nail bed, and the capillaries beneath it would not show through as well.

Function: None.

The hyponychium

The **hyponychium** is part of the epidermis under the free edge of the nail.

Function: To protect the nail bed from infection.

The nail grooves

The **nail grooves** run alongside the edge of the nail plate.

Function: To keep the nail growing forward in a straight line.

The perionychium

The **perionychium** is the collective name given to the nail walls and the cuticle area.

Function: To protect the nail.

The nail walls

The **nail walls** are the folds of skin overlapping the sides of the nails.

Function: To protect the nail plate edges.

The eponychium

The **eponychium** is the extension of the cuticle at the base of the nail plate, under which the nail plate emerges from the matrix.

Function: To protect the matrix from infection.

The cuticle

The **cuticle** is the overlapping epidermis around the base of the nail. When in good condition, it is soft and loose.

Function: To protect the matrix from infection.

ACTIVITY

Recognising nail structure
With a colleague, try to identify the structural parts of each other's nails. Write down both the parts that you can see and the parts that you cannot.

Nail growth

Cells divide in the matrix and the nail grows forward over the nail bed, guided by the nail grooves, until it reaches the end of the finger or toe, where it becomes the free edge. As they first emerge from the matrix the translucent cells are plump and soft, but they get harder and flatter as they move toward the free edge. The top two layers of the epidermis form the nail plate; the remaining three form the nail bed.

The nail plate is made up of a protein called keratin, and the hardening process that takes place in the nail cells is known as **keratinisation**.

The nail bed has a pattern of grooves and furrows corresponding to those found on the underside of the nail plate: the two surfaces interlock, holding the nail in place.

Fingernails grow at approximately twice the speed of toenails. It takes about 6 months for a fingernail to grow from cuticle to free edge, but about 12 months for a toenail to do so.

THE MUSCLES

Muscles are responsible for the movement of body parts. Each is made up of a bundle of elastic fibres bound together in a sheath, the **fascia**. Muscular tissue contracts (shortens) and produces movement. Muscles never completely relax – there are always a few contracted fibres in every muscle. These make the muscles slightly tense and this tension is called muscle tone.

Muscle tissue has the following properties:

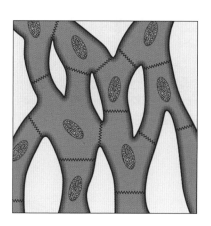

Cardiac muscle tissue

- It has the ability to contract
- It is extensible (when the extensor muscle in a joint contracts the corresponding flexor muscle will be stretched or lengthened)
- It is elastic – following contraction or extension it returns to its original length
- It is responsive – it contracts in response to nerve stimulation.

A muscle is usually anchored by a strong tendon to one bone: the point of attachment is known as the muscle's origin. The muscle is likewise joined to a second bone: the attachment in this case is called the muscle's **insertion**. It is this second bone that is moved: the muscle contracts, pulling the two bones towards each other. (A different muscle, on the other side of the bone, has the contrary effect.) Not all muscles attach to bones, however: some insert into an adjacent muscle, or into the skin itself. The muscles with which we are concerned here are those of the face, the neck and the shoulders.

Muscle tissue

There are three different types of muscle tissue:

- **cardiac muscle tissue**: found only in the heart and responsible for keeping the heart beating rhythmically
- **involuntary muscle tissue**: carries out automatic functions in the body such as maintaining blood pressure, movement of substances by peristalsis and controlling the size of the pupil of the eye

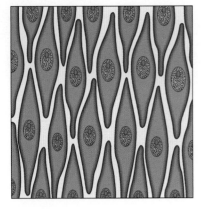

Involuntary muscle tissue

- **voluntary muscle tissue**: usually attached to the skeleton, causing movement of parts of the skeleton. This type of muscle tissue is made up of many strands lying parallel to one another. The small muscle fibres may be up to 30 cm long and around 10 to 100 thousandths of a mm in diameter. Each fibre is composed of even smaller strands called myofibrils and when these are examined closely, the mechanism of how muscles contract can be deduced.

How do voluntary muscles contract?

Voluntary muscles contract by a system of sliding filaments. Each myofibril is made up of two types of filament – thin ones composed mainly of a protein called **actin** and thick ones composed mainly of a protein called **myosin**. These filaments partially overlap. When the muscle is stimulated to contract the filaments pull over each other and overlap more. This shortens the muscle and increases its tension. The more the fibres pull together and overlap (until the actin fibres touch) the more tension is produced. Force increases as the muscle gets shorter and shorter.

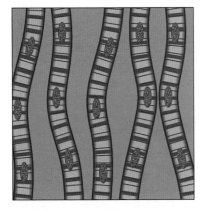

Voluntary muscle tissue

TIP	✔

Measuring microscopic structures

If you look at your ruler you will see that it is marked off in centimetres. Each centimetre is divided into ten parts. Each one of these is a millimetre. You will not see any divisions smaller than a millimetre on a ruler. Cells and small structures of the body are measured in **micrometers** (μm). There are 1000 μm in one mm. If you laid the muscle fibres across your ruler there would be between ten and one hundred in each one millimetre gap.

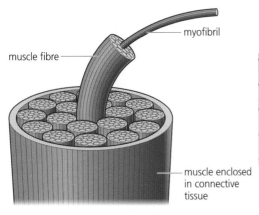

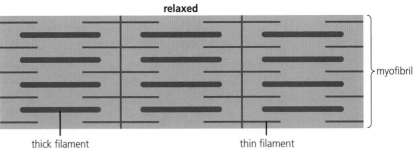

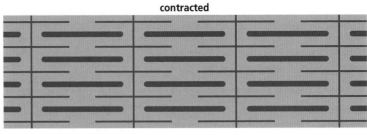

Muscle enclosed in connective tissue

The sliding filament theory of muscle contraction

THE NERVE SUPPLY

All muscles are made to work by electrical stimulation via the nerves. These, together with the **brain** and the **spinal cord**, form the nervous system.

Neurones

Nervous tissue is made up of nerve cells or neurones. These cells connect all parts of the body to the **central nervous system** (CNS – the brain and spinal cord) and conduct impulses throughout these organs.

Sensory receptors are found in many areas of the body, including the dermis of the skin, muscles, tendons and joints, nose, mouth, eye and ear. When stimulated, impulses pass from the receptor along the fibre of a **sensory (receptor) neurone** to the CNS, giving us sensations such as touch, taste, smell and hearing. Being fed such information about our environment enables us to make suitable responses.

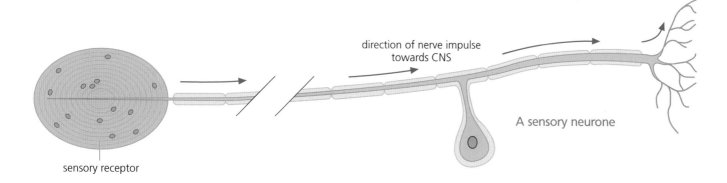

direction of nerve impulse
towards CNS

A sensory neurone

sensory receptor

Motor (effector) neurones conduct impulses from the CNS to muscles or glands of the body. Motor neurones that initiate voluntary muscle contractions form motor end plates on the muscle fibres. Each neurone stimulates between 10 and 2000 muscle fibres depending on whether the muscle makes very precise, fine movements or gross ones.

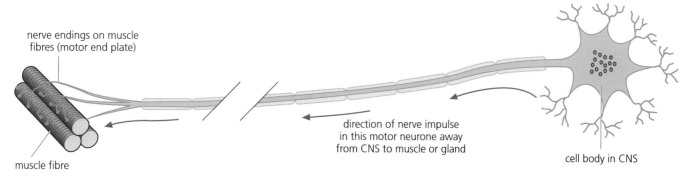

nerve endings on muscle
fibres (motor end plate)

muscle fibre

direction of nerve impulse
in this motor neurone away
from CNS to muscle or gland

cell body in CNS

A motor neurone with detail of a
motor end plate

A **nerve** is a collection of single neurones surrounded by a protective sheath. Sensory nerves contain only sensory neurones, motor nerves contain only motor neurones and mixed nerves contain both sensory and motor neurones.

HEALTH AND SAFETY

Nerve damage
Nerve cells do not reproduce; when damaged, only a limited repair occurs.

Kinds of nerve

There are two types of nerve: *sensory nerves* and *motor nerves*. Both are composed of white fibres enclosed in a sheath.

- **Sensory nerves** These receive information and relay it to the brain. They are found near to the skin's surface and respond to touch, pressure, temperature and pain.
- **Motor nerves** These are situated in muscle tissue and act on information received from the brain, causing a particular response, typically muscle movement.

Nerves of the face and neck

These nerves link the brain with the muscles of the head, face and neck.

There are 12 pairs of **cranial nerves**. Those of concern to the beauty therapist when performing a facial massage are as follows:

- the 5th cranial nerve, or **trigeminal**
- the 7th cranial nerve, or **facial**
- the 11th cranial nerve, or **accessory**.

5th cranial nerve

This nerve carries messages to the brain from the sensory nerves of the skin, the teeth, the nose and the mouth. It also stimulates the motor nerve to create the chewing action when eating. The 5th cranial nerve has three branches:

- the **ophthalmic nerve** serves the tear glands, the skin of the forehead, and the upper cheeks
- the **maxillary nerve** serves the upper jaw and the mouth
- the **mandibular nerve** serves the lower jaw muscle, the teeth and the muscle involved with chewing.

ophthalmic

maxillary

mandibular

5th cranial nerve

7th cranial nerve

This nerve passes through the temporal bone and behind the ear, and then divides. It serves the ear muscle and the muscles of facial expression, the tongue and the palate.

The 7th cranial nerve has five branches:

- the **temporal nerve** serves the orbicularis oculi and the frontalis muscles
- the **zygomatic nerve** serves the eye muscles

- the **buccal nerve** serves the upper lip and the sides of the nose
- the **mandibular nerve** serves the lower lip and the mentalis muscle of the chin
- the **cervical nerve** serves the platysma muscle of the neck.

11th cranial nerve

This nerve serves the sternomastoid and trapezius muscles of the neck and its function is to move the head and shoulders.

temporal
zygomatic
buccal
mandibular
cervical

7th cranial nerve

THE NERVOUS SYSTEM

Central nervous system

The central nervous system (CNS) is composed of the brain and spinal cord. The brain is protected by being surrounded by the bones of the cranium. The spinal cord is protected by passing through the bones (vertebrae) of the spinal column.

The brain is composed of several parts, each of which perform specific functions as described in the table.

Brain function

Part of the brain	Position	Function
Cerebrum	Consists of two hemispheres; the major part of the forebrain	Initiates and controls all voluntary muscular movement; receives sensory information (enabling us to feel, see, smell, hear and taste); the centre of thought, memory and intelligence
Cerebellum	Situated at the back of the brain; butterfly-shaped with two lateral wings	The motor coordinating centre, maintaining posture and controlling motor skills
Medulla oblongata	A continuation of the spinal cord	Controls the autonomic nervous system (e.g. heart rate and movement of food through the body); also controls involuntary reflex actions such as coughing, sneezing and swallowing
Hypothalamus	Situated above the pituitary gland to which it is linked	Contains centres controlling body temperature, thirst and hunger
Ventricle	A cavity in the brain containing cerebrospinal fluid	The fluid acts as a shock absorber, delivers nutrients and removes waste

Epilepsy

Epilepsy is a common disorder which occurs as a result of abnormal discharges of electricity across the brain. The symptoms vary from short lapses of attention to violent seizures (fits) resulting in unconsciousness. It does not affect intelligence, and seizures can successfully be prevented by drug therapy.

Nerves

A nerve is a collection of nerve fibres. All nerves emerge from the CNS. Sensory (receptor) nerves are linked to sensory receptors, while motor (effector) nerves end in a muscle or gland.

Twelve pairs of cranial nerves emerge from the brain. Some cranial nerves are sensory nerves. The second cranial nerve (the optic nerve) contains only sensory nerve fibres. It supplies the eye and is the nerve of sight. The twelfth cranial nerve is primarily a motor nerve. It contains mainly motor fibres and supplies the tongue muscles. (The sensory fibres in this nerve transmit information about the position of the tongue.) Other cranial nerves such as the fifth (trigeminal) nerve are called mixed nerves as they contain both motor fibres (to supply muscles) and sensory fibres (to relay sensations).

Thirty-one pairs of spinal nerves emerge from between the vertebrae of the spinal column. All the spinal nerves are mixed nerves.

A vertical section through the brain

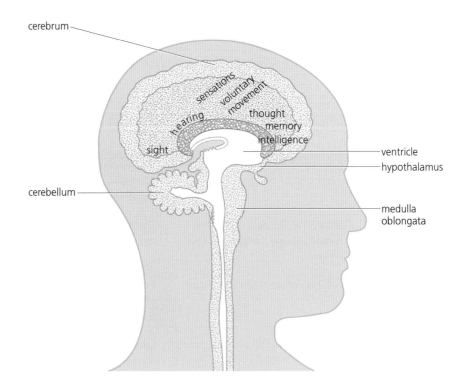

Transmission of nerve impulses

Nerve fibres are individual neurones. Messages pass along nerve fibres as electrical impulses. These electrical impulses are the result of changes to the charges present on the inside and outside of the membrane of the nerve

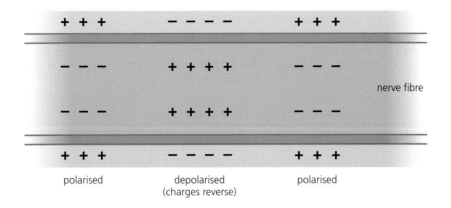

Conduction of nerve impulses

nerve fibre

polarised   depolarised   polarised
(charges reverse)

fibre. The membrane of a resting nerve fibre is said to be polarised when there are more positive ions present on the outer surface and more negative ions present inside the membrane. Sodium and potassium ions present in all body fluids are positively charged while chloride ions are negatively charged. When the neurone is stimulated, a wave of depolarisation passes along the fibre as the charges become temporarily reversed.

Local anaesthetics block the passage of electrical impulses by preventing depolarisation. Some medical terms which relate to the nervous system are:

- anaesthesia: the loss of sensation
- analgesia: the loss of sensation to pain
- hyperaesthesia: over-sensitisation to touch.

Passage of impulses from one neurone to another

Information passes along neurones to and from the CNS. Inside the CNS, impulses pass from one neurone to another even though individual neurones never touch. When an impulse reaches the end of the nerve fibre a chemical is released. This chemical is called a **neurotransmitter substance**. An example is acetylcholine. The chemical passes across a tiny gap and is taken up by an adjacent neurone, generating an electrical impulse in that neurone. The gap between adjacent neurones is called a **synapse**.

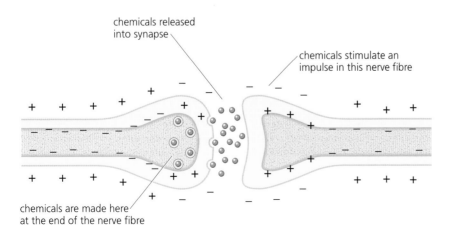

chemicals released into synapse

chemicals stimulate an impulse in this nerve fibre

chemicals are made here at the end of the nerve fibre

Passage of an impulse across a synapse

Passage from a neurone to a muscle fibre

This is similar to passage across a synapse and takes place with the use of chemical transmitter substances. These are released from the end of the motor neurone into the muscle. All muscle fibres stimulated by that neurone will then contract.

The **motor point** is where a motor nerve enters a muscle. A muscle only contracts if stimulated by a motor nerve. Each individual neurone branches, making contact with individual muscle cells. One neurone together with the muscle fibres it stimulates is called a **motor unit**. The area of contact between the neurone and the muscle fibre is called the **motor end plate** or **neuromuscular junction**.

Diagram of the synapse and neuromuscular junction (motor end plate)

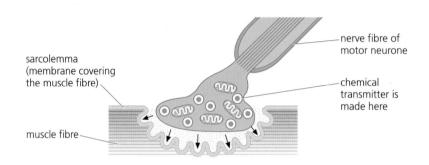

Voluntary and reflex actions

Voluntary actions are always initiated by the brain and we can control these actions. Examples are speaking and walking. A reflex action is a quick involuntary response to a stimulus. For example, on picking up an unexpectedly hot plate you may quickly drop it. This happens because pain receptors in your hand have been stimulated. Impulses pass via sensory nerve fibres to the spinal cord and are transmitted via relay neurones to

Diagram of a simple reflex arc

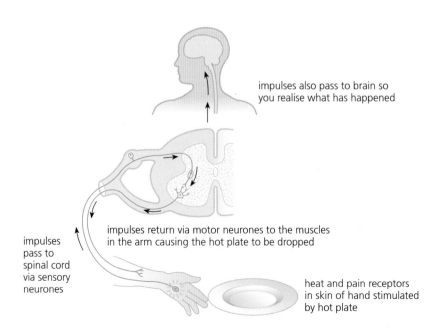

motor neurones. Impulses pass to the arm muscles which are stimulated to contract and the plate is dropped. A reflex involving the spinal cord is called a **spinal reflex**. Impulses will also pass up the spinal cord to the brain so you become aware of what you have done. This may stimulate a secondary response such as yelling OW!

Coughing, sneezing, blinking and swallowing are also reflexes but these are cranial (involving the brain) rather than spinal reflexes.

The olfactory system

The first cranial nerve is called the olfactory nerve. It is a sensory nerve, giving us our sense of smell. Olfactory receptors are present in the upper nasal passages which are coated with watery mucus. Some chemicals dissolve in this watery mucus and stimulate the receptors of the sensory cells. Nerve fibres from the receptors join to form the olfactory nerves which pass through the ethmoid bone into the olfactory bulbs. These lie below the frontal lobes of the cerebrum.

Position of olfactory centre and diagram of olfactory nerve and receptors

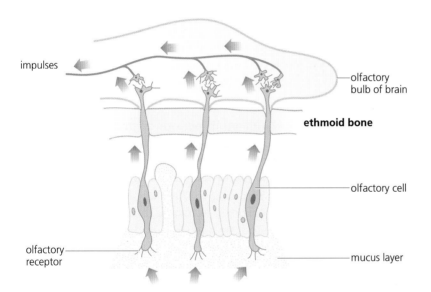

impulses

olfactory bulb of brain

ethmoid bone

olfactory cell

olfactory receptor

mucus layer

stimulus
(chemical to be smelled)

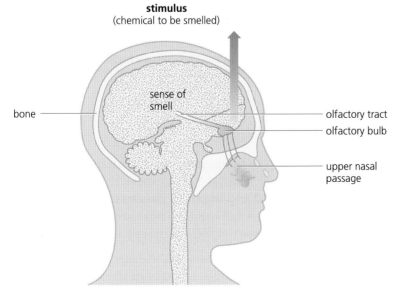

sense of smell

bone

olfactory tract
olfactory bulb

upper nasal passage

From the olfactory lobes, nerve fibres run to the olfactory centre of the cerebral cortex along the olfactory tract. Here in the olfactory centre, the impulses are interpreted as sensations of smell.

Smells may influence the behaviour of a person. Pheromones are scents given off by animals (including humans) to encourage sexual attention. They may be responsible for male–female attraction and male–male acts of aggression. Food must have a pleasant aroma for us to enjoy it.

The **limbic system** is involved in emotions such as pain, pleasure, anger, fear, sorrow, sexual feelings and affection. It consists of a group of structures that encircle the brain stem. It also plays a part in memory and behaviour. Aromatherapy takes advantage of this limbic response using the effects of the aroma of essential oils to produce a range of responses. These may involve feelings of relaxation and well-being.

The autonomic nervous system

The autonomic nervous system controls the involuntary activities of smooth muscle, cardiac muscle and glands. It therefore regulates the size of the pupil, vasodilation and vasoconstriction (see below), the heart rate, movements of the gut and the secretion of most glands. There are two divisions, called the **sympathetic** and **parasympathetic**. Many organs receive a supply from each division. Fibres from one division stimulate the organ while fibres from the other division inhibit it.

The sympathetic division is stimulated in periods of stress or danger and prepares the body for physical activity in case fighting or escape becomes necessary. Fibres of the sympathetic division will therefore increase the rate and force of the heartbeat, dilate the bronchioles of the lungs, dilate the pupils of the eyes and increase sweating. Blood supply through the muscles is increased and blood sugar levels rise. Activities that are not essential in this stressful situation are inhibited, so digestion and gut movements are slowed and urine production is decreased.

The Parasympathetic division is stimulated in times of relaxation. Fibres of this division stimulate digestion and absorption of food.

Although this system is called autonomic, suggesting that we exert no conscious control over its activities, research has shown that transcendental meditation (yoga) seems to inactivate the sympathetic division and has a calming effect on the body.

The effect of heat on the body

Our body attempts to keep its temperature at a constant 37°C whatever the environmental temperature. When the skin experiences high temperatures, skin receptors are stimulated and impulses pass to the hypothalamus of the brain to bring about cooling mechanisms. These are involuntary actions beyond our control and are part of the autonomic nervous system.

The skin reddens as vasodilation occurs. Vasodilation involves opening up of the skin capillaries near the surface so that hot blood can flow through

TIP

The Sympathetic division is associated with Stress. The Parasympathetic division is associated with Peace.

Yoga/meditation

HEALTH AND SAFETY

Heat treatments to even a small area of the body will eventually cause heating of the whole body, as blood passing through the treated area will be warmed and will distribute heat elsewhere.

them and radiate excess heat to the outside. (Radiation of heat from the skin will only take place if the environmental temperature is less than body temperature.)

We also sweat more. When sweat evaporates it cools the skin surface. If the surrounding air is very dry, causing evaporation to take place quickly, the body can tolerate temperatures of up to 130°C for as long as 20 minutes. If the air is moist, reducing the rate of evaporation, then a person can only tolerate a temperature of 46°C for a few minutes only.

FLUIDS OF THE BODY

All cells need a constant supply of energy and raw materials, and a means of removing waste products.

- Epidermal cells need energy to continue dividing, and supplies of raw materials to manufacture new cells.
- Muscle cells need energy to contract, and become fatigued if their waste products are not removed efficiently.
- Neurones need energy in order to transmit impulses.

The fluids of the body are responsible for delivering whatever the cells require, and for removing any waste products. The three principle body fluids are:

- **blood**
- **tissue fluid**
- **lymph**.

Blood

Blood circulates through the blood vessels (arteries, capillaries and veins), collecting oxygen from the lungs and delivering it to the cells of the body. Glucose is also carried in the blood to be used by the cells together with the oxygen to supply energy. Blood supplies other raw materials to build or maintain cells or to manufacture products such as secretions. Inside the tissues, some fluid leaks from the capillaries as blood passes through them. When this fluid leaves the capillaries to enter the tissues it becomes tissue fluid.

> **TIP**
>
> Blood helps to maintain the body temperature at 36.8°C: varying blood flow near to the skin surface increases or diminishes heat loss.

The main constituents of blood

Blood consists of the following:

- **Plasma** A straw-coloured liquid: mainly water, with foods and carbon dioxide.
- **Red blood cells (erythrocytes)** These cells appear red because they contain **haemoglobin**; it is this that carries oxygen from the lungs to the body cells.

- **White blood cells (leucocytes)** There are several types of white blood cells: their main role is to protect the body, destroying foreign bodies and dead cells, and carrying away the debris (a process known as **phagocytosis**).

- **Platelets (thrombocytes)** When blood is exposed to air, as happens when the skin is injured, these cells bind together to form a clot.

- **Other chemicals** Hormones also are transported in the blood.

Tissue fluid

This fluid carries essential oxygen and nutrients to the cells. These useful substances are taken up by the cells and exchanged for waste products such as carbon dioxide. Some of the fluid containing waste products will then re-enter the capillaries and be carried by the blood back to the heart.

Lymph

It is not as easy for the fluid to get back into the blood capillaries as it is to leave them, so excess fluid, together with waste products, collects in **lymph capillaries** and is carried though lymph vessels. Lymph passes through lymph nodes for processing before it is emptied back into the blood circulation close to the heart.

Tissue fluid as an electrolyte

Tissue fluid is a solution of many salts carried in the form of ions. It conducts electricity. When a direct current, such as that used in galvanism, is applied to the body, the ions present in tissue fluid move. Positive ions like sodium, potassium and calcium move towards the negative electrode, making this region alkaline. Negative ions like chloride and hydroxide ions move towards the positive electrode, making this region acidic.

The diagram illustrates the exchange of blood, tissue fluid and lymph as blood flows through the capillaries.

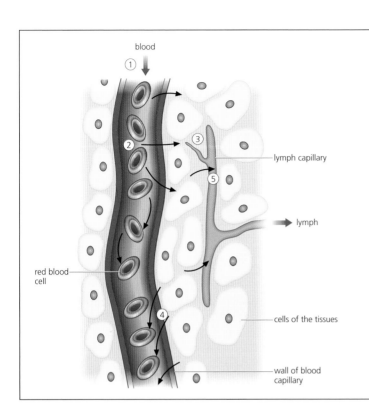

1 The blood flowing into the capillary network is under high pressure. The liquid part of the blood is forced through the walls of the capillary.
2 Larger proteins and blood cells remain in the capillaries.
3 The fluid has now become tissue fluid. It supplies the cells and removes the waste.
4 Some fluid will be drawn back into the capillaries.
5 Other fluid, together with large molecules like proteins from the cells, is drawn into the very porous lymph capillaries.

Exchange of blood, tissue fluid and lymph

ORGAN SYSTEMS OF THE BODY

Organ system	Functions	Diagram
Skeletal	Forms a strong framework which supports the softer tissues and maintains the shape of the body. Internal organs are suspended from the skeleton which keeps them anchored in position. Together with the muscles and joints, the skeleton allows movement. Many organs are surrounded by a protective cage of bone. Many of the blood cells are made in bone marrow (found inside the bones).	

The position of the primary bones of the skeletal system

Organel system	Functions	Diagram

Organ system	Functions	Diagram
Nervous	Coordinates the activities of the body by responding to stimuli received by sense organs	

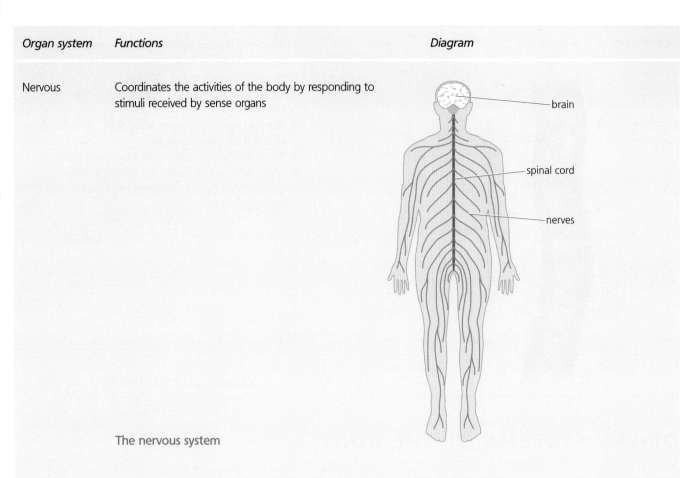

The nervous system

Urinary	Filters waste products from the blood, maintaining its normal composition	

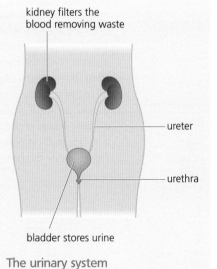

kidney filters the blood removing waste

ureter

urethra

bladder stores urine

The urinary system

TIP ✔

Excretion of liquids
The kidneys are two bean-shaped organs that filter waste from the blood which passes through them.

Waste is carried through two tubes, the ureters, to the bladder, which stores the liquid, called urine, until it is passed from the body. The waste is the end product of cellular metabolism.

Urine leaves the body via the urethra.

Organic system	Functions		Diagram

Digestive   Digests food so that nutrients can be absorbed by the body

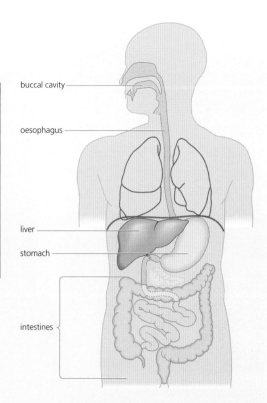

> **TIP**
>
> **The digestive process**
> Food is digested in the alimentary canal, which is divided into several regions.
> - The buccal cavity, the space where food is chewed in the mouth and which connects to the pharynx.
> - The pharynx (throat) links with the oesophagus, a muscular tube which passes food to the stomach. Food spends a few hours in the stomach before it passes to the intestines, small and large, before finally leaving the alimentary canal via the anus.

The digestive system

Respiratory   Ensures oxygen collected from the lungs by the blood reaches all cells of the body where it can be used to provide energy by cell respiration. The waste product from cell respiration, carbon dioxide, is breathed out through the lungs

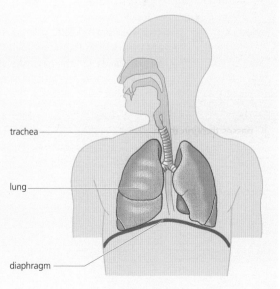

The respiratory system

Organ system	Functions	Diagram
Circulatory	Transports materials around the body so that it can function properly	

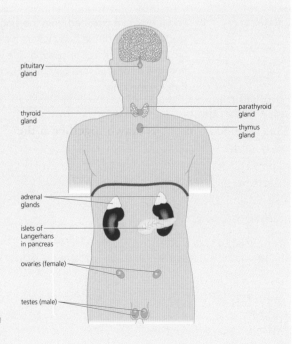

head and forelimbs

vena cava

lungs

aorta

pulmonary artery

pulmonary vein

heart

liver

gut

vena cava

kidneys

trunk and lower limbs

The circulatory system

| Endocrine | Co-ordinates and regulates processes in the body by means of chemicals (hormones) released by endocrine glands into the bloodstream | |

pituitary gland

thyroid gland

parathyroid gland

thymus gland

adrenal glands

islets of Langerhans in pancreas

ovaries (female)

testes (male)

The endocrine system

Organ system	Functions	Diagram
Reproductive	Produces new humans.	

TIP ✔

The sex glands
The testes are two organs lying outside the body which produce the male sex hormones – androgens (testosterone). These hormones stimulate the development of male characteristics, hair growth, deepening of the voice and development of the male physique. They also produce sperm, which is required for sexual reproduction.

The ovaries produce female sex hormones – oestrogen and progesterone – which stimulate the development of the female physique and are important in the menstrual cycle and pregnancy. They produce the egg required for sexual reproduction.

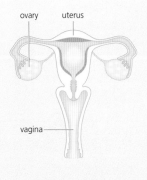

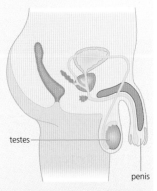

The female reproductive system

The male reproductive system

THE SKELETAL SYSTEM

General structure

The body is covered by the epidermis. Beneath the epidermis is the dermis (a layer of connective tissue). In a few areas of the body, such as the scalp, bone can be felt through these layers, but more usually a padding of fat (adipose tissue) covers bony areas.

ACTIVITY ⬅➡

Straighten your fingers and stretch them apart. Can you see and feel the tendons that pass over the back of your hand?

Muscles can also be felt under the skin – those near the surface are called **superficial muscles**. While these are the muscles you can feel when massaging, deeper muscles lying beneath these may be equally important at producing movement. Most muscles are attached to bones at either end. When used normally, the stationary end of the muscle is called the origin and the end that moves is called the insertion. Connective tissue is used to wrap bundles of muscle fibres and to surround the entire muscle. This connective tissue is drawn together at the ends of the muscle to form **tendons** which attach the muscles to the bones. These are very strong attachments. Tuberosities (thickened and strengthened areas of bone) develop where the muscles are attached.

Bones get stronger when they are moved regularly by muscles. Load-bearing activity is useful in helping to prevent osteoporosis (thinning and weakening of the bone tissue) in older people. Muscular work also increases muscle size. With lack of use, muscles lose their strength and waste away.

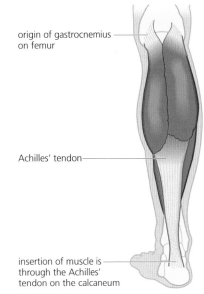

origin of gastrocnemius on femur

Achilles' tendon

insertion of muscle is through the Achilles' tendon on the calcaneum

The skeleton and types of bone

The tissue of a tendon consists of bundles of collagenous fibres together with columns of collagen secreting cells (fibroblasts)

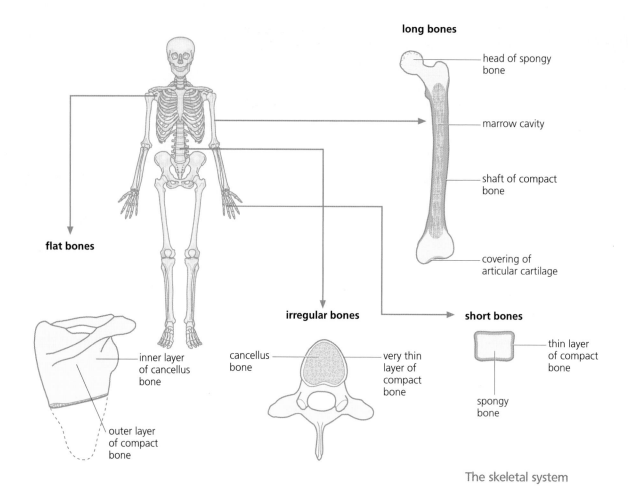

long bones

head of spongy bone

marrow cavity

shaft of compact bone

covering of articular cartilage

flat bones

inner layer of cancellus bone

outer layer of compact bone

irregular bones

cancellus bone

very thin layer of compact bone

short bones

thin layer of compact bone

spongy bone

The skeletal system

Bones and joints

The skeleton is made up of many bones to facilitate movement. Each bone is connected to its neighbour by connective tissue. Fibrous connective tissue is used for immovable joints such as those in the cranium. Fibro-cartilage is used for semi-moveable joints such as those between the bodies of the vertebrae. The most common joints are freely moveable. They are called **synovial joints** and are loosely held together by a form of connective tissue called a **ligament**.

Synovial joints

In a typical synovial joint a sleeve-like ligament joins one bone loosely to the next. This forms a fibrous **capsule** which is flexible enough to permit free movement, but strong enough to resist dislocation.

Lining this capsule is the **synovial membrane** which secretes synovial fluid into the joint. Synovial fluid looks and feels like egg white. It lubricates the joint, becoming less viscous as movement at the joint increases. It also contains phagocytic cells to remove debris caused by wear and tear at the joint and it nourishes the **articular cartilage** that covers the ends of each bone. Articular cartilage provides a smooth coating at the ends of the bones, protecting them from wear by reducing friction.

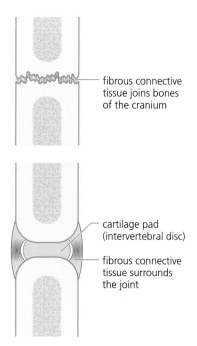

fibrous connective tissue joins bones of the cranium

cartilage pad (intervertebral disc)

fibrous connective tissue surrounds the joint

Bone connections

Extra ligaments may run around the outside of the articular capsule or inside the joint, providing extra strength. Some joints may also contain discs of cartilage to help maintain their stability.

The main support for joints is provided by the muscles that surround it. Very mobile joints such as the shoulder rely heavily on muscles as well as ligaments to hold the joint together.

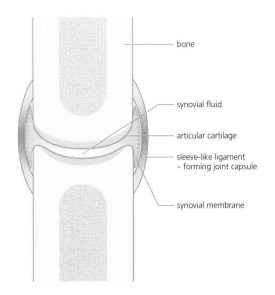

bone

synovial fluid

articular cartilage

sleeve-like ligament – forming joint capsule

synovial membrane

A synovial joint

Specific synovial joints in the body

Position	Type	Movement
Hip	Ball and socket: the head of the femur forms the ball which fits into a socket on the pelvis	Abduction, adduction, extension, flexion, rotation
Shoulder	Ball and socket: the head of the humerus forms the ball that fits into a shallow socket on the scapula	As hip Arm circling involves movement of this joint together with that of the shoulder (pectoral girdle)

Hip:
intracapsular ligament
socket (pelvis)
ball (head of femur)

Shoulder:
shallow socket (scapula)
ball (head of humerus)
tendon of biceps muscle runs through the joint capsule
humerus

Position	Type	Movement
Knee 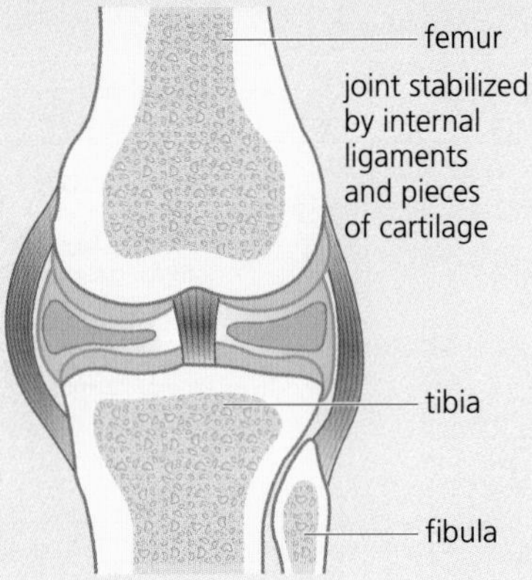	Hinge: formed between the femur and the tibia	Flexion, extension

femur
joint stabilized by internal ligaments and pieces of cartilage
tibia
fibula

Position	Type	Movement
Elbow 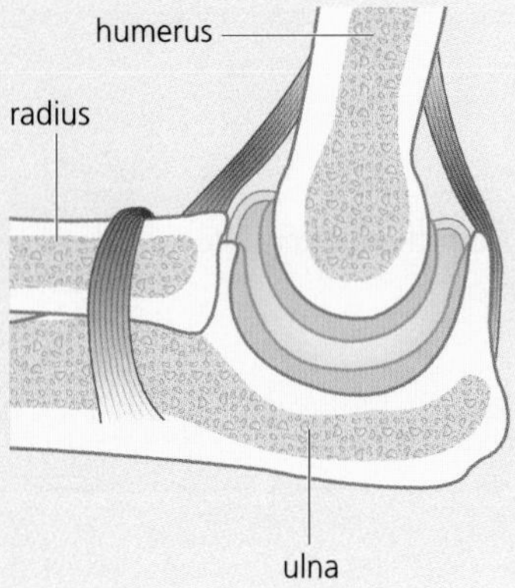	Hinge: formed between the humerus and the ulna	As knee

humerus
radius
ulna

Position	Type	Movement
Forearm	Pivot: formed between the ulna and head of the radius	Supination (turning the hand palm up), pronation (turning the hand palm down)
Ankle	Hinge: formed between the bones of the lower leg (tibia and fibula) and the talus of the foot)	Dorsiflexion (foot pulled up towards knee), plantar-flexion (pointing the foot
Wrist	Condyloid: formed between the bones of the lower arm (radius and ulna) and the bones of the wrist (carpals)	Flexion, extension, abduction, adduction
Foot	Gliding	Inversion, eversion
Hand	Gliding	Flexion or clenching, extension or stretching
Toe	Hinge	Flexion, extension the joint at the base of the toes allows abduction and adduction
Finger	Hinge	As toe

Bones of the head

The bones which form the head are collectively known as the **skull**. The skull can be divided into two parts, the face and the cranium, which together are made up of 22 bones:

- the 14 facial bones form the face
- the 8 cranial bones form the rest of the head.

As well as forming our facial features, the facial bones support other structures such as the eyes and the teeth. Some of these bones, such as the nasal bone, are made from **cartilage**, a softer tissue than bone.

The cranium surrounds and protects the brain. The bones are thin and slightly curved, and are held together by connective tissue. After childhood, the joints become immovable, and are called **sutures**.

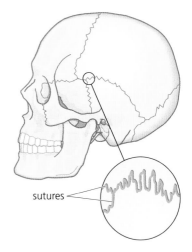

Sutures

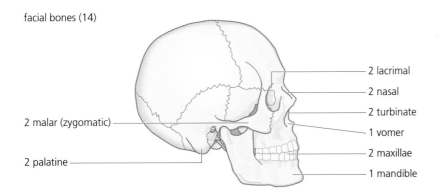

facial bones (14)

2 lacrimal
2 nasal
2 turbinate
1 vomer
2 maxillae
1 mandible

2 malar (zygomatic)
2 palatine

Bones of the face

Facial bones

Bone	Number	Location	Function
Nasal	2	The nose	Form the bridge of the nose
Vomer	1	The nose	Forms the dividing bony wall of the nose
Palatine	2	The nose	Form the floor and wall of the nose and the roof of the mouth
Turbinate	2	The nose	Form the outer walls of the nose
Lacrimal	2	The eye sockets	Form the inner walls of the eye sockets; contain a small groove for the tear duct
Malar (zygomatic)	2	The cheek	Form the cheekbones
Maxillae	2	The upper jaw	Fused together, to form the upper jaw, which holds the upper teeth
Mandible	1	The lower jaw	The largest and strongest of the facial bones; holds the lower teeth

ACTIVITY

Facial expressions
In front of a mirror, move the muscles of your face to create the expressions that you might form each day.

   What expressions can you make? Which part or parts of the face are moving? Which facial muscles do you think have contracted to create these expressions?

HEALTH AND SAFETY

Crow's feet
To avoid the premature formation of 'crow's feet':
- avoid squinting in bright sunlight – wear sunglasses
- have your eyes tested regularly
- if you use a visual display unit, ensure that you take regular breaks, and have a protective filter screen to remove glare.

Bones of the cranium

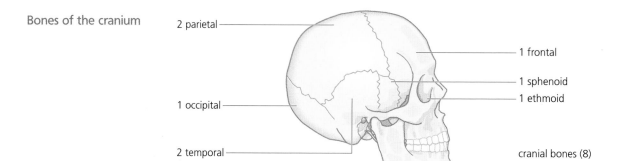

cranial bones (8)

Cranial bones

Bone	Number	Location	Function
Occipital	1	The lower back of the cranium	Contains a large hole called the *foramen magnum*: through this pass the spinal cord, the nerves and blood vessels
Parietal	2	The sides of the cranium	Fused together to form the sides and top of the head (the 'crown')
Frontal	1	The forehead	Forms the forehead and the upper walls of the eye sockets
Temporal	2	The sides of the head	Provide two muscle attachment points: the mastoid process and the zygomatic process
Ethmoid	1	Between the eye sockets	Forms part of the nasal cavities
Sphenoid	1	The base of the cranium the back of the eye sockets	A bat-shaped bone which joins together all the bones of the cranium

Bones of the neck, chest and shoulder

Bone	Number	Location	Function
Cervical vertebra	7	The neck	These vertebrae form the top of the spinal column: the *atlas* is the first vertebra, which supports the skull; the *axis* is the second vertebra, which allows rotation of the head
Hyoid	1	A U-shaped bone at the front of the neck	Supports the tongue
Clavicle	2	Slender long bones at the base of the neck	Commonly called the *collar bones:* these form a joint with the sternum and the scapula bones, allowing movement at the shoulder
Scapula	2	Triangular bones in the upper back	Commonly called the *shoulder blades*: the scapulae provide attachment for muscles which move the arms. The *shoulder girdle*, which allows movement at the shoulder, is composed of the clavicles and the scapulae
Humerus	2	The upper bones of the arms	Form ball-and-socket joints with the scapulae: these joints allow movement in any direction
Sternum	1	The breastbone	Protects the inner organs; provides a surface for muscle attachment; and supports muscle movement

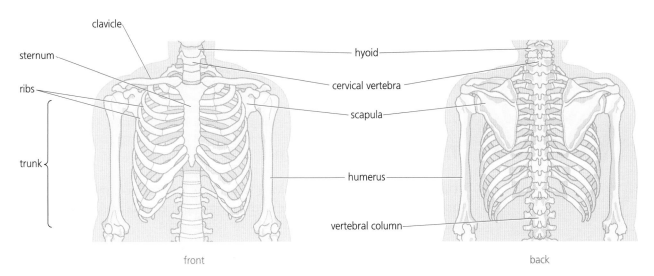

front

back

Bones of the neck, chest and shoulder

THE HAND AND THE FOREARM

The bones of the hand

The wrist consists of eight small **carpal** bones, which glide over one another to allow movement. This is called a **condyloid** or **gliding joint**.

There are then five **metacarpal** bones that make up the palm of the hand.

ACTIVITY

Identifying bones in the hand
Look very closely at your hand. Can you identify where the bones are? Try feeling the bones with your other hand. How many can you feel?

Bones of the hand

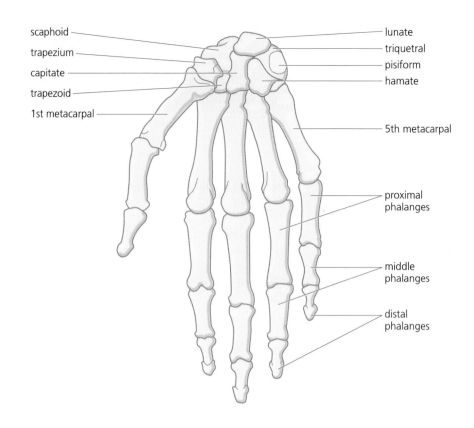

The fingers are made up of 14 individual bones called **phalanges** – two in each of the thumbs, and three in each of the fingers.

The bones of the arm

The arm is made up of three long bones: the **humerus** is the bone of the upper arm, from the shoulder to the elbow; the **radius** and **ulna** lie side by side in the lower arm, from the elbow to the wrist.

Having two bones in the lower arm makes it easier for your wrist to rotate. This movement that causes the palm to face downwards is called **pronation**; the movement that causes it to face upwards is called **supination**.

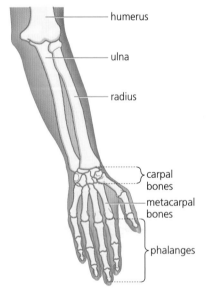

Bones of the arm

THE FOOT AND THE LOWER LEG

The bones of the foot

The foot is made up of 7 **tarsal** bones, 5 **metatarsal** bones, and 14 **phalanges**. These bones fit together to form arches which help to support the foot and to absorb the impact when we walk, run and jump.

Bones of the foot

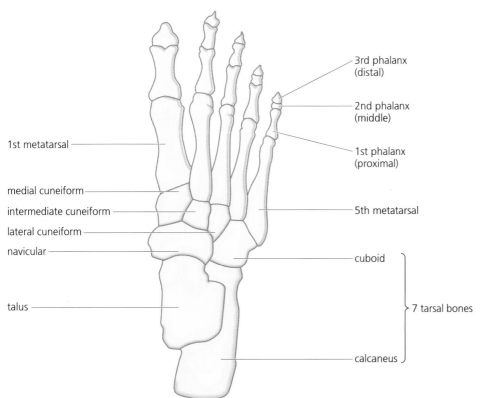

1st metatarsal

medial cuneiform
intermediate cuneiform
lateral cuneiform
navicular

talus

3rd phalanx
(distal)

2nd phalanx
(middle)

1st phalanx
(proximal)

5th metatarsal

cuboid

7 tarsal bones

calcaneus

The arches of the foot

The **arches** of the foot are created by the formation of the bones and joints, and supported by ligaments. These arches support the weight of the body and help to preserve balance when we walk on even surfaces.

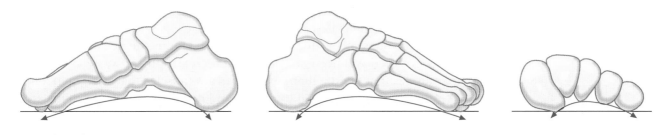

Arches of the foot

The bones of the lower leg

The lower leg is made up of two long bones, the **tibia** and the **fibula**. These bones have joints with the upper leg (at the knee) and with the foot (at the ankle). Having two bones in the lower leg – as with the forearm – allows a greater range of movement to be achieved at the ankle.

Bones of the lower leg

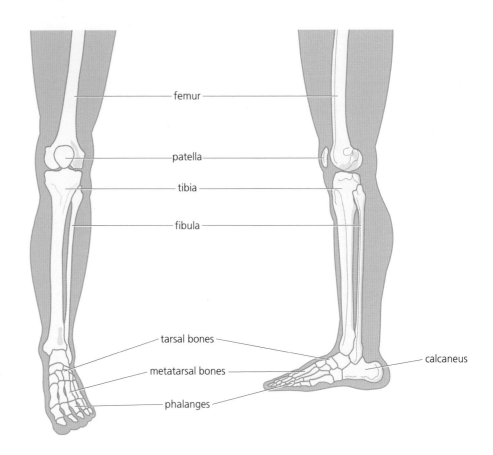

femur

patella

tibia

fibula

tarsal bones

metatarsal bones

phalanges

calcaneus

VOLUNTARY MUSCLES

Muscle tone

Muscles never completely relax – there are always a few contracted fibres in every muscle. These make the muscle slightly tense and this muscular tension is called **muscle tone**.

Muscle tone helps the body to stand upright and keeps the muscles prepared for immediate action. A flaccid muscle is one with less than normal tone. Sometimes this is due to damage to the motor nerve supply. A muscle that is not used will become flaccid and then atrophy or waste away. **Flexors** are muscles that bend a limb; **extensors** are muscles that straighten a limb. We can only keep upright if the flexor and extensor muscles of joints are both partially contracted to keep the joints steady.

- **Good posture**: the body is held upright with little muscular effort as the head is balanced on top of the spine, all the vertebrae are balanced on each other, the spine is balanced on top of the hip bone and the feet are square on the ground.

- **Poor posture**: if the body is not balanced then the muscles must work harder to keep the unbalanced posture and can start to tire and ache. The back and neck muscles are the ones most likely to be affected by stooping or sitting over a desk. Poor posture also compresses the internal organs and affects their function. This can cause breathing difficulties and digestive problems. Poor posture can be corrected by conscious effort and by regular exercise.

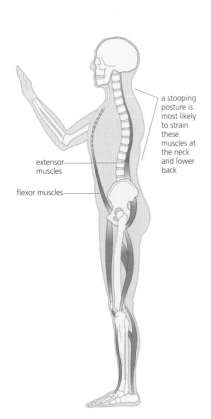

a stooping posture is most likely to strain these muscles at the neck and lower back

extensor muscles

flexor muscles

Main extensors and flexors used in posture

The properties of muscle tissue

- it has the ability to contract (shorten)
- it is extensible (when the extensor muscle in a joint contracts, the corresponding flexor muscle will be stretched or extended)
- it is elastic (it can return to its original length following contraction or extension)
- it is responsive (it contracts in response to nerve stimulation.

Voluntary muscles contract only when stimulated by their nerve supply. Muscle contraction requires energy and this is supplied by tissue respiration taking place inside muscle cells. In this reaction, glucose and oxygen are used to supply the energy, and carbon dioxide and water are released as waste products. Muscles need a good blood supply when a person is exercising, in order to bring the oxygen and glucose and to carry away the waste products.

The muscles can respire anaerobically (without oxygen), for short periods if the blood cannot supply enough oxygen. Glucose is then broken down to lactic acid. As it builds up in muscle tissue lactic acid causes fatigue. When muscles become fatigued they stop contracting and become painful.

It is essential that the muscle receives a good blood supply after anaerobic exercise as oxygen is required to complete the breakdown of lactic acid to carbon dioxide and water, and to remove all traces of lactic acid which can cause stiffness in muscles if allowed to remain.

Massage helps to warm and relax muscles and improve their blood flow. When a muscle is warmer it responds more quickly and more strongly, giving a stronger contraction. Warming-up exercises are always advised before more vigorous activity in order to improve the blood flow through the muscles and prepare the muscles for more vigorous action.

Disorders of the muscular system

- **Fatigue**: lack of response by a muscle to continuous stimulation (i.e. it stops working) due to a lack of oxygen or the build up of lactic acid and carbon dioxide.
- **Cramps**: an involuntary complete tetanic contraction in a muscle.
- **Shivering**: tone increases as the muscles become colder. Shivering is due to these 'prepared' muscles contracting spasmodically. This produces heat and therefore helps to raise the body temperature.

TIP

Muscle attachment
Muscles are attached at both ends to ligaments, tendons, bones, skin and even each other. The origin is the part of the muscle that is attached to a bone; the insertion is the other end, which is attached to a moveable part. During muscle contraction this part of the muscle moves.

TIP

Cooling-down exercises are also useful in maintaining a good blood supply to the muscle following strenuous exercise. This ensures that the accumulated waste products continue to be removed quickly so will not cause cramps.

Massage

ACTIVITY

Hold one hand above your head and the other by your side. Make a fist with each hand and then release. Keep doing this until you have to stop – until your muscles become fatigued. Do the muscles in the arm above your head, with a slower blood supply (because you are holding it up) become fatigued first?

Hypothermia
As muscle tissue is cooled the chemical reactions slow and contractions take longer to occur. In hypothermia, the body temperature is so low that the muscles may become rigid, preventing the person moving.

plantar flexion
(toe pointing)

dorsi flexion
(foot raised)

adduction – muscles
pull limb towards
body/fingers together
to their usual position

pronation

supination

abduction – muscles
move limb, etc. from
usual position

extension

flexion

Diagrams showing the main muscle actions

Facial muscles

Many of the muscles located in the face are very small and are attached to ('insert into') another small muscle or the facial skin. When the muscles contract, they pull the facial skin in a particular way: it is this that creates the facial expression.

With age, the facial expressions that we make every day produce lines on the skin – frown lines. The amount of tension, or **tone**, also decreases with age. When performing facial massage, the aim is to improve the general tone of the facial muscles.

Muscles of facial expression

Muscle	Expression	Location	Action
Occipitofrontalis	Surprise	The forehead	Raises the eyebrows
Corrugator	Frown	Between the eyebrows	Draws the eyebrows together
Orbicularis oculi	Winking	Surrounds the eyes	Closes the eyelid
Risorius	Smiling	Extends diagonally, from the corners of the mouth	Draws mouth corners outwards
Buccinator	Blowing	Inside the cheeks	Compresses the cheeks
Zygomaticus	Smiling, laughing	Extends diagonally from the corners of the mouth	Lifts the mouth corners upwards and outwards
Zygomaticus, major and minor	Smiling, laughing	Extend diagonally upwards from the corners of the mouth	Lifts the corners of the mouth
Procerus	Distaste	Covers the bridge of the nose	Wrinkling of the skin over the bridge of the nose
Nasalis	Anger	Covers the front of the nose	Opens and closes the nasal openings
Quadratus labii superioris	Distaste	Surrounds the upper lip	Raises and draws back the upper lips and nostrils
Depressor labii	Sulking	Surrounds the lower lip	Depresses the lower lip and draws it slightly to one side
Orbicularis oris	Pout, kiss, doubt	Surrounds the mouth	Purses the lip, closes the mouth
Triangularis	Sadness	The corner of the lower lip extends over the chin	Draws down the mouth's corners
Mentalis	Doubt	Chin	Raises the lower lip, causing the chin to wrinkle
Masseter	Anger/aggression	Cheeks	Raises the jaw and clenches the teeth
Platysma	Fear, horror	The sides of the neck and chin	Draws the mouth's corners downwards and backwards

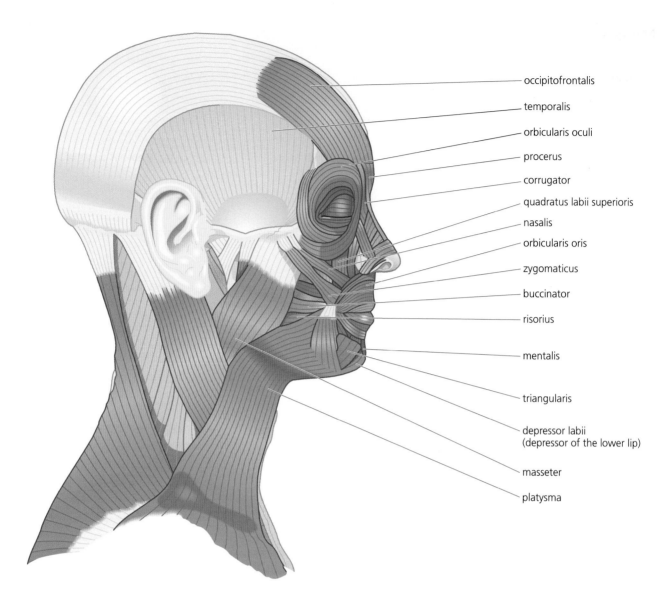

occipitofrontalis

temporalis

orbicularis oculi

procerus

corrugator

quadratus labii superioris

nasalis

orbicularis oris

zygomaticus

buccinator

risorius

mentalis

triangularis

depressor labii
(depressor of the lower lip)

masseter

platysma

Muscles of the face

Muscles of mastication

The muscles responsible for the movement of the lower jawbone (the **mandible**) when chewing are called the **muscles of mastication**.

Muscle	Location	Action
Masseter	The cheek area: extends from the zygomatic bone to the mandible	Clenches the teeth; closes and raises the lower jaw
Temporalis	Extends from the temple region at the side of the head to the mandible	Raises the jaw and draws it backwards, as in chewing

Muscles that move the head

Muscle	Location	Action
Sterno-cleido-mastoid	Runs from the sternum to the clavicle bone and the temporal bone	Flexes the neck; rotates and bows the head
Trapezius	A large triangular muscle, covering the back of the neck and the upper back	Draws the head backwards and allows movement at the shoulder
Occipitalis	Covers the back of the head	Draws scalp backwards

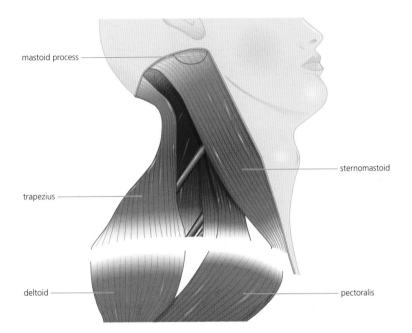

Muscles that move the head

mastoid process

sternomastoid

trapezius

deltoid

pectoralis

Superficial muscles of the body

Abdominal muscles

Muscle	Location	Action
Rectus abdominis	Front of abdomen from the pelvis to the sternum and costal cartilages of the lower ribs	Flexes the spine, compresses the abdomen, tilts the pelvis upwards
Obliques	The internal obliques lie to either side of the rectus abdominis, running downwards and outwards; the external obliques lie on top of the internal obliques, running downwards and forwards	Both compress the abdomen and twist the trunk, the left internal oblique working with the right external oblique

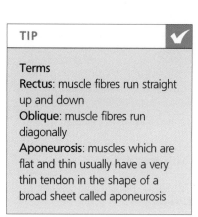

TIP ✔

Terms
Rectus: muscle fibres run straight up and down
Oblique: muscle fibres run diagonally
Aponeurosis: muscles which are flat and thin usually have a very thin tendon in the shape of a broad sheet called aponeurosis

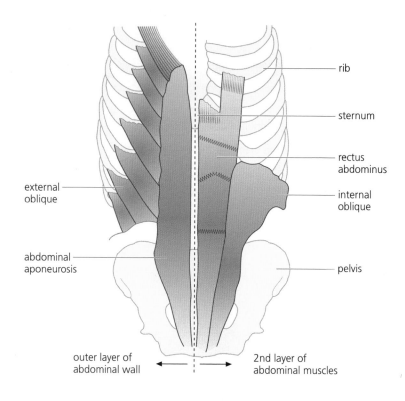

rib

sternum

rectus abdominus

internal oblique

external oblique

pelvis

abdominal aponeurosis

outer layer of abdominal wall

2nd layer of abdominal muscles

Abdominal muscles

Muscles of chest and upper arm

Muscle	Location	Action
Pectoralis major	Across the upper chest (underneath the breasts) from the clavicle, sternum and ribs to the top of the humerus, forming the front wall of the axilla	Used in throwing and climbing to adduct the arm, drawing it forwards and rotating it medially
Pectoralis minor	Underneath the pectoralis major. Its origin is the third, forth and fifth ribs and it inserts into the outer corner of the scapula	Draws the shoulder downwards and forwards
Deltoid	Over the top of the shoulder from the clavicle and scapula to the upper part of the humerus	Abducts the arm to a horizontal position; aids in further abduction and in drawing the arm backwards and forwards
Biceps	Lies over the front of the upper arm. Its two origins are on the scapula and its insertion is on the radius	Flexes the elbow; supinates the forearm and hand
Triceps	The only muscle at the back of the upper arm. It has three origins – one on the scapula and two on the humerus. It inserts into the ulna	Extends the elbow
Brachialis	Under the biceps at the front of the humerus from halfway down its shaft to the ulna near the elbow joint	Flexes the elbow

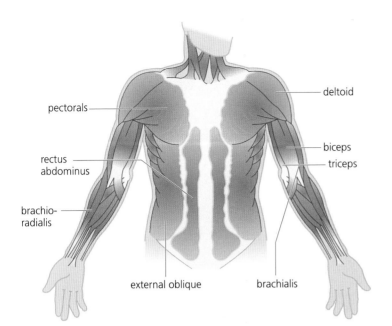

Anterior muscles of the arm and trunk

- deltoid
- pectorals
- biceps
- triceps
- rectus abdominus
- brachio-radialis
- external oblique
- brachialis

Muscle	Location	Action
Brachio radialis	On the thumb side of the forearm, its origin is at the shaft of the humerus, its insertion is at the end of the radius bone	Flexes the elbow
Flexors	Middle of the forearm	Muscles that flex and bend the wrist, drawing it towards the forearm
Extensors	Little finger side of the forearm	Muscles which extend and straighten the wrist and hand
Thenar muscles	In the palm of the hand, below the thumb	Flexes the thumb and moves it outwards and inwards
Hypothenar muscles	In the palm of the hand, below the little finger	Flexes the little finger and moves it outwards and inwards

The muscles of the hand and arm

The hand and fingers are moved primarily by muscles and tendons in the forearm. These muscles contract, pulling the tendons, and thereby move the fingers much as a puppet is moved by strings.

The muscles that bend the wrist, drawing it towards the forearm, are **flexors**; other muscles, **extensors**, straighten the wrist and the hand.

ACTIVITY

Observing the tendons
Hold your palm face upwards, with your sleeve pulled back so that you can see your forearm. Move the fingers individually towards the palm. Can you see the tendons moving?

Muscles of the arm and hand

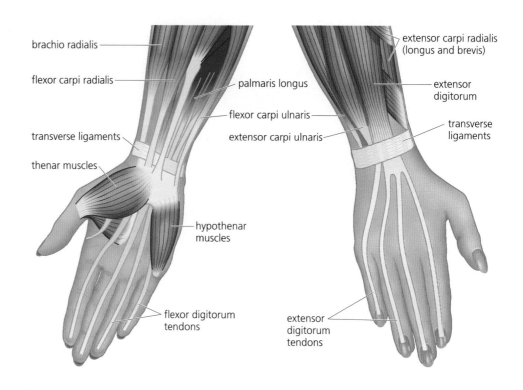

brachio radialis

flexor carpi radialis

transverse ligaments

thenar muscles

palmaris longus

flexor carpi ulnaris

extensor carpi ulnaris

hypothenar
muscles

flexor digitorum
tendons

extensor carpi radialis
(longus and brevis)

extensor
digitorum

transverse
ligaments

extensor
digitorum
tendons

Muscles of the back (shoulder and trunk)

Muscle	Location	Action
Trapezius	The back of the neck and chest with its origin running from the base of the skull (the occipital bone) down the spines of the thoracic vertebrae. It inserts into the scapula and clavicle	Moves the scapula up, down and back; raises the clavicle; can also be used to extend the neck
Latissimus dorsi	Crosses the back from the lumbar region up to insert into the top of the humerus. It forms the back wall of the axilla (arm pit)	Used in rowing and climbing; it adducts the shoulder downwards and pulls it backwards
Erector spinae	Three groups of overlapping muscles which lie either side of the spine from the neck to the pelvis	Extends spine; keeps the body in an upright position
Rhomboids	Between the shoulders originating from the thoracic vertebrae and inserting to the scapula bone	Braces the shoulder, and rotates the scapula, moving the shoulder

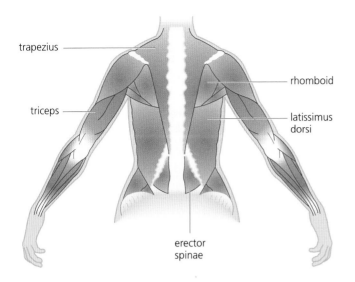

Posterior muscles of the arms and trunk

trapezius

rhomboid

triceps

latissimus dorsi

erector spinae

Muscles used in breathing

Muscle	Location	Action
External intercostals	Connect the lower border of one rib to the one below with the muscle fibres running downwards and forwards	Used in breathing movements to draw the ribs upwards and outwards when breathing in
Internal intercostals	Between the ribs with the fibres running upwards and forwards to the rib above (both sets of intercostals maintain the shape of the wall of the thorax)	Draw the ribs downwards and inwards when breathing out
Diaphragm	Divides the thorax from the abdomen	Contraction of this muscle increases the volume of the thorax

Diagrams to illustrate inspiration and expiration

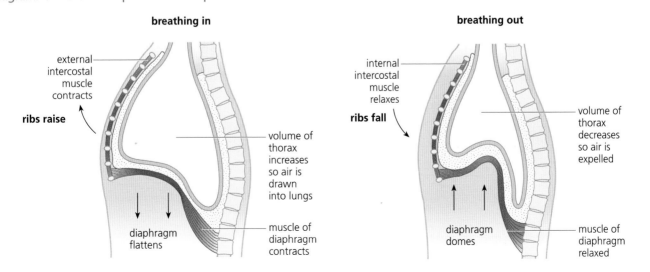

breathing in

external intercostal muscle contracts

ribs raise

diaphragm flattens

volume of thorax increases so air is drawn into lungs

muscle of diaphragm contracts

breathing out

internal intercostal muscle relaxes

ribs fall

diaphragm domes

volume of thorax decreases so air is expelled

muscle of diaphragm relaxed

Muscles of the buttocks and legs

Muscle	Location	Action
Gluteals	In the buttock connecting the pelvis and femur. There are three layers of gluteal muscles	Abduct and rotate the femur; used in walking and running and to raise the body to an upright position
Hamstrings	Back of the thigh from the pelvis and the top of the femur to the bones of the lower leg below the knee	Flex the knee; extend the thigh; used in walking and jumping
Gastrocnemius	Calf of the leg	Flexes the knee; plantar-flexes foot
Soleus	Calf of the leg, below the gastrocnemius (both calf muscles insert through the Achilles' tendon into the heel)	Plantar-flexes foot both calf muscles are used to push off (when walking and running)
Quadriceps extensor	Front of the thigh. A group of four muscles running from the pelvis and top of femur to the tibia through the patella and patellar ligament	Extend the knee; used in kicking. The rectus fibres from the pelvis help to flex the hip
Sartorius	Crosses the front of the thigh from the outer front rim of the pelvis to the tibia at the inner knee	Flexes the knee and hip; abducts and rotates the femur; used to sit cross-legged
Adductors	Inner thigh	Adducts the hip; flex and rotate the femur
Tibialis anterior	Front of the lower leg	Inverts the foot; dorsiflexes the foot; rotates foot outwards

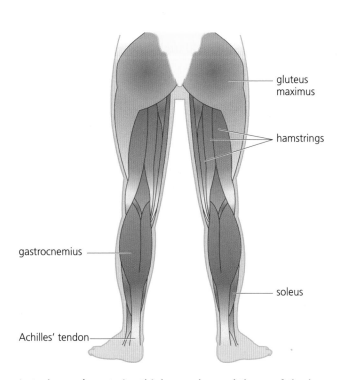
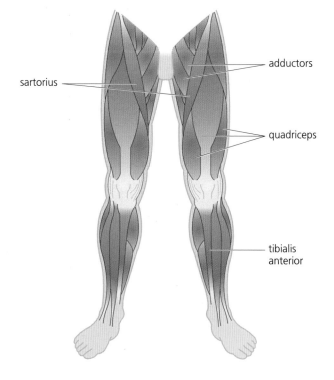

Anterior and posterior thigh muscles and those of the lower leg

The muscles of the foot

The muscles of the foot work together to help move the body when walking and running. In a similar way to the movement of the hand, the foot is moved primarily by muscles in the lower leg; these pull on tendons, which in turn move the feet and toes.

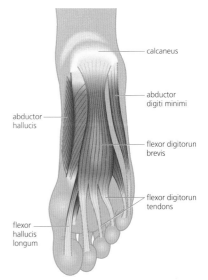

calcaneus

abductor digiti minimi

abductor hallucis

flexor digitorun brevis

flexor digitorun tendons

flexor hallucis longum

Muscles of the foot

THE CIRCULATORY SYSTEM

The heart

The heart is a muscular pump which keeps the blood circulating. During diastole, the heart fills with blood from the veins. At systole, forceful contractions of first the atria and then the ventricles force blood out of the heart through the arteries. The pulmonary artery carries blood from the right ventricle to the lungs to absorb oxygen, while the aorta carries oxygenated blood from the left ventricle around the rest of the body.

diastole – heart fills with blood

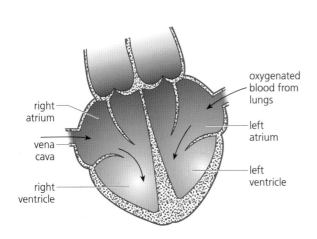

right atrium

vena cava

right ventricle

oxygenated blood from lungs

left atrium

left ventricle

ventricular systole

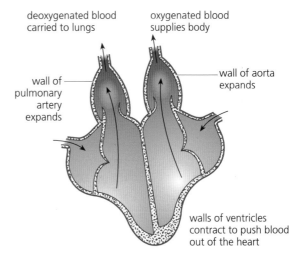

deoxygenated blood carried to lungs

oxygenated blood supplies body

wall of pulmonary artery expands

wall of aorta expands

walls of ventricles contract to push blood out of the heart

Stages of the heartbeat

Blood vessels

There are three main kinds of blood vessel: **arteries**, **veins** and **capillaries**. Arteries are thick, elastic-walled vessels that carry blood away from the heart. Every time the heart contracts to pump blood around the body, the elastic walls become stretched and then recoil. This absorbs and smoothes the surges from the heart and helps to push the blood forward. This stretching and recoiling is felt as a pulse.

TIP ✓

If your occupation requires you to sit or stand for long periods, you may get swollen feet and ankles or even varicose veins. Keep the blood circulating by exercising those leg muscles.

Arteries lead into the main organs where they divide into smaller and smaller vessels. The smallest blood vessels are called capillaries. Capillaries are about the size of a hair. They are close to all the cells of the body, bringing supplies of oxygen and nutrients and carrying away products from the cells.

The capillary network then reforms into larger vessels called veins to deliver blood back to the heart. The blood flows much more slowly and evenly in veins. They do not pulsate like arteries. The veins often pass through the muscles. Each time muscles contract, veins are squeezed and blood is pushed along. To make sure the blood is squeezed along in the right direction, many veins have valves to stop blood flowing backwards. The veins have much thinner walls than arteries. This means that they are more easily compressed by the muscles they pass through.

Blood vessels

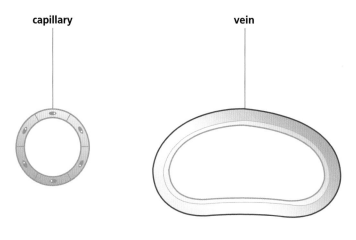

artery   capillary   vein

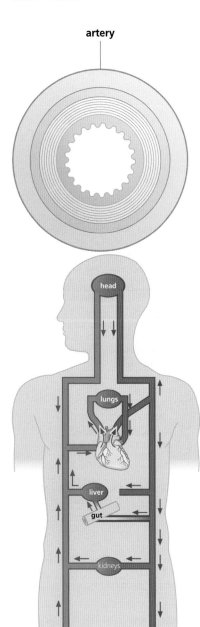

Diagram of the circulatory system

Flow of blood in arteries

The flow of blood in the arteries is maintained by blood pressure caused by the forceful contractions of the ventricles of the heart pushing blood into them. Blood pressure is maintained by the elastic walls of the large arteries, which stretch to accept the blood from the ventricles and then recoil to push the blood on its way.

Blood pressure is measured in the arteries. Normal blood pressure has a value of about 115 mm mercury over 70 mm mercury. The first value refers to the pressure reached when the heart is contracting and pushing blood around the body, and the second to the pressure when the heart is relaxed and filling up with blood. The blood pressure is always higher when someone is standing rather than lying down, and it increases with exercise or anxiety. A value of 100 over 60 would be low; a value of 160 over 100 would be high. A person with high blood pressure is said to be suffering from **hypertension**.

Hypertension needs to be treated as it can damage the heart, brain and kidneys. It is often without symptoms and can only be detected by routine blood-pressure checks. Low blood pressure may cause a person to faint easily.

Heat treatments may cause dizziness and fainting as blood is diverted to the skin (to reduce the rising body temperature) causing a fall in blood pressure and reduced flow to the head and brain. This fall in blood pressure can also occur when a client stands up following a treatment in the prone position.

Blood flow through the organs

Arterioles are the smaller arteries which feed the capillary networks. Capillary networks are found through each major organ of the body including the skin. Arterioles are very important because they control blood flow through the organs. They have smooth muscle fibres in their walls which can contract to constrict the size of the lumen and reduce blood flow, or relax to cause dilation of the lumen and increase blood flow. The lumen is the cavity through which the blood flows.

Blood flow through the muscles is controlled by this process. It is increased during exercise when muscles are contracting, in order to bring supplies of oxygen and glucose and to carry away the waste products – mainly carbon dioxide and heat and perhaps lactic acid.

Blood flow through the skin

Normal body temperature is 37°C. Blood circulating through the internal organs or through working muscles therefore becomes warm. If the body temperature starts to rise, then allowing blood to pass near the skin surface releases some of this heat to the environment. This will check the rise in temperature. The skin will appear red and may feel warm to the touch.

The blood vessels in the skin are organised so that blood can either flow near the skin surface or can pass through shunt vessels which lie deeper in the dermis. The skin capillaries are used to help regulate body temperature. If the body temperature begins to drop, then blood flows deeper through the dermis, releasing less heat to the environment. This process of **vasodilation** and **vasoconstriction** is controlled by the autonomic nervous system – nerves control the arterioles that feed the capillary networks through the skin.

blood flow through skin when hot   and when cold

blood flows close to epidermis

epidermis

capillaries constricted

shunt vessel constricted

blood flows deep in dermis

Vasoconstriction and vasodilation

TIP

Pulse rate relates to the speed of the heartbeat. The strength of the pulse relates to the pressure of blood flow leaving the heart.

Blood pressure increases during activity and decreases during rest.

Relaxing treatments such as Indian head massage lower blood pressure.

TIP

Thrombosis
Thrombosis is the formation of a thrombus (a clot) in the blood vessels. A thrombus in a deep vein of the leg may cause pain in the calf. Pieces of the thrombus can break off and get carried through the blood stream until they wedge in tiny capillaries. If this happens in the lungs, oxygen absorption decreases and breathing is affected. A coronary thrombosis (blockage of coronary arteries supplying blood to the heart) can cause a heart attack.

Erythema is reddening of the skin caused by dilation of the blood vessels controlling local capillary networks in areas of the skin affected by injury or infection.

Flow of blood in veins

The flow of blood in veins is slower and under less pressure than the flow in arteries. Veins tend to pass through muscles of the body where they can be squeezed so that the blood is helped along. This is especially important in the legs, where blood is being returned against gravity.

Varicose veins are a result of incompetent valves which allow blood to flow backwards, stretching and weakening the walls of the vein. The veins on the surface of the leg (and therefore not surrounded by muscle tissue) are the ones most commonly affected as gravity forces the blood back down the leg.

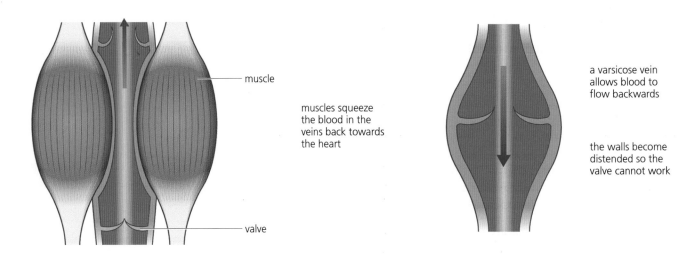

muscle

muscles squeeze the blood in the veins back towards the heart

valve

a varsicose vein allows blood to flow backwards

the walls become distended so the valve cannot work

Control of blood flow by valves

The circulation

The circulation of blood is under the control of the **heart**, a muscular organ which pumps the blood around the body.

As previously stated, blood leaving the heart is carried in large, elastic tubes called **arteries**. The blood to the head arrives via the **carotid arteries**, which are connected via other main arteries to the heart. There are two main carotid arteries, one on each side of the neck.

These arteries divide into smaller branches, the *internal carotid* and the *external carotid*. The **internal carotid artery** passes the temporal bone and enters the head, taking blood to the brain. The **external carotid artery** stays outside the skull, and divides into branches:

- the **occipital branch** supplies the back of the head and the scalp;
- the **temporal branch** supplies the sides of the face, the head, the scalp and the skin
- the **facial branch** supplies the muscles and tissues of the face.

These arteries also divide repeatedly, successive vessels becoming smaller and smaller until they form tiny blood **capillaries**. These vessels are just one cell

THE ENDOCRINE SYSTEM

Endocrine glands secrete chemicals called **hormones** directly into the bloodstream where they circulate around the body and affect certain organs. The organ affected by a particular hormone is called a **target organ**. The endocrine system works with the nervous system to bring about coordination. Hormones tend to be associated with long-term changes, such as growth, rather than the quick response expected from nerve stimulation.

Endocrine glands and their functions

Name of gland	Hormones secreted	Function
Pituitary gland	Trophic hormones	Act on other endocrine glands
	FSH (follicle stimulating hormone) and LH (luteinizing hormone)	Control reproduction
	ADH (anti-diuretic hormone)	Affects water balance
Thyroid gland	Thyroxine	Controls the rate of metabolism
Parathyroid	Parathormone	Controls blood calcium levels
Thymus gland (both an endocrine and lymphatic gland)	Various hormones	Stimuates lymphoid cells responsible for antibody production against disease
Pancreas (islets of Langerhans)	Insulin	Controls blood sugar levels
Adrenal (medulla)	Adrenalin	Prepares the body for sudden stressful events
Adrenal (cortex)	Glucocorticoids	Reduce stress responses such as inflammation
	Aldosterone	Controls level of sodium and potassium in the blood
	Oestrogens and androgens	As other sex hormones
Ovary	Oestrogens and progesterones	Control female reproductive events including puberty, menstruation, pregnancy and the menopause
Testes	Testosterone (an androgen)	Controls male fertility

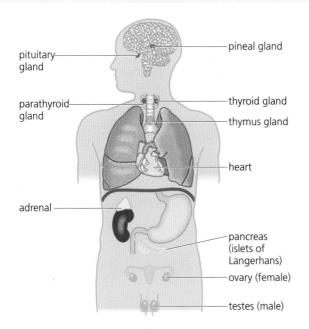

Glands of the endocrine system

The effect of hormones on hair, skin and body shape

Gland	Name of hormone	Effect
Pituitary	GH (growth hormone)	Excess (in adults) causes coarsening of skin, increased hair growth and more muscular appearance
Thyroid	Thyroxine	Excess causes a warm, moist, flushed skin with thin hair and loss of body weight; deficiency causes swelling and puffiness of the face, weight gain and muscular weakness
Parathyroid	Parathormone	Lack of hormone not only affects the bones but causes abnormal production of keratin, affecting hair, skin and nails
Adrenal	Glucocorticoids	Excess causes Cushing's syndrome, characterised by a redistribution of fat producing a 'moon face', 'buffalo hump', large abdomen and thin limbs; purple stretch marks and bruises may appear on the skin; deficiency causes Addison's disease with weight loss and darkening of the skin
	Aldosterone	Excess can cause oedema
	Corticosteroids (sex hormones)	Excess of androgens causes virilism in women (deepening of the voice, growth of facial and body hair, muscle development and sometimes male pattern baldness); excess of oestrogens causes feminisation in men – breasts will enlarge
Ovary	Oestrogen and progesterone	Keep skin and hair in good condition; control distribution of body hair at puberty and influence the typical 'female' shape by causing fat to be stored in breasts, hips and thighs
Testes	Testosterone	Causes growth of facial and body hair at puberty; causes muscular development influencing 'male' body shape; encourages fat to be deposited around the waist and abdomen

Typical male and female body shapes

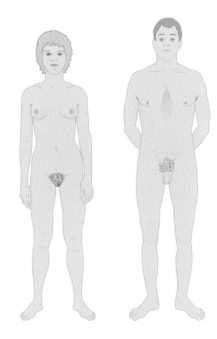

breasts

waist

wider hips

body hair
in axilla
(armpit) and
pubic region

muscular chest
and limbs

thicker waist

narrower hips

body hair
in axilla
(armpit) and
pubic region

thicker growth
may also be
present on back,
chest and limbs

THE REPRODUCTIVE SYSTEM

Male reproductive system

Sperm are continually being made in the testes of males from puberty onwards. At ejaculation, during sexual intercourse, the sperm travel along the sperm duct, mix with secretions from the reproductive glands, and are deposited in the vagina of the female. To fertilise an ovum one of these sperm must travel through the cervix and uterus to the oviduct and penetrate an ovum.

Female reproductive system

Ova or eggs are released from the ovary. Usually, in women of child-bearing age, one ovum is released approximately every four weeks. The ovum travels down the oviduct. This is where it may be fertilised if sexual intercourse has taken place and sperm are present. A fertilised ovum embeds in the wall of the uterus where it will develop until birth in approximately 38 weeks. An unfertilised ovum will travel through the uterus and be shed with the next menstrual flow.

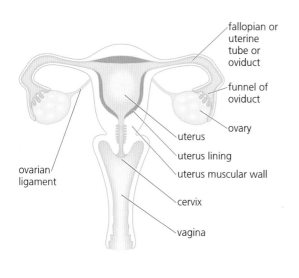

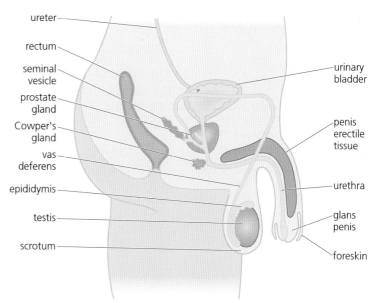

Male and female reproductive organs

Menstruation

This occurs from the onset of puberty until the menopause. Each menstrual cycle lasts on average for 28 days and involves changes in the ovaries and uterus controlled by hormones released from the ovary (oestrogen and progesterone) and from the pituitary gland (FSH and LH).

The menopause

After the menopause the menstrual cycle ceases, ovaries become inactive and atrophy (shrink) and ovarian production of the hormones oestrogen and progesterone ceases. The other reproductive organs (uterus, vagina, oviducts, breasts) also begin to atrophy. Bones become more brittle. Blood cholesterol levels and the risk of suffering a heart-attack increase. Hormone replacement therapy (HRT) delays these changes.

Female reproductive disorders

- **Amenorrhoea**: the absence of menstruation. Extreme weight changes or excessive exercise can inhibit menstruation. People suffering from anorexia or taking part in strenuous athletic training often find that their periods stop.
- **Dysmenorrhoea**: painful menstruation. This may be due to reproductive disorders but also affects young adults while the hormone changes affecting menstruation and the response by reproductive organs are becoming fully established.
- **Ovarian cysts**: a cyst is a fluid-filled swelling. Ovarian cysts are common and often without symptoms. They can, however, become infected, twist and cause pain, bleed, or grow to an uncomfortable size causing swelling of the abdomen.
- **Pre-menstrual tension**: a collection of symptoms which appear a few days before the onset of menstruation each month when progesterone levels are high. Symptoms may include headaches, irritability, fluid retention and sore breasts.

The breasts

The main function of the breasts or mammary glands is to produce milk for the offspring. The glandular tissue of the breast is similar to that found in

Vertical section showing breast tissues

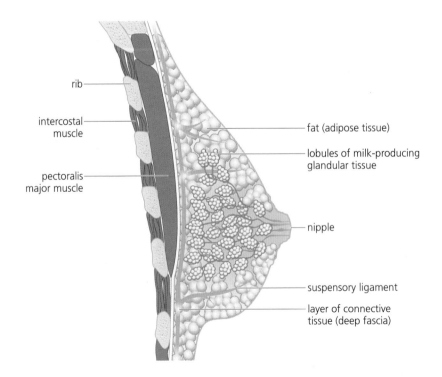

rib

intercostal muscle

pectoralis major muscle

fat (adipose tissue)

lobules of milk-producing glandular tissue

nipple

suspensory ligament

layer of connective tissue (deep fascia)

sweat glands. The milk-secreting cells (acini) are embedded in connective tissue and arranged as lobules separated by adipose (fat) tissue. The amount of adipose tissue present determines the size of the breast. Milk is produced under the influence of the hormone prolactin and passes through ducts to the nipple. It is ejected during breast-feeding in response to the hormone, **oxytocin**, produced as the baby starts to suckle. Oxytocin also causes uterine contractions, so breast-feeding can help the uterus return to its normal size more quickly following birth.

The breasts lie over the pectoral and serratus anterior muscles. They are attached to them by a layer of connective tissue. Strands of connective tissue called suspensory ligaments run through the breast tissue, anchoring the skin to the connective tissue layer covering the muscles. This support is relatively fragile.

Breast tumours

Breast tumours are felt as lumps in the breast tissue. Benign tumours are very common. They remain only in the breast and can be removed easily by minor surgery. Cysts are hollow tumours containing fluid. Fibroadenomas feel firm and rubbery.

Malignant tumours occur in breast cancer. A malignant tumour can spread quickly and easily to other tissues of the body when small parts of it break off and travel via the lymph system (metastasis). Early detection and treatment is vital. It is rarely painful so any breast changes including thickening, swelling, lumps, dimpling of the skin, nipple changes, discharge, scaliness or skin irritation should be reported to a doctor.

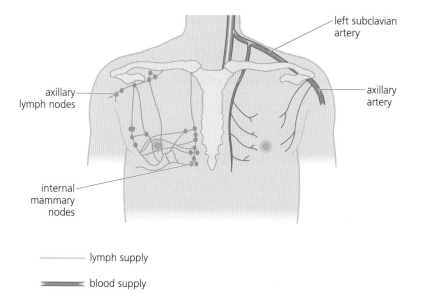

Lymph and blood supply to breast area

AGEING

Ageing is associated with a loss of body cells. Cells reproduce more slowly, die more quickly and malfunction more often. This means that all body tissues and organ systems deteriorate and the body responds less well in all situations. The maximum force generated by a muscle decreases by 30–40% between the ages of 30 and 80 years, and muscles adapt less easily to increased activity. (In a young person, muscle performance improves rapidly in response to training.)

Reproductive function decreases with age. This is a gradual process in men as testosterone secretion slowly declines from about the age of 40; in women the changes are more dramatic. The menopause occurs around the age of 50. Menstruation stops and there is a significant decline in the amount of oestrogen circulating in the body. Reproductive organs, including breast tissue, start to atrophy (shrink.) There is also a loss of bone mass. Connective tissues become less elastic, affecting skin, blood vessels, ligaments and even the lens of the eye.

Assessment of knowledge and understanding

You have now learnt about the related anatomy and physiology for the beauty therapy units with an essential knowledge requirement.

To test your level of knowledge, answer the following short questions. These will prepare you for your summative (final) assessment.

1 Make a large, labelled diagram to show the structure of the skin. Include on your diagram the five layers of the epidermis, a hair follicle, sweat and sebaceous glands, nerve endings and capillaries.

2 Describe the connective tissue of the dermis.

3 Which structures are found beneath the dermis?

4 What is the endocrine system?

5 Name the three main types of blood vessels.

6 Which type of blood vessel carries blood away from the heart?

7 Why do veins have valves?

8 Why do all cells in the body need a blood supply?

9 Where does lymph come from and where does it go?

10 Name the lymph nodes on this diagram.

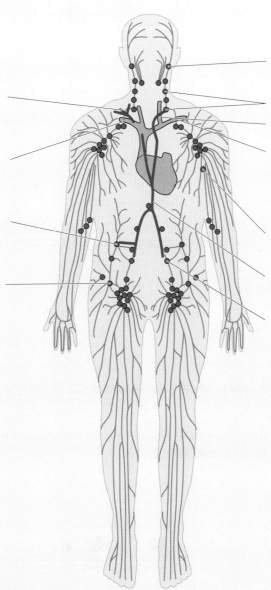

11 a. Describe erythema.
   b. What are its possible causes?

12 Label the organs on this diagram of the digestive system.

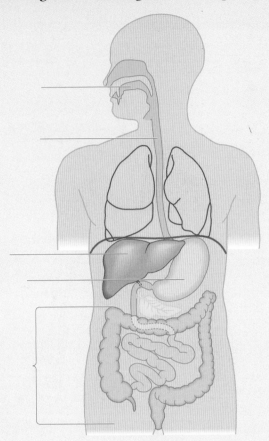

13 a. Label the kidneys and bladder on this diagram of the renal system.
    b. What is the function of each?

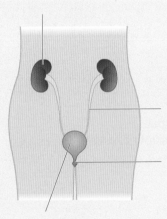

14 In which areas of the body would you find each of the following bones?
    tibia, carpal, vertebra, sternum, scapula, humerus, clavicle, femur, phalange, cranium.

15 a. In which areas of the body would you find each of the following
        muscles?
        deltoid, gastrocnemius, pectorals, hamstrings, tibialis anterior,
        gluteals, quadriceps, rectus abdominus, latissimus dorsi.
    b. State an action for each.

16 How is a tendon different from a ligament?

17 Describe the structure of voluntary muscle tissue.

18 What is meant by muscle tone and how can tone be lost or
    improved?

1 Name the type of joint found (a) in the cranium, (b) at the hip,
   (c) at the elbow.

2 At a synovial joint, what are the functions of the synovial fluid,
   ligaments and articular cartilage?

3 How do nerve impulses pass along nerve fibres?

4 How do nerves stimulate muscles to contract?

5 What is meant by the autonomic nervous system?

6 Name the main organs on the diagram of the respiratory system.

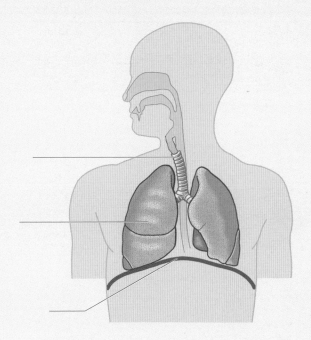

7 Where are the olfactory bulbs situated and what is their function?

8 Which area of the brain interprets the sensation of smell?

9 What is the importance of the limbic system to an aromatherapist?

10 a. Name the organs of the endocrine system on the diagram.
   b Name the hormones produced by each.
   c. What effect does each hormone have in the body?

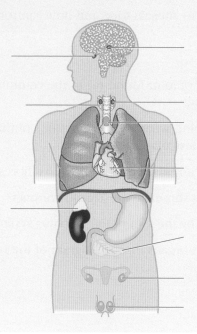

client treatments

chapter 5

Client treatments

ASSESSING THE CLIENT AND PREPARING TREATMENT PLANS

Before any treatment plan is decided upon, a thorough consultation with the client must be carried out by the therapist. An effective consultation, analysis or diagnosis is vital to enable the therapist to make an accurate assessment of the client's needs.

Professional consultation

Through the consultation process you assess the needs of the client and ascertain the treatment objectives. As a Level 3 therapist you will be performing many different treatments. The objectives of these treatments will be generally:

- to improve skin/nail condition and appearance
- to improve contour and muscle condition
- to aid relaxation and reduce symptoms of stress.

Consultation

Ellisons

Assessment techniques

Often there may be an underlying cause not immediately obvious that will only become apparent through:

- questioning
- observation and diagnostic assessment
- skin analysis
- body analysis.

Questioning techniques

It is necessary to ask the client a series of questions before the treatment plan can be finalised. This is carried out in a private area and the details are recorded on the client record card. The information is confidential and should be stored in a secure area following client treatment. This is enforced through the **Data Protection Act 1998** – legislation designed to protect the client's privacy and confidentiality.

The client should understand the reason behind the questions asked and feel comfortable when answering them. As such, she should be asked in a sensitive and supportive manner. Avoid technical terms, choosing commonly understood words to ensure client understanding. Ask 'open' questions which will encourage the client to give more than a one word response of 'yes' or 'no'.

If, after the consultation, you are unsure of the client's suitability for treatment, tactfully explain to the client why this is and ask her to seek permission from her GP before the treatment is given. The expectations of some clients may be unrealistic. If this is the case, tactfully explain why and aim to agree to a realistic treatment programme.

> **TIP**
>
> Designing an effective treatment plan includes:
> - completion of the client record card
> - checking for client suitability to treatments
> - diagnostic techniques
> - design of a suitable agreed treatment plan.

> **TIP**
>
> Open questioning techniques may begin with 'how', 'what', 'when' or 'where', for example 'How do you want to improve your skin's appearance?' 'What skin-care products do you use currently?'

> **HEALTH AND SAFETY**
>
> If there is a contra-indication, you will require a letter of consent from your client's GP before commencing any treatment.
> Never diagnose contra-indications when referring a client to her GP. This is not within your professional area.
> The health of the client should be checked at each treatment as her health or medication may change at any time.

Suitable questions for consultation and assessment

Questions for the client	Information required
What is your treatment need? (e.g. slimming, hair removal, improved facial muscle tone)	Is this realistic for this client? The therapist can consider appropriate treatments.
What area requires treatment?	Never presume the area to be treated! The treatment area may require an intensive approach through selected treatments in order to achieve maximum results.
	A longer treatment time and cost may be necessary, i.e. the removal of superfluous hair with epilation.

Questions for the client	Information required
What treatments have you received previously? Were you satisfied with the treatment results? If not, why?	Discuss the benefits of the treatment choice you are able to offer to meet her treatment needs.
(A client may be nervous of electrical treatments because of a previous bad experience.)	Where necessary, reassure the client and regain her confidence in the treatment through your professionalism.
Are you undergoing any current treatment for the area? (e.g. temporary methods of hair removal, current skin-care routine.)	You may find that the area of treatment has become worse through neglect or inappropriate treatment methods. Advise the client accordingly.
Describe your lifestyle.	These factors will directly affect the client's health.
Do you take regular exercise?	It may be necessary for the client to take regular exercise to improve fitness, muscle tone and increase calorie expenditure.
What is your occupation?	The client's occupation may be stressful or contribute to poor posture, muscle fatigue, etc. Discuss relevant treatments and supportive home-care advice.
Are there any external factors which may limit your commitment to the treatment programme?	The client's domestic situation may present restrictions to the programme.
Describe your diet.	Is the client's diet healthy and balanced? If not, offer a healthy alternative which is relevant to her needs.
Do you take part in any leisure activities?	Are these offering an effective means of relaxation? Offer suggestions where relevant, such as relaxation exercises.
Do you smoke?	Smoking has a detrimental effect on health and fitness. Tactfully discuss these issues.
Check the client's suitability for treatment – the client may have known contra-indications or contra-actions to treatments.	The client's health may contra-indicate treatment, i.e. medical history, current medication, recent operations, allergies, etc. Explain the reason and offer alternatives.
Inspect the treatment area and question the client if there are any evident conditions which cause concern.	There may be visible contra-indications to treatment application.
Suggest a realistic treatment plan and discuss treatment attendance, period of time and cost.	You need to know if the client can commit herself to the plan, in terms of time and cost.
Question the client to ensure she understands all aspects of the treatment plan, i.e. aims, outcomes.	This should provide an opportunity to answer relevant questions and will ensure client satisfaction.

HEALTH AND SAFETY

If the client's expectations from the treatment are unrealistic, tactfully advise her why this is so. For example, the client is seriously overweight and the slimming treatment will not be of beneficial effect unless there is substantial weight loss.

Remember, there are always alternative treatments that can be offered which will support the client in achieving her treatment goal.

Lifestyle factors

After questioning, consider whether the client's current lifestyle habits have contributed to the condition.

- **Alcohol**: Alcohol is a toxin (poison) and deprives the body of its vitamin reserves, especially vitamin B and C which are necessary for a healthy skin. It also causes skin dehydration.

- **Smoking**: Smoking interferes with cell respiration and slows down the circulation. This makes it more difficult for nutrients to reach the skin cells and for waste products to be eliminated. As such, the skin looks dull with a tendency towards open pores. Cigarette smoking also releases a chemical that destroys vitamin C. This interferes with the production of collagen and elastin and contributes to premature ageing of the skin. Nicotine is also a toxic substance.

- **Stress**: Stress can occur any time a person becomes pressurised. The symptoms of stress are seen in many different forms, including insomnia, poor digestion, headaches, muscular tension, and skin disorders such as psoriasis and eczema. If someone is suffering from stress, she may drink more alcohol and smoke more cigarettes, causing further stress to the skin. At the consultation, try to determine if the client is suffering from symptoms of stress. Very often the client will offer this information and the treatment objective will be to induce relaxation through its therapeutic effect.

- **Sedentary lifestyle**: Lack of exercise results in poor blood and lymph circulation and poor muscle tone, resulting in slack contours and weight gain due to inactivity. A feeling of well-being is achieved when taking part in exercise. Lack of exercise also results in lethargy. Aim to improve the client's motivation by educating her in the benefits to be achieved from a balanced diet, regular exercise and specific salon treatments.

- **Diet**: A nutritionally balanced diet is vital to the health of the body and the appearance of the skin. A healthy diet contains all the nutrients we need for health and growth. Lack of energy, skin allergies and disorders are, in part, the result of a poorly balanced diet.

- **Health**: The diagnosis of the client's health is important before considering any treatment plan. Medication and ill health can contra-indicate certain treatments or be a contributory cause of the problem. Always confirm the client's general health whilst completing the record card.

- **Ageing**: With ageing, there is a decrease in bone density (osteoporosis) so that bones become brittle and are easily fractured. Exercise and a diet containing plenty of calcium-rich foods can both guard against this. The change in appearance of women's skin during ageing is closely related to the altered production of the hormones oestrogen, progesterone and androgen at the menopause. The skin loses its elasticity, becomes dry, appears thinner, and the facial contours become slack. Treatments which accelerate the skin's natural functioning by nourishing and firming are recommended.

- **Exposure**: Unprotected exposure to the environment allows evaporation from the epidermis which results in a dry, dehydrated skin condition. Ultraviolet exposure causes premature ageing of the skin as the UVA rays

HEALTH AND SAFETY ✚

Miscarriage is most likely during the first three months of pregnancy. Regular monitoring of the client's health is important before every treatment, as medical conditions may occur such as blood pressure and diabetes.

penetrate the dermis. Free radicals – highly reactive molecules which can cause skin cells to degenerate – are also formed. These molecules disrupt the production of collagen and elastin that give skin its strength and elasticity. Environmental pollutants such as lead, mercury and aluminium can accumulate in the body where they attack protein in the cells. The skin should always be protected. Advise the client on suitable skin care and cosmetics that offer maximum protection. Anti-oxidant nutrients in the form of C, E and beta-carotene are beneficial in that they reinforce the effects of the skin-care routine and treatment plan.

- **Pregnancy**: Pregnancy is a time when clients may feel they need pampering. It is a time when the body undergoes significant bodily changes which can cause sensitive and pigmented skin, fluid retention, insomnia, nausea, constipation and back ache. Caution is needed in the choice of treatments, but there are many treatments available which may be of significant help to the client.

Observation and diagnostic assessment

Specific diagnostic procedures will enable you to identify any underlying condition or cause which may be creating or contributing to the condition identified. These must be carried out in a way that ensures the client's modesty and privacy is maintained at all times.

Skin analysis

Following facial cleansing, inspect the skin's surface using a magnifying lamp.

Assessing skin type

The skin is the largest organ of the body. Its basic structure does not vary from person to person, but the physiological functioning of its different features does, and it is this that gives us different skin types.

Skin reflects general health and responds quickly to any changes. This must be taken into consideration. For example, hormonal change at puberty or pregnancy may cause the sebaceous glands to become more active, resulting in a greasier skin. During this time, the treatment routine must therefore be altered to suit the skin's needs. However, when the hormonal balance is settled, the skin type may change completely.

Skin tone

A healthy young skin will probably have good skin tone and will be supple and elastic. This is because the collagen and elastin fibres in the skin are strong. The skin loses its strength with age and poor muscle tone is recognised by the appearance of facial lines and wrinkles. To test skin tone, gently lift the skin at the cheeks between two fingers and then let go. If the skin tone is good, the skin will spring back to its original shape.

Sorisa

A magnifying lamp

Stretch marks (striations)

Stretch marks appear on the skin as long, faint scars. They occur as a result of the skin breaking beneath the surface, in the dermal layer. Stretch marks are permanent and are caused by fluctuations in body weight as the skin stretches with weight gain, i.e. pregnancy. They are commonly seen on the breast, abdomen, inner upper arm and inner thigh.

Treatments which improve skin tone through firming will improve the appearance of stretch marks. For example microcurrent body application supported by the application of skin-strengthening creams or oils. Pregnant clients, clients with fine skin or sun-damaged skin should be encouraged to keep the skin supple with regular application of skin-care emollients.

Muscle tone

Observe the facial contours when the client is semi-reclined on the treatment couch. Poor muscle tone will be recognised by slack facial contours. The treatment aim will be to strengthen the muscles by shortening them which will tighten and firm the muscles and contours. Suitable treatments include facial electrical muscle stimulation and microcurrent, supported by facial exercises which the client can perform at home.

A healthy diet, effective skin-care routine and supportive beauty treatment plan all help to delay the effects of ageing.

Body analysis

Body analysis follows the completion of personal details on the client record card. Further details are recorded from each stage of the analysis.

Body type

There are three main body types, but most people are a combination of these.

- **ectomorph** – long limbs, slender, slim
- **mesomorph** – muscular build, well-developed shoulders and slim hips; an inverted triangle shape

Body types

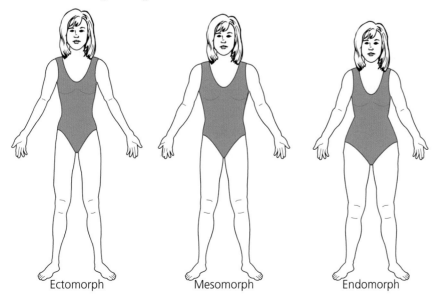

Ectomorph   Mesomorph   Endomorph

- **endomorph** – short limbs, plump, rounded body, often pear-shaped.

Specific target areas for treatment and figure correction will be common to each figure type.

Muscle tone

Exercising a muscle causes it to become firm, with improved metabolism, responsiveness and blood supply. Lack of exercise results in the muscle becoming stretched and slack. It is also less responsive and has a reduced rate of metabolism. Even when relaxed, a muscle which is regularly exercised will appear toned. Many treatments will require the muscle to have its tone improved. This will involve the client physically exercising or passive exercise where the use of electrical equipment causes the muscles to contract and relax, thus improving their tone.

To assess muscle tone, simple exercises may be performed either on the treatment couch or on the floor. Sample exercises are described in the table.

Simple exercises to assess muscle tone

Area	Exercise
Abdominals	Ask the client to perform a sit-up (legs bent at knee) from the lying position.
	Ask the client to breathe in – the abdomen should become flatter, possibly concave.
Legs	Whilst lying on her back, ask the client to perform leg raises, slowly lifting one leg at a time and holding each at its raised position.
Arms	The client holds her hand to her shoulder whilst the therapist attempts to move the arm from position.

Body fat

The amount of body fat stored underneath the skin will depend upon the weight of the client. This is not always evenly distributed, leading to problem areas – usually the thighs and bottom in women.

Body mass index

The body mass index (BMI) is a height–weight measure often used to determine if a client is overweight.

A formula used to calculate this is as follows:

- Weight in kilograms divided by height in meters squared.

The average adult BMI is between 20–25, in excess of 26 is considered a health risk.

$$BMI = \frac{wt}{ht^2}$$

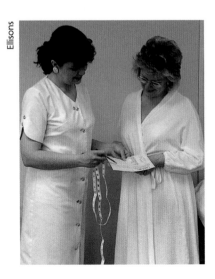

Ellisons

Measuring

Cellulite

Cellulite is a term used to describe fatty tissue that causes the overlying skin to appear dimpled, like 'orange peel' in appearance. Common places for the occurrence of cellulite are thigh, buttock, knee and triceps area.

To assess for cellulite, gently squeeze the client's skin. If cellulite is present, small lumpy nodules will be seen. In advanced cases this will be obvious without squeezing the skin.

Cellulite is caused by:

- poor venous and lymphatic circulation, providing poor elimination of waste products
- a sedentary lifestyle, resulting in weight gain caused by low energy expenditure and sluggish circulation due to inactivity
- poor diet and metabolism problems due to hormonal imbalance.

However, slim women who exercise regularly can also be affected. Therefore a specific treatment course should be advised, with supporting retail products. The treatment plan will be to stimulate the lymphatic circulation, increase exercise and improve the diet, with a reduction in processed foods and toxins, and an increase in water consumption to flush out excess toxins.

Beauty therapy treatments which are beneficial for the treatment of cellulite are those which improve circulation, mobilise fatty tissue and generally improve skin appearance. These include manual and mechanical massage, aromatherapy, vacuum suction, galvanic body therapy and microcurrent.

Advise the client on the application of any retail preparations recommended. Often the cost of the treatment will include the supporting home-care preparations.

> **TIP** ✔
>
> Specific types of massage, such as manual lymphatic drainage (MLD), improve the efficiency of the lymphatic system. Cypress, lemon and lavender are essential oils which may be used in conjunction with massage on a cellulite condition.

Fluid retention

Tissue fluid can accumulate, causing swelling (oedema). The therapist must assess if this has a medical or non-medical cause. This will be determined at the consultation stage whilst completing the client record card.

Normal swelling can occur around the ankles if a person stands for long periods. It is common before menstruation, affecting the abdomen and breasts. Fluid retention can also be caused by allergies and a diet with excessive processed foods, high salt intake and insufficient water. To test for fluid retention, press the client's skin. If it remains indented and does not immediately spring back, this is a sign of fluid retention.

> **HEALTH AND SAFETY**
>
> Fluid retention may be symptomatic of a serious underlying cause requiring medical attention, such as cardiac, kidney or metabolic problems.

Weight

When weighing the client, ideally weigh her at the same time of day in the same clothing. Usually this will be with the client in her underwear but if not, allow 2 lbs (1 kg) for outer clothing. Record the weight on the client record card. The weight should then be measured against the desirable weight range tables for the client's height and frame size.

If the client wishes to lose weight, a realistic target should be set. This should be monitored weekly to maintain motivation.

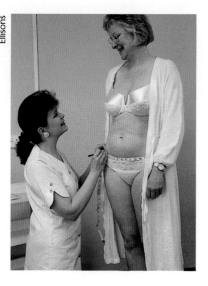

Taking measurements

Height

Using a fixed scale attached to the wall, measure the client's height without shoes, heels together and the back as straight as possible. The shoulders should touch the wall whilst the client looks ahead.

Taking measurements

Measurement records provide evidence of inch loss, the aim of many figure body treatments. They may be performed before and immediately after certain body treatments where the aim is to achieve immediate inch loss, e.g. a slimming body wrap. Normally, if the client is regularly attending the salon, once a week is sufficient. Frame size is identified by measuring the size of the client's bones – small, medium or large.

> **TIP**
>
> For accuracy when measuring, always take measurements from the same place – ideally fixed bony points. For example, any vertebrae may be used as these points remain static. Record the results on the client record card.

> **TIP**
>
> Another method of checking postural alignment is to use a weighted plumb-line (a string with an attached weight). This line is the line of gravity, and should appear to pass through the centre of the earlobe, the centre of the shoulder, behind the hip joint, in front of the knee joint and in front of the ankle joint.
>
> The client is checked from the side, front and back for any exaggerated protrusion against the line of gravity created by the weighted plumb-line.

Assessing posture

Posture varies from person to person and is affected by the client's:

- occupation
- health
- psychological state
- muscular strength.

Good posture is recognised when the body is in alignment:

- head held up
- arms loose at the sides of the body
- back held straight but not stiff
- abdomen pulled in
- hips held at the same level

- bottom pulled in
- feet – body weight equally distributed.

Observe your client from the front, side and back. Make notes on the record card of any exaggerated curves or alignment imbalance of the body. Areas of postural imbalance will result in muscle strain, tightening and fatigue.

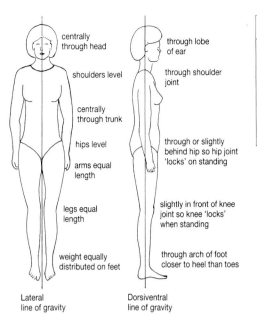

centrally through head

shoulders level

centrally through trunk

hips level

arms equal length

legs equal length

weight equally distributed on feet

Lateral line of gravity

through lobe of ear

through shoulder joint

through or slightly behind hip so hip joint 'locks' on standing

slightly in front of knee joint so knee 'locks' when standing

through arch of foot closer to heel than toes

Dorsiventral line of gravity

Good posture

HEALTH AND SAFETY +

Whilst some postural disorders are caused through bad habits, others are genetic postural deformities which cannot be corrected or remedied.

Common figure faults

Fault	Cause	Treatment
Poking chin: If the head pokes forwards it distorts the ligaments of the neck, leading to neck and shoulder pain. Headaches, tiredness and backache can result due to unnecessary strain on the ligaments and muscles.	High heels, which alter balance, throwing the body weight forwards; occupation, where the head protrudes forwards for long periods; associated postural problems – round shoulders.	Heat treatment to the upper back followed by manual massage; stretching and mobility exercises for the shortened muscles; education of correct posture.
One shoulder higher than the other: This can lead to the postural condition 'scoliosis' where there is a sideways deviation of the vertebral column. This is commonly seen with one hip being higher than the other.	Uneven distribution of weight when carrying loads, e.g. carrying a bag on one shoulder; standing with the weight on one hip, affecting postural alignment.	Shortened muscles will require lengthening and lengthened muscles will require shortening to correct the lateral deviation; stretching and mobility exercises; education of correct posture.

Scoliosis

Fault	Cause	Treatment	
Rounded shoulders: The shoulders sag forwards, shortening the chest muscles and lengthening the muscles of the upper back. This leads to sagging breasts in women and often a dowagers hump occurs in old age. Here, fatty deposits accumulate over the thoracic and cervical area of the upper back and neck. This is commonly associated with the postural condition 'kyphosis' where there is an exaggerated outward curve in the thoracic area of the vertebral column.	Occupation, where the shoulders tend to be rounded for long periods, i.e. computer operators, hairdressers; psychological, e.g. lack of confidence or a postural attempt to disguise a large chest or minimise height.	Mechanical massage or vacuum suction may be of benefit following a preheating treatment applied to the area; stretching and mobilising exercises; muscle-toning treatments for the stretched muscles; education of correct posture.	 Kyphosis
Forwards or backwards tilt of the pelvic girdle: This pelvic deviation affects body alignment, causing back strain and muscle fatigue. A forward pelvic tilt is commonly referred to as the postural condition 'lordosis', where the client will appear to have a hollow back in the lumbar region.	Poor posture, e.g. slouching; poor muscle tone of the anterior abdominal walls; post-pregnancy or operation in the area.	Manual massage to stretch the tightened muscles and increase mobility; active exercise or passive exercise using electrical muscle stimulation or microcurrent treatment to strengthen the abdominal muscles.	
Hips not level: This is also commonly seen as one hip and one knee being higher than the other. This can lead to or be caused by the postural condition 'scoliosis' where there is a sideways deviation of the vertebral column to the left or right.	Standing with the body weight on one hip; uneven distribution of weight when carrying loads.	Shortened muscles will require lengthening and lengthened muscles will require shortening to correct the lateral deviation; education of correct posture.	Lordosis

Sitting, standing and walking

Assess and correct the client's sitting, standing and walking stance:

- **Sitting**: Ensure the knees are parallel to the floor. Ideally the knees should be higher than the hips; this avoids unnecessary back strain. The bottom should be pressed against the back of a chair. Feet should be flat on the floor.

- **Standing**: The body should be held upwards yet not stiff. Spinal curvatures must not be exaggerated. The weight should be balanced between both feet. Hips should be level, with the stomach and bottom pulled in. Shoulders should be relaxed and set back a little; arms loosely at the sides.

- **Walking**: The body should be tilted slightly forwards as each step is taken. The toes should point forward and the heel should be lifted well off the ground as the weight is transferred to the front foot. Arms should swing freely.

Postural education requires emphasising to the client poor postural habits which require correction. To improve posture, strengthening and stretching exercises may be recommended which tone weak muscles, increase mobility and support salon treatments.

HEALTH AND SAFETY

Certain spinal curvatures and postural disorders require medical attention and cannot be treated by the therapist. If unsure, always recommend GP approval before treatments are given.

HEALTH AND SAFETY

Pregnancy
Avoid leaning back. Keep the back straight which is less tiring. Strengthen the muscles following the birth, avoiding slouching.

beauty
therapy
units

chapter 6

BT16 Epilate the hair follicle using diathermy, galvanic and blend techniques

Learning objectives

This unit describes how to epilate the hair permanently using diathermy, blend and galvanic techniques. It describes the competencies required to enable you to:

- **Consult with the client**

- **plan the treatment**

- **prepare for the treatment**

- **treat hair follicles using diathermy, galvanic and blend epilation**

- **complete the treatment**

When providing electrical needle epilation techniques it is important to use the skills you have learnt in the following core mandatory units:

Unit G1   Ensuring your own actions reduce the risks to health and safety

Unit G6   Promote additional products or services to clients

Unit G11 Contribute to the financial effectiveness of the business

INTRODUCTION

Electrical needle epilation is used to permanently remove unwanted superfluous (excess) hair. A fine needle is used to deliver an electrical current into the hair follicle to destroy the hair root and this eventually destroys the hair follicle tissue, preventing the hair from regrowing.

This is a popular salon treatment and is usually carried out for cosmetic reasons. It is used on occasions to remove excessive hair growth resulting from certain medical conditions and has psychological benefits, as clients can often be very distressed by the hair growth. Clients experience great improvement in self-esteem and self-confidence following treatment.

Superfluous hair is perfectly normal at certain stages of a woman's life, such as during puberty, pregnancy and menopause. Hair found during these times can disappear once the normal balance has returned. However, hair newly formed during the menopause is often permanent. Unwanted hair on the face is the area most often treated by epilation, but body hair can be removed from areas such as the breasts, underarms, bikini lines and legs. Male clients may also have hair permanently removed either for cosmetic reasons or because of irritation or ingrowing hairs. Clients undergoing gender reassignment from male to female may also want to change their hair growth pattern into a more female one.

ANATOMY AND PHYSIOLOGY

Endocrine system

The endocrine system is made up of glands, which are situated around the body with no direct links to one another. They are known as ductless glands because the hormones they secrete go directly into the bloodstream.

A hormone is a chemical substance which is made in one gland and carried by the blood to an organ (target organ) or tissue where it will influence nutrition, growth and activity. The body is regulated partly by hormones and partly by the autonomic nervous system.

The endocrine system consists of the following glands:

- Pituitary gland and hypothalamus
- thyroid gland
- parathyroid glands (4)
- adrenal glands (2)
- Islets of Langerhans in the pancreas
- pineal gland
- ovaries (2) female
- testes (2) male.

The structure of the hair follicle

Hair follicles are formed from the epidermis before birth. The developing follicle extends as a sheath down through the dermis into the subcutaneous tissue. The hair follicle, in combination with its sebaceous gland, is known as the pilosebaceous unit. The follicle develops from epithelial cells and differentiates into specific components. These are:

- dermal papilla
- outer root sheath
- inner root sheath
- bulb
- dermal cord
- vitreous membrane
- connective tissue.

Cross-section through the hair follicle and hair

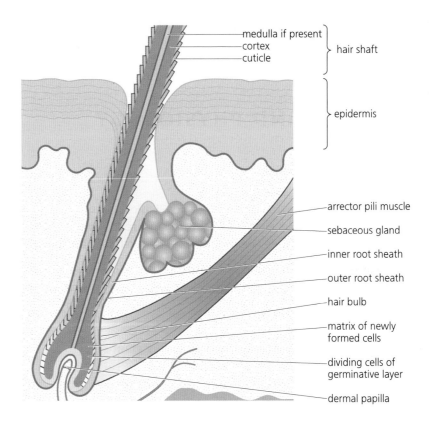

medulla if present
cortex
cuticle
hair shaft

epidermis

arrector pili muscle
sebaceous gland
inner root sheath
outer root sheath
hair bulb
matrix of newly formed cells
dividing cells of germinative layer
dermal papilla

Dermal papilla

This is the connective tissue sheath surrounded by the hair bulb. It is not part of the hair follicle but a separate organ that serves the follicle. It has an excellent blood supply which is necessary for the growth of the hair. Hormones secreted by the endocrine glands are transported via the bloodstream, therefore follicle sensitivity to these hormones can lead to increased hair growth.

Outer epithelial root sheath

This is a continuation of the germinative layer of the epidermis and forms the follicle wall. It is a constant source of hair germ cells from which the new follicles grow when stimulated by circulating hormones. It contains glycogen (a water-soluble animal starch) which attracts the electrical current in treatment. The outer root sheath is always present and not removed in epilation.

Inner root sheath

The inner root sheath grows from the bottom of the follicle with the hair, to the level of the sebaceous gland, where it disintegrates. It consists of three layers:

- Henle's layer, the outer layer
- Huxley's layer, the middle layer
- Cuticle, the inner layer.

The cuticle layer of the inner root sheath interlocks with the cuticle of the hair and anchors it in place.

Bulb

The bulb is the expanded base of the hair root and surrounds the dermal papilla. Its lower part is where the cells multiply and divide (mitosis) to create the hair shaft: this is the matrix. The hair continues to develop as it passes through the regions of the upper bulb and root.

Connective tissue

This surrounds the follicle and sebaceous glands, providing necessary sensory and blood supplies. The connective tissue sheath includes and is a continuation of the papilla.

Vitreous membrane

The vitreous membrane is a non-cellular hyaline membrane which lies next to the outer root sheath.

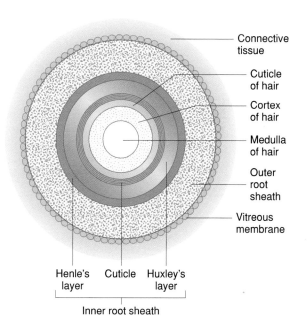

The layers of the hair and follicle

Dermal cord

This is present in the first stage of hair growth (anagen). It is a thin cord of hair germ cells which maintain contact with the dermal papilla, enabling a new hair to develop by mitosis. It grows until it covers the dermal papilla and forms the bulb.

Hair types

Lanugo hair

Lanugo hair is found on the unborn foetus and usually shed at the eighth month of pregnancy or within two weeks of birth. Lanugo hairs are soft and lack pigmentation due to the absence of a medulla.

Vellus hair

Vellus hairs are very fine, downy and soft hairs found on the face and body. These primary hairs develop follicle sensitivity to hormone-related conditions and become thicker, darker and coarser resulting in terminal hair. Often, vellus hairs do not contain a medulla.

Terminal hair

These are deep-rooted, thick, coarse, pigmented, visible hairs which replace vellus hair in specific regions of the body. They vary greatly in shape, diameter, length, colour and texture. Terminal hair can be found on the scalp, underarms, pubic region, eyelashes and eyebrows. In men they are also present on the chest and beard areas.

Terminal hairs can be divided into three types, as shown in the table.

Terminal hair types

Name	Characteristics	Examples
asexual	genetic hair, present at birth	eyelashes, eyebrows, scalp, arms and legs
ambisexual	develops in both sexes at puberty	axilla, pubic area, lower limbs and forearms
sexual	influenced by androgen hormones	beard, moustache, nasal hair, ears, back and chest

Hair growth cycle

Hair growth can be divided into three stages: anagen, catagen and telogen.

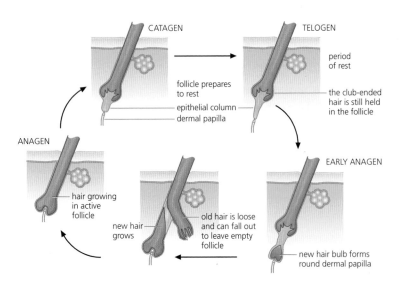

Hair growth cycle

Anagen

This is the active hair growth stage which occurs when the hair follicle is at its maximum depth. Nourishment is gained from the dermal papillae, whilst the hair germ cells multiply by mitosis to produce the bulb in the follicle. If a hair is epilated in the anagen stage, the inner root sheath and bulb will be visible. Anagen can last for several years in scalp hair.

Catagen

This is a brief transitional phase between anagen and telogen, lasting from only a few days up to a few weeks. The hair starts to travel up in the follicle and becomes detached from the dermal papillae. It receives nourishment from the follicle walls and transforms itself into a club hair; the lower follicle begins to shrivel and collapse whilst the dermal cord maintains contact with the lower follicle to continue the hair growth cycle.

Telogen

The club hair remains in the follicle for several months until a newly regrowing anagen hair pushes it out.

Hair structure

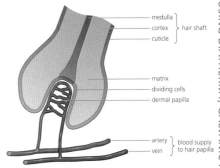

Cross-section of terminal hair

Hair shape is determined by the shape of the follicle – straight hairs grow from straight follicles whereas curly hairs grow from curved follicles. Terminal hair, whether straight or curly, has three layers:

- **Cuticle**: a single layer of overlapping cells which interlocks with the cuticle of the hair follicle. It anchors the hair in place and provides protection for the cortex, and gives the hair its elasticity.
- **Cortex**: this forms the bulk of the hair and contains elongated keratinised cells cemented together. The pigment melanin can be found in this layer and is responsible for giving the hair its colour.
- **Medulla**: found in the centre of the hair but not always present. It can appear continuous or broken and is responsible for the sheen of the hair.

Hair growth

Hair growth is usually inherited. The amount of facial and body hair and the basic pattern of its distribution varies with each racial group.

- People of North European and Caucasian extraction tend to have light to medium body and facial hair growth.
- People of Latin and Indian extraction tend to possess heavier body and facial hair.
- People of Eastern extraction tend to possess very little or no body and facial hair.
- People of African-Caribbean extraction tend to have little body or facial hair.

Types of hair growth

Superfluous hair can be described as either **hypertrichosis** or **hirsutism**. Hirsutism is a term used to describe a pattern of hair growth that is abnormal for that person's sex, such as when a woman's hair growth follows a man's hair growth pattern. The hairs become thicker in diameter and the hair growth cycle is speeded up. It may be due to **primary hirsutism**, where the client has follicle sensitivity to circulating androgen (male) hormones. In **secondary hirsutism** the adrenal glands and ovaries produce too much androgen due to an endocrine disorder. This condition can be treated by medical help and epilation.

> **TIP**
>
> Hereditary factors must be taken into account when assessing what is normal for a particular client.

Hypertrichosis is an abnormal growth of excess hair. It is usually due to abnormal conditions brought about by disease or injury. This condition is found in both sexes and is determined by a general overgrowth of vellus and terminal hair.

All hair growth, whether normal or abnormal, is regulated by hormones. It is the over-secretion of male hormones that causes excessive hair growth.

Normal hair growth occurs during periods of life where the endocrine system changes naturally, causing an increase in hair growth, i.e. puberty, pregnancy and menopause. This is often classed as **normal systemic hair growth**.

Changes during puberty, pregnancy and the menopause

Oestrogen and progesterone bring about the female characteristics whilst androgens produce the male characteristics, i.e. pubic and underarm hair. At puberty, females start to develop breasts and menstruation begins. If there is an imbalance in the hormones the client may develop male hair growth characteristics. When the client is pregnant, large amounts of progesterone are secreted which thicken and maintain the lining of the uterus. This stimulates androgen production which may result in excessive hair growth.

Pregnancy and the menopause

Hypertrichosis (excess hair) which develops during pregnancy usually diminishes once the child has been born, therefore the client should be informed of this at the consultation.

During the menopause, oestrogen and progesterone secretions from the ovaries diminish and circulating androgens stimulate the hair follicles. This can result in a thickening of vellus hair producing a thicker, coarser growth. Excess hair may develop and epilation will be necessary to remove the hair growth permanently.

Abnormal hair growth

Abnormal hair growth is often the result of an abnormal change in the endocrine system causing a hormonal imbalance. This may be due to illness, tumours, dietary disorders or medication.

Virilisation

With virilisation, the female body becomes more masculine and as result, heavy facial and body hair growth can be seen in a masculine pattern. A hormone imbalance which may be due to a tumour of the adrenal cortex or a tumour of the ovaries will influence the hypersecretion of androgens and the reduction in the secretion of oestrogen. This will produce the male pattern of hair growth in females. This condition is known as **abnormal systemic hair growth**.

Polycystic ovary syndrome (Stein–Leventhal syndrome)

A variety of symptoms can result from this condition, including infertility, heavy periods, irregular periods and excessive growth of facial and body hair. The cause is cysts, or growths, on the ovaries which develop due to non-completion of the ovulation process. This is not uncommon.

Cushing's syndrome

This condition is often due to tumours on the adrenal cortex, where too much cortisol is produced. There is an associated over-production of androgens as a result and a heavy masculine hair growth can be seen. Other symptoms include a thickened trunk, round face, dowager's hump and thin legs and arms.

Anorexia nervosa

People suffering from the eating disorder anorexia nervosa become very thin and undernourished. It is quite common to see excessive hair growth all over the face and body. This is a result of a shutdown in the ovaries, reducing the oestrogen level and stimulating the circulating androgens. Also, women and girls who have a high level of athletic training with low levels of body fat (i.e. gymnasts) may also be affected by the ovaries shutting down. Both processes will result in varying degrees of virilisation.

Effects of medication

Certain prescribed drugs, such as androgens and anabolic steroids, have a secondary effect of causing excessive hair growth. The therapist needs to determine the effect of the drug with the client's doctor so that an effective treatment plan can be devised.

Unusual hair growth

- **Ingrowing hairs**: These are hairs which have not grown above the surface of the epidermis and are still in the follicle. If left, the hairs can become infected so they need to be freed.

HEALTH AND SAFETY
To free an ingrowing hair the skin's surface should first be sanitised. Wearing disposable gloves, the therapist should gently pierce the surface of the skin to free the hair using a sterile disposable needle. The hair should then be cut, not removed, to allow the skin to heal around it.

TIP
Women under considerable stress have excessive hair growth due to high levels of adrenalin which also stimulates androgen production.

- **Embedded hairs**: These again are hairs which have become trapped below the skin. They should be treated as ingrowing hairs. When the skin is pierced, the hair usually will uncoil from underneath.
- **Pili multigemini hairs**: Here, two or more hairs grow out of a single follicle. Beneath the opening there are separate papillas for each hair, and the hairs have their own outer and inner root sheath.
- **Corkscrew hairs**: This hair is curved due to the follicle being distorted in shape. Over-treatment using temporary or permanent hair removal methods can cause this condition.

● **Tombstone hairs**: If the therapist treats a telogen hair and there is an early anagen hair also growing in the follicle, the anagen hair will work its way to the skin's surface and will appear dull and thicker than normal. It will eventually fall out.

ELECTRICAL SCIENCE

Direct or galvanic current

A direct current is one where electrons flow in one direction.
This current uses the negative pole (cathode) and positive pole (anode) to complete a circuit.

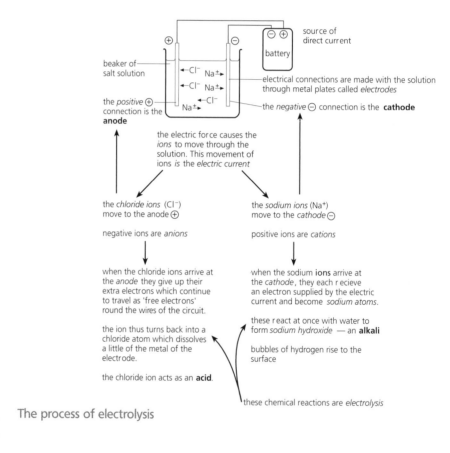

The process of electrolysis

Galvanic current action occurs throughout the length and width of the follicle (indicated by a dark line)

The client holds the indifferent electrode (anode) and the needle holder is attached to the negative outlet (cathode). The negative pole is the active pole and the positive pole is used to attract and complete the circuit.

When direct current electrons go through a salt water solution, the salt and water molecules become chemically rearranged and form new substances. The salt and water are changed into sodium hydroxide and hydrogen gas. This reaction is called **electrolysis**.

Ellisons

A diathermy machine

Carlton Professional

Blend epilator

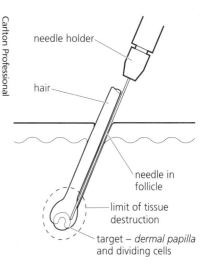

needle holder

hair

needle in follicle

limit of tissue destruction

target – *dermal papilla* and dividing cells

Diathermy current action is restricted to the base of the hair follicle

The needle from the direct current electrical epilation machine is inserted into the follicle; direct current flows out over the length of the needle. Because of the moisture in the follicle, sodium hydroxide (lye) is formed within it. This chemically decomposes the follicle tissue and then remains in the follicle to continue to destroy the cells.

High frequency current or short wave diathermy

Short wave diathermy uses a high frequency alternating current oscillating at millions of cycles per second. High frequency epilating machines work on 13.56 and 40.68 MHz (the higher the frequency the more comfortable the sensation).

A high frequency alternating current is introduced into the skin via a needle, which produces heat as the water molecules in the cells are agitated by the high frequency energy.

The needle itself is not hot. Low level tissue destruction occurs as proteins in the cells coagulate on heating, called electro-coagulation, and blood vessels in the area are cauterised.

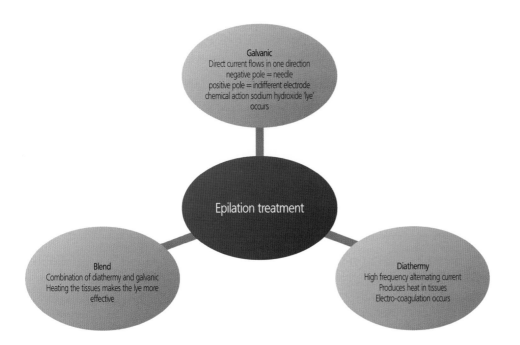

Galvanic
Direct current flows in one direction
negative pole = needle
positive pole = indifferent electrode
chemical action sodium hydroxide 'lye'
occurs

Epilation treatment

Blend
Combination of diathermy and galvanic
Heating the tissues makes the lye more
effective

Diathermy
High frequency alternating current
Produces heat in tissues
Electro-coagulation occurs

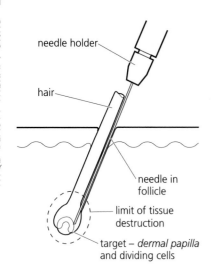

needle holder

hair

needle in follicle

limit of tissue destruction

target – *dermal papilla* and dividing cells

Blend current action combines the effects of galvanic and diathermy, producing both heat (dashed line) and lye (dark line)

Blend current

In the blend method, both high frequency and direct currents flow from the needle at the same time. Both currents still retain their individual effects in the skin follicle.

The direct current produces sodium hydroxide (lye) that chemically decomposes the follicle, while the high frequency current coagulates the follicle. The interaction of the two currents produces better results than either current on its own. The heating of the tissue makes the sodium hydroxide more effective.

RECEPTION

When booking the initial appointment for epilation treatment, sufficient time should be allocated to perform the consultation, which normally takes 15 minutes. This is usually complimentary. This is followed by a test treatment of the area to assess skin tolerance to the treatment and check the client's suitability for the treatment. It also gives the client an indication of the sensation to expect during the treatment process. After the first consultation, treatment times will vary according to the area to be treated and the amount of hair to be removed.

- Small treatment areas such as the upper lip and chin are usually treated within 10 to 15 minutes.
- Larger areas such as the back, forearm and lower limbs may take up to an hour.

The client should be advised to wear loose-fitting clothing if body hair is to be removed, to prevent rubbing and irritation of the area following treatment.

If the facial area is to be treated, advise the client to avoid wearing heavy facial make-up and high-necked clothes or scarves, which may irritate the area. The skin must be kept clean to avoid infection. Advise against activities such as swimming or skin treatments such as exfoliation on the same day, as these may cause skin sensitisation.

Skin healing intervals must be allowed between treatments. This will prevent infection and scarring. Dependant upon the area to be treated, hair growth and skin type this may be between one and two weeks.

Consultation

The consultation is an important part of a successful electrical epilation treatment. The information gained will allow you to assess whether the client is suitable for treatment and devise a treatment plan to suit each client.

The therapist will consider the client's medical history, emotional condition, general health and well-being, any contra-indications present, current hair growth and her suitability for treatment. Time should be spent explaining the treatment procedure and what is achievable with regular treatments, so that the client is aware of her commitment in relation to time and costs.

Planning the treatment

- Discuss and plan the treatment programme with the client
- Suitable for client's hair growth
- Suitable for client's skin type and condition
- Management of hair growth during treatment
- Discuss possible contra-actions
- Home-care advice
- Diathermy, galvanic or blend

Explain the sensation of the treatment to the client:

- High frequency – short wave diathermy technique: a slight stinging 'irritating' sensation will be experienced.

- Direct current – galvanic technique: there will be a sensation of warmth which will gradually increase in intensity.

- Blend technique: a slight stinging 'irritating' sensation will be experienced.

During the consultation, the client should be encouraged to discuss the treatment and ask questions. The following questions should be asked of the client during the consultation in order to obtain relevant information:

- *When did the problem start?* This will give an indication of the cause of the unwanted hair growth, i.e. common times for unwanted hair to appear for a female are during puberty, pregnancy and the menopause. Such hair, although unwanted, is normal. If the hair appears for no apparent reason it may indicate an underlying medical cause.

- *How is your general health?* This may give you an indication as to the cause of hair growth. Details of the client's medical history and medication taken need to be recorded. This is necessary because some medication may cause unnatural hair growth and her medical history may indicate the cause.

- *Is your menstrual cycle normal?* An unusual menstrual cycle may indicate a medical problem resulting in unwanted hair growth.

ACTIVITY

State how your consultation questions would differ when treating a female client and a male client.

- *How many children? What are their ages?* Occasionally pregnancy can initiate an unwanted hair growth problem due to hormonal imbalance. This usually diminishes after the birth, but the client may require temporary removal.

- *Which methods of hair removal have you used previously?* Removing hair from the root with temporary methods of hair removal, such as tweezing and waxing, can increase hair growth due to stimulation of the dermal papillae and blood supply. These measures may also have distorted the follicle, therefore it may take longer to achieve success with this treatment. Such methods must be stopped as soon as treatment commences.

- *Which area do you want to have treated?* This will allow you tactfully to determine the problem area and the psychological effect on the client. Never presume the area to be treated!

- *Have you had epilation before?* The therapist needs to know when, why and what method was used and how successful it has been. Be professional and discreet at all times when discussing other therapists.

- *Name, address and telephone number* This is necessary in case the client needs to be contacted in order to change her appointment.

Client record card

A client record card should always be completed prior to the treatment being given. This enables the therapist to ensure that the client is suitable for treatment. Once the client has verified the details given she must sign the card. This protects the therapist and client from undesirable treatment outcomes caused by misinformation. An evaluation of the information will form the basis of the treatment plan.

Once the consultation is completed, make sure that the client is satisfied with the information given and the treatment plan, and encourage the client to ask any further questions. Full and accurate record cards are necessary for insurance purposes.

TIP

Before contacting a client by telephone you must confirm that this is acceptable. Some clients may wish to keep their treatments confidential.

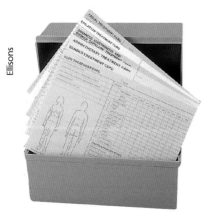

Ellisons

Record cards

CONTRA-INDICATIONS

If, whilst completing the record card or on visual inspection of the skin, the client is found to have any of the following in the treatment area, then electrical epilation treatment must not be carried out.

Contra-indications requiring medical referral

- epilepsy – a fit would put the client at risk of injury
- diabetes – poor skin healing makes the client vulnerable to infection
- hormone imbalance (abnormal hair growth) – the treatment will be ineffective unless the hormonal imbalance is treated and controlled

HEALTH AND SAFETY

Diabetes
In diabetes sufferers, the skin is slow to heal. To enable effective skin healing, treatment time should be shorter and over longer periods. Treatment applications must be well spaced.

- cardio-vascular conditions – the anti-coagulant drugs prescribed for these conditions interfere with the effectiveness of the treatment as coagulation is required in the follicle

- nervous system dysfunction or highly nervous clients – it is important that the client is able to detect sensations in order that the skin is not over-treated

- pregnancy – after the birth of the child, any excess hair growth often disappears naturally as the hormones stabilise

- metal plates and pins in the area being treated – if being treated with galvanic technique, current concentration may occur causing tissue burning around the metal

- skin disorders such as psoriasis, eczema, naevi, keloids, scarring, cuts, abrasions, recent wounds, bruising – there is a risk of infection or further skin damage

- skin disease, infectious conditions such as herpes simplex and scabies – there is a risk of cross-infection

- pre-malignant moles – the cells may become damaged and become malignant as a result

- blood disorders such as hepatitis B and AIDS caused by the virus HIV (human immunodeficiency virus) – there is a risk of cross-infection as the viruses are transmitted by body fluids

- loss of skin sensation or hypersensitive skin – the skin may become damaged

- asthma – the stress of the treatment may cause an attack

- electrical implants such as a pace-maker – their efficiency may be affected by the electrical current, i.e. the high frequency current.

Clients who have contra-indications must be referred to their GP prior to treatment. This must be done without specifically naming a condition and must not cause concern or alarm. The GP will diagnose professionally and will be able to determine whether the client is able to have electrical epilation treatment. A note from the GP is then needed before the treatment commences. These contra-indications apply to all three types of electrical epilation.

ACTIVITY

Explain when you would decide that treatment could not be carried out. Discuss the ways in which you should explain to your client that you would like her/him to seek medical advice.

HEALTH AND SAFETY

Areas not recommended for treatment
Areas which are not recommended for treatment are inside the ear, inside the nose and genitals. These areas are all very sensitive and also may have healing and infection problems.

TIP

GP referral
Acknowledge a GP referral with thanks. This will maintain a positive, professional relationship between yourself and the medical profession.

EQUIPMENT AND MATERIALS

General equipment

- couch, with adjustable height
- stool, with adjustable height
- trolley
- magnifying lamp (normally .3 diopter fluorescent) – this allows a slight magnification of three-quarters the normal size and a clear cold light
- record card
- pre-sterilised needles in assorted selection sizes – 002–006

EQUIPMENT LIST

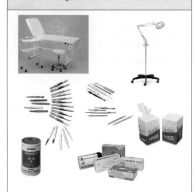

couch, with adjustable height

stool, with adjustable height

trolley

magnifying lamp

record card

needles in assorted sizes

stainless steel tweezers

kidney bowl (for needle holder and tweezers)

sharps box

antiseptic cleanser or swabs

antiseptic soothing lotion or gel

cotton wool

tissues

disposable surgical gloves

bowls (for jewellery)

covered, lined foot pedal bin

hand mirror

antiseptic wipes

cold sterilising solution (and small container to hold it and to keep tweezers etc. sanitary)

autoclave (to sterilise tweezers etc.)

Additional equipment for direct galvanic treatment

galvanic/direct current epilation unit

indifferent hand-held electrode

needle holder with finger button or foot switch

Additional equipment for diathermy high frequency treatment

diathermy/high frequency epilation unit

needle holder with finger button or foot switch

Additional equipment for blend treatment

blend epilation unit

hand-held indifferent electrode

needle holder with finger button or foot switch

- stainless steel tweezers – six pairs are required to allow for sterilisation between each client
- kidney bowl, to store the sterile tweezers and needle holder
- sharps box, for the disposal of used needles
- pre-treatment antiseptic skin cleanser or swabs
- post-treatment antiseptic soothing lotion or gel
- cotton wool to apply skin-treatment preparations (stored in a covered container)
- tissues, to blot the skin dry after cleansing and to shield the eyes from the magnification lamp (stored in a covered container)
- disposable surgical gloves (latex or vinyl) to avoid cross-infection to the client or therapist. A fresh pair is used for each client
- bowls, to hold client jewellery as necessary
- covered, lined, foot pedal bin for contaminated waste
- hand mirror, to show the client the facial area before and after treatment
- antiseptic wipes (unscented) to sanitise the treatment area
- cold sterilising solution such as sodium hyperchlorite and small container to hold it in, to keep tweezers and scissors sanitary
- autoclave, used to sterilise tweezers and chuck caps for epilation treatment.

Additional equipment for direct current galvanic treatment

- galvanic/direct current epilation unit
- indifferent hand-held electrode
- needle holder with finger button or foot switch to control current application.

Additional equipment for diathermy high-frequency treatment

- diathermy/high frequency epilation unit
- needle holder with finger button or foot switch to control current application.

Additional equipment for blend treatment

- blend epilation unit
- hand-held indifferent electrode
- needle holder with finger button or foot switch to control current application.

STERILISATION AND SANITISATION

As electrical epilation involves possible blood contact, and a high standard of hygiene and sterilisation should be adhered to at all times to prevent infection. Hepatitis and AIDS are common today and stringent measures must be followed to prevent cross-infection of the virus to the clients and therapist. Bacterial and viral strains can be prevented from spreading by sterilising equipment effectively and keeping all surfaces clean.

The couch, trolley, magnifying lamp and floor should be cleaned daily with disinfectant. Manufacturers' instructions should be followed for diluting substances for effective destruction of bacterial and viral spores. The couch should not have a cover, but be protected with clean disposable bed roll for each client.

Antiseptic wipes should be available to clean the couch or equipment before and during treatment as necessary.

Tweezers and scissors

These should be made of good quality stainless steel to prevent rusting and be placed in the autoclave to sterilise prior to treatment.

Probe and chuck

The probe should be cleaned with disinfectant before each client. Several chuck caps should be available, sterilised in the autoclave and placed in the UV cabinet for the recommended time. Place the needle holder on clean cotton wool in the kidney bowl.

HEALTH AND SAFETY

Tweezers and chuck caps are sterilised between clients using an autoclave. These must be washed in a soapless cleanser and carefully rinsed in cold water before being placed in the autoclave. Use an ultrasound cleaning bath to ensure all microscopic debris is removed before sterilising.

Needles

Needles can be bought from different companies but all come pre-packed and sterilised and are disposed of after each client.

The needle has three parts – the shank, shaft and tip. Most needles are made from stainless steel. If the client has very sensitive skin, a 24 carat gold-plated, stainless steel needle is available which is considered to reduce irritation and thought to facilitate insertion.

HEALTH AND SAFETY

The Environmental Health Officer (EHO)

EHOs are inspectors appointed to verify standards of hygiene and safety in the salon. They will advise and support the implementation of the necessary bye-laws relating to skin piercing. A copy of all the local bye-laws and regulations can be obtained from the Local Council area you are registered in.

HEALTH AND SAFETY

When removing the sterilised tweezers from the autoclave, use the appropriate tool for this purpose. Never handle them as not only will this contaminate them, but they will also be extremely hot.

HEALTH AND SAFETY

Sufficient resources should be available for effective sterilisation of equipment between clients.

ACTIVITY

Draw and describe the different types of needle (one-piece, two-piece, insulated, surgical steel, gold plated) available for epilation treatment. Research the cost of each of the different types of needle and state for which hair and skin types they are most suitable.

Parts of a needle

Insulated needles are available for the treatment of diabetic clients but can only be used with short-wave diathermy. These have a coating covering the shaft, leaving only the tip exposed, which concentrates the current at the base of the hair follicle. Many needles are supplied with a protective plastic covering which prevents contamination of the needle during loading.

Care should be taken when loading the needles to prevent contamination. Needles must always be in perfect condition.

All other aseptic methods are followed as for all beauty therapy treatments.

PREPARATION OF THE TREATMENT AREA

- The treatment area should be clean.
- All towels should be replaced with clean ones after each client.
- Clean paper tissue roll should cover the surface of the treatment couch.
- Time should be spent cleaning the couch, magnifying lamp and trolley.
- The needle holder, lamp edges and any other surface touched during the previous treatment should be wiped over with disinfectant.
- Sterile equipment should be collected in a clean kidney bowl lined with a clean paper tissue.

Positioning of the equipment

The treatment trolley should be placed on the side that the operator is working from. This prevents trailing wires or leads stretching across the client when adjusting machine settings. The magnifying lamp should be placed so that it can illuminate the area without being knocked when the therapist is working, or spring back because it has been over-stretched. A pedal bin should be placed under the couch within the therapists reach, lined with a disposable bin bag. If possible, the couch should be pulled away from the wall at the head so that the therapist can move around the top when epilating the eyebrows or when wishing to work from the opposite side. This creates minimal disturbance to the client when working.

The trolley should be prepared with all the equipment required.

PREPARATION OF THE THERAPIST

The therapist should present a professional, clean appearance at all times. Creating a good impression promotes a good working practice.

- A clean overall and tights should be worn daily.
- Minimal perfume should be worn to avoid client allergy and overpowering the client whilst in close contact.
- Nails should be short, clean and free of enamel.
- Long hair should be tied back at the nape of the neck to prevent it falling forward.

PREPARATION OF THE CLIENT

The therapist should greet the client and put her at ease. The client record card should be collected and completed if this is the consultation, or referred to if this is a follow-up treatment.

Positioning of the client is important for effective treatment. Depending on the area being treated, the client should be positioned on the couch comfortably and any clothing removed from the body part to be treated as relevant. If the face is to be treated, any make-up or lotions should be cleansed from the face by wiping over with antiseptic pre-electrolysis lotion.

Disposable eye-pads can be used to cover the eyes to protect them from the bright light of the magnifying lamp. This also encourages the client to relax.

Disposable bed roll should be placed in the area to be treated so that it protects the client's modesty and area being treated.

TREATMENT APPLICATION

For effective treatment, the following factors need to be taken into consideration:

- Analysis of the client's skin type – this will affect the selection of current intensity and duration of application.
- Follicle size – this should be observed because it will determine the choice of needle size and length for effective destruction of the lower follicle and destruction of the dermal papillae. Having chosen the correct needle size, the therapist will need to only stretch the skin lightly without distorting the hair follicle. This enables ease of insertion. Sufficient current needs to be applied for the correct amount of time for effective destruction of the lower follicle. The hair should then slide out of the follicle easily without any traction.

HEALTH AND SAFETY

Correct needle choice for the follicle size
- If the needle chosen is too large it can stretch the follicle and cause bruising and burning.
- If the needle chosen is too small the current will not destroy the dermal papilla, and ineffective treatment will occur.

- Correct analysis of the hair type – hairs vary in length and thickness according to race and different parts of the body. Consider this when selecting needle size and needle insertion.
- Positioning of the client and therapist – this is important because it can hinder effective removal. The therapist should be able to achieve ease of insertion without compromising the treatment.
- Therapist's technique, rhythm and continuity should be accurate. Misprobing can lead to the client's skin becoming damaged and scarred.

Current application for different skin types

Oily skin

This skin is thick and coarse with follicles that will appear open. Excess sebum present on the skin's surface will act as an insulator to the current, maintaining the intensity of the current in the lower follicle. With the follicles being slightly wider this gives the therapist ease of insertion.

There will usually be a higher level of moisture in the skin's lower tissues making treatment more effective.

TIP

The area which has been wiped and cleansed with antiseptic lotion should be dried before epilation is performed. If this is not done, the moisture can conduct a sudden surge of current up the follicle which may cause surface burning.

TIP

Needle choice is determined by the size of the follicle, hair type being treated, i.e. vellus or terminal, and the thickness and diameter of the hair.

ACTIVITY

When working on different types of hair, note how the treatment needs to be varied in order to successfully epilate them. Describe the current intensities, treatment times and the types of epilation treatment that seem to suit each type of hair best.

Dry skin

The upper layers of the epidermis can be dry or dehydrated due to lack of sebum or moisture. Dead skin cells can build up and block the follicle opening, making needle insertion more difficult. The current intensity must be set at a level to avoid burning in the upper follicle where there is a lack of moisture.

Sensitive skin

This type of skin is thin and very fine. It has a translucent appearance and red, broken capillaries may be present. When using high-frequency epilation technique, the application of heat can make the skin react quickly, creating a sudden erythema. Sensitive skin can be associated with both dry and oily skin so care should be taken when choosing current intensity.

Moist skin

This has a high water content through the epidermis and dermis layers. The therapist should be careful when applying the current because it can have a tendency to shoot back up the follicle to the surface of the skin, causing surface burning. Accuracy needs to be maintained on application of current and duration of treatment as different parts of the body have differing moisture gradients.

HEALTH AND SAFETY

If the client is warm when being treated, check that there is no sweat on the skin's surface which could result in surface burning.

Therapist's posture

The therapist should maintain a good working position throughout the treatment to avoid fatigue and postural problems. A height-adjustable stool should be placed at the correct height and side of the couch. This will enable the therapist to maintain a steady position to facilitate accurate insertion into the hair follicle. Leaning on the client should be kept to a minimum as the client may become uncomfortable. If right-handed, the therapist should work from the left side and if left-handed, from the right side.

Positioning of the client

The client should be placed on the couch in a position which enables ease of insertion in the area being treated. If the client suffers from respiratory disorders, the head of the couch must be elevated into a sitting position to enable the client to breathe properly. The client must feel comfortable and relaxed throughout the treatment. Depending on the area to be treated, a pillow or bolster may be required for support.

Lip

The client lies on the couch in a comfortable position and the therapist works from the side. The client is treated from the corners of the mouth alternately until the middle is reached under the nose. This area is treated last because it is very sensitive, and the client will have become more accustomed to the current intensity.

Chin

The client is positioned on the couch. If the client has a thick neck, a roll can be placed behind the neck to extend the chin upwards. Hairs normally grow at random, so the coarser darker hairs should be removed first to thin the area out.

Eyebrows

These can be treated from the head of the couch or the side. The client's hair must be secured away from the face with a clean headband. The therapist should work from the outside of the brows inwards towards the nose. Care should be taken when epilating between the brows because it is very vascular and moist. If incorrect technique is used, bruising or a black eye can occur.

Chest/nipple

The hair on the chest grows either towards the face or towards the waist. The client should be positioned with pillow support. The therapist may work from the top of the couch or at the side. Observe the client for sensitivity at all times. The breast and chest area are extremely sensitive areas but are suitable to treat.

> **TIP**
>
> **Consultation**
> On a client's first treatment session, space out the epilation. Do not attempt to clear an area – this will occur over future treatments. Explain this to the client.

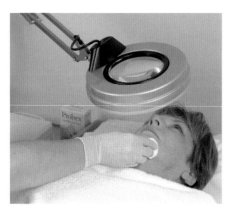
Preparing the client

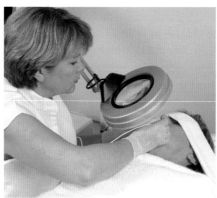
Upper lip

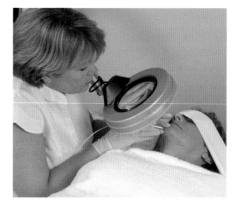
Chin

Eyebrow

Chest

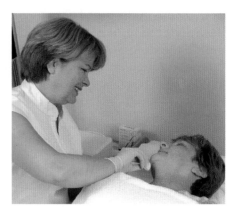
Aftercare

Legs

Support the limb being treated with a pillow. Hairs grow in varying directions dependant upon the area and are normally embedded in deep follicles.

Underarm

Support the arm with the client's hand placed behind her head on the side being treated. For comfort, support the arm being treated on a pillow. The armpit is very moist so care should be taken when selecting the current intensity. The hairs under the arm grow in different directions so the therapist will have to change her positioning to gain accurate insertion.

High frequency – short-wave diathermy technique

1 Check the client for contra-indications.

2 Ensure the record card is up to date and signed.

3 Wash the hands using an antiseptic wash and dry thoroughly using a warm air hand drier or disposable paper roll.

4 Protect the hands with clean disposable gloves.

5 Sanitise the area with pre-epilation lotion.

6 Using a magnifier, assess the skin type and follicle size. Blot the skin surface dry with a clean tissue as necessary.

7 Place the selected disposable needle into the needle holder. Ensure the needle is securely fastened into the probe.

8 Switch the machine on at the mains and unit.

9 Stretch the follicle open slightly with the index and middle finger of the left or right hand without distorting the follicle.

10 Probe the follicle, inserting the needle underneath the hair with the direction and angle of hair growth. This will prevent you piercing the follicle wall.

TIP	✔

Selection of hair
For the first few minutes, remove finer hairs. This will enable the client to adjust to the treatment sensation. Coarser hairs require a higher current intensity.

Needle insertion

Correct probing

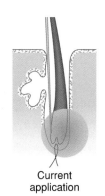

Current application

Tissue destruction

Correct probing technique

Incorrect probing technique

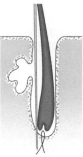
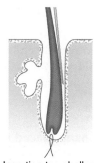
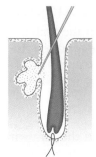

Insertion too deep

Incorrect probing

Insertion too shallow

Incorrect current discharge

Probe into the
sebaceous gland opening

TIP	✔

Technique
Transfer the tweezers into the working hand to remove the treated hair, keeping the skin taut. Do not lose sight of the hair to be removed!

11 When the needle is at the base of the hair follicle apply the HF current to enable the hair to be removed from the hair follicle without traction. The current should be set at the lowest intensity setting possible, using the shortest amount of time to effectively remove the hair. The client should not feel too uncomfortable during the treatment.

12 Remove the epilated hair using the tweezers and place on tissue or cotton wool kept within range of the area being treated. The hair should slide easily from the follicle.

13 Treat the area, observing skin reaction and adjust the current intensity to correspond with differing hair types and treatment areas.

14 Check client satisfaction with the area treated.

15 At the end of the treatment period, reduce the current intensity to zero and switch the unit off.

16 Remove the contaminated needle and place in the sharps box. Place the contaminated waste in the lined waste bin.

HEALTH AND SAFETY ✚

The current should be adjusted throughout the treatment for effective removal of different types of hair growth. If the hair cannot be removed after the second attempt, assess the area for any reaction. If it is not sensitised, a third insertion may be performed although this is not desirable. If the hair still cannot be removed, tweeze the hair to avoid infection caused by the tissue destruction that has occurred.

17 Apply post-epilation lotion to the treatment area with clean, sterile cotton wool.

18 Discuss aftercare with the client.

19 Complete details of the treatment on the record card, including: date; area treated; treatment duration; needle type and size; current intensity; skin reaction; your signature.

20 Help the client from the couch. Book the next appointment for the client to ensure continuity of treatment.

21 File the record card at reception.

Direct current – galvanic technique

1 Repeat steps 1 to 8 from page 189.

2 The client must hold the indifferent electrode in her hand. Protect this with a dampened tissue or as directed by the manufacturer.

3 Attach the needle holder to the negative pole.

4 Set the current intensity to 0.10 milliamps and the duration to 10 seconds.

5 Insert the needle into the follicle, apply the current intensity by pressing the foot-pedal. Most equipment will automatically switch off after the allotted time.

6 Remove the probe from the follicle, use the tweezers to remove the hair from the follicle and place it onto a clean piece of tissue or cotton wool.

7 The treatment effect continues after the current stops because of the chemical action on the tissues in the follicle. To maximise this effect you may leave a treated hair in place whilst treating another to ensure effective removal.

   It may be necessary to increase the intensity or lengthen the time to allow the hairs to be easily removed.

8 Continue working across the area until treatment has been completed.

9 Repeat steps 14 to 21 from page 190.

Blend technique

1 Repeat steps 1 to 8 from page 189.

2 The client will hold the indifferent electrode protected with a dampened tissue or as advised by the manufacturer's instructions.

HEALTH AND SAFETY

Some manufacturers do not require the indifferent electrode to be covered. Check the manufacturer's instructions for recommended settings.

---

3 Set the blend machine with the high frequency on low and the galvanic current on 0.10 milliamps. Set the timer for five seconds.

4 Insert the needle into the follicle.

5 Apply the current using the foot-pedal, wait for the time to be completed, then switch the current off. (Some machines automatically switch the current off.) It will be necessary to adjust the current intensity and treatment time to treat different strengths of hair growth.

6 Remove the needle from the follicle and gently remove the hair from the follicle. Place the hair onto a dry piece of tissue or cotton wool.

7 Repeat steps 14 to 21 from page 190.

ACTIVITY

Plan and write up the full treatment programme for a client with fine upper lip hair and coarse chin hair.

UNITS OF LYE CHART AND RECOMMENDED SETTINGS

A unit of lye is a tiny quantity of lye solution made in the follicle. The formula for assessing how much lye is made is: one-tenth of a milliampere of galvanic current flowing for one second will produce one 'unit' of lye, *or* tenth milliamperes × seconds = units of lye. The table shows approximately how much lye is needed to destroy which size of follicle. The intensity and duration for each follicle can then be calculated.

Approximate units of lye for different follicle sizes

Follicle size/treatment area	Units of lye
Shallow insertion: vellus hairs on upper lip, eyebrows, face, arms	15
Medium insertion: side of face (cheeks), chin, eyebrows, arms, stomach, medium leg hair	45
Deep insertion: chin, back, legs, thigh, underarms, bikini, shoulders	60
Very deep insertion: man's beard, back, shoulders, thighs	80

HAIR REGROWTH

This occurs after epilation and the growth eventually becomes weaker and finer. There are several reasons for the occurrence of regrowth.

Hormonal imbalance

If the client has a medical condition and is taking hormonal tablets or steroids, these can influence the blood supply to the follicle. The hairs will be nourished and continue to grow so medical advice should be sought to help determine an effective treatment plan and outcome as appropriate.

Partial destruction of the follicle

If the hair was not in the anagen stage of hair growth only partial destruction will occur because the bulb was not attached to the dermal papillae. Alternatively, the therapist may not have applied sufficient current to effectively destroy the dermal papillae.

Incorrect technique

- Incorrect probing – the therapist has not probed to the base of the follicle therefore insufficient current has been distributed to effectively destroy the blood supply.
- Incorrect needle size – if the needle size is too small, insufficient current will disperse to effectively destroy the dermal papilla and follicle, therefore regrowth will occur.
- Previous methods of removal – if the client has previously had the hairs removed by temporary measures this can cause distortion of the follicle. This makes it harder for the therapist to effectively probe the follicle, so reducing the treatment effectiveness.

AFTERCARE

Following epilation treatment, the skin will be prone to infection because of the heat and tissue destruction. To avoid infection the area should be kept clean following treatment. The following aftercare procedures must be explained to the client:

- Apply the recommended soothing lotion for 48 hours following each treatment. The skin should be treated gently and carefully. Always wash hands before touching the area.
- Report any scabbing or pustular infection to the therapist. Do not pick or rub the skin. Do not expose the area to ultraviolet light, either through sunbathing or use of sunbeds because this will possibly cause skin pigmentation. Protect the area with sun protection factor (SPF) 15 lotion but do not apply self-tanning lotion or heavily perfumed creams to the area.
- Do not pluck or wax the area in-between treatments because this will stimulate the hair growth making them appear thicker and coarser. If necessary, trim the hairs.
- Facial hair can be trimmed with scissors or, if necessary, shaved between treatments but not within 48 hours of the next treatment. Bleaching the hair is a useful method of disguising the remaining growth between treatments.
- For body treatments, keep the area clean and fresh. Do not wear tight or constricting clothing which may rub or irritate the area.
- Some scabbing may occur occasionally when strong hairs, such as those in the bikini line, are being treated. Do not remove any such scabs otherwise scarring may occur. The therapist should be advised if any scabbing does occur.
- Do not use heat treatments such as sauna, and do not swim for 48 hours after treatment.
- Do not have a hot bath or shower for the following 48 hours due to skin sensitivity. Wash in lukewarm water no hotter than body temperature.

These aftercare instructions need to be explained after every treatment and the client must be advised to follow them to prevent infection or scarring.

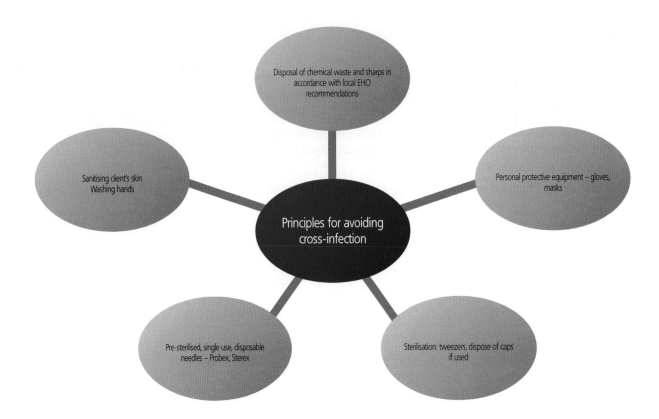

Epilation irritates the skin which can easily become infected if proper procedures are not followed.

Keep the working area clean and tidy for each client. Discard waste, sanitise surfaces, sterilise equipment, and renew towels and paper tissue roll.

CONTRA-ACTIONS

These are effects which might occur particularly if the area is very delicate or the therapist's technique is incorrect. The table describes some common contra-actions.

Common contra-actions following epilation

Contra-action	Cause	Action
Bleeding – a spot of blood appears at the follicle opening	This may be as a result of the needle having been mis-probed, piercing the follicle wall or base of the follicle and breaking blood capillaries	Wearing disposable gloves, apply dry cotton wool with a light pressure to stop the bleeding. Contaminated waste must be incinerated or placed in a sharps box. Take care to make sure insertions are accurate

Common contra-actions following epilation (continued)

Contra-action	Cause	Action
Small white pus-filled spots	Usually a bacterial infection (staphylococcus) introduced either during the treatment or by the client after treatment	Advise the client to use an antiseptic cream to aid healing. Review your sterilisation, disinfection and sanitising techniques to make sure they are in place. Explain the aftercare to the client again and make sure she understands the importance of looking after her skin properly to avoid infection
Bruising – a blue lump appears under the skin where the insertion has been made	The needle has gone through the base of the follicle or the side of the follicle, causing bleeding into the dermis	A cold compress with ice or witch hazel can be applied to reduce swelling and bruising. Make sure insertions are accurate
Erythema (redness) – a reaction to injury being caused to the skin during treatment	While some redness is inevitable, too much, together with associated swelling, indicates over-treatment	Apply a soothing compress such as witch hazel. A shorter treatment time and spacing insertions are needed for the next treatment
Brown scabs or crusts	High intensity high-frequency currents can cause scabbing, often seen on treatment areas such as the bikini line and abdomen. Scabbing can also be caused by incorrect placement of the electrical current in the hair follicle, e.g. too shallow, and applying the current when entering or leaving the hair follicle	Advise the client to continue to apply a soothing antiseptic cream as the skin heals. The client must not remove the scabs or scarring may occur. Keep the current intensity levels low whilst still maintaining effectiveness. Ensure the insertions are deep enough
Blanching – immediate whitening of the skin around the needle when a high intensity of current is applied	The skin has dried too quickly	Apply a soothing cool compress. In future, make sure the current intensity is kept lower, or is applied for a slightly shorter time
Weeping follicles – the follicles weep clear tissue fluid after treatment	Too much galvanic current, either on its own or when using blend, will result in weeping follicles	Keep the current intensity lower or the time shorter
Brown spots or hyper-pigmentation – the pigment layer is disrupted and the skin becomes darker in the treated areas	This happens when the current intensity is too high using any of the methods	Keep the current intensity lower; make sure the probe insertion is deep enough. Asian and Afro-Caribbean clients are particularly prone to hyper-pigmentation
White spots or hypo-pigmentation – the pigment layer is disrupted and the melanocytes are damaged, resulting in small white spots around the treated follicles	This occurs when the current intensity is too high	Keep the intensity lower and make sure the probe depth is correct
Keloids – raised, shiny scarring	Caused by incorrect needle insertion and current application. Afro-Caribbean clients are susceptible to these	With clients with a predisposition assess skin tolerance and healing by performing shorter treatments; identify the most suitable current intensity to promote safe skin healing

Common contra-actions following epilation (continued)

Contra-action	Cause	Action
Pitting and dermal contraction scars – small, round indentations, giving the skin a pitted look; sometimes described as orange peel in texture	This is caused by scars in the dermis. Over-treatment and too high current intensities are the usual causes	Keep current intensities and treatment time to the minimum necessary
Indifferent electrode rash – reddening and irritation of the skin on the palm of the hand in which the indifferent electrode has been held	The positive electrode produces hydrochloric acid	Make sure the indifferent electrode is covered with dampened tissue or as recommended by the manufacturers

Assessment of knowledge and understanding

You have now learnt about the about the business resources available and how they can be effectively utilised to meet the financial targets of the business.

To test your level of knowledge and understanding, answer the following short questions. These will prepare you for your summative (final) assessment.

Organisational and legal requirements

1 What are your responsibilities under the relevant health and safety legislation?

2 Why is it important to maintain standards of hygiene? Give examples of how to avoid cross-infection and what sort of personal protective equipment you must wear.

3 What is repetitive strain injury and how can you avoid it?

4 How would you dispose of the clinical waste from an epilation treatment?

5 What problems might occur if you do not complete your epilation treatments within the allocated time?

Client consultation

1 How can you measure a nervous client during the consultation?

2 State ways in which you can maintain your client's confidentiality and privacy.

3 How would you describe the treatment to a client who had never had epilation before?

4 When would you decide that a doctor's referral or approval is required and how would you encourage you client to obtain this?

5 When dealing with gender dysphoria clients why do you think extra sensitivity is required?

6 Some skincare treatments can affect epilation treatments. Give three examples of these and state why and how they do this.

Preparation for treatment

1 It is necessary for the environmental conditions to be right for the epilation treatment. Describe how you would make sure that you had these right and what would they be?

2 Why would you always check the record card for previous treatments?

3 How would you prepare yourself and your client for treatment?

4 What factors would you take into consideration when choosing the size and type of needle?

5 How would you prepare the area for treatment?

6 List three methods of preventing cross-infection and describe how they would be used during the epilation treatment.

Anatomy and physiology

1 Draw and describe the structure and function of the skin.

2 Draw and describe the structure of the pilosebaceous unit.

3 What is the hair growth cycle and how does this influence epilation treatments?

4 Define three types of hair growth.

5 List and describe four types of endocrine system malfunction which have an effect on hair growth.

6 How are hormones circulated through the body?

Contra-indications

1 List three contra-indications to epilation treatment and explain how you would recognise them.

2 Which conditions would require medical referral and approval before treatment could commence?

3 Which conditions could restrict your epilation treatment?

Equipment and materials

1 Describe how you would prepare, maintain and use the equipment and materials for the blend treatment.

2 Describe the different types of needles available for epilation treatments (one-piece, two-piece, stainless/surgical steel, gold-plated, insulated) and state why you would choose each type for different treatments.

3 Lighting and magnifying are important for the treatment area. How do you decide which methods are best and what level of magnification you need?

Treatment-specific knowledge

1 What sort of contra-actions may occur during treatment and how would you deal with them?

2 How would you adjust your treatment in order to remove hairs from different types of follicle – single, compound, ingrowing?

3 How does short wave diathermy achieve its destructive effect on the skin and describe a normal skin reaction to this?

4 When using the blend technique describe the currents which are used and explain the benefits in comparison with other methods of epilation.

5 How does galvanic current affect the hair follicle? Explain why this is the least commonly used method of epilation.

6 Describe fully the actions taken in order to successfully insert the needle into the hair follicle.

7 What is the general aftercare advice you must give to your client?

8 Why is it important to give full aftercare advice?

9 What problems may occur if the client has not been given or does not follow the aftercare advice?

10 Why is it useful to take photographs before, during and on completion of the treatment programme?

chapter 7

Provide head and body massage treatments

Learning objectives

This unit describes how to provide the service head and body massage treatment. This may be performed *manually*, where the therapist's hands manipulate the client's skin, tissue and muscle, or *mechanically* using a machine.

It describes the competencies to enable you to:

- **consult with the client**
- **plan the treatment**
- **prepare for the treatment**
- **massage the client's head and body using suitable massage techniques**
- **perform mechanical massage techniques**
- **complete the treatment**

When providing head and body massage treatment it is important to use the skills you have learnt in the following core mandatory units:

Unit G1 – Ensure your own actions reduce risks to health and safety

Unit G6 – Promote additional products or services to clients

Unit G11 – Contribute to the financial effectiveness of the business

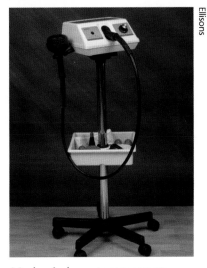

Mechanical gyratory massage machine

Ellisons

Manual massage has been practiced for thousand of years and benefits the client both physiologically and psychologically. The treatment manipulates the soft tissue of the body, producing heat and stimulating the vascular and nervous system. Massage manipulations either have a relaxing or stimulating effect and create a feeling of well-being.

There are also different electrical appliances manufactured to create similar effects to manual massage. These treatments may be combined wth manual massage to enhance the effect achieved.

Mechanical gyratory massage is a hand-held electrical body massage treatment which provides a deep stimulating massage from a vibratory head

Attachment heads

Ellisons

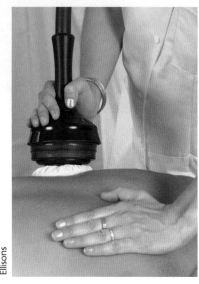

Ellisons

Gyratory massage application

Carlton Professional

Audio sonic machine

to which different applicator heads are attached. This massage treatment is often used to soften fatty tissue and stimulate the lymphatic system.

Audio sonic is a hand-held electrical vibratory machine which gently compresses and decompresses the soft tissues caused using sound waves which are created as the machine head passes over the skin. This vibratory treatment creates a deep stimulating action without irritating the skin surface.

The knowledge and understanding for gyratory and audio sonic massage is found in unit **BT18, Improve body condition using electro-therapy**.

To treat clients using effective head and body massage techniques you will need to show competence in manual and gyratory massage and audio sonic technique.

HEAD AND BODY MASSAGE

Effects of manual massage

Physiological effects

- increases the blood circulation, bringing fresh nutrients and oxygen to the body cells and systems
- warms the tissues and produces an erythema
- superficial and deeper layers of the skin are stimulated, increasing cellular function and regeneration of body cells
- aids desquamation – the removal of dead skin cells
- sebaceous secretions of the skin are increased, moisturising the skin
- reduces fibrous growth formation such as skin tags (verruca filiformis) and aids the dispersion of milia
- increases lymphatic flow, aiding the removal of waste products and toxins
- relaxes tense and contracted muscles, improving muscle tone
- stimulates the nerve endings, relieving muscular pain and fatigue
- softens and breaks down localised fatty deposits
- loosens scar tissue
- improves venous and arterial circulation. relieving congestion.

Psychological effects

Each massage performed is adapted to the client's psychological needs; these are identified at the client consultation. A stimulating massage application will invigorate a client, whilst a slow, deep massage will relax and help to relieve tension and stress. The client will also feel energised as the body systems such as blood and lymphatic circulation are stimulated. A feeling of well-being can increase client confidence and positive thoughts.

> **TIP** ✔
>
> **Pre-blended massage medium to create therapeutic effects**
> Pre-blended massage oils and creams can be used for massage. When inhaled and absorbed through the skin they help with relaxation.

ANATOMY AND PHYSIOLOGY OF HEAD AND BODY MASSAGE

Circulatory and lymphatic systems

The circulatory system is improved with massage. The blood flow in the arteries is increased by effleurage and petrissage manipulations and the vessels dilate (vasodilation), bringing about an erythema to the skin. The arteries aid the transportation of oxygen and nutrients to the cells. Massage improves the gaseous exchange, helping to promote healthier cells. The venous return helps to eliminate waste products, toxins and carbon dioxide from the cells, creating a feeling of well-being.

Lymph capillaries have a single layer of cells, composed of endothelial tissue. They begin as blind-ended tubes in areas that contain tissue fluid and eventually join together to form lymph vessels. Some waste products and toxins pass into lymph vessels via the lymph capillaries, which have larger pores than those in the blood capillaries. Before re-entering the bloodstream, lymph passes through lymph nodes where many toxins are eliminated by the actions of white blood cells.

Muscular system

The increased blood circulation feeds the muscle tissue, bringing extra oxygen and nutrients and aiding the removal of waste products in the venous return. This helps muscles to function to their full potential, keeping them toned and maintaining their elasticity and extensibility. The increased production of heat created by vasodilation produces a warming effect and the skin's surface temperature is raised. Muscles which are tense and shortened can be relaxed and stretched; weakened muscles can increase in tone.

Nervous system

The peripheral nerve endings can be either soothed or stimulated, depending on the massage movements being performed. Vigorous manipulations can have a stimulating effect – tissues and organs can be influenced to work more efficiently. Slow, rhythmic manipulations can induce relaxation and sleep. Massage can also have a soothing effect on the nerves when performing effleurage and vibrations, causing temporary pain relief.

The skin

Massage helps the skin to perform its various functions. Stimulation of the sebaceous glands by general massage manipulations produces more sebum, which helps to soften the skin and make it more resistant to infection due to its anti-bacterial property. The vasodilation action creates warmth in the

HEALTH AND SAFETY

The skin will gain an erythema during massage due to increased blood flow. However, excessive erythema could indicate skin intolerance – a contra-action. Cease treatment and identify the cause.

skin, increasing the output of the sudoriferous glands. This helps to remove the waste products and urea from the body more efficiently. Frictions used in the massage routine will aid desquamation of the dead skin cells, leaving the skin smoother and softer. Sensory nerve endings can either be soothed or irritated depending on the massage manipulation used, i.e. effleurage or tapotement (percussion).

The lungs

Percussion movements have an effect on the lung tissue. The circulation to the bronchioles is increased, helping to feed and nourish the tissues. This in turn promotes good elasticity and gaseous exchange within the lungs.

Pre-heating treatment

To increase the treatment objectives of the massage, such as relaxation, a pre-heating treatment may be given. This will increase the circulatory response to massage.

These treatments include infra-red paraffin wax therapy, steam or sauna treatment.

Infra-red

Infra-red lamps emit infra-red rays which have a heating therapeutic effect on the epidermal tissue. The skin becomes warmer and blood circulation will increase locally in the area as the blood vessels dilate. The reddening of the skin is called hyperaemia. A soothing effect on the sensory nerve endings in the area occurs due to the heating action.

Infra-red is applied to a skin that is clean and free from any products. It is important that a tactile and thermal skin sensitivity test is performed before treatment application. General body electro-therapy contra-indications should be checked for.

The infra-red lamp is heated in advance of treatment application and then applied at a distance of 20–40 cms dependant upon skin sensitivity and the body part being treated. The rays from the bulb must strike the skin perpendicularly (at right angles) for maximum penetration. Always refer to manufacturers' instructions for treatment application.

As a pre-heating treatment infra-red is usually applied 10 minutes before massage application.

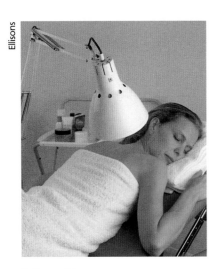

Ellisons

Infra-red lamp

HEALTH AND SAFETY

Infra-red treatment over exposure
Incorrect treatment technique can result in:
● burns
● headaches
● fainting.

MASSAGE MOVEMENTS

There are several different massage movements which are selected according to the desired effect. These are described below.

Effleurage (stroking)

Effleurage movements have a sedating and relaxing effect on the skin. They are performed with the whole palm and depending on the pressure applied, can either be superficial or deep movements. Effleurage always commences and completes a massage routine.

Effects of effleurage:

- increases lymphatic and blood circulation
- relieves tension
- helps reduce non-medical oedema
- aids desquamation
- induces relaxation.

Effleurage to the arm

TIP

Deep effleurage movements are always directed towards the heart and bring about a physical change to the surface capillaries, producing an erythema. Superficial effleurage is used to bring the therapist's hands back to the starting position.

Petrissage (compression)

Petrissage manipulations include kneading, knuckling, lifting, rolling, pinching and wringing. Intermittent pressure is applied smoothly and firmly to the tissues of the skin, lifting it from the underlying structures. This is then followed by relaxation. These movements help to tone and relieve muscular fatigue, leading to an improvement in elasticity within the muscle.

Effects of petrissage:

- increases lymphatic and blood circulation
- increases venous return
- breaks down tight nodules in the muscles
- aids removal of waste products from the tissues
- promotes relaxation in the client
- helps to soften and mobilise fat.

Petrissage skin-rolling movement

Tapotement (percussion)

Tapotement movements are used for general toning and should not be included in a relaxing massage. Tapotement movements include beating, clapping/cupping, hacking and pounding. The client must have suitable body mass to receive this treatment (the client's weight needs to be within the correct range for their height) otherwise it can be very uncomfortable.

Effects of tapotement/percussion:

- increases sluggish circulation
- stimulates the sensory nerve endings
- improves muscle tone and response

TIP

Tapotement movements should be avoided on thin or elderly clients because they could lead to bruising. They should also be avoided over the abdomen due to lack of bony support.

- helps to loosen mucus in chest conditions
- helps to reduce obesity
- improves spotty skin.

Tapotement movements are particularly beneficial for stimulating the surface and underlying tissues to give a better appearance.

Gluteal beating

Vibrations

Vibrations are used to help relieve pain and fatigue, stimulate the nerves and produce a sedative effect. The movements are fine, trembling movements, performed with one or both hands. They can vary between static and running vibrations. The palmar surface of the hand, the pads of the fingertips and the distal phalanx of the thumb can all be used for vibrations.

Effects of vibrations:

- relieve tension in the neck and long muscles of the back
- increase the action of the lungs
- help to increase peristalsis (muscular contractions of the gut which move food along) in the colon.

Frictions

Frictions cause the skin and superficial structures to move together over the deeper, underlying structures. They are concentrated in a particular area and applied with regulated pressure. The movements help to break down fibrous thickening and fat deposits, and aid the removal of any non-medical oedemas.

Effects of frictions:

- aid relaxation
- break down tight nodules
- increase lymph and blood circulation.

Any massage treatment should include a full range of movements chosen to suit the client's needs. For example, if the client is particularly tense in the neck and shoulders, the therapist should adapt the manipulations to benefit the client. More time should be spent concentrating on this area and correspondingly less on other parts of the body.

Frictions to the back

Pressure points

Pressure points is the application of pressure on specific points of the head, face or body using fingertips and thumbs. This helps to release blocked energy channels flowing through the body, improving circulation, stimulating the nervous system, improving the bodies ability to function and repair.

Reception

Massage treatments in the salon can range from a full body massage to treatments for specific areas of the body, e.g. a back massage or a neck and shoulder massage. The receptionist should identify the client's requirements at the time of booking so that a suitable time can be allocated for the treatment required. An hour and 15 minutes should be allocated for a full body massage, to include consultation; approximately 30 minutes for a back treatment. Treatment times for other specific areas will vary according to the size of the area being treated.

A full body and head massage with consultation and aftercare advice should last for approximately 75 minutes, with each area receiving attention as illustrated in the following table. Allow 60 minutes for a full body massage without head massage.

Massage times for specific areas

Area	Time (minutes)
arms, each	5
neck/chest	5–8
abdomen	5–8
legs, each	5
buttocks	5–8
back	20
head and face	15

Contra-indications to massage

These are divided into three categories as illustrated in the table: general, local and temporary. **General** contra-indications affect the whole body or part of the body; **local** contra-indications are concentrated in a particular area; the symptoms of **temporary** contra-indications have only a short life span and clear up quite quickly. The massage treatment will be adapted to suit the client's needs. If the therapist has any concern over the client's health or well-being, medical advice should be sought prior to the treatment.

Contra-indications to massage

General	Local	Temporary
heart conditions	recent operations	medication
high and low blood pressure	recent scar tissue	bruising
certain medication	psoriasis or eczema	skin abrasions
diabetes	skin diseases	pregnancy
cancer	skin disorders	medical oedema
rheumatism		skin diseases
undiagnosed lumps, bumps or swelling		skin disorders
loss of skin sensation		during chemotherapy
postural deformities		or radiotherapy
over bulbous varicose veins		product allergies
phlebitis		
deep vein thrombosis		
high temperature		
epilepsy		

Consultation techniques

The therapist needs to obtain relevant details from the client before commencing a massage treatment. For this reason a full consultation should be performed. The therapist must be professional in her manner and make the client feel welcome. The client should feel at ease throughout the treatment and a good rapport should be built up between client and therapist. Personal details should be taken and recorded on a record card. These should include medical history, doctor's details, any contra-indications that may be present and the treatment required. There are very few contra-indications that will prevent the therapist from performing manual massage (refer to contra-indications table), but if in doubt, a letter of approval should first be obtained from the client's doctor.

BEAUTY WORKS

Date	Beauty therapist name	
Client name		Date of birth (identifying client age group)
Address		Postcode
Evening phone number	Day phone number	
Name of doctor	Doctor's address and phone number	

Related medical history (conditions that may restrict or prohibit treatment application)

Are you taking any medication (this may affect the condition of the skin or skin sensitivity)

CONTRA-INDICATIONS REQUIRING MEDICAL REFERRAL
(Preventing head and body massage treatment application)

☐ skin disorders – active   ☐ skin disease
☐ high or low blood pressure   ☐ severe bruising
☐ recent head and neck injury   ☐ severe cuts and abrasions
☐ severe varicose veins   ☐ medical conditions
☐ recent scar tissue   ☐ epilepsy
☐ pregnancy   ☐ diabetes
☐ heart disease
☐ dysfunction of the nervous system

TREATMENT AREAS

☐ neck   ☐ face
☐ head   ☐ chest and shoulders
☐ arms and hands   ☐ abdomen
☐ back   ☐ legs and feet
☐ full body   ☐ gluteals

LIFESTYLE

☐ occupation   ☐ family situation
☐ dietary and fluid intake   ☐ sleep patterns
☐ exercise habits   ☐ smoking habits
☐ hobbies, interests, means of relaxation

MASSAGE TECHNIQUES

☐ effleurage   ☐ petrissage
☐ tapotement (percussion)   ☐ frictions
☐ vibrations   ☐ pressure points

LUBRICANT (IF USED)

☐ oil   ☐ cream
☐ powder   ☐ gel
☐ emulsion

CONTRA-INDICATIONS WHICH RESTRICT TREATMENT
(Treatment may require adaptation)

☐ skin disorder
☐ high or low blood pressure
☐ recent scar tissue (avoid area)
☐ recent scar tissue
☐ cuts and abrasions
☐ mild eczema/psoriasis
☐ undiagnosed lumps, bumps, swellings
☐ asthma
☐ product allergies
☐ recent injuries to the treatment area
☐ certain medication
☐ abdomen during menstruation
☐ migraine
☐ epilepsy

PHYSICAL CHARACTERISTICS

☐ weight   ☐ size
☐ muscle tone   ☐ age
☐ health   ☐ skin condition

OBJECTIVES OF TREATMENT

☐ relaxation
☐ sense of well being

EQUIPMENT AND MATERIALS

☐ couch/chair/stool   ☐ gyratory massager
☐ towels   ☐ audio sonic
☐ spatulas   ☐ infra-red
☐ protective covering
☐ consumables
☐ oil removal medium

Beauty therapist signature (for reference)

Client signature (confirmation of details)

TREATMENT ADVICE

This information includes:
- What products have been used in the Head and Body Massage treatment as appropriate
- Advice re products that would be suitable for the client to use at home
- Advice on how to gain maximum benefit from product use
- Postural advice
- Advice to follow immediately following the treatment to include:
  - Possible reactions to the treatment and recommended action to take
  - Suitable rest period following treatment
  - General advice re food and drink intake
  - Avoidance of stimulants
- Contra action advice, action to be taken in the event of an unwanted reaction (aching, tiredness, heightened emotional state)
- Recommendations for further Head and Body Massage treatments and the benefits of continuous treatments
- Recommendations for further treatments including heat treatments and electrical massage treatments
- The recommended time intervals between treatments

Questioning the client on expectations and outcomes can ensure the client gains satisfaction from the treatment. The client will also require a postural check at the time of consultation. This is to assess whether the client has any postural conditions which the therapist may advise exercise for, or whether the therapist needs to adapt the massage treatment in any way for the comfort of the client.

Once the consultation is complete, the therapist should ensure that all the details are recorded and that the client has signed her record card. This enables continuity of treatment and up-to-date tracking of the treatments received.

TIP

Examples of postural conditions which the therapist will be looking for are kyphosis, lordosis and scoliosis.

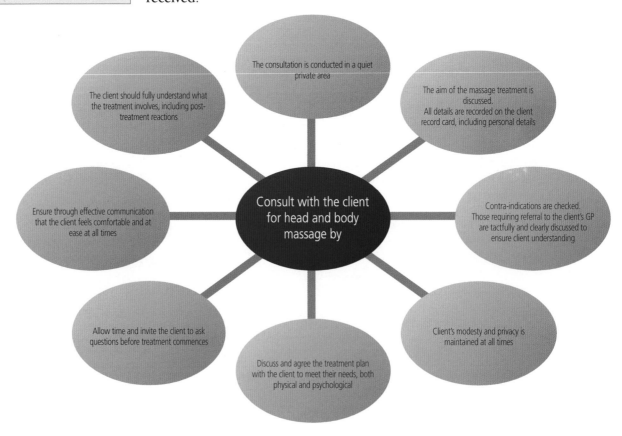

Consult with the client for head and body massage by

- The consultation is conducted in a quiet private area
- The aim of the massage treatment is discussed. All details are recorded on the client record card, including personal details
- Contra-indications are checked. Those requiring referral to the client's GP are tactfully and clearly discussed to ensure client understanding
- Client's modesty and privacy is maintained at all times
- Discuss and agree the treatment plan with the client to meet their needs, both physical and psychological
- Allow time and invite the client to ask questions before treatment commences
- Ensure through effective communication that the client feels comfortable and at ease at all times
- The client should fully understand what the treatment involves, including post-treatment reactions

Equipment and materials

A massage treatment is relatively inexpensive to provide and does not require a lot of expensive products or equipment. You will need the following items of equipment:

- massage couch
- massage chair/stool
- removable protective couch cover
- trolley for equipment/consumables
- two large and two small towels
- disposable bedroll
- purified talc
- massage oil
- massage cream
- massage emulsion
- massage gel
- gyratory massager
- audio sonic massager
- infra-red unit
- witch hazel or eau de cologne to cleanse the area being massaged and remove excess massage medium
- cosmetic cleansing preparations to remove facial make-up
- dry cotton wool and tissues
- jar of petroleum jelly
- spatulas
- four plastic bowls – two large and two small
- client's record card.

EQUIPMENT LIST

massage couch

massage chair/stool

trolley for equipment/consumables

large and small towels (2 of each)

large towel or bathrobe (for client)

disposable bedroll

purified talc

massage oil

massage cream

massage envision

massage gel

witch hazel or eau de cologne

cosmetic cleansing preparations (to remove facial make up)

dry cotton wool and tissues

jar of petroleum jelly

spatulas

plastic bowls

client's receord card

gyratory massage

audio sonic massager

infra-red unit

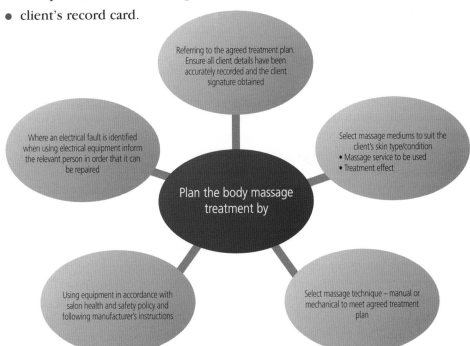

Plan the body massage treatment by

Referring to the agreed treatment plan. Ensure all client details have been accurately recorded and the client signature obtained

Where an electrical fault is identified when using electrical equipment inform the relevant person in order that it can be repaired

Select massage mediums to suit the client's skin type/condition
- Massage service to be used
- Treatment effect

Using equipment in accordance with salon health and safety policy and following manufacturer's instructions

Select massage technique – manual or mechanical to meet agreed treatment plan

Sterilisation and sanitisation

Manual massage

Prior to the massage treatment, make sure the couch and trolley have been wiped over with warm soapy water. Plastic spatulas should be cleaned and placed in an ultraviolet cabinet prior to use to ensure they are free from bacteria. Clean towels and bedroll should be provided for each client to prevent cross-infection.

HEALTH AND SAFETY

It is important that you comply with all relevant health and safety legislation whilst performing body massage.
Examples include:
Workplace (Health, Safety and Welfare) Regulations 1992
Control of Substances Hazardous to Health Regulations (COSHH) 1999
Electricity at Work Regulations 1989
Remember to use the knowledge and skills you have learnt in **Unit G1**. Ensure your own actions reduce risks to health and safety

Gyratory massage

Attachments should be washed in warm soapy water to remove talc, dead skin cells and sebum. They should then be dried and sanitised in the ultraviolet cabinet. Disposable protective attachment covers may be purchased from larger wholesalers.

Audio sonic

Heads should be cleaned with a spirit-based cleaner after use and sanitised in the ultraviolet cabinet.

Preparation of the treatment area

The treatment area should be clean and at a comfortable working temperature for both the client and therapist, between 18 and 21°C. One large towel should be placed over the length of the couch and a small towel over the head end. The remaining towels should be used as appropriate to preserve the client's modesty. All products and utensils should be placed on the trolley prior to the treatment, so that the therapist does not need to break the continuity of the massage to go in search of them.

If the client is receiving the treatment while sitting on a treatment chair/stool, make sure you position them correctly. Adequate ventilation should be provided to create a hygienic environment, preventing cross-infection through viral airborne spores, drowsiness through carbon dioxide-saturated air and the removal of stale smells and odours. The treatment area should induce relaxation and client comfort. Lighting should be soft, decor subtle and non-gender biased. Sound levels should be low for relaxation. An electric point should be available for electrical equipment.

Preparation of the therapist

The therapist should wear an overall which does not restrict movement. Full, enclosed shoes should be worn with low or medium-height heels. Very high heels can lead to serious foot and postural problems for the therapist. The client's record card should be collected prior to her arrival and the therapist should identify the client's massage requirements. A full consultation, including a postural check, should be carried out before the treatment commences.

Therapist's hands

The therapist should always sanitise her hands prior to the treatment. The hands also need to be flexible in order to fit the contours of the client's body. Mobilising the joints of the hands and fingers will loosen the hands and facilitate good manipulations. Hand exercises should be practised on a regular basis. Examples of some the therapist can practice are illustrated.

HEALTH AND SAFETY

When performing massage you will strengthen certain muscles used to perform the massage movements. To avoid a repetitive strain injury, your muscles must be stretched, especially those of the neck, shoulders, back, arms and hands. Stretching exercises should be performed slowly to avoid muscle fibre damage.

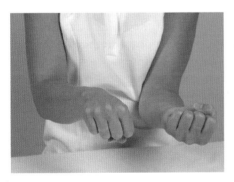

Rotate wrists clockwise then anti-clockwise to loosen the wrists

Clench the fingers together with backs of hands facing. Pull fingers apart but maintain contact

Rotate fists in a circular motion

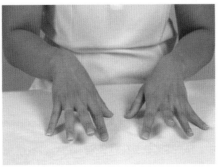

Finger-pad resistance – press the fingers against each other one by one

Place alternate fingers down on a hard surface as if playing a piano

Place palms together and apply slight pressure, maintaining the contact

Preparation of the client

- Instruct the client to remove her clothing down to the undergarments. It is important that you maintain the client's modesty at all times.
- Provide a private changing area for the client. A large towel or bathrobe may be provided for the client to wear.
- Ask the client to remove all jewellery and accessories and store it in a safe place – either in a bowl on the bottom of the trolley or pass to the client for safekeeping.
- Position the client for treatment. Instruct the client to lie on the couch in a supine position for body massage.
- Place towels over the client in a way which will allow minimal interruption to the treatment and keep her warm.
- Cover any minor skin defects, cuts or abrasions with an adhesive dressing prior to the treatment.
- If the client has long hair it may need to be secured in a clip while you treat the neck area.

TIP

The supine position is lying on the back, facing upwards.

BODY AND HEAD MASSAGE TREATMENT PROCEDURES

A thorough consultation will have included details of the client's age, weight, size and muscle tone. This will help to determine whether the massage is to be provided for relaxation, toning or maintenance of physical health. (Maintenance of physical health refers to such things as relief of muscle tension and fatigue, improvement of blood and lymph circulation, and improvement of skin conditions.)

The massage routine should be planned before you start, so that it provides for continuity of treatment. The sequence that is normally followed is:

- left arm
- right arm
- chest
- abdomen
- right leg
- left leg, with the client lying supine.

The client then lies prone for the gluteals, back and shoulders to be massaged. The massage movements should be adapted to suit the needs of each client.

The correct stance for massaging the body

Therapists need to ensure they are correctly positioned when massaging. This will prevent strain and fatigue to the therapist whilst working. Failure to

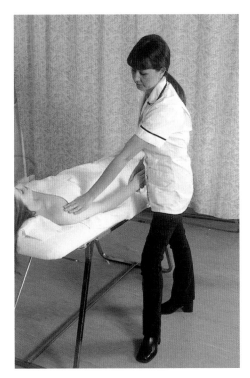

Walk standing

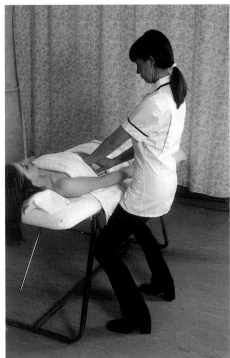

Stride standing

adopt the correct stance will result in the therapist being unable to work a full day and eventually serious back injury could occur. Working positions are walk standing and stride standing (see table and illustrations).

Working positions for the therapist

Name	Description
Walk standing	This stance enables the therapist to work longitudinally over the body. The therapist stands with one foot in front of the other and moves her body weight forwards and backward through the ball and heel of the foot with the massage.
Stride standing	This enables the therapist to work transversely across the body. The therapist faces the couch with her back upright and knees slightly bent.

Selecting the massage medium

The choice of massage medium is important in order to provide an effective treatment. This will be determined by the skin type of the client but on occasion the client will state which medium she prefers. The massage medium chosen should be used sparingly and always applied to the therapist's hands first and not directly onto the client's skin.

Types of massage media

Name	Use
Massage cream	Used for normal to dry skin; helps to soften and nourish the skin; is readily absorbed.
Massage oil	Good for normal to dry skin; helps to nourish and lubricate the skin; helps the therapist to provide a deeper massage and prevents the skin from tearing whilst being stretched.
Purified talc powder	Used on combination and oily skins; helps to absorb excess sebum and perspiration on the skin; allows the hands to slide over the skin and provides adequate slip.
Massage emulsion	Massage emulsion, an oil and water-based medium, may be used. This is easily absorbed by the skin and further application may be necessary to avoid dragging the skin.

HEALTH AND SAFETY

Aromatherapy oils
Undiluted aromatherapy essential oils can be highly irritant or poisonous. Oils should be blended and used *only* by a qualified aromatherapist.

Once you have decided on the type of massage the client requires and have selected a suitable massage medium, you should wipe over with witch hazel or eau de cologne, applied with clean cottonwool, each part of the client's body to be massaged, in order to sanitise it. Dry the skin, blotting with a clean tissue.

Adapting the massage

There are several reasons why you might need to adapt your massage. These will become evident whilst you are performing your consultation.

- **Relaxing massage**: avoid all stimulating movements and concentrate on effleurage movements. The pressure should be firmer and the rhythm slower.

- **Tight or contracted muscles**: tapotement movements should be avoided, and slow and rhythmical movements should be used to help stretch the muscle.

- **Slack muscles**: elasticity of the muscles has been lost and the circulation needs to be improved. Stimulating tapotement massage movements should be used to help to tone and firm the area being treated.

- **Massage for weight problems**: stimulating movements on the areas of excess fat and cellulite are used with increased pressure. This helps to mobilise the fat deposits. The massage should be combined with a low fat diet and exercise program if the client wants to gain maximum benefits from weight loss.

- **Massage for males**: muscle bulk in men is larger and stronger than in women. The muscles are firmer, the skin thicker and there is less fatty tissue. The therapist's full body weight is used and the massage should be firmer. When massaging men, the femoral triangle is avoided.

- **Skin condition**: Dead skin cells are removed during massage, blood circulation is increased and sebaceous gland activity is increased. The skin appears healthier and functions more efficiently. This is particularly beneficial for all skin types. However, if the client has a greasy skin type with pustules and papules present, avoid over-stimulating the skin and select a purified talc massage medium. In some cases, it will be necessary to avoid the area to prevent client discomfort and secondary infection. If the skin lacks elasticity e.g. stretch marks or aged skin, avoid stretching massage manipulations such as wringing and rolling and incorporate toning massage manipulations.

- **Older clients**: As the client ages the skin becomes thinner: bony areas may become more prominent and possibly brittle and the skin reduces in elasticity and tone. Avoid over-stimulating the skin, unnecessarily stretching the skin and excessive pressure during massage application. Check with the client to ensure they are comfortable during the treatment.

TIP

The femoral triangle refers to the area covering the space on the medial side of the upper thigh, and can be seen as a slight depression.

TREATMENT APPLICATION

Arms

1 Support the client's arm with one hand and effleurage the whole arm from the wrist to the shoulder with the free hand. Repeat this step at least three times and up to six times until the client feels relaxed.

2 Still supporting the client's arm, deep effleurage the deltoid muscle ensuring the palm of the hand is contoured around the muscle. Rotate the movement three times clockwise and then repeat three times anti-clockwise.

3 Supporting the arm, use alternate palmar kneading to the biceps and triceps muscles, working upwards with the movement three times and then sliding back to the elbow.

4 On completion of alternate kneading, slide your hands down from the elbow to the wrist joint to remain supporting the client's arm. Pick up the extensors and flexors three times, working from elbow to wrist, and slide back up to the elbow. Support the client's arm at the wrist and thumb knead along the interosseous membrane up to the elbow. Work up in small controlled movements three times and slide back down to the wrist.

5 With the arm still supported, thumb knead the metacarpals down each bone, adapting the pressure so as not to cause discomfort.

6 Supporting the client's arm, place the hand to the opposite shoulder and on the lateral aspect of the upper arm, perform hacking up and down the arm from shoulder to elbow.

7 Complete the arm routine by effleurage as before. Place the client's arm back onto the couch and repeat the movements on the other arm.

> **TIP**
>
> If the client is heavy, support the arm on a pillow or a plinth so that the massage movements can be applied with ease.

> **TIP**
>
> The interosseous membrane is the gap between the radius and ulna bones of the arm.

> **TIP**
>
> Only perform tapotement movements if the client has enough tissue present in the area. Hacking will increase the circulation and lymphatic drainage in the area, promoting a better appearance and texture.

Effleurage to the arm

Single-handed kneading of triceps

Picking up extensors

Picking up flexors and extensors

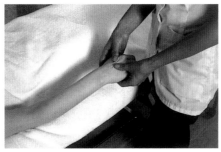

Metacarpal kneading

Effleurage to complete the sequence

Neck and chest

1 Facing the client, effleurage across the clavicle, around the shoulders and up behind the neck, ensuring that the pressure is adapted to suit the client. Keeping the hands in contact with the client, slide back to the sternum, cross the hands over and effleurage to the deltoids, pausing for a few seconds with a slight stretch on the movement, keeping the palms of the hands on the deltoids.

2 Apply superficial stroking across the chest with alternate hands from axilla to axilla, ensuring that one hand begins as the other is leaving the body.

3 Follow with double-handed kneading over the chest repeated three times, making sure the pressure is appropriate for the client. With the hands still in contact with the client, walk round to the top of the bed and thumb knead the trapezius muscle, working inwards from the shoulders up to the occiput and sliding back round. Repeat the procedure three times or, if the client is tense, up to six times.

4 Working from the front of the client, knead the clavicle three times with index and middle finger.

5 Repeat effleurage movements three to six times to complete the neck and chest massage.

Effleurage movements to the neck and chest

Effleurage movements to the neck and chest

Finger-kneading the clavicle

Abdominal massage

1 Ensure the client's modesty is maintained by placing a small towel over the bust area and pulling the large towel down to the hips. Place the palms of the hands at the waist and effleurage up to the sternum, back to the waist and then down to the pubic symphysis. This is known as diamond effleurage. Repeat this movement slowly three times.

2 Place the hands on the lateral walls of the abdomen and alternate knead three times. Follow the kneading movement with wringing to the lateral walls three times, ensuring the client has enough subcutaneous tissue to manipulate, otherwise it can be uncomfortable for the client.

3 Progress from the movement in Step 2 to skin rolling, applied with the palms of the hands underneath the posterior aspect of the abdomen and the thumbs placed on the anterior aspect of the abdomen. Roll the thumbs down towards the palms of the hands with visible skin movement underneath the thumbs.

4 Complete the abdominal routine with three diamond effleurage sequences (Step 1). Cover the client back up and proceed to the leg routine.

Kneading to lateral walls of the abdomen

Kneading to colon

TIP	
If the client is constipated, trace and knead the colon to stimulate peristalsis.	

Legs

1 Uncover the leg you are going to work on and place a towel in the middle of the legs so that the other leg remains covered.

2 Effleurage the entire leg, covering the anterior, lateral and medial walls three times from the tarsals up to the femoral triangle. Pressure should be applied towards the heart with superficial effleurage to return the movement back to the tarsals.

3 Alternate hand-knead three times from the hip to the patella, starting at the lateral aspect of the thigh – when both hands are parallel they will knead alternately.

4 Slide the palms of the hands around the anterior and posterior aspect of the legs so that they are positioned on the quadriceps and hamstrings. Alternate hand-knead the muscles three times. If the movement is difficult because the client is large, place a bolster underneath the patella to aid movement. If the client suffers from poor circulation or cellulite on the upper lateral aspect of the thigh, tapotement movements will be beneficial to stimulate the circulation. Standing in stride stance, use hacking and clapping movements three times, working from the patella to the groin area and back.

5 Effleurage the upper thigh three times, and then around the patella three times in slow rhythmical movements.

6 Flex the client's knee up and down the gastrocnemius muscle three times and then follow with palmar kneading. Support the client's lower leg and palmar knead the lateral side of the leg three times.

7 Slide the palm down to the ankle on the last kneading movement and thumb-knead the tibialis anterior on the outer shin three times, working upwards.

8 Thumb knead the top of the foot down each metatarsal and slide back to the ankle. Scissor the plantar region of the foot three times, scissoring down and pulling back up.

9 Place the hands either side of the toes; gently press together and rotate all the toes three times clockwise and three times anticlockwise (phalange circling). Effleurage the foot three times, including Swiss chop to the arch of the foot.

10 Change the working stance and complete the leg massage with effleurage to cover the whole leg three times.

TIP	

When scissoring, enough pressure needs to be applied to prevent irritation to the client.

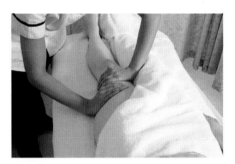

Effleurage to leg

Hacking to upper, outer thigh

Clapping to outer thigh

Kneading to the gastrocnemius

Scissoring to plantor region of foot

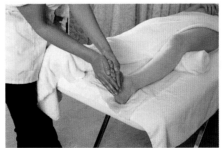

Phalange circling

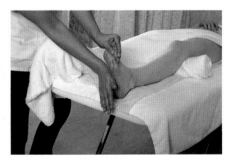

Swiss chop to the arch of the foot

Buttocks (gluteals)

1 Work on one side of the gluteals at a time. Cover the other side with a small towel so minimal exposure is achieved. Stand on the opposite side to the gluteals being massaged. This will enable you to work inwards with the movements performed.

2 Effleurage inwards with one hand to cover the buttocks. The free hand can be placed on the towel on the other buttock to keep it in place. Knead the gluteals three times with deep movements then use reinforced kneading to follow.

3 To stimulate the area, use hacking, clapping, beating and pounding in that order (see table), ensuring that the whole buttock is covered. This will help to improve the area.

4 Effleurage the area to complete the routine.

5 Cover the client's buttock with the towel and change positions to enable you to work on the other side. Uncover the buttock and repeat the procedure.

TIP

Couch with face hole
For client comfort, some couches have an optional face hole so that when the client receives back massage they can breathe easily without strain on the neck.

Tapotement movements

Name	Description
Hacking 	Hands are placed at right angles to the wrist with palms facing. The movement is applied with a light, fast action and the fingers are flicked against the skin.
Clapping 	This is a stimulating movement and is used over adipose tissue. The hands are formed into cups and strike the body rhythmically; a hollow sound can be heard.

Tapotement movements (continued)

Name		Description
Beating	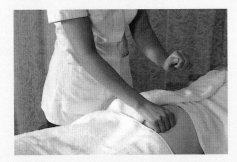	The hands are held in loose fists and moved rhythmically, either quickly or slowly, depending on the response required. The hands are moved from shoulder height and alternately placed on the buttocks and brought back to the starting position.
Pounding		A stimulating movement used over adipose tissue and the deep gluteal muscle. The hands are loosely closed and as one hand strokes the area it is closely followed by the other in a rapid rhythmical manner.

Back and neck

1 With the client still in the prone position, effleurage up the back from the sacrum, splitting the hands at the scapula and massaging to the deltoid muscles. Slide the hands back down the same channel to the starting position. Repeat the effleurage movement, covering the trapezius muscle.

2 Single-hand knead from the scapula to the sacrum in three channels on either side of the spine, placing the non-working hand behind your back for support.

3 Continue with double-handed kneading three times down either side of the spine.

4 Place the thumbs at the posterior aspect of the shoulders and thumb knead along the trapezius muscle to the base of the neck. Depending on how tense the client is, repeat the movement three to six times.

5 Knead around the sacrum and then knead up towards the scapula on either side of the spine. Repeat the movement one to three times.

6 Follow with thumb frictions down either side of the spine three times, covering the whole of the back. Thumb friction down from scapula to sacrum and slide the thumbs back up.

7 Wring the lateral walls, working around the back. Roll the lateral walls around the back.

8 Follow with gentle hacking three times.

9 Complete the back routine with effleurage three to six times.

Wringing to lateral walls of the back

Effleurage to the back

Double-handed kneading to the back

Thumb frictions to the back

Head massage technique

Scalp massage to the head may follow body massage. Allow approximately 10 minutes to complete if incorporated. If preferred a treatment oil may be applied to the scalp, use approximately 4 mls. This will nourish the skin of the scalp and the hair. As part of the aftercare advice it is recommended that the treatment oil is left on the hair for the remainder of the day, if practicable, to continue its conditioning effect.

Discuss if the client wishes to have oil applied to the scalp during the consultation and explain the benefits.

1 Interlock fingers and place joined hands on the forehead. Using the heel of the hands simultaneously perform circular, petrissage movements moving the hands to cover the scalp.

2 Place the thumbs on the scalp at the hair line and gently apply pressure point technique. This helps to relieve stress and tension as the pressure points are on the meridians of energy pathways that connect the body. This in turn stimulates the nerve pathways, frees blockages on the meridian lines of the body and helps to balance the body.

3 Place one thumb above the other. Each thumb alternately applies pressure in a 'C' shape moving from the hairline towards the crown area.

4 Position both thumbs at the crown area. Rotate both thumbs simultaneously in a clockwise direction, increasing pressure with each rotation: check pressure with client for comfort. Follow by rotating thumbs anti-clockwise, reducing pressure with each rotation.

5 Apply petrissage movement over the scalp as if shampooing the scalp, using the fingertip pads to move the scalp gently.

6 Place the knuckles of each hand against the scalp and apply gentle pressure, rotating the knuckles of each finger to cover the scalp.

7 Grasp sections of hair between the fingers of each hand and gently pull the hair at the roots.

8 Alternating the fingers of each hand, use the fingers to slowly comb through the hair from the scalp to the end of the hair. Cover the scalp.

9 Using the third finger of each hand alternately stroke the forehead from above the nose towards the hairline.

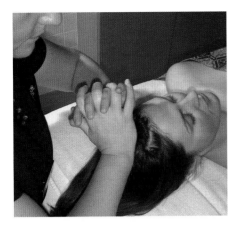

Petrissage to scalp

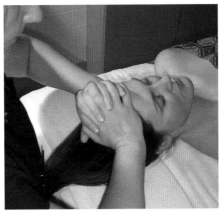

Using heel of hands

Pressure point technique to scalp

Thumb pressure from hairline to crown

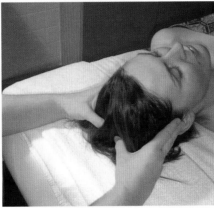

Thumb rotations to crown area

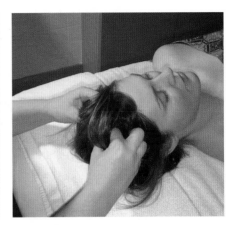

Shampooing movement to scalp

Knuckling to scalp

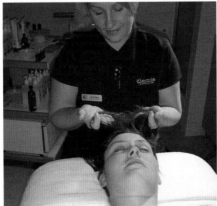

Gentle pulling of hair

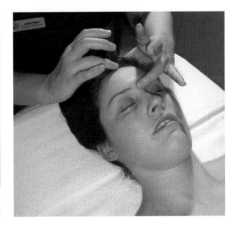

Alternate handed stroking using third finger from nose to hairline

To conclude the massage apply gentle pressure at the temples, cradling the sides of the head with each hand. Slowly remove hands.

In a gentle manner, quietly inform the client that the treatment has ended. Advise her to rest and get up slowly to avoid feelings of dizziness. A glass of water may also be provided for the client.

Wash your hands as necessary following client preparation
Washing your hands demonstrates to the client that you work hygienically

When performing body massage it is important to correctly position yourself, observing good postural technique and stance to prevent pain, fatigue and the risk of permanent injury

Allow the client to dress in a private changing area
Provide facilities for personal grooming

Adapt massage technique to meet the aims of the agreed treatment plan
• Depth of pressure
• Speed of application
• Choice of massage manipulations
• Choice of massage medium

Leave the treatment area in a safe and hygienic state ready for further use
Waste should be disposed of in a sealed polythene bag and towels laundered

Vary the pressure according to the area being treated, client comfort and skin reaction to treatment

Ensure that the client's records are up-to-date and accurate. This enables continuation of the treatment to be tracked and any adverse reactions noted

Carry out head and body massage by

Ensure there is sufficient massage medium to provide adequate slip to perform massage techniques effectively and efficiently

Ensure that the treatment is cost-effective and completed in a commercial time

Conclude the treatment maintaining the correct atmosphere
Avoid startling the client if asleep!
Ensure client satisfaction and that the results meet the agreed treatment plan

Where excess medium has been applied, remove

If a contra-action occurs discontinue the treatment and provide appropriate action and advice

Monitor client satisfaction/comfort during treatment
Observe client body language to monitor satisfaction
Cover body parts when not being treated to maintain the physiological effect achieved

HEALTH AND SAFETY

A hydrotherm massage cushion filled with warm water and maintained at a constant temperature enables the therapist to slide her hands between the client and cushion when the client is lying in a supine position on the bed. This is beneficial for clients who cannot lie in a prone position, e.g. pregnant clients. The warmth of the water soothes the nerves and warms the muscles, enabling the client to receive a relaxing massage.

Faults during massage

If the therapist does not apply the correct pressure and her massage is too light or too heavy, the client will not feel the benefits. Inconsistent massage will not relax the client and will not feel as though it is flowing.

The therapist should ensure that the client is appropriately positioned to prevent discomfort and that the massage treatment provided is not too rough.

Ensure that the correct massage medium is selected and that adequate medium is applied. Too little may cause client discomfort, too much will make the skin too slippery to manipulate correctly.

AFTERCARE AND HOME CARE ADVICE

Before the client gets up from the couch, gently remove any remaining massage medium with a small clean towel or soft strong tissues. Eau de cologne may be applied to remove excess oil. The client should be covered with a towel and allowed to rest for a few minutes to allow the blood circulation to return to normal. If she were to get up immediately she might feel light-headed as the brain is temporarily starved of blood. She might even faint.

This resting time could be used to discuss with the client suitable aftercare and home care to complement the massage. This might involve advice on

Provide advice to clients by

- Encouraging the client to rest for a short period following treatment
  Offer a glass of water to avoid dizziness

- Discuss aftercare and homecare with the client to complement the massage

- For 24 hours avoid
  – Stimulants such as alcohol and caffeine
  – Heavy meals
  – Strenuous exercise

- Where possible the massage medium should be left upon the skin to condition and regulate for several hours

- Ask the client how they feel to establish if the treatment has achieved the objectives set

- Explain the benefits of ongoing regular treatment

- Recommend additional/further treatments that would be of benefit to the client
  Discuss timings/duration and cost

- Discuss recommendations to lifestyle changes
  • Increased exercise
  • Dietary advice
  • Increased intake of natural water (8 glasses per day recommended)
  • Relaxation techniques

- Treatment should be recommended as follows:
  – Body massage 1–2 times per week
  – Mechanical massage 2–3 times per week
  – Audiosonic 1–2 times per week
  Above recommendations will vary according to treatment plan/aim

- Body and head massage warn the client of post-treatment reactions including:
  – Sickness
  – Emotional anxiety
  – Headaches
  This reaction normally subsides in 24 hours

- Contra-actions
  Where an unnamed reaction occurs the client should inform the therapist immediately for advice on appropriate action to take

- Any contra-action should be noted on the client's records

healthy eating and exercise, including specific exercises that might be necessary to alleviate any postural problems. You should also advise the client to rest for a few hours when she gets home, and not to eat a heavy meal and to avoid alcohol.

As the client's circulation continues to return to normal, the blood vessels will constrict, resulting in a need to visit the toilet frequently. Advise the client to drink plenty of fluids to replace the fluids lost, preferably water.

If the massage was for relaxation, you might give advice on relaxing bath products and massage techniques that could be used at home. The massage could, of course, form part of a comprehensive treatment plan, including heat treatments such as infra-red, paraffin wax treatments and electrical treatments which will further benefit the client.

CONTRA-ACTIONS

These might include:

- sickness, caused by the increased circulation of waste products transported in the lymphatic system
- fainting, caused by dilation of the blood capillaries, altering blood-pressure levels
- skin reactions, such as an allergy to the massage medium used
- bruising, caused by incorrect application of the technique, i.e. excessive pressure during tapotement application.

If the client suffers any contra-action, you must assist the client before letting her leave the salon:

- Ensure the client can breathe properly and that the room is well ventilated.
- Offer the client a glass of water if she feels sick.
- Apply a cold compress if a skin reaction occurs.
- Advise the client to seek medical advice if the symptoms persist.

You should complete the client's record card fully so that continuation of the treatment can be tracked and any adverse reactions noted for future reference.

Mechanical massage treatments

Refer to unit **BT 18** to learn the techniques for performing mechanical massage treatment.

The following knowledge and understanding questions will include assessment for these areas.

Assessment of knowledge and understanding

You have now learnt about the effects of body and head massage and how to select and adapt your massage technique both manually and mechanically to meet the client's treatment requirements. These skills will enable you to professionally treat clients using effective head and body massage techniques.

To test your level of knowledge and understanding, answer the following short questions. These will prepare you for your summative (final) assessment.

Anatomy and physiology questions required for this unit are found on pages 146–50.

Organisational and legal requirements

1 Which health and safety legislation are you responsible for implementing when body massage treatment?

2 When using electrical equipment such as gyratory massage, what are your responsibilities under the Electricity at Work Act?

3 How can cross-infection be avoided when carrying out body massage treatment?

4 What is the commercially acceptable timing for the following:
   - a back massage?
   - a full body massage?

5 Why is it important to allow sufficient time to complete a service?

6 Why is it important to obtain the clients signature and keep detailed records of the clients treatment/s?

7 Why is it important to maintain correct posture when performing body massage?

Client consultation

1 What information should be recorded on the client record card before treatment application?

2 What is the purpose of the consultation before body massage treatment?

3 What contra-actions may occur when using body massage techniques?

4 Why is it important to discuss potential contra-actions with a client at the consultation?

Preparation for treatment

1 How should the treatment environment be prepared to ensure client comfort and maximum benefit from the treatment? Consider temperature, lighting and sound.

2 Why can it be beneficial to perform a pre-heating treatment before body massage treatment?

3 How should the client be prepared before the body massage treatment commences?

4 What considerations should be given to support and positioning of the client during treatment?

5 How would you recognise the following skin types/conditions:
- dry
- oily
- sensitive
- aged.

6 Which massage medium would be most suitable for the skin types/conditions above? Also, explain how you would adapt your massage technique for each.

Contra-indications

1 Why is it important to refer clients to their GP if you identify a contra-indication?

2 When would you need to refer a client to their GP before treatment could be given?

3 State three contra-indications that *prevent* body massage treatment.

4 State three contra-indications that *restrict* body massage treatment.

Equipment and materials

1 How is the following equipment cleaned and sanitised to prevent cross-infection:
- gyratory massage heads
- audio sonic attachment heads
- treatment couch

2 How can hygiene be maintained in the body massage treatment room?

3 Name a suitable product to use with mechanical massage to provide slip.

Treatment-specific knowledge

1 What do you understand by the term *erythema*, and what is its cause?

2 What effect does massage have on the following:
- skin
- bones
- muscle
- blood system

- lymph system
- nervous system.

3 What do you understand by the term muscle tone? How may this be affected by body massage?

4 How would body massage techniques, choice of medium, speed of application and pressure be adapted for the following clients:
- a young, athletic male client
- a female client with poor skin tone and stretch marks
- an overweight client on a weight reducing client
- an elderly client requiring a relaxation massage?

5 How would an allergic reaction to a massage medium be recognised?

6 Give four physiological benefits that the client may expect from the following treatments:
- body massage
- gyratory massage
- audio sonic treatment.

5 In which direction and at what systems of the body is body massage application directed towards?

6 How can client satisfaction be assessed during treatment application?

Treatment advice

1 Why is it important to gain feedback from the client and give relevant advice to her following treatment?

2 Why is it important to record any contra-action either during or following treatment on the client record card?

3 State three contra-actions that could occur during or following body massage.

4 What aftercare products may be recommended to your client?

5 How often would you recommend a client receives body massage?

6 What other treatment/s could be recommended to a client who was following a weight reduction programme?

7 What recommendations to lifestyle habit would enable a client to continue to benefit from the treatment for:
- relaxation
- sense of well-being.

chapter 8

Improve body condition using electro-therapy `BT18`

Improve the face and skin condition using electro-therapy `BT19`

Improve the appearance of the skin using micro-dermabrasion `BT36`

ELECTRICAL AND MECHANICAL TREATMENTS FOR THE FACE AND BODY

Introduction

Electrical and mechanical treatments – electro-therapy – produce intensified results in a short period of time compared with those that can be achieved manually.

Treatment objectives for electrical and mechanical treatments for the face and body include:

- Improved skin condition
- Improved contour and muscle condition
- Lymphatic drainage
- Relaxation.

> **HEALTH AND SAFETY**
>
> **Manufacturer's instructions**
> Always read the manufacturer's instructions provided with each piece of electrical equipment before you attempt to use it.

TIP

Exhibitions are ideal places to visit to view equipment, talk directly to the suppliers and compare benefits and costs with other suppliers in order to reach the best deal.

Choosing your equipment

Electro-therapy equipment is costly and careful consideration should be made before purchase. Always:

- purchase from a reputable company, whose equipment has proved suitable for its purpose
- check that the machine is safe; look for the CE mark awarded only if electrical safety standards have been reached
- check that it carries a guarantee.
- consider whether it is financially viable
- question whether the equipment supplier will support you with advertising and training
- ask if a temporary replacement will be provided should the equipment become faulty
- ensure you are provided with sufficient materials. Often materials may need to be washed or sterilised between clients, therefore have several sets available. This will also reduce wear and tear.

Obviously, care and consideration are necessary when using any piece of equipment to ensure a safe and effective treatment is received.

The CE mark

HEALTH AND SAFETY

Do not:
- use equipment from a socket where the mains lead is likely to be over-stretched
- use a twisted, torn flex or cable
- handle plugs or sockets with wet hands
- overload a socket.

General electrical safety precautions

The following safety guidelines should always be followed:

- Always keep water away from electrical equipment to avoid electrical shock.
- Avoid trailing wires, to prevent damage to the machine and personal injury caused through tripping over them.
- Always check that the current controls are at zero before treatment commences, to avoid accidental current transfer.
- Store and place all equipment on a sturdy surface.

HEALTH AND SAFETY

A fire extinguisher must be available to deal with electrical fires. This will usually be of a dry powder type colour coded blue.

- Position equipment so that the current intensity reading is clearly visible.
- Check the performance of the machine on yourself if possible before use on a client, to make sure it is in good working order.
- Sufficient plug sockets should be provided to avoid overloading and possible fire.

Legal requirements

The **Electricity at Work Act 1989** imposes duties on employers and self-employed persons to comply with specific health and safety regulations within their control and responsibility. Electrical equipment must be safe; equipment must therefore be regularly inspected by a qualified electrician. Accurate records listing the date of inspection, the test results and next test date must be available for inspection by the Environmental Health Officer (EHO).

The **Health and Safety at Work Act 1974** states that:

- all equipment should meet safety standards, be regularly checked and be in good working order
- consideration of handling and application of equipment is the responsibility of the employer to avoid possible employee injury, and adequate training should be given
- trailing leads should not pose a threat to the welfare of employees or clients.

Reception

When booking a client for an electrical/mechanical facial or body treatment you must select equipment that will achieve the results that you require. The application of each treatment may need to be adapted for differing skin or body types, whilst also selecting appropriate cosmetic therapeutic ingredients.

There are certain conditions which may be present that will prevent you from selecting a piece of electrical equipment. These contra-indications must be checked for before booking the client for an appointment and an alternative treatment offered in such cases.

Several different electrical and mechanical treatments may be selected when planning a treatment programme for your client in order to achieve optimum results and to add variety to the programme.

Preparation of the treatment area

The treatment area should be clean and warm; a comfortable working temperature for both client and therapist is between 18 and 21°C.

Adequate ventilation should be provided to create a hygienic environment, preventing cross-infection through viral airborne spores, drowsiness through carbon dioxide-saturated air and the removal of stale smells and odours.

HEALTH AND SAFETY

Many pieces of electrical equipment now have a safety feature whereby the current will not flow if any amplitude dials are not set at zero.

HEALTH AND SAFETY

- Infrequently used equipment should be tested every 12 months.
- Frequently used equipment should be checked every 6 months.

EQUIPMENT LIST

couch or beauty chair

beauty stool (with or without backrest)

trolleys (2 are necessary)

magnifying lamp

towels (small and large)

gown for client

headband

cotton wool

tissues

petroleum jelly

container for jewellery

spatulas

waste bin

record card

The treatment area should induce relaxation and comfort. Lighting should be soft, the decor subtle and non-gender biased. Sound levels should be low and chosen for relaxation.

Before the client is shown through to the cubicle, it should be checked to ensure that it is clean and tidy and that all the required equipment, accessories and consumables are available.

The following guidelines describe the basic preparation of the treatment cubicle:

- **Couch or beauty chair**: with sit-up and lie-down positions and an easy-to-clean surface. For the therapist's comfort it should be adjustable in height to avoid future postural problems and muscle strain.

- **Beauty stool**: this may or may not have a back rest; in some designs the back rest is removable. For the comfort of the therapist it should be adjustable in height; to allow mobility it should be mounted on castors.
- **Trolleys**: two trolleys are necessary – one to display treatment products and consumables; the other to place small pieces of electrical equipment on.
- **Magnifying lamp**: this is used to magnify the skin's surface during facial treatments.

TIP

You may prefer to purchase a multi-unit which will offer a wider treatment choice for the client and will also save space. However, if the machine becomes faulty, the disadvantage is that you can not offer any of the other treatments until it is repaired!

- **Towels**: these should be clean for each client. Small and large towels must be available to drape across the client as necessary.
- **Hand towel**: easily accessible for the therapist to wipe her hands on.
- **Gown**: a clean gown should be provided for each client to maintain client modesty.
- **Headband**: a clean headband is used to protect the client's hair from cosmetic creams.
- **Cotton wool**: there should be a plentiful supply of both damp and dry cotton wool, sufficient for the treatment to be carried out. Dry cotton wool should be stored in a covered container; damp cotton wool is usually placed in a clean bowl.
- **Tissues**: these should be large and of a high quality. They should be stored in a covered container.

Ensure that the treatment area creates the right environment to ensure client relaxation to gain maximum treatment benefit.
Consider temperature, lighting, decor , sound and smells

Follow organisational and legal requirements to prepare the treatment area/equipment

Prepare for the electro-therapy treatment by

Ensure that all equipment products and consumables are available in the treatment area to select from to ensure efficient work practice procedures

Ensure that your appearance is both professional and conforms to hygiene and health and safety requirements

- **Petroleum jelly**: this should be available to protect the client's skin where necessary, forming a barrier to electric current.
- **Container for jewellery**: this may be provided for the safe storage of removed jewellery.
- **Spatulas**: several clean spatulas (preferably disposable) should be provided for each client. These are used mainly to remove products from their containers.
- **Waste bin (covered)**: this should be placed unobtrusively within easy reach. It should be lined with a disposable bin-liner.
- **Record card**: for facial and body treatments.

Preparation of the client

By the time the client is shown through to the treatment cubicle, her record card will have been partly filled in at reception by the receptionist. The card should be collected by the beauty therapist, who will add to it during and after the treatment.

Consultation

In the privacy of the treatment cubicle, carry out a treatment consultation and assess the client's needs, following accepted codes of practice. This should take place when the client first meets the therapist and again whenever a new treatment is to be carried out. All details must be recorded on the client record card.

Consultation techniques to assess client's needs and suitability for treatment include questioning the client and examining the client both visually and manually as necessary.

The client is prepared for the electro-therapy treatment, which may include:

HEALTH AND SAFETY

Jewellery in contact with electrical current can cause the current to concentrate as metal is a good conductor of electricity. Also, burning could occur to the client's skin if receiving a pre-heating treatment such as in infra-red treatment application. Always ensure jewellery is removed in the treatment area.

Face treatment

- *Cleansing*: to remove dead skin cells, sebum debris and make-up if worn.
- *Exfoliation*: this may include an exfoliating facial cosmetic, or facial brush to remove debris and dead skin cells which would act as a barrier offering initial resistance.
- *Pre-heating treatment*: such as steam. The increase in skin temperature makes the skin more receptive.

Body treatment

- *Exfoliation*: may include an exfoliating body cosmetic or body brush.
- *Pre-heat treatment*: may include, infra-red, steam, sauna, spa treatment.
- It may be necessary to shower before treatment to cleanse the skin, remove other body products, apply an exfoliant or remove a body preparation.

Sample record cards are shown for body and face electro-therapy treatments.

Contra-indications

The consultation will draw your attention to any specific contra-indications to electrical therapy or aspects which require special care and attention. The following contra-indications are relevant to all electrical therapy treatments:

- cuts and abrasions: if the skin is broken, the electrical current will concentrate in that area as body fluid is a conductor of electricity
- severe bruising would make treatment uncomfortable and harmful to the client
- skin disease/disorder: may be contagious or could be aggravated by treatment
- recent scar tissue: scar tissue will have less strength than healthy skin; avoid treatments that will involve stretching the skin
- malignant melanoma, cancer of the skin making cells abnormal in the area
- inflammation or swelling of the skin: the condition could be made worse
- operation in the treatment area: if recent, wait for 6 months
- high or low blood pressure: this could be made worse
- circulatory disorder
- hepatitis, inflammation of the liver caused by a virus, can make the client feel very ill
- defective sensation: the client *must* be able to tell you of the sensation experienced
- metal plates or pins within the treatment area
- heart disease/disorder
- electronic implants: can be affected by the electric current
- spastic condition: dysfunction of the nervous system.
- epilepsy
- botox (botolinum toxin) is a neurotoxin which affects the nervous system paralysing muscles temporarily, reducing the appearance of lines and

HEALTH AND SAFETY

Contra-indications
In the event of a client having a contra-indication:
- Encourage the client to seek medical advice, never make a personal judgement
- Explain professionally why the treatment cannot be carried out: because you would not wish to harm the client or make the condition worse. If contagious there is also a risk of cross-infection!
- Treatment may be possible if the treatment is adapted, e.g. avoiding areas such as a mild bruise. If GP consent is obtained after medical advice has been sought, treatment may be given.

BEAUTY WORKS

Date		Beauty therapist name	
Client name		Date of birth (identifying client age group)	
Address		Postcode	
Evening phone number		Day phone number	
Name of doctor		Doctor's address and phone number	

Related medical history (conditions that may restrict or prohibit treatment application)

Are you taking any medication (this may affect the condition of the skin or skin sensitivity)

CONTRA-INDICATIONS REQUIRING MEDICAL REFERRAL
(Preventing **body electro-therapy** treatment application)

- ☐ bacterial infection e.g. impetigo
- ☐ viral infection e.g. herpes simplex
- ☐ fungal infection e.g. tinea corporis
- ☐ skin disorders
- ☐ skin disease e.g. malignant melanoma
- ☐ high or low blood pressure
- ☐ heart disease/disorder
- ☐ medical conditions under supervision
- ☐ pacemaker
- ☐ recent scar tissue
- ☐ dysfunction of the nervous system
- ☐ epilepsy
- ☐ botox treatment
- ☐ HIV

TREATMENT AREAS

- ☐ trunk   ☐ limbs   ☐ full body

SKIN SENSITIVITY TEST
- ☐ thermal   ☐ tactile

EQUIPMENT
- ☐ direct high frequency   ☐ galvanic unit
- ☐ faradic unit   ☐ microcurrent unit
- ☐ gyrator massager   ☐ vacuum suction
- ☐ micro-dermabrasion

CLIENT PREPARATION
- ☐ exfoliation   ☐ pre-heat treatments
- ☐ skin cleansing   ☐ showering

CONTRA-INDICATIONS WHICH RESTRICT TREATMENT
(Treatment may require adaptation)

- ☐ cuts and abrasions
- ☐ bruising and swelling
- ☐ recent scar tissue (avoid area)
- ☐ undiagnosed lumps, bumps, swellings
- ☐ recent injuries to the treatment area
- ☐ mild eczema/psoriasis
- ☐ high or low blood pressure
- ☐ history of thrombosis/embolism
- ☐ menstruation, over the abdomen
- ☐ varicose veins
- ☐ medication   ☐ diabetes
- ☐ metal pins or plates   ☐ pregnancy
- ☐ body piercings   ☐ highly anxious client

LIFESTYLE
- ☐ occupation   ☐ family situation
- ☐ dietary and fluid intake   ☐ sleep patterns
- ☐ exercise habits   ☐ smoking habits
- ☐ hobbies, interests, means of relaxation

BODY TYPES AND CONDITION
- ☐ endomorph   ☐ mesomorph
- ☐ ectomorph   ☐ cellulite
- ☐ poor muscle tone   ☐ sluggish circulation
- ☐ blemish/congested skin

OBJECTIVES OF TREATMENT
- ☐ improved skin and body condition
- ☐ improved contour and muscle condition
- ☐ lymphatic drainage
- ☐ relaxation

Beauty therapist signature (for reference)

Client signature (confirmation of details)

TREATMENT ADVICE

This information includes:
- Advice on products that would be suitable for the client to use at home
- Advice on how to gain maximum benefit from product use
- Record samples provided, to evaluate effectiveness at next treatment with the client
- Advice to enhance the effectiveness of the treatment including:
  - Postural advice
  - Exercise advice
  - Dietary advice
- Advice to follow immediately following the treatment to include:
  - Possible reactions to the treatment and recommended action to take
  - Suitable rest period following treatment
  - General advice re food and drink intake
  - Avoidance of stimulants
- Contra-action advice on action to be taken in the event of an unwanted reaction (e.g. a skin reaction)
- Recommendations for further body electro-therapy treatments and the benefits of continuous treatments
- The recommended time intervals between treatments

wrinkles in the area of application. Immediate side effects include redness and swelling at the site of botox injection. As the treatment paralyses the muscle, treatments to exercise muscle would be ineffective.

- HIV (human immunodeficiency virus) damages the body's defence system so that it cannot fight certain infections. Certain side effects of the disease would contra-indicate treatment. Cross-infection can occur if there is contact with infected blood or serum.

- history of thrombosis or embolism, as the formation of a thrombus (blood clot) can occur. Pieces of the thrombus can break off and are transported in the bloodstream becoming wedged in capillaries, affecting the lungs or heart. Blockage of the coronary arteries can lead to a heart attack!

- metal pins of plates, which may cause electrical current concentration

- piercings in the area, which may cause electrical current concentration

- highly anxious client, the treatment may be ineffective or too uncomfortable for the client

- certain medication may cause an unwanted skin reaction or be the cause of the skin/body condition

If you are unsure about the suitability of a client's skin sensitivity, perform a skin sensitivity test. This is necessary to test if the client's sensory nerve endings are responsive to stimuli such as heat and touch.

Skin sensitivity test

Using a sharp and smooth object, lightly stroke this over the skin (usually the limb). This is called a tactile skin sensitivity test. Hold a test tube containing warm water followed by cold water next to the skin. This is called a thermal skin sensitivity test. Ask the client to differentiate between the different sensations.

Once the consultation is complete, the therapist should ensure that all details are recorded accurately and that the client has signed her record card. This enables continuity of treatment and up-to-date tracking of the treatments received.

BEAUTY WORKS

Date	Beauty therapist name	
Client name		Date of birth (identifying client age group)
Address		Postcode

Evening phone number	Day phone number
Name of doctor	Doctor's address and phone number

Related medical history (conditions that may restrict or prohibit treatment application)

Are you taking any medication (this may affect the condition of the skin or skin sensitivity)

CONTRA-INDICATIONS REQUIRING MEDICAL REFERRAL
(Preventing **facial electro-therapy** treatment application)

☐ bacterial infection e.g. impetigo
☐ viral infection e.g. herpes simplex
☐ fungal infection e.g. tinea corporis
☐ skin disorders
☐ skin disease e.g. malignant melanoma
☐ high or low blood pressure
☐ heart disease/disorder
☐ medical conditions under supervision
☐ pacemaker
☐ recent scar tissue
☐ dysfunction of the nervous system
☐ epilepsy
☐ botox treatment
☐ HIV

SKIN SENSITIVITY TEST
☐ thermal   ☐ tactile

EQUIPMENT
☐ high frequency direct/indirect   ☐ galvanic unit
☐ faradic unit   ☐ microcurrent unit
☐ vacuum suction   ☐ micro-dermabrasion

CLIENT PREPARATION
☐ exfoliation   ☐ pre-heat treatments
☐ skin cleansing

CONTRA-INDICATIONS WHICH RESTRICT TREATMENT
(Treatment may require adaptation)

☐ cuts and abrasions
☐ bruising and swelling
☐ recent scar tissue (avoid area)
☐ undiagnosed lumps, bumps, swellings
☐ recent injuries to the treatment area
☐ high or low blood pressure
☐ history of thrombosis/embolism
☐ menstruation, over the abdomen
☐ mild eczema/psoriasis   ☐ varicose veins
☐ medication   ☐ diabetes
☐ metal pins or plates   ☐ pregnancy
☐ body piercings   ☐ highly anxious client

LIFESTYLE
☐ occupation   ☐ family situation
☐ dietary and fluid intake   ☐ sleep patterns
☐ current skincare routine   ☐ smoking habits
☐ hobbies, interests, means of relaxation

SKIN TYPES AND CONDITIONS
☐ oily   ☐ dry
☐ combination   ☐ sensitive
☐ mature   ☐ dehydrated
☐ poor skin tone   ☐ poor muscle tone
☐ blemish/congested skin

OBJECTIVES OF TREATMENT
☐ improved skin condition
☐ improved contour and muscle condition
☐ lymphatic drainage
☐ relaxation

Beauty therapist signature (for reference)

Client signature (confirmation of details)

TREATMENT ADVICE

This information includes:
- Advice on products that would be suitable for the client to use at home
- Advice on how to gain maximum benefit from product use
- Record samples provided, to evaluate effectiveness at next treatment with the client

- Advice to enhance the effectiveness of the treatment including:
  - Skin care advice
  - Facial exercise advice
  - Dietary advice
- Advice to follow immediately following the treatment to include:
  - Possible reactions to the treatment and recommended action to take
  - Avoidance of make-up application following a deep cleansing facial
- Contra-action advice on action to be taken in the event of an unwanted reaction (e.g. a skin reaction)
- Recommendations for further facial electro-therapy treatments and the benefits of continuous treatments
- The recommended time intervals between treatments

Equipment

The pieces of equipment that the NVQ Level 3 beauty therapist may become competent in using are as follows:

- **Mechanical massage equipment**: vibrators which use electricity (via electric motors) to produce mechanical movement, gyratory massage, audio sonic and vacuum suction.
- **Electro-therapy equipment**: (pass various types of electric current through the client for a variety of effects) high frequency, galvanic, faradic, microcurrent, epilation.
- **Ray therapy equipment**: (use electricity to produce electromagnetic rays to treat the client) infra-red, ultraviolet lamps, sunbeds/booths.
- **Heat treatment equipment**: (use electricity to produce heat to treat the client) saunas, steam baths, spa pools.

The beauty therapy Units that assess electro-therapy are:

BT18 Improve body condition using electro-therapy
BT19 Improve face and skin condition using electro-therapy

EQUIPMENT LIST

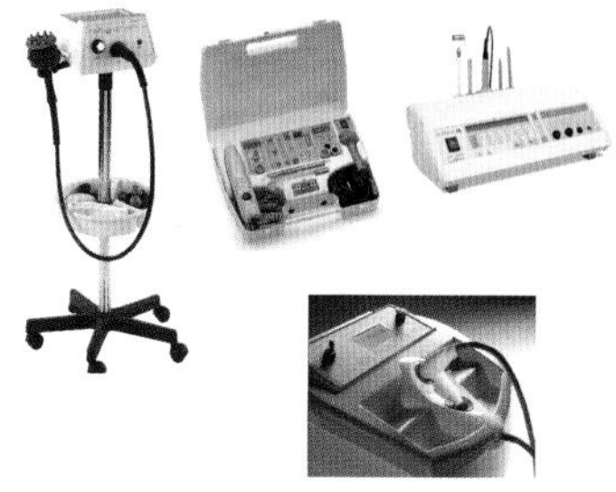

mechanical massage equipment

electro-therapy equipment

ray therapy equipment

heat treatment equipment

BT18 IMPROVE BODY CONDITION USING ELECTRO-THERAPY

Learning objectives

This unit describes how to provide electro-therapy treatment selecting and using different equipment to improve figure appearance and skin condition.

It describes the competencies to enable you to:

- **prepare for the body treatment**
- **consult and plan the treatment with the client**
- **perform electro-therapy treatments**
- **complete the treatment**

It also covers the knowledge requirements for Unit **BT36** Improve the appearance of the skin using micro-dermabrasion

BT19 IMPROVE FACE AND SKIN CONDITION USING ELECTRO-THERAPY

Learning objectives

This unit describes how to provide the service electro-therapy treatment selecting and using different equipment to improve face and skin condition.

It describes the competencies to enable you to:

- **prepare for the facial treatment**
- **consult and plan the treatment with the client**
- **perform electro-therapy treatments**
- **complete the treatment**

When providing an electro-therapy treatment to the face and body it is important to use the skills you have learnt in the following core mandatory units:

Unit G1 ensure your own actions reduce risks to health and safety
Unit G6 promote additional products or services to clients
Unit G11 contribute to the financial effectiveness of the business

Both BT18 and 19 are discussed below, explaining the differences in application between body and face.

Equipment to be studied includes:

- High frequency
- Galvanic
- Faradic
- Microcurrent
- Gyratory massager (body application only)
- Vacuum suction

* Audio sonic treatment is discussed and is referenced to BT17 provide head and body massage treatments. It is recommended as a pre-heating treatment for massage but is not assessed as part of units 18, 19 and 36.

FARADIC TREATMENT

Faradic treatment, or electro-muscle stimulation, is an electrical treatment, applied to both the face and body. An electrical current is used to simulate the effect of isometric exercise, that is exercise requiring repetitions. Specific muscles are repeatedly exercised by stimulation by the electrical current, which creates a tightening, toning effect.

General effects:

- improved tone of specific muscles, producing a reshaping effect for figure correction and face lifting
- increased metabolism of the stimulated muscles
- waste products are more readily eliminated from muscles by the pumping action on the lymph vessels and veins as the muscles contract and relax.

Body use:

- increased fluid and waste elimination through an improved lymphatic circulation, beneficial to improve the appearance of a cellulite condition
- posture improvement achieved through increasing muscle tone in over-stretched muscles
- improved appearance of the body contour as the muscles tighten, having a slimming effect
- beneficial for clients contra-indicated to active exercise.

Facial use:

- improved firmness of slack facial muscles
- improved skin colour through improved blood circulation.

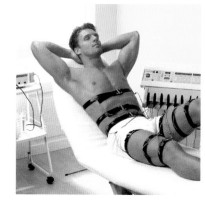

A male receiving treatment

Anatomy and physiology

Muscles are composed of bundles of muscle fibres. Each fibre is supplied with many nerves which, when stimulated by the electrical current, cause the muscle fibres to shorten and the muscle to contract. The nerves creating movement are called motor nerves, and repeated stimulation by the electrical current causes the muscle fibres to improve in tone. The result is increased firmness of the tissues and a reshaping of body contours.

The positioning of the electrode which passes the electrical current is important. It should be as close as possible to the muscles **motor point**. This is the point where the motor nerve enters it. This ensures that stimulation occurs with minimum current intensity.

Initially, the skin will resist the current as the surface epidermal cells contain little moisture and the underlying adipose layer is also a poor conductor of electric current. Once the current has overcome the skin's resistance, the electrical pulses bring about muscle contraction.

Electrical science

The faradic current uses a low frequency interrupted direct current. The current is applied through paired electrodes.

A typical machine has the following features:
- **Mains switch**: for turning the machine on and off.

TIP	

With advances in technology, certain units now are computerised and produce quite complex routines programmed by their microprocessors to suit different parts of the body.

- **Pulse control**: this varies the length of time for which the stimulation and relaxation periods occur. This is variable between 0.5–2.5 seconds. In the stimulation period, the current flows and the muscle fibres contract. In the interval period, the current ceases to flow and the muscle is allowed to rest.

TIP

The stimulation period must be long enough for the muscle fibres to be stimulated and shorten. The interval period must be of a sufficient duration to allow all the muscle fibres to relax and lengthen or muscle fatigue will occur. A client with poor muscle tone or excessive adipose tissue will require longer stimulation and relaxation periods to achieve a full contraction of the muscle fibres being stimulated.

- **Frequency control**: controls the number of electrical pulses per second. This is commonly adjustable between 65–135 pulses per second. The frequency setting alters the depth of stimulation and the stimulation of different groups of fibres within the muscle. Therefore the lower frequency is selected for the treatment of deeper muscles and for clients with excessive adipose tissue. The higher frequency is selected for superficial fascia and muscle.
- **Amplitude**: regulates the intensity of power to each electrode/s. This is usually adjustable from 0–10.
- **Pulse width**: this changes the width of each pulse, which affects the period of stimulation within the muscle. The higher the setting of the pulse, the greater the stimulation. A lower pulse is selected for facial application and a higher setting for body application.
- **Mode control**: this is used to select the polarity. There are usually two options. In unidirectional or monophasic mode, pulses are of the same polarity. One electrode has a negative charge and the other a positive charge; the current flows in one direction between the two. In **bi-directional** or **bi-phasic** mode, impulses are of reversed polarity. This minimises the skin's resistance, making it possible to stimulate the muscles with a lower current intensity. Each electrode can have the same polarity, the current flows in one direction and then the other. A pull sensation is experienced after each contraction.
- **Gain control**: this dial increases all the intensity dials without the need for turning them up individually.
- **Variable control**: a feature which randomly changes the pattern of the stimulation and interval period. This ensures that the client can relax as she will not be able to anticipate the contraction period.
- **Electrodes**: these enable the current to flow to selected muscles.

Reception

- Complete personal details on the client record card.
- Question the client to check for possible contra-indications.

Facial treatment

Allow 15 minutes for the treatment application itself. As the treatment is usually applied following other preparatory facial treatments, a 45 minute appointment is normally booked. The client should attend twice a week for a course of 10 and then continue with a maintenance facial once every month.

Body treatment

An initial treatment assesses the client's tolerance to the treatment and should be given for 15–20 minutes. Future treatment time increases to 30–40 minutes. The client should attend the salon 2 to 3 times per week for a course of 10 treatments. She should then continue with a maintenance treatment once every 1–2 weeks.

Contra-indications

During the client assessment, if you find any of the following in the treatment area, faradic treatment must not be carried out:

- broken skin
- defective sensation
- metal plates or pins in the treatment area
- excessive dental fillings
- nerve or muscular disorders
- thrombosis or phlebitis
- heart disorders
- pacemaker
- IUD coil
- varicose veins
- pregnant client.

> **HEALTH AND SAFETY**
>
> Wait approximately 6 months before treating a client following any surgery such as a caesarean section. If in doubt always consult the client's GP.

Equipment and materials

- record card
- faradic facial/body or combined unit
- electrodes, commonly composed of electrically conductive carbon impregnated plastic. The electrodes are used in pairs for body application. Small, one-piece twin electrodes are used to stimulate the muscles for facial treatment or a facial mask electrode may be used to treat several facial muscles at once

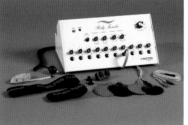

Faradic unit

Carlton Professional

> **TIP** ✔
>
> The facial electrode has a twin electrode, as two connections are necessary to complete a circuit.

EQUIPMENT LIST

record card

faradic facial/body combined unit

electrodes

elasticated straps

- elasticated straps to hold the electrodes in place for body application

> **TIP**
>
> If the client is obese it may be necessary to place sponge dampened with warm water underneath each body electrode to ensure even contact with the skin and to guard against a concentration of current. This technique may also be used if the client is allergic to the surface of the electrodes. This would be recognised by red circles of erythema.

- electrical leads, to transport the electric current to the electrodes
- skin-care preparations to cleanse the skin
- ionised solution applied directly to the skin or surface of the electrode to ensure good conduction of the current
- unperfumed talc to soothe the skin after body application if necessary.

Sterilisation and sanitisation

After use, clean the surface of the electrodes in warm, soapy water. Dry naturally and sanitise in an ultraviolet sterilising cabinet. Additional electrodes are necessary to allow for effective sterilisation between the treatment of clients.

Wash the elasticated straps in warm soapy water and dry.

Preparation of the treatment area

- Cover the treatment couch with a clean towel.
- Check all general electrical safety precautions.
- Test the electrode/s to ensure they are in good working order.
- Dampen the surface of the electrode/s and hold against the palm of one hand. With the other hand, turn up the current intensity until you can feel a mild tingling sensation indicating that the current is flowing.

Sorisa

Applying ionised solution

HEALTH AND SAFETY ✚

Ensure that the leads are firmly attached to the electrodes to be certain of effective current transfer.

> **TIP** ✔
>
> Testing the electrodes before application ensures that treatment is not delayed after padding if an electrode is not working.

Facial application

- Prepare the facial electrode for treatment.
- Secure the electrode firmly to the electrical leads.
- Insert the lead into the relevant connection.

Body application

- Place the elasticated straps on the couch, ready for positioning for the treatment.
- Prepare the electrode/s for treatment.
- Secure the electrodes firmly to the electrical leads.
- Insert the leads into the relevant outlet/s of the unit.
- Select the frequency required for the client according to the client requirements.

TIP ✔

The elasticated straps must not be too tight. Have spare straps available if those selected are unsuitable.

Preparation of the therapist

- Collect the client's record card.
- Sanitise your hands before handling the client.
- Assess the client, discuss the clients lifestyle and objectives for the treatment if this is the initial treatment. Agree on an appropriate treatment plan.
- If a treatment has a slimming requirement it will be necessary to measure the client at the beginning of the treatment course and once every week.
- If this is a repeat treatment, check the client's progress against targets set and provide support and advice as necessary.

Preparation of the client

Facial application

1 Perform a skin sensitivity test in the area to be treated.

2 Remove all jewellery from the treatment area.

3 Cleanse and tone the skin of the face and neck. Blot the skin dry with a soft facial tissue.

4 Analyse the client's skin using a magnifying lamp, and question the client further where necessary to check information in relation to the client's skin condition.

5 Explain the treatment sensation to the client. The client will initially feel a prickling sensation as the sensory nerve endings in the skin are stimulated, followed by a gentle tightening of the skin as the muscle contracts. Explain to the client that the skin may appear reddened in the area following treatment. This is a reflex action causing the capillaries in the area temporarily to dilate.

 Sorisa

Facial application

TIP ✔

It is beneficial to perform a preheating treatment before the faradic treatment as this will maximise the response to the current. For the face this may be a steam treatment, for the body it may be a dry or wet heat treatment such as sauna or spa.

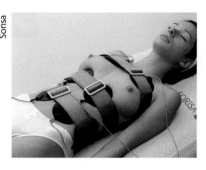

Body application

Body application

1 Perform a sensitivity test in the area to be treated.

2 Remove all jewellery from the area.

3 Instruct the client to remove all clothing except underwear.

4 Measure the client.

5 Position the client on the treatment couch. This will be in a supine or prone position depending on the padding layout selected.

6 Cleanse the skin using a non-oily detergent cleanser to remove body creams, etc. Cover any minor cuts or abrasions with petroleum jelly or a small surgical plaster to form a barrier to the electric current.

7 Secure the elasticated straps around the parts to be treated. These must not be too tight.

8 Apply the ionised solution to the surface of each electrode. Select the appropriate padding technique for the body part to be treated. Place in position and secure with the straps.

9 Set the stimulation, interval, frequency, pulse sequence and mode according to the needs of the client.

10 Explain the treatment sensation to the client. The client initially will feel a prickling sensation as the sensory nerve endings in the skin are stimulated, followed by a tightening of the muscle as it contracts. A visible contraction of the muscle will be seen as it is stimulated.

HEALTH AND SAFETY

Ensure the client does not have any metal contained in underwear in contact with the electrodes.

TIP

It is important that the pairs of electrodes do not touch each other in body application as the current will not enter the muscle efficiently if this happens.

Treatment application

Facial application

1 Position the client in a semi-reclined position. It is easier to exercise the muscles in this position.

2 Ensure all intensity dials on the unit are at zero.

3 Switch the machine on at the mains.

4 Select the frequency according to the treatment requirements.

5 Apply a conducting solution to the electrode surface.

TIP

- As facial muscles insert into the facial skin or other adjacent muscles it is often difficult to treat individual muscles. Therefore, appropriate facial nerves are stimulated to ensure an effective treatment of groups of muscles.
- Because the facial muscles are difficult to isolate, the pair of facial electrodes are small and close together.
- By stimulating the facial nerve by placing the electrode at the side of the face below the ear, all the superficial muscles of facial expression may be stimulated at the same time.

6 Place the electrode on the first motor point to be stimulated. Increase the current intensity slowly, during the stimulation period. When the intensity gauge registers, wait approximately 30 seconds to allow the current to overcome the skin's resistance.

HEALTH AND SAFETY

A gentle pulling of the skin in the area of stimulation is sufficient. Exaggerated facial movements should be avoided, especially around the eye area.

7 Increase the current intensity until the client experiences the prickling sensation. Continue increasing the current until a visible contraction can be seen.

8 Exercise each muscle motor point 6–10 times.

9 Treat each area three times.

10 Turn the intensity control to zero and switch the unit off.

11 Complete details of the treatment on the client's record card.

Body application

This treatment is usually aimed at general muscle toning. The therapist is able to concentrate on improving problem areas of particular concern to the client. This is commonly known as **spot reduction**. Other treatments may also be offered which achieve a different complimentary effect.

1 Place the electrodes in pairs, secured with the elasticated straps, selecting the padding technique to achieve the required results:
Longitudinal: an electrode is placed near the origin and insertion of a particular muscle. This method specifically shortens muscles but is less economical on electrodes.
Split motor point: an electrode is placed on the motor point of the same muscle but on each side of the body. This method is suitable for treating smaller muscles where the actual motor point is difficult to locate. It is efficient on electrodes so more areas of the body can be treated at once.
Duplicate: an electrode is placed on the motor point of two different muscles that are adjacent to each other. This allows for differing muscle strengths on either side of the body.

2 Select the most appropriate frequency.

> **HEALTH AND SAFETY** ✚
>
> It is important to know the position of different muscles motor points or the treatment will be less effective and possibly uncomfortable for the client.

3 Ensure all dials are at zero and then turn on the current at the mains.

4 Switch the machine on.

5 Increase the intensity of each electrode outlet during each stimulation period until the client feels the tingling sensation. The current continues to be increased until visible, even contractions are achieved.

6 Apply the treatment according to the treatment plan. At the end of the treatment, reduce the level of current intensity simultaneously until all outlets are at zero.

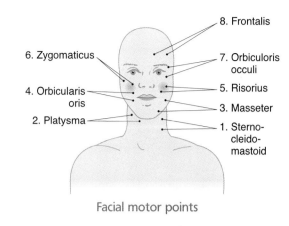

6. Zygomaticus
8. Frontalis
7. Orbiculoris occuli
5. Risorius
3. Masseter
1. Sterno-cleido-mastoid
2. Platysma
4. Orbicularis oris

Facial motor points

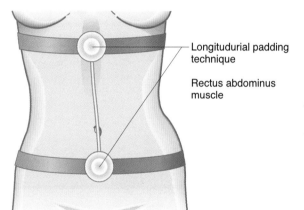

Longitudurial padding technique

Rectus abdominus muscle

Padding technique – rectus abdominus

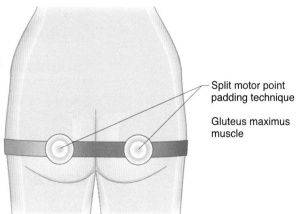

Split motor point padding technique

Gluteus maximus muscle

Padding technique – gluteus maximus

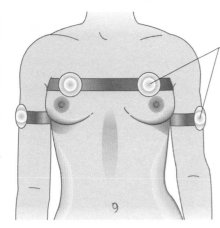

Padding technique – pectoralis major and triceps

Duplicate padding technique

Pectoralis major and triceps muscles

7 Switch off the machine at the mains.

8 If the client's skin appears reddened in the treatment area, explain that this is a reflex action causing the capillaries in the area to temporarily dilate.

9 Complete details of the treatment on the client's record card.

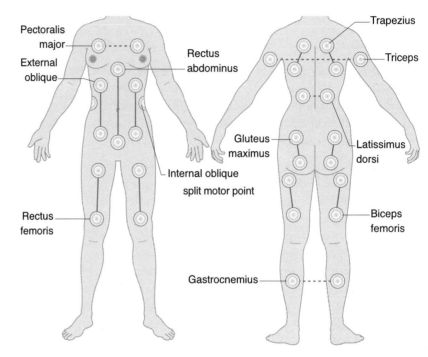

Pectoralis major

External oblique

Rectus abdominus

Internal oblique split motor point

Rectus femoris

Trapezius

Triceps

Gluteus maximus

Latissimus dorsi

Biceps femoris

Gastrocnemius

Sample padding techniques to anterior and posterior body

Aftercare

Advise the client on the the purchase and correct application of commercial face and body cosmetic skin-care preparations. Nutritional advice should be given if the client is on a weight-reducing diet. Supportive exercises for the face or body may also be given.

The treatment should be seen as a support to active exercise rather than a replacement.

Contra-actions

- Muscle fatigue caused by over-stimulation of weak disused muscles. This can be recognised by erratic contractions of the muscles or poor response to the stimulation. The muscles will feel sore and stiffened following treatment. This can be avoided by ensuring an effective consultation and communication with the client during treatment.
- Excessive reddening of the skin caused by allergic reaction to the graphite electrode. Action: place a dampened sponge beneath the electrode to enable the treatment to continue.
- Erythema caused by reflex vasodilation of the blood capillaries. Action: apply unperfumed talc to soothe the skin.

GALVANIC TREATMENT

Galvanism is an electrical treatment which can be applied to both the face and body. Therapeutic substances are introduced into the skin using a direct current to create specific effects upon the surface and underlying tissues.

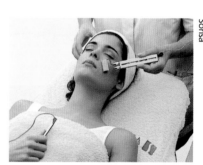

Galvanic treatment

General effects:

- increased blood and lymphatic circulation
- reduction of non-medical swelling and puffiness by improving the dispersal of accumulated tissue fluids and waste products from the area
- improved function and appearance of the skin by introduction of water-soluble substances.

Body use:

- used in slimming treatments as fat is more readily transported for utilisation in the increased lymphatic flow
- to improve the appearance of a cellulite condition.

Facial use:

- improved skin texture through removal of the surface dead skin cells (desquammation)
- introduction into the skin of regulating therapeutic ingredients enables different skin types and conditions to be treated.

Sorisa

Anatomy and physiology

The chemical effects of the substances produced beneath the electrodes are used to improve the general functioning of the skin. Acids are produced under the positive pole (the anode), and alkalis are formed under the negative pole (the cathode).

The irritant effect of the alkaline chemical formation stimulates the blood flow and causes the superficial blood capillaries to dilate, thus causing the deeper blood vessels to dilate as a reflex action. The astringent effect of the acid chemical formation reduces redness of the skin and firms the tissues.

The propelling of ionised cosmetics into the skin is called **iontophoresis**. The cells are nourished by the improved circulation and the skin benefits from the therapeutic effects of the substances which have been introduced.

Electrical science

The galvanic unit produces a smooth-flowing, uninterrupted direct electric current (d.c.). It converts the mains alternating current at 230 volts to a smooth direct current at up to 100 volts. This is achieved in three stages:

- a **transformer** reduces the voltage of the a.c. mains
- a **rectifier** changes a.c. to d.c.
- a **capacitor** smoothes any irregularities in that d.c.

A **rheostat** is used to set the required intensity. A **milliameter** shows the flow of current through the client and an **electronic circuit** keeps the current at the required level, even though the skin's resistance will change during the course of the treatment.

A low-intensity direct current is used, measured in milli-amps (mA – one thousandth of an amp) to introduce into the skin electrically charged, water-based solutions containing therapeutic ingredients from plants, herbs, flowers and fruit. These solutions are known as **electrolytes**. They contain acids and salts which increase electrical conductivity, helping to break down the skin's resistance and create chemical changes when the galvanic current is passed through them.

When dissolved in water, an electrolyte partly splits and forms ions which carry either a positive charge (cation) or negative charge (anion). When electrodes carrying a continuous direct current are introduced into the electrolytic solution, the ions in the solution begin to move and are attracted to either the positive pole (anode) or negative pole (cathode).

The treatment effectiveness works upon the electrical principle:

- like charges repel
- opposite charges attract

The tissue fluids of the human body have electrolytic properties. They contain ions and therefore allow the current to pass through the human body. Both positive and negative connections are required when performing the treatment. You select the appropriate pole according to the effect you want to create upon your client's tissues. The electrode then creates the chemical effects of this pole and is known as the **active** electrode. The other

> **TIP**
>
> Because the superficial layers of the epidermis have a low water content and are coated with sebum, they offer resistance to the current. The current applied must be sufficient to pass through them. As the treatment progresses, sebum will be cleansed from the skin and the resistance will fall.

electrode is known as the **indirect** or **indifferent** pole and is used to complete the electrical circuit.

The polarity of the active ingredients in galvanic solutions is usually indicated with a ⊕ or ⊖ symbol. The solutions are repelled into the skin by the active electrode which must be the same polarity as the solution.

Chemical effects created at the poles

Effects at the anode (positive pole)	Effects at the cathode (negative pole)
Acid reaction	Alkaline reaction
Vasoconstrictive, decreases blood supply which reduces redness of the skin	Vasodilative, increases blood supply which increases the redness of the skin
Astringent effect – pores tighten	Pores relax
Soothing effect on nerve endings	Stimulating effect on nerve endings
Firms tissues	Softens tissues

Reception

- Complete personal details on the client record card.
- Question the client to check for possible contra-indications.

Facial treatment

Explain that it is inadvisable to wear make-up for at least 8 hours after treatment due to its cleansing action. Other facial treatments may be received between treatments according to the client's requirements. Allow one hour when booking the treatment.

Body treatment

Explain that it is inadvisable to receive ultraviolet or a heat treatment directly after this treatment. It is recommended that the client undergoes treatment 2–3 times per week for a course of 10 sessions. Allow 30 minutes when booking the treatment.

Contra-indications

During the client assessment, if you find any of the following in the treatment area, galvanic treatment must not be carried out:

- excessive fillings
- broken skin

HEALTH AND SAFETY
Any skin disorder where the skin is broken, such as eczema, should not be treated as the skin's resistance to the current would be reduced, resulting in a concentration of current in the area.

HEALTH AND SAFETY ✚

Internal metal may cause a localised concentration of current, possibly resulting in internal burning.

EQUIPMENT LIST

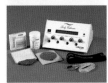

record card

galvanic facial/body combined unit

electrodes

- defective sensation
- metal plates or pins within the area
- pacemaker
- IUD coil
- varicose veins
- pregnant client.

Body galvanic treatment should not be applied over the kidney, sciatic nerve or breast area.

Equipment and materials

- record card
- galvanic facial/body or combined unit
- electrodes – a number of different electrodes are used in galvanic therapy which act as active or indifferent electrodes; the electrodes may be composed either of rubber impregnated with carbon or stainless steel

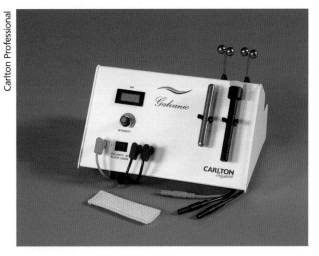

Galvanic facial unit

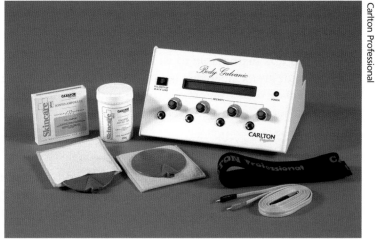

Galvanic body unit

Electrodes for galvanic therapy

Electrode	Illustration	Use and effect
Indifferent metal bar electrode		A metal bar contained within a damp sponge envelope is held by the client; this completes the electrical circuit. Used in facial treatment

Electrodes for galvanic therapy (continued)

Electrode	Illustration	Use and effect
Indifferent metal plate electrode	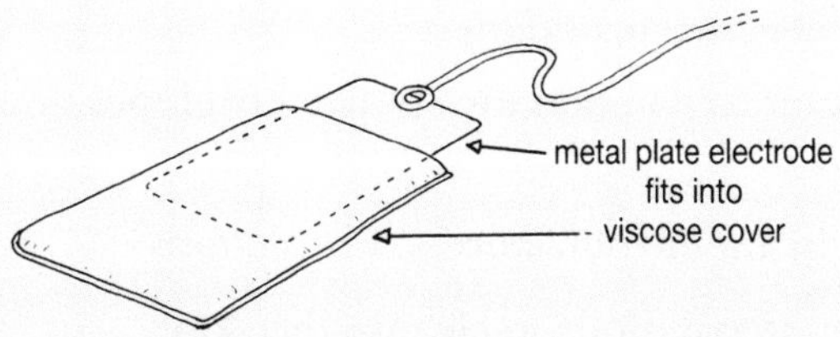 metal plate electrode fits into — viscose cover	A small metal plate contained in a damp sponge envelope completes the electrical circuit. This is placed firmly in contact with the client's skin, usually behind the shoulder. Used in facial treatment
Ball electrode	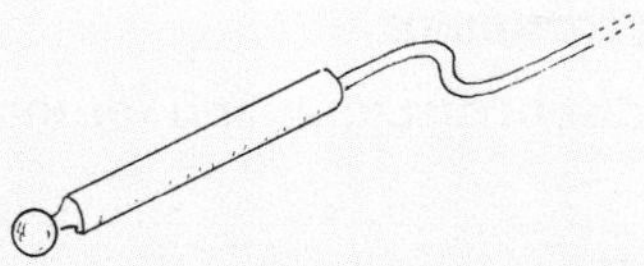	Used to treat smaller areas in facial treatment such as the sides of the nose and chin area
Roller electrode	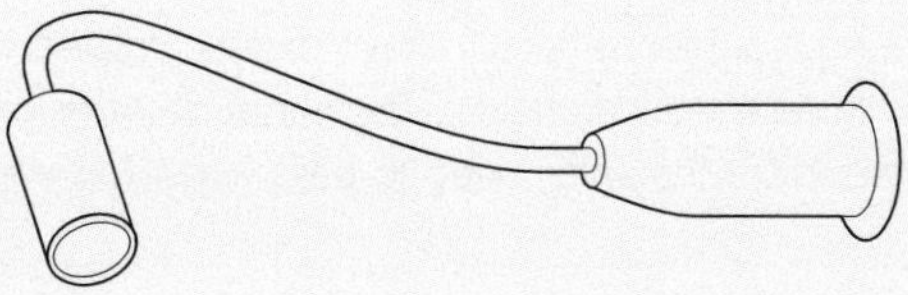	The most frequently used electrodes for the face and upper body; held one in each hand, they move over the skin surface with a slow even rhythm
Tweezer electrode	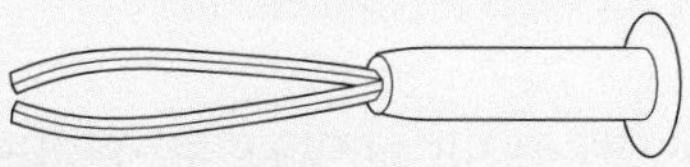	Used for desincrustation; its points are protected with cotton wool or lint soaked in disencrustation solution
Carbon-impregnated electrodes	 Sorisa	Used in pairs for treatment of the body
Metal plate electrodes	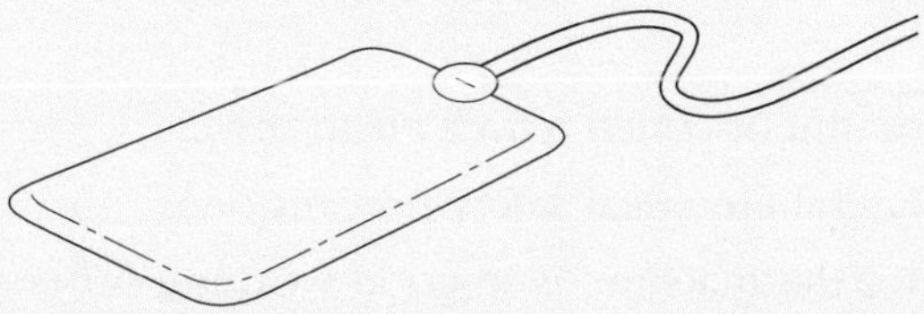	Larger plate electrodes used in pairs covered with damp sponge envelopes for treatment of the body

- dampened sponge envelopes or cotton wool selected to cover the electrodes according to the type of electrode and the area of treatment

---

HEALTH AND SAFETY ✚

Metal electrodes can suffer in time from corrosion and should be replaced when this becomes obvious. Cracked electrodes should not be used as they would not maintain good contact with the skin or ensure even current application.

- elasticated straps as necessary to hold electrodes in place
- leads which attach to the electrodes and connect to the machine. These are often colour coded as follows:
  red = positive (anode)
  black = negative (cathode)
- warm water to dampen the sponge envelopes and to remove facial products.

As advised by the manufacturers' instructions:

- skin-care preparations to cleanse the skin
- soothing and moisturising skin-care preparations to apply to the skin following treatment
- ionised solution for disencrustation and iontophoresis.

Sterilisation and sanitisation

After each treatment, wash the sponge envelopes in warm, soapy water. Dry naturally, and sanitise in an ultraviolet sterilising cabinet. Store in polythene bags to keep clean.

Clean the electrodes thoroughly, removing any cosmetic preparations and chemical formations with warm, soapy water. Dry, and place in an ultraviolet sterilising cabinet. Wash the elasticated straps in warm soapy water and dry.

Preparation of the treatment area

- Cover the treatment couch with a clean towel.
- Check all general electrical safety precautions.
- Test to ensure the machine is in good working order.
- For galvanic test button machines: switch the machine on, turn the amplitude dials up slightly and press the test buttons. The mA gauge should rise, showing the machine is working. Return the amplitude to zero.
- Dampen the sponge coverings evenly in warm water.

Facial application

- Prepare the electrodes for the treatment area. All metal electrodes except the roller electrodes should be covered with dampened sponge sleeves or cotton wool.
- Secure the electrodes firmly to the electrical leads.
- Insert the leads into the relevant connections.

Body application

- Place the elasticated straps on the couch in position for the treatment.
- Prepare the electrodes for the treatment. All electrodes should be covered with dampened sponge sleeves.
- Secure the electrodes firmly to the electrical leads.
- Insert the leads into the relevant connections.

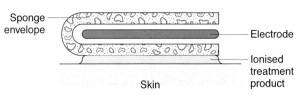

Preparation of electrodes

 HEALTH AND SAFETY

A galvanic burn, caused by current concentration, may be caused due to poor preparation of the electrodes such as:
- tucks or folds in the covering
- unevenly moistened viscose covers
- inadequate electrode insulation
- exposure of skin to metal points of facial tweezer electrodes.

 HEALTH AND SAFETY

The client must not come into contact with the metal frame of the couch. As a safety precaution you may choose to drape an insulating fabric over the couch underneath the towel.

Preparation of the therapist

- Collect the client's record card.
- Sanitise your hands before handling the client.
- Assess the client. Discuss the client's lifestyle and objectives of the treatment if this is the initial treatment. Agree on an appropriate treatment plan.
- If a treatment has a slimming requirement it will be necessary to measure the client at the beginning of the treatment course and once every week.
- If this is a repeat treatment, check the client's progress against targets set and provide support and advice as necessary.

Preparation of the client

Facial application

1 Remove the client's upper clothing to underwear. Position the client comfortably on the couch in a supine position and cover with a clean towel.
2 Remove all jewellery from the treatment area.
3 Perform skin sensitivity and thermal tests if it is the client's first treatment. Record the results on the client's record card.
4 Cleanse and tone the skin of the face and neck. Blot the skin dry with a soft facial tissue.
5 Analyse the client's skin using a magnifying lamp. Question the client further where necessary to check information in relation to the client's skin condition.

 TIP

The skin will have increased resistance if it is dehydrated, very dry or very greasy as lack of moisture, dead skin cells and sebum act as an initial barrier to current flow. A mild exfoliating skin preparation may be applied before treatment commences to remove dead skin cells, sebum and cosmetic ingredients' residue. This will reduce the skin's resistance initially to the electric current and facilitate absorption of the galvanic solution.

HEALTH AND SAFETY

Broken skin exposes the living tissues of the epidermis. Unless protected, the higher water content of these tissues will encourage a concentration of the current in the area and may cause a burn.

HEALTH AND SAFETY

The client should not feel any 'hot spots'. These may be chemical burns. Question the client during treatment to check.

HEALTH AND SAFETY

Broken skin exposes the living tissues of the epidermis. Unless protected, the higher water content of these tissues will encourage a concentration of the current in the area and may cause a burn.

6 Cover any minor cuts or abrasions with petroleum jelly or a small surgical plaster to form a barrier to the electric current.

7 Explain the treatment sensation to the client. A slight prickling sensation in the skin will be experienced as the skin resistance drops and the lotion penetrates the skin. This will be followed by a feeling of warmth as the skin becomes stimulated and the circulation increases.

Body application

1 Perform a skin sensitivity and thermal test if it is the client's first treatment. Record the results on the client's record card.

2 Remove all jewellery from the treatment area.

3 Instruct the client to remove all clothing except underwear.

4 Measure the client.

5 Position the client on the treatment couch. This will be in a supine or prone position depending on the padding layout selected.

6 Cleanse the skin using a non-oily detergent cleanser and blot dry with paper tissue.

TIP

Question the client further where necessary to check information in relation to the client's skin condition. You will then be able to offer supportive advice and recommend the sale of commercial body treatment products for home use.

7 Cover any minor cuts or abrasions with petroleum jelly or a small surgical plaster to form a barrier to the electric current.

8 Explain the treatment sensation to the client. A slight prickling sensation in the skin will be followed by a feeling of warmth.

Treatment application: Facial

After analysing the client's skin you may select to chose either the positive or negative pole. The **positive pole** is used to:

● close the pores

● reduce skin redness

● introduce acid preparations into the skin.

The negative pole is used to:

● improve circulation – the current passing through the skin acts as an irritant, causing the superficial blood vessels to dilate

● remove the surface dead skin cells and sebum

● open the pores

● introduce alkaline preparations into the skin.

The treatment techniques are described as **desincrustation** and **iontophoresis**.

- **Desincrustation**: the negative pole is selected. As the solution is ionised, alkalis form which soften the dead skin cells and fatty acids of sebum. This has a cleansing action upon the skin's surface which is suitable for most skin types except those which are highly sensitive.

- **Iontophoresis**: manufactured water-soluble preparations are introduced into the skin. These may be either creams or gels which assist rehydration and increase cellular metabolism in the area.

> ### HEALTH AND SAFETY
>
> Avoid excessive application of desincrustation treatment or the skin's sebaceous glands will become over-stimulated, producing more sebum as a result!

Treatment technique is given according to the skin type and the results to be achieved.

> ### HEALTH AND SAFETY
>
> A metallic taste may be experienced by the client. Through the initial consultation reassure the client that this is simply a reaction between the saliva in the mouth and the electric current.

Desincrustation treatment

1 The client firmly holds a clean, damp, sponge envelope containing the indifferent electrode, or alternatively the indifferent electrode is secured in contact with the client's body, usually the upper arm.

2 Dependant upon the electrodes used, the desincrustation solution is applied directly to the skin of the face and neck with a mask brush, or by cotton wool soaked in a desincrustation solution which then covers the active electrode.

> ### HEALTH AND SAFETY
>
> Apply sufficient solution to provide even current flow. A solution provided in an ampoule is usually liquid. This is best poured over gauze in a bowl, then the gauze is placed directly over the face. This is not necessary with gels providing a thick enough layer is applied.

3 Switch on the machine at the mains. Select the negative pole and switch the machine on.

4 Place the electrode/s on the skin's surface and keep it moving whilst the current intensity is gradually increased until the amperage meter registers. Then increase the intensity further until the client experiences a mild tingling sensation. The skin's resistance varies for this treatment but the current should not exceed 1.5 mA. The electrode(s) should not break contact with the skin whilst the current flows or discomfort may be experienced by the client.

> **TIP**
>
> This is not a suitable treatment to have immediately before a special occasion as it is inadvisable to wear make-up for 8 hours afterwards and a few pustules may also occur.

Desincrustation application

Smart buy

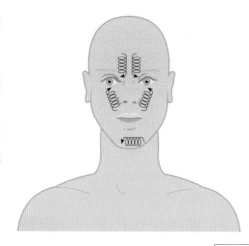

Desincrustation application using tweezer or ball/probe electrode – commonly treated areas

5 Apply the current to the skin for between 3–5 minutes. The treatment should not be uncomfortable and the client's comfort should be checked during application. Suggested desincrustation application technique using the tweezer or ball electrode is illustrated:

6 Reduce the current intensity slowly with one hand. Remove the active electrode(s) from the skin. Switch off the machine.

7 Remove the indifferent electrode from the client.

8 Switch off the machine at the mains.

9 Remove the remaining solution from the client's skin using damp sponges or damp cotton wool.

HEALTH AND SAFETY ✚

Although most machines can adapt the current to within 5% of the initial setting, it may be necessary to manually reduce the current over bony areas which offer less resistance to the electrical current.

10 As the skin's pores are relaxed, gentle comedone removal may be performed.

11 Iontophoresis may follow, selecting suitable treatment products for the client's skin type.

TIP ✔

The application of the electrodes should follow movements which will induce client relaxation. Be firm in application but without applying unnecessary pressure.

TIP ✔

You may recommend the benefits of the cleansing and healing action of galvanic therapy for the treatment of a congested, pustular or mild acne vulgaris condition.

TIP ✔

If using a combined electrical unit, high frequency may be applied following desincrustation or iontophoresis if appropriate to the client's treatment needs.

12 A facial mask may be applied, followed by the application of toning lotion and a treatment moisturiser.

13 Record the treatment details on the client's record card.

HEALTH AND SAFETY ✚

The intensity of the current and the timing of the treatment are important. Too low a current intensity and too short an application renders the treatment ineffective. Too high a current intensity and too long an application can sensitise the skin resulting in possible skin injury.

Iontophoresis treatment

1 The client firmly holds a clean, damp, sponge envelope containing the indifferent electrode, or alternatively the indifferent electrode is secured in contact with the client's body, usually the upper arm.

2 An appropriate iontophoresis solution is applied to the skin of the face and neck in accordance with its opacity.

3 Switch the machine on at the mains. Select the relevant pole according to the iontophoresis solution chosen and switch the machine on.

Sorisa

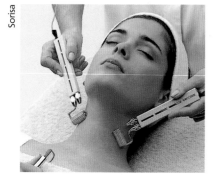

Iontophersis application

4 Place the active electrode/s on the skin's surface and reassure the client of the treatment sensation to be experienced. Increase the current intensity gradually until the mA meter gauge registers, keeping the electrode moving all the time. Wait 30 seconds before increasing the current until the client experiences a tingling sensation. Then gradually increase the current to a level where the tingling sensation subsides. The current should not exceed 1.5 mA.

5 Continue the treatment, moving the electrodes slowly over the skin's surface. Suggested iontophoresis application using roller electrodes is illustrated.

6 Apply the treatment for between 5–7 minutes, depending on the treatment effect required and the client's skin tolerance.

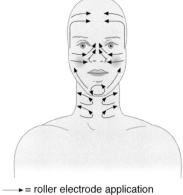

——→ = roller electrode application

Iontophersis application using roller electrodes – treatment area

---

TIP ✔

Combining galvanic therapy followed by high-frequency currents produces a skin-toning effect when used with skin-firming ingredients. A small electrode is used to introduce the gel into the skin. This is followed by a low-intensity application of high frequency. This may be offered as a treatment for the eye tissue.

HEALTH AND SAFETY ✚

- Never increase the current until the electrode is in contact with the skin's surface.
- Turn up the current very slowly until the amperage meter begins to register. The client's skin offers an initial resistance to the current through its dead skin cells and adipose tissue.

---

7 Reduce the current very slowly to allow the chemical effects to be completed. When using the roller electrode it is necessary to remove one hand to reduce the current intensity whilst keeping the other electrode in contact with the skin. You may reverse the polarity and apply the current on the reverse pole for a further 2 minutes. This will neutralise any chemical residue on the skin's surface which may cause sensitivity.

8 Switch off the machine.

9 Switch off at the mains.

10 Remove the indifferent electrode from the client.

11 Remove remaining solution from the skin's surface with clean, damp sponges or cotton wool.

12 A facial mask may be applied, followed by the application of toning lotion and a treatment moisturiser.

13 Record the details of the treatment on the client's record card.

HEALTH AND SAFETY ✚

If a client finds the treatment is causing intolerable irritation of the skin, reduce the current very slowly and cease treatment. You may wish to reverse polarity and apply the current on the reverse pole for a few moments to neutralise the chemicals which are causing the irritation.

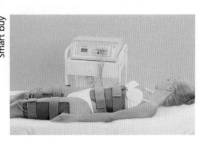

Treatment of the body

Treatment application: Body

Body galvanic treatment is usually applied for the treatment of cellulite and a sluggish lymphatic circulation. The combination of the physiological effects created and the penetration of active therapeutic ingredients gives an immediate improvement to skin appearance. The galvanic current stimulates the metabolism in the tissues and the localised movement of tissue fluids through the cell membranes. Tissue fluids are drawn towards the negative pole (known as **electro-osmosis**) which may help improve the appearance of lumpy tissue.

The deeper blood vessels dilate due to a reflex action to the stimulation of the superficial capillaries. The whole area becomes warm but the erythema is greater under the negative electrode due to the alkaline skin irritant effect.

After assessing the client's skin condition and treatment needs you may select either the positive or negative pole according to the physiological effects required.

The positive pole is used to:

- reduce skin redness
- introduce acid preparations into the skin.

The negative pole is used to:

- open the pores to enable penetration of the active ingredients
- stimulate blood and lymph circulation to help improve a sluggish circulation
- introduce alkaline preparations into the skin which claim to break down the metabolites by ionisation
- improve the appearance of cellulite – the increased tissue fluids to the active pole plump out the skin and improve circulation.

1 The appropriate active solution should be placed under the negative or active electrode – this is usually the area requiring attention. A suitable conducting solution must be placed at the positive or indifferent electrode. This is placed opposite the active pad.

2 Firmly strap the electrodes in place so that they make firm, even contact with the skin. The electrodes must not touch each other or the treatment will be ineffective as the current will pass straight from one to the other without ionisation occurring. Sample padding arrangements are illustrated.

3 Switch the machine on at the mains.

4 Select the negative pole and switch the machine on.

5 Slowly increase each intensity dial until the mA meter registers and the skin's resistance is reduced, causing the client to feel a tingling sensation. Wait approximately 30 seconds before increasing the current intensity. The tingling sensation will disappear as the current intensity is increased, being replaced by a feeling of warmth. A final amperage reading of 4.25 mA is not normally exceeded.

Sample padding techniques

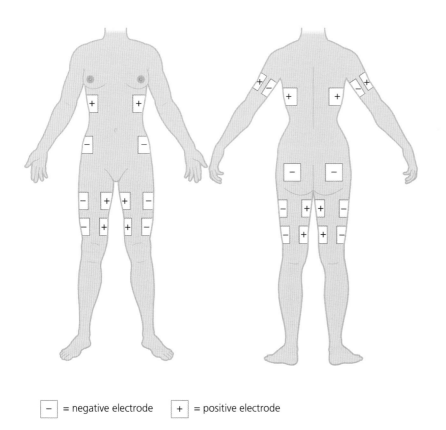

| $-$ | = negative electrode | $+$ | = positive electrode |

6 Increase the treatment time from an initial 10 minutes to 20 minutes for future treatments. The polarity may be reversed for the final 2–3 minutes to neutralise the chemicals which have been formed in order to reduce skin irritation.

7 At the end of the treatment, slowly reduce the current intensity to zero to avoid client discomfort. A noticeable erythema will be seen on the skin when the electrodes are removed as a result of chemical formation.

8 Switch the machine off at the mains.

9 Remove the straps and electrodes from the treatment area.

10 Wash the skin in warm water to remove the galvanic solution and acids and alkalis which will have formed.

11 A light application of unperfumed talc may be applied to soothe the skin and reduce the erythema.

12 Record details of the treatment on the client's record card.

HEALTH AND SAFETY

The intensity of the current and the timing of the treatment are important. Too low a current intensity and too short an application renders the treatment ineffective. Too high a current intensity and too long an application can sensitise the skin resulting in possible skin injury.

TIP

If the client has a noticeable hyperaemia following treatment, explain that this is due to increased blood stimulation which will reduce in a few hours. Explain also that exposure to warmth directly after treatment will increase the colour further.

Aftercare

Following facial treatment, advise the client to avoid face make-up for up to 8–12 hours to support the skin-cleansing effect.

Following body treatment, the client should be advised to drink plenty of water. The client may need to pass urine immediately after treatment because of increased fluid elimination.

Advise the client on the purchase and correct application of commercial body and skin-care preparations appropriate to her needs. Advice should also be given on a supportive nutritional and exercise plan as necessary.

Contra-actions

- **Galvanic burn**: this is a chemical burn caused by a concentration of alkali formation on the skin. It is recognised by a darkish split in the skin surrounded by a red, inflamed ring.
  Action: sterile, cold water should be applied to the area followed by a sterile, dry dressing.

- **Sensitisation**: if the facial skin shows a strong erythema it is indicating a release of histamine showing that the skin is distressed.
  Action: cease treatment, or reverse the current for a short time and apply a cosmetic containing a cooling, soothing ingredient.

HIGH-FREQUENCY TREATMENT

This is a popular treatment in the salon. High frequency may be applied directly or indirectly to the skin of the face or body to stimulate, sanitise and heal the skin.

Direct high-frequency application

In the direct method, the therapist places a high-frequency electrode in contact with the client's skin in the treatment area.

Direct high-frequency treatment

Effects:

- warms the skin's tissues
- increases blood circulation resulting in erythema
- increases lymph circulation resulting in absorption of waste products
- increases metabolism in the area
- stimulates superficial nerve endings
- generates ozone which has a germicidal action on the surface of the skin.

Uses:

- treatment of a greasy skin type
- treatment of mild acne vulgaris
- treatment of dry skin – stimulates sebaceous gland activity.

Indirect high-frequency application

In the indirect method the client holds an electrode whilst the therapist massages her skin. The high-frequency current is then transferred between the client's skin and the therapist's fingers.

Effects:

- increases the activity of the sebaceous and sudoriferous glands
- improves blood circulation, nourishing the skin
- improves the lymphatic circulation, speeding up the elimination of waste products.

Uses:

- treatment of a dry and dehydrated skin type
- tightening effect to improve the appearance of fine lines and wrinkles
- improving the appearance of the skin.

Anatomy and physiology

The high-frequency current generates warmth in the skin and stimulates the nerve endings. This in turn causes reflex vasodilation of the blood capillaries leading to increased blood circulation.

Metabolism in the area is increased which encourages healthy cell function and promotes skin healing. With the direct method of application, sparking beneath the electrode generates ozone which has a mild antiseptic, drying effect making the direct method beneficial for the treatment of a blemished skin.

A dry skin benefits from the stimulation of the sebaceous and sudoriferous glands with indirect high frequency, through its skin-warming effect.

Electrical science

A high-frequency current is an electrical current which moves backwards and forwards at very high speed. The current is termed as an **alternating** or **oscillating** current. This rapid backwards and forwards movement creates high-frequency vibrations over the skin's surface of between 10 000 and 250 000 vibrations per second. We say it has a frequency of 100 000 to 250 000 cycles per second or **hertz**. The result is a heating, stimulating effect.

Reception

Complete personal details on the client record card. Question the client to check for possible contra-indications.

High frequency may be offered as an individual treatment or may be incorporated into a programme with other treatments. As such, one hour is usually allowed when booking this treatment. The treatment should be received once every 4–6 weeks.

Contra-indications

During the client assessment, if you find any of the following in the treatment area, high-frequency treatment must not be carried out:

- skin inflammation
- skin disorder or disease
- excessive dental metalwork
- hypersensitive skin
- acne rosacea
- oedema
- migraine
- lack of tactile sensation
- severe headaches
- nervous client.

TIP

Although most skin disorders contra-indicate treatment, mild infections such as pustules and papules benefit from high-frequency treatment.

Equipment and materials

- record card
- high-frequency unit
- selection of both glass and metal high-frequency electrodes – the electrodes have a metal cap which inserts into the electrode holder; this allows conductivity of the current. Inside the glass electrodes is a near vacuum. A tiny amount of a gas allows the current to pass through and create energy in the form of light and ultraviolet rays. When the current passes through the glass electrode and the oxygen on the skin's surface, ozone is created
- cosmetic preparation for direct high-frequency – for example oxygenating cream which encourages the production of oxygen, or talc. The cream has a soothing, nourishing effect on the skin whereas talc is more stimulating and drying
- massage medium for indirect high-frequency – for example a cream emulsion.

EQUIPMENT LIST
record card
high-frequency unit
selection of both glass and metal high frequency electrodes
cosmetic preparation for direct high-frequency
massage medium for indirect high-frequency – cream emulsion

High-frequency unit

TIP ✔

High-frequency glass electrodes may show different colours when in use. This depends on the gas they contain:
- violet – electrode containing air
- blue – electrode containing mercury vapour
- orange – electrode containing neon.

Electrode	Illustration	Use and effect
Mushroom electrode	ø 30 mm ø 47 mm	A glass electrode available in different sizes, selected according to the part to be treated – the smaller the electrode the more stimulating the effect.
Horseshoe electrode		A glass electrode shaped to contour the neck area. Moved over the skin of the neck, it has a sedative effect on the nerve endings.
Saturator electrode		A metal bar which is placed into the high-frequency applicator. Held by the client and used in indirect high frequency.

Electrode	Illustration	Use and effect
Spiral intensifier electrode		A metal coil contained in a cylindrical glass electrode which intensifies the effect. Held by the client and used in indirect high frequency.
Roller electrode		Glass roller-shaped electrodes which may be freely moved along the skin's surface. Used for general treatment application to the face and body.

Sterilisation and sanitisation

After use:

- the electrodes should be cleaned according to their type
- glass electrodes should have any massage medium removed and be wiped with disinfectant
- the electrodes should then be placed in an ultraviolet sterilising cabinet, turning the electrodes to ensure thorough sanitisation after 20 minutes.

Preparation of the treatment area

- Cover the treatment couch with a clean towel.
- Check all general electrical safety precautions.
- Test the equipment and machine to ensure they are in good working order.
- Select a suitable electrode for the treatment area and effect to be created.
- Switch on the machine and place the electrode directly on your skin's surface.
- Gradually increase the current intensity until a low buzzing noise occurs.
- Return the current intensity to zero.
- Sanitise the surface of the electrode after testing, before client application.

Preparation of the therapist

- Collect the client record card.
- Sanitise your hands before handling the client.
- Assess the client's skin and determine the objectives of the treatment.

HEALTH AND SAFETY	

It is essential to make sure that any moisturising creams or talcum powder are cleaned off the electrode holder. Both are very conductive to high frequency and can result in the therapist feeling more of the high frequency current than she should.

Preparation of the client

- Instruct the client to remove upper clothing to underwear.
- Position the client comfortably on the treatment couch in a supine position and cover her with a clean towel.
- Remove all jewellery from the treatment area.
- Cleanse and tone the area of skin to be treated, and apply a suitable therapeutic cosmetic skin preparation.
- Analyse the skin using a magnifying lamp. Question the client further where necessary to check information in relation to the client's skin condition.
- Explain the treatment procedure. A new client will need to be reassured of the buzzing noise, glowing colour of the electrode and the mild ozone smell.
- If performing indirect high frequency, ask the client to remove all jewellery from the hand and wrist area.

> **HEALTH AND SAFETY**
>
> Wedding bands and metal nail jewellery must be covered with an insulating material if they cannot be removed.

Direct high-frequency treatment application

1 Switch on the power at the mains.
2 Switch on the machine.
3 Hold the selected active electrode in contact with the treatment area, increase the current intensity to the desired level.
4 Move the electrode over the skin's surface in a rotary fashion, creating a stimulating, warming effect.
5 The treatment is applied according to the needs of the client's skin. Generally, the electrode is applied to the skin for 8–10 minutes for an oily skin type, and 5 minutes for a dry skin type.
6 Check the client's comfort and observe skin reaction during treatment application.

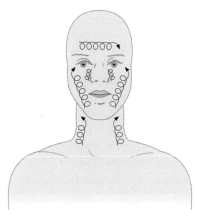

Facial direct high-frequency application

> **TIP**
>
> **Sparking**
> 'Sparking' may be incorporated to dry up and sanitise any pustules that might be present. The electrode is lifted approximately 7 mm away from the skin, and then quickly replaced on the skin's surface. This is repeated in a gentle tapping motion approximately 6–8 times. The oxygen in the air becomes ionised and creates ozone which destroys bacteria, promoting skin healing.

> **HEALTH AND SAFETY**
>
> Do not spark near the client's eyes where the skin is delicate.

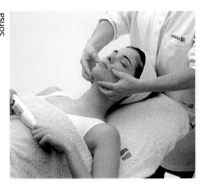

Indirect high-frequency
application

7 Remove excess cream or talc from the client's skin.

8 Follow with a treatment mask, toner and suitable moisturiser.

9 Record details of the treatment on the record card.

Indirect high-frequency treatment application

1 Switch on the power at the mains.

2 Place the saturator electrode into the handle and place firmly into the client's hand.

3 Place one hand on the client's face, performing small circular massage movements. With the other hand switch on the machine.

4 Increase the current slowly until the client experiences a tingling sensation and gentle warmth as your hands act as the electrode and the current flows from the client to your fingers.

5 Place both hands on the client's face and perform a face, neck and shoulder massage using effleurage and petrissage movements but omitting tapotement movements. When massaging over bony areas and around the eye area, remove one hand from the client's face and reduce the current intensity.

6 Check the client's comfort and skin reaction during treatment application.

7 Treatment times will differ according to skin type and skin tolerance. Generally the massage is performed for 8–10 minutes with the electrical current.

8 At the conclusion of the treatment, remove one hand whilst keeping the other hand in contact with the client's skin. Remove massage medium from this hand before slowly reducing the current intensity.

9 Switch the machine off.

10 Switch the power off at the mains.

11 Remove the saturator from the client's hand and continue with a light massage without electrical current for a further 5–8 minutes.

12 Remove all massage medium from the electrodes, particularly the electrode holder, to avoid the current going astray and giving you accidental shocks.

13 Remove excess cream from the skin's surface.

14 Follow with a treatment mask, toner and suitable moisturiser.

15 Record details of the treatment on the record card.

HEALTH AND SAFETY ✚

Tapotement must be avoided as it would cause the current to jump between the gap created between the therapist's hands and the client's skin, causing a sparking effect and irritation.

HEALTH AND SAFETY ✚

Areas with little fatty tissue offer less resistance to the current, intensifying the sensation experienced by the client in these areas. Therefore always reduce the current intensity accordingly.

Aftercare

The client should be advised against applying make-up for up to 8 hours following treatment, to support the skin-cleansing effect. Advise on the correct application of skin-care preparations appropriate to her needs.

Contra-actions

- Excessive erythema, indicating over-stimulation of the skin.
- Tissue destruction caused by sparking for too long or electrode held too far from the skin's surface.

GYRATORY VIBRATORY TREATMENT

Gyratory vibratory treatment is an electrical body massage treatment which produces friction on the skin's surface, creating a heating effect. It provides a deep massage and is often used as a slimming treatment where the aim is to soften fatty tissue and stimulate the lymphatic circulation. The benefits resemble those created by manual massage but with less effort required by the therapist!

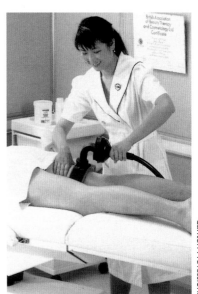

Carlton Professional

Gyratory vibratory treatment

General effects:

- increased blood circulation which improves the skin colour and transports nutrients and oxygen to the skin cells and muscles
- increased venous blood and lymph circulation which increases the removal of toxins and waste materials
- improved skin texture by removal of the surface dead skin cells (desquammation)
- relaxing of tense muscles due to the heating effect
- softening of areas of soft and hard adipose tissue
- stimulation of sensory nerve endings
- stimulation of skin function, increasing sebaceous gland activity.

Body use:

- to reduce localised fatty deposits. This is commonly referred to as 'spot reduction'
- to improve areas of cellulite
- to stimulate a sluggish lymphatic and blood circulation, improving cellular metabolism
- to improve a dry skin condition by removing dead skin cells and improving sebaceous-gland activity.

Anatomy and physiology

The warmth generated by the treatment increases metabolic activity in the treatment area. The combination of warmth and the stimulation of superficial nerve endings causes reflex vasodilation – the blood vessels and capillaries expand and there is an immediate increase in the blood flow producing an erythema. Muscles are relaxed by the warmth of the increased

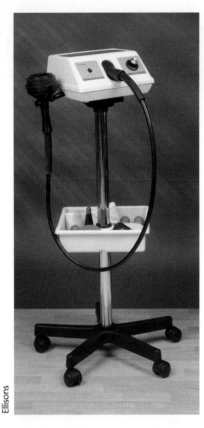

Floor standing vibratory machine

blood circulation through the area. The increase in skin temperature stimulates the sweat glands and sebaceous glands.

Electrical science

The gyratory vibrator machine may be floor-standing or hand-held. The gyratory vibration of the massage head is driven by a powerful electric motor. An internal fan draws air through the motor to keep it cool. The air vents on the motor unit must not be obstructed.

Floor-standing vibratory machine

The electric motor is supported on a pedestal. A flexible drive shaft connects the motor to the vibratory head. Various applicators are attached to the head – these simulate the therapeutic effects of manual massage. The applicators may be made from sponge, rubber or polyurethane.

Hand-held vibratory machine

The hand held vibratory massage has a variable speed controller that creates either a deeper, soothing massage or a more superficial, stimulating effect.

TIP
The hand-held gyratory vibratory massager is suitable for the mobile therapist. It has less choice in applicator heads than the floor-standing type.

Reception

- Complete personal details on the client record card.
- Question the client to check for possible contra-indications.

The effects, although similar to manual massage, are created much more quickly therefore treatment time is shorter. Allow 30–45 minutes for a full-body application and 20 minutes for specific areas such as the thighs and gluteals. The client should attend 2–3 times per week for treatment.

Contra-indications

HEALTH AND SAFETY
Mechanical massage is indicated for larger areas of the body and areas of excess adipose tissue and muscle bulk. It is not suitable for the chest area and other bony areas.

During the client assessment, if you find any of the following in the treatment area, mechanical massage treatment must not be carried out:

- skin inflammation
- broken skin
- highly vascular skin

- hypersensitive skin
- painful joints
- recent fractures
- excessively hairy areas
- bony areas
- varicose veins
- senile skin
- skin tags, moles.

Mechanical massage treatment must not be carried out over the abdomen of a pregnant client or during menstruation.

Equipment and materials

- record card
- gyratory vibration machine – floor-standing or hand-held
- a selection of applicators appropriate for the treatment (see tables)
- purified, unperfumed talc to allow the applicator to move easily across the skin's surface
- clean cotton wool to cleanse the skin and apply talc to the treatment area
- witch hazel or eau de cologne to cleanse the skin
- clean tissues to blot the skin dry.

EQUIPMENT LIST

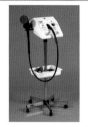 

| record card |
| gyratory vibration machine |
| a selection of applicators |
| talc |
| cotton wool |
| witch hazel or eau de cologne |
| tissues |

Common applicator attachments for floor standing model

Name of attachment	Illustration	Use and effect
Round smooth rubber applicator		Client who has sensitive skin which may be irritated by sponge; used for effleurage and petrissage effects.
Round smooth water massage head		Warm or cold water creates a stimulating/invigorating or relaxing effect; used for effleurage and petrissage effects.
Round sponge applicator		Used on the trunk to induce relaxation at the start and end of massage of the treatment part; used for effleurage effect.
Curved sponge applicator		Used on the arms and legs to induce relaxation at the start and end of massage of the treatment part; used for effleurage effect.
'Eggbox' rubber applicator		Used on bulky muscular areas and fatty tissue such as the gluteals and thighs; used for petrissage effect.

Common applicator attachments for floor standing model (continued)

Name of attachment	Illustration	Use and effect
'Pronged' rubber applicator		Used on bulky muscular areas and fatty tissue such as the gluteals and thighs; used for petrissage effect.
'Football' rubber applicator		Used on loose flabby areas of the skin such as the abdominal walls; also used over the colon to promote **peristalsis**; used for petrissage effect.
'Spiky' rubber applicator		Used generally over the body to stimulate the nerve endings and create a rapid hyparemia; improves a dry skin condition by removing surface dead skin cells; used for percussion effect.
'Lighthouse' rubber applicator		Used to treat tension nodules on the upper trapezius and may be used either side of the spine and around the knee; used for friction effect.

Common applicator attachments for hand-held model

Name of attachment	Illustration	Use and effect
'Egg box' applicator		Used on bulky muscular areas and fatty tissue such as the gluteals and the thighs.
'Spiky' applicator	Depilex	Used generally over the body to stimulate the nerve endings and create a rapid hyparemia.
'Smooth' applicator		Used for effleurage and petrissage effects.

Sterilisation and sanitisation

After use, attachments should be washed in warm soapy water to remove talc, dead skin cells and sebum. They should then be dried and sanitised in an ultraviolet cabinet. Disposable protective attachment coverings may be purchased from larger wholesalers.

Preparation of the treatment area

- Cover the treatment couch with clean towels.
- Check all general electrical safety precautions.
- Select applicator attachments for the area/s to be treated. These should be placed on a trolley or in the equipment tray provided if using the floor-standing unit.

Preparation of the therapist

- Collect the client record card.
- Sanitise your hands before handling the client.
- Assess the client, discuss the client's lifestyle pattern and the objectives for the treatment.
- Agree on an appropriate treatment plan.
- If this is a repeat treatment, check the client's progress against targets set and provide support and advice as necessary.

Preparation of the client

- Remove all jewellery from the treatment area.
- Explain the treatment sensation to the client, explaining how the skin will become warm and reddened. Demonstrate to the client the noise of the motor.
- Expose the part of the body to be treated and cover all other areas.
- Cleanse and dry the client's skin.
- Apply a dry medium, such as an unperfumed talc, to aid treatment application.

TIP

A preheating treatment is beneficial before application as the therapeutic effects are created more rapidly when the tissues have been warmed.

Treatment application

The order of treatment application is usually as follows: arms, abdomen, front of the legs. The client then turns over and the back of the legs, gluteals and back are treated.

Attachments must be securely fixed to the head before switching the motor on.

1 Switch the machine on at the mains and at the mains switch on the machine.
2 Commence treatment with the effleurage applicators in the direction of lymphatic and venous flow. When treating the limbs, always apply effleurage strokes towards the trunk in one direction.
3 Apply 4–6 strokes to cover the whole treatment area. One hand may be used to lead or follow the applicator head to soothe the skin.
4 Switch off the machine to change applicator heads.
5 Cover each part as treated with a clean towel for modesty and to keep the client warm.

TIP

Treatment technique
Ensure each part of the applicator is in contact with the part being treated to avoid uneven pressure of application, which could result in bruising. Support the tissues with one hand to maximise the treatment effect.

Application to the body

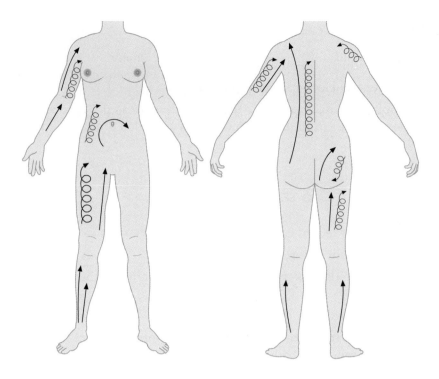

↑	Gliding strokes towards the venous return lymphatic nodes	⟨ Rotary movements along muscle length or localised area
↑	Round smooth sponge applicator	↑ Round smooth applicator
↑	Round smooth massage head	Eggbox rubber applicator
	Curved sponge applicator	Pronged rubber applicator
	Spiky rubber applicator	Football rubber applicator
		Lighthouse rubber applicator (used on upper fibres of trapezius muscle)

6 Follow with the petrissage applicators. Petrissage commences at the upper treatment part and descends in a rotary application.

7 Lift and guide the tissues under the applicator head with one hand.

8 Continue application until a mild erythema is created upon the skin's surface.

9 Follow with the friction applicator. Small, localised rotary movements are applied to the treatment area. Common areas of treatment include:
- the upper fibres of the trapezius – to relieve tension
- either side of the spine – to stimulate and induce relaxation
- around the knee – for the mobilisation of adhesions or stiffness.

10 Follow with the percussion applicator. Percussion is applied in one direction in a flowing stroke as with effleurage. Use one hand to lead or follow each application stroke. Complete each treatment area with the effleurage applicator head to soothe the skin.

11 Switch off the machine.

12 Remove the massage medium as necessary on completion of treatment.

13 Switch off and unplug the machine at the mains.

14 Complete details of the treatment on the client's record card.

HEALTH AND SAFETY

Avoid application over the kidneys and breast area.

Hand-held model

1 Attach the applicator head according to the treatment effect required and the area to be treated. The machine should be switched off so that it is not accidentally turned on during fitting.

2 Select the variable speed control according to the treatment effect required.

3 Apply the massage head to the treatment area.

4 Switch off the machine.

5 Remove the massage medium as necessary on completion of treatment.

6 Switch off and unplug the machine at the mains.

7 Complete details of the treatment on the client's record card.

Aftercare

Manual massage may be applied to soothe the skin following treatment application. This will also increase the lymphatic drainage effect. Other treatments may also be offered which achieve a different complimentary effect.

The use of skin-care preparations designed to increase skin firmness or tone a localised problem area should be encouraged to support the salon treatment. These include gels and creams which are applied in light circular movements, working in an upwards direction. Nutritional advice should be given if the client is on a weight-reducing diet. Supportive exercises for the body may also be given.

Contra-actions

Bruising, caused by:

- too heavy an application
- incorrect choice of applicator head for treatment area
- too lengthy a treatment application.

Skin scratching and irritation caused by:

- incorrect choice and application of applicator head (usually the sponge and spiky applicator).

AUDIO SONIC

Audio sonic is a hand-held electrical massage treatment which is applied to localised areas of the face or body. The equipment produces sound waves, heard as a humming noise, which vibrate through the skin's cells and tissues. The vibrations travel approximately 5 cms into the skin without any tissue damage. It is particularly beneficial for the treatment of sensitive areas or hypersensitive skin, because no surface friction is created as with other massage treatments.

Carlton Professional

Audio sonic machine

General effects:

- Increases blood circulation, which improves skin colour and transports nutrients and oxygen to the skin's cells and muscles.
- Increases venous and lymph circulation which enhances the removal of waste and toxins.
- Improves skin texture by removal of surface skin cells (desquamation).
- Relaxation of tense muscles.
- Softening of areas of soft adipose tissue.
- Stimulation of skin function, increasing sebaceous gland activity.

Body use:

- Cellulite, particularly soft fat which offers less resistance than hard fat.
- Deep relaxation of contracted muscle tissue.
- Fibrositis nodules in the trapezius muscle.

Facial use:

- Hypersensitive or vascular skin conditions.
- Mature skin.

Anatomy and physiology

Nodules are shaken and vibrated by the sound waves. These compress and decompress the soft tissues. During compression the cells press together, moving tissue fluid including waste and toxins. Decompression of the tissues allows fresh blood to circulate through the area bringing fresh oxygen and nutrients.

Electrical science

An electro magnet is used. The current flows in one direction and then the other, which causes a coil of the electro magnet to move backwards and forwards. This movement passes to the head of the appliance which, when applied to the skin, transmits to the tissues as a vibration. The depth of sound pitch creating the vibrations can be increased or decreased affecting the depth of travel into the tissues. Intensity is controlled by an adjustment knob. Frequency is the number of vibrations per second.

Reception

- Complete personal details on the client record card.
- Question the client to check for possible contra-indications.

The treatment is usualy applied to localised areas and effects are achieved quickly. Allow 10 minutes for treatment depending on the treatment area. The client may receive the treatment as necessary.

Contra-indications

During the client assessment, if you find any of the following in the treatment area, audio sonic treatment must not be carried out:

- skin inflammation
- skin disorder such as psoriasis and eczema
- excessive broken veins
- bony area
- very slim clients
- broken skin
- painful inflamed joints
- varicose veins
- metallic implants
- recent fractures
- the eye area because the skin is fine and sensitive so bruising may occur.

Equipment and materials

- record card
- audio sonic machine and attachment heads
- skincare preparation to cleanse the skin
- talc, oil or cream to allow the attachment head to move easily across the skins surface
- clean cotton wool to cleanse the skin and apply talc to the treatment area
- clean tissue to blot the skin dry
- surgical spirit to clean heads after use.

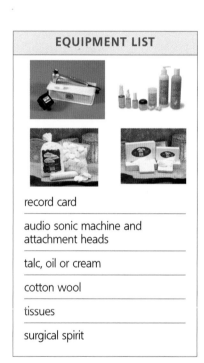

EQUIPMENT LIST

record card
audio sonic machine and attachment heads
talc, oil or cream
cotton wool
tissues
surgical spirit

Attachment heads for audio sonic

Name of attachment	Use and effect
Flat plate or disc	Facial and body use. Used over larger areas.
Hard ball	Fibrositis nodule and deep body treatment. Used over smaller areas for an intensified effect.

Sterilisation and sanitisation

After use, attachment heads should be washed in warm soapy water to remove talc/cream, dead skin cells and sebum. Wipe over the heads with surgical spirit applied with clean cotton wool. They should then be sanitised in the ultraviolet cabinet.

Preparation of the treatment area

- Cover the treatment couch if used with clean towels and disposable paper roll.
- If the client is to be seated, ensure the seat is at the correct height and placed in an area close to the electrical point.
- Check all electrical safety precautions.
- Select applicator heads for the area/s to be treated. These should be placed on a clean trolley surface.

Preparation of the therapist

- Collect the client record card.
- Sanitise your hands before handling the client.
- Assess the client, discuss the client's lifestyle pattern and objectives for the treatment.
- Agree on an appropriate treatment plan.
- If this is a repeat treatment, check the client's progress and provide advice as necessary.

Preparation of the client

- Remove all jewellery and accessories from the treatment area.
- Explain the treatment sensation to the client, and how the skin will become warm and slightly reddened. Demonstrate to the client the noise the equipment will make.
- Expose the treatment area: all other areas should be covered.
- Cleanse and dry the client's skin.
- Apply a medium to the skin to aid treatment application.

Treatment application

Attachments must be securely fixed to the head before switching the motor on.

1 Switch the machine on at the mains and at the switch on the machine.
2 Test the machine and adjust the intensity as appropriate. Clean the attachment head with surgical spirit.
3 Select the head to be used and attach it securely to the equipment.
4 For full body application commence treatment with the soles of the feet, calves, thighs, hand, forearm and upper arm.
5 Apply the head to the skin and follow the muscle length where tension is present, moving in a vertical or horizontal direction in straight lines or in a circular movement upwards towards the heart.
6 Increase or decrease sound frequency as you work over different areas using the adjustment control. It is necessary to reduce the frequency over bony areas.

HEALTH AND SAFETY

Application pressure
Never apply pressure, this is unecessary and may cause skin irritation.

TIP

Treating bony areas
Place your free hand over the treatment area and apply the applicator head over the hand. This will reduce the vibrations and avoid irritation.

This is particularly beneficial when treating the facial area.

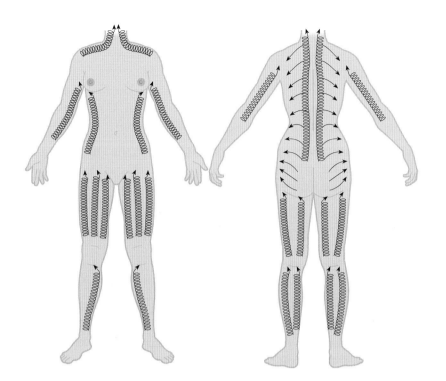

Audio sonic application to body – front and back

7 Switch off the machine to change applicator heads.

8 Cover the body part when treated, for modesty and to keep the client warm.

9 Switch off the machine.

10 Remove the massage medium as necessary on completion of the treatment. If applied as part of a facial treatment you may wish to apply a mask.

11 Switch off and unplug the equipment at the mains.

12 Complete details on the client's record card.

Aftercare

The use of facial and body skin-care preparations designed to treat the skin should be encouraged to support the treatment. Advice on correct posture and exercises may be given when this is the cause of the problem, such as tension nodules in muscles. If the treatment was for relaxation, you might give advice on relaxing bath products and massage techniques that could be used at home.

Contra-actions

- Discomfort caused by insufficient protection and incorrect frequency when treating bony parts.

- Excessive erythema caused by too lengthy treatment of the skin.

- Skin irritation caused by excessive pressure during application.

VACUUM SUCTION TREATMENT

Vacuum suction is a mechanical treatment which can be applied to either the face or the body. External suction is applied to the surface tissues causing lift and stimulation of the underlying structures.

There are two methods of application, **static**, where the cup is held in one position, and **gliding**, where the cup is moved in the direction of the local lymphatic flow to the nearest lymph node.

General effects:

- The blood and lymphatic vessels dilate, improving blood and lymphatic circulation.
- Non-medical swelling and puffiness is reduced, by improving the dispersal of accumulated tissue fluids and waste products from the area.
- Localised fatty deposits can be softened. The fat is more readily transported for utilisation in the increased lymphatic flow.
- Skin texture is improved by removing the surface dead skin cells (desquamation).

Body use:

- to reduce fatty deposits on the thighs, abdomen and buttocks
- to improve areas of 'cellulite'
- to treat areas of non-medical swelling; this tissue fluid accumulation is described as **oedema**.

Facial use:

- cleansing action, to remove surface cells and to gently draw out sebum, make-up and impurities
- to improve the appearance of skin and reduce fine lines
- to stimulate a sluggish lymphatic circulation and promote skin respiration
- to treat a dry skin condition by stimulating the activity of the sebaceous glands.

Anatomy and physiology

Vacuum suction is aimed at improving the circulation of **lymph**. Lymph fluid, which is transported in the lymphatic system, is composed of water, salts and waste products and fatty materials of body metabolism and digestion.

Lymph vessels have valves at intervals along their length to prevent backflow. Under normal circumstances lymph flow is caused by pressure applied on the vessels as nearby muscles contract and relax, either in normal movement or when exercising. As vacuum suction treatment is applied, it too alternately applies and releases pressure over the lymphatic vessels, thereby moving the lymph.

Directing the gliding movements in the direction of the lymphatic flow towards the nearest lymph node (gland) enhances the effect and result. Therefore, when applying the treatment to the face or body it is necessary to know where the relevant lymph nodes are situated (see Chapter 4, page 139).

Electrical science

The vacuum suction unit comprises a vacuum pump driven by an electric motor. Dome-shaped glass cups are attached to the machine by plastic tubing. As the vacuum pump reduces atmospheric pressure, air is sucked out of the cup which draws the skin and subcutaneous tissues into the cup. The degree of suction is indicated by a gauge, and the vacuum level should be set according to the part being treated. This is set by the control valve.

In some machines, the static vacuum suction is pulsed in differing levels of vacuum intensity, causing the skin and subcutaneous tissue to rise and fall underneath each cup.

Some machines blow air, which is used to apply cosmetic oils and liquids. This feature, created by a pulsation valve, can also be used to create the effect of 'air massage' where the vacuum is pulsed and the degree of suction rises and falls as it travels over the skin's surface, creating a toning effect.

Reception

Vacuum treatment is usually given as part of a programme in conjunction with other treatments as planned by the therapist. Generally, 20–40 minutes is allowed for body application, 5–12 minutes for facial application.

Body vacuum is usually booked as a course of 10 treatments, applied 2–3 times per week. Facial vacuum suction treatment may be applied every 4–6 weeks.

Contra-indications

If the client has any of the following, vacuum suction treatment should not be carried out:

- reduced skin elasticity (including stretch marks and scar tissue) – the skin will be damaged by the stretching action on the tissues
- broken veins – as the skin is delicate the condition may be worsened
- senile skin – as the skin ages it loses both strength and elasticity and the treatment may cause discomfort and damage
- hypersensitive skin
- varicose veins – the treatment would put unnecessary pressure on the veins
- thrombosis, phlebitis.

Vacuum suction treatment should not be carried out on breast tissue.

EQUIPMENT LIST

vacuum suction facial/body or combined unit

record card

glass cups of various sizes

plastic tubing

oil or cream

tissues

cotton wool

Equipment and materials

- vacuum suction facial/body or combined unit
- record card
- glass cups of various sizes – glass apertures known as ventouses are also available for facial application. The cups must be clear to allow you to see the degree of suction at all times

TIP

Cups should be selected according to the size of the part being treated; the larger the part, the greater the diameter of the cup.

TIP

Some glass cups have finger holes. By covering the holes, the vacuum is created and the tissue is lifted. By removing the finger the vacuum is released and the tissue is lowered.

TIP

Less effort is required by the therapist when performing static pulsating vacuum suction treatment, although practice is required to select the correct pressure in each individual cup.

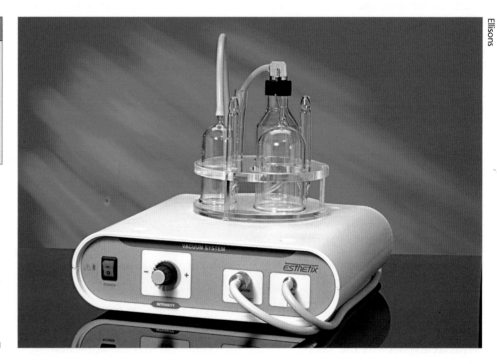

Vacuum system

HEALTH AND SAFETY

Always remember to release the vacuum before removing the cup from the skin to avoid skin damage such as bruising and thread veins.

Different types of vacuum cup

Glass cup	Illustration	Use and effect
Body cup: various diameters available from 2–10 cm		All areas of the body including the back where muscular tension may also be relieved
Facial cup: various diameters available from small to medium		General skin cleansing; lymphatic drainage of the face and neck; treatment of fatty deposits (double chin condition)
Comedone ventouse		Mechanical comedone extraction; congested areas around the chin and nose
Flat ventouse		Treatment of expression lines; can also be used for general skin cleansing

- plastic tubing
- oil or cream to act as a lubricant and provide movement of the cup, and to act as a seal between the skin and the cup
- tissues for protection of the client's clothes (body treatment)
- damp cotton wool to cleanse skin and remove excess lubricant.

Sterilisation and sanitisation

After treatment, remove oil from the cups and plastic tubes with warm water and detergent. The cups should then be thoroughly rinsed, dried and sanitised in an ultraviolet sterilising cabinet.

HEALTH AND SAFETY ✚

Use a small, flexible spiral brush to clean the inside of facial ventouses where dead skin cells and oil will readily accumulate. Glass cups may be sterilised in the autoclave.

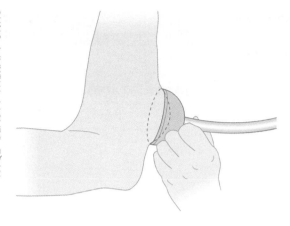

Checking the vacuum setting

Preparation of the treatment area

- Cover the treatment couch with a clean towel.
- Check all general safety precautions.
- Test the machine to ensure it is in good working order.
- Select cups of appropriate size and type to treat the client's needs. Ideally this should be one size smaller than the part to be treated. Attach the cups and tubing to the machine.
- Switch on the machine at the mains and check the vacuum setting of the unit on your own skin; this is usually done on the relaxed upper arm for a body cup or on the lower arm for a facial cup. Slowly increase the intensity until the skin visibly rises into the cup.
- Return the vacuum intensity to zero and switch off the machine.
- Clean the ventouse with a disinfectant agent after testing.

Preparation of the therapist

- Collect the client's record card.
- Sanitise your hands before handling the client.
- Assess the client; discuss the client's lifestyle and the objectives for the treatment.
- Agree on an appropriate treatment plan.
- If this is a repeat treatment, check the client's progress against targets set and provide support and advice as necessary.

Preparation of the client

Facial treatment

- Instruct the client to remove upper clothing to underwear. Position the client comfortably on the couch in a supine semi-reclined position and cover with a clean towel.
- Remove all jewellery from the treatment area.
- Check the area of treatment for visible contra-indications.
- Cleanse and tone the skin of the face and neck. Blot the skin dry with a soft facial tissue.
- Analyse the client's skin using a magnifying lamp. Question the client further where necessary to check information in relation to the client's skin condition.
- Discuss the treatment effect and explain the treatment sensation to the client, i.e. a gentle pulling of the skin, creating a warming, stimulating effect.
- Usually a preheating treatment is carried out to prepare and stimulate the treatment area so that it is more receptive. If a client has had a preheating treatment, ensure that she is kept warm to maximise the effect.

TIP

A preheating treatment to prepare for facial vacuum treatment may be vapour; for body treatment, a sauna or steam treatment may be given. Remember, though, that the vacuum effects will be achieved more quickly so treatment time must be reduced accordingly.

- Apply sufficient lubricant to the treatment area to allow easy movement across the skin.

Body treatment

- Remove all jewellery from the treatment area.
- Instruct the client to remove all clothing except underwear.
- If the purpose of the treatment is for body contouring, measure the client and record this on the client's record card.
- Position the client on the treatment couch. This will be in a supine or prone position depending on the part to be treated.
- Cleanse the skin using witch hazel and blot dry with paper tissue.
- Discuss the treatment effect and explain the treatment sensation to the client, i.e. a gentle pulling of the skin, creating a warming, stimulating effect.

Treatment application

Facial gliding technique

Facial vacuum suction may be applied for the purpose of facial cleansing, skin toning, improving skin functioning and facial contouring.

1 Select a suitable cosmetic lubricant and apply this in an even layer to the face and neck.

2 Switch the machine on at the mains.

3 Select the vacuum intensity for the part to be treated. Always begin the treatment on the lowest degree of vacuum until a comfortable level is reached (usually the cup is 20% full with flesh), moving the cup at all times. Remember, less suction is required over the neck and bony areas of the face as there is less subcutaneous tissue here.

4 Starting at the base of the neck, direct each stroke in an upwards direction towards the relevant lymphatic node. Release the vacuum at the end of the stroke before removal of the cup.

5 Repeat each stroke on average four times.

6 Depending on the cup or ventouse used, break the vacuum by inserting the fingertip of the opposite hand underneath the cup, or lift the finger over the hole to release the vacuum.

Vapour preheating

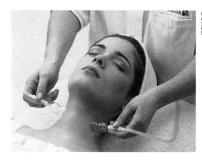

Facial vacuum suction

HEALTH AND SAFETY ✚

Avoid treatment around the delicate eye tissue to prevent stretching.

TIP ✔

Technique
- Strokes should be rhythmical and flowing.
- Do not apply the strokes too fast as this will make the results less effective.
- Do not apply strokes directly over lymph nodes.
- Overlap each stroke by half the previous stroke.
- If contact with the skin is broken during the application of a stroke, commence the stroke again.

Removal of comedones

7 Move the cup by half a width each time, repeat the stroke and continue application upwards to cover the facial area.

8 Return the vacuum intensity dial to zero and switch the machine off at the mains.

9 Remove the massage medium from the skin or follow the treatment with another complimentary treatment such as facial massage. Complete the treatment with a face mask, toning lotion and treatment moisturiser.

Skin blockages

To remove signs of congestion such as comedones, select a small ventouse. The small diameter of the aperture increases the suction effect on the skin and the comedone is loosened.

HEALTH AND SAFETY

The facial comedone ventouse must *not* be moved in a gliding action over the skin's surface. Hold it static whilst operating the vacuum and release the vacuum before removal to avoid bruising or stretching the skin.

Face and neck applications

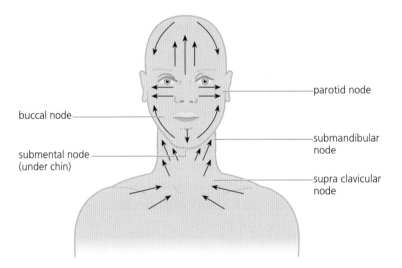

Body gliding technique

A poor diet, sedentary lifestyle and stress can cause sluggish lymphatic circulation. Toxins become stored, causing puffy and tender tissue.

The body gliding technique is used to increase dispersal of accumulated fluid in the tissues and to soften areas of fatty tissue, improving the general functioning and appearance of the skin.

1 Place tissues along the edges of underwear to prevent staining with the lubricant.

2 Apply oil to the area to be treated, either manually or with the vacuum spray attachment if available.

3 Switch on the machine at the mains.

4 Place the cup on the border of the area to be treated and increase the vacuum suction intensity until the tissue fills the cup by 20%.

5 Starting at the boundary of the area to be treated, gently lift the cup away from the skin without breaking the seal and glide it in a straight line towards the nearest lymphatic node.

6 At the end of the strip, depending on the cup chosen, break the seal by inserting the tip of a finger of the opposite hand underneath the edge of the cup or uncovering the hole which releases the vacuum. Return the cup to the beginning of the strip.

7 Perform the gliding action over each strip of skin 4–6 times, then move onto the next strip, overlapping the previous strip by half its width.

8 Adjust the vacuum intensity according to the area being treated; the suction may be increased or decreased during application.

9 Continue until all the treatment area has been covered.

10 Return the vacuum intensity to zero and switch the machine off at the mains. The skin should have become warm with a visible mild erythema and the area should feel smooth and invigorated.

11 At the end of the treatment you may perform a manual massage effleurage stroke to reinforce the lymphatic drainage effect.

> **TIP** ✔
>
> Avoid the use of excessive oil as this will make the cup difficult to control.

> **HEALTH AND SAFETY** ✚
>
> If the suction is too high, break the seal immediately to avoid a contra-action, i.e. bruising.

> **TIP** ✔
>
> Loose, soft-fat areas of tissue require less suction than other areas.

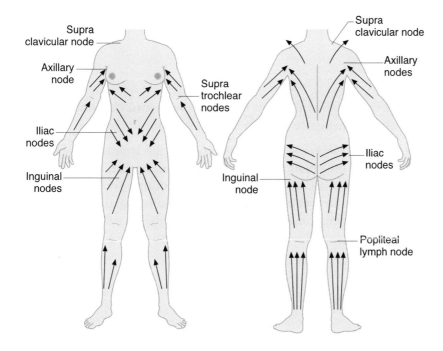

Application to body – front and back

Body pulsating multi-cup vacuum technique

With multi-cup vacuum suction, up to eight cups are placed on the skin's surface. These operate simultaneously. This method is suitable for larger clients and for specific problem areas of stubborn fat such as the abdomen and thighs.

1 Switch on the machine at the mains.

2 Switch on the pulsation control operated by the pulsation valve. This controls the degree of suction and also the length of pulsation periods.

TIP

When treating the abdominal area of slimmer clients, select the gliding technique, as suction will become difficult on the low-pulsed vacuum periods.

TIP

Other treatments you may offer:
- Microcurrent machines are aimed at the effective drainage of the lymphatic system. The current is directed at the problem areas.
- Inflatable air-pressure massage body envelopes treat localised cellulite and poor lymphatic-drained areas. External pressure on the tissues increases the flow of lymph.

3 Place the cups on the skin, not too close together, ensuring the seal of the cup makes good contact with the skin's surface and the vacuum created draws the tissues into the cup.

4 The lower degree of pulsation must be sufficient to ensure the cups remain in contact with the skin. During the release period the cup may be moved along the area being treated.

5 Increase the degree of lift (intensity) and duration of pulsation period according to the effect required.

6 The cups may be moved to other treatment areas during application. Gliding technique may be used to reinforce the removal of tissue fluid in the area.

7 Apply the treatment for 10–15 minutes.

8 Remove the cups during the lower degree pulse.

9 Return the vacuum intensity to zero and switch off at the mains.

10 Remove the oil thoroughly from the skin and follow with further complimentary treatment if required.

Aftercare

Complete details of the treatment on the client record card and include details of home-care advice and any product samples provided.

Advise the client to increase fluid intake to help the lymphatic cleansing effect. Also advise the client of an effective treatment plan combining diet and exercise appropriate to her needs. Retail products support the effectiveness of the treatment. These include exfoliating and body contour products. These often contain anti-diuretic ingredients such as seaweed, ivy, ginseng and horsetail which aim to increase the skin's metabolism and lymphatic circulation.

Contra-actions

Bruising and thread veins caused by:

- pulling the cup off without reducing the vacuum
- vacuum pressure being too high
- over-treatment of an area
- cup too small for area of treatment
- increasing the vacuum whilst the cup is stationary (gliding technique).

Over-stretching of the skin caused by:

- over-treatment of the area
- failure to reduce vacuum over looser areas of skin.

Sorisa

Inflatable air pressure massage envelope

MICROCURRENT TREATMENT

Microcurrent therapy is an electrical treatment with an immediate skin toning and firming effect. It may be offered as a treatment for either the face or body and is available as a single or combined treatment unit. It is very popular as its results are immediate. It may be offered to a wide client group, including those who wish to use the treatment as a preventative measure against premature ageing as well as to re-educate and strengthen muscles.

General effects:

- stimulation of cellular functioning of the epidermal and dermal layers – this naturally slows through the ageing process
- improved blood circulation, increasing the transportation of oxygen and nutrients to the skin's cells
- improved lymphatic circulation, speeding the elimination of waste and toxins which accumulate, causing puffy skin tissue (non-medical oedema)
- shortening of muscles and improvement in tone.

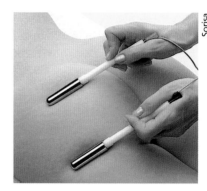

Microcurrent therapy

Sorisa

Body use:

- for its skin rejuvenation effect
- to improve the appearance of a cellulite condition
- to improve the appearance of skin tone in specific problem areas, being especially beneficial for scar tissue
- to improve the appearance of stretch marks by the effect of skin tightening
- to improve the bust contour.

Facial use:

- skin rejuvenation through an improved muscle and skin tone; lines and slack facial contours will appear less obvious
- frown lines resulting from tense muscles are softened if the current is used to relax the muscles
- skin type characteristics may be treated specifically, such as the open pores of a greasy skin type which may be tightened
- skin colour is improved by the improved blood circulation and improved elimination of waste products and toxins
- dark circles and puffiness around the eyes may be treated.

Anatomy and physiology

Cells degenerate with ageing, resulting in reduced nutrition and oxygen which affects the cellular metabolism. The electrical current stimulates cell metabolism and increases the permeability of cell membranes to improve movement of materials in and out of the cells. The application of a small

HEALTH AND SAFETY

Microcurrent equipment for convenience may operate from a rechargeable battery; the client may see it psychologically as safer because it is not directly connected to the mains.

electrical current directly stimulates the muscle fibres, but because the microcurrent operates at a low intensity it does not cause visible contraction as seen in faradic treatment.

Electrical science

Microcurrent is based on a modified direct current and as such creates the same effects as a galvanic current. It is basically a direct current interrupted at low frequencies of one to a few hundred times per second.

The modern microcurrent delivers currents which are measured in microamps (millionths of an amp) shown as μA. Outputs are typically 300–600 μA (0.3–0.6 milliamps), although in alternating mode 1200 μA (1.2 mA) can be reached. The voltage adjusts itself to give the required safe current level.

A negative polarity stimulates the nervous response and dilates the vessels of the blood and lymphatic circulatory systems. This has a beneficial warming effect on the tissues. In the treatment of a cellulite condition, sluggish circulation is increased, causing waste toxins to be eliminated more rapidly. To eliminate the effects of the galvanic current, each alternate electrical pulse can be modified to an alternating current. Other machines operate on alternating current and then electronically reverse each alternate pulse. The microcurrent therefore oscillates back and forth between positive and negative charges.

A very low, computerised microcurrent sends electrical impulses which stimulate the skin's nerve endings. This causes the muscles to contract and shorten, which strengthens them and increases tone. This results in a firmer facial skin appearance.

A d.c. galvanic current may be incorporated to stimulate the blood and lymph circulation to treat the general functioning of the skin and cellulite conditions.

Reception

- Complete personal details on the client's record card.
- Question the client to check for contra-indications.
- The number of sessions required will vary for each client.
- It is important that the client first receives a one-off treatment to observe the result. A course of treatment should then be recommended.

Facial treatment

Allow 30–60 minutes for a facial application, depending on the treatment application technique chosen. The client should attend 2–3 times per week. Usually the treatment is given as a course of 12.

Body treatment

Allow half an hour for a body application. The client should attend on average 2–3 times per week. The treatment is usually given as a course of 10.

For both facial and body treatments, once the contours have been improved in tone, a general maintenance plan of 2–3 courses a year is advised.

Contra-indications

During the client assessment, if you find any of the following in the treatment area, microcurrent treatment must not be carried out:

- skin disorder or disease – these could be aggravated by the treatment or cross-transfer of infection could occur
- electrical implants, e.g. pacemakers – the microcurrent could cause interference with other electrical sources
- metal plates and pins – these will conduct the current and cause discomfort
- severe varicose veins
- excessive dental metalwork – these conduct minute current transfer to the tooth nerve.
- loss of tactile skin sensation.

Clients who suffer from migraines should not be treated around the eye or forehead area.

HEALTH AND SAFETY

If the client has dental work such as fillings which may cause possible discomfort, place the electrodes above or below the gum area.

Equipment and materials

- record card
- microcurrent unit
- facial leads
- probes, double or single/pad electrodes
- conductive gloves (if required)

TIP
Some machines use needles to pass the current directly in to the skin. The needle is inserted into the epidermis and this transmits the current to the muscle for a few minutes. Probes are usually made of stainless steel as it is a good conductor of electrical current.

- conducting ionised gel – this may contain specific therapeutic ingredients to enhance the effects achieved
- disposable cotton buds – cut to 1.5 cm (if required).

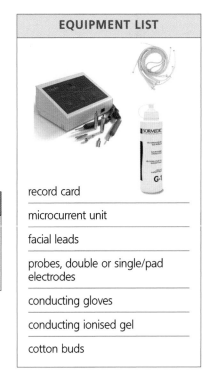

EQUIPMENT LIST

record card

microcurrent unit

facial leads

probes, double or single/pad electrodes

conducting gloves

conducting ionised gel

cotton buds

Sterilisation and sanitisation

Disposable cotton buds must be used for each client. After each treatment the probes should be cleaned thoroughly, removing the conduction gel with surgical spirit. Place in an ultraviolet sterilising cabinet. Facial pads, if used, should be replaced after each client.

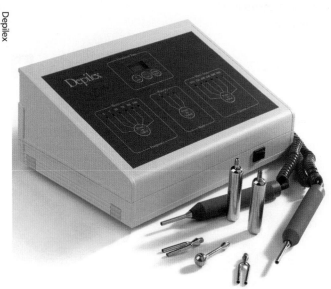

Microcurrent unit

Preparation of the treatment area

- Cover the treatment couch with a clean towel.
- Check all electrical safety precautions.
- Test the machine to ensure it is in good working order. If battery operated, the equipment will only work if the unit is fully powered up.

Facial application

- Prepare the cotton buds for facial treatment if used. These are cut and shortened for insertion into the facial electrode probes.
- Prepare the facial electrode pads for face and neck treatment.
- Select the probes according to the area to be treated.
- Secure the probe electrodes firmly to the electrical leads.
- Insert the leads into the relevant connections.

Body application

- Collect clean conductive gloves.
- Select the probes according to the area to be treated.
- Secure the probe electrodes firmly to the electrical leads.
- Insert the leads into the relevant connections.

Preparation of the therapist

- Collect the client's record card.
- Sanitise your hands before handling the client.
- Assess the client; discuss the client's lifestyle and objectives of the treatment if this is the initial treatment. Agree an appropriate treatment plan.
- If a treatment has a slimming requirement it will be necessary to measure the client at the beginning of the treatment course and once every week thereafter.
- If this is a repeat treatment, check the client's progress against targets set and provide support and advice as necessary.
- Often with a course of facial treatment a 'before' and 'after' photograph may be taken.

Preparation of the client

- After an initial consultation, the correct treatment for the client's needs is identified. This consultation evaluates the client's lifestyle. Effectors such as smoking, alcohol and stress are discussed and a relevant treatment programme is reached.

- Discuss the aims of the treatment with the client.
- For facial application, a photograph could be taken before to show the results that have been achieved after the microcurrent therapy treatment.
- Instruct the client to remove upper clothing to underwear. Position the client comfortably on the couch in a supine position and cover with a clean towel.
- Perform a skin sensitivity test to ensure the client can detect different skin sensations.
- Record the results on the client's record card.
- Remove all jewellery from the treatment area.
- Cleanse the skin area with cleanser and toner and blot the surface dry. A facial exfoliation is beneficial before the treatment to allow the current to flow easily.
- Analyse the client's skin using a magnifying lamp. Question the client where necessary to check information in relation to the client's skin condition.
- Cover any minor cuts or abrasions with petroleum jelly or a small surgical plaster to form a barrier to the electrical current.
- Explain the treatment sensation to the client. A slight prickling sensation will be experienced in the skin.
- It is advisable to recommend a pre-treatment of facial peeling to reduce the skin's resistance to the current.

> **TIP**
>
> If used in the treatment, facial pads will fail to stick to the skin if the skin is not dry. This will result in treatment interference and uneven current application.

> **TIP**
>
> The wave forms produced may be an alternating current or a direct current. The benefit of the direct current is that it has both muscle stimulation and galvanic treatment effects.

Treatment application

The current intensity, frequency (pulses per second), wave form and duration should be selected as appropriate to treat the client's skin condition and for client comfort. This may need to be varied for each side of the face or body. The current levels may be kept low, intensity does not have to be high to achieve the best results.

Facial application

1 Apply an electrolyte such as ionised gel to the skin's surface.
2 Select the treatment electrode. These will be either probes or facial pads.
  The specific application of the single probes in various strokes, or placement of the facial pads over the skin's surface achieve increased blood and lymph circulation. Also, specific muscles are tightened and relaxed as the electric current flows, creating an immediate lifting effect. Probes are normally used on delicate areas such as around the eye area. Application must be firm to ensure effective current application.
  Dual probes may be used on larger muscles of the face and are especially beneficial along the jaw area in the treatment of jowls.

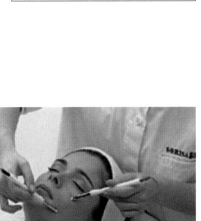

Single probes

HEALTH AND SAFETY ✚

In contrast to faradic treatment there will be no visible contraction of the muscle with the electrical current application. It is important to consider this when using facial electrodes. Also warn the client that flashing lights can be experienced when working around the eye area. This is not harmful!

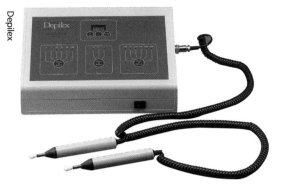

Dual probes

3 Place and move single large and small probes in a gliding motion – the large probe towards the smaller – to firm the face and neck muscles. The process also helps to soften the appearance of lines and wrinkles.

4 After treatment using electrode pads or facial probes, return all control settings to zero.

5 The facial may be completed with ionisation, where ionised substances are passed into the epidermis with an uninterrupted direct current.

6 Remove excess conducting gel from the skin's surface.

7 Record the treatment details on the client's record card.

Body application

1 Select the current, frequency and wave form appropriate to part of the body to be treated.

2 Apply conductive gel to the skin.

3 Apply probes or conductive gloves. The application of the probes or conductive gloves over the skin firms the tissues and soft fatty areas are broken down. Application must be firm to ensure effective current application.

4 Stretch marks and scar tissue improve in appearance as the microcurrent tightens the collagen fibres that give strength to the skin and stimulates cell and collagen renewal. The tissues will appear firmed.

5 Often, a manual massage is used to conclude the treatment to ensure the absorption of all the treatment gel.

6 Alternatively a specialised skin-toning treatment product may be applied with the aim of improving a cellulite appearance.

TIP ✔

More gel may be applied if the skin drags as the gel absorbs and dries during application.

TIP ✔

The glove system is useful on the face, hips and thighs where specific muscles are stimulated by electric pulses emitted through silk-like gloves. The gloves are dampened with water.

Aftercare

To continue the treatment process the therapist should discuss the benefits of home care with the client. Ideally, facial cosmetic creams and make-up must not be applied directly after treatment. The skin needs to be able to 'breathe'. However, as some treatments only take 30 minutes some clients may wish to take advantage of receiving their treatment during a lunch-break. The negative effects on the skin of alcohol, smoking and ultraviolet radiation should be discussed with the client. The drinking of natural, uncarbonated water should be encouraged following treatment to help remove toxins, and the benefits of a healthy diet should also be discussed.

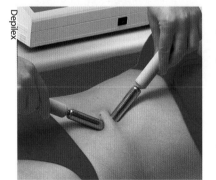

Application of probes

Simple, facial exercises should be recommended to the client. These will continue to firm the facial muscles and reinforce the firming effects of the microcurrent treatment.

Clients should be offered retail cosmetic skin-care preparations to support and enhance the effects achieved. Alpha hydroxy acid (AHA) treatments are beneficial to cosmetically remove surface dead skin cells and improve the skin's appearance, reducing the skin's resistance to the treatment.

Contra-actions

- Muscle fatigue caused by incorrect choice of current intensity, frequency and wave form.

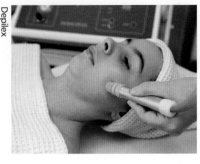

Depilex

Derma peel (micro-dermabrasion)

BT36 IMPROVE THE APPEARANCE OF THE SKIN USING MICRO-DERMABRASION

Micro-dermabrasion is a mechanical exfoliating or skin-peeling facial and body treatment where a controlled high-speed flow of microcrystals is applied under pressure over the skin's surface through an applicator probe which gently breaks down the skin cells. An immediate vacuum effect then occurs: whilst applying the crystals to the skin the applicator probe also removes dead skin and excess microcrystals. The treatment also has a cellular regenerative effect, improving both cellular renewal and repair and the tone and elasticity of the skin.

General effects

Face and body

- Desquamation effect, due to the exfoliation of the skin surface, specifically improving the appearance of:
  - coarse skin with open pores – regular treatment will help remove excess dead skin cells and cleanse the pores
  - fine lines and wrinkles around the eyes, lips and neck
  - scar tissue e.g. acne scarring, stretch marks – their appearance will be less noticeable
  - superficial hyperpigmentation, (only if the pigmentation is located in the epidermis)
- Improved blood circulation locally, increasing the transportation of oxygen and nutrients to the skin's cells
- Stimulation of cellular functioning of the epidermal and dermal layers – (this naturally slows as part of the ageing process) creating a skin rejuvenating effect
- Improved lymphatic circulation locally, speeding the elimination of waste and toxins which cause puffy skin tissue when they accumulate (non-medical oedema).

Anatomy and physiology

> **TIP**
>
> **One single treatment**
> When promoting micro-dermabrasion, remind the client that one single treatment will remove excess dead skin cells and sebum, making the skin appear brighter and healthier, whatever the skin type.

The treatment is termed mechanical because the microcrystals mechanically remove cells from the skin's surface, removing 0.06 mm (superficial dermabrasion) to 0.45 mm (medium dermabrasion) of skin in a single treatment. The applicator probe stimulates cells called fibroblasts in the connective tissue of the dermis, held in a substance called the ground substance. These cells are responsible for the production of collagen and elastin protein fibres. Elastin gives the skin elasticity, whilst collagen fibres give it strength. Thus the treatment improves the strength and elasticity of the skin. The vacuum suction feature stimulates both blood and lymphatic circulation locally.

Electrical science

A compressor, a device that compresses gas, draws atmospheric air through the hole in the applicator when not in contact with the skin. A vacuum occurs when the applicator is then placed in contact with the skin. This causes the microcrystals located at the other end of the system to be sucked by negative pressure until they reach the applicator probe. When the applicator head is in contact with the skin, this closes the air outlet hole. Microcrystals will only flow when the outlet hole is closed onto the treatment area.

Reception

Allow 50–60 minutes for treatment application depending upon the treatment area. A course of 10–20 treatments is generally recommended every 7–10 days. The length of course and interval will depend upon the condition being treated, skin sensitivity and the reaction of the skin to treatment. Following the course maintenance treatment should be recommended once per month. As the skin continuously renews and replaces, treatment must be repeated in order to maintain the result. When booking this service advice should be given as to aftercare requirements.

Contra-indications

During the client assessment, if you find any of the following micro-dermabrasion treatment must not be carried out:

- Skin disorder or disease – these could be aggravated by the treatment or cross-transfer of infection could occur.
- Recent laser surgery or chemical peel.
- Hypersensitive skin.
- Highly vascular skin, e.g. acne rosacea or broken capillaries: as the skin is delicate the condition may be worsened.
- Erythema caused by recent UV exposure.
- Loss of tactile skin sensation.
- Anti-coagulation drugs as prescribed to treat cardio-vascular conditions as these will interfere with the skin coagulation process.
- Diabetic condition: poor skin healing makes the client vulnerable to infection.
- Pigmentation disorders such as moles and birthmarks.
- Keloid scarring: this could make the condition worse.
- Blood disorders such as hepatitis B and AIDS caused by the virus HIV (human immunodeficiency virus) – there may be a risk of cross-infection as the viruses are transmitted by body fluids.

HEALTH AND SAFETY

Medication
Some oral and topical medication can cause increased skin sensitivity. Examples include Retin A and certain antibiotics.

EQUIPMENT LIST

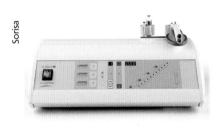

record card

micro-dermabrasion unit

applicator probe

disposable applicator heads for the probe

microcrystals, made of aluminium oxide (corundum)

Sorisa

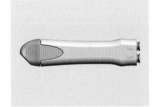

Micro-dermabrasion unit

Sorisa

Applicator probe attachment

Equipment and materials

- Record card.
- Micro-dermabrasion unit.
- Applicator probe.
- Disposable applicator heads for the probe.
- Microcrystals, made of aluminium oxide a hard mineral referred to as corundum.

HEALTH AND SAFETY

Storage of microcrystals
These must be kept dry. Store in a dry atmosphere to avoid them becoming damp, which would affect flow of crystals during treatment application.

- Protective eyeshields, ie. damp cotton wool.
- Facial sponges to remove skin care preparations.
- Complimentary skin care cosmetic skin care preparation, i.e. treatment mask, skin calming, strengthening preparations.

Sterilisation and sanitisation

The crystals are sterile; once applied to the skin they are returned with any waste materials from the skin to the waste crystal container. The used crystals should be placed in a strong waste disposal bag before disposal. Replace the active probe cap after each client treatment.

Preparation of the treatment area

- Cover the treatment couch with a clean towel.
- Check all electrical safety precautions.
- Test the machine to ensure it is in good working order.
- Ensure the crystal level in the active container is filled with sterile crystals, observing the minimum and maximum levels as a guide. Remove any crystal residue from the cap of the bottle with a dry brush, insert the suction tube in the crystals and close cap securely.
- The waste crystal bottle must be emptied regularly, observing the maximum level as a guide. Empty the used crystal bottle before use and clean its filter following manufacturer's instructions.

Preparation of the therapist

- Collect the client's record card.
- Sanitise your hands before handling the client.
- Assess the client; discuss the client's lifestyle and the objectives of the treatment if this is the initial treatment. Agree an appropriate treatment plan.

- Features of this treatment may include taking a photograph to show skin appearance comparison before and after treatment.

Preparation of the client

- After an initial consultation, the correct treatment for the client's skin needs is identified and agreed with the client.
- Instruct the client to remove clothing according to the area being treated.
- Position the client comfortably on the couch and cover with a clean towel.
- All jewellery must be removed from the treatment area.
- Question the client further where necessary to check information in relation to the client's skin condition.
- Cleanse and tone the client's skin using appropriate skin care preparations and then blot the skin dry. *A dry skin is essential* to ensure effective exfoliation.
- For safety test the compressor suction power setting on your inner wrist before use on the client.
- Inform the client of the noise.
- Inform the client of the sensation and expected appearance of the skin following treatment.
- Provide protective eyeshields to prevent irritation of the eyes from the crystals and any skin debris during facial application.

Treatment application

- Start equipment.
- Select the programme according to the area being treated and the pressure required.

HEALTH AND SAFETY

Avoid overworking an area by moving the applicator too slowly or applying the suction pressure too high or skin bleeding may occur as excessive skin cells are removed.
   On a sensitive skin increase the speed of application, resulting in superficial exfoliation. This will allow you to assess skin tolerance.

- The attachment probe is continuously moved over the skin's surface, following lymphatic flow. The crystals are directed onto the skin's surface and a mild suction is applied. The slower the movement the greater the degree of abrasion in the area.
- For general facial treatment movements are from the centre of the face outwards.
- For pigmentation marks, wrinkles and scarring, treat each individually.
- For stretch marks work over the skin at the outside of the scar first as the stretched skin has less resistance and will readily bleed.

Sorisa

Cleaning the crystal containers

Sorisa

Cleaning the crystal containers

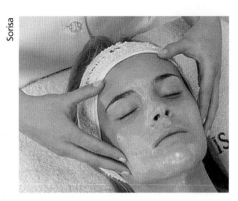
Sorisa

Skin cleansing and make-up removal

Sorisa

Protect the eyes

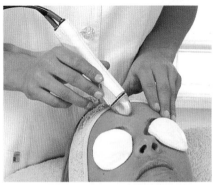
Sorisa

Facial application: General facial micro-dermabrasion

Sorisa

Facial application to problem areas

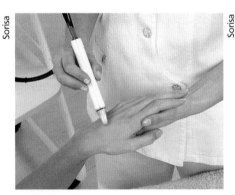
Sorisa

Appplication to the hands for treatment of pigmentation marks

Sorisa

Application to the limbs for treatment of scars

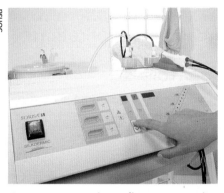
Sorisa

Compressor suction adjustment setting

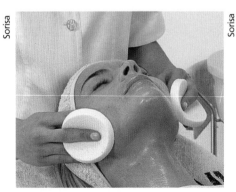
Sorisa

Facial cleansing following micro-dermabrasion treatment

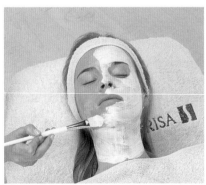
Sorisa

Face mask application

Avoid treatment on delicate eye tissue.

- Compressor suction setting should be selected according to the skin condition being treated, effect to be achieved and skin sensitivity. The higher the suction, the stronger the speed of crystal abrasion.

- Treatment time varies according to the area of the body being treated. Clean the skin's surface whilst dry after treatment application to observe the results achieved, further treatment may be required.

- Allow between 10–20 minutes for the face and 5–10 minutes for the hands.

- Excess crystals may be gently removed from the skin surface using cleansing lotion and damp sponges.

- A calming treatment mask is applied to the skin to calm and desensitise. As the skin is more permeable following exfoliation and vacuum treatment the products will work more efficiently.

Medication
If the client is taking medication to thin the blood, treatment pressure must be lighter as the blood will reach the skin's surface much quicker.

Aftercare

Inform the client that following the treatment they may experience signs of skin irritation such as redness, dryness and itching. This will vary according to the treatment application technique applied or the skin type treated. Soothing, nourishing skin-care preparations should be recommended and the client must not scratch the skin.

Promote other electro-therapy treatments such as facial/body faradic therapy or micro-current or body wraps. Encourage the retail sale of sun protection creams and relevant skincare.

If a contra-action occurs advise the client to contact the salon immediately to receive appropriate professional advice.

The client should:

- Avoid UV exposure for up to seven days following treatment, as the skin is more susceptible to sun damage.

- Wear a UV sunblock on exposure to sunlight at all times.

- Use recommended retail products to care for the skin at home, to soothe and nourish the skin.

- Avoid full make-up application for 24 hours following treatment: eye and lip make-up may be worn.

Provide advice to clients for electro-therapy by

- Discuss aftercare and homecare products with the client to complement the treatment
- For 24 hours as applicable avoid:
  – Stimulants such as alcohol and caffeine
  – Make-up for up to 8 hours following a deep cleansing treatment – if worn, eye make-up and lipstick may be worn
- Discuss recommendations to lifestyle changes. Facial/body exercises may be recommended to aid muscle strengthening electro-therapy treatments
- Special aftercare may be provided for different electro-therapy treatments as advised by the manufacturer, including the use of specialised skin care products
- Nutritional advice should be provided for client's whose regular diets show poor nutritional balance
- Ask the client how they feel to establish if the treatment has achieved the objectives set
- Evaluate and modify the treatment plan accordingly in relation to:
  – client satisfaction
  – treatment outcome results
  – an alternative treatment being more suitable to meet the clients treatment needs
  – contra-action to treatment provided
- Explain the importance of ongoing regular treatment
- When additional treatments are recommended discuss client commitment in terms of cost, timing and duration
- Inform the client of post-treatment reactions such as skin blemishes following deep cleansing facial treatments
- Any contra-action following treatment should be discussed with the therapist so appropriate advice is given. This should be noted on the client's records
- Make a further treatment appointment as appropriate

Contra-actions

- Excessive erythema, skin irritation.
- Excessive skin bleeding.

Do not treat the skin again until skin healing has occurred. In cases of extreme skin reaction to treatment it will be advisable that the client does not receive the treatment again due to unsuitability.

HEALTH AND SAFETY

Care should be taken when treating fair skin types as this skin has less tolerance and may suffer from excessive erythema.

Do not treat a client who has post-acne scars if there are any pustules present to avoid sensitisation and infection.

Assessment of knowledge and understanding

You have now learnt about the effects of electro-therapy and how to select and adapt your technique of application to meet the client's treatment requirements. These skills will enable you to improve face, body and skin condition using electro-therapy.

To test your level of knowledge and understanding, answer the following short questions. These will prepare you for your summative (final) assessment.

Anatomy and physiology questions required for this unit are found on pages 146–50.

Organisational and legal requirements

1 Which legislation are you responsible for implementing when performing electro-therapy treatments?

2 How can cross-infection be avoided when carrying out electro-therapy treatment?

3 What action should be taken to safeguard others in the event of faulty equipment?

4 How often should electrical equipment be checked and by whom?

5 State four general electrical safety precautions which should be taken when using electro-therapy equipment.

6 Why is it important to allow sufficient time to complete a service?

7 Why is it important to keep detailed records of the clients treatment/s?

Client consultation

1 To perform an effective consultation you need the client to feel confident about providing you with positive, honest answers to your questions. You should have good:
   a. communication skills
   b. questioning techniques
   c. listening skills
   d. answering techniques.
   Give examples of what you understand by good skills and techniques for each of the above.

2 What details are required on your client record card?

3 Why is it important to discuss the client's lifestyle?

4 How would you recognise the following skin types/conditions:
   - dry
   - oily
   - sensitive
   - congested
   - dehydrated?

5 How would you recognise:
- poor muscle tone of the abdomen
- kyphosis
- cellulite
- fluid retention
- the body type mesomporph?

Preparation for treatment

1 How should the treatment environment be prepared to ensure client comfort and maximum benefit from the treatment? Consider temperature, lighting and sound.

2 Why is it beneficial to perform a pre-heating treatment before certain electro-therapy treatments?

3 How should the client be positioned to gain maximum benefit from:
- micro-current treatment to the face
- audio sonic treatment to the shoulders?

4 Why is it important to discuss the expected treatment sensation with the client?

Contra-indications

1 Why is it important to refer clients to their GP if you identify a contra-indication?

2 When would you need to refer a client to their GP before treatment could be given?

3 State three contra-indications to facial electro-therapy treatment.

4 State three contra-indications to body electro-therapy treatment.

Equipment and products

1 How is the following equipment cleaned to prevent cross-infection:
- vacuum suction ventouses
- gyratory massage heads
- faradic pad electrodes?

2 Why are water-based solutions used for galvanic treatment?

3 Name a suitable product to use for facial vacuum suction treatment.

Treatment-specific knowledge

1 Why is a skin sensitivity test performed before treatment application?

2 How should the skin be prepared for:
- audio sonic body application
- body galvanic iontophoresis

- facial indirect high frequency
- facial micro-dermabrasion?

3 How would the following contra-actions be recognised:
- galvanic burn
- faradic or microcurrent muscle fatigue
- bruising from a vacuum suction treatment
- skin bleeding from a micro-dermabrasion?

What action should be taken?

4 Considering the differences between male and female skin, how would this affect the application of facial vacuum suction in terms of vacuum intensity?

5 What type of electric current is used for the following treatments:
- faradic
- galvanic
- high frequency?

6 Give four physiological benefits that the client may expect from the following treatments:
- gyratory massage
- faradic treatment
- facial ionto-phoresis
- micro-dermabrasion.

7 In which direction and at what system of the body is facial vacuum suction treatment directed?

8 Over what areas of the face may galvanic current intensity have to be produced and why?

Treatment advice

1 Why is it important to gain feedback from the client and give relevant advice to her following treatment?

2 Why is it important to record any contra-action either during or following treatment on the client record card?

3 After the electro-therapy treatment the client should be given advice to follow to ensure that she gains maximum benefit from the treatment. Discuss the advice to be given following:
- facial galvanic desincrustation
- facial micro-current
- body gyratory massage
- body faradic treatment.

4 What recommendations to lifestyle habit would enable a client to continue the benefits from the treatment for:
- body faradic, the client wishes to improve her muscle tone
- facial vacuum suction, the client wishes to improve her sluggish, congested skin type
- micro-dermabrasion?

5 How often would you recommend a client receive micro-current electro-therapy treatment for rejuvenation?

6 What intervals would you recommend between micro-dermabrasion treatments?

chapter 9

Provide Indian head massage treatment

Learning objectives

This unit explains how to provide Indian head massage treatment.

It describes the competencies to enable you to:

- **consult with the client to establish needs and expectations**
- **plan the treatment**
- **prepare the treatment area for Indian head massage**
- **carry out procedure for Indian head massage**
- **provide aftercare advice**

When providing Indian head massage treatment it is important to use the skills you have learnt in the following core mandatory units:

Unit G1 ensure your own actions reduce risks to health and safety
Unit G6 promote additional products or services to your clients
Unit G11 contribute to the financial effectiveness of the business

INTRODUCTION

Indian head massage is a treatment applied to the upper part of the body (the shoulders, upper arms, neck and head) using the hands. It helps to relieve stress and tension, and creates a feeling of well-being. This type of massage has developed over a thousand years from traditional techniques practiced in India. The family tradition of massage plays a central role in daily life in India and dates back to the beginnings of Hinduism, the main religion of that country. Indian head massage is known as 'champissage' in India and is part of the system of Ayurveda – the science of life – an ancient form of medical treatment which is nearly 4000 years old. Ayurveda is a method of relieving pain and healing through the balance of the body.

The Ayur-veda (Art of life), a sacred Hindu text, was written around 1800 BC. In Ayurveda life consists of body, mind and spirit and each person is different. Massage is included amongst its principles of achieving balance of the body. By restoring balance and harmony of the body, mind and spirit the health of the individual improves.

As the therapeutic effects of massage become more popular, Indian head massage is an ideal treatment to offer and has many advantages that can meet the needs of different clients. There is no need for the client to undress, it is relatively quick to perform, can be performed almost anywhere and does not require expensive equipment.

The massage is adapted to the client's physiological and psychological needs. These are determined during the client consultation and are termed as the objectives of the treatment.

These objectives may include:

- Relaxation.
- Maintaining a feeling of well-being.
- To improve the condition of the scalp and hair.

Physiological effects of Indian head massage include:

- The muscles receive an improved supply of oxygenated blood, essential for cell growth. The tone and strength of muscles are improved.
- The increased blood circulation in the area warms the tissues. This induces a feeling of relaxation, which is particularly beneficial when treating tense muscles.
- As the blood capillaries dilate and bring blood to the skin's surface, the skin colour improves.
- The lymphatic circulation and the venous blood circulation increase. These changes speed up the removal of waste products and toxins. The removal of excess lymph improves the appearance of a puffy oedematous skin.
- Sensory nerve endings can be soothed or stimulated, depending on the massage manipulations selected.
- Massage stimulates the sebaceous and suderiferous glands and increases the production of sweat and sebum. This increases the skin's natural oil and moisture balance.
- Applying oil to the head (optional) adds moisture and improves the condition of dry hair or scalp.

The psychological effects of massage are broad, and when performed on a regular basis, can relieve stress and tension in the client. The client may feel fresh, invigorated and healthier.

TIP

Emotional effect
Clients may become tearful following Indian head massage. This is because clients relax, and they may then wish to talk about their problems.

If this happens *listen* – unless qualified you should not counsel.

Psychological effects of Indian head massage include:

- helps to improve concentration – increased oxygen to the brain
- relieves tension
- induces relaxation
- relieves stress
- confidence-raising following the removal of tension.

ANATOMY AND PHYSIOLOGY

For Indian head massage the necessary anatomy and physiology you need to know and understand is listed for you on pages 75–6.

Massage movements

Indian head massage is based on a series of classic Westernised and Indian massage movements, used to create different effects. There are six basic types of movement/s:

- effleurage
- petrissage
- percussion
- frictions
- vibrations
- pressure point.

The therapist can adapt the way each of these movements is applied, according to the needs of the client. Either the *speed* of application or the *depth of pressure* can be altered.

Effleurage

Effleurage is a stroking movement, used to begin the massage, as a link manipulation, and to complete the massage sequence. This manipulation can be applied lightly or briskly, has an even pressure and is applied in a rhythmical, continuous manner to induce relaxation. The speed of application depends upon the effect to be achieved and according to the underlying structures and tissue type, but it must *never* be unduly heavy. Movements also includes stroking. Effleurage has the following effects:

- desquamation (skin removal) is increased
- arterial blood circulation is increased, bringing fresh nutrients to the area
- venous circulation is improved, aiding the removal of congestion from the veins
- lymphatic circulation is increased, improving the absorption of waste products
- the underlying muscle fibres are relaxed.

Uses in treatment: to relax tight and contracted muscles.

Petrissage

Petrissage involves a series of movements in which the tissues are lifted away from the underlying structures and compressed. Pressure is intermittent, and should be light yet firm. Petrissage has the following effects:

- improvement of muscle tone, through the compression and relaxation of muscle fibres

- improvement in blood and lymph circulation, as the application of pressure causes the vessels to empty and fill
- increased activity of the sebaceous glands, due to the stimulation.

Movements include picking up, kneading, pinching and rolling

Uses in treatment: to stimulate a sluggish circulation; to increase sebaceous gland and suderiferous gland activity when treating a dry skin condition.

Percussion

Percussion, also known as **tapotement**, is performed in a brisk, stimulating manner. Rhythm is important as the fingers are continually breaking contact with the skin; irritation or damage can occur if this movement is performed incorrectly. Percussion has the following effects:

- a fast vascular (skin reddening) reaction because of the skin's nervous response to the stimulus – this reaction, erythema, is a sign of skin stimulation
- increased blood supply, which nourishes the tissues
- improvement in skin and muscle tone in the area.

Movements include hacking and tapping. When performed on the scalp, only light pressure should be used. In facial massage only light tapping should be used.

Uses in treatment: to tone areas of loose skin and improve circulation in the area.

Frictions

Frictions cause the skin and superficial structure to move together over the underlying structures. These movements are performed with either the fingers or the thumbs and concentrated in a particular area, applied with regulated pressure. Frictions have the following effects:

- gentle stimulation of the skin and superficial tissues
- improved lymphatic and blood circulation
- breaks down tight nodules (tension in the muscle fibres).

Uses in treatment: to help break down fatty deposits, fibrous thickening and the removal of non-medical oedema (fluid retention). To stimulate, and improve a dry skin condition.

Vibrations

Vibrations are applied on the nerve centre. They are produced by a rapid contraction and relaxation of the therapist's arm, resulting in a fine trembling movement. Vibration has the following effects:

- stimulation of the nerves, inducing a feeling of well-being
- gentle stimulation of the skin.

Movements include *static* vibrations, in which the pads of the fingers are placed on the nerve and the vibratory effect created by the therapist's arms and hands is applied in one position; and running vibrations, in which the vibratory effect is applied along a nerve path.

Uses in treatment: to stimulate a sensitive skin in order to improve the skin's functioning without irritating the surface blood capillaries.

Pressure point technique

Pressure point application is also incorporated into Indian head massage. It is based on the principles and practices of *Marma*. Pressure is applied to nerve junctions which stimulates vital energy points on the head, face and ears to improve circulation, relieve tiredness and induce relaxation. Marma pressure point technique also balances the body.

RECEPTION

Indian head massage can be carried out as required, but is usually recommended once or twice a week, and preferably as a course for maximum effect. Regularity of treatment will depend upon the client's personal circumstances including her financial position and time constraints. When a client is booking for this treatment, allow 45 minutes, which includes consultation, practical treatment and aftercare advice. The Indian head massage treatment itself should take 30 minutes. Warn the client that they may have a reaction after treatment. Symptoms can include sickness, tiredness, emotional anxiety and headaches. These contra-actions can be termed a *healing crisis*. This reaction will normally subside after 24 hours. If the client is wearing a false hair piece warn them that this will have to be removed.

> **TIP** ✔
>
> **Treatment timing**
> It is important to complete service in the given time. This will ensure that:
> - Each client receives a competent treatment meeting their treatment requirements.
> - Clients are not disadvantaged by receiving a hurried treatment.
> - A relaxing treatment environment in which clients are not made to feel anxious or stressed due to treatment delay is maintained.

CONTRA-INDICATIONS

Certain contra-indications preclude Indian head massage. These can be divided into three categories: general, local and temporary. **General** contra-indications affect the whole body or part of the body; **local** contra-indications are concentrated in a particular area; the symptoms of **temporary** contra-indications have only a short time span and clear up quite quickly. If the therapist has any concern over the client's health or well-being, medical advice should be sought prior to the treatment. A doctor's note should be obtained before treatment is carried out.

> **HEALTH AND SAFETY**
>
> **Pregnancy**
> It is best not to treat a client in the early stages of pregnancy, as the side effects may include feelings of nausea. This is a common symptom in the early stages of pregnancy and could cause a client to feel worse.

General	Local	Temporary
Heart conditions	Recent operations*	Medication
High or low blood pressure	Recent scar tissue (up to 6 months)*	Severe bruising*
Medication	Psoriasis or eczema*	Skin cuts and abrasions*
Diabetes	Skin disease	Pregnancy
Cancer	Skin disorder	Medical oedema
Rheumatism and arthritis (especially of the neck)	Recent injury*	Skin disease
Undiagnosed, lumps, bumps and swelling		Skin disorder
Loss of skin sensation		Intoxication
High temperature		Flu, cold symptoms
Migraine or severe headaches		
Disorders of the nervous system		

* Only apply if located in the area.

Check for contra-indications at the consultation, and if present do not proceed with the treatment.

EQUIPMENT LIST

stool/chair with adjustable height, low back without an arm rest

trolley or other surface on which to place everything

clean towels

paper tissue disposable bedroll

dry cotton wool and tissues

skin cleansing agent such as witch hazel or eau de cologne

organic massage oil

bowls or lined pedal bin for waste materials

comb

hair clip

cliient's record card

EQUIPMENT AND MATERIALS

Before beginning the massage, check that you have to hand the necessary equipment and materials.

- *Stool/chair* with adjustable height, low back without an arm rest
- *trolley* or other surface on which to place everything
- *clean towels* freshly laundered for each client
- *paper tissue disposable bedroll*
- *dry cotton wool* and *tissues*
- *skin cleansing agent* such as witch hazel or eau de cologne
- optional choice of *organic massage oil*, e.g. almond, mustard or coconut oil
- *bowls* or *lined pedal bin* – for waste materials
- *comb* – sanitised, to allow the client to comb her hair following treatment
- *hair clip* – used to secure long hair away from the neck area
- *client's record card.*

HEALTH AND SAFETY

Check that all products are clean and that the 'use by' date has not expired. Ensure all bottles are wiped over and lids are securely replaced after use to prevent spillage and the spread of bacteria.

Sterilisation and sanitisation

Prior to the massage treatment, make sure that the work area is hygienic. Clean towels and bedroll should be provided for each client to prevent cross-infection.

Preparing the treatment area

The treatment area should be clean and at a warm, comfortable working temperature for both the client and the therapist, between 18 and 21°C. Adequate ventilation should be provided to create a hygienic environment, preventing cross-infection through viral airborne spores, drowsiness through carbon dioxide-saturated air and the removal of stale smells and odours. The treatment area should induce relaxation and client comfort. Lighting should be soft, the colour of the decor should be subtle and non-gender biased. Sound levels should be low and selected for relaxation. Pillows or towels should be placed over the couch (covered with disposable paper roll). These support the client during treatment application to ensure client comfort. Place all the equipment and materials required on the trolley prior to the treatment.

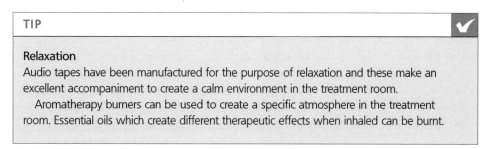

TIP	✔

Relaxation
Audio tapes have been manufactured for the purpose of relaxation and these make an excellent accompaniment to create a calm environment in the treatment room.
  Aromatherapy burners can be used to create a specific atmosphere in the treatment room. Essential oils which create different therapeutic effects when inhaled can be burnt.

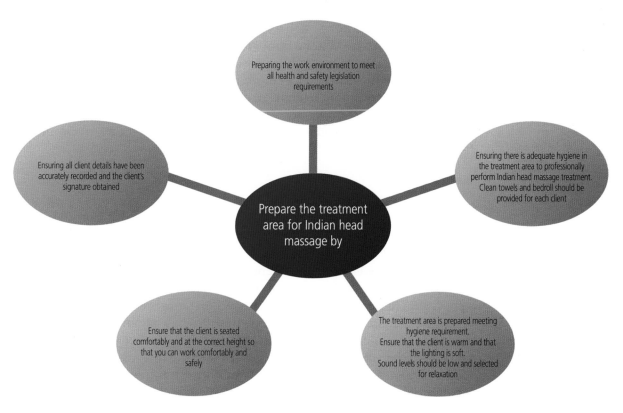

Preparing the work environment to meet all health and safety legislation requirements

Ensuring all client details have been accurately recorded and the client's signature obtained

Ensuring there is adequate hygiene in the treatment area to professionally perform Indian head massage treatment. Clean towels and bedroll should be provided for each client

Prepare the treatment area for Indian head massage by

Ensure that the client is seated comfortably and at the correct height so that you can work comfortably and safely

The treatment area is prepared meeting hygiene requirement. Ensure that the client is warm and that the lighting is soft. Sound levels should be low and selected for relaxation

Preparation of the therapist

The therapist should wear a professional work uniform which does not restrict movement. Full, enclosed shoes should be worn with low or medium-height heels. Optionally shoes may be removed when performing the massage to assist energy flow. Jewellery must be removed from the hands and wrists.

Before preparing the client for the treatment, wash your hands. The hands need to be flexible in order to fit the contour of the client's upper body. Shake the hands to remove any tension from the wrists and hands. Practice deep slow breathing technique before applying massage. This will help you to relax and focus your concentration on the massage treatment.

Collect the client's record card from reception prior to her arrival. A full client consultation should be carried out before the treatment commences.

PREPARATION OF THE CLIENT

Take the client through to the treatment area. The client may need to remove any outdoor clothing such as a coat or jacket. Footwear should be removed and the feet placed flat on the floor. Clients generally receive Indian head massage through their outdoor clothing, but bulky clothing which may restrict treatment application should be removed. Shirt or blouse collars should be loosened to allow access to the neck region. If oil is to be used for the massage, upper clothing should be removed and the client provided with a towel. Any jewellery in the area of massage application should be removed – this includes earrings, necklaces, bracelets and watches. Other accessories such as glasses should also be removed. False hairpieces will also need to be removed before treatment. If you are using screens, ensure that these are fully closed to maintain the client's privacy. This will enable the client to feel more comfortable and relaxed – essential if they are to gain treatment benefit. Seat the client on a stool or low-backed chair facing the treatment couch. If the client is in a wheelchair it may be possible to treat them whilst sitting in their chair, which means minimum disturbance to the client.

Client consultation

The therapist needs to obtain relevant details from the client before starting the Indian head massage treatment. The therapist must ensure that her communication skills make the client feel welcome and comfortable. The client should be at ease throughout the treatment and a good, professional rapport should be built between client and therapist. Personal details taken from the client are recorded on a record card. These should include medical history, doctor's details, and contra-indications that may be present. If in doubt as to the client's suitability for treatment the therapist should first obtain a letter of approval from the client's doctor. It is important to find out about the lifestyle habits of the client. These include:

Consult with the client for Indian head massage treatment to establish needs and expectations by

Taking the client to the treatment area. Outdoor clothing is removed

Bulky clothing which restricts treatment application should be removed. Shirt or blouse collars should be loosened to allow access to the neck region. The face may be cleansed to remove facial make-up if desired.

Maintaining client privacy at all times

The client should fully understand what the treatment involves, including possible post-treatment reactions

Recording personal details on the client record card: name, address, etc. Check that there are no contra-indications to Indian head massage treatment. Check for known allergies to products

Allow time and invite the client to ask questions before treatment commences

Ensuring through communication that the client feels comfortable and at ease at all times

Treatment objectives include:
– Relaxation
– Maintenance of health and well-being
– Stress relief
– Improved hair/scalp condition

Assessing the client's treatment requirements. Question the client on lifestyle and desired expectations and outcomes to ensure they gain treatment satisfaction

Looking for contra-indications: do not provide treatment if present. This prevents harm to the client, therapist or other clients, for example in the case of a contagious disease or disorder

Plan the treatment by

Discussing and advising the client on further suitable treatments and products

Preparing the client for the treatment considering the use of massage medium and the client's treatment requirements

Discussing how the treatment will be carried out to benefit the client

Ensuring all equipment is positioned to ensure that a safe, efficient treatment is carried out without unnecessary disruptions

Selecting suitable equipment and materials to meet the client's treatment needs

- *Occupation* – the client's occupation may be stressful or contribute to poor posture and muscle fatigue.

- *Family situation* – the client's domestic situation may affect their stress levels and limit their opportunities to take exercise or relax.

- *Dietary and fluid intake* – a nutritionally balanced diet is vital to the health of the body and the appearance of the skin. Lack of energy, skin allergies and disorders are, in part, the result of a poorly balanced diet. A healthy diet contains all the nutrients we need for health and growth. *Caffeine*, which is a stimulant, is found in tea, coffee and some fizzy drinks. Excessive amounts can interfere with digestion and block the absorption of vitamins and minerals. *Water* is important to avoid dehydration of the body and *at least* one litre of natural water should be drunk per day.

- *Alcohol* – alcohol is a toxin (poison) and deprives the body of vitamin reserves, especially vitamin B and C. It also causes dehydration.

- *Hobbies and interests* – these leisure activities can be a form of relaxation and method to alleviate stress.

- *Exercise taken and regularity* – a lack of exercise leads to poor lymph and blood circulation and poor muscle tone, resulting in slack contours and weight gain due to inactivity. Lack of exercise also results in lethargy.

- *Smoking habits* – smoking interferes with cell respiration and slows down the circulation. This makes it more difficult for nutrients to reach the skin cells and for waste products to be eliminated. The skin looks dull with a tendency towards open pores. Nicotine is a toxic substance.

- *Sleeping patterns* – disturbed sleeping patterns are often a result of raised stress levels. Disturbed sleep can result in exhaustion, fatigue, irritability and poor concentration.

Questioning the client on expectations and outcomes ensures that the client gains satisfaction from the treatment. Listen carefully to make sure you fully understand the client's treatment requirements. Indian head massage treatment should be adapted in application to meet the client's needs and physical characteristics obtained at the consultation.

TIP

Frame size
Look at the client's frame size: this will guide you on how to adapt your massage.
Small frame
If the client has a small frame avoid heavy pressure, especially over bony areas.
However, pressure must be firm if that is required.
Large frame
If the client has a large frame pressure will be firmer, especially over fatty areas.

With all clients, check their comfort with regard to the pressure you apply during the massage.

Once the consultation is complete, the therapist should ensure that all details are recorded accurately and that the client has signed her record card. This enables continuity of treatment and up-to-date tracking of the treatments received. An example of a typical record card is shown opposite.

BEAUTY WORKS

Date	Beauty therapist name	
Client name		Date of birth (identifying client age group)
Address		Postcode
Evening phone number	Day phone number	
Name of doctor	Doctor's address and phone number	
Related medical history (conditions that may restrict or prohibit treatment application)		
Are you taking any medication (this may affect the condition of the skin or skin sensitivity)		

CONTRA-INDICATIONS REQUIRING MEDICAL REFERRAL
(Preventing Indian head massage treatment application)

☐ bacterial infection e.g. impetigo
☐ viral infection e.g. herpes simplex
☐ fungal infection e.g. tine ungium
☐ skin disorders
☐ skin disease
☐ high or low blood pressure
☐ recent head and neck injury
☐ severe bruising
☐ severe cuts and abrasions
☐ hair disorders
☐ medical conditions
☐ recent scar tissue
☐ dysfunction of the nervous system
☐ epilepsy

TREATMENT AREAS

☐ scalp   ☐ head   ☐ face
☐ neck   ☐ shoulders ☐ upper back
☐ arms   ☐ hands   ☐ primary chakra areas

MASSAGE TECHNIQUE
☐ effleurage   ☐ petrissage
☐ tapotement   ☐ frictions
☐ vibrations   ☐ pressure points

LUBRICANT (IF USED)
organic oil – type [＿＿＿＿]   ☐ cream

CONTRA-INDICATIONS WHICH RESTRICT TREATMENT
(Treatment may require adaptation)

☐ cuts and abrasions   ☐ bruising and swelling
☐ recent injuries to the treatment area
☐ medication   ☐ mild eczema/psoriasis
☐ recent scar tissue (avoid area)
☐ undiagnosed lumps, bumps, swellings
☐ migraine   ☐ allergies

LIFESTYLE
occupation [＿＿＿＿＿＿]
family situation [＿＿＿＿＿＿]
dietary and fluid intake [＿＿＿＿＿＿]
(including allergies)
hobbies, interests, means of relaxation [＿＿＿＿]
exercise habits [＿＿＿＿＿＿]
smoking habits [＿＿＿＿＿＿]
sleep patterns [＿＿＿＿＿＿]

PHYSICAL CHARACTERISTICS
☐ weight   ☐ size
☐ muscle tone ☐ age

OBJECTIVES OF TREATMENT
☐ relaxation   ☐ maintenance of health and well-being
☐ improvement of hair and scalp condition

EQUIPMENT AND MATERIALS
☐ towels   ☐ comb
☐ spatulas   ☐ protective covering
☐ consumables ☐ hair clip
☐ stool

Beauty therapist signature (for reference)
Client signature (confirmation of details)

TREATMENT ADVICE

This information includes:
- What products have been used in the Indian head massage treatment as appropriate
- Advice on hair and scalp care
- Advice on products that would be suitable for the client to use at home
- Advice on how to gain maximum benefit from product use
- Postural advice
- Advice to follow immediately after the treatment, to include:
  - Possible reactions to the treatment and recommended action to take
  - Suitable rest period following treatment
  - General advice re food and drink intake
  - Avoidance of stimulants
- Contra-action advice, action to be taken in the event of an unwanted reaction (aching, tiredness, heightened emotional state)
- Recommendations for further Indian head massage treatments and the benefits of continuous treatments
- The recommended time interval between treatments

Allow time and invite the client to ask any questions before treatment commences. Be honest and concise in your answers. Confirm the objectives of the treatment. Remember to remove jewellery, spectacles and hair accessories. Ensure the client is seated comfortably: correct positioning opens up the central channel energy flow.

Before the Indian head massage is applied, the face may be cleansed to remove facial make-up.

After preparing the client, and before touching the skin, wash your hands again.

HEALTH AND SAFETY

Allergies
Refer to the record card to check for any known allergies to products, which could cause a contra-action i.e sesame oil can cause skin irritation, where possible select an alternative such as olive oil.

Selecting massage oil

Suitable massage oils

Organic oils are the most suitable oils when massaging the scalp. High in polyunsaturated fats, they are very soft and liquid at room temperature. They absorb easily through the skin, and have both an internal and external effect. Approximately 2–5 ml are required for the scalp massage, this will, of course, vary according to the length of the client's hair and condition of the scalp. The choice of oil depends on its texture, smell and specific properties. Popular oils are sesame, mustard, almond, olive and coconut.

Name		Use
Sesame oil		This oil is high in minerals which nourish the skin and hair. Sesame oil has a high lecithin content (a fat-like substance) thought to relieve swelling and muscular pains. Sesame oil may irritate sensitive skin and scalps.
Mustard oil		A strong-smelling oil which creates an intense heating, invigorating action. Popular for use in winter due to its warming action. The increase in body heat relieves pain, swellings and relaxes stiff muscles. The skins' pores open and a cleansing action is created. Not suitable on sensitive skin and scalps as it may cause irritation.
Almond oil		A light-textured oil, it is warm pressed and good to moisturise dry skin and hair as it is high in unsaturated fatty acids (essential fats derived from food), protein and vitamin A, B, D and E.
Olive Oil		Cold pressed from olives, it has a thick consistency high in unsaturated fatty acids, suitable for excessively dry hair and skin. It also creates a heating action which helps to relieve pain, swellings and relax stiff muscles.
Coconut oil		A medium to light oil with skin and hair moisturising properties; particularly suitable for dry, brittle, chemically-treated hair. Popular for use in summer as it induces a cooling action on the scalp.

Massage stance

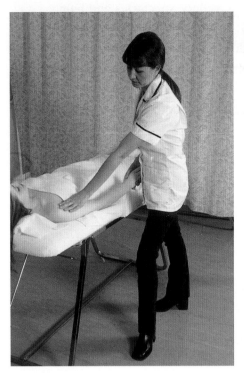 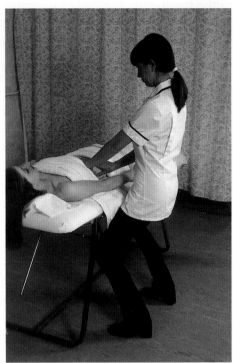

Walk standing   Stride standing

When performing the Indian head massage it is important to position yourself correctly. This will prevent pain and fatigue whilst working. Working positions are *walk standing* and *stride standing*.

Walk standing

The therapist stands with one foot in front of the other. This enables the therapist to work longitudinally (along the length) of the body.

Stride standing

The therapist works transversely (across) the body.

APPLICATION TECHNIQUE

The treatment commences by *grounding* or *levelling*, a technique to balance the bodies *chakras*. Chakras are non-physical energy centres, located about an inch away from the physical body, which cannot be seen. If energy levels become blocked due to stress negative energy becomes stored in the chakra and it becomes unbalanced. This can then result in physical or mental illness. An imbalance in one energy centre can affect others. Grounding is where the therapist and client begin to communicate, energy channels open, and healing begins.

Chakras

In ancient Eastern belief the body is said to have seven major chakra centres, each with a function, which all work together in balance with each other. Chakras have many associations including flower representation, differing in petal number depending upon the chakra. They are also associated with different colours and elements and these are listed below.

1   The **base** chakra, also known as root, associated colour red, element earth. Concerned with connection to earth, health and survival.

2   The **sacral** chakra, associated colour orange, element water. Concerned with relationships, especially sexual relationships.

3   The **solar plexus** chakra, associated colour yellow, element fire. Concerned with personal harmony and energy.

4   The **heart** chakra, associated colour green, element air. Concerned with empathy with others.

5   The **throat** chakra, associated colour blue, element sound or ether. Concerned with communication and expression.

6   The **brow** chakra, associated colour indigo, element light. Concerned with inner vision.

7   The **crown** chakra, associated colour white, element spirit. Concerned with imagination and thought.

TIP	

Massage and chakras
When working on a chakra you may feel heat or cold in your hands from the energy channels opened.

Seven principle chakras

In Indian head massage we are concerned with restoring balance of the higher chakras: the throat, brow and crown.

At the end of the treatment the therapist may sometimes feel tired. Through energy channels created during massage, energy may have been taken from the therapist to the client.

Grounding or levelling

1 With both feet placed firmly on the floor, place the hands on the client's shoulders. Ask the client to close their eyes and relax. At this point outside energies pass through your body to the client.

2 Place your hands on the client's scalp on the crown area.

3 Then place the hands, one on the forehead and one on the occiput, hold this position for two minutes.

4 Rest your forearms on the client's shoulders – ask the client to breathe in and then breathe out. This will cause the client to relax and feel calmer. As the client breathes out apply gentle pressure with your forearms onto the client's shoulders.

If oil is to be used when performing the scalp massage this is applied now, selected according to the treatment effect required. The hair is gently parted and oil is applied to the partings.

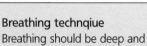

> **TIP** ✔
>
> **Breathing technqiue**
> Breathing should be deep and slow, not shallow and rapid. Encourage the client to breathe in slowly through the nose – the stomach should move out slightly – and out through the mouth.

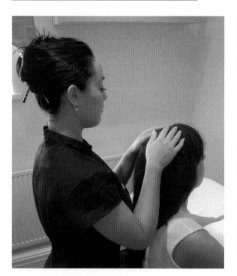

Hands placed on client's crown area of scalp

Hand placed on client's forehead and occiput

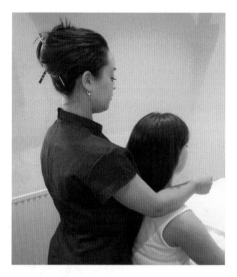

Resting forearms on client's shoulders

> **TIP** ✔
>
> **Long hair**
> If the client has long hair it may be necessary to secure it with a clip whilst performing massage to the neck, shoulder and back.

Shoulder and back

5 Ask the client to place her head forwards supported by pillows or towels.

6 Frictions are applied over the tops of the shoulder area, small circular movements are applied with the thumbs to the muscle fibres of the trapezius.

7 Kneading is applied to the shoulder and back, the heels of the hand apply pressure gently in a rotary movement along the trapezius and either side of the spine.

8 Picking up is applied along the trapezius; the muscle is lifted and gently squeezed using the whole hand.

9 Hacking is applied across the top of the shoulders.

10 Lurching is applied down either side if the spine. The hands are placed flat on the shoulders and then swiftly drawn down the body, either side of the spine, flicking off the body at the base of the spine.

TIP ✓

Checking body language for effectiveness
The client posture should become more relaxed during treatment application. The shoulders should drop and breathing should become deeper allowing energy to flow more freely through the body.

Encourage the client to relax if they appear stiff.

Frictions to the tops of the shoulders

Kneading to shoulders

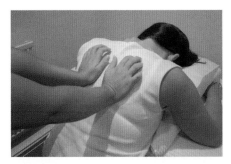

Kneading to either side of spine

Picking up to trapezius

Hacking to top of shoulders

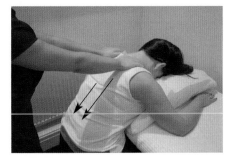

Lurching down either side of spine

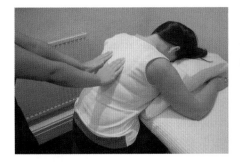

Lurching

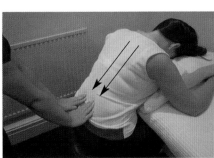

Lurching

Neck

11 Pick up the muscle and skin at the back of the neck. Gently lift the tissue with each hand alternately.

12 Apply frictions under the occiput. Using both thumbs apply gentle pressure in a circular movement.

13 Apply petrissage under the occiput. Using the heel of one hand, apply a gentle circular pressure.

14 Apply pressure points with both thumbs in a triangular movement under the occiput.

Petrissage under the occiput

Pressure points using thumbs under the occiput

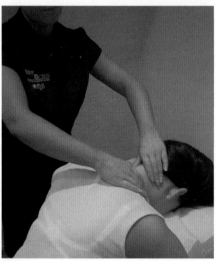

Picking up to the neck

Arms

15 Ask the client to slowly lift her head.

16 Place your hands flat on the upper shoulders. Swiftly draw the hands down the length of the upper arm and flick off hands at the client's elbow.

17 Knead the upper arm.

18 Place your hands firmly on the upper arms. Ask the client to fold her arms in front of her, ask her to breathe in deeply, gently apply a lifting pressure as she does this. Ask the client to breathe out, remove your hands from their supporting position and the client's body will gently drop.

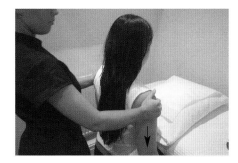

Hands drawn swiftly down the length of the upper arm and removed at the elbow

Kneading to the upper arm

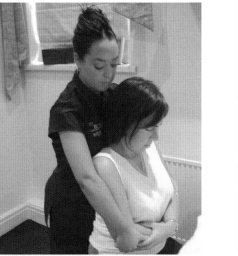

Client's arms folded, breathing in

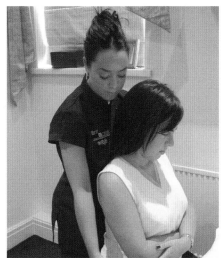

Client breathing out, arms have relaxed and dropped slightly

Scalp

19 Apply effleurage strokes to the scalp. Place each hand alternately on the hair line and stroke hand upwards, covering the whole scalp.

20 Apply frictions to the scalp – using the pads of the fingers apply small circular movements.

21 Apply finger stroking, place the fingertips on the hairline and draw them in a combing action through the hair.

22 Apply vibrations: gently grasp the hair and pull in a vibrating manner.

23 Apply hacking using both hands to cover both sides of the head.

24 Using flat hands, place one hand on the forehead and the other over the occipital bone and gently lift the head. Move the hands, place one hand over the corner of the forehead the other over the corner of the back of the skull and lift. Repeat on remaining corners of the head.

25 Stroke over the forehead using alternate hands.

26 Finally, apply effleurage to the scalp.

Wash your hands following scalp massage

Frictions to the scalp

Finger stroking through the hair

Vibrations

Gentle lifting of the head

Pressure points

Place a folded or rolled towel behind the client's head and ask the client to lean their head against your body.

27 Apply pressure points: using the index and middle finger apply firm pressure upwards from the top of the nose to the forehead.

28 Apply pressure points along the zygomatic (cheek) bone.

29 Gently pinch the length of both eyebrows simultaneously, using the finger and thumb of each hand.

30 Gently hold the tip of each ear using the finger pads and simultaneously apply a pinching and rolling movement to cover the outside of each ear.

31 Using the pads of the fingers apply a light tapping movement to cover the face.

32 Apply circular pressure to the temples simultaneously using the fingertips.

33 Finally, place the hands, one on the forehead and one on the occiput, and hold this position briefly. This will indicate to the client that the massage has finished.

34 Wash your hands.

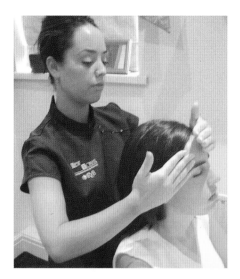
Stroking to the forehead

Pressure points to the zygomatic (cheek) bone

Pinching along the eyebrow

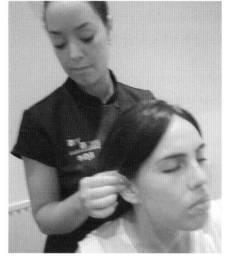
Pinching and rolling to the outer ear

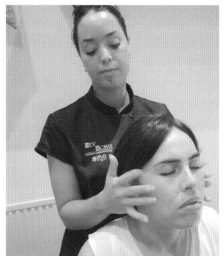
Tapping to cover the face

Circular pressure to the temples

Adapting the massage

Relaxing massage: avoid stimulating movements and incorporate more effleurage, light petrissage movements. Pressure should be firm and rhythm slower.

Tight or contracted muscles: avoid excessive use of percussion movements. Slow, rhythmical movements should be used to stretch the muscles.

Slack muscles: stimulating percussion massage movements should be used to help to tone and firm the area being treated.

Massage for excess weight: incorporate stimulating movements over fatty areas, to help mobilise adipose (fatty) tissue.

Massage for males: muscle bulk tends to be larger and firmer. The skin is thicker and generally there is less fatty tissue. The massage usually needs to be firmer.

Hands placed on forehead and occiput to conclude massage

> **TIP**
>
> **Faults during massage**
> - Incorrect pressure applied. If it is too light or too heavy the client will not feel the benefits.
> - Avoid placing excessive pressure on top of the client's head: this can cause discomfort to the head and neck.
> - Inconsistent massage movements will not relax the client and the massage will not flow.
> - Ensure the client is appropriately positioned. This prevents discomfort to yourself and the client.

CONTRA-ACTIONS

These might include:

- Sickness, caused by increased circulation of waste products transported in the lymphatic system. This is often termed a 'healing crisis'.
- Fainting caused by dilation of the blood capillaries, altering blood pressure levels.
- Tiredness caused by release of toxins and increased energy channels.
- Skin reactions, such as an allergy to the massage oil.
- Heightened emotional state including tearfulness.
- Flu-like symptoms, including raised temperature.
- Aching muscles, caused by the release of toxins.

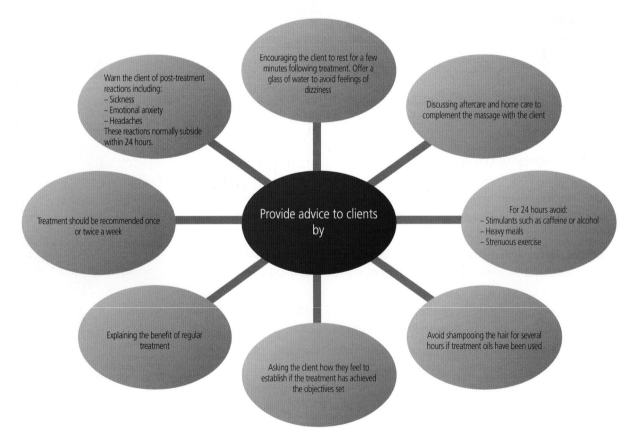

If the client suffers any contra-action, you must assist the client before letting her leave the salon:

- Ensure the client can breathe properly and that the room is well ventilated.
- Offer the client a glass of water if she feels sick.
- Apply a cold compress if a skin reaction occurs.
- Advise the client to seek medical advice if the symptoms persist.

You should complete the client's record card fully so that continuation of the treatment can be tracked and any adverse reactions noted for future reference.

AFTERCARE AND ADVICE

Before the client gets up, encourage her to rest for a few minutes to allow the blood circulation to return to normal. A deep relaxation massage can leave the client feeling light-headed. Sudden movement may result in a light-headed feeling as the brain is temporarily starved of blood; she may even faint.

As the client's circulation returns to normal, the blood vessels will constrict.

Whilst resting, use the time to discuss with the client suitable aftercare and homecare to complement the massage. The client will probably feel extremely relaxed at this point.

If the massage was for relaxation, you might give advice on relaxing bath products and massage techniques that could be used at home. Recommend the client increases her water intake to help detoxification and encourage good eating habits.

Provide hair and scalp care advice, including the avoidance of excessive chemical hair treatments, the importance of hair protection when exposed to UV, and the application of specialised hair/scalp treatment products.

For the following 24 hours avoid:

- stimulants such as caffeine or alcohol
- heavy or highly spiced meals
- strenuous exercise.

For several hours:

- avoid shampooing the hair, especially if treatment oils have been used to maximise treatment effects.

Ask the client how they feel to establish if the treatment has achieved the outcome agreed at consultation. Explain the benefits of regular treatment to achieve maximum benefit.

HEALTH AND SAFETY

It is a good idea to offer the client a glass of water following treatment and to allow a suitable rest period to avoid feelings of dizziness.

ACTIVITY

As part of the client's home care programme, simple massage techniques could be taught.
Think of three simple self-massage techniques that the client could use at home.

Assessment of knowledge and understanding

You have now learnt about the effects of Indian head massage and how to adapt your technique to meet the client's treatment requirements. These skills will enable you to provide Indian head massage treatment.

To test your level of knowledge and understanding, answer the following short questions. These will prepare you for your summative (final) assessment.

Anatomy and physiology questions required for this unit are found on pages 146–50.

Consult with the client

1 How should the client be greeted for treatment? Why is this important?

2 To perform an effective consultation you need the client to feel confident about providing you with positive, honest answers to your questions. You should have good:
   a. communication skills
   b. questioning techniques
   c. listening skills
   d. answering techniques.
   Give examples of what you understand by good skills and techniques for each of the above.

3 What details are required on your client's record card?

4 Why is it important to discuss the client's lifestyle?

5 Name three contra-indications identified at the consultation which would prevent treatment being carried out.

6 Name three contra-indications that may restrict treatment application.

7 Give four physiological/psychological benefits that the client can expect from the treatment.

8 When would you need to refer a client to their General Practitioner before treatment could be given?

Plan the treatment

1 What is the purpose of a treatment plan?

2 How long should be allowed to perform an Indian head massage treatment?

3 How should the client be prepared prior to treatment?

4 How can the massage treatment be adapted to achieve different treatment effects?

Prepare for the treatment

1 How should the treatment environment be prepared to ensure client comfort and maximum benefit from the treatment? Consider temperature, lighting, colour, smells and sound.

2 What is the importance of self-preparation when delivering Indian head massage?

3 How should the client be positioned to gain maximum benefit from the Indian head massage treatment?

4 How should the client be prepared to receive Indian head massage?

5 Oils may be used as a massage medium for Indian head massage. Name four oils that you could use for Indian head massage, giving a brief description of each.

Carry out Indian head massage treatment

1 Name the main massage techniques performed with Indian head massage and their effect.

2 Name the three primary chakra areas treated when performing Indian head massage.

3 How can cross-infection be avoided when carrying out Indian head massage treatment?

4 How should the client be advised to breathe to induce relaxation?

5 What should be checked with the client during treatment application?

6 Why is it important to observe body language during treatment?

7 What should be offered to the client at conclusion of treatment?

8 What is the suitable rest period following Indian head massage? Why is this necessary?

Provide aftercare advice to the client

1 Why is it important to gain feedback from the client and give relevant advice to her following treatment?

2 What is a healing crisis? What reactions should you advise the client she may experience from a healing crisis?

3 Why is it important to record any contra-action either during or following treatment on the client record card?

4 After the Indian head massage the client should be given advice to follow to ensure that she gains maximum benefit from the treatment. Discuss the advice to be given.

5 What recommendations to lifestyle habits would enable her to continue the benefits from the treatment?

6 How often would you recommend a client receive Indian head massage treatment?

chapter 10

BT21 Provide massage using pre-blended aromatherapy oils

> ### Learning objectives
>
> This unit describes how to provide and adapt massage using pre-blended aromatherapy oils to meet the client's requirements. It also discusses how essential oils are selected and blended to meet the needs of your client.
>
> It describes the competencies to enable you to:
>
> - **consult with the client**
> - **plan the treatment**
> - **prepare for the treatment**
> - **massage client head and body using suitable massage techniques**
> - **complete the treatment**
>
> When providing massage using pre blended aromatherapy oils it is important to use the skills you have learned in the following core mandatory units:
>
> **Unit G1** ensure your own actions reduce risks to health and safety
> **Unit G6** promote additional products or services to your clients
> **Unit G11** contribute to the financial effectiveness of the business

INTRODUCTION

Aromatherapy could be defined as the use of aromas (or smells) for their healing qualities. Essential oils are used to bring about a feeling of well-being. The oils may be used in a number of ways including massage, inhalation, compresses and air sprays. Aromatherapy has been used for thousands of years by people from many different cultures across the world. In Babylon, essential oils were used to perfume building materials for temples. Egyptians used oils for cleansing and embalming. Essential oils and the use of aromatic substances are mentioned in many historical texts and scriptures which allows their historical uses to be dated with some accuracy, some as early as 2000 BC.

In today's fast-paced society, stress is a major contributory factor in many diseases and disorders such as heart disease, high blood pressure and tension, and many people are looking to alternative methods to help them to achieve a better quality of life. The beauty therapist plays a major role here – using essential oils and massage to help reduce the symptoms of modern day living. Aromatherapists can be found working in a variety of environments including doctors' surgeries, hospitals, beauty salons and alternative therapy clinics.

ESSENTIAL OILS

Essential oils are the aromatic substances used in aromatherapy. They have an infinite range of aromas and also come in a variety of colours including yellow, green, brown, blue and red. Being extracted from the many parts of plants, including flowers, seeds, roots, fruits and bark, these organic compounds have a multitude of uses.

Essential oils are made up largely of three elements: **carbon**, **hydrogen** and **oxygen**. The molecular structure of essential oils is relatively small, and this explains why they are able to penetrate the skin and enter the bloodstream. Their fat solubility also helps them to penetrate more easily. Although the individual components of an oil are relatively simple in structure, an oil can be made up of hundreds of components, some of them being present in very small amounts. It may be these trace components of a natural oil which have the therapeutic effect; these may not be present in a synthetic oil, which is why chemically reproduced or synthetic oils may have the same smell as the natural oil but not the same therapeutic properties. It is also said that naturally occurring oils have a 'life force' that cannot chemically be reproduced.

Ellisons

Essential oils and carrier oils

Essential oils have only a simple molecular structure, yet the active constituents which make up each oil are complex. The complexity of these active constituents gives the oils their own distinctive aromas and therapeutic qualities. The active constituents work **synergistically**, that is, they are more powerful when combined than if each were used separately.

Essential oils are not only used in aromatherapy, in fact of all the essential oils produced commercially, only a tiny percentage is actually used by aromatherapists. The majority of the oils are used in food flavourings, with the remainder being used in perfumes and the pharmaceutical industry.

Properties of essential oils

All essential oils have the same basic properties that identify them as an essential oil. These are that they:

- do not mix with water
- mix with alcohol

- mix with mineral oil
- mix with vegetable oil
- evaporate
- have an aroma
- are not greasy.

All essential oils are volatile, but their evaporation rates vary. These evaporation rates can be used to group certain types of essential oils together. Oils with rapid evaporation rates are known as **top notes**. Oils with moderate evaporation rates are known as **middle notes** and those with very slow rates of evaporation are known as **base notes**.

Top notes

Top notes have the highest evaporation rates of all essential oils. They last on the skin for about 24 hours, and are absorbed into the skin very quickly. They commonly have a very sharp aroma and a stimulating effect. Examples of top notes are citrus oils like orange, lemon and grapefruit, and herb oils such as peppermint and clary sage.

Middle notes

Middle notes evaporate moderately quickly, and last for about two to three days on the skin. Once applied, they are absorbed into the skin moderately quickly. Middle notes are generally produced from herbs, having a recognisable herby aroma. Their effect is generally therapeutic. Examples of middle notes are lavender, camomile and geranium.

Base notes

Base notes have the slowest evaporation rate of all essential oils. Lasting for about seven days, they are absorbed slowly into the skin, taking up to 100 minutes to be fully absorbed. Base notes tend to be produced from gums and resins, and have a rich, heavy aroma with relaxing, sedating effects. Examples of base notes are sandalwood, rose and jasmine.

Classification of essential oils

Top note	Middle note	Base note
Clary sage	Camomile Roman	Neroli
Eucalyptus	Geranium	Rose bulgar
Grapefruit	Lavender	Ylang-ylang
Lemon	Marjoram	
Lemongrass	Rosemary	
Tea tree		

ACTIVITY

Put a few drops of a base essential oil on a piece of blotting paper and place in a cupboard. Go back each day to see if the oil still has an aroma. How many days did the base oil keep its aroma?

TIP

Never buy oils from a supplier who charges the same price for every oil. The yield of essential oil when extracted from its source will be reflected in the price of the oil.

Storage of essential oils

Essential oils can be spoiled if incorrectly stored, and this can lead to evaporation which causes loss of therapeutic properties, fragrance and colour. The ideal storage conditions for essential oils would be a cool, dark place, away from sunlight. The storage container should be airtight and made of dark-coloured glass. Bottles should be well labelled to avoid misuse and pure, unblended essential oils should be fitted with a dropper cap for careful measuring during blending.

Purchasing essential oils

To avoid waste, essential oils should not be purchased in bulk unless they are to be used often. Large quantities of oil should be divided into small bottles because the air in a part-used bottle can oxidise very quickly – particularly with citrus oils. Do not use plastic bottles as these are permeable to essential oils. Some essential oils have a shorter shelf-life than others. Citrus oils tend to lose their therapeutic properties quite quickly but may still be used for their aroma, for example as a room freshener.

HEALTH AND SAFETY

As polythene is basically a solid oil, essential oils can escape from polythene bottles!

Essential oils should always be purchased from a reputable supplier who has a quick turnaround of stock; this way you can be relatively confident that the essential oil has not been left on a shelf for many months before purchasing. A good supplier of essential oils will be able to show you a gas–liquid chromatogram. This identifies the components of an essential oil on a percentage basis and is used to clarify its purity. The gas liquid chromatograms are carried out by independent bodies such as agricultural laboratories and the results of the tests will carry their stamp to show validity.

Extraction of essential oils

There are a number of different ways to extract essential oils from plants. The yield of essential oil per tonne of plant material reflects the price of the oil. For example, it takes 5 tonnes of rose-flower petals to produce 1 kilogram of rose oil; it is therefore very expensive to produce. Many kilograms of lemon oil may be obtained from 1 tonne of lemon rind, making lemon oil relatively inexpensive.

Essential oils can be extracted from different parts of the plant, such as flowers, leaves and stems:

- Lavender, ylang-ylang, rose, camomile and jasmine essential oils are all extracted from the flowers of the plants.
- Sandalwood and cedarwood essential oils are extracted from the woody parts of the plants.
- Frankincense essential oil is extracted from a gum which is present in the plant.
- Rosemary, clary sage and thyme essential oils are all extracted from the leaves of the plants.
- Lemon, bergamot, orange and grapefruit essential oils are extracted from the rind of the fruits.

Methods of extracting essential oils include: distillation, enfleurage, comminution, maceration, solvent extraction and expression.

Distillation

Steam distillation is the most common method of extraction of essential oils from plants. The process involves heating the plant material with steam. The steam evaporates out the essential oil and a condenser turns the vapour to a liquid made up of essential oil and water. The essential oil floats on the surface of the water and is then siphoned off. The water that is left is known as **flower water**. Oils produced by distillation include rose, lavender and ylang-ylang.

Water distillation involves heating the plant material in water to boiling point then condensing the steam. Essential oils are extracted in this way from hard seeds, fruits and woods which have been thoroughly chopped

Enfleurage

Enfleurage is a method that is now largely outdated. It involves the use of cold fat and is used for flowers which continue to produce essential oils after they have been picked. Fatty substances can easily absorb essential oils and the fat which is used in this process is pure and odourless. A thin layer of the fat is spread on a glass frame and the fresh flowers are put in layers on top of this. The essential oils are absorbed into the fat. Periodically, the dead flowers are taken off and new flowers are re-spread on the fat. At this stage the fat and essential oil mixture is known as a **pomade**. When the fat has become saturated with essential oils (i.e. has absorbed the maximum amount) it is washed in alcohol and the essential oils pass into the alcohol. The pomade and alcohol mixture is known as an **absolute**. The alcohol is then evaporated, leaving pure essential oil. Enfleurage is used to extract essential oils from delicate flowers that cannot be heated, e.g. jasmine.

Comminution

During this method, the whole fruit is liquidised for 'whole fruit' drinks and left to stand. The oil rises to the top and is skimmed off.

Maceration

Maceration is a method whereby essential oils are extracted from plants by dipping them into hot fat. The process is repeated with fresh flowers until the fat is saturated. It is then washed in alcohol, which evaporates, leaving pure essential oil. The type of plants used in this method are those which do not produce essential oils after they have been harvested. This method is rarely used today to produce pure essential oil but is used to produce infused oils.

Solvent extraction

During solvent extraction, plants are covered with a solvent such as ether, benzene, petroleum or acetone and then heated gradually until the solvent extracts the essential oils from the plant. After filtration, the dark paste or

---

ACTIVITY

Dig your finger nail into the peel of a ripe orange. You will be able to smell the essential oil being released.

'concrete' is mixed with alcohol and cooled. The essential oil dissolves in the alcohol which then evaporates, leaving the essential oils. Gums and resins which are dissolved in acetone, produce resinoids. Flowers which are dissolved in ether, benzene or petroleum, produce an absolute.

Expression

Expression is the most common method of extraction used to obtain citrus oils such as lemon and orange essential oil. Machines are used to crush, grate or express the essential oil from the rind of the fruit.

Methods of entry of essential oils into the body

Essential oils enter the body via four basic routes: the skin, the lungs, the olfactory system and the digestive system.

Skin

Essential oils penetrate the skin when they are applied via massage. The warmth and pressure of the hands during massage speeds up the penetration of the essential oils, which may take up to 100 minutes. The most likely places of entry are sebaceous glands, sudoriferous glands and hair follicles. The lipophilic (fat-loving) nature of essential oils allows penetration between the cells via the lipid or glue that holds cells together, and even through the lipid component of cell membranes.

Some areas of the skin are more permeable than others – the palms of the hands, soles of the feet, forehead, forearms and scalp are more permeable than the abdomen, legs and trunk. Essential oils penetrate to the dermis where they then pass through the capillary walls into the bloodstream. The blood then transports the essential oils all around the body which may take only about 28 seconds! Other substances with a small molecular structure that can be absorbed through the skin to the dermis include hormones, vitamins and certain types of drugs. Carrier oils, like acids, alkalis and alcohols, can only penetrate to the epidermis as their molecular structure is too large to allow them to penetrate further.

Lungs

Essential oils, being volatile substances, penetrate the lungs when they are inhaled. They pass through the lining of the lung tissue, through the capillary walls and into the bloodstream where they are then transported around the body.

Olfactory system

The olfactory system is located high up inside the nose and is responsible for the sense of smell. When we smell something, the nerve endings in the olfactory system are stimulated and relay messages to the brain, which then causes the body to respond. For example, the smell of freshly baked bread may cause a person to salivate. The smell of a particular substance may also trigger certain memories or emotions associated with a particular smell:

ACTIVITY

Smell an open bottle of lemon oil. Immediately you will begin to salivate more. This is the olfactory system in action!

- The primary olfactory cortex and higher olfactory areas in the brain are responsible for recognising what we have smelled and associating it with other information. For example, lavender oil may remind you of a favourite aunt who wears a lavender fragrance.
- The limbic system activates instinctual behaviour and emotion. For example, smelling grapefruit oil may cause you to salivate and desire food.

The volatile essential oils penetrate the olfactory system when they are inhaled through the nose. The olfactory surface (the ends of the olfactory nerves) is coated with a very thin layer of mucus. The essential oils pass through the mucous membranes and fatty tissues, where they bond temporarily to register their odour and stimulate the olfactory nerves. If the mucous membranes are blocked, for example during the common cold, substances have difficulty passing through and we therefore find it difficult to identify different smells. An illustration of the olfactory system and associated nerves can be found on page 105.

Digestive system

HEALTH AND SAFETY

Due to the toxic nature of some essential oils, all essential oils should be stored out of the reach of children.

Essential oils pass into the digestive system when they are taken orally. Clients should be warned against using this method as essential oils have a high risk of toxicity and irritation of the delicate membranes lining the digestive system.

Elimination of essential oils

Although essential oils may stay in the body for some time, especially in the deeper organs, eventually they are eliminated from the body in several ways. The skin helps with elimination through perspiration. Essential oils (garlic, for example) are eliminated in the breath during exhalation and traces of essential oils may also be found in the urine.

Physiological effects of essential oils

Essential oils can affect the body physiologically in a number of ways:

- The cardiovascular system can be stimulated by rosemary, eucalyptus and black pepper, resulting in increased local circulation.
- Camphor can raise the body temperature, while camomile can help to lower it.
- Blood pressure can be decreased by lavender and heart rate can be stimulated by camphor.
- Most oils have an antibacterial effect.
- Phagocytosis is stimulated by camomile, lemon and thyme.
- Fennel, peppermint, rose and clary sage have an antispasmodic effect on the respiratory system, which helps to lessen muscle spasms.
- An expectorant effect can be produced by eucalyptus, lemon and benzoin.
- Lavender, rosemary, sandalwood and rose have an antispasmodic effect on the digestive system, while marjoram and rosemary have a laxative effect.
- The pH of gastric juices can be raised by clove oil.

- Lemon, fennel, cinnamon and cardamom have a stimulating effect on the nervous system, while melissa, lavender, sandalwood and ylang-ylang have a sedative effect.
- Peppermint has an analgesic effect.
- Juniper, sandalwood, fennel and rosemary all have diuretic properties.
- Jasmine, ylang-ylang and rose are said to have an aphrodisiac effect.
- Aniseed, garlic and fennel oil stimulate oestrogen production.

Essential oils

Name of oil and plant/s of origin	Details
Camomile *Chamaemelum noblie Matricaria recutita Ormenis mixta* 	Camomile has three sources: Roman camomile (*Chamaemelum nobile*) – yellow/brown; German camomile (*Matricaria recutita*) – deep blue; Moroccan camomile (*Ormenis mixta*) – yellow. German camomile essential oil is distilled from the flowers and seeds of the camomile plant – a small daisy-like flower with feathery green leaves. Roman camomile is distilled from the flowers only. Grown commercially in Europe, North Africa and Asia, this middle note essential oil is best known for its calming and anti-inflammatory properties. The oil has a sweet smell and is ideal to use in massage blends for clients suffering from tension and stress. Due to its high azulene content, German camomile turns blue in colour during distillation. Azulene is a fatty substance responsible for the soothing, anti-inflammatory effect of camomile.
Clary sage *Salvia sclarea* 	Clary sage is a top note and comes from a plant with broad, wrinkled, green/purple/blue flowers similar to common sage. This herb is grown commercially in France and Russia and the essential oil is obtained by distillation from the flowers. Its sedative properties make clary sage the ideal choice for clients who have difficulty relaxing. Clary sage may induce feelings of euphoria and should be used with care.

HEALTH AND SAFETY

Clients should not drink alcohol before or after treatment with clary sage as its enhancing effect on alcohol may produce unpleasant side effects.

Eucalyptus *Eucalyptus globulus* 	Eucalyptus is a tall tree with whitish, papery bark and long, pointed leaves. A native plant of Australia and Tasmania, the leaves of the eucalyptus are distilled to obtain the essential oil. It is a good antiseptic and expectorant and is effective for colds, catarrh, flu and sinus problems. Eucalyptus is a top note and is good to use in blends for clients with oily skin.

HEALTH AND SAFETY

Essential oils are flammable. Never leave used towels, bedlinen or tissues near a heat source as they pose a fire hazard.

Geranium *Pelargonium odoratissimum Pelargonium robertianum* 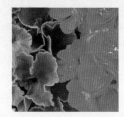	The geranium plant comes in a variety of shapes and sizes, but in its most recognisable form it is about 2 feet high with pink and red flowers. The leaves of this plant are distilled to produce the sweet, floral, middle note essential oil. Geranium has sedative and antiseptic qualities and is often used in skin-care preparations. It also has an uplifting, antidepressant effect and is ideal for use with clients suffering from stress or those who want an uplifting massage. Geranium is grown commercially in Africa, southern France and Spain.

Essential oils (continued)

Name of oil and plant/s of origin	Details
Lavender *Lavandula* *officinalis* 	Lavender is the most widely used and versatile of all essential oils. Distilled from the lavender plant, a bush with green-blue leaves and lavender/blue flowers, this essential oil has a multitude of uses and effects. It is an excellent antiseptic and in emergencies can be used undiluted on the skin for bites and stings, etc. Lavender is an oil that will enhance the effect of other oils that are blended with it. It has a balancing and harmonising effect on the body and is therefore useful for all kinds of conditions. The oil is distilled from the flowers, which are grown in southern Europe and many other parts of the world.
Lemon *Citrus limon* 	Lemons grow on a small tree that has dark-green, shiny leaves and produces white flowers before the fruit. Lemon is a stimulating top note, expressed from the skin of the fruit. Grown in northern India, Europe, California and Australia, this inexpensive essential oil has a sharp, tangy, distinctive aroma. Lemon has strong antiseptic and antibacterial properties, and has an invigorating effect. It is ideal in blends designed to uplift clients or for those with oily or acnefied skin types.
Lemongrass *Cymbopogon* *citratus* 	This top note has a sharp, lemon-scented aroma and is extracted from the grass itself. Grown in Brazil, Sri Lanka, USA and China, it has a deep yellow colour. The plant is a common ingredient in oriental cooking. Lemongrass has sedative, antiseptic, anti-fungal and insect-repelling properties. It is often used as a general tonic to stimulate the circulation in cellulite conditions.
Marjoram *Origanum* *majorana* 	Marjoram oil is extracted from the leaves of the plant. It is pale yellow in colour and is grown commercially in Europe and Egypt. Its calming, relaxing and sedative properties make it useful in blends for rheumatism and arthritis.
Neroli *Citrus* *aurantium* 	Neroli oil is obtained from the flowers of the bitter orange tree and is an ingredient of eau de cologne. It is useful in blends for insomnia, stress, muscular tension and nervousness, and is soothing for dry, sensitive skin. The rejuvenating properties of neroli make it a popular choice for blends used on stretch marks and scars.
Rose Rosa damascena Rosa centifolia 	The rose is a well-known, beautiful, scented flower with numerous white to red petals on a thorny stem. The plant is grown all over the world, but most commercially grown roses come from Bulgaria, France and North Africa. The flowers are used in the steam distillation process to produce rose essential oil. A base note, rose's many properties include antidepressant, antiseptic, aphrodisiac, astringent and sedative. It is useful in massage blends needed to relax clients and for those with dry or mature skin types.
Rosemary *Rosmarinus* *officinalis* 	Rosemary is a top note essential oil with a camphorous aroma that is distilled from the plant and its roots. A shrub with needle-like leaves and pale blue flowers, Rosemary is grown in southern Europe, northern Africa and the Mediterranean. Its rubefacient and stimulating properties make it a good oil for use in massage prior to exercise. Its astringent properties also make it useful for clients with oily skin.
Sandalwood Santalum album 	Sandalwood essential oil is obtained by distillation from the wood of the small, evergreen sandalwood tree that is grown commercially in India and Australia. Sandalwood is particularly useful when treating male clients as it has a masculine fragrance. It is a base note with relaxing and antiseptic properties and is also said to be a strong aphrodisiac. Sandalwood is beneficial to dry and dehydrated skins.

Essential oils (continued)

Name of oil and plant/s of origin		Details
Tea tree *Melaleuca alternifolia*		The tea tree plant is a native of Australia and is a small tree with frond-like leaves. It has very good anti-fungal, anti-viral, antibacterial and antiseptic properties due to its high terpene content, making it invaluable for many kinds of problems. Like lavender, tea tree may be used directly on the skin with safety in emergencies. This essential oil is distilled from the leaves of the plant and is a top note.
Ylang-ylang *Cananga odorata*		The ylang-ylang is a tree that grows to about 50 feet tall and produces yellow flowers, from which the essential oil is distilled. A base note oil is produced that has a very rich, sweet, floral fragrance. Native to Indonesia and the Philippines, ylang-ylang has sedative, calming properties which make it an ideal choice for insomnia. It is also reputed to be an excellent aphrodisiac.

Essential oil safety

The use of essential oils on the skin may present a potential hazard to both the client and the therapist if not used correctly. There is a particular risk if essential oils are used undiluted. These risks include toxicity, irritation and sensitisation.

- **Toxicity** is often termed 'poisoning'. If an oil is toxic, it means that at a certain level it becomes fatal whether taken orally or applied to the skin. Toxicity is dose-dependant and varies according to the size of the person concerned. Babies and children should be exposed to a much lower percentage of essential oils per carrier oil, e.g. 10 times lower, and treatments should be less frequent. Some oils are known to be phototoxic, which means that they make skin more sensitive to sunlight.
- **Irritation** from essential oils is localised and may affect the skin or mucous membranes. Irritation is also dose-dependant.
- **Sensitisation** is an allergy to an essential oil. Only a small amount of oil is needed to trigger a response, therefore it is not dose-dependant.

It is important to keep very detailed records of essential oil blends used on every client so that if any problems are reported such as irritation or sensitivity, the therapist can identify the oil or quantity involved and change it accordingly for the next treatment.

CARRIER OILS

As essential oils are not actually oily in texture, an oily medium is needed in which to mix the essential oils before they can be massaged into the skin. The skin will absorb fat-soluble substances more readily than water-soluble substances, therefore essential oils will penetrate more efficiently if applied to the skin via a carrier oil. This efficiency will be enhanced by the use of an oil with a low viscosity.

TIP

Unsafe oils
The following essential oils should never be used in aromatherapy:
Bitter almond
Boldo leaf
Calamus
Horseradish
Jaborandi leaf
Mugwort
Mustard
Pennyroyal
Rue
Sassafras
Savin
Southernwood
Tansy
Thuja
Wintergreen
Wormseed
Wormwood
Yellow camphor

TIP

If you wish to use an essential oil simply for its fragrance, mix three drops of your favourite essential oil in 6 ml of mineral oil and apply sparingly to your pulse points as with perfume. The mineral oil will hold the fragrance on the surface of the skin.

The most effective medium for this purpose is a vegetable carrier oil. Mineral oils such as baby oil are not suitable for use in aromatherapy as their molecular structure is too large to allow penetration of the epidermis and they would therefore not assist the penetration of essential oils.

Almost any vegetable oil can be used as a carrier oil, but an oil that has been cold pressed and not processed is most suitable as it contains valuable nutrients for the body and will not adversely affect the therapeutic properties of the essential oils diluted in it.

The properties of carrier oils are that they:

- have a medium viscosity
- have little or no aroma
- are not soluble in water or alcohol
- have low volatility.

Carrier oils that are high in polyunsaturates absorb more readily into the skin than those high in monounsaturates or saturates.

Extraction of carrier oils

Cold pressing

Cold pressing is a method of extraction that is most desirable for carrier oils used in aromatherapy massage. The plant material is crushed using great pressure, literally squeezing the oil from the plant. No chemicals or solvents are used, resulting in a pure, unrefined oil.

Solvent extraction

Solvents such as petroleum are heated and washed through the plant material to dissolve any oil that is present. The solvents are then evaporated, leaving a refined oil that is unsuitable for aromatherapy massage.

Choosing a carrier oil

The choice of your carrier oil depends on its texture, smell and specific properties. For dry skin use an oil with a thicker consistency, and for an oily skin, or fine skin such as that on the face, use a finer or lighter oil with a lower viscosity.

Carrier oils

Name of oil and plant of origin	Details
Aloe vera *Aloe barbadenesis*	Aloe vera is a low-viscosity carrier and is therefore often blended with thicker oils to improve its texture for massage treatments. Its soothing, anti-inflammatory properties make it ideal for use on sensitive skins.
Apricot kernel oil *Prunus armenica*	Apricot kernel oil is a pale yellow colour and is an ideal facial massage oil due to its nourishing and protective properties.

Carrier oils (continued)

Name of oil and plant of origin	Details
Avocado oil *Persea americana*	In its refined state avocado oil is a pale yellow colour, but cold-pressed avocado oil is green. It is a very rich oil which penetrates to the deep epidermis, making it ideal for very dry skin. Its high vitamin E content also makes it a good antioxidant. Due to its cost and thick consistency, avocado oil is usually blended with other lighter carrier oils before use.
Evening primrose oil *Oenothera biennis*	Evening primrose oil is a pale yellow oil which is ideal for use on dry, irritated skin conditions such as eczema and chapped hands. Due to its cost, evening primrose oil is usually blended with a cheaper carrier oil.
Grapeseed oil *Vitis vinifera*	Grapeseed oil is a very inexpensive, light oil commonly used in aromatherapy. It has a very pale yellow-green colour and can be used on all types of skin.
Hazelnut oil *Corylus avellana*	Hazelnut oil is obtained from the kernel. It is a yellow, fine-textured oil that is particularly suitable for dry sensitive skin.
Jojoba *Simmondsia chinesis*	Jojoba is cold pressed and is semi-solid at room temperature. It therefore needs to be warmed in the hands prior to use. Jojoba is very expensive but very stable, and is therefore often blended with cheaper oils.
Macadamia nut oil *Macadamia ternifolia*	Macadamia nut oil has a slight odour and is pale yellow in colour. It is easily absorbed and is particularly suitable for mature dry skin.
Olive oil *Olea europea*	Olive oil is cold pressed and green in colour with soothing properties. As its consistency is quite thick, it is often blended with a lighter oil prior to massage.
Rose-hip oil *Rosa canina*	Rose-hip oil is produced by solvent extraction and is a warm golden colour.
Safflower oil *Carthamus tinctorius*	Safflower oil is pale yellow in colour. It is not very stable so needs the addition of an antioxidant such as avocado or wheatgerm to prevent it spoiling quickly.
Sunflower oil *Helianthus annus*	Sunflower oil has a light texture and pale yellow colour. It contains vitamins A, B, C, D and E.
Sweet almond oil *Prunus amygdalus*	Sweet almond oil is a light-textured, pale yellow oil that is good for facial massage as it soothes and protects the skin. It is warm pressed and is particularly good for dry, sensitive skin.
Wheatgerm oil *Triticum vulgare*	Wheatgerm oil is a warm orange colour and is rich in vitamins E and C. It is a cold-pressed oil that is a very good antioxidant due to its high vitamin E content. It is often added to other blends in small quantities to prolong their shelf life. Wheatgerm oil is very thick and has a strong wheatgerm smell, so it should be blended with a lighter oil prior to massage.

HEALTH AND SAFETY

Wheatgerm carrier oil should not be used on clients with wheat allergies.

Creams can also be used to blend essential oils prior to application on the skin. Although not as good as vegetable oil for body massage, cream bases are ideal for use on smaller areas – hands or feet for example. Any unperfumed and unmedicated cream can be used for this purpose and there are many bland creams designed for use by aromatherapists. These are known as base creams. Less essential oils are needed when blending with base creams due to their denser consistency. Use approximately one drop of essential oil per 5 grams of cream. Mix thoroughly with a clean glass rod before use.

TYPES OF MASSAGE USED IN AROMATHERAPY

The reasons for using massage in aromatherapy treatments are threefold. The pressure from the hands helps to spread and push the oils into the skin, heat helps the oils to be absorbed more easily and the effects of the manual manipulations help the client to relax.

There are three basic types of massage used in aromatherapy treatments:

- Swedish
- neuromuscular
- shiatsu.

TIP

If a client desires a relaxing treatment, minimize or completely omit tapotement movements.

Swedish massage

Swedish massage uses effleurage, petrissage, tapotement and vibrations to increase the blood supply generally to muscles and skin and to improve the efficiency of the lymphatic system by increasing drainage to the lymph nodes. It can be either a relaxing or stimulating massage depending on the movements used, with emphasis placed on the smooth continuity of strokes.

Neuromuscular massage

Neuromuscular massage uses strokes that are designed to affect the nerves rather than blood and lymphatic flow. The pressure is much firmer than Swedish strokes and the direction is related to the direction of the sensory nerve roots rather than the direction of blood and lymphatic flow. As the pressure is very firm it may cause mild discomfort. The overall effect of these strokes is to stimulate the nerves.

Shiatsu massage

Shiatsu is an Oriental massage technique with strokes which relate to energy paths within the body rather than nerves, blood flow or lymphatic flow. Adapted forms of shiatsu are often incorporated in aromatherapy massage and the strokes are designed to either increase or decrease energy levels within the body. The massage is performed with long flowing strokes along meridians or with pressures on the tsubo points. The pressures are quite firm and may sometimes be quite uncomfortable.

TIP

If the client experiences sharp or sudden pain stop applying pressure immediately.

During aromatherapy massage, tsubo points should be pressed with the fingertips using the therapist's body to apply pressure. Apply pressure for three to five seconds, and five to seven seconds on the back when the client is breathing out. Pressure applied to these points helps to unblock the energy flow along the meridian, promoting greater well-being of the client.

Contra-indications

Contra-indications to aromatherapy massage are:

- cuts and abrasions
- contagious diseases
- fever
- varicose veins
- soon after or before alcohol consumption
- immediately after heat treatment such as sauna or steam bath
- inflammation
- pregancy (to a large extent)
- chemotherapy patients
- radiotherapy patients.

Contra-indicated essential oils

Some essential oils are contra-indicated to particular conditions
as shown in the table. However, this is not an exhaustive list. The therapist
should always check for contra-indicated essential oils associated with any
conditions that the client may have.

Condition	Contra-indicated oil
pregnancy	aniseed, basil, camphor, carrotseed, cinnamon, clove, cedarwood, clary sage, cypress, fennel, hyssop, juniperberry, jasmine, lemongrass, marjoram, origanum, nutmeg, parsley, peppermint, rose, rosemary, sage, savoury, thyme
high blood pressure	hyssop, rosemary, sage, thyme
epilepsy	hyssop, fennel, sage
prior to exposure to sunlight	angelica, bergamot, lemon, lime, orange

Contra-actions

After an aromatherapy massage, some clients may feel excessively sleepy or
relaxed, depending upon the essential oils used. Clients reacting in this way
must be recommended not to drive or operate dangerous machinery until
they feel more alert. Some clients may also experience a feeling of light-
headedness or headaches, depending on which oils were used and the
degree of sensitivity of the client. Clients with very sensitive skin may
experience skin irritation if stimulating essential oils are used. The therapist
should encourage clients to report any adverse effects to them immediately
so that notes can be made on their record cards and future treatments
adjusted accordingly.

EQUIPMENT LIST

treatment couch

pillows

towels

trolley

small bowls

tissues

record card and pen

gown

glass rod

glass measuring jug

blending bottles

damp cotton wool

range of carrier oils

range of essential oils

cleansing lotion

toner or flower water

headband

bin

Essential Aromatherapy
Tel: 01706 1112222

*Relaxing Rose
& Lavender Bath
Oil*
Add 6-8 drops to running water

Example of a hand-written label

Preparation of the treatment area

The use of subdued lighting and gentle relaxing music may help to enhance the mood of the treatment cubicle. Listed below is everything that your working area should contain to carry out a full body aromatherapy massage.

- **Treatment couch**: The massage couch should be of a height that allows you to work comfortably and allows the client to get on safely. The couch should have a removable cover made from a material that is both comfortable for the client to lie on and easy to clean.

- **Pillows**: Two pillows are used during treatment. One supports the head and the other is used to support the limbs. Each pillow should be covered with a clean, removable pillow case.

- **Towels**: Two small towels are required to protect the pillows and two large towels are used to cover the client during treatment. Towels should be soft and clean. Additional towels may be used during the treatment for client comfort and support.

- **Trolley**: Used to hold working materials.

- **Small bowls**: These may be used to hold tissues and damp cotton wool, and to blend oils.

- **Tissues**: A small number of split tissues should be placed on the trolley. These may be used to wipe excess oil from the client's skin or the therapist's hands, or to remove toner or flower water after cleansing.

- **Record card and pen**: To record details of the client and treatments given.

- **Gown**: To protect the client's modesty if required.

- **Glass rod**: To mix essential oils with carrier oils. Wooden spatulas should not be used as they may absorb too much of the essential oils from the blend.

- **Glass measuring jug**: To accurately measure the quantity of carrier oil.

- **Blending bottles**: A small range of glass bottles are used to thoroughly blend the carrier oil with the essential oil. They may also be used to store remaining oil after a treatment or given to the client to take home.

- **Damp cotton wool**: To remove make-up and cleansing lotion.

- **Range of carrier oils**: For blending with essential oils.

- **Range of essential oils**: To include top, middle and base notes.

- **Cleansing lotion**: To remove make-up prior to facial massage.

- **Toner or flower water**: To freshen the skin after cleansing.

- **Headband**: To keep the client's hair away from the face during cleansing if required.

- **Bin**: This should have a foot-operated lid to avoid contact with the hands during treatment. A disposable liner should also be used for hygiene.

HEALTH AND SAFETY

Always label blended oils thoroughly. State the type and quantity of carrier oil, number of drops and type of essential oil, the date and the client's name.

The following table gives details of sterilisation and sanitation procedures.

Sterilisation and sanitisation

Equipment item	Procedure
Treatment couch	The surfaces should be wiped with surgical spirit. During treatment, the couch may be covered with disposable tissue, towels or a loose cover
Couch cover	Machine wash in hot, soapy water
Pillows	Protect with washable covers and towels during treatment
Towels	Machine wash in hot, soapy water
Trolley	The surfaces should be wiped with surgical spirit at the beginning of each session, then covered with disposable tissue
Bowls	Wash in hot, soapy water
Gowns	Machine wash in hot, soapy water
Glass rods	Wash in hot, soapy water
Glass measuring jug	Wash in hot soapy water
Glass blending bottles	Wash in hot soapy water and dry thoroughly. Store with lids off
Headband	Machine wash in hot, soapy water
Bin	Use a disposable liner and wipe regularly with disinfectant

The treatment room should be warm, quiet, private, well-ventilated and with soft lighting, and must be kept clean and tidy at all times. The working area should be adequately screened to allow the client privacy.

Presentation of the therapist

In order to promote professionalism, and to promote a healthy and safe working environment, the therapist must:

- maintain a high standard of personal hygiene
- have fresh breath, free from cigarette or food odours
- wear a clean, pressed overall
- wear clean, low-heeled shoes
- not wear rings or any jewellery on the arms, including watches. Plain wedding bands, however, are acceptable
- ensure that any earrings or necklaces are discreet
- ensure that any make-up is discreet and expertly applied
- style long hair neatly away from the face and shoulders
- ensure that nails are short, smooth, clean and free from nail polish
- ensure that any cuts are covered with a clean plaster
- ensure that hands are washed immediately before and after physical client contact.

The therapist should adopt a calm and professional manner at all times.

Preparation of the client

Consultation

When the client arrives she should be treated with courtesy and respect. Always address the client by her name and inform her of yours. Advise the client which articles of clothing she needs to remove and show her the gown that she may wear if she prefers. Allow the client to undress in private.

Help the client onto the couch and allow her to get comfortable in a prone (face down) position. Cover her with towels and ensure that she is warm and comfortable before beginning the verbal consultation. This step is important, not only to elicit information but also to help the client to relax in the knowledge that she is being treated by a professional.

First, ask for basic details such as name, address, date of birth, etc., and record them on the client's record card. Second, ask the client about her general lifestyle, hobbies, work, eating patterns, smoking, etc. This will help you to take a more holistic approach to her treatment. By knowing and understanding the client's lifestyle you can perhaps discover not only the correct help for her problems but also gain an understanding of how the problems may have arisen in the first place. For example, if a client suffers with headaches and eyestrain, a contributory factor to these conditions could be that she watches a lot of television,

ACTIVITY

A client presents for a full body aromatherapy massage treatment but has a broken wrist in plaster. What action do you take?

BEAUTY WORKS

Date	Beauty therapist name	
Client name		Date of birth (identifying client age group)
Address		Postcode

Evening phone number   Day phone number

Name of doctor   Doctor's address and phone number

Related medical history (conditions that may restrict or prohibit treatment application)

Are you taking any medication (this may affect the condition of the skin or skin sensitivity)

CONTRA-INDICATIONS REQUIRING MEDICAL REFERRAL
(Preventing aromatherapy massage treatment application)

☐ bacterial infection e.g. impetigo
☐ viral infection e.g. herpes simplex
☐ fungal infection e.g. tinea corporis
☐ systemic medical conditions
☐ severe skin conditions
☐ chemotherapy patients
☐ radiotherapy patients

CLIENT
☐ male
☐ female

PHYSICAL CHARACTERISTICS
weight
height
muscle tone
age
skin condition

CONTRA-INDICATIONS WHICH RESTRICT TREATMENT
(Treatment may require adaptation)

☐ cuts and abrasions
☐ bruising and swelling of known origin
☐ recent scar tissue
☐ pregnancy
☐ during lactation
☐ epilepsy
☐ post epilation
☐ allergies

LIFESTYLE
occupation
family situation
dietary and fluid intake
(including allergies)
hobbies, interests, means of relaxation
exercise habits
smoking habits
sleep patterns

OBJECTIVES OF TREATMENT
☐ relaxation
☐ sense of well-being
☐ uplifting

Beauty therapist signature (for reference)

Client signature (confirmation of details)

or that she reads a lot but does not wear glasses, and may need to seek the advice of an optician. Ask what her motivations are for attending a beauty salon. Does she want to be relaxed or uplifted?

The verbal consultation will also reveal whether any medication is being taken and whether the client is suffering from conditions that cannot be seen with the eye, e.g. period pain or premenstrual tension. Other conditions which are visually obvious, such as varicose veins, can be identified during the visual part of the consultation.

Ask the client to sit up straight. Look at her spinal column to see if it is straight. If not, is it due to poor posture, trauma or a genetic condition? Check her skin visually and physically for colour and texture. Encourage the client to ask questions as these may lead to further discussions about her needs. Record all relevant details on the client's record card. An example of a typical record card is illustrated.

SELECTING PRE-BLENDED ESSENTIAL OILS

For this unit you are required to select a suitable pre-blended aromatherapy oil to meet the client's needs. The table of compatibility will help you easily to select oils that are required for particular outcomes. You will find it of great help when selecting oils for clients before you have gained experience and become competent enough to select oils on your own.

Compatibility of essential oils

Relaxing	Uplifting	Sense of well-being
Camomile Roman	Eucalyptus	Camomile Roman
Clary sage	Grapefruit	Clary sage
Geranium	Lemon	Geranium
Lavender	Lemongrass	Lavender
Marjoram	Rosemary	Neroli
Neroli	Tea tree	Rose bulgar
Rose bulgar		Ylang-ylang
Ylang-ylang		

For body massage the oils should be mixed in a 2 per cent blend, i.e. one drop of essential oil to each 2 ml of carrier oil, or 12 drops of essential oil into 24 ml of carrier oil. For a full body massage, use 25–30 ml of carrier oil. For a facial massage use 5–8 ml of carrier oil with essential oils in a 1 per cent dilution, i.e. one drop of essential oil for every 4 ml of carrier oil.

There are approximately 20 drops of essential oil per millilitre. This is useful to know if you are blending oils for clients to take home as it allows you to work out exactly how much the blend will cost you.

Treatment procedures

Greet the client and introduce yourself. Carry out a full verbal, visual and tactile consultation as described on pages 350–2. Inform the client which clothing to remove then offer to help the client onto the couch.

- Choose the appropriate pre-blended oils, then tell the client which oils you are using and why.
- Ask if she has a particular dislike of, or allergy to, any particular essential oil.
- Measure out and mix the chosen blend.
- Wash your hands.
- Apply aromatherapy massage using the procedure outlined on the following pages, ensuring client comfort and discretion at all times.
- At the end of the treatment, offer the client home-care advice.
- Ask the client if she has any queries that you may be able to answer.
- Offer to assist the client in getting off the couch.
- Tell the client where you are going then leave them to dress in privacy.

Patch Testing

A patch test should be carried out 24 hours prior to treatment. This will help to determine the client's suitability for treatment. Carry out the patch test in the crook of the elbow. Ensure that the skin is clean and then apply an essential oil blend to the area using a 2% blend e.g. 2 drops of essential oil in 2 mls of carrier oil. Ask the client to inform the salon immediately if any contra-actions are identified e.g. redness, itching or swelling. If any contra-actions occur treatment must not be carried out.

HEALTH AND SAFETY

It is necessary to wear disposable gloves when blending oils to avoid skin contact with neat essential oils.

TIP

A client may receive treatment for the head and neck whilst sitting in a chair, leaning over a couch or leaning against the therapist.

This is a popular de-stressing massage and is suitable for clients who are unable to get on to the beauty couch.

TIP

Remember that irritation or sensitivity to essential oils may be dose-dependent, so contra-actions may not show up in patch test but could appear in treatment.

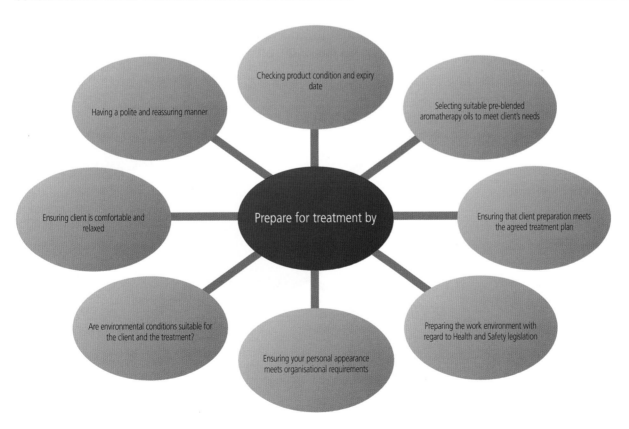

Order of aromatherapy massage

If the client is wearing make-up and desires a facial massage, cleanse the face prior to treatment then massage with a suitable pre-blended aromatherapy oil. Massaging the face first allows the client to breathe in the aromas quickly.

Start the full body massage with the back. As this is the largest area, the oils will begin to penetrate the skin and enter the bloodstream quickly, therefore allowing a more immediate effect of the treatment. Then proceed in this order:

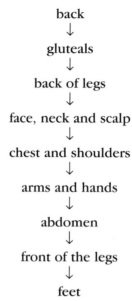

back
↓
gluteals
↓
back of legs
↓
face, neck and scalp
↓
chest and shoulders
↓
arms and hands
↓
abdomen
↓
front of the legs
↓
feet

Before commencing treatment on each body part, carry out a friction rub. Using the flat palms of both hands, quickly rub back and forth a number of times. This will help to warm the skin and brush off dry, superficial skin cells, aiding the absorption of the oils.

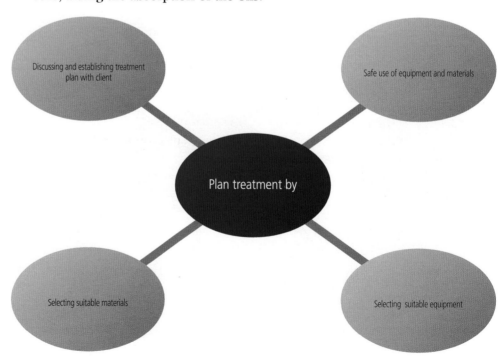

Massage routine for the back

1 **Effleurage** From the base of the back, effleurage up the erector spinae area, across the shoulders and back down to the base of the spine. Repeat this step a further two times.

2 **Reverse effleurage** Standing at the client's head, effleurage from the back of the neck, down over the erector spinae area, across the base of the back, and back up to the back of the neck. Repeat this step a further two times.

3 **Double-handed kneading** Starting at one shoulder, place the hands side by side and knead together, compressing the tissue between the hands. Work down to the base of the back, then move the hands slightly towards the trapezius area, and finally work down again to the base of the back. Continue until the whole of the back has been treated. Repeat this step a further two times.

4 **Reinforced kneading** Starting at one shoulder, place one hand on top of the other and knead the tissues. Work down to the base of the back, then move the hands slightly towards the trapezius area, and finally work down again to the base of the back. Continue until the whole of the back has been treated. Repeat this step a further two times.

5 **Kneading to the intercostal nerves** Starting at the base of the spine, on either side of the spinal column, work outwards with both hands simultaneously. Using the first and middle fingers of each hand, knead in small circles, gradually working to the sides of the body. Slide the fingers back to the original position then move up slightly and repeat the movement. When the fingers reach the ribs, the kneading should be done between the ribs on the intercostal nerves and the fingers should slide back on the rib. This movement is continued up to the occiput.

6 **Single-handed stroking to intercostal nerves** Starting at the top of the spine, use the whole of the hands to alternately stroke away from the spine in the direction of the intercostal nerves. Stroke down one side of the spine, then repeat on the other side. Work with moderate to slow speed.

7 **Thumb kneading to erector spinae** Starting at the base of the spine, place the thumbs one in front of the other on the erector spinae muscle. Slowly slide the thumbs back and forth whilst also moving slowly up the muscle. Continue to the top of the back then repeat on the other side of the muscle.

8 **Double-handed stroking to intercostal nerves** – Place both hands either side of the spine, then gently stroke both hands outwards simultaneously in the direction of the intercostal nerves. Repeat the movement whilst working down towards the base of the spine.

9 Repeat step 1 a further three times.

10 Apply pressure to the tsubo points shown in the diagram.

11 Repeat step **1** a further three times.

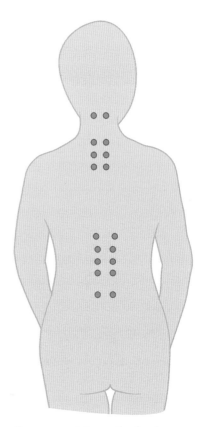

Pressure points on the back

HEALTH AND SAFETY

Never massage directly on the spinal column.

Reverse effleurage

Double-handed kneading

Thumb kneading to erector spinae

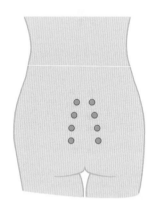

Pressure points on the gluteals

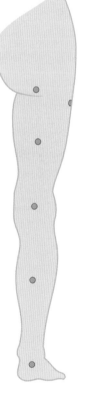

Pressure points on the back of the leg

Massage routine for the gluteals

1   Effleurage to whole of one side of gluteals. Use the whole of the hand and work from the lateral aspect to the mid line. Repeat this step a further two times.

2   Kneading to whole of one side of gluteals. Knead in a circular motion from the lateral aspect to the midline. Repeat this step a further two times.

3   Apply pressure to the tsubo points as shown in the diagram opposite.

4   Repeat step **1** a further three times.

Massage routine for the back of the legs

1   **Effleurage to whole leg** Starting at the tips of the toes, use the whole of the hands to apply effleurage over the whole posterior aspect of the leg, finishing at the gluteal area. Repeat this step a further two times.

2   **Alternate kneading to whole leg** Start at the top of the thigh with the hands on either side. Knead the tissues in an alternate movement, applying pressure on the upward movement. Work down to the foot and include the plantar aspect of the foot. Repeat this step a further two times.

3   **Effleurage to lower leg (with knee bent)** With one hand, raise the lower leg and support it at the ankle. With the other hand, apply effleurage strokes from the ankle to the knee. Repeat this step a further five times.

4   **Four-finger stroking to hamstring area** Place both hands on the upper thigh just below the gluteals. Stroke both hands away from the midline in a diagonal movement. Bring the hands back to the midline just below their previous position and repeat the movement. Carry the movement on to the knee.

5   **Thumb stroking of sciatic nerve** Place the thumb over the base of the Achilles tendon and gently slide the thumb up the centre of the calf towards the knee. Use a firm, even pressure and stop just below the knee. Repeat this step a further two times.

6   Apply pressure to the tsubo points as shown in the diagram opposite.

7   **Effleurage to whole leg** Repeat step 1 a further three times.

TIP	
Two large, folded towels may be used to support the raised leg, instead of the therapist holding the foot.	

Massage routine for the face, neck and scalp

1 **Effleurage to front of neck, face, scalp and back of neck** Repeat step **1** a further two times.

2 **Finger kneading to scalp** Starting at the temple, use the finger tips to slowly but firmly knead the scalp all over. This movement is similar to that of shampooing the hair, but with a slower action.

3 **Effleurage to neck and cheeks** Place both hands on the sternum and effleurage up the neck to the chin, out across the jawline, up over the cheeks to the temples. Apply a slight vibration to the temple with the fingertips before lifting the hands. Repeat step **3** a further two times.

4 **Effleurage across chin** Support the side of the head with one hand, and with the other hand apply a smooth effleurage stroke from one angle of the jaw to the other. Swap hands and repeat on the other side. Repeat step **4** a further three times.

5 **Finger kneading to jawline** Starting on the chin apply effleurage over the jawline to the ears with both hands simultaneously. With the fingertips apply circular kneading movements back across the jawline to the chin. Repeat step **5** a further three times.

6 **One finger effleurage around lips** With the ring fingers of both hands placed beneath the centre of the lower lip, apply a light effleurage stroke around the mouth to the nose. Take the fingers off the skin and repeat the movement three times.

7 **Drain from nose to ears** Place the first and middle finger of each hand on either side of the nostrils. With a light even pressure sweep across the cheeks beneath the cheekbones to the ear. repeat step **7** a further two times.

8 **Circle around eyes** Place both thumbs on the forehead with one hand placed on the side of the head for support. With the fingers of the other hand, circle around the eyes towards the nose. Repeat three times. Keeping the thumbs in contact with the skin, support the other side of the head with the other hand and draw circles around the eye with the fingers of the free hand. Repeat three times. Repeat step **8** a further two times.

9 **Alternate stroking to forehead** Place one hand on the forehead and stroke from the eyebrows to the hairline. Repeat with alternate hands covering the whole forehead. Use a slow controlled effleurage movement.

10 **Finger curtains to eyes** Slide the fingertips of both hands down the bridge of the nose, relax the fingers onto the cheeks and slowly draw the hands over the eyes. Hold for a count of three. Slide finger tips out to the temples, apply a slight vibration then remove.

11 Apply pressure to the tsubo points shown in the diagrams opposite.

12 Repeat step **1** a further three times.

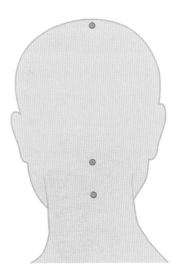

Pressure points on the scalp

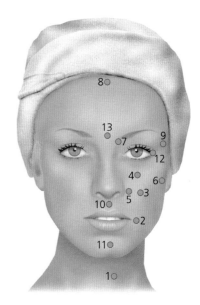

Pressure points on the face

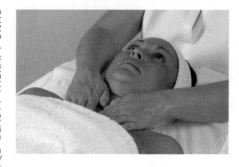

Effleurage to neck and chest

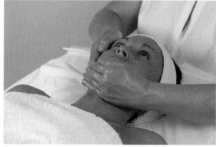

Effleurage across chin

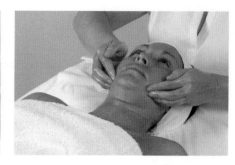

Finger kneading to jawline

One finger effleurage around lips

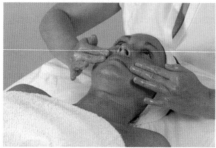

Drain from nose to ears

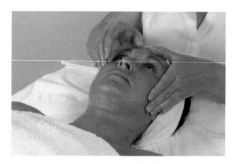

Circle around eyes

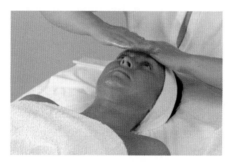

Alternate stroking to forehead

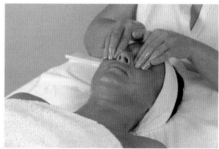

Finger curtains to eyes

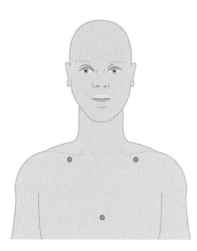

Pressure points on the chest and shoulders

Massage routine for the chest and shoulders

1   **Effleurage to chest and shoulders** Place both hands on the sternum and effleurage out across the chest, behind the shoulders and up the back of the neck. Repeat step **1** a further two times.

2   **Kneading to chest and shoulders** Place both hands on the sternum in a relaxed fist with fingers underneath the hand. Using circular movements knead out across the chest, behind the shoulders, over the upper trapezius area and back of the neck. Repeat step **2** a further two times.

3 **Effleurage to chest and shoulders** Place both hands on the sternum and effleurage out across the chest, behind the shoulders and up the back of the neck. Repeat step **3** a further two times.

4 Apply pressure to the tsubo points shown in the diagram on page 358.

5 Repeat step **1** a further three times.

Massage routine for the abdomen

1 **Effleurage** Place both hands on the abdomen just below the sternum. Stroke outwards to the waist then inwards down towards the pubic bone. Repeat the stroke in reverse. Repeat this step a further two times.

2 **Single-handed stroking to rectus abdominus** Place one hand just below the sternum and apply a smooth effleurage stroke down the rectus abdominus muscle. Repeat the movement using alternate hands. Repeat this step a further five times.

3 **Kneading to abdominal walls** Place the hands either side of the waist just below the ribcage. Using upward, circular movements, knead down towards the hip. Effleurage back to the ribcage. Repeat this step a further two times.

4 Apply pressure to the tsubo points shown in the diagram below.

5 Repeat step **1** a further three times.

Pressure points on the abdomen

Single-handed stroking to the abdomen

Kneading to colon

Massage routine for the front of the legs

1 **Effleurage to whole leg** Starting at the tips of the toes, use the whole of the hands to apply effleurage over the whole anterior aspect of the leg, finishing at the inguinal gland area. Repeat this step a further two times.

2 **Alternate kneading to whole leg** Start at the top of the thigh with the hands on either side. Knead the tissues in an alternate movement, applying pressure on the upward movement. Work down to the foot and include the plantar aspect of the foot. Repeat this step a further two times.

Pressure points on the front of the leg

3 **Reverse diagonal stroking across thigh** Standing with your back towards the client's upper body, stroke from the medial aspect of the knee, across the thigh to the hip, with alternate hands. Use a light pressure and moderate speed. Repeat this step a further three times.

4 **Reverse double kneading to thigh** Stand with your back towards the client's upper body with the hands on either side of the thigh just above the knee. Knead the tissues in an alternate movement, applying pressure on the upward movement, working towards the hip. Repeat this step a further two times.

5 **Effleurage around knee** After crossing your wrists, place the hands on either side of the knee and effleurage around the knee until the thumbs meet again at the front. Using the thumbs, stroke towards the back of the knee. Repeat this step a further two times.

6 **Thumb kneading to tibialis anterior** Starting just below the knee, use the thumb to apply small, circular kneading movements to tibialis anterior. The fingers may be used to steady the thumb in this movement but do not use them to apply pressure. Work down towards the ankle. Repeat this step a further two times.

7 **Cross-thumb kneading to dorsal aspect of foot** Hold the foot with both hands, fingers supporting the plantar surface and thumbs on the dorsal surface. Keeping the fingers still, push the thumbs back and forth across the foot with moderate speed, covering the whole surface from toes to ankles.

8 **Palm kneading to sole of foot** Supporting the dorsal aspect of the foot with one hand, use the base of the other hand to apply deep circular kneading to the plantar surface of the foot. Movement should be slow with moderate to deep pressure to avoid tickling the client.

9 Apply pressure to the tsubo points as shown in the diagram opposite.

10 Repeat step **1** a further three times.

Effleurage to whole leg

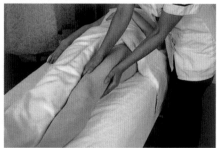

Reverse double kneading to thigh

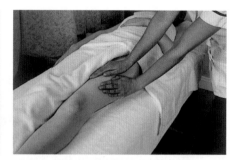

Reverse diagonal stroking across thigh

Massage routine for the arms

1 **Effleurage to whole arm** Starting at the fingertips, use both hands to apply alternate effleurage strokes up to the shoulder. Repeat this step a further two times.

2 **Alternate kneading to whole arm** With the hands on either side of the arm, just below the shoulder, apply alternate kneading movements with pressure on the upward movement. Work down over the forearm to the hand. Repeat this step a further two times.

3 **Picking up over forearm** Using both hands, alternately pick up the tissues of the forearm. Repeat this step a further two times.

4 **Thumb kneading to palms** Repeat this step a further two times.

5 **Cross-thumb kneading to backs of hands** Repeat this step a further two times.

6 Apply pressure to the tsubo points shown in the diagram opposite.

7 Repeat step **1** a further three times.

Pressure points on the arm

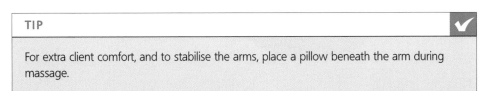

TIP	✔
For extra client comfort, and to stabilise the arms, place a pillow beneath the arm during massage.	

Effleurage to whole arm

Picking up over forearm

Kneading to palm

Aftercare

After the massage treatment it is important to give the client aftercare advice. This will ensure that she gets the maximum benefit from her treatment and will also promote retail sales. Aftercare advice should include the following:

- a recommendation against bathing for at least 6 hours to allow the oils to penetrate the skin completely
- a recommendation to drink plenty of fluids, e.g. water and herb tea, to promote a cleansing effect on the body
- recommendation of suitable relaxation techniques
- methods of using essential oils at home.

> **TIP** ✔
>
> **After scalp massage treatment**, advise the client to add shampoo to her hair before she adds water, as this will make the oil easier to wash out.

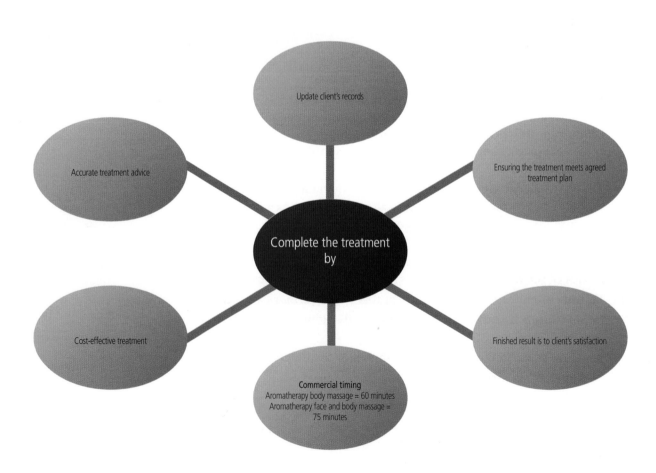

Update client's records

Accurate treatment advice

Ensuring the treatment meets agreed treatment plan

Complete the treatment by

Cost-effective treatment

Finished result is to client's satisfaction

Commercial timing
Aromatherapy body massage = 60 minutes
Aromatherapy face and body massage = 75 minutes

Bathing

As essential oils are not soluble in water it is important to dissolve them in a carrier oil such as vegetable oil or alcohol, prior to adding to bath water. This will prevent the concentrated oils from irritating the skin. Use approximately 6–8 drops in a full bath of water. Add the oils to the bath just before getting in to obtain maximum benefits.

Vaporisation

Essential oil burners are now widely available in a variety of shapes and colours. They usually contain a small dish in which to place the essential oils, with a space beneath for a small candle. When lit, the candle heats the oil, speeding up the evaporation rate and filling the room with fragrance.

RETAILING FOR THE AROMATHERAPIST

Aromatherapy is a very caring profession and its practitioners must have a very sympathetic and understanding nature. It could almost be said that aromatherapy is a vocation, much in the same way as that of doctors and teachers. However, a love of one's profession is only one of the reasons for working. In order to live, everyone needs money. Some need a lot and some need very little, but there is a need all the same.

Aromatherapists, being the caring people that they are, seem reluctant to make money from their profession and see the word 'profit' as being alien to their very existence. However, one's work will soon become tiresome if the financial rewards do not meet basic needs. Retailing is a means of improving this 'financial reward'.

Many aromatherapists are self-employed with their own practice, usually a room at home or in a clinic. However, most of the principles applied here would be just as suited to the employed aromatherapist working in a large clinic with other practitioners. An aromatherapist can only carry out so many treatments in the working week. This means that there is a maximum amount of money that it is possible to earn. For example, if an aromatherapist treats 15 clients per week at £45 per person she will earn £675. Take away any costs that are incurred, such as premises, heat and light, oils, etc., deduct tax and National Insurance payments, and this will leave her with her take-home pay. Unless the number of clients treated increases, the amount of money earned will always be the same. To increase earnings while still working the same hours and treating the same number of clients, retailing must be introduced.

Retailing must not be looked upon as an unnecessary chore, forcing the client to buy products that they do not want. How does the therapist know that the client does not want the product until she has been given the opportunity to buy in the first place?

Own blends or pre-packaged products?

Once the decision has been made to introduce retailing into the aromatherapy clinic then the therapist will need to decide whether to sell own-blended products or oils packaged and manufactured by an aromatherapy supplier. There are a number of differences between the two that may influence the choice.

Comparing own blends with pre-packaged products

	Ready-made products	*Own-blended products*
Advantages	<ul><li>brand name instantly recognisable by your client, e.g. Tisserand</li><li>large companies advertise in magazines, etc. which is free advertising for your product</li><li>wide range of products from which to choose</li><li>glossy promotional material</li><li>no messy filling up of bottles</li></ul>	<ul><li>can be personalised for your client</li><li>you know exactly what's in each product</li><li>satisfaction from knowing that you created the product</li></ul>
Disadvantages	<ul><li>high cost minimum orders</li><li>therapist has no say in product ingredients</li></ul>	<ul><li>time-consuming and messy to blend products</li><li>time-consuming to decide on product range and ingredients</li><li>no national advertising campaigns</li><li>no 'independent' quality control</li></ul>

Product marketing

Once the aromatherapist has decided which type of products she is going to sell in her clinic, she needs to look at how she is going to market them to her clients. The first item that will be required is a retail display unit. This will display all of the products available for sale to the client. It's no good buying a range of products then hiding them away in a corner of the clinic where no one will see them – if a product cannot be seen then it cannot be bought! Each product should be labelled with a price so that the client is aware of its cost. The products should be displayed at eye level so that the client does not have to make undue effort to see the product.

If a product has a short shelf life, it should not be stocked in large quantities, unless of course it sells very quickly.

Assessment of knowledge and understanding

You have now learnt how to apply aromatherapy massage using pre-blended oils.

To test your level of knowledge and understanding, answer the following short questions. These will prepare you for your summative (final) assessment.

Consult with the client

1 State four types of consultation technique.

2 How can a sensitive a supportive manner be demonstrated to the client?

3 Why is it important to determine the clients' lifestyle pattern prior to treatment planning?

4 Why is it important to agree the objectives of treatment prior to treatment planning?

5 Why is a patch test carried out?

6 State three conditions that would contra-indicate aromatherapy massage treatment.

7 State three conditions that would require treatment adaptation.

8 Why is it important to agree the content of the consultation record with the client before asking for their signature?

9 Why is it important to ensure that records are kept accurate and up-to-date?

Plan the treatment

1 Give two reasons for discussing the treatment plan with the client.

2 What equipment and materials are required for a full body aromatherapy massage?

3 Why is it important to have all equipment and materials to hand during the treatment?

Prepare for the treatment

1 Why is the environment of the treatment area important when performing aromatherapy massage?

2 How would you prepare the treatment area?

3 State two ways in which you could help the client to relax during treatment preparation.

4 How is the quantity of oil selected for a client?

5 Name three oils that you could select for each of the following outcomes:
- relaxing
- uplifting
- sense of well-being

6 If the client disliked the smell of the oil you had chosen what would you do?

7 State two conditions that would affect your choice of carrier oil.

8 List three problems associated with the use of a product that has reached its expiry date.

9 Why is it important to follow the agreed treatment plan whilst preparing for treatment?

Massage the body using pre-blended aromatherapy oils

1 List three ways that you can minimise cross-infection during treatment.

2 How do essential oils enter the body?

3 Describe how the olfactory system is affected by the inhalation of aromatherapy oils.

4 How does massage assist in the penetration of oils?

5 What are the properties of essential oils?

6 What is a commercially acceptable time for a full body massage?

7 What are the risks associated with using undiluted oils on the skin?

8 How would you adapt massage technique for a densely muscled client?

9 List five different types of massage technique that can be used in aromatherapy massage.

10 How can massage be adapted to suit the area of the body being treated?

11 Give three reasons why is it important to use the correct quantity of oil.

12 State two contra-actions that may occur during treatment.

Complete the treatment

1 State the aftercare advice that should be given to a client following aromatherapy massage treatment.

2 How can you ensure that the treatment is carried out cost-effectively?

3 State three ways that you can identify whether or not a client is satisfied with the treatment.

4 How might a client use aromatherapy oils at home?

5 State two products that may be recommended for retail to a client after aromatherapy massage treatment.

6 Why must detailed records be kept on the essential oil blends used with clients?

ACTIVITY

Case studies

Look at the four record cards shown on pages 367 to 370. If these clients presented themselves for treatment what action would you take?
What questions would you ask when preparing their treatment plan?
Which oils would you choose?
How much oil would you use?
How would you adapt the treatment?
What aftercare advice would you give?

BEAUTY WORKS

Date 10.3.03	Beauty therapist name MAXINE

Client name IRENE HARDING	Date of birth 21.5.51 (identifying client age group)
Address 1 OLD AVE, OLD TOWN	Postcode

Evening phone number 891 0123	Day phone number 891 0123

Name of doctor DR BROWN, OLD TOWN   Doctor's address and phone number 891 4567

Related medical history (conditions that may restrict or prohibit treatment application)

HIATUS HERNIA

Are you taking any medication (this may affect the condition of the skin or skin sensitivity)

MEDICATION EVERY DAY FOR HERNIA

CONTRA-INDICATIONS REQUIRING MEDICAL REFERRAL
(Preventing aromatherapy massage treatment application)

☐ bacterial infection e.g. impetigo
☐ viral infection e.g. shingles
☐ fungal infection e.g. tinea corporis
☐ systemic medical conditions
☐ severe skin conditions
☐ chemotherapy patients
☐ radiotherapy patients

CLIENT
☐ male
☑ female

CONTRA-INDICATIONS WHICH RESTRICT TREATMENT
(Treatment may require adaptation)

☐ cuts and abrasions
☐ bruising and swelling of known origin
☐ recent scar tissue
☐ pregnancy
☐ during lactation
☐ epilepsy
☐ post epilation

LIFESTYLE

pattern	SEDENTARY
occupation	SHOP ASSISTANT
family situation	MARRIED, GRANDMOTHER
dietary and fluid intake	ALWAYS ON LATEST FAD DIET
hobbies, interests, means of relaxation	SWIMMING, CARAVANNING
exercise habits	SWIMS 3X WEEK
smoking habits	GAVE UP 5 YEARS AGO
sleep patterns	FAIRLY GOOD

OBJECTIVES OF TREATMENT
☐ relaxation
☑ sense of well-being
☐ uplifting

Beauty therapist signature (for reference)

Client signature (confirmation of details)

BEAUTY WORKS

Date   20.7.03   Beauty therapist name   MAXINE

Client name   CRAIG MITCHELL   Date of birth   14.5.71
                                    (identifying client age group)

Address   1 SCHOOL STREET, OLD TOWN   Postcode

Evening phone number   456 7789   Day phone number   456 7789

Name of doctor   DR JONES, OLD TOWN   Doctor's address and phone number   456 1234

Related medical history (conditions that may restrict or prohibit treatment application)

   ASTHMA

Are you taking any medication (this may affect the condition of the skin or skin sensitivity)

   VENTOLIN INHALER

CONTRA-INDICATIONS REQUIRING MEDICAL REFERRAL
(Preventing aromatherapy massage treatment application)

- ☐ bacterial infection e.g. impetigo
- ☐ viral infection e.g. herpes simplex
- ☐ fungal infection e.g. tinea corporis
- ☐ systemic medical conditions
- ☐ severe skin conditions
- ☐ chemotherapy patients
- ☐ radiotherapy patients

CLIENT
- ☑ male
- ☐ female

CONTRA-INDICATIONS WHICH RESTRICT TREATMENT
(Treatment may require adaptation)

- ☐ cuts and abrasions
- ☐ bruising and swelling of known origin
- ☐ recent scar tissue
- ☐ pregnancy
- ☐ during lactation
- ☐ epilepsy
- ☐ post epilation

LIFESTYLE

pattern	ACTIVE
occupation	TEACHER
family situation	SINGLE NO CHILDREN
dietary and fluid intake	VERY HEALTHY DIET – EXCEPT HIGH ALCOHOL INTAKE
hobbies, interests, means of relaxation	FOOTBALL
exercise habits	GYM 4X WEEK
smoking habits	NEVER SMOKED
sleep patterns	REGULAR INSOMNIA

OBJECTIVES OF TREATMENT
- ☑ relaxation
- ☐ sense of well-being
- ☐ uplifting

Beauty therapist signature (for reference)

Client signature (confirmation of details)

BEAUTY WORKS

Date   1.5.03   Beauty therapist name   MAXINE

Client name   ELIZABETH PETERS

Date of birth   11.1.64
(identifying client age group)

Address   30 WILTON STREET, OLD TOWN

Postcode

Evening phone number   345 6789   Day phone number   345 6789

Name of doctor   DR SMITH, OLD TOWN   Doctor's address and phone number   567 8998

Related medical history (conditions that may restrict or prohibit treatment application)

NONE

Are you taking any medication (this may affect the condition of the skin or skin sensitivity)

CONTRACEPTIVE PILL

CONTRA-INDICATIONS REQUIRING MEDICAL REFERRAL
(Preventing aromatherapy massage treatment application)

- ☐ bacterial infection e.g. impetigo
- ☐ viral infection e.g. herpes simplex
- ☐ fungal infection e.g. tinea corporis
- ☐ systemic medical conditions
- ☐ severe skin conditions
- ☐ chemotherapy patients
- ☐ radiotherapy patients

CLIENT
- ☐ male
- ☑ female

CONTRA-INDICATIONS WHICH RESTRICT TREATMENT
(Treatment may require adaptation)

- ☐ cuts and abrasions
- ☐ bruising and swelling of known origin
- ☐ recent scar tissue
- ☐ pregnancy
- ☐ during lactation
- ☐ epilepsy
- ☑ post epilation   HAD 1/2 LEG WAX TODAY

LIFESTYLE

pattern	SEDENTARY
occupation	PUBLIC RELATIONS
family situation	SINGLE NO CHILDREN
dietary and fluid intake	UNHEALTHY DIET, EXCESS ALCOHOL
hobbies, interests, means of relaxation	TV, THEATRE, DINING OUT
exercise habits	NONE
smoking habits	NEVER
sleep patterns	GOOD

OBJECTIVES OF TREATMENT
- ☐ relaxation
- ☐ sense of well-being
- ☑ uplifting

Beauty therapist signature (for reference)

Client signature (confirmation of details)

BEAUTY WORKS

Date	10.6.03	Beauty therapist name	MAXINE

Client name ANDREW RICHARDS	Date of birth 6.3.69 (identifying client age group)
Address 1 OLD ROAD, OLD TOWN	Postcode

Evening phone number 012 345 677	Day phone number 012 345 677

Name of doctor DR BROWN, OLD TOWN   Doctor's address and phone number 456 7891

Related medical history (conditions that may restrict or prohibit treatment application)

NONE

Are you taking any medication (this may affect the condition of the skin or skin sensitivity)

NONE

CONTRA-INDICATIONS REQUIRING MEDICAL REFERRAL
(Preventing aromatherapy massage treatment application)

- ☐ bacterial infection e.g. impetigo
- ☐ viral infection e.g. herpes simplex
- ☐ fungal infection e.g. tinea corporis
- ☐ systemic medical conditions
- ☐ severe skin conditions
- ☐ chemotherapy patients
- ☐ radiotherapy patients

CLIENT
- ☑ male
- ☐ female

CONTRA-INDICATIONS WHICH RESTRICT TREATMENT
(Treatment may require adaptation)

- ☑ cuts and abrasions ON BOTH SHINS
- ☐ bruising and swelling of known origin
- ☐ recent scar tissue
- ☐ pregnancy
- ☐ during lactation
- ☐ epilepsy
- ☐ post epilation

LIFESTYLE

pattern	FAIRLY ACTIVE
occupation	LAWYER
family situation	MARRIED ONE YOUNG SON
dietary and fluid intake	FAIRLY HEALTHY, NO ALCOHOL
hobbies, interests, means of relaxation	FOOTBALL – PLAYING AND WATCHING
exercise habits	WEIGHTS & AEROBIC GYM 3X WEEK
smoking habits	NEVER SMOKED
sleep patterns	ERRATIC DUE TO YOUNG SON

OBJECTIVES OF TREATMENT
- ☑ relaxation
- ☐ sense of well-being
- ☐ uplifting

Beauty therapist signature (for reference)

Client signature (confirmation of details)

chapter 11

Enhance the appearance of natural nails using artificial nail systems

Learning objectives

This unit describes how to enhance the appearance of natural nails using acrylic, UV gel and wrap artificial nail systems. It describes the competencies to enable you to:

- **consult with the client**
- **plan the treatment**
- **prepare for the treatment**
- **apply artificial nails using acrylic liquid and powder systems**
- **apply artificial nails using UV gel system**
- **apply artificial nails using the wrap system**
- **complete the treatment**

When providing artificial nail systems it is important to use the skills you have learned in the following core mandatory units:

G1 ensure your own actions reduce risks to health and safety
G6 promote additional products or services to clients
G11 contribute to the financial effectiveness of the business

INTRODUCTION

Nail extensions are an important area of treatment in the beauty industry and it is the duty of the professional beauty therapist to be aware of current trends. In the last few years the UK has been flooded with many types of nail extension, including the following:

Acrylic liquid and powder systems

This method involves the use of a powder and liquid mixed to form a strong acrylic. The mixture is built up over the nail plate and extends past the free edge on a nail form or tip. Skill is required to obtain a natural shape; often an abrasive drill is used to speed up shaping and filing.

Approximate application time – 1 hour 15 minutes.

UV gel systems

This method is the same as that for acrylic nails but uses a gel, rather than liquid and powder. Gels need to be cured (set) with an ultraviolet light.

Approximate application time – 1 hour.

Nail tips

This method uses pre-formed nail tips applied to the natural nail tip only. The seam area is then buffed to disguise the join.

Approximate application time – 45 minutes.

Fibre systems

This method involves applying a nail tip as above, then overlaying with fibre for added durability.

Approximately application time – 1 hour 30 minutes.

ACTIVITY

Nail extensions
Write down any other reasons you can think of for applying nail extensions.

Clients demand a high level of service when they attend a salon for nail extensions, so thorough product training is essential. A good supplier will offer training courses and full back-up support. As a nail-extension service is quite expensive the client must be happy if she is to return regularly for her infills. Remember, an unhappy client will tell twice as many people about the salon as a happy one! The methods outlined in this chapter are a general guide to the application of nail extensions. Due to the vast number of products available, however, specific application techniques may vary. To ensure a completely safe and professional-looking application, always follow the manufacturer's instructions.

What are the uses of false nails? They are applied:

- to make hands look more attractive
- as an aid to help the client stop biting her nails
- to match an odd broken nail
- to give aesthetic appeal to a deformed nail.

Reception

When a client makes an appointment for a nail extension service, the receptionist should ask a few simple questions in order to ascertain her needs. Information obtained from the client will help the nail technician to set up the working area with the appropriate equipment and materials, and will save time when the client arrives for treatment. The basic questions that the receptionist should ask are these:

- Why does she want a nail extension treatment? Is it for a special occasion, for example, or to help stop nail biting?
- Has she had nail extensions applied before?

TIP

Because of the need for maintenance procedures with nail-extension treatments, the client's appointments should be booked in advance. This ensures that maintenance can be carried out as required.

ACTIVITY

Reception
Write down any other questions you can think of that the receptionist could ask to ensure that the client receives the treatment most appropriate for her needs.

Record cards

As with all other beauty treatments, accurate record cards must be kept for clients having nail-extension services. If a client has had such services before, the receptionist should consult the card and tell the nail technician about these. This will give the nail technician a good idea of what to expect when the client arrives. For example, if the client has not attended for over three weeks, her nails may need a lot of maintenance work and extra time could be booked out to allow for this.

Information on the client's record card will include the following:

Occupation

The client's occupation will help the nail technician to decide which type of nail system to use and how long to leave the free edge. A client with a very physically demanding occupation, for example, will need a very strong nail extension with a medium to short free edge.

Condition of natural nails and cuticles

The condition prior to extension will be relevant later when the nail extensions are removed. The client cannot expect her nails to be in perfect condition later if they were not so at the outset.

Type of nail system used

Should the nail technician be away for any reason, other technicians must know what type of nails to apply. The record card will tell assisting staff which products to set out at the working area.

ACTIVITY

What advice would you give to clients who displayed each of the following nail conditions prior to treatment?
- severely bitten nails
- hook-shaped nails
- spoon-shaped nails
- crooked nails
- very flat nails
- discoloured nails e.g. yellowing, stained, bruised or white spots

A client's record card – front and back

Fancy Fingers Nail Salon
Client Record Card

Name	Address
Mrs Irene Brown	11a New Street, Newtown

Tel No	Date of Birth	Occupation
Home: 456456	21 June 1951	Housewife
Work: 498798		

Conditions of natural nails on first salon visit

Cuticles soft and in good condition

Details of previous nail treatment prior to attending Fancy Fingers Nail Salon

None

Details of nail care carried out at home

Hand cream applied occasionally. Nails painted for special occasions. Rough edges are filed if nails break

Size of nail tips

Right Hand   Left Hand

Signature of client JBrown	Date
	4.5.00

Date	Treatment Details	Homecare Advice	Retail	Nail Technician	Client Signature
4.5.00	Full set of sculptured acrylic nail extensions. Applied clear enamel only.	Gave client aftercare advice leaflet for acrylic nails. Discussed it with her so that she understood why the home care was important	Small bottle of non-acetone nail polish remover	Hayley	JBrown
18.5.00	Maintenance on full set of nails. Repair to thumb on left hand. Crack in free edge due to minor accident.	As previous	Rose Pink nail enamel	Hayley	JBrown

Size of nail tips (if used)

A record of the size of tip will save time during repairs and maintenance – the technician will know which tip size to use, and won't have to measure each time to get the right size.

Allergies to products

Knowing which products, if any, the client is allergic to is crucial so that these products can be avoided.

Reason for having nail extensions

This information helps the technician to assess whether to recommend temporary or permanent nail extensions.

Client signature

The client must confirm that she has been informed of the treatment details and possible contra-actions.

Contra-indications

Some clients may not be suited to a nail extension service. If they have a disease or disorder of the hand or nail it is in the interests of both the nail technician and the client not to proceed with treatment. Treating a client with a contra-indication may lead to cross-infection or a worsening of the client's condition. It is important to advise the client to seek medical advice to ensure a correct diagnosis and treatment for her condition.

Contra-indications to nail extensions are as follows:

- **Onychophagy** Severely bitten nails do not allow sufficient nail plate for adhesion of a nail tip. Also, the bulbous skin at the fingertip would cause the result to be a spoon-shaped application.
- **Onychorrexis** Thin, peeling nails do not provide a secure enough base for artificial nails.
- **Tinea unguium** This condition may spread unnoticed beneath the artificial nail. As it is contagious, it may also infect the nail technician and the manicure instruments.
- **Paronychia** Inflammation and infection of the nail fold would cause discomfort for the client during any nail treatment. The products used might further irritate the condition.
- **Certain occupations** Some heavy, manual occupations, such as gardening, preclude nail extension applications: the nails would be too easily broken. However, application in such cases would not be detrimental to the client's well-being, so is at the discretion of the nail technician.
- **Allergies** If a client has suffered an allergy after previous nail extension application, do not repeat the application.
- **Cuts and abrasions in the specific area** Applying nail extensions to a client with these conditions could result in discomfort during treatment and might lead to subsequent infection.

workstation or table

lamp for workstation

waste bin (with lid)

plastic glasses

manicure pads or disposable tissue

cotton buds

nail wipes or tissue

tissues

orange sticks

glass bowl

3 bowls

dappen dish

scissors

tip cutters

coarse file

medium file

fine file

4 sided buffer

towels

antiseptic

nail steriliser

acetone

cuticle oil

non-acetone nail enamel remover in pump dispenser

mid antiseptic cleaner for hands

nail tips

aftercare leaflets

- **Eczema** This condition may be irritated by the chemicals used in the nail extension treatment.
- **Psoriasis** As with eczema, clients with psoriasis on the hands and fingers may find that the condition is irritated by the products used.
- **Broken bones** Pressure applied during treatment would cause pain and discomfort to a client with broken bones in the hands, arms or fingers.

Equipment and materials

The equipment and materials listed below are general to all applications of nail extensions. Additional specialised items are listed with the individual techniques.

- workstation or table
- lamp for workstation use
- waste bin (with lid)
- plastic glasses
- manicure pads or disposable tissue
- nail wipes or tissue
- cotton buds
- tissues
- orange sticks
- glass bowl
- three bowls
- dappen dish
- scissors
- tip cutters
- coarse file (100-grit) – for reducing length of artificial free edge
- medium file (180-grit) – for blending in seam areas
- fine file (240-grit) – to smooth nail and remove scratches
- four-sided buffer – to bring nail surface to a shine
- medium-sized towels (three)
- antiseptic
- nail steriliser
- acetone
- cuticle oil
- non-acetone nail enamel remover (in a pump dispenser)
- mild antiseptic cleanser for hands
- nail tips in assorted styles and sizes
- client record card
- aftercare leaflets.

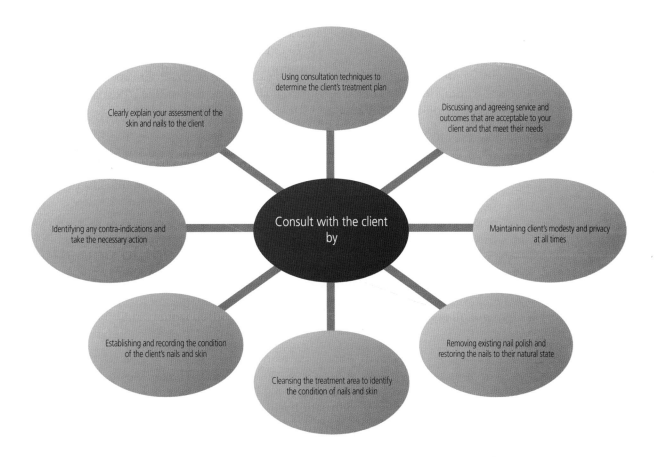

Consult with the client by

- Using consultation techniques to determine the client's treatment plan
- Discussing and agreeing service and outcomes that are acceptable to your client and that meet their needs
- Maintaining client's modesty and privacy at all times
- Removing existing nail polish and restoring the nails to their natural state
- Cleansing the treatment area to identify the condition of nails and skin
- Establishing and recording the condition of the client's nails and skin
- Identifying any contra-indications and take the necessary action
- Clearly explain your assessment of the skin and nails to the client

Sterilisation and sanitisation

For the health and safety of both the nail technician and the client, and to uphold the standards of the profession, you should ensure that all tools and materials are sterilised prior to use.

Prior to treatment, both the client and the technician should wash their hands with a mild antiseptic cleanser and then dry them on soft, disposable paper towels. This will help to prevent cross-infection and make the working area pleasant for both.

Before artificial nails are applied, the natural nail should be sterilised using an appropriate solution such as **methylated spirits** or **isopropyl alcohol**. This reduces the risk of infection from bacteria and fungi (such as *Tinea unguium*).

Allow the client to see cleaning and sterilising procedures taking place; they will instil in her confidence in your work and professional competence as well as reassure her about her own personal safety.

Preparing the treatment area

The working area should contain all the equipment and materials necessary for the treatment: this avoids unnecessary disturbance to the client during treatment. It should be well ventilated, warm and with a good source of light. When carrying out nail extension services you will need a lamp on the work surface in addition to general room lighting. This reduces shadows and allows you to work with precise detail.

Work surfaces should be covered with a clean, dry material capable of absorbing liquid if spilt. The material should be disposable or capable of being sterilised. Ideal materials are towels or disposable tissues.

Towels must be clean, dry and soft to ensure client comfort. Fresh towels must be used for each client. Place one towel flat to cover the work surface; fold the other towel into a small pad and place it beneath the client's forearm. This supports the client's arm during treatment and helps to keep her comfortable. Disposable tissue should be placed over the top of the towel. It should be changed two or three times during treatment to keep the dust from filing to a minimum.

The chairs for both the client and nail technician should be comfortable – they will be in use for approximately one and a half hours. The client will not be happy with her nails if she has had to sit in discomfort whilst they were being applied.

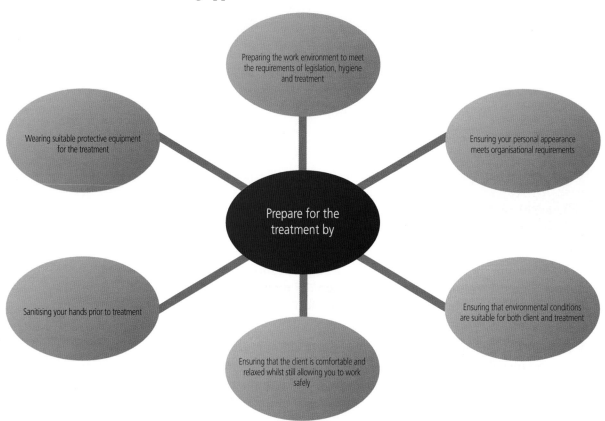

Preparing the client

The client should be given a light protective gown to wear during treatment. This will protect her clothes from the dust that is created during filing and from accidental spillages.

When artificial nails are cut, they occasionally flick towards the client's face. This could prove to be uncomfortable or dangerous should clippings get into the client's eyes, so plastic glasses should be available to the client whilst nail clipping is taking place. Advising the client to wear the glasses also assures her that you taking all possible precautions to safeguard her health.

Planning the treatment

Before applying nail extensions to a client, you should first discuss why she requires this treatment. This will help you to decide which nail system best matches her needs. Points to discuss include these:

- Is the client very busy and active? If so she will need her nails to be shorter and very strong.
- Is she allowed to wear nail polish at work? If not she will need a nail system that looks natural without nail polish.
- How long does she want the nails to last? Temporarily or semi-permanently?

Discovering your client's motivation in choosing nail extensions will help you to offer her the best possible service to meet her needs.

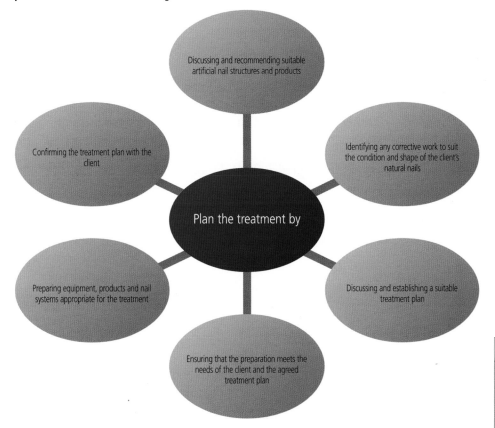

Discussing and recommending suitable artificial nail structures and products

Identifying any corrective work to suit the condition and shape of the client's natural nails

Confirming the treatment plan with the client

Plan the treatment by

Discussing and establishing a suitable treatment plan

Preparing equipment, products and nail systems appropriate for the treatment

Ensuring that the preparation meets the needs of the client and the agreed treatment plan

PRE-FORMED NAILS

Pre-formed nails are a temporary way of producing attractive nails as they are designed to last only 7–14 days. Made of plastic, these nails come in many shapes and sizes and are also available in colours to eliminate the need for nail polish.

HEALTH AND SAFETY

Adhesives
Artificial nail adhesives will bond skin in seconds. If this happens, use a cotton bud to apply acetone to the bonded area to dissolve the resin, and gently ease the skin apart. If this does not work, or if the skin is sore, seek medical attention immediately. Always read manufacturers' instructions and follow them carefully.

NAIL TIPS

Nail tips are a very natural looking type of nail extension, but they are also very weak. As the name suggests, nail tips are applied only to the tip of the natural nail (approximately halfway down the natural nail) and this leaves the cuticle area free. Nail tips can be strengthened by the overlay application of gel, fibreglass or acrylic.

Advantages	Disadvantages
1 Very natural-looking.	1 The weakest form of nail extension.
2 Ideal for special occasions such as weddings where the hands are on show.	2 Only last 7–10 days.
3 Easy to remove.	3 Easily broken.
4 Ideal for matching odd broken nails.	
5 Odourless during application.	

Kinds of nail tips

There are many different styles of nail tip, but generally they fall into two categories: cut-out tips and full tips. **Cut-out tips** are used for a client:

- with a small nail plate area
- with an exaggerated transverse arch of the nail plate
- who only desires short nail extensions.

Full tips are used for a client:

- who desires long nail extensions
- who has a medium to large nail-plate area
- who has a regular transverse arch to the nail plate.

Creative Nail Design

Nail tips

Equipment and materials

In addition to the basic equipment and materials (page 376), you will need the following:

- nail tips in assorted styles and sizes
- resin and nozzle
- selection of nail polish, including base and top coats.

EQUIPMENT LIST

nail tips

resin and nozzle

selection of enamels

Application

1 Wash your hands and ask your client to wash hers.
2 Check for contra-indications.

3 Sterilise the nail plate. Wiping or spraying the nails with an appropriate nail steriliser will inhibit the growth of bacterial and fungal infections.

4 Check the size of the nail tips. When the nail tips have been sized up correctly, lay them out on the work surface in order of application. For clients with very small nail plates, such as nail-biters, use a tip with a cut-out well area.

5 Dehydrate the nails (to remove surface oils and moisture) by wiping with a cotton bud that has been dipped in acetone.

6 Lightly buff the distal end of the natural nail, where the tip is to be applied, with a medium-grade file. e.g. 180-grit. Buff the nail surface gently with the file to remove remaining surface oils: this promotes better adhesion of the nail tip.

TIP ✔

When practising, carry out steps 6–11 for each nail (one nail at a time).
When proficient, carry out each step for *all* nails before moving to the next step (one step at a time).

---

7 Apply a small drop of adhesive to the natural nail tip. Adhesive should be applied only in the area that the well of the nail tip is to cover.

8 Apply the nail tip, at a 90° angle to the natural nail. Hold the edge of the well against the free edge, then gently press down and rock into position, squeezing out all air bubbles until the tip is flat against the nail surface.

If air bubbles appear or if the nail tip is not straight, remove it immediately before the adhesive starts to set, then re-apply. If the adhesive has set, the nail will have to be carefully removed and then re-applied.

9 Apply a small amount of adhesive to the seam area and allow to set. This is to ensure that the edge of the tip is securely bonded: it also allows blending to be done more quickly.

10 Blend the seam area. Begin with a coarse-grit file to reduce the bulk, then work through to a fine-grit file to remove scratches. Hold the board at a slight angle and blend the seam area without touching the nail plate excessively.

11 Buff the nail to a shine with a four-sided buffer, using the coarse side first and working through to the smooth side.

12 Cut the nail tip to the desired length and file to shape, first with a coarse-grit file to reduce the length, then with a fine grit-file to smooth. The client's choice must always be taken into consideration, but remember to *advise* on length – for instance, a mother with a young child would find very long nails most inconvenient.

13 Apply cuticle oil to soften the cuticles and surrounding skin.

14 Ask the client to wash her hands to remove the cuticle oil and dust particles. Wash your own hands. Change the towel on the work surface for a fresh one at this stage. This keeps dust to a minimum and prevents dust particles from spoiling the nail polish application.

ACTIVITY

Contra-indications
Make a list of all the conditions that you feel would contra-indicate the application of nail tips.

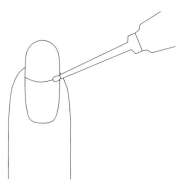

Applying adhesive to the seam area

HEALTH AND SAFETY

Artificial nail adhesives will bond skin in seconds. If this happens use a cotton bud to apply acetone to the bonded area to dissolve the resin and gently ease skin apart. If this does not work, or if the skin is sore, seek medical attention immediately. Always read manufacturers' instructions and follow them carefully.

TIP

The artificial free edge should be no longer than the nail plate from the cuticle to the flesh line. This will ensure that the nail is balanced and reduces the chance of the nail popping off.

15 Apply base coat over the entire nail plate.

16 Nails may be left natural or painted with a coloured nail polish as desired.

Aftercare and advice

Give your client the following instructions:

- Use rubber gloves when cleaning or washing up.

- Do not use the fingernails as tools.

- Use only 'non-acetone' nail polish removers. Acetone will soften the artificial nails, leading to lifting.

- Caution should be exercised when near any naked flame, including cigarettes, as nail adhesives are inflammable and plastic nails can melt.

ACTIVITY

Research the different products available with fibreglass systems and make yourself familiar with the chemical reactions that are taking place at each stage of the application.

FIBREGLASS SYSTEMS

Fibreglass nail extensions are possibly the most natural-looking nail extension system: the finished nail is transparent over the nail bed, allowing the pink colour to show through. The nails are also very thin and flexible, similar to natural nails. Fibreglass nails are also the least damaging to the natural nails because no primer is needed during application. This makes them an ideal choice for clients who wish to grow their own nails to wear without artificial products.

Advantages	Disadvantages
1 Very natural-looking.	1 Not suitable for clients with very little nail plate, principally nail-biters, as not enough nail plate is available for adequate adhesion of the nail tip and fibreglass overlay.
2 Ideal for matching odd, broken nails.	
3 Very strong and flexible.	
4 Not porous, so does not stain.	2 More expensive to apply than other nail systems.

TIP

As with gel and acrylic nail extensions, fibreglass nails may go yellow after sunbed use or after long periods in the sun, such as on holiday. Yellowing is only temporary and will fade once exposure has ceased. Discolouration can be stopped by covering the nails with coloured nail polish or a product designed for this purpose before exposure to the sun.

Equipment and materials

In addition to the basic equipment and materials (page 376) you will need the following:

- nail tips in assorted styles and sizes
- scissors for fibreglass
- resin and nozzle
- resin activator
- fibreglass mesh
- a selection of nail polish, including base and top coats.

EQUIPMENT LIST
nail tips
scissors for fibreglass
resin and nozzle
resin activator
fibreglass mesh
selection of enamels

Application

In the procedure below, each step is carried out for all ten nails before proceeding to the next step.

1 Wash your hands and ask your client to wash hers.

2 Remove any nail polish and check for contra-indications.

3 Sterilise the nail plate. Wiping or spraying the nails with an appropriate nail steriliser will help to inhibit the growth of bacterial and fungal infections.

4 Push back the cuticles and cut the free edge to approximately 3 mm. The cuticles must be pushed back gently with a cotton wool-tipped orange stick or hoof stick. This is to ensure that as much as possible of the nail plate is uncovered to allow optimum adhesion of the nail extension. It also ensures that the nails look their best after treatment.

5 Choose which type of tip is required, and check the sizes of the nail tips.

6 Lightly buff the nail surface to remove shine. Use a fine grit file to remove surface oils and to roughen the nail plate slightly. This allows better adhesion of the nail extension.

7 Apply resin down the centre of the nail plate and spread it over the whole nail using the extender nozzle. Leave a small gap all around the nail plate to avoid resin touching the cuticle or the nail walls.

8 Spray with activator. An activator is used not only to speed up the drying time of the adhesive but also to make the surface non-porous: this helps to prevent staining from nail enamel or other dyes. Activator must be sprayed from at least 30 cm away to ensure an even application and client comfort. Depress the pump fully to ensure a fine mist of activator. Failure to do so will result in large droplets of activator falling on the nail plate. This could cause a heat reaction, making application uncomfortable for the client and giving pitting in the resin, which would prevent even application.

9 Lightly buff the distal end of the nail plate.

10 Apply a small drop of adhesive to the natural nail tip. Adhesive should be applied only in the area that the well of the nail tip is to cover.

11 Apply the nail tip, at a 90° angle to the natural nail. Hold the edge of the well against the free edge then gently press and rock into position, squeezing out all air bubbles until the tip is flat against the nail surface.

TIP
Use nail wipes or tissues during treatment, not cotton wool. Cotton wool may shed its fibres onto the nail extension, spoiling the finished result.

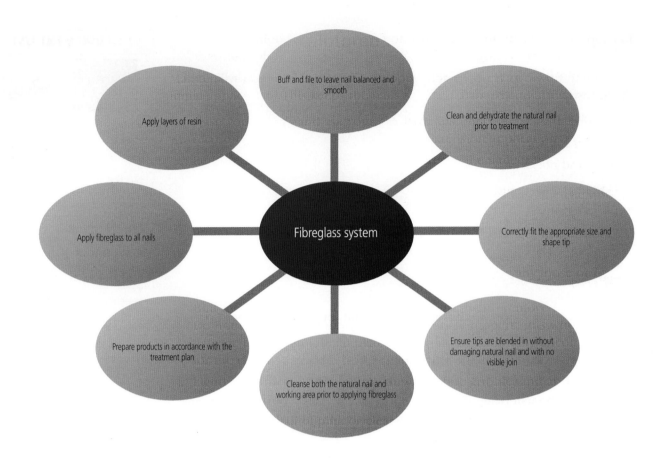

Apply layers of resin

Buff and file to leave nail balanced and smooth

Clean and dehydrate the natural nail prior to treatment

Apply fibreglass to all nails

Fibreglass system

Correctly fit the appropriate size and shape tip

Prepare products in accordance with the treatment plan

Cleanse both the natural nail and working area prior to applying fibreglass

Ensure tips are blended in without damaging natural nail and with no visible join

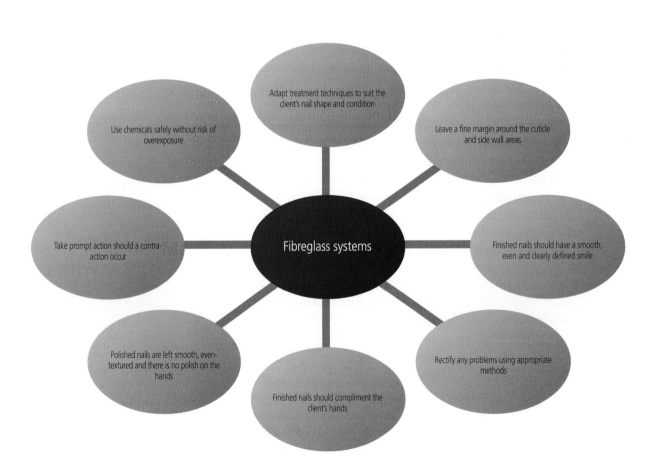

Use chemicals safely without risk of overexposure

Adapt treatment techniques to suit the client's nail shape and condition

Leave a fine margin around the cuticle and side wall areas

Take prompt action should a contra-action occur

Fibreglass systems

Finished nails should have a smooth, even and clearly defined smile

Polished nails are left smooth, even-textured and there is no polish on the hands

Finished nails should compliment the client's hands

Rectify any problems using appropriate methods

12 Apply a small amount of adhesive to the seam. This is done to ensure that the edge of the tip is securely bonded: it also allows blending to be done more quickly.

13 Spray with activator.

14 Cut the nail tip to the desired length and file it to shape.

15 Blend the seam area. Begin with a coarse emery board, then work through to a fine one. Hold the board at a slight angle and blend the seam area without touching the nail plate excessively. Do not buff to a shine as this would prevent further resin from adhering properly.

HEALTH AND SAFETY

Some fibreglass nail systems may use an ultraviolet light or brush-on activator to set the resin. Always follow the manufacturer's instructions carefully.

HEALTH AND SAFETY

Remove excessive dust from the nail plate using a dry tissue or nail wipe. Do not use a brush: brushes are difficult to sterilise and may encourage cross-infection.

---

16 Apply adhesive to the nail plate and spread it over the nail. This must be done carefully to avoid touching the cuticle and surrounding skin. Any product touching the skin will allow natural oils to get underneath, resulting in lifting later.

17 Spray with activator.

18 Apply fibreglass mesh. Very sharp scissors must be used to cut the mesh, or fraying will result. Cut the fibreglass to fit the whole nail surface, leaving approximately 3 mm gap around the edges. Apply the mesh with the tacky side to the nail plate and ensure that it is completely smooth with no frayed edges.

19 Repeat steps **16** and **17** twice. Allow the resin to soak into the fibreglass mesh for a few seconds before spraying with activator. This reduces the chance of the mesh showing through the finished application.

20 Gently buff the surface to remove shine. This allows step **21** to be carried out effectively. If the surface is buffed too much the fibreglass mesh will show through. If this happens, repeat steps **16** and **17** twice before continuing as usual.

21 Buff the surface to a shine. Using a four-sided buffer, bring the now dull surface to a shine. Begin with the coarsest side of the buffer and work down to the smooth.

22 Apply cuticle oil. This is to re-introduce moisture to the area, which may have become dehydrated with all the buffing and filing. It also gives a luxurious glossy finish. Apply oil to the cuticle and the nail walls then massage in with thumbs.

23 Ask the client to wash her hands to remove all dust particles and leave the hands feeling fresh and comfortable.

24 Nail polish may be applied if required. Treat the nails as if they were natural: apply a base coat to avoid staining from dark colours. Remember that only *acetone-free* nail polish remover may be used. Ordinary nail polish remover would result in a softening of the nails.

TIP

After each use, the sides of the resin bottle should be squeezed to allow any resin in the applicator nozzle to flow back into the bottle. A burping sound will be heard from the bottle if this has been done correctly. Failure to do this will result in the nozzle becoming blocked, making application difficult.

HEALTH AND SAFETY

If resin flows onto the skin, wipe it off immediately, before it dries, with the corner of a tissue or a nail wipe soaked in acetone. Allowing the resin to dry on the skin will irritate the client's skin and may cause the nail to lift later.

TIP

Fibreglass nails are not porous and therefore do not need a base coat under coloured polish. It is a good idea to advise the client to use it anyway, however, as this gets her into a good habit for the future when she is applying nail polish to her natural nails.

TIP

Do not spray activator towards the adhesive bottle as it may set inside.

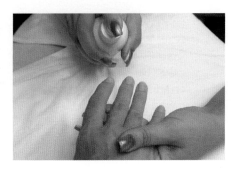

Sterilising the nail

Buffing the nail to remove shine

Applying the nail tip

Cutting the nail tip

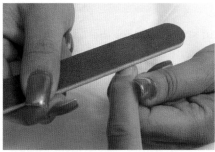

Blending the seam

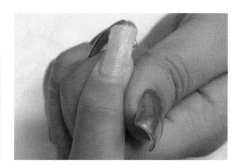

Applying fibreglass mesh

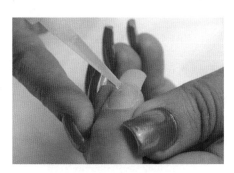

Apply adhesive to nail plate

Spray with activator

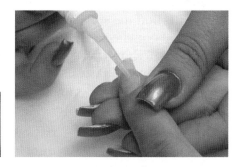

Applying resin over the fibreglass

Buffing the nail to a shine

Applying cuticle oil

Completed fibreglass nail extensions

Stress strip application

A **stress strip** is simply a narrow piece of fibreglass mesh placed across the nail where the nail tip is blended into the natural nail. This is the weakest area of the nail extension and is usually where breaks will occur if the client is careless with her nails.

Stress strips should be used on the nails of clients:

- who desire very long nail extensions
- who are careless or clumsy with their hands.

To apply a stress strip, simply apply the nails in the usual way but stop prior to the application of the fibreglass mesh, i.e. before step 18.

18 Now apply the stress strip across the nail, and coat with a layer of resin and spray activator. Then continue in the usual way, applying mesh over the whole nail plate without touching the cuticle or nail walls:

18a Apply the fibreglass strip.

18b Apply resin over the whole nail and spray with activator.

18c Apply fibreglass mesh over the whole nail without touching the cuticle or nail walls.

18d Proceed with application in the usual way.

A fibreglass stress strip

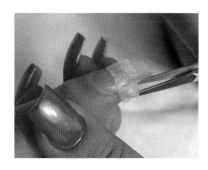

Fibreglass mesh being placed over the whole nail

Aftercare and advice

These are the same as for pre-formed nails – page 382.

TIP ✔

Clients can still have a regular manicure whilst they are wearing nail extensions. Recommending a regular manicure will help to keep the client's skin and cuticles in good condition, whilst allowing the nail technician to keep a check on the condition of the nail extensions.

TIP ✔

Alternate maintenance procedures so that one maintenance is with fibreglass, the next without. This avoids unnecessary use of fibreglass and build-up of product around the cuticle area.

Acrylic products

Problem-solving

- **White areas under the nail tip** This could be due to air bubbles trapped during application of the nail tip. Remove the tip and start again. Use slightly more adhesive to give more time before the nail bonds.
- **Fibreglass mesh shows through the finished nail** This can happen if the first coat of adhesive did not soak through properly before the activator was sprayed, or if the fibreglass was handled too much prior to application.
- **Lifting of the fibreglass overlay** This may be due to products touching the cuticle or nail wall. Too much adhesive, or not enough, may also cause this problem.
- **Burning** If the client complains of a burning sensation, hold the activator further away to avoid this heat reaction.
- **Frayed fibreglass mesh** If the mesh has frayed through the adhesive, it could be that the scissors were not sharp enough, or that the fibreglass was not pressed smooth to the nail before the adhesive was applied.

SCULPTURED ACRYLIC NAILS

Liquid and **powder acrylic** can be used in two ways to produce strong, natural-looking nail extensions. They can be sculpted over a nail form, or they can be sculpted over a nail tip. Which method is used depends on the client's needs and the therapist's preference. With nail tips:

- application takes longer, as time is needed to apply and blend in the tips
- less sculpting skill is required, as the tip provides the basis of a natural shape
- the method is more expensive, due to the use of tips
- less filing is required, as the need for sculpting is minimal.

With nail forms:

- once the application skill has been mastered, sculpting over a form is quicker than with the application of a tip
- the method is cheaper, as no nail tips are required
- the technique is more difficult to learn
- if the form is incorrectly applied or is moved during application, extensive filing is required to achieve a natural shape.

Acrylic nails are very strong and durable, and are therefore ideal for clients who are rough with their hands.

Advantages	Disadvantages
1 Very strong.	1 The need for primer means that the natural nails are weak when acrylic nails are removed. However, this weakness is not permanent and will grow out as the nails grow forward.
2 Suitable for nail-biters, due to the strong adhesive qualities of acrylic and the fact that a large nail plate is not needed.	2 Acrylic nails are not suitable for clients who wish to grow their own nails without artificial products to strengthen them.
3 The moulding qualities of acrylic allow sculpting to be adapted to any size or shape of natural nail.	3 Nails need to be 'infilled' every 2–3 weeks.
	4 Products have a strong, unpleasant odour.

Equipment and materials

In addition to the basic equipment and materials (page 376) you will need the following:

- acrylic powder in a variety of colours, including white, pink and clear
- acrylic liquid
- primer
- nail forms
- brush
- dappen dish
- a selection of enamels, including base and top coats.

Application: sculptured acrylic nail extensions

1   Wash your hands and ask your client to wash hers.
2   Remove any nail enamel and check for contra-indications.
3   Sterilise the natural nail plate with sterilising solution. This prevents the growth of bacterial and fungal infections beneath the artificial nail.
4   Lightly buff the nail plate with a fine-grit board, to remove shine.
5   Apply primer to the nail plate and allow this to dry. Do not allow primer to touch the cuticle or the nail walls.
6   Apply the nail form to the fingertip, beneath the free edge of the natural nail. This is the base for the extended acrylic tip. Check from all angles that the form is in the most natural position.

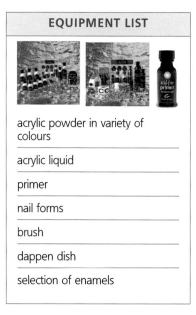

EQUIPMENT LIST

acrylic powder in variety of colours

acrylic liquid

primer

nail forms

brush

dappen dish

selection of enamels

TIP

Acrylics are now also available in a variety of bright colours and glitters.

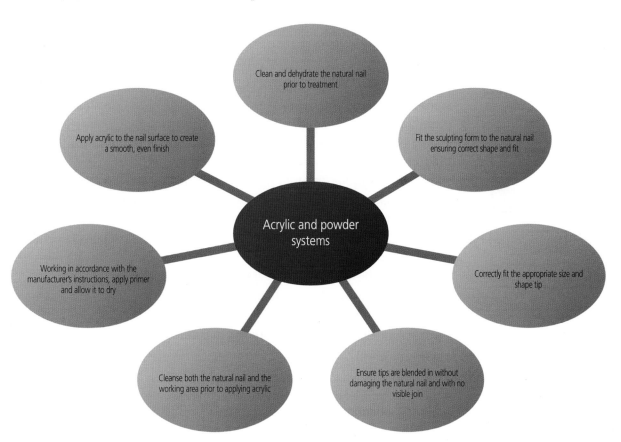

Clean and dehydrate the natural nail prior to treatment

Fit the sculpting form to the natural nail ensuring correct shape and fit

Apply acrylic to the nail surface to create a smooth, even finish

Acrylic and powder systems

Correctly fit the appropriate size and shape tip

Working in accordance with the manufacturer's instructions, apply primer and allow it to dry

Ensure tips are blended in without damaging the natural nail and with no visible join

Cleanse both the natural nail and the working area prior to applying acrylic

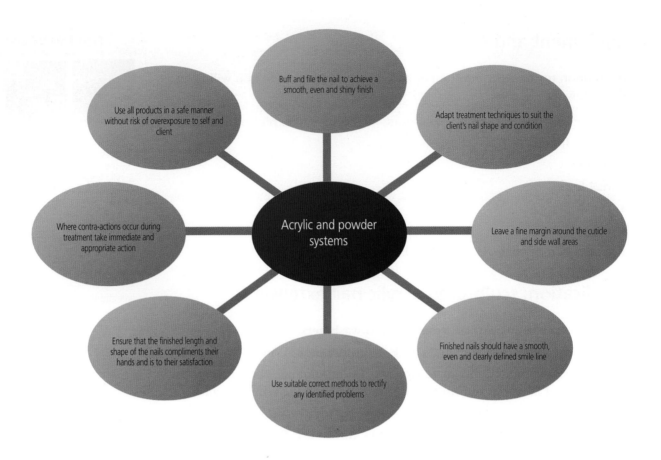

Acrylic and powder systems

- Buff and file the nail to achieve a smooth, even and shiny finish
- Adapt treatment techniques to suit the client's nail shape and condition
- Use all products in a safe manner without risk of overexposure to self and client
- Leave a fine margin around the cuticle and side wall areas
- Where contra-actions occur during treatment take immediate and appropriate action
- Finished nails should have a smooth, even and clearly defined smile line
- Ensure that the finished length and shape of the nails compliments their hands and is to their satisfaction
- Use suitable correct methods to rectify any identified problems

TIP

Tidy the work area and cleanse nails to prevent dust from spoiling the finish.

TIP

Take immediate action should a contra-action occur during treatment.

7 To achieve a natural look when applying acrylic nails, use pink or white acrylic for clients with light skins and ivory and peach acrylic for clients with dark skins.

  Dip the brush in the liquid, then in acrylic powder to form a ball the size of a small pea. Apply this to the nail form to create a free edge. Smooth and shape the acrylic using the flat side of the brush.

8 Dip the brush in liquid, then in powder, as before, and apply to the middle of the nail plate. Use the sides of the brush to blend the acrylic towards the free edge and sides of the nail.

9 Dip the brush in liquid, then powder, and apply the acrylic near the cuticle. This should be a wetter, thinner application to avoid a ridge and give a more natural-looking application.

10 When the desired shape has been created, allow it to set hard. To check whether the acrylic has set, tap it with an orange stick: listen for an audible click rather than a dull sound.

  Once set, remove the nail form and shape the free edge with a coarse-grit file.

11 Using a four-sided buffer, smooth the nail surface to a shine.

12 Apply cuticle oil.

13 Wash your hands, and the client should wash hers. This step is very important: you both need to remove any acrylic dust that might otherwise become irritating on the skin.

Remove the towel from the workstation and replace it with a clean one. This prevents dust particles from ruining the nail enamel application and makes the working environment more pleasant.

14 Enamel the nails as usual. Always ensure a base coat, as acrylic is a porous substance and nail enamel might stain it.

TIP

Every 2–3 months the nails should be removed and a new set applied. This allows the new nail growth to be properly dehydrated with acetone. Failure to do this will result in repeated problems with nails lifting in the cuticle area.

HEALTH AND SAFETY

Ventilation
Because of the volatile nature of acrylic liquids and the dust created from filing, you must always work in a well-ventilated room. Specially designed extractor fans are available for use at the workstation.

Forming the free edge

Forming the nail plate

Completed acrylic nail extensions

Application: nail tips with acrylic overlay

Follow the instructions for nail tip application up to and including step 12 (page 380–1). Then follow this procedure:

13 Apply primer to the natural nail area only.

14 Dip the brush in liquid, then in clear powder, to form a ball the size of a large pea.

15 Apply the acrylic ball to the centre of the nail plate. Use the sides of the brush to blend acrylic over the entire nail plate, ensuring that application is thinner at the cuticle, the nail wall and the free edge areas, to give a natural appearance.

Nail tape

Ellisons

TIP ✔

Natural nails may be overlaid with gel, fibre or acrylic in order to make them stronger without increasing their length.

16 Re-apply acrylic if necessary to ensure adequate coverage of the nail plate.

17 Check the nail from all angles to ensure that the shape is natural.

18 Once the desired shape has been created, allow the product to set hard.

19 Remove any surface irregularities using a coarse-grit file.

20 Buff the surface to a shine with a four-sided buffer.

21 Apply cuticle oil to the skin around the nail.

22 Wash your hands, and your client should wash hers.

23 Apply nail polish as desired.

Aftercare and advice

These are the same as for nail extensions – see page 382.

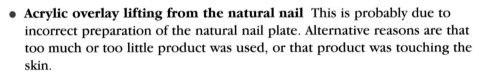

HEALTH AND SAFETY

Working with acrylic
The dust created during the filing of acrylic nails can lead to skin allergies and respiratory problems. Keep dust to a minimum by using an extractor fan near the workstation and changing towels on the workstation during treatment.

Problem-solving

- **Acrylic overlay lifting from the natural nail** This is probably due to incorrect preparation of the natural nail plate. Alternative reasons are that too much or too little product was used, or that product was touching the skin.

- **Infills are obvious** Ensure a thorough blending in of the previous application before applying new acrylic.

- **Nails break at the flesh line** Not enough product was applied in the area, or it was over-buffed.

- **Acrylic liquid is solid in the bottle** The liquid has been contaminated with powder. Never pour products back into the bottle, or put the brush in the bottle.

- **Acrylic appears frosty when set** The room is too cold. The room should be quite warm if the product is to set correctly.

- **The finished nail points upwards or downwards** This results from incorrect placing of the nail form or incorrect application of the nail tip. Check regularly from all angles during application.

Nail pointing up

Nail pointing down

left Too much product at the sides
centre Too much product in the middle
right Too much product at one side

- **The transverse arch of the nail is irregular** The acrylic was applied unevenly:
  - too much product at the sides of the nail
  - too much product on the middle of the nail
  - too much product at one side – the clients fingers were tilted before the product set, or the application was too wet, causing the product to run.
- **The longitudinal arch of the nail is irregular** The acrylic was applied unevenly:
  - too much product at the cuticle area
  - too much product in the centre of the nail
  - too much product at free edge.

If you make a mistake, remove the nail using the correct procedure and re-apply it.

top Too much product in the cuticle area
centre Too much product in the middle
bottom Too much product at the free edge

UV GEL SYSTEMS

Gel can be applied over a tip or can be sculpted over a nail form as with acrylic. Application methods are very similar to those with acrylic, but due to the self-levelling nature of the gel, the procedure is easier. Because gel is clear, the finished nail is very natural-looking and does not require nail polish. Coloured gels are also available, giving a permanently enamelled look that doesn't chip or fade: however, clients may get bored wearing the same colour all the time. UV gel systems require the use of an ultraviolet light to set the gel, others may use a spray activator similar to that used in the fibreglass application process.

Advantages	Disadvantages
1 Very natural-looking.	1 Not as strong as acrylic or fibreglass.
2 Easier to apply than acrylic or fibreglass.	2 Methods using ultraviolet light are more expensive than other systems.
3 Self-levelling gel means less filing.	
4 Less filing means less dust, so the environment is more pleasant for the client and nail technician.	

Equipment and materials

In addition to the basic equipment and materials (page 376) you will need the following:

- manicure table
- gel
- gel-setting spray or ultraviolet light

EQUIPMENT LIST

manicure table

gel

gel-setting or ultra-violet light

primer

nail forms

nail tips

adhesive

brushes

selection of enamels

- primer
- nail forms
- nail tips
- adhesive
- brushes
- a selection of polish, including base and top coats.

Application: the tip and overlay method

1 Wash your hands and ask your client to wash hers.
2 Remove any nail enamel and check for contra-indications.
3 Sterilise the nail plate.
4 Push back the cuticles and cut the free edge to approximately 3 mm.
5 Size up the nail tips.
6 Lightly buff the natural nail to remove shine.
7 Apply a small drop of adhesive to the tip of the natural nail.
8 Apply the nail tip.
9 Cut the nail tip to the desired length and file it to shape.
10 Blend the seam area.
11 Apply primer to the natural nail plate area.

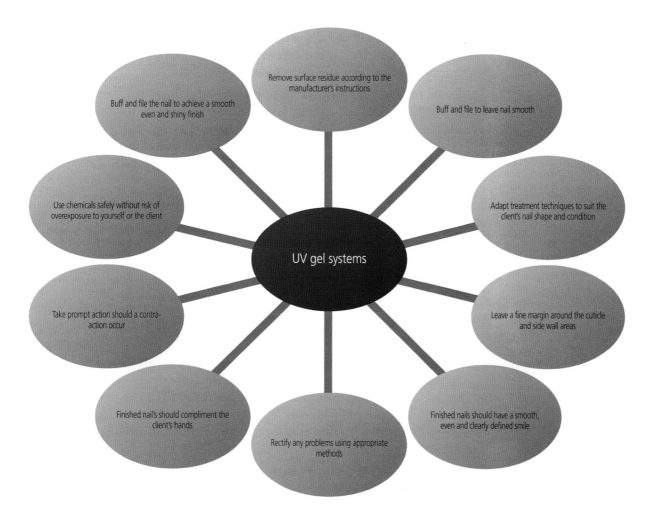

Central node: **UV gel systems**

Surrounding nodes:
- Remove surface residue according to the manufacturer's instructions
- Buff and file to leave nail smooth
- Adapt treatment techniques to suit the client's nail shape and condition
- Leave a fine margin around the cuticle and side wall areas
- Finished nails should have a smooth, even and clearly defined smile
- Rectify any problems using appropriate methods
- Finished nail's should compliment the client's hands
- Take prompt action should a contra-action occur
- Use chemicals safely without risk of overexposure to yourself or the client
- Buff and file the nail to achieve a smooth even and shiny finish

12 Apply gel according to the manufacturer's instructions. Some gels need an ultraviolet light source to cure them; others may be set with an activator spray or brush-on setting liquid.

13 Remove any sticky residue with a nail wipe soaked in non-acetone nail polish remover.

14 Buff the surface to a shine.

15 Apply cuticle oil.

16 Ask the client to wash her hands.

17 Apply nail polish if desired.

> **TIP**
>
> Because gel is semi-liquid, ask client to keep her fingers flat until the gel is set, otherwise the gel will slide to one side of the nail resulting in an uneven application. Apply gel to the fingers and thumbs separately, so that the client can keep them level.

Application: sculptured gel nail extensions

1 Wash your hands and ask your client to wash hers.

2 Remove any nail enamel and check for contra-indications.

3 Sterilise the natural nail plate with sterilising solution. This prevents the growth of bacterial and fungal infections beneath the artificial nail.

4 Lightly buff the nail plate with a fine-grit board to remove the shine.

5 Apply primer to the nail plate and allow it to dry. Do not allow primer to touch the cuticle or nail walls.

TIP

Some systems use three different gels, others only one. Always read the manufacturer's instructions carefully.

6 Apply a nail form to the fingertip beneath the free edge of the natural nail. This is the base for the extended gel tip. Check from all angles that the form is in the most natural position.

7 Dip the brush in gel to form a ball the size of a small pea. Apply this to the nail plate near the cuticle, and pull the gel towards the free edge with the brush. (Do not apply like nail enamel as this will result in too thin an application of gel.) Gel is self-levelling: push it over the nail plate, avoiding the cuticle and nail walls. Shape the gel over the nail form to create the free edge.

8 When you have created the desired shape, allow the gel to cure according to the manufacturer's instructions.

9 Once set, remove the nail form and shape the free edge with a coarse-grit file.

10 Remove any sticky residue on the gel with a nail wipe soaked in non-acetone nail polish remover.

11 Using a four-sided buffer, smooth the nail surface to a shine.

12 Apply cuticle oil.

13 You and your client should now wash your hands. This step is very important: it removes any dust or gel residue that might otherwise become irritating on the skin. Remove the towel from the workstation and replace it with a clean one. This prevents dust particles from ruining the nail polish application and makes the working environment more pleasant.

14 Apply polish to the nails as usual. Always use a base coat to prevent the polish staining the gel.

TIP

Every 2–3 months, the nails should be removed and a new set applied. This allows the new nail growth to be properly dehydrated with acetone. Failure to due this will result in recurring problems with nails lifting in the cuticle area.

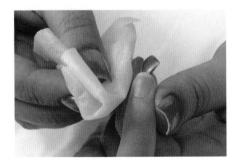

Sterilising the nail plate

Buffing the nail plate to remove shine

Fitting the nail forms

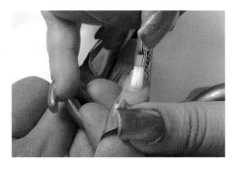

Applying the base coat gel

Curing the gel

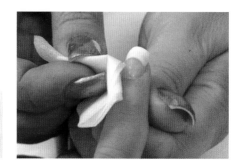

Wiping with acetone

Shaping the nail

Applying cuticle oil

Completed gel nail extensions

Aftercare and advice

It is important when carrying out a nail-extension treatment that the client knows how to care for her nails at home. It is up to you to give her the correct advice, otherwise she may unwittingly undo the work done during treatment.

As you give home-care advice you can also recommend products such as nail polish or hand cream, enhancing retail sales and your profit.

Home-care advice will differ slightly for each client, but basically will be as follows:

- Use only non-acetone nail polish remover to avoid softening the nails.
- Have the nails regularly maintained (infilled) to keep them attractive and strong.
- Always use a base coat under nail polish to avoid yellowing.
- Do not pull the nails off if they start to lift. Have them removed professionally and safely.

ACTIVITY

Designing an aftercare leaflet
Design an attractive aftercare leaflet to be given to the clients after their nails have been applied. Include any home-care advice and recommended retail products that you think would be useful.

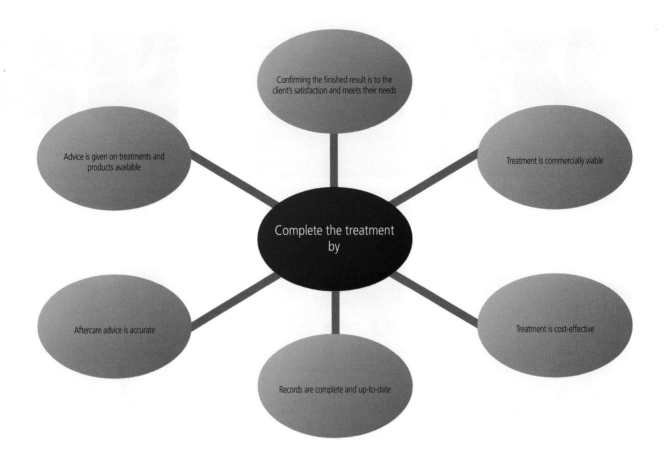

Assessment of knowledge and understanding

You have now learnt about how to enhance the appearance of natural nails using artificial nail structures.

To test your level of knowledge and understanding, answer the following short questions. These will prepare you for your summative (final) assessment.

Anatomy and physiology questions required for this unit are found on pages 146–50.

Consult with the client

1 State three contra-indications to nail extension application.

2 Why is it important to remove any nail polish during the consultation?

3 What is the importance of identifying the condition of the skin and nails during consultation?

4 Why is it important to record the condition of the client's skin and nails prior to continuing with treatment?

5 How would you recognise a fungal infection?

Plan the treatment

1 State three differences between pre-formed nail extensions and sculptured nail extensions.

2 What advice should you give a client regarding the length of the artificial free edge?

3 Why is it important to recommend suitable products to your client?

4 How is the client's nail shape important when considering corrective work?

5 Why is the condition of the client's nail important when considering treatment?

6 Why is it important to discuss the treatment plan with the client?

Prepare for the treatment

1 Which file is most coarse: a 100 grit or a 240 grit?

2 What is nail tape used for?

3 Why is it important to always read the manufacturer's instructions prior to using nail extension products?

4 Why is good ventilation important in the working area?

5 How can you encourage the client to relax during treatment?

6 What protective equipment should you wear during treatment?

Apply artificial nails using acrylic liquid and powder system

1 What is the action of a primer on the natural nail plate?

2 What home-care advice should you give to a client regarding the maintenance of acrylic liquid and powder nail extensions?

3 What contra-actions are applicable to nail extension application?

4 Why is it important to keep the cuticle and nail walls free of product?

5 What is a smile line?

6 Why is it important to keep the work area free from dust?

Apply artificial nails using the UV gel system

1 Why should the client's nail plate be free of oil and moisture prior to nail extension application?

2 What home-care advice should you give to a client regarding the maintenance of UV gel nail extensions?

3 What may be the result of fitting incorrectly sized tips?

4 What may occur if nails are buffed too aggressively when blending the seam area?

Apply artificial nails using the wrap system

1 What home-care advice should you give to a client regarding the maintenance of wrap system nail extensions?

2 What advice would you give the client with regard to the length of the free edge?

3 What is activator used for?

4 How can you prevent the resin nozzle from becoming blocked during use?

5 When is a stress strip used?

Complete the treatment

1 State three products that should be recommended to the client for home use.

2 How often should the client be recommended to return to the salon for infill/maintenance routines?

3 Why is cuticle oil applied at the end of the treatment?

Case study

The following clients require nail extension services. Which type of nail extension system would you choose for each client? Give reasons for your answer.

a. A bride who would like very natural-looking nails for her wedding day and honeymoon but who must take them off soon after as her occupation does not permit her to wear them.

b. A client who bites her nails and would like her nails to look nice for her two-week summer holiday.

c. A client who has three broken nails and would like the short nails extended to match the naturally long nails.

chapter 12

Maintain, repair and enhance artificial nail structures BT23

Learning objectives

This unit describes how to maintain and repair damage to artificial nail systems, and to enhance and camouflage damaged nails. It describes the competencies to enable you to:

- **consult with the client**
- **plan the treatment**
- **prepare for the treatment**
- **maintain and repair artificial nail structures**
- **cosmetically enhance damaged nails**
- **remove artificial nail structures**
- **complete the treatment**

When providing artificial nail systems it is important to use the skills you have learned in the following core mandatory units:

G1 ensure your own actions reduce risks to health and safety
G6 promote additional products or services to clients
G11 contribute to the financial effectiveness of the business manicure
BT22 enhance the appearance of natural nails using artificial nail systems

THE NAIL

The structure and function of the nail

Nails grow from the ends of the fingers and toes and serve as a form of protection. They also help when picking up small objects.

Nails and nail art by Gina Wallace

Nails and Nail Art by:
Gina Wallace

The nail plate

The **nail plate** is composed of compact translucent layers of keratinised cells: it is this that makes up the man body of the nail. The layers of cells are packed very closely together, with fat but very little moisture.

The nail gradually grows forward over the nail bed, until finally it becomes the free edge. The underside of the nail plate is grooved by longitudinal ridges and furrows, which help to keep it in place.

In normal health the plate curves in two directions:

- transversely – from side to side across the nail;
- longitudinally – from the base of the nail to the free edge.

There are no blood vessels or nerves in the nail plate: this is why the nails, like hair, can be cut without pain or bleeding. The pink colour of the nail plate derives from the blood vessels that pass beneath it.

Function: To protect the nail bed.

The free edge

The **free edge** is the part of the nail that extends beyond the fingertip; this is the part that is filed.

Function: To protect the fingertip and the hyponychium (see below).

The matrix

The **matrix**, sometimes called the **nail root**, is the growing area of the nail. It is formed by the division of cells in this area, which is part of the germinating layer of the epidermis. It lies under the eponychium (see below), at the base of the nail, nearest to the body. The process of keratinisation takes place in the epidermal cells of the matrix, forming the hardened tissue of the nail plate.

Function: To produce new nail cells.

The nail bed

The **nail bed** is the portion of skin upon which the nail plate rests. it has a pattern of grooves and furrows corresponding to those found on the underside of the nail plate; these interlock, keeping the nail in place, but separate at the end of the nail to form the free edge. The nail bed is liberally supplied with blood vessels, which provide the nourishment necessary for continued growth; and sensor nerves, for protection.

Function: To supply nourishment and protection.

The nail mantle

The **nail mantle** is the layer of epidermis at the base of the nail, before the cuticle.

Function: To protect the matrix from physical damage.

The lunula

The **lunula** is located at the base of the nail, lying over the matrix. It is white, relative to the rest of the nail, and there are two theories to account for this:

- newly formed nail plates may be more opaque than mature nail plates;
- the lunula may indicate the extent of the underlying matrix – the matrix is thicker than the epidermis of the nail bed, and the capillaries beneath it would not show through as well.

Function: None.

The hyponychium

The **hyponychium** is part of the epidermis under the free edge of the nail.

Function: To protect the nail bed from infection.

The nail grooves

The **nail grooves** run alongside the edge of the nail plate.

Function: To keep the nail growing forward in a straight line.

ACTIVITY

Recognising nail structure
With a colleague, try to identify the structural parts of each other's nails. Write down both the parts that you can see and the parts that you cannot.

The perionychium

The **perionychium** is the collective name given to the nail walls and the cuticle area.

Function: To protect the nail.

The nail walls

The **nail walls** are the folds of skin overlapping the sides of the nails.

Function: To protect the nail plate edges.

The eponychium

The **eponychium** is the extension of the cuticle at the base of the nail plate, under which the nail plate emerges from the matrix.

Function: To protect the matrix from infection.

The cuticle

The **cuticle** is the overlapping epidermis around the base of the nail. When in good condition, it is soft and loose.

Function: To protect the matrix from infection.

Nail growth

Cells divide in the matrix and the nail grows forward over the nail bed, guided by the nail grooves, until it reaches the end of the finger or toe, where is becomes the free edge. As they first emerge from the matrix the translucent cells are plump and soft, but they get harder and flatter as they move toward the free edge. The top two layers of the epidermis form the nail plate; the remaining three form the nail bed.

The nail plate is made up of a protein called keratin, and the hardening process that takes place in the nail cells is known as **keratinisation**.

The nail bed has a pattern of grooves and furrows corresponding to those found on the underside of the nail plate: the two surfaces interlock, holding the nail in place.

Fingernails grow at approximately twice the speed of toenails. It takes about 6 months for a fingernail to grow from cuticle to free edge, but about 12 months for a toenail to do so.

Reception

When a client makes an appointment for a nail extension maintenance service the receptionist should ask a few simple questions in order to ascertain her needs. Information obtained from the client will help the nail technician to set up the working area with the appropriate equipment and materials and will save time when the client arrives for treatment. The basic questions that the receptionist should ask are these.

● What type of extension does she have i.e. acrylic, gel etc.?

● What is the extent of the damage to the nails (if any)?

Record cards

As with all other beauty treatments, accurate record cards must be kept for clients having nail extension maintenance and repair services. As the client has had nail services before, the receptionist should consult the card and tell the nail technician about these.

This will give the nail technician a good idea of what to expect when the client arrives. For example, if the client has not attended for over three weeks her nails may need a lot of maintenance work and extra time could be booked out to allow for this.

Information on the client's record card will include the following.

Condition of natural nails and cuticles

The condition prior to extensions being applied may be relevant later if the nail extensions are removed. The client cannot expect her nails to be in perfect condition later if they were not so at the outset. The amount of damage and wear and tear will give an indication as to how well the client is caring for her nails.

Type of nail system used

Should the nail technician be away for any reason, other technicians must know what type of nails to apply and what repairs have been done. The record card will tell assisting staff which products to set out at the working area.

Size of nail tips [if used]

A record of the size of tip will save time during repairs and maintenance – the technician will know which tip size to use, and won't have to measure each time to get the right size.

Allergies to products

Knowing which products, if any, the client is allergic to is crucial so that these can be avoided.

Maintenance and repair

Specific details of the type of maintenance carried out, which nails have been repaired and how, should be kept.

Client signature

The client must confirm that she has been informed of the treatment details and possible contra-actions.

A client's record card – front and back

Fancy Fingers Nail Salon
Client Record Card

Name	Address
Mrs Irene Brown	11a New Street, Newtown

Tel No	Date of Birth	Occupation
Home: 456456	21 June 1951	Housewife
Work: 498798		

Conditions of natural nails on first salon visit
Cuticles soft and in good condition

Details of previous nail treatment prior to attending *Fancy Fingers Nail Salon*
None

Details of nail care carried out at home
Hand cream applied occasionally. Nails painted for special occasions. Rough edges are filed if nails break

Size of nail tips

Right Hand   Left Hand

Signature of client	Date
IBrown	4.5.04

Date	Treatment Details	Homecare Advice	Retail	Nail Technician	Client Signature
4.5.04	Full set of sculptured acrylic nail extensions. Applied clear enamel only.	Gave client aftercare advice leaflet for acrylic nails. Discussed it with her so that she understood why the home care was important	Small bottle of non-acetone nail polish remover	Hayley	IBrown
18.5.04	Maintenance on full set of nails. Repair to thumb on left hand. Crack in free edge due to minor accident.	As previous	Rose Pink nail enamel	Hayley	IBrown
31.5.04	Backfills in pink and white. New nail applied to left thumb. Reduced length of all nails.	Recommended a full manicure between maintenance visits.	Hand cream	Hayley	IBrown

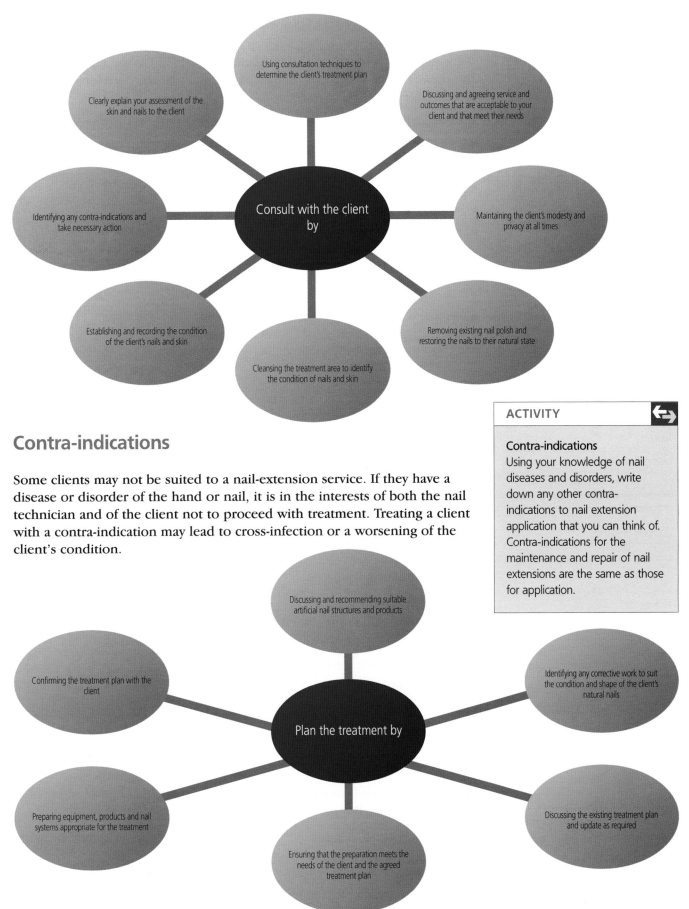

Using consultation techniques to determine the client's treatment plan

Clearly explain your assessment of the skin and nails to the client

Discussing and agreeing service and outcomes that are acceptable to your client and that meet their needs

Identifying any contra-indications and take necessary action

Consult with the client by

Maintaining the client's modesty and privacy at all times

Establishing and recording the condition of the client's nails and skin

Removing existing nail polish and restoring the nails to their natural state

Cleansing the treatment area to identify the condition of nails and skin

Contra-indications

Some clients may not be suited to a nail-extension service. If they have a disease or disorder of the hand or nail, it is in the interests of both the nail technician and of the client not to proceed with treatment. Treating a client with a contra-indication may lead to cross-infection or a worsening of the client's condition.

ACTIVITY

Contra-indications
Using your knowledge of nail diseases and disorders, write down any other contra-indications to nail extension application that you can think of. Contra-indications for the maintenance and repair of nail extensions are the same as those for application.

Discussing and recommending suitable artificial nail structures and products

Confirming the treatment plan with the client

Identifying any corrective work to suit the condition and shape of the client's natural nails

Plan the treatment by

Preparing equipment, products and nail systems appropriate for the treatment

Discussing the existing treatment plan and update as required

Ensuring that the preparation meets the needs of the client and the agreed treatment plan

EQUIPMENT LIST

workstation or table

lamp for workstation

waste bin (with lid)

plastic glasses

manicure pads or disposable tissue

cotton buds

nail wipes or tissue

tissues

orange sticks

glass bowl

3 bowls

dappen dish

scissors

tip cutters

coarse file

medium file

fine file

4 sided buffer

towels

antiseptic

nail steriliser

acetone

cuticle oil

non-acetone nail enamel remover in pump dispenser

mid antiseptic cleaner for hands

nail tips

aftercare leaflets

Equipment and materials

The equipment and materials listed below are general to the maintenance and repair of nail extensions. Additional specialised items are listed with the individual techniques.

- workstation or table
- lamp for workstation use
- waste bin (with lid)
- plastic glasses
- manicure pads or disposable tissue
- nail wipes or tissue
- cotton buds
- tissues
- orange sticks
- glass bowl
- three bowls
- dappen dish
- scissors
- tip cutters
- coarse file (100-grit) – for reducing length of artificial free edge
- medium file (180-grit) – for blending in seam areas
- fine file (240-grit) – to smooth nail and remove scratches
- four-sided buffer – to bring nail surface to a shine
- medium-sized towels (three)
- antiseptic
- nail steriliser
- acetone
- cuticle oil
- non-acetone nail polish remover (in a pump dispenser)
- mild antiseptic cleanser for hands
- nail tips in assorted styles and sizes
- client record card
- aftercare leaflets.

Sterilisation and sanitisation

Sterilisation and sanitisation procedures for the maintenance and repair of nail extensions are the same as those for application.

Preparing the treatment area

Preparing the treatment area for the maintenance and repair of nail extensions is the same as the scheme for application.

TIP

Ensure that the nail technician's chair is very comfortable and at a suitable height: you could be sitting in it for up to forty hours a week!

Preparing the client

The method of preparing the client for the maintenance and repair of nail extensions is the same as for application.

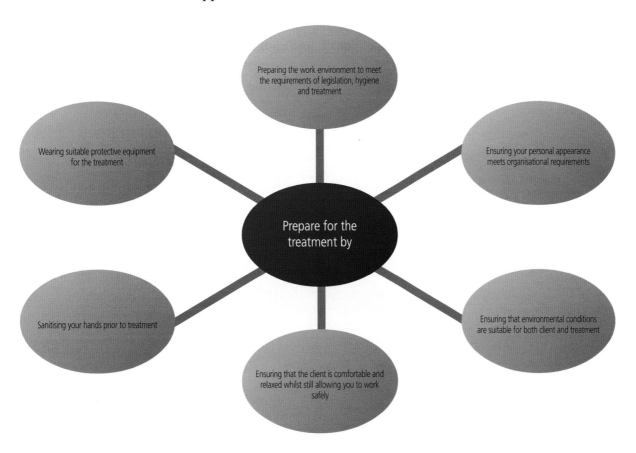

Prepare for the treatment by

- Preparing the work environment to meet the requirements of legislation, hygiene and treatment
- Ensuring your personal appearance meets organisational requirements
- Ensuring that environmental conditions are suitable for both client and treatment
- Ensuring that the client is comfortable and relaxed whilst still allowing you to work safely
- Sanitising your hands prior to treatment
- Wearing suitable protective equipment for the treatment

Maintenance of nail tips

Due to the very temporary nature of nail tips, maintenance is not necessary. If tips crack or break, they should be removed using the correct procedure, then re-applied.

Equipment and materials

In addition to the basic equipment and materials (page 408), you will need the following:

- nail tips in assorted styles and sizes
- resin and nozzle
- selection of nail polish, including base and top coats.

EQUIPMENT LIST

nail tips

resin and nozzle

selection of enamels

Maintenance of fibreglass nail extensions

Equipment and materials

In addition to the basic equipment and materials (page 408) you will need the following:

- nail tips in assorted styles and sizes
- scissors for fibreglass
- resin and nozzle
- resin activator
- fibreglass mesh
- a selection of nail polish, including base and top coats.

Buff and file to leave the nail balanced and smooth

Clean and dehydrate the natural nail prior to treatment

Apply layers of resin

Fibreglass system

Correctly fit the appropriate size and shape tip

Apply fibreglass to all nails

Ensure tips are blended in without damaging the natural nail and with no visible join

Prepare products in accordance with the treatment plan

Cleanse both the natural nail and the working area prior to applying fibreglass

Maintenance

Two weeks after the initial application

1 Cleanse the hands and nails.

2 Remove any nail polish with acetone-free polish remover and check for any signs of infection. If any infection is present, remove the nails immediately and advise the client to see her doctor.

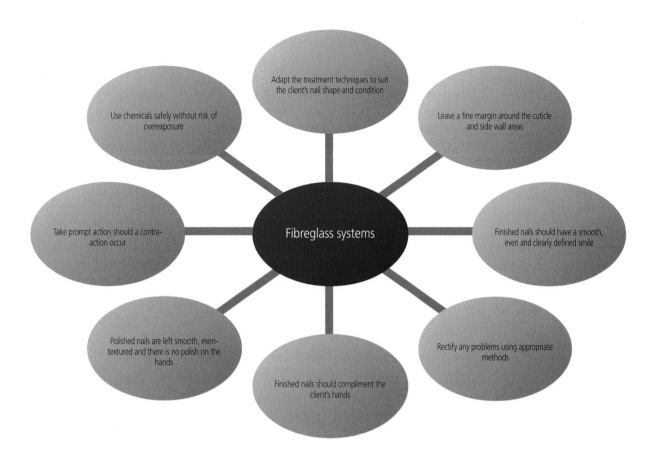

3 Push back the cuticles with a cotton wool-tipped orange stick or hoof stick.

4 Buff the seam area using a medium-grit file to remove any loose or lifting fibreglass, then buff with a fine-grit file until the seam becomes invisible. Buff the whole nail plate with a fine-grit file to remove shine.

   Do not use cuticle nippers to remove loose or lifting fibreglass: these would cause discomfort to the client and would damage the natural nail.

5 Apply a small amount of adhesive to the regrowth area and spread it with the nozzle to cover the whole regrowth area.

6 Spray with activator from at least 30 cm away.

7 Apply adhesive to the whole nail surface, including the regrowth area.

8 Spray with activator.

9 Buff gently with a fine-grit file to remove shine.

10 With a four-sided buffer bring the nails to a shine.

11 Apply cuticle oil.

TIP

Alternate maintenance procedures so that one maintenance is with fibreglass, the next one without. This avoids unnecessary use of fibreglass and build-up of product around the cuticle area.

TIP

Clients can still have a regular manicure whilst they are wearing nail extensions. Recommending a regular manicure will help to keep the client's skin and cuticles in good condition, whilst allowing the nail technician to keep a check on the condition of the nail extensions.

Four weeks after the initial application

1 Cleanse the hands and nails.

2 Remove any nail enamel with acetone-free polish remover, and check for any signs of infection. If any infection is present, remove the nails immediately and advise the client to see her doctor.

3 Push back the cuticles with a cotton wool-tipped orange stick or hoof stick.

4 Buff the seam area using a medium-grit file to remove any loose or lifting fibreglass, then buff with a fine-grit file until the seam becomes invisible. Buff whole nail plate with a fine-grit file to remove shine.

   Do not use cuticle nippers to remove loose or lifting fibreglass: these would cause discomfort to the client and will damage the natural nail.

5 Apply a small amount of adhesive to the regrowth area and spread it with the nozzle to cover the whole regrowth area.

6 Spray with activator from at least 30 cm away.

7 Apply a small piece of fibreglass to the regrowth area, slightly overlapping the old application.

8 Apply adhesive over the new fibreglass.

9 Spray with activator.

10 Repeat steps **7** and **8**.

11 Apply adhesive to the whole nail surface, including the regrowth area.

12 Spray with catalyst from at least 30 cm away.

13 Buff gently with a fine-grit file to remove shine.

14 With a four-sided buffer, bring the nails to a shine.

15 Apply cuticle oil.

EQUIPMENT LIST

acrylic powder in variety of colours
acrylic liquid
primer
nail forms
brush
dappen dish
selection of enamels

Equipment and materials needed for the maintenance and repair of sculptured acrylic nail extensions and tips with acrylic overlays

In addition to the basic equipment and materials (page 408) you will need the following:

- acrylic powder in a variety of colours, including white, pink and clear
- acrylic liquid
- primer
- nail forms
- brush
- dappen dish
- a selection of nail polish, including base and top coats.

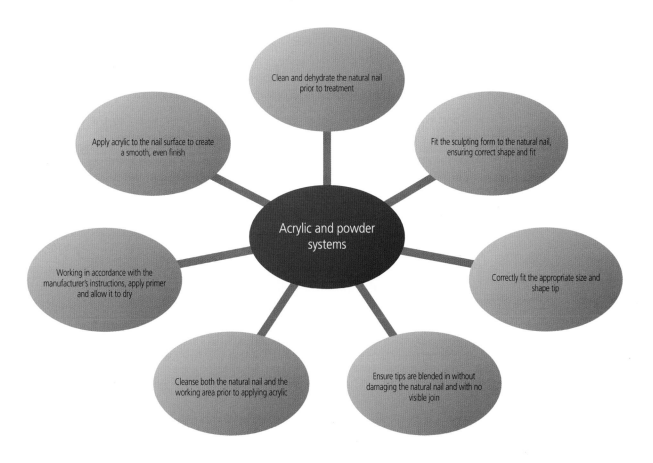

Acrylic and powder systems

- Clean and dehydrate the natural nail prior to treatment
- Fit the sculpting form to the natural nail, ensuring correct shape and fit
- Correctly fit the appropriate size and shape tip
- Ensure tips are blended in without damaging the natural nail and with no visible join
- Cleanse both the natural nail and the working area prior to applying acrylic
- Working in accordance with the manufacturer's instructions, apply primer and allow it to dry
- Apply acrylic to the nail surface to create a smooth, even finish

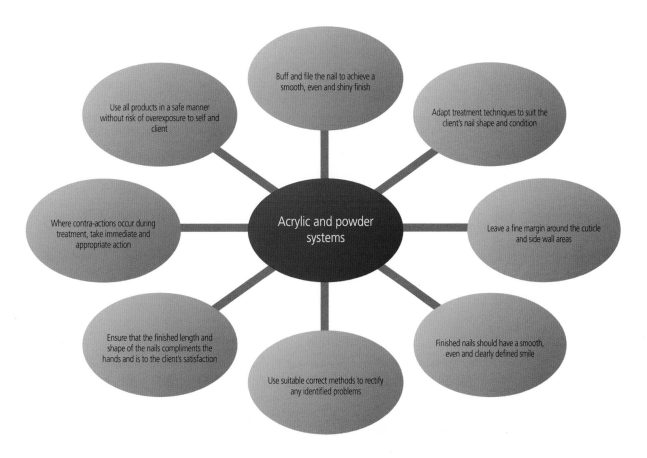

Acrylic and powder systems

- Buff and file the nail to achieve a smooth, even and shiny finish
- Adapt treatment techniques to suit the client's nail shape and condition
- Leave a fine margin around the cuticle and side wall areas
- Finished nails should have a smooth, even and clearly defined smile
- Use suitable correct methods to rectify any identified problems
- Ensure that the finished length and shape of the nails compliments the hands and is to the client's satisfaction
- Where contra-actions occur during treatment, take immediate and appropriate action
- Use all products in a safe manner without risk of overexposure to self and client

Maintenance: sculptured acrylic nail extensions

Maintenance should be carried out approximately every two weeks after the initial application. This keeps the nails strong, balanced and attractive.

1 Wash your hands and ask your client to wash hers. Refer to the client's record card for details of previous nail-extension applications.

2 Remove any nail enamel with acetone-free nail enamel remover and check for any signs of infection. If infection is present, such as *Tinea unguium*, remove the extensions immediately and advise the client to see her doctor.

3 Push back the cuticles with a cotton wool-tipped orange stick or hoof stick.

4 Buff the seam area with a medium-grit file to remove any loose or lifting acrylic, then buff with a fine grit file until the seam becomes invisible. Buff the whole nail plate with a medium-grit file to remove the shine. Do not try to cut off loose acrylic with cuticle nippers: this would cause damage to the natural nail plate and would be extremely uncomfortable for the client.

5 Lightly buff the new nail regrowth with a fine-grit file, and apply primer to this area only.

6 Apply a small ball of pink or clear acrylic near the cuticle. This should be a thin application, to avoid a ridge and to give a more natural-looking finish.

Blend in the new application by brushing the acrylic down towards the free edge.

Dip the brush into liquid and wipe it clean on a tissue regularly throughout application. This will prevent acrylic from setting on the brush.

7 When the infill is finished, allow it to set hard.

8 Using a four-sided buffer, smooth the nail surface to a shine.

9 Apply cuticle oil.

10 Both of you should now wash your hands.

11 Polish the nails as usual.

Maintenance tips with acrylic overlay

This procedure is carried out using exactly the same method as for sculptured acrylic nails.

TIP

The white free edge moves forward with the growing nail, and soon the natural nail's free edge can be seen through the acrylic. To disguise this, file the surface of the artificial free edge to form a step at the natural flesh line. Be careful not to file right through. Fill in this step with white acrylic. Use a fine layer of clear acrylic to strengthen the join.

Repair to acrylic nails

Due to the strength of a correctly applied acrylic nail, repairs are seldom necessary. If nails are cracked, chipped or broken, however, repairs may be carried out using the following methods.

Lifting or cracking of the product around the cuticle area

1 Repair using the general maintenance procedure.

Chip or crack in the free edge

1 Use the edge of a course-grit file to widen and roughen the crack. This makes filling it in easier.
2 Place a nail form beneath the free edge and 'fill in' the chip or crack with matching coloured acrylic. Wetting the old acrylic nail with acrylic liquid will help to improve adhesion.
3 File and buff the new acrylic as in original application.

Free edge broken off

1 Roughen the nail surface with a medium-grit file.
2 Place a nail form beneath the free edge. Dampen the free edge with acrylic liquid and sculpt the free edge with white powder as in original application. Secure the free edge with a thin layer of clear acrylic over the entire nail.
3 Finish off as in original application.

HEALTH AND SAFETY

Lifting acrylic
Do not use nippers to clip away lifting acrylic. This is extremely uncomfortable for the client and may cause bruising to the nail plate and further lifting of the existing acrylic.

Equipment and materials needed for the maintenance and repair of gel nails

In addition to the basic equipment and materials (page 408) you will need the following:

- manicure table
- gel
- gel-setting spray or ultraviolet light
- primer
- nail forms
- nail tips
- adhesive
- brushes
- a selection of nail polish, including base and top coats.

EQUIPMENT LIST

manicure table

gel

gel-setting or ultra-violet light

primer

nail forms

nail tips

adhesive

brushes

selection of enamels

Home-care advice

The advice given to a client at the end of a repair or maintenance treatment is the same as that given to the client at the end of the initial application.

Aftercare and advice

Maintenance to the nail extensions should be carried out approximately every two weeks after the initial application. This keeps the nails strong, balanced and attractive.

1 Wash your hands and ask your client to wash hers. Refer to the client's record card for details of previous nail-extension applications.

2 Remove any nail enamel with acetone-free nail enamel remover and check for any signs of infection. If infection is present, such as *Tinea unguium*, remove the extensions immediately and advise the client to see her doctor.

3 Push back the cuticles with a cotton wool-tipped orange stick or hoof stick.

4 Buff the seam area with a medium-grit file to remove any loose or lifting gel, then buff with a fine-grit file until the seam becomes invisible. Buff the whole nail plate with a medium-grit file to remove the shine and to avoid build-up of product.

   Do not try to cut off loose gel with cuticle nippers. This would cause damage to the natural nail plate and would be extremely uncomfortable to the client.

5 Lightly buff nail regrowth with a fine-grit file, and apply a primer to this area only.

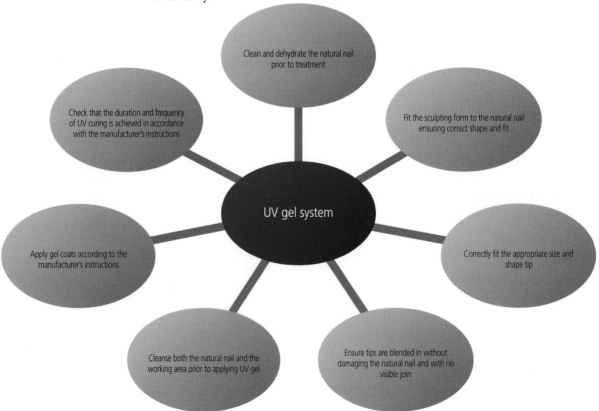

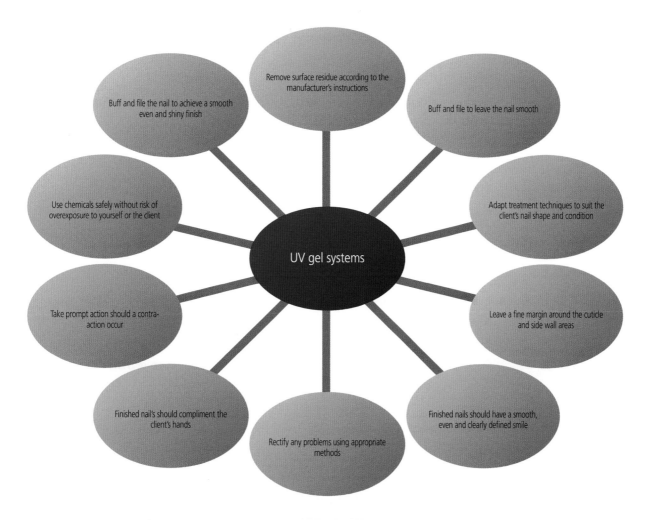

6 Apply a small ball of gel near the cuticle. This should be a thin application to avoid a ridge and to give a more natural-looking finish. Blend in the new application by brushing the gel down towards the free edge.

7 When the infill is finished, cure it with ultraviolet light or activator spray.

8 Remove any sticky residue with non-acetone nail polish remover.

9 Using a four-sided buffer, smooth the nail surface to a shine.

10 Apply cuticle oil.

11 You and your client should now wash your hands.

12 Polish the nails as usual.

Contra-actions

A contra-action to artificial nail application is an adverse condition that appears after nails have been applied. Examples are:

- thinning of the natural nail plate
- allergies
- infection
- softening of the nail plate
- physical trauma to the nail plate, bed or cuticle.

Thinning of the natural nail plate

Appearance

When artificial nails are removed, the natural free edge is very thin. It can easily be bent or torn using very light pressure.

Causes

- excessive filing of the nail plate during preparation
- excessive filing whilst blending in the nail tip
- incorrect removal of the nails.

Treatment

1 Keep the free edge short.
2 Allow the thin nail plate to grow out.
3 Apply nail strengthener to the nails.
4 Do not re-apply artificial nails until the thin nails have grown out.

Allergies

Appearance

Redness, blisters, inflammation and itching. These may appear on the cuticle or skin around the nails, or on the face and neck which the nails regularly touch.

Cause

- Exposure to a product to which the client is allergic. Allergies are specific to individual people, so what may irritate one client may prove harmless to another.

Treatment

1 Remove the artificial nails immediately, using the correct procedure. If the allergic reaction is severe, advise the client to seek medical attention.
2 Once the allergy has cleared, alternative nail systems may be applied to single nails to test the client's tolerance. Do not test products on the client's skin: they are not designed for such use and will cause an allergic response in many clients and therefore give inaccurate results.

Infection

Appearance

Redness, inflammation and pus in the cuticle area and surrounding skin; separation of the nail plate from the nail bed at the flesh line; or dark spots between the artificial nail plate and the natural nail plate.

HEALTH AND SAFETY

There are many suppliers of nail-extension products. If a product regularly causes allergies among clients, and it is being used correctly, inform the manufacturer and try alternative products to discover one that is less irritating.

Causes

- lack of hygiene in the salon during application
- incorrect home care.

Treatment

1 Remove the artificial nails immediately, using the correct method.
2 Advise the client to seek medical attention.

Softening of the nail plate

Appearance

When the nails are removed, the natural nail plate is very soft and easily torn at the free edge.

Cause

- Prolonged exposure to the products used in artificial nail application, particularly primer.

Treatment

1 Allow the softened nail to grow out, keeping the free edge short. Apply nail strengthener, and do not re-apply artificial nails until the soft nails have grown out.

Physical trauma

Appearance

Bruising; ridges in the nail plate; and cuts and abrasions to the cuticle and surrounding skin.

Causes

- **Bruising** – too much pressure applied to nails during treatment.
- **Ridges** – excessive filing in one place, causing thinning of the nail plate.
- **Cuts and abrasions** – careless use of files and buffers.

Treatment

1 Apply antiseptic to cuts and abrasions. Allow bruises and ridges to grow out. Extreme care should be taken during application. Use tools correctly and do not apply too much pressure. Ensure that tools are of a high quality with no rough or sharp edges.

> **HEALTH AND SAFETY**
>
> If nails start to lift, moisture will get underneath: this creates an ideal breeding ground for bacteria. Always advise clients to return to the salon immediately the nails start to lift, so that the appropriate treatment can be carried out at once to avoid infection.

> **HEALTH AND SAFETY**
>
> If the sides of files are rough or sharp, use a fine-grit file to gently smooth them down. This will reduce the risk of cutting the client's cuticles, and will also make the files more pleasant for the nail technician to work with.

REPAIRING THE NATURAL NAIL

If a natural nail is broken, split or cracked, it is sometimes possible to repair the damage so that the client doesn't lose the free edge of her nail. Repairs can be done with different types of materials, the strongest being, silk, fibreglass, linen and acrylic. Once repaired, nails should be treated in the same way as artificial nails, for example, non-acetone nail polish remover must be used.

Types of nail damage that can be repaired are:

- flaking nails
- free-edge or flesh-line break
- severed free edge.

Flaking nails

1 Remove any nail polish and dehydrate the nail plate by wiping it with a cotton bud soaked in acetone.
2 Place a piece of mending material over the whole nail plate, extending over the free edge.
3 Apply a layer of resin over the material and allow this to dry. Use a resin activator, if available, to reduce the drying time. If using acrylic, allow it to dry before proceeding to step 5.
4 Repeat step 3.
5 Use a four-sided buffer to bring the nails to a shine.

TIP

Coating the whole nail with any of the materials used in repairs or extensions is known as 'capping'. This service can be offered to clients who don't want artificial nails but need something to keep their own nails from breaking. Capping needs to be maintained in the same way as semi-permanent nails.

Free-edge or flesh-line break

1 Remove any nail polish and dehydrate the nail plate by wiping it with a cotton bud soaked in acetone.
2 Place a small piece of mending material over the break.
3 Apply a layer of resin over the material and allow this to dry. Use a resin activator, if available, to reduce the drying time.
4 Repeat step 3.
5 Use a four-sided buffer to smooth the repair application and bring the nails to a shine.

Severed free edge

1 Place the severed free edge into a bowl of hot water to soften the nail. Soak for approximately 3 minutes, then dry with a tissue.

2 Remove any nail polish and dehydrate the nail plate by wiping it with a cotton bud soaked in acetone.

3 Lightly buff the whole nail plate to remove the shine.

4 Place a small drop of resin close to the free edge.

5 Apply the severed nail tip to the nail plate, overlapping it slightly.

6 Blend the join with a medium-grit file.

7 Place a small piece of mending material over the join.

8 Apply a layer of resin over the material and allow this to dry. Use a resin activator, if available, to reduce the drying time.

9 Apply mending material to the whole nail plate.

10 Repeat step 8 twice.

11 Use a four-sided buffer to smooth the repair application and bring the nails to a shine.

If the client did not keep her severed free edge, the broken fingernail could be matched to the others by applying a nail extension.

Removing artificial nails

1 The client should wash her hands.

2 Remove any existing nail polish.

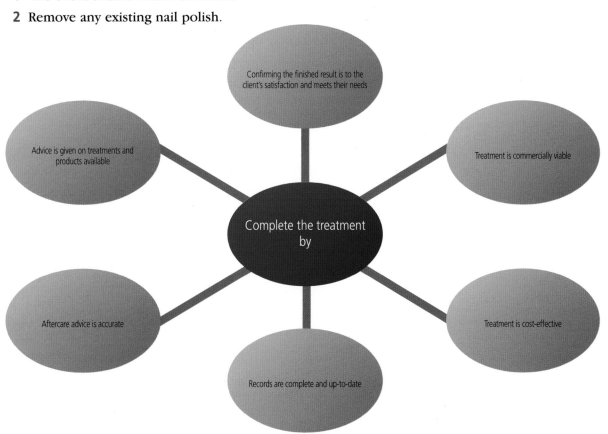

3 Cut off the artificial free edge, being careful not to cut the natural free edge.

4 Slightly roughen the surface of the nail with a medium-grit file, to encourage absorption of the solvent by the nail.

5 Place the fingertips in a glass bowl containing acetone and a teaspoon of vegetable oil. To ensure client comfort, place the hands in separate bowls. (Acetone dehydrates the skin and nail plate: the vegetable oil helps to soften and lubricate the skin and nails as they are taken from the bowl.)

6 Every 2–3 minutes, remove the fingers and wipe away the dissolving artificial nail with a tissue soaked in acetone.

7 When the nail has completely dissolved – which takes approximately 10–15 minutes – a full manicure, including the application of a nail strengthener, should be carried out to ensure that the client leaves the salon with her nails in the best possible condition.

TIP

Always recommend after nail extension removal that the client purchase a nail strengthener for home use.

HEALTH AND SAFETY

Never try to re-stick nails that are coming loose by applying adhesive under the false nail. This could trap bacteria beneath the nail, leading to infection.

Aftercare and advice

It is important when carrying out a nail-extension treatment that the client knows how to care for her nails at home. It is up to you to give her the correct advice, otherwise she may unwittingly undo the work done during treatment.

As you give home-care advice you can also recommend products such as nail enamel or hand cream, enhancing retail sales and your profit.

Home-care advice will differ slightly for each client, but basically will be as follows:

- Use only non-acetone nail enamel remover to avoid softening the nails.
- Have the nails regularly maintained (infilled) to keep them attractive and strong.
- Always use a base coat under nail enamel to avoid yellowing.
- Do not pull the nails off if they start to lift. Have them removed professionally and safely.

ACTIVITY

Designing an aftercare leaflet
Design an attractive aftercare leaflet to be given to the clients after their nails have been applied. Include any home-care advice and recommended retail products that you think would be useful.

Assessment of knowledge and understanding

You have now learnt about how to enhance the appearance of natural nails using artificial nail structures.

To test your level of knowledge and understanding, answer the following short questions. These will prepare you for your summative (final) assessment.

Anatomy and physiology questions required for this unit are found on pages 146–50.

Consult with the client

1 Why is it important to disscuss the client's needs?

2 Why is it important to remove any existing nail polish prior to planning the treatment?

3 It is important to record the condition of the client's skin and nails prior to treatment. Why is this?

4 State two contra-indications that would prohibit treatment.

5 State two conditions that would require treatment adaptation.

Plan the treatment

1 Why should the shape of the client's nail be considered before planning any corrective work?

2 What products would be required for a routine maintenance of sculptured acrylic nails?

3 How much time would be required for a routine maintenance of gel nails?

4 Do some research of salon prices in your area. What is the average price for nail extension maintenance?

Prepare for the treatment

1 Why does the working area need to be hygienic prior to treatment commencing?

2 Why is it important for the therapist's chair to be comfortable?

3 Why is it important for the client to be comfortable?

4 What kind of protection should be worn by the therapist during treatment?

Maintain and repair artificial nail structures

1 A client is attending for her second maintenance on fibre nails. Describe the procedure.

2 Why should the natural nail be clean prior to treatment?

3 Why is it important to closely follow the manufacturer's instructions on products?

4 Why should you read the manufacturer's instructions each time you purchase a product?

5 What steps can you take to prevent overexposure of products to both yourself and your client?

Cosmetically enhance damaged nails

1 What is meant by cross-infection?

2 How could you enhance the appearance of nails that are ridged due to ageing?

3 How might you adapt your technique on a client with spoon-shaped nails?

4 Why is it important to keep products away from the skin?

Remove artificial nail structures

1 State two conditions that would prohibit the removal of nail extensions.

2 Why should nails be shortened prior to removal?

3 What precautions should be taken when buffing product from the natural nail plate?

4 Why is it important that the client thoroughly washes their hands at the end of the nail removal?

5 Why should a manicure be carried out after nail removal?

Complete the treatment

1 State two ways in which you can identify if the client is happy with the treatment.

2 What is a commercially acceptable time for a routine maintenance on fibre nail extensions?

3 What aftercare advice would you give to a client?

4 State two retail products that you could recommend to a client.

5 Why should you suggest that the client makes an appointment for her next maintenance before she leaves the salon?

chapter 13

Plan, design and provide nail art services to clients

BT24

Design and create images incorporating nail art techniques

BT25

Learning objectives

This unit describes how to plan and provide nail art services to clients and how to design and create images incorporating nail art techniques.

It describes the competencies to enable you to:

- **consult with the client**
- **plan and design the service**
- **prepare for the service**
- **provide nail art services to clients**
- **complete the service**
- **plan and design a range of images**
- **create a range of images**
- **evaluate your results against the design plan objectives**

When providing nail art services it is important to use the skills you have learned in the following core mandatory units:

G1 ensure your own actions reduce risks to health and safety
G6 promote additional products or services to clients
G11 contribute to the financial effectiveness of the business

INTRODUCTION

Nail art is an exciting service to offer the client and can be catered to suit everyone's tastes, from the wild and wacky to the quiet and conservative. It's fun to do and allows you to be as creative as you wish.

Nail art should be priced as a stand alone service, not just included in the cost of a manicure or nail extension service. Depending on the complexity of the design, nail art can take 20 minutes or more and your pricing should reflect this.

THE NAIL

The structure and function of the nail

Nails grow from the ends of the fingers and toes and serve as a form of protection. They also help when picking up small objects.

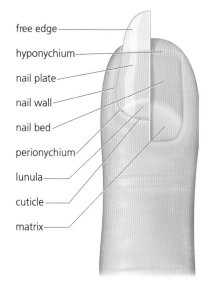

free edge
hyponychium
nail plate
nail wall
nail bed
perionychium
lunula
cuticle
matrix

The structure of the nail

The nail plate

The **nail plate** is composed of compact translucent layers of keratinised cells: it is this that makes up the man body of the nail. The layers of cells are packed very closely together, with fat but very little moisture.

The nail gradually grows forward over the nail bed, until finally it becomes the free edge. The underside of the nail plate is grooved by longitudinal ridges and furrows, which help to keep it in place.

In normal health the plate curves in two directions:

- transversely – from side to side across the nail;
- longitudinally – from the base of the nail to the free edge.

There are no blood vessels or nerves in the nail plate: this is why the nails, like hair, can be cut without pain or bleeding. The pink colour of the nail plate derives from the blood vessels that pass beneath it.

Function: To protect the nail bed.

The free edge

The **free edge** is the part of the nail that extends beyond the fingertip; this is the part that is filed.

Function: To protect the fingertip and the hyponychium (see below).

The matrix

The **matrix**, sometimes called the **nail root**, is the growing area of the nail. It is formed by the division of cells in this area, which is part of the germinating layer of the epidermis. It lies under the eponychium (see below), at the base of the nail, nearest to the body. The process of keratinisation takes place in the epidermal cells of the matrix, forming the hardened tissue of the nail plate.

Function: To produce new nail cells.

The nail bed

The **nail bed** is the portion of skin upon which the nail plate rests. It has a pattern of grooves and furrows corresponding to those found on the underside of the nail plate; these interlock, keeping the nail in place, but separate at the end of the nail to form the free edge. The nail bed is liberally supplied with blood vessels, which provide the nourishment necessary for continued growth; and sensor nerves, for protection.

Function: To supply nourishment and protection.

The nail mantle

The **nail mantle** is the layer of epidermis at the base of the nail, before the cuticle.

Function: To protect the matrix from physical damage.

The lunula

The **lunula** is located at the base of the nail, lying over the matrix. It is white, relative to the rest of the nail, and there are two theories to account for this:

- newly formed nail plates may be more opaque than mature nail plates;
- the lunula may indicate the extent of the underlying matrix – the matrix is thicker than the epidermis of the nail bed, and the capillaries beneath it would not show through as well.

Function: None.

The hyponychium

The **hyponychium** is part of the epidermis under the free edge of the nail.

Function: To protect the nail bed from infection.

The nail grooves

The **nail grooves** run alongside the edge of the nail plate.

Function: To keep the nail growing forward in a straight line.

The perionychium

The **perionychium** is the collective name given to the nail walls and the cuticle area.

Function: To protect the nail.

ACTIVITY

Recognising nail structure
With a colleague, try to identify the structural parts of each other's nails. Write down both the parts that you can see and the parts that you cannot.

The nail walls

The **nail walls** are the folds of skin overlapping the sides of the nails.

Function: To protect the nail plate edges.

The eponychium

The **eponychium** is the extension of the cuticle at the base of the nail plate, under which the nail plate emerges from the matrix.

Function: To protect the matrix from infection.

The cuticle

The **cuticle** is the overlapping epidermis around the base of the nail. When in good condition, it is soft and loose.

Function: To protect the matrix from infection.

ACTIVITY

What questions could the receptionist ask to ascertain the client's needs?

Reception

When a client makes an appointment for nail art services the receptionist should ask a few simple questions in order to ascertain her needs. Information obtained from the client will help the nail technician to set up the working area with the appropriate equipment and materials and will save time when the client arrives for treatment.

Record cards

As with all treatments and services, accurate record cards must be kept for clients having nail art services. If the client has had nail art services before, the receptionist should consult the record card and inform the nail technician about these. This will give the nail technician a good idea of what to expect when the client arrives.

Contra-indications

HEALTH AND SAFETY

Do not try to make a medical diagnosis yourself. The client may then apply inappropriate treatment that may fail to cure or worsen the condition.

Contra-indications for the application of nail art are the same as for any other nail service. If the client has a disease or disorder of the hand or nail it is in the interests of both the nail technician and of the client not to proceed with the service. Treating a client with a contra-indication may lead to cross-infection or a worsening of the client's condition. It is important to advise the client to seek medical advice to ensure a correct diagnosis and treatment for her condition.

Severe bruising

The client may experience pain and a possible worsening of the condition if a nail art service is carried out.

Severe eczema

This condition may be irritated by products used during the nail art service.

Psoriasis

As with eczema, clients with psoriasis on the hands and fingers may find that the condition is irritated by the products used.

Broken bones

Pressure applied during treatment would cause pain and discomfort to a client with broken bones in the hands, arms or fingers.

Infection

Clients with an infection of any kind, whether its fungal, bacterial or viral, should not be treated due to the risk of cross-infection.

Some conditions will require restriction and adaptation of the nail art service. These include mild eczema and psoriasis, minor nail separation and severely bitten nails.

ACTIVITY

Do some research and find out at least one type of fungal, bacterial and viral infection that the nail technician may come across in her work.

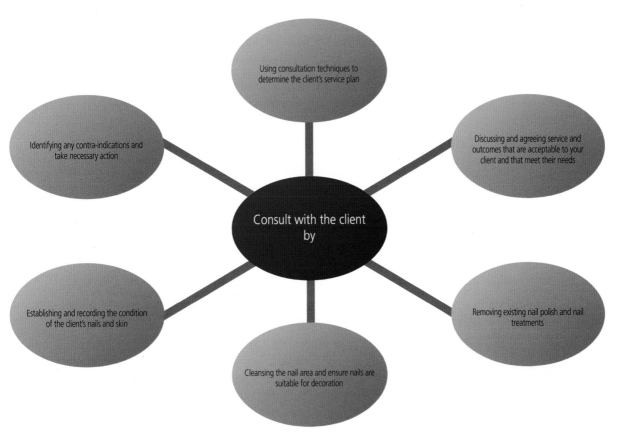

Equipment and materials

The equipment and materials used in nail art will vary depending on the design. Below is a list of commonly used nail art materials, but the items that can be used are not limited to those sold commercially. You can use various materials – in fact anything that your imagination allows.

Selection of paints and brushes

Brushes

Nail art brushes come in many different shapes and sizes and each one can be used to create a different effect with nail paint. Some brushes are also available in the form of a pen, which makes them easier to work with.

Nail paints

Instead of using nail enamels, nail artistry uses special acrylic nail art paints. The advantages of these are:

- being water-based they are easy to remove if mistakes are made
- they can be diluted to create different effects
- colours can be mixed to create endless designs
- brushes are easily cleaned with soap and water
- fine texture makes detail easier to apply
- they are generally non-toxic
- they dry quickly

The only apparent disadvantage of acrylic nail paint is that it must be sealed in order to prevent it from washing or wearing off quickly.

Paints are also available in a ready-loaded pen form which makes them quicker, if slightly more expensive, to work with.

Coloured gels and acrylics

To create a more permanent art work, coloured acrylics or gels may be used. Nail paints can be used over a coloured a coloured gel base, for example, or permanent designs such as marbling can be created with the products themselves. The permanency of this method means that the client might get bored, but the advantage is that the design won't chip or fade off. The client can also apply a coloured enamel or other nail art over the top if they fancy a change!

Gemstones

Gemstones

These come in a variety of shapes and colours. The uppermost side is raised and the underside is flat. This flat surface is stuck to the nail using wet enamel. Gemstones and shapes are sometimes referred to as 'polish secures' as they are secured by polish. Designs can include a single stone as a highlight or a multitude of gem-encrusted sparkles!

Transfers

Transfers create instant designs that can be applied to the nail in seconds. In two basic formats – water-release and self-adhesive – transfers can be used alone or with other nail art products to produce spectacular results.

Sealer or top coat

This is applied like nail polish at the end of the service to protect the nail art design. The sealer is a good product to recommend for home use so that the client can re-apply it every few days. This protects the nail art, making it last longer. Some nail art products require specific sealers. Always follow the manufacturer's instructions.

Foils

Foils come in a number of different colours and patterns, on rolls or sheets, and may be self-adhesive or require sticking to the nail with foil adhesive. This is applied to the nail as a white product and clears as it is ready to have the foil applied.

Glitter polish

These are applied like nail enamel using a brush over the whole nail. They can be used alone or to enhance an underlying design.

Glitter dusts

These come in powder form and need to be mixed with an adhesive to stick to the nail. They can be applied to the whole nail or as a highlight to a design. Glitter dust gives a much denser colour than glitter polish.

Tape

Tape comes in rolls of many different colours. It is very fine and self-adhesive and is used to create stripes. Simply apply to nails and cut to length.

Marbling tool

Also known as a dotting tool, this has small metal balls at each end in different sizes. It is used to apply paint to the nails to create dots, or to mix paints together on the nail, creating a marbled effect.

Nail jewellery

Nail jewellery is found in three basic types: adhesive, post and nut, or ringed. Adhesive nail jewellery is quite flat and is either attached with polish or nail glue.

Compressors

Compressors use either the air around you or compressed air in a can. Air is compressed to around 30 psi (pounds per square inch). A regulator attached to the compressor will allow the pressure to be set and a gauge will allow you to check the pressure before use. There are many different compressors on the market, each with its own advantages. Shop around to find one that suits you. If you are a mobile technician your needs will be very different to those of a busy salon where the compressor will be supplying air to more than one airbrush. Following the manufacturer's instructions carefully regarding maintenance of the machine will ensure that you can work trouble free.

Airbrushes

Airbrushes

These are attached to the compressors by a hose and are held in the hand. It is in the airbrush that the air is mixed with the paint before being forced out under pressure to create a colour spray.

The amount of paint sprayed is determined by a needle that fits into the tip or nozzle of the airbrush. As the trigger is pressed the needle is pulled back and paint sprays out. The further back the needle, the greater the amount of paint is sprayed.

Airbrushes may be single or double action. Single action brushes have a predetermined distance that the needle is pulled back. When the trigger is pressed, air is released and paint is sprayed.

Dual action airbrushes use two actions to control both airflow and paint flow. This allows more variety in the use of the paint therefore widening the scope of designs. The dual action airbrush can also be used to spray air only which can be used to speed up drying.

There are numerous designs of airbrush, so try them out to see which feels most comfortable in your hand.

Airbrushes use acrylic paints with a runny consistency that helps to produce a fine spray and prevents clogging up of the machine. Always check that the paints you want are compatible with your particular airbrush before buying. It is very important to keep your airbrush clean as it may clog up, resulting in a blockage. Your machine should have detailed cleaning instructions with it when purchased.

Sterilisation and sanitisation

All tools and materials used during nail art should be either sterilised or disposable. Prior to nail art application, both client and nail technician should wash their hands to minimise cross-infection.

Preparing the working area

Ensure that the workstation is well lit, preferably with a magnifying lamp for detailed work. Always ensure that any dust and clippings from a previous nail treatment, e.g. a manicure or extensions that may have been carried out on the client, are completely removed. Cover the work station with disposable paper towel.

Decorative materials required will depend upon the design, but for most designs the following basic equipment will be required:

- paints
- brushes
- base coats
- top coats/sealers
- nail polish remover
- orange sticks

- cotton buds
- paper towels
- airbrush and compressor
- decorative materials

If used, it is very important that the airbrush is kept clean, and this should be done between each client. Blockages may arise if dried paint builds up and this may result in a poor performance from your equipment. Always follow the manufacturer's cleaning instructions carefully.

Preparing the client

Ensure that the client is sitting comfortably.

When airbrushing a design, ensure that the client's clothes are protected and any jewellery is removed or covered up. It is also advisable for the client to wear protective glasses to ensure that paint spray does not accidentally get into her eyes.

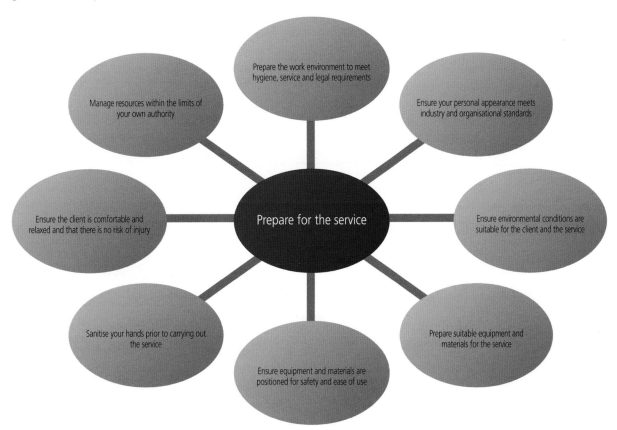

Manage resources within the limits of your own authority

Prepare the work environment to meet hygiene, service and legal requirements

Ensure your personal appearance meets industry and organisational standards

Ensure the client is comfortable and relaxed and that there is no risk of injury

Prepare for the service

Ensure environmental conditions are suitable for the client and the service

Sanitise your hands prior to carrying out the service

Ensure equipment and materials are positioned for safety and ease of use

Prepare suitable equipment and materials for the service

PLANNING NAIL ART DESIGNS

Before applying any kind of nail art it is necessary to carry out a thorough consultation with the client. What are her likes and dislikes? How adventurous is she? Does she have specific ideas for a design or is she prepared to give you a free reign?

TIP

Always carry a camera with you in your nail art kit so that you can photograph your work to go in your portfolio. It will become a great catalogue of your work and a source of inspiration for both you and your clients.

TIP ✔

Be prepared to adapt the design plan in case circumstances change.

As well as the salon client, there are numerous opportunities for creating nail art. These include photographic work and fashion shows.

The images that you create in the salon will usually be mild to moderately adventurous in nature. They need to be practical for the client. However, for work outside of the salon environment, your nail images may be more avant-garde.

When you have an idea for a new design it is a good idea to write a design plan. This will include your notes, sketches, pictures torn from magazines, photos, examples of texture on leaves or fabric, ideas for colours and materials to use. You could also practise your idea on some nail tips and include these in your plan.

When working outside of the salon environment, on a fashion show for example, your design plan may be needed by other colleagues/team members. Your nail art may form part of an overall image and so must work with clothes, make-up and accessories. If you are working with others such as make up artists etc. you must ensure that your plan is clear and accurate.

When creating a design, your ideas may be influenced by a number of factors such as client's needs, time and budgetary constraints. Products and equipment available to you may also influence your creations.

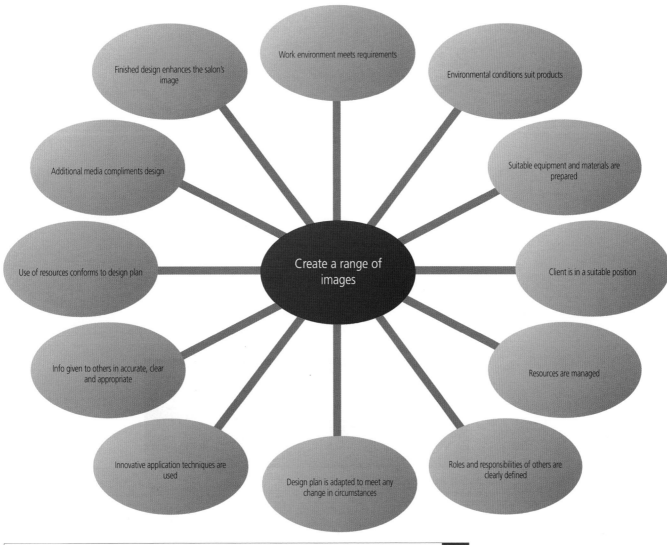

ACTIVITY

Create a design plan for each of the following, including the created design on a nail tip or a photograph[s] of your creation.
1 A design for a photographic shot using a fantasy image. The image is to appear on the CD cover of a rock band called 'Heavenly'.
2 A design to be used on all the female models of a bridal fashion show.
3 A design for a client who is going to a Christmas party. She has asked for a design that includes snow and Rudolph!
4 A design for a mature client who will be celebrating her ruby wedding with a big family party.

Applying nail art

Freehand painting

Pictures and designs applied freehand with paint are limited only to your imagination. They can be as simple as a daisy or a complex character or scene. Before the painting begins, a base coat must first be applied. This is usually nail polish and forms the background of your design. The colour of this background cannot be mixed or blended with the nail paints.

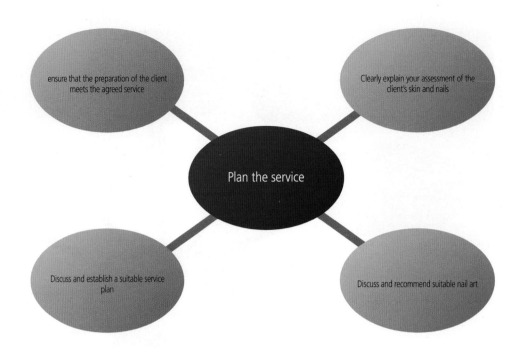

ensure that the preparation of the client meets the agreed service

Clearly explain your assessment of the client's skin and nails

Plan the service

Discuss and establish a suitable service plan

Discuss and recommend suitable nail art

Freehand designs

Nails and nail art by Gina Wallace

Step by step – simple daisy design

1 Apply a base coat.

2 Apply two coats of lilac enamel and allow to dry.

3 Using a small brush or dotting tool, pick up a small amount of white paint and place four dots diagonally across the nail.

4 Using a small brush or dotting tool, pick up a small amount of lilac paint and place five dots around each white dot.

5 Using a small brush, pick up a small amount of green paint and apply 'leaves' to join the daisies together.

6 Seal with a top coat.

This simple design looks very effective for spring and can be built upon to create a myriad of daisy type designs. Experiment with different colours and sizes of dots.

TIP	
Dotting/marbling tools are available with a variety of sized balls on the end to help create dots of different sizes.	

Step by step daisy chain design

Step by step – striping

Brushes with long hairs are used to create a striped effect on the nail. The finer the brush the finer the stripe will be.

1 Apply a base coat and allow to dry.
2 Apply a coat of red nail polish and allow to dry.
3 Use a striping brush and paint three white stripes diagonally across the nail.
4 Use a striping brush and paint two blue stripes between the white ones.
5 Seal with a top coat.

Marbling can be used to decorate the whole nail or may used as part of a different decorative design. The procedure below uses marbling to create a fingertip flame design.

Step by step – marbling flames

1 Apply a base coat and allow to dry.
2 Apply a coat of red nail polish and allow to dry.
3 Use a dotting tool and place 3 drops of orange paint close to the free edge.
4 Use a dotting tool and place 3 drops of gold paint near the orange paint.
5 Use a dotting tool and place two drops of white paint near the gold paint.
6 Use a marbling tool or small brush to swirl the paints together from the free edge towards the cuticle.
7 Seal with a top coat.

TIP ✔

Some nail paints come in a bottle with a striping brush attached, similar to ordinary nail polish. These are quick to use as there is no washing of brushes after use.

ACTIVITY

Create a range of images on nail tips and display attractively to use as examples for clients. Stencils can be used to create geometric designs that are difficult to obtain with a free hand. They are also useful if you are not very artistic and need a little help with your creations.

TIP

Use nail paint sparingly within the stencil as this will give a cleaner sharper edge to the design.

TIP

Nail polish must be completely dry before applying the stencil, otherwise the base coat may be spoiled.

TIP

Gemstones are easy to pick up by using an orange stick dipped in water.

Transfers

TIP

Create any design or picture by 'painting' with adhesive. The foil will stick only to this design creating instantly dramatic results.

Step by step stencilling

1 Apply a base coat and allow to dry thoroughly.
2 Apply two coats of polish and allow to dry.
3 Remove the stencil from its backing and apply to the nail.
4 Fill in the stencil with nail paint, glitter dust, adhesive for foil etc.
5 Seal with top coat.

Step by step – gemstones

1 Apply a base coat and allow to dry.
2 Apply two coats of polish.
3 Whilst this is still wet, place the gemstones into position.
4 Seal the design with three coats of sealer or top coat.

Step by step – water-release transfers

1 Apply a base coat and allow to dry.
2 Apply two coats of coloured nail polish and allow to dry thoroughly.
3 Cut the design from the sheet and soak in water for 30 seconds.
4 Use an orange stick or finger to slide the transfer off the paper and onto the nail. Smooth with finger tip.
5 Remove any excess water carefully with a tissue.
6 Seal with a top coat.

Step by step – self-adhesive transfers

1 Apply a base coat and allow to dry.
2 Apply two coats of coloured nail polish and allow to dry thoroughly.
3 Peel transfer design from the backing sheet and apply to the nail.
4 Seal with a top coat.

Step by step – foil designs

1 Apply a base coat and allow to dry.
2 Apply a coat of coloured nail polish and allow to dry.
3 Cut out the design with sharp scissors.
4 Peel off the foil from its backing paper.
5 Press the foil onto the nail then carefully peel off the plastic protector.
6 Seal with a top coat.

Step by step – gold French manicure – foil on a roll

1 Apply a base coat and allow to dry.
2 Apply two coats of pink nail polish and allow to dry.
3 Paint adhesive across the free edge and allow to clear.
4 Apply foil to the adhesive and rub gently with a cotton bud.
5 Apply sealer.

Post and nut jewellery is attached to a small post that is inserted through a hole in the free edge. It is then secured with a tiny nut on the underside of the free edge. This type of jewellery usually sits on the surface of the nail.

A nail drill is used manually to pierce or create a hole in the free edge of the nail in which to attach nail jewellery. Piercing is most successful on artificial nails, however it is possible to pierce natural nails if they are strengthened first with a nail extension product such as acrylic, gel or fibreglass and resin.

Ringed jewellery is also attached to the free edge through a piercing, but instead of a post and nut, the item is attached with a ring. The ring usually has a ball or sliding piece to cover the join, which helps to prevent snagging. This type of jewellery usually dangles from the free edge.

The client must have sufficient free edge to allow the piercing to be away from the hyponychium and the tip of the nail plate. Piercing too close to the hyponychium may result in discomfort and too close to the tip may result in the jewellery breaking away.

How to use a nail drill

1 Turn the clients hand so that the palm faces up.
2 Rest the nail on a soft surface. A large ball of blu tac covered with a tissue is ideal.
3 Place the drill where the piercing is required.
4 Turn the drill until the nail is pierced. Withdraw the drill by turning it in the opposite direction.
5 Smooth any rough surfaces using a buffer.
6 Fix the required jewellery into place.

Nail drill and jewellery

United Beauty Products Ltd

Embedding

Embedding or encasing involves the use of acrylic or gel to act as both an adhesive and protector of various nail art items. This results in a three-dimensional design. Many items can be embedded into the nail such as gemstones, shapes, flat jewellery or any tiny decorative item that you can think of. The beauty of this type of art is that it is attractive when only clear polish (or none!) is worn, and the client can then ring the changes by applying a coloured enamel over the top.

To create embedded art, apply acrylic or gel in the usual way and before it cures, press the nail art items into it with an orange stick, then apply a small amount of product over the top to seal it in. This method is only suitable with clear tips, gels and acrylics, otherwise the results will be poor.

> **TIP**
>
> Exercise caution when buffing the nail. Overthinning the product may result in reducing the life of the design by causing the embedded items to break loose and drop out.

Cut out

Cut out designs involve using a tip which has pieces 'cut out' of it to create different shapes. It is an impractical design for every day wear as it will tend to snag: however, it will add a new dimension to fantasy designs for photographic and competition work. Create the cut-outs by using a nail drill.

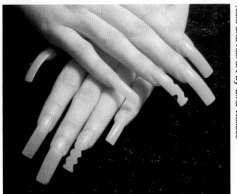

Cut out design

Nails and nail art by Gina Wallace

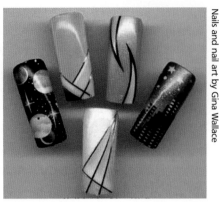

Airbrush designs

Nails and nail art by Gina Wallace

Airbrushing

Airbrushing is a method of applying or spraying a fine mist of colour, in layers, to the nails using compressed air. It is not an easy skill to learn but once mastered will open up your design possibilities, speed up your design applications and add to your service menu, hopefully increasing your profit.

This method requires equipment that is very expensive compared to all the other nail art products – airbrushing machines (compressors) can be hundreds of pounds.

The advantages of airbrushing over free hand designs are:

- Drying time is quicker
- Lines are more accurate
- Very smooth finish
- Increased variety of effects achievable

Different airbrushing systems will each have their own particular methods of use. Most suppliers will offer training in their own products and it is advisable for you to take the training to master the skill of using the system that you purchase. However, the following guidelines will apply regardless of the system chosen:

- Load the airbrush with paint according to the manufacturer's instructions and practice spraying onto a paper towel prior to applying colour to the client.
- Plenty of practice on nail tips will save time and mistakes on paying clients.
- Build up colour with a number of fine layers rather than one heavy one.
- Always completely remove one colour from the airbrush before refilling with a different one.

Many different effects can be achieved with airbrushing and a commonly used one is colour fading. This involves applying a base colour, then with a complimentary or contrasting colour applying the paint in graded intensity,

TIP

Wearing nail art designs yourself will encourage interest from clients to do the same.

usually from the tip. This results in a concentrated colour that appears to fade away with no apparent joining of the two colours. This method may be used on its own or as a base for other designs.

If the surface or top colour is required to be true e.g. yellow on blue, paint out the area underneath the yellow with white paint first. This will stop the colours mixing i.e. turning green in this case.

Stencils are ideal to use with airbrushing and provide almost instant results. By varying the distance that the stencil is held from the nail you can create soft or sharp edges: the closer the stencil is held to the nail the sharper its edges will be. Overlapping, rotating, repeating shapes etc. means that as with all other nail art media, airbrushing designs created from stencils are limitless.

You can make your own stencils from masking tape or sticky-back plastic. Draw your design onto the masking material and cut out using a sharp craft knife. Always ensure that the base coat is completely dry when using self-adhesive stencils.

Step by step airbrushed design

1 Apply a base coat and allow to dry.
2 Spray pale pink base onto the whole nail.
3 Mask the nail base exposing the chevron at the free edge. This can be done with a stencil or other masking material.
4 Spray the exposed area with white paint.

> **TIP**
>
> When buying an airbrushing system ensure that you purchase paints and other products that are compatible with it.

Airbrushed design

Nails and nail art by Gina Wallace

> **TIP**
>
> A base coat should always be applied prior to airbrushing as the paint will not adhere properly to a bare tip.

- Confirm the client's choice of nail art prior to commencing
- Use products according to the manufacturer's instructions
- Seal the nail art effectively leaving the cuticle free of product
- **Provide nail art to clients**
- Ensure the free edge is smooth and shaped to the required length
- Apply the appropriate base for the nail art being carried out
- Use tools and techniques appropriate for the nail art being carried out
- Ensure that nail and cuticle are clean and undamaged

5 Remove the stencil.

6 Apply gold striping tape where the colours join.

7 Apply a top coat.

8 Whilst the top coat is still tacky, apply a gold teardrop shape to the centre of the chevron.

9 Apply two coats of top coat.

10 Allow nails to dry then remove paint that has been sprayed onto the surrounding skin. This can be done either by the client washing her hands – ensure polish is very dry and take great care – or with a cotton-wool tipped orange stick dipped in nail polish remover.

Contra-actions

Contra-actions to nail art are few as the products used are generally non-toxic. However, some clients are very sensitive and it is wise to be aware of possible contra-actions and how to deal with them.

Allergy

This is most likely to happen when products touch the skin surrounding the nail, as they do in airbrushing. Symptoms may include redness, rash, itching or blistering. Remove the offending product immediately with water. If symptoms persist advise the client to see her doctor.

Stained nails

This is caused by not using a base coat prior to applying colour to the nails. Always make a note on the client's record card of any contra-actions and detail any action taken by the nail technician.

Aftercare and advice

The advice given to clients after the application of nail art should include:

● Re-apply top coat every few days to maintain the life of the design.
● How to remove nail jewellery where appropriate e.g. for washing hair, putting on tights etc.
● Use rubber gloves when cleaning or washing up.
● Do not use the fingernails as tools.

Toenail art

Some clients may want creative finger nails but are restricted by work, lifestyle etc. There is no reason for them to be disappointed though – suggest that they have creative toenails instead. This is obviously a seasonal trend as toes tend to disappear during the cold months, but come spring and summer there is no reason for toenails not to have their moment. Designs may be restricted to the big toenails due to the small size of the other nails, but almost any of the methods outlined in this chapter can be used to create funky feet!

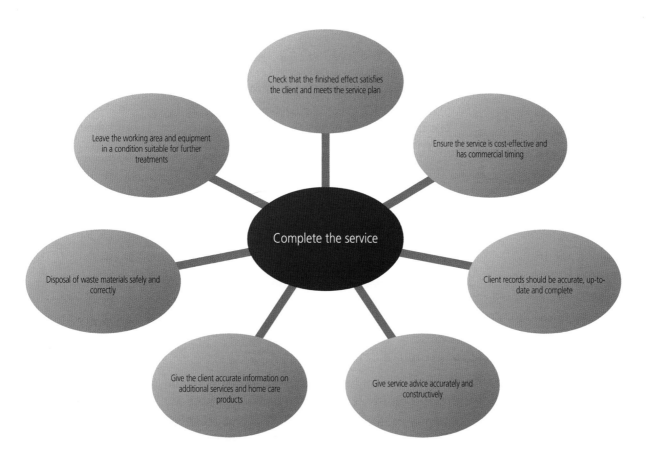

Assessment of knowledge and understanding

You have now learnt about how to enhance the appearance of natural nails using artificial nail structures.

To test your level of knowledge and understanding, answer the following short questions. These will prepare you for your summative (final) assessment.

Anatomy and physiology questions required for this unit are found on pages 146–50.

Organisational and legal requirements

1 Why is it important to discuss the client's requirements prior to beginning the service?

2 How can consultation techniques help to determine the client's service plan?

3 Why is it important to remove all of the clients existing nail polish and treatments prior to beginning the service?

4 Why should the nail area be cleansed prior to the nail service being carried out?

5 State two contra-indications to providing a nail art service.

6 Why is it important to record the condition of the client's nails and surrounding skin prior to beginning the service?

7 State three ways in which the preparation of the working environment should meet legal and hygiene requirements.

8 List five ways in which your personal appearance should meet the accepted standards in industry.

9 Why is it important that equipment and materials are appropriately positioned for service?

10 How is the risk of cross-infection minimised prior to nail art services being carried out?

11 Why is it important for the client to be sitting comfortably for the nail art service?

12 State three ways in which you can ensure that the environmental conditions are suitable for the client.

13 Why is it important for you to be comfortable whilst working?

Client consultation

1 Why is the condition of the client's nails and surrounding skin important when planning a nail art service?

2 A client with mid length nails in good condition is going to a wedding. What types of nail art might you recommend?

3 A busy business client requests nail art services. She works in a very conservative industry. What nail art services would you not recommend and why?

4 How can the colour of the client's skin affect your choice of nail art?

5 List three things that may be included in a design plan.

6 List two factors that may influence your designs.

7 Why is it important for your design plan to be clear and accurate?

8 What opportunities are available for creating nail art?

Nail art requirements

1 List five methods of applying nail art.

2 Why is it important to read the manufacturer's instructions prior to using a product?

3 Why is it important to ensure that the nails are appropriately prepared prior to nail art application?

4 Why is it necessary to seal nail art?

5 Why is it important that your work is of a high standard?

6 How might you need to adapt your design plan in changed circumstances?

7 Why is it important that the environment is appropriate for the products used?

8 What types of additional media are available to complement nail art designs?

chapter 14

Enhance appearance using cosmetic camouflage

Learning objectives

This unit describes how to enhance appearance using cosmetic camouflage applications that do not involve medical consultation. It describes the competencies you will need to enable you to:

- **consult with the client**
- **planning the camouflage application**
- **prepare for the camouflage application**
- **preparing the area to be camouflaged**
- **applying camouflage products to restore skin colouration**
- **instruct and advise the client in camouflage application**

When providing treatment to enhance the appearance using cosmetic camouflage it is important to use the skills you have learned in the following core mandatory units:

G1 ensure your own actions reduce risks to health and safety
G6 promote additional products or services to clients
G11 contribute to the financial effectiveness of the business manicure

INTRODUCTION

Specialist techniques are required for **corrective** make-up and **camouflage** make-up. People asking for this treatment are often distressed about some aspect of their appearance. This can vary from a dislike of their normal face shape or feature/s, through to disfigurement from disease or injury. Corrective and camouflage make-up application techniques are usually carried out using products specifically made for the purpose.

- Corrective make-up is applied to conceal areas or change the appearance of the facial features.
- Camouflage make-up is opaque and is used to conceal and disguise an area completely.

| TIP | |

A skin graft is where skin is moved from one part of the body to another for skin repair. This may result in differing skin tones and scarring.

Problem areas which may be camouflaged

- **Scars**: injury, post operative, burns, keloid (lumpy scar tissue forming at the site of wounds), acne vulgaris, raised or discoloured.
- **Burns**: scars which are ridged or discoloured.
- **Skin grafts**: where the skin is a different colour from the surrounding area and may also be hairy.
- **Birth marks**: strawberry naevus, capillary naevus (port wine stain), darker pigmented areas.

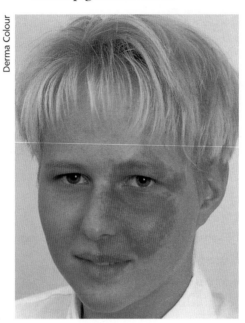

A birthmark

- **Bruising**: temporary post-operative or post-injury bruising.
- **Pigment disorders**: hypopigmentation (reduced melanin production), e.g. vitiligo (white patches), hyperpigmentation (increased melanin production), e.g. chloasmata (brown patches).

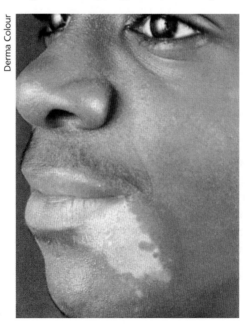
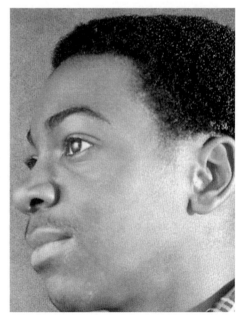

Vitiligo

- **Vascular disorders**: acne rosacea (chronic inflammation of the skin on the nose and cheeks caused by dilation of the blood capillaries), telangiectasia (dilated capillaries appearing on the face, body or legs) varicose veins (deep blue and purple veins on the legs), and erythema, redness possibly caused by acne rosacea or general high colour.

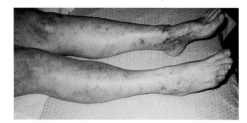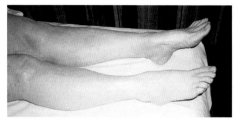

Varicose veins

- **Tattoos**: these may be professional or amateur but both are permanent.

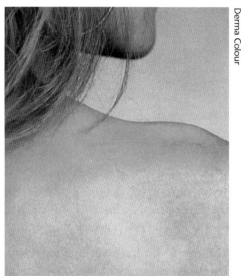

Derma Colour

Tattoo

- **Age spots**: darker areas of pigmentation on the face, body and hands.
- **Moles**: large brown naevi on the face and body.
- **Dark skin around eyes**: dark circles due to illness, stress, lack of sleep, hereditary causes.

Facial areas which may be corrected

- **Face shapes:** e.g. heavy jawline, wide forehead.
- **Facial features**: e.g. prominent nose, small eyes, thin lips.

Reception

Both camouflage make-up and corrective make-up sessions will often take the form of a lesson. This will enable the client to apply make-up in the future for the purpose of correction.

The client will have her make-up applied by the therapist, showing each step. One hour is booked for this, which allows for instruction to be conducted in a relaxed manner. It is not always possible for the beauty therapist immediately to match the client's skin tone, so time must be allowed for experimentation. Once successfully completed, should the client then want to return to the salon to have professional application for a special occasion, then 30 to 45 minutes is normally allocated. Treatment times will vary dramatically according to client needs and treatment requirements.

If the client has a sensitive skin, a skin test may be recommended to test for allergy to the camouflage make-up.

The projected costs and treatment duration should be agreed with the client.

Consultation

The consultation should be confidential and relaxed, in order for the client to feel comfortable in discussing the area requiring attention. Often the client may be psychologically upset and as such the consultation should be tactful and reassuring.

Ask the client why she wants the area to be corrected – it may be for a special occasion, photograph or for disguise during normal day wear. It is important to establish whether the client's expected outcomes from the treatment are realistic.

A case history of the blemish is required. Ask questions such as:

- How long has the blemish been there? Congenital abnormalities, i.e. capillary haemangioma (port wine stain) are present at birth. Pigmentation abnormalities, i.e. chloasmata (brown patches) or vitiligo (white patches) will have developed as the person aged.

- If scars are present, what was their cause? They may be due to accidental injury, i.e. cuts, burns or surgery.

- Is surgery or laser treatment being carried out in the area? When was your last treatment done?

- For how long has healing been taking place?

- Is there any soreness or lack of sensitivity in the area?

If it is a facial feature that is disliked, then explain how it might be disguised and always give the client a realistic expectation of the result obtainable. Clients who have unrealistic expectations should be accurately and tactfully advised of achievable outcomes.

ACTIVITY

The type of light that a camouflage make-up is seen in makes a difference as to how it will look. Experiment with three different light sources to see how your make-up will look in each, e.g. daylight, fluorescent light, incandescent light.

Lighting

You need to know the *type* of light in which the proposed make-up will be seen. This is important when deciding on the correct choice of make-up colours, because the appearance of colours may change according to the type of light. Is the make-up to be seen in daylight, in a fluorescent-lit office, or a softly lit restaurant?

White light (natural daylight) contains all the colours of the rainbow. When white light falls on an object, some colours are absorbed and others reflected: it is the *reflected* colours that we see. Thus, an object that we see as red is one that absorbs all the colours in white light *except* for red. A *white* object reflects most of the light that falls on it; a *black* object absorbs most of the light that falls on it.

If the make-up is to be worn in natural light, choose subtle make-up products as daylight intensifies colours.

If the make-up is to be worn in the office, it will probably be seen under **fluorescent light**. This contains an excess of blue and green, which have a 'cool' effect on the make-up: the red in the face does not show up and the face can look drained of colour. Reds and yellows should be avoided, as these will not show up; blue-toned colours will. Don't apply dark colours, as fluorescent light intensifies these.

Evening make-up is usually seen in **incandescent light** – light produced by a filament lamp. This produces an excess of red and yellow light, which creates a warm, flattering effect. Almost all colours can be used in this light, except that browns and purples will appear darker. Choose a lighter foundation than normal to reflect the light, and use frosted highlighting products where possible for the same reason.

TIP

If working under artificial light, use warm fluorescent light for day make-up, as this closely resembles natural light.

Planning and preparation for treatment

- Preparing the work environment to meet health and safety legislation requirements
- Book at least 1 hour for the first treatment
- Check if this is for a special occasion or if it will be an application lesson
- Consultation must be relaxed, confidential with a thorough case history
- Have the right lighting available to ensure effective treatment application
- Treatment area clean, comfortable and ventilated with all resources required available
- Trolley fully prepared: skin preparations, make-up, applicators, sponges, brushes, cotton wool, tissues

TIP

Further consultations may be recommended to select differing cosmetic colours, as skin colour changes on exposure to ultraviolet light.

TIP

Photographs of 'before' and 'after' make-ups are useful at the consultation to illustrate the results obtainable.

HEALTH AND SAFETY

The department of health has issued strict hygiene recommendations in the application of skin camouflage products

Because it is necessary to choose brighter colours and to emphasise facial features using contouring cosmetics, evening make-up will appear very obvious and dramatic in daylight.

Treatment plan

The content of the treatment plan discussed should be agreed by the client and her signature recorded on her treatment record card.

Contra-indications

If, whilst completing the record card, or on visual inspection of the skin, the client is found to have any of the following in the treatment area, specialist make-up should not be applied. If in doubt, then the client must be referred to her doctor as to her suitability for treatment.

- broken skin, unhealed wounds
- eye infections (e.g. conjunctivitis)
- skin disorders or disease
- skin swelling, irritation, soreness
- suspicious moles (showing signs of growing, changing colour, itching, soreness or weeping).

If camouflage make-up is to be used to cover post-operative bruising (e.g. after face lifting), then the client must provide evidence of the surgeon's permission before treatment.

Sterilisation and sanitisation

Make-up must be removed from containers using clean, sanitised spatulas. Colours can be mixed on a sanitised colour-mixing palette. Applicators such as brushes and sponges can either be disposable, or alternatively should be thoroughly washed using a soap-free antibacterial cleanser, rinsed in cold, clean water, allowed to dry and then stored in an ultraviolet cabinet.

Professional make-up brush cleaner can be sprayed onto the brushes, dried and then removed onto tissue along with the make-up. The quick anti-bacterial action allows the brushes to be used again almost immediately.

Short nails are important when applying the make-up by hand to avoid make-up collecting underneath the nails during application.

Brush cleaner

HEALTH AND SAFETY	+

Brushes and sponges kept damp will encourage bacterial growth, possibly resulting in skin irritation and cross-infection. Wash thoroughly and store dry, preferably in a UV cabinet.

HEALTH AND SAFETY	+

Do not put directly in the make-up containers any applicators that have been in contact with the client's skin. The make-up may then become contaminated with bacteria, resulting in cross-infection.

Equipment and materials

- couch or beauty chair, with a reclining back and a headrest, and an easy to clean surface
- trolley or other surface on which to place everything
- disposable tissue such as bedroll – to cover the work surface and the couch or beauty chair
- towels (two), freshly laundered for each client – one to be placed over the head of the couch, the other over the area to be treated to protect the client's garments
- specialised cleansing and toning preparations, efficient at removing waterproof make-up
- moisturiser
- magnifying lamp – to inspect the area after cleansing
- cotton wool, dry and damp, prepared for each client
- large white facial tissues – to blot the skin after cleansing and moisturiser application
- bowls to hold the prepared cotton wool
- range of concealing and camouflage make-up
- range of contouring and general make-up products to treat a variety of skin types and colours

ACTIVITY	

Research which types of camouflage make-up are available and how you would buy them. Compare the costs of setting up a range for the salon.

EQUIPMENT LIST

couch or beauty chair, with a reclining back and headrest and an easy to clean surface

trolley or other surface on which to place everything

disposable tissue such as bedroll – to cover work surface and the couch or beauty chair

towels

specialised cleaning or toning preparations

moisturiser

magnifying lamp

cotton wool

large white facial tissues

bowls to hold cotton wool

range of concealing and camouflage and contouring and general make up (specialist make up products)

make-up application brushes

spatulas, disposable

concealing creams

foundations

eyelash curlers

false eyelashes

loose powder

general range of facial make up cosmetics

mirror

record card

bright lighting

- fixing powder, essential for a matt finish, which absorbs facial oils and perspiration, giving the make-up durability
- make-up applicator brushes (assorted) and disposable sponges

TIP

Fine brushes are required when disguising small scars and blemishes.

HEALTH AND SAFETY

Prevention of cross-infection
Three sets of make-up brushes are required to allow for effective sanitisation between clients. Have a pencil sharpener available for lip and eye pencils – sharpening will allow a fresh surface for each client. Never apply make-up over broken skin, and only scar tissue when it is completely healed.

- spatulas, disposable
- concealing creams
- foundations, light to dark
- eyelash curlers and false eyelashes
- loose powder
- general range of facial make-up cosmetics
- mirror
- record card
- bright lighting, ideally daylight.

TIP

Vitiligo is commonly seen around the eyes, mouth and hands; chloasmata are commonly seen on the forehead, cheek area and around the lips.

TIP

Common racial skin problems:
- Caucasian – easily damaged by exposure to high temperatures and ultraviolet light, leading to broken veins and pigmentation disorders.
- Oriental – prone to uneven pigmentation on ultraviolet light exposure.
- Asian – often has uneven pigmentation skin tones; darker skin is often found around the eyes.
- Afro-Caribbean – greater protection against ultraviolet light as melanin is present in all layers of the epidermis; tends to scar easily, possibly leading to uneven pigmentation, vitiligo and keloids.

Preparation of the treatment area

The treatment room should have good ventilation so that the client's skin does not become too warm. The treatment couch or make-up chair should be clean and covered with fresh towels, and/or disposable bed roll as required. The trolley should display all the required make-up, applicators (including sponges, spatulas and brushes) and skin cleansers, toners and moisturisers ready to use. Cotton wool, tissues and protective make-up capes are normally used. A pedal bin with removable bin liner is ideal for waste.

Preparation of the therapist

Complete a record card during the consultation, or if this is a repeat visit, have the client's record card ready. Hands must be sanitised before handling the client.

Presentation of the therapist must meet the organisation's and the industry's professional standards. A clean, fresh uniform and smart appearance, preferably wearing make-up, will make the client feel relaxed and reassured that she/he is in capable hands.

Preparation of the client

The client must be made to feel relaxed and confident on the treatment couch or make-up chair. Protect the client's clothing with tissue or a make-up cape.

The area to be treated should be cleansed and toned with the appropriate skin-care preparations. If moisturiser is to be used, it must be absorbed before make-up is applied. This usually takes about 10 minutes. Before make-up application, any excess moisturiser may be blotted off using a clean tissue.

Have a mirror ready to use through the stages of the make-up, so that the client can see what it looks like as you progress, and how to apply it.

> **TIP**
>
> Do not use moisturiser on an area that is to be camouflaged, unless it is very dry. It may change the colour of the make-up or prevent it from setting properly.

> **TIP**
>
> Check the manufacturer's instructions on how to apply the camouflage make-up. Brands vary and some may require different preparation or setting techniques.

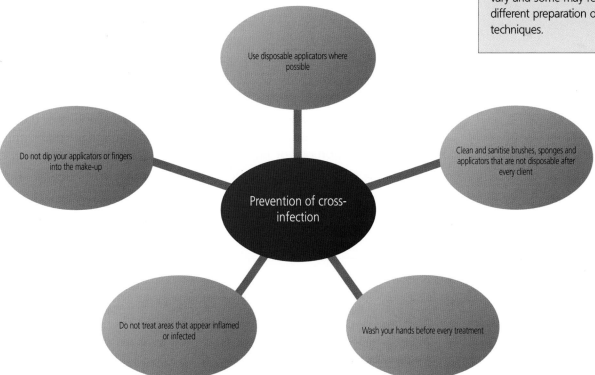

ACTIVITY

Research the principles of colour theory and make a colour wheel. Experiment to see what colours best suit which skin conditions.

HEALTH AND SAFETY

If using make-up in containers, remove it with a clean spatula.

CAMOUFLAGE MAKE-UP

Treatment application

1 Select the chosen colour or colour mixture which best matches the skin tone surrounding the area to be treated.

2 Using your ring and middle fingers in a patting motion, or using a dry sponge, blend the make-up thinly over the problem area, extending it approximately 2 cm past the edge. If disguising scars, a brush may be used to feather the make-up at the edges to create a natural effect. The sponge may be dampened if needed to facilitate extra blending.

3 Build up the colour depth to ensure the blemish is completely covered, thinning the colour at the edge to blend in. A small make-up brush can be used to blend in the edges of the make-up.

4 Once the required result has been achieved, apply the fixing powder generously with a large powder puff.

5 Leave the make-up to set for 5–10 minutes.

6 Gently brush off any excess fixing powder with a large, soft make-up brush, e.g. blusher/powder brush. Blot off excess powder if required with damp cotton wool. The make-up is now waterproof and rub resistant, and should not be detectable.

TIP

It is preferable to build up several layers to achieve the desired effect, rather than applying a thick layer.

TIP

Copy the surrounding skin tone carefully to ensure the most natural effect, i.e. add freckles or shade the camouflage make-up to match darker or lighter areas.

7 If the camouflage has been applied to the face, a full make-up may now be applied. The foundation colour selected should match the colour of the camouflage make-up.

8 Apply foundation up to the area of camouflage make-up and blend so that an invisible finish is created. Putting an oily cream foundation over the camouflage make-up will only move or remove the camouflage make-up: it is best to use a non-oily or liquid foundation.

9 Record on the client record card the make-up products selected and application technique used.

TIP

- **Covering a deep red mark**: use a green pigmented make-up first, then apply make-up which matches the skin tone over the top.
- **Covering a dark brown mark**: use white, opaque make-up first, then apply make-which matches the skin tone over the top.
- **Covering a lighter mark**: commence with a darker foundation and apply make-up which matches the skin tone over the top.

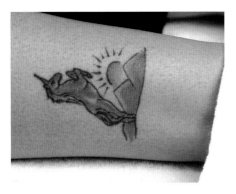

The tattoo to be camouflaged

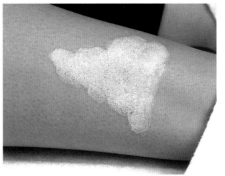

Applying the make-up

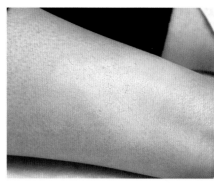

Blending the colour

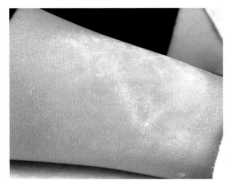

Applying fixing powder

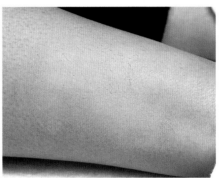

The finished cosmetic camouflage make-up

Derma Colour

Covering a deep red mark

Derma Colour

Covering a deep red mark

CORRECTIVE MAKE-UP

Before applying these products, decide on the effect you wish to achieve. Study the client's face from the front and side profiles, and determine what facial corrective work is necessary.

Contouring

Contour cosmetics

Changing the shape of the face and the facial features can be achieved with the careful application of **contour cosmetics**. These products draw attention either towards or away from facial features, and can create the optical illusion of perfection.

Contour cosmetics include **highlighters**, **shaders** and **blushers**. They are available in powder, liquid and cream forms.

- Highlighters draw attention towards – they emphasise.
- Shaders draw attention away – they minimise.
- Blushers add warmth to the face, and emphasise the facial contours.

Each face differs in shape and size, so each requires a different application technique.

Applying blusher

Applying blusher

Some blushers appear very vibrant in the container, yet when they are applied to the skin they appear very subtle.

Powder blushers

1 Stroke the contour brush over the powder blusher. Tap the brush gently to dislodge excess blusher.

2 Apply the blusher to the cheek area, carefully placing the product according to the effect you wish to create. The direction of brush strokes should be upwards and outwards, towards the hairline. Keep the blusher away from the nose, and avoid applying blusher too near the outer eye.

3 Apply more blusher if necessary. The key to successful blusher application is to build up colour slowly until you have achieved the optimum effect.

Cream blushers

1 Apply the cream blusher after foundation application, then place a loose, translucent powder over the cream blusher.

2 If liquid or cream cosmetics are used, these must be applied on top of a liquid or cream foundation, before powder application. (If powder contour products are used, these should be applied after the application of loose face powder. The rule of contour cosmetic application is: powder on powder; cream on cream.)

Treatment application

1 Apply suitable moisturiser base, i.e. anti-shine product, skin firming product, eye gel.

2 Apply foundation to the whole face.

3 If using cream concealers, apply directly on top of the foundation. A dark colour will make a feature less prominent; a light colour will make a feature more prominent; a light cover over a dark area, i.e. under eyes, will help to conceal it.

4 Fix foundation with translucent loose powder using a clean powder puff. Remove excess powder with a powder brush.

5 If using powder highlighters or shaders, apply on top of powdered foundation.

6 Record on the client record card, make-up products selected and application technique used.

> **TIP** ✔
>
> It is important to experiment with different applications to ensure the best result.

> **TIP** ✔
>
> Choose a foundation suitable for the skin problem, i.e. light-reflective, long lasting, concealing lines.

> **TIP** ✔
>
> Make-up to disguise or enhance facial features must be subtle and applied in the lighting the client is going to be seen in. Daytime make-up is the most subtle finish of all. Stronger make-up can be applied for evening or photographic looks.

Concealing

Before you begin to apply make-up to the face, inspect the skin and identify the areas that require concealing, such as blemishes, uneven skin colour or shadows.

Foundation may be used to disguise minor skin imperfections, but where extra coverage is required it is necessary to apply a special **concealer** – a cosmetic designed to provide maximum skin coverage. The concealer may be applied directly to the skin after skin moisturising, or following application of the foundation.

Choose a concealer that matches the client's skin tone as closely as possible. If the concealer is to be applied *after* the foundation, it should match the colour of the *foundation*.

Concealer can contain pigment to help correct skin tone:

- **green** helps to counteract high colouring, and to conceal dilated capillaries
- **lilac** counteracts a sallow skin colour and disguises dark circles
- **white** or **cream** helps to correct unevenness in the skin pigmentation
- light-reflecting and line concealing.

Applying concealer

Remove a small quantity of the concealer from its container, using a clean, disposable spatula. Apply the concealer to the area to be disguised, using

Applying concealer

either a clean make-up sponge or a soft make-up brush. Blend the concealer to achieve a realistic effect.

Correcting face shapes

To assess the client's face shape, take the hair away from the face – hairstyles often disguise the face shape. Study the size and shape of the facial bone structure. Consider the amount of excess fat, skin condition and the muscle tone.

Oval

This is regarded as the perfect face shape. Corrective make-up application usually attempts to create the *appearance* of an oval face shape.

Draw attention to the cheekbones by applying shader beneath the cheekbone, and highlighter above. Blusher should be drawn along the cheekbone and blended up towards the temples.

Round

- *Bone structure*: broad and short.
- *Corrective make-up*: Apply highlighter in a thin band down the central portion of the face, to create the illusion of length. Shader may be applied over the angle of the jaw to the temples. Apply blusher in a triangular shape, with the base of the triangle running parallel to the ear.

Square

- *Bone structure*: A broad forehead and a broad, angular jawline.
- *Corrective make-up*: Shade the angles of the jawbone, up and towards the cheekbone. Apply blusher in a circular pattern on the cheekbones, taking it towards the temples.

Heart

- *Bone structure*: A wide forehead, with the face tapering to a narrow, pointed chin, like an inverted triangle.
- *Corrective make-up*: Highlight the angles of the jawbone and shade the point of the chin, the temples and the sides of the forehead. Apply blusher under the cheekbones, in an upward and outward direction towards the temples.

Diamond

- *Bone structure*: A narrow forehead, with wide cheekbones tapering to a narrow chin.
- *Corrective make-up*: Apply shader to the tip of the chin and the height of the forehead, to reduce length. Highlight the narrow sides of the temples and the lower jaw. Apply blusher to the fullness of the cheekbones, to draw attention to the centre of the face.

Oval

Round

Square   Heart   Diamond

Oblong

- *Bone structure*: Long and narrow, tapering to a pointed chin.
- *Corrective make-up*: Apply shader to the hairline and the point of the chin, to reduce the length of the face. Highlight the angle of the jawbone and the temples, to create width. Blend blusher along the cheekbones, outwards towards the ears.

Pear

- *Bone structure*: A wide jawline, tapering to a narrow forehead.
- *Corrective make-up*: Highlight the forehead, and shade the sides of the chin and the angle of the jaw. Apply blusher to the fullness of the cheeks, or blend it along the cheekbones, up towards the temples.

Oblong

Correcting facial features

Noses

- If the nose is *too broad*, apply shader to the sides of the nose.
- If the nose is *too short*, apply highlighter down the length of the nose, from the bridge to the tip.
- If the nose is *too long*, apply shader to the tip of the nose.
- If there is a *bump* on the nose, apply shader over the area.
- If there is a *hollow* along the bridge of the nose, apply highlighter over the hollow area.
- If the nose is *crooked*, apply shader over the crooked side.

Pear

TIP

An Asian face may appear as a rather flat plane. The skilful application of shading and highlighting products can create highs and lows.

TIP

Foreheads can be improved by a flattering hairstyle.

Foreheads

- If the forehead is *prominent*, apply shader centrally over the prominent area, blending it outwards towards the temples.
- If the forehead is *shallow*, apply highlighter in a narrow band below the hairline.
- If the forehead is *deep*, apply shader in a narrow band below the hairline.

Chins

- If the jaw is *too wide*, apply shader from beneath the cheekbones and along the jawline, blending it at the neck.
- If the chin is *double*, apply shader to the centre of the chin, blending it outwards along the jawbone and under the chin.
- If the chin is *prominent*, apply foundation to the tip of the chin.
- If the chin is *long*, apply shader over the prominent area.
- If the chin *recedes*, apply highlighter along the jawline and at the centre of the chin.

Necks

- If the neck is *thin*, apply highlighter down each side of the neck.
- If the neck is *thick*, apply shader to both sides of the neck.

Correcting eye shapes

Make-up is applied to the eye area to complement the natural eye colour, to give definition to the eye area, and to enhance the natural shape of the eye.

Dark circles

1 Minimise the circles by applying a concealing product.

Dark circles

Wide-set eyes

1 Apply a darker eye colour to the inner portion of the upper eyelid.
2 Apply lighter eyeshadow to the outer portion of the eyelid.
3 Apply eyeliner in a darker colour to the inner half of the upper eyelid.
4 Eyebrow pencil may be applied to extend the inner browline.

Wide-set eyes

Close-set eyes

1 Lighten the inner portion of the upper eyelid.
2 Use a darker colour at the outer eye.
3 Apply eyeliner to the outer corner of the upper eyelid.
4 Pluck brow hairs at the inner eyebrow – this helps to create the illusion of the eyes being further apart.

Close-set eyes

Round eyes

1 Apply a darker colour over the prominent central upper lid area.
2 Elongate the eyes by applying eyeliner to the outer corners of the upper and lower eyelids.

Round eyes

Prominent eyes

1 Apply dark matt eyeshadow over the prominent upper eyelid.
2 Apply a darker shade to the outer portion of the eyelid, and blend it upwards and outwards.
3 Highlight the browbone, drawing attention to this area.
4 Eyeliner may be applied to the inner, lower eyelid.

Prominent eyes

TIP	✔
False eyelashes may be effective in enhancing the eye's natural shape.	

> **TIP** ✔
>
> To make the eyes appear less prominent, select matt eyeshadows – pearlised and frosted eyeshadows will highlight and emphasise the eye.

Overhanging lids

1 Apply a pale highlighter to the middle of the eyelid.
2 apply a darker eyeshadow to contour the socket area, creating a higher crease (which disguises the hooded appearance).

Overhanging lids

Crepey skin on eyelids

1 Use a light matt eyeshadow powder as a base.
2 Use matt eyeshadow powder colours to minimise the crepey look. (Shiny, pearlescent shadows will emphasise the crepey skin.)

Deep-set eyes

1 Use light-coloured eyeshadows.
2 Eyeshadow may also be applied in a fine line to the inner half of the lower eyelid, beneath the lashes.
3 Apply eyeliner to the outer halves of the upper and lower eyelids, broadening the line as you extend outwards.

Deep-set eyes

Downward-slanting eyes

1 Create lift by applying the eyeshadow upwards and outwards at the outer corners of the upper eyelid.
2 Apply eyeliner to the upper eyelid, applying it upwards at the outer corner.
3 Confine mascara to the outer lashes.

Downward-slanting eyes

Small eyes

Small eyes

1 Choose a light colour for the upper eyelid.

2 Highlight under the brow, to open up the eye area.

3 Curl the lashes before applying mascara.

4 Apply a light-coloured eyeliner to the outer third of the lower eyelid.

5 A white eyeliner may be applied to the inner lid, to make the eye appear larger.

Narrow eyes

Narrow eyes

1 Apply a lighter colour in the centre of the eyelid, to open up the eye.

2 Apply a shader to the inner and outer portions of the eyelid.

Eye make-up for the client who wears glasses

If the client wears glasses, check the function of the lens, as this can alter the appearance and effect of the eye make-up.

- If the client is **short-sighted**, the lens makes the eye appear *smaller*. Draw attention to the eyes by selecting brighter, lighter colours. When applying eyeshadow and eyeliner, use the corrective techniques for small eyes. Apply mascara to emphasise the eyelashes.

- If the client is **long-sighted**, the lens will *magnify* the eye. Make-up should therefore be subtle, avoiding frosted colours and lash-building mascaras. Careful blending is important, as any mistakes will be magnified!

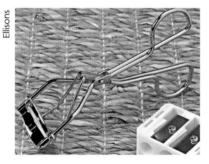

Ellisons

Standard eyelash curlers

Curling the eyelashes

To emphasise the eyelashes, making them appear longer temporarily, curl them using **eyelash curlers**.

1 Rest the upper lashes between the upper and lower portions of the eyelash curlers.

2 Bring the two portions gently together with a squeezing action.

3 Hold the lashes in the curlers for approximately 10 seconds, then release them.

4 If the lashes are not sufficiently curled, repeat the action.

5 Heated lash curlers are also available.

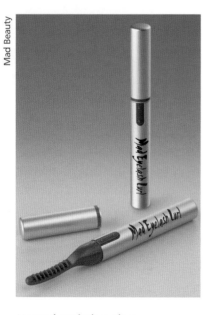

Mad Beauty

Heated eyelash curlers

TIP	
Eyelash curling is beneficial for oriental clients who have short lashes that grow downwards.	

Correcting lip shapes

It is not uncommon for the lips to be out of proportion in some way. Using lip cosmetics and corrective techniques, symmetrical lips can be created. A careful choice of product and accurate application are required to achieve a professional effect.

The main lip cosmetics are lip pencils, lipsticks and lip glosses. Sometimes the lips may be unevenly pigmented. The application of a lip toner or foundation over the lips corrects this.

There are a number of products available that are specifically for conditioning lips. Some act as a base for lipsticks, others are applied around the lips to prevent feathering, when lip cosmetics run into the lines around the lips.

Thick lips

Select natural colours and darker shades, avoiding bright, glossy colours.

1 Blend foundation over the lips to disguise the natural lip line.
2 Apply a darker lipliner inside the natural lip line to create a new line.

Thick lips

Thicker upper or lower lip

1 Use the technique described above to make the larger lip appear smaller.
2 Apply a slightly darker lipstick to the larger lip.
3 If the lips droop at the corners, raise the corners by applying lipliner to the corners of the upper lip, to turn them upwards.

Thicker upper lip

Thin lips

Select brighter, pearlised colours. Avoid darker lipsticks, which will make the mouth appear smaller.

1 Apply a neutral lipliner just outside the natural lip line.

Thicker lower lip

Small mouth

1 Extend the line slightly at the corners of the mouth, with both the upper and the lower lips.

Thin lips

Uneven lips

1 Use a lipliner to draw in a new line.
2 Apply lipstick to the area.

Small mouth

Lines around the mouth

1 Apply lipliner around the natural lip line.
2 Apply a matt cream lipstick to the lips. (Don't use gloss, which might bleed into the lines around the mouth.)

Uneven lips

Lines around the mouth

Airbrushing

Airbrushing techniques are used for all types of camouflage and corrective make-up. The technique involves using an air-powered (by compressor) airbrush which sprays extremely tiny droplets of make-up in a water suspension over the area. Several sweeps of the airbrush are used to carefully build up the colour and amount needed. The make-up is especially formulated for the airbrush.

Preparation

The skin is prepared by cleansing, toning and blotting with a tissue. Moisturiser is not normally used as it may interfere with the result of the airbrushing. Very dry skins that need moisture have a fine layer of jojoba oil air brushed onto the make-up when it is completed.

The order of work is the same as normal for the application of make-up. Mascara and lipstick are applied in the normal way once the airbrushing is complete.

Airbrushing has the following benefits:

- A sheer, flawless coverage can be achieved.
- It is hygienic as the skin is not touched with brushes or sponges.
- The seamless blending and long-lasting properties make it suitable for covering blemishes and tattoos.
- It is suitable for all skin types and colours.
- The application is very quick.
- It is both rub and water resistant.
- It sets on contact with the skin.

Airbrushing

Aftercare

- All the make-up must be thoroughly removed using the appropriate cleansers and toners. Camouflage make-up manufacturers normally specify their own makes. These are often oily, in order to help remove the waterproof make-up effectively. The client must have the right cleanser and toner for use at home. Recommend a good skin-care routine and stress the importance of hygiene and keeping make-up and applicators clean.

- Care should be taken if the area covered becomes wet. Advise the client to pat the area dry gently with a soft towel.

- Corrective make-up should not be left on for longer than 24 hours at a time as it may clog the skin and cause irritations and spots.

- Once you have shown the client how to apply the make-up, she can apply it for herself at home. Recommend that the client applies the make-up in good light.

ACTIVITY

How would you apply make-up to conceal a red-coloured birthmark on the cheek and dark shadows under the eyes? Describe the treatment from start to finish. Include the method and order of applying the make-up.

- The client's current skin-care routine should be discussed as incorrect skin care routines can affect the condition of the skin.
- The client should be advised to wear regular sun protection in the case of pigmentation disorders.

Contra-actions

Irritation, soreness, erythema

Camouflage make-up is formulated to be used on sensitive and delicate skin types, so allergic reactions are rare. However, if skin irritation occurs, cleanse all traces of make-up from the skin and advise the application of a soothing lotion. If skin irritation continues, ask the client to seek her GP's advice.

Blocked pores, pustules

The client may not be following the aftercare advice. Discuss how to cleanse the skin thoroughly and advise against wearing the make-up for longer than 24 hours at a time.

Assessment of knowledge and understanding

You have now learnt about how to enhance the appearance using cosmetic camouflage.

To test your level of knowledge and understanding, answer the following short questions. These will prepare you for your summative (final) assessment.

Anatomy and physiology questions required for this unit are found on pages 146–50.

Organisational and legal requirements

1 Which Health and Safety legislation is relevant to cosmetic camouflage treatments?

2 It is important to maintain standards of hygiene and to avoid cross-infection. How would you do this?

3 Why is it important to position your clients in a comfortable and suitable way?

4 How is it possible to injure yourself if this is not done?

5 Why is it essential to keep records of your camouflage treatments and how does the Data Protection Act affect this?

6 Why would you only offer camouflage treatment to a client once they have asked about it?

Client consultation

1 When going through the consultation procedure with a new client, how can you make sure you are using effective communication and consultation techniques?

2 How would you go about encouraging your client to seek medical advice about a contra-indication to treatment? Why is it important not to name specific contra-indications?

3 It is necessary to maintain your client's modesty and privacy at all times. How can you make sure this is done?

4 How would you go about gathering the necessary information required for the consultation? For instance, the client's camouflage requirements, relevant medical and medication information, current and recent lifestyle?

Preparation for camouflage application

1 How would you prepare the plan for the camouflage application?

2 What sort of environmental conditions would you consider when planning the camouflage treatment?

3 How would you make sure both yourself and your client were properly prepared for the treatment or lesson?

Anatomy and physiology

1 Draw and label a detailed diagram of the skin.

2 Describe the functions of the skin.

3 Describe how skin structure differs in differing racial groups.

4 How do you recognise contra-indications to cosmetic camouflage treatment?

5 What sort of skin conditions would restrict camouflage application?

Products

1 Describe two different ranges of camouflage make-up and explain how you would go about purchasing them for use in the salon and for retailing to clients.

2 Each cosmetic camouflage application or lesson is very different. How would you go about selecting the right products for the treatment?

3 Describe the positive aspects of camouflage make-up and the possible negative aspects.

4 How would you ensure that the products and applicators are always kept in a clean and hygienic condition?

The treatment

1 Describe the appearance and state the causes of the wide range of skin conditions that may need cosmetic camouflage treatment.

2 Erythema is a common condition that people often ask about camouflaging. When would an erythema be a contra-indication to cosmetic camouflage treatment?

3 What sort of contra-action could you observe during and after treatment? How can you minimise the possibility of contra-actions?

4 How would you demonstrate the methods of application to your clients and how can you make sure the clients understand and can do it for themselves?

5 What advice should you give the client about keeping the camouflage make-up on and then removing it in the correct way with the right products?

6 What are the main principles of colour theory?

7 How would you test for colour match and why is this important?

8 Why is it useful to show the client the difference between the made-up area and an untreated area? How could you do this during the treatment?

chapter 15

Design and create images for use in fashion and photographic make-up

BT27

Learning objectives

This unit is about developing your artistic make-up skills by planning and designing images that are suitable for their intended purpose. During this process you must develop a professional profile by researching and developing your knowledge of past and current fashion trends. You also need to communicate the design concepts effectively to others involved in the project.

It describes the competencies to enable you to:

- **plan and design a range of images**
- **produce a range of images**
- **evaluate your results against the design plan objectives**

When designing and creating images for use in fashion photographic contexts, it is important to use the skills you have learnt in the following core mandatory units:

G1 ensure your own actions reduce risks to health and safety
G6 promote additional products or services to clients
G11 contribute to the financial effectiveness of the business

INTRODUCTION

The world of the fashion photographic make-up artist is an exciting and ever-changing one. It is of the utmost importance to keep up-to-date with current fashion and trends. What may be fashionable one season can change the next, and quickly look outdated. You can produce some looks which are classic and never really date, or design high fashion images which will look terrific on a professional model, but not so good on a member of the general public as a special occasion make-up.

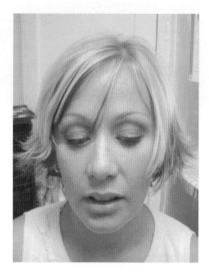

Special occasion make-up (client specification)

Work closely with the other people involved in the process so you all work towards, and aim for, the same end result. Detailed and accurate planning is important so that no misunderstandings and subsequent waste of time and money occur.

Your work in this area will include make-up for photographic shoots, catwalk shows, pop videos, bridal and special occasion make-ups.

PREPARATION

By talking to the client, fashion editor, fashion designer etc., you should get a pretty good idea of what they are looking for. You may need to do some sketches, worksheets, or discuss what they and you have in mind for the overall look. You may need to research extensively for the shoot, utilising magazines, books and the Internet. You must communicate effectively with the others before you agree to a final design plan and have your work checked over again at the end. It must then be checked under the final lighting and on the set, with any props if required.

Make sure you have acquired any relevant props, make-up and hair equipment before you arrive at the job. If you need any other additions to your kit, allow plenty of time to source them, contacting suppliers. Make-up can be sourced from professional make-up suppliers and department stores.

You may wish to take your own Polaroids, although most good photographers will use them to check the lighting effects anyway, and then pass them to you to check make-up and hair. Always check with the relevant people that you will have the resources you need such as good lighting, seating, a mirror if possible and space to work. If you have any problems at all, do not ignore them hoping they will go away, but communicate with the relevant people as soon as possible.

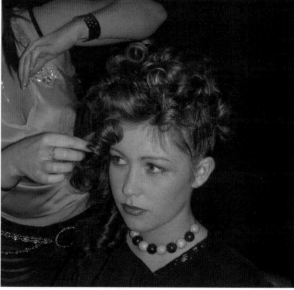

Catwalk make-up

WORKING AREAS AND ENVIRONMENTS

Make sure you are prepared, have everything you could possibly need, and your kit is clean. When you arrive at the studio there may or may not be a designated area for make-up application. Most good studios have an area with seating and a make-up mirror, others can be less than ideal and you just have to make the most of what you have. Make sure the area is safe, comfortable and clean before you lay out your equipment. If you are in a dingy corner without natural daylight, ask the photographer to set up some extra lights to illuminate your model's face while you are working. When you have finished your make-up, you will need to keep a few products on hand, such as powder and a powder puff, cotton buds, tissues and lipstick. For changes of costume and make-up, you should be able to take your model back to the designated make-up area.

If on location you must make the most of the environment you are in. Try to keep make-up at a regular temperature, so it does not freeze, or melt in the heat. A cool bag is a good place to store your make-up. If working in windy conditions, make sure your make-up box has a lid, so it does not end up full of sand or leaves etc. Set bags as used when filming (see page 551) are very useful when on location, when you need to find products quickly. Some products can be decanted into plastic bottles, which can reduce breakages, especially on flights.

Be aware that the client may have not been on a shoot before. Advise them about health and safety, and any potential danger areas in the studio or on location. Items such as trailing cables, light boxes and stands and reflector boards are all hazards that you must look out for. You must be aware of legislation and any local by-laws that are likely to affect you.

Catwalk make-up

ROLES AND TASKS OF OTHERS ON A PHOTOGRAPHIC SHOOT

Adding finishing touches to the hair

- **Photographer** takes the photographs.
- **Photographer's assistant** sets up for the photographs, holds reflector boards, takes light readings. They are responsible for anything involving camera equipment.
- **Model** changes poses, models clothing, make-up and hair. Essential, as you would not have the work without them!
- **Fashion stylist** selects the clothing, dresses the model, and checks that the clothing ties in with the overall look.
- **Hairstylist** creates the models hairstyle/s. Sometimes there can be many changes throughout the day.
- **Make-up artist** responsible for creating the make-up.
- **The client/Art director** the person who is commissioning the shoot. Occasionally they may not be present, or they may bring an entourage of additional people with them. Remember your role and do not step into other colleague's roles unless asked to do so.

All the above people work closely together to finalise the image. It is important to note that sometimes the make-up artist can also be responsible for the hair and styling. This depends on budgets (which should be decided and agreed prior to the shoot) and the size of the shoot.

Depending on where in the world this all takes place, you may have a location guide and interpreters who travel with you too.

Fashion shoot

Natural make-up for cosmetic promotion

WORKING TO A BRIEF

If you need any special resources, make sure you have budgeted for them, and make sure you are able to adapt the design plan if any circumstances change. Give out accurate information to others, making sure it is clear, and delivered at a pace suitable for the event. You could be working on a catwalk show where time is limited and you need to get over information calmly and quickly, having to interrupt someone else. Make sure you apologise for interrupting. It is very important that you communicate and work closely with the rest of the team so that no misunderstandings take place and the overall design plea is realised.

Check that the use of your resources conforms to the design plan, and use additional media wherever possible to enhance the image and complement it, such as painting nails to colour co-ordinate, along with clothing, accessories (props, jewellery) and hairstyling. Carefully chosen accessories can really improve the look of the overall shot.

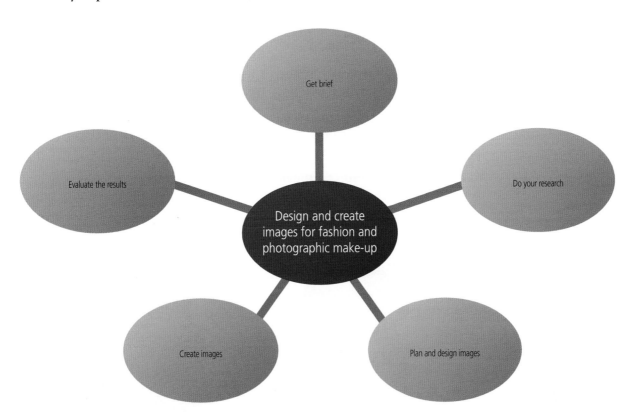

DESIGNING AND DEVELOPING IMAGES

When you create an image it is often advertising something, e.g. jewellery or clothing, and the make-up should not distract from whatever you are selling. In an advertising make-up, do not distract from the subject of the advert with too many other fussy accessories. Also consider design, scale and proportion. As the shoot progresses, you may see an opportunity for

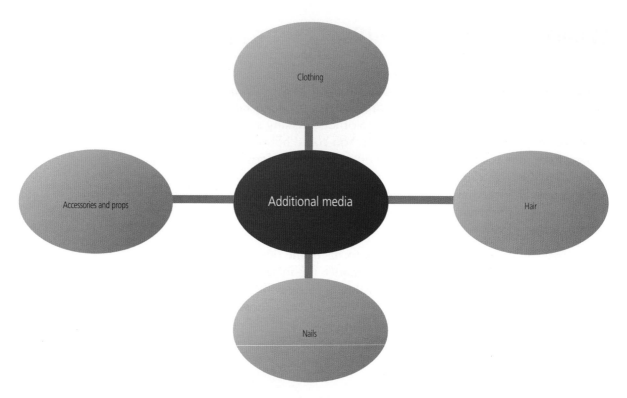

developing the initial image slightly. Check with the rest of the team before you go ahead and change anything.

Products can be adapted to suit effects required, for example you may wish to dilute a creme foundation to make it into a tinted moisturiser, and lipstick could be used on eyelids etc.

You may need to interpret a theme, e.g. an icy winter scene could imply using colours such as silvers, blues, greys and white. Or the client may want a make-up designed in brighter colours to 'warm up' a winter's day.

Fantasy make-up for cosmetic promotion

Medusa with blocked out eyebrows and gold body make-up

LIGHTING AND CAMERA EFFECTS

Various different effects can be achieved with changes in lighting, camera lenses, types of film, and even in the film development process.

A strong directional light which has had its beam broken by placing a transparent white sheet of material between it and the subject can bleach out the make-up and skin tones. If you are photographing a model with a blemished skin, this type of lighting can help create a smooth, even skin texture.

The standard lens on most cameras is around 50 mm, which is roughly the same field of view as the human eye. If you change the lens to say 100 mm, this has the effect of making the subject appear larger on film as well as foreshortening facial perspective, which will show the subject in a more flattering way.

There are numerous film types available to the photographer who can use one sort of film to create a grainy effect on the image and another to emphasise contrast. The variations are vast, and are best discussed with the photographer before shooting the images. These same effects can also be achieved by varying conditions and chemical combinations during the processing of the film.

Coloured gels can also be applied over the lights to create various effects. For example, if you are using black and white film the colour of the gel in use will darken the same colour on the subject. So if your model is wearing red lipstick and you either cover the lens with a red filter, or place a red gel over the light, the red lipstick will appear darker when the film is processed. You will also find this has an effect when working on catwalk or runway shows. Coloured lighting will affect the shades of your make-up and you may need to adapt your colours accordingly.

Black and white studio portraiture

Dramatic studio lighting effects for black and white film

Location work in New York

SOURCING WORK

To get work you will have to visit photographers, model agencies and any other potential clients. You will need to take your portfolio of pictures along. This is the only way they can check your work is what they are looking for at that time, without asking you to do a test make-up or you being recommended by word of mouth. Presentation of your photographs and designs should be in a professional-looking portfolio. The photographs should flow from one to another and offer a variety of images, including studio and exterior shots and both colour and black and white shots. Specialist make-up artist agencies like you to have a certain image to your work – natural, funky, avante-garde – because they find it easier to market you in this way, and only take on experienced make-up artists.

EVALUATION

- Ask for feedback from the rest of the team, but in particular the client, as to the overall effectiveness and impact of your make-up, checking that it is conforming to the original design plan. If you are not 100 per cent sure of something, ask 'What do you think about this?'

- For your own self-development, check, evaluate and compare the development process and final result with the original client specification to identify opportunities for improvement in your design and application techniques. Is there anything you could have improved on? How? Have you used the products correctly to get the desired outcome?

- If you have done a good job then the client will no doubt use you again. The final design should enhance your professional profile.

- Record the results of your evaluation for future reference. When you see the final image check everything carefully again.

Step by step make-up

1 Make sure your working area is comfortable, clean and hygienic for your client.
2 Wash your hands and gown up your client to protect their clothing.
3 Check for contra-indications; assess your client's skin type, tone and face shape.
4 Cleanse, tone and moisturise according to skin type.
5 Colour correct areas if necessary, e.g. use green to counteract any redness.
6 Apply foundation with a sponge or brush.
7 Apply concealer over any blemishes and to shadows under the eyes.
8 Apply translucent powder to set the base using a powder puff. Brush off excess using a powder brush.
9 Apply powder blusher using a blusher brush. If you want to use a cream or gel blusher, apply it before the powder stage.

10 Brush through the eyebrows and fill in any gaps with an eyebrow pencil or powder eyeshadow. Eyebrow gel will smooth down any stray hairs.

11 Apply eyeshadow colours. Use various sizes of brushes according to the area involved and the colours. If using strong or dark colours, you can apply a dusting of loose powder under the eyes to catch speckles of eye shadow.

12 Apply eyeliner using a brush or pencil.

13 Brush mascara onto the lashes.

14 Apply false lashes if the design brief requires them.

15 Apply lip pencil to outline the lips and prevent the lipstick from 'bleeding' into the lines around the mouth.

16 Apply lipstick, stain and/or gloss.

17 Add any finishing touches such as glitter.

18 Check the overall result and make amendments as necessary.

Sarah before

Foundation, powder, blusher and eyeshadow base applied

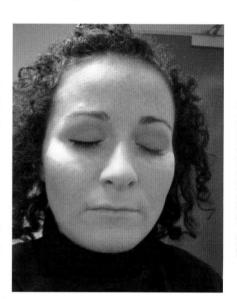

Application of eyeliner

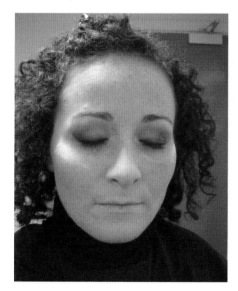

Eyeshadow colour darkened and mascara added

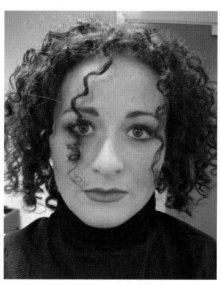

Extra blusher and red lipstick applied for finished effect

Assessment of knowledge and understanding

You have now learnt about fashion photographic make-up. To test your level of knowledge and understanding, answer the following short questions. These will prepare you for your summative (final) assessment.

Planning

1 Why should you plan prior to the job?

2 Why is it important to communicate clearly with the client and colleagues?

3 Why should you discuss the budget and come to an agreement on it?

4 Why should you specify the resources you need to do the job properly?

5 Why is it important to have some knowledge of lighting and camera effects?

6 Why is it important to gain as much information as possible about the venue beforehand?

Designing and developing images

1 How do you use the basic principles of design, scale and proportion when creating an image?

2 Explain how you would go about researching for an image.

3 How should you present your design plans and images?

4 How should you present your final images, when sourcing work?

5 Where would you obtain your resources?

6 How should the working environment be prepared prior to starting work?

7 What is 'additional media' and how can it be used to complement the overall design image?

8 Name two ways of adapting your make-up products to suit changing circumstances.

Evaluation

1 Why is it important to evaluate your performance at the end of a shoot?

2 In which particular areas should you collect feedback?

3 How should you seek constructive feedback?

4 How would you identify any areas for improvement?

chapter 16

Set up, monitor and shut down water, temperature and spa facilities

BT28

Provide specialist spa treatments

BT29

Learning objectives

This unit describes how to set up, monitor and shut down water, temperature and spa facilities and provide specialist spa treatments

It describes the competencies to enable you to:

- **prepare, clean and maintain the spa environment**
- **consult with, and prepare, the client for treatment**
- **provide body wrapping treatments**
- **provide flotation treatments**
- **provide hydrotherapy treatments**
- **monitor water, temperature and spa treatments and environments**
- **provide aftercare advice**
- **complete shutdown of treatment areas and spa environments**

When providing spa treatment it is important to use the skills you have learnt in the following core mandatory units:

G1 ensure your own actions reduce risks to health and safety maintaining health, safety and hygiene practice throughout
G6 promote additional products or services to clients
G11 contribute to the financial effectiveness of the business

Dalesauna Ltd. Photographer: Nicholas Gentill. Interior design: Corporate Edge.

INTRODUCTION

Spa treatments are used for their beneficial effects upon the whole body. The spa environment and spa treatments induce a physical and mental sense of well-being.

The term spa is derived from a village near Liege, in Belgium called *Spau*, which had mineral hot springs that people would visit to improve their health and ailments.

The choice of spa treatments offered in the workplace will depend on the space available and the nature of other treatment services offered.

Health farms commonly offer a comprehensive range of spa treatments; leisure centres and gyms popularly offer heat treatments such as sauna, steam and spa pools.

Spa treatments studied here include:

- **Sauna**, a dry heat treatment where air is heated.
- **Relaxation room**, sometimes referred to as a *tepidarium*, a room of ambient temperature (close to body temperature).
- **Steam**, a wet heat treatment where water is heated.
- **Cold therapy**, treatments that use temperatures lower than body temperature, i.e. cold water showers for stimulating the circulation.
- **Hydrotherapy**, where water is used for its therapeutic effect.
- **Flotation**, in which the body is suspended (wet flotation), or supported (dry flotation) inducing relaxation.
- **Body wrapping**, where the body is wrapped in bandages, plastic sheets or thermal blankets for different therapeutic effects. Ingredients such as marine minerals or clay are applied to the bandages or directly to the skin to achieve different results.

TIP

Before adding spa treatments to the services available, consider client usage and profitability. If you do not have a shower facility you will be limited in the range of spa services you can offer.

TIP

Spa treatments as a preparatory service
Spa treatments are beneficial when applied before other body treatments as they make the body tissues and systems more receptive.

Spa treatments as a rehabilitation service
Water is used for the treatment of medical conditions such as rheumatism and rehabilitation after injury.

GENERAL EFFECTS OF SPA THERAPY TREATMENTS

Spa treatments and therapeutic skin conditioning treatments

Treatments which raise the body temperature:

- Induce relaxation, increasing the blood circulation generally, which soothes sensory nerve endings and causes muscle relaxation. Heat therapy is a popular de-stressing treatment.
- Blood pressure falls as the superficial capillaries and vessels dilate.
- Heart rate and pulse rate increase.
- Blood circulation is improved. Vaso-dilation occurs which increases the blood flow through the area, supplying oxygen and nutrients to the cells.
- Lymphatic circulation is increased, assisting with the elimination of toxins and waste materials.
- Increased activity of the sebaceous and suderiferous glands improves skin condition. This also creates a deep skin-cleaning action.
- Metabolism may be increased or decreased depending on the treatment received.
- Flotation treatments cause a fall in heart and pulse rate due to its relaxation effect.
- Body wrapping treatments cause a rise in pulse rate due to an increase in body temperature.

Treatments which lower the skin temperature:

- Metabolism is increased if prolonged shivering to increase the body temperature, occurs.
- Stimulation of the sympathetic nervous system which accelerates the heartbeat, as in times of fear.

Iceroom

- vaso-constriction occurs which decreases blood flow through the area and causes the skin to become paler.
- contra-action of the arector pili muscles attached to the hair follicle, seen as goose bumps.

ANATOMY AND PHYSIOLOGY

Heat treatments: sauna, steam, relaxation room

When heat treatments are applied, there is an increase in body temperature generally, that is, the treatments affects the whole body by 1–2°C. Vasodilation of the blood capillaries occurs to lower the body temperature by increasing heat loss. This vasodilation effect causes erythema, where the skin becomes reddened. This effect soon subsides after application. The increase in body temperature causes a corresponding increase in the heart and pulse rates. There is a fall in blood pressure as the resistance of the capillary walls is reduced when the capillaries dilate.

The dilation of the blood capillaries enables the blood to transport increased nutrients to the skin, enhancing its function and appearance.

The maximum temperature that the body can tolerate varies according to the type of treatment – dry or wet.

Dry air holds less heat than water vapour, and body sweat is able to evaporate in dry heat, thus cooling the skin. This enables the body to tolerate a higher temperature.

Air which is saturated with water vapour is able to hold more heat, and body sweat is unable to evaporate so the body cannot cool itself. The body therefore cannot tolerate very high temperatures in wet heat.

Hydrotherapy treatment

Hydrotherapy uses water to induce physical and mental well-being. Hydrotherapy treatments include spa pools and hydro baths.

Vasoconstriction and vasodilation

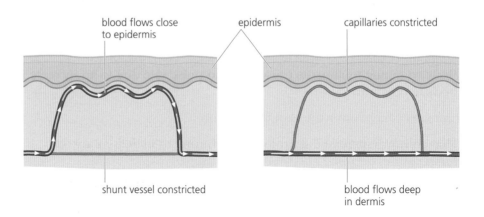

blood flows close to epidermis   epidermis   capillaries constricted

shunt vessel constricted   blood flows deep in dermis

Spa pool

Stimulation of the circulation is caused by the thermal stimulation of the water and mechanical stimulation, created by air being forced through the water after passing through small openings in the bath.

This thermal and mechanical stimulation increases blood and lymphatic circulation generally. The rise in body temperature causes the pulse to increase.

Muscular pain and fatigue is reduced as accumulated toxins and waste are dispersed in the improved circulation.

Hydro bath

The bath is fitted with water jets which massage the tissues of the body as the compressor aerates the water. A hose may also be used to manually direct air over the body.

Body temperature is increased, which causes muscles to relax due to the rise in body temperature and increased blood circulation.

Metabolism – a series of chemical reactions which utilises the nutrients required for growth and body repair – is also increased.

Flotation treatments

During flotation treatment total relaxation occurs, affecting the autonomic nervous system, which has two divisions: the *parasympathetic* and *sympathetic* division.

● The parasympathetic division is stimulated in periods of relaxation.

● The sympathetic division is stimulated in periods of stress.

During flotation treatment, the sympathetic system is deactivated and the parasympathetic division is stimulated. A calming effect on the body occurs as the pulse slows, metabolism reduces, and there is a relaxation of the muscles.

Body wrapping

Body wrapping results in an increase in body temperature, blood circulation generally, and pulse rate. The dilation of the blood capillaries enables the blood to transport increased nutrients to the skin, enhancing its function and appearance.

As the skin warms, therapeutic ingredients are absorbed by the skin and have a skin conditioning effect. They are absorbed through the pores, hair follicles and the epidermis (stratum corneum).

The increase in body temperature also increases perspiration and waste elimination. Ingredients used, such as clay, help to draw out toxins.

Hydro bath

Image courtesy of Cosmopro Inc.

Flotation treatment

Floataway (www.floataway.co.uk)

Body wrapping

Finders International Ltd (www.findershealth.com)

The lymphatic circulation increases, which aids the elimination of excess fluid and toxins in the improved circulation.

Where heating is an effect of the body wrap this helps to relax tense muscles.

SPA OPERATION

Sauna – dry heat treatment

Sauna treatment is a dry heat treatment where the air is heated. There are alternative methods including traditional the Finnish or Tyrolean sauna and the Laconium sauna.

Finnish or Tyrolean sauna

The sauna is usually a timber construction, usually made from pine, which is a porous wood. This allows the condensation created to be absorbed and the internal furnishing walls to breathe.

The sauna air is usually heated by an electric stove, which contains coals, to between 70–110°C. Steam is created by pouring water onto the hot coals. An air inlet is situated at floor level and an outlet is found near the top of the cabin.

This high temperature is tolerable because the heat is reduced on contact with the skin and the sweat induced rapidly reduces the skin temperature.

Laconium sauna

This sauna creates an evenly distributed mild dry heat. The temperature in the Laconium sauna is approximately 55°C and it usually uses underfloor heating as opposed to heat created from a stove.

Laconium is suitable for gently heating the skin for the purpose of cleansing and purifying. Some clients will prefer this sauna type as the heat is less intense.

Electricity is used to produce the heat. A sauna is operated by the mains supply because of the high power rating used.

Additional therapeutic effects of dry heat

- Elimination of metabolic waste is increased.
- Skin cleansing occurs as the pores dilate, secreting sweat onto the skin's surface, thereby eliminating waste products.
- Respiratory congestion can be relieved.
- Increased sweating can cause temporary weight loss. However, this loss is quickly replaced with fluids consumed following treatment.
- Muscles are relaxed due to the rise in body temperature and increased blood circulation.

Sauna (traditional wood)

Dalesauna Ltd

Laconium sauna

TIP ✓

Infrared sauna
An infrared sauna heats the body directly, rather than heating the air which in turn heats the body. Infrared radiators penetrate the body tissues; this stimulates the cardio-vascular system which improves cellular metabolism, muscular fatigue and tension. The positive effect of colour as a therapy – *phototherapy* – can be combined with this treatment.

NVQ2 SPA FACILITIES/PROVIDE SPECIALIST SPA TREATMENTS BT28/BT29

Relaxation room

The relaxation room enables the client to rest between experiencing different spa treatments. This allows the body temperature and blood pressure to lower.

The air is ambient, the same as the body's temperature and is dry air, to enhance the body's immune system and relieve stress.

It is important that this area is very quiet to induce relaxation. Heated couches warmed by a heat-conducting hot mortar may be found in this room. These are ideal for clients unsuitable to receive heat treatments, which significantly increase blood circulation, e.g. sauna treatment.

Additional therapeutic effects

- The heating effect sooths the sensory nerve endings.
- Helps relive muscular aches and pains.
- Increases blood flow and removes waste products and improves the delivery of nourishment to the body.
- The relaxing environment reduces stress and tension.

Electricity is used to produce the heat. The room is operated by the mains supply because of the high power rating used.

Image courtesy of Pevonia UK

Relaxation room

HEALTH AND SAFETY ✚

Humidity in the sauna
Water can be sprinkled onto the stones in the sauna to raise the moisture content of the air (humidity).

Steam

A wet heat treatment where water is heated. Steam treatment can be received individually in a steam bath, or communally in a steam room.

Steam bath

This is constructed from fibreglass. A hinged door allows access and encloses the client. An opening at the top of the bath exposes the client's head. The client sits on a seat inside the bath which is adjustable for the height of each client and for her comfort.

Water is heated in a small tank inside the bath, situated underneath the seat. On boiling, the water produces steam. The steam mixes with the air in the bath and produces water vapour which circulates inside the cabinet. The temperature inside the cabinet is most comfortable at between 45–50°C.

Dalesauna Ltd

Steam room

TIP ✔

Steam cubicles
These are filled with steam and offer an alternative to the steam bath. The air is gently heated to 45°C and usually diffused with herbal aromatic oils, used for their therapeutic effect.

   Treatment time is usually 15 minutes and clients can listen to their favourite music or even specialised motivational CDs to assist the client with lifestyle improvements such as giving up smoking and weight management.

Caldarium

Hamman

Dalesauna Ltd

Steam room

To provide steam for a room, the water is heated in a boiler. The steam created is passed through tubes which enter the steam room. The water vapour created circulates inside the room. Adequate ventilation is important to ensure the efficient production of steam.

The *caldarium* is a steam room that uses natural herbal essences to create an aromatic steam room.

The *hamman* is a steam bath with a hot, moist aromatic atmosphere to purify and detox. Traditionally a communal bath, the bath-house has a dome-shaped central chamber and further chambers of differing temperatures leading from it. The hottest room is heated from the floor.

TIP
Bath houses have been used for thousands of years. The ancient Romans used hot rooms.

Additional therapeutic effects of steam heat

- Muscles are relaxed due to the rise in body temperature and increased blood circulation.

To produce steam, water is heated to 100°C. This then mixes with air to produce water vapour. Electricity is used to produce the heat. The room is operated by the mains supply because of the high power rating used.

HEALTH AND SAFETY
Temperature in the steam room   As the air in the steam bath/room is saturated with water vapour (that is, it is unable to hold more water), the sweat created on the skin's surface is unable to evaporate to create the skin-cooling effect. For this reason, the temperature for steam treatment is lower than that for sauna to avoid the body overheating.

TIP 
Hydrotherapy bath water may have seaweed, sea salt or essential oils added to enhance its therapeutic effect.

Hydrotherapy

In hydrotherapy water is used for its therapeutic effect.

Spa pool

A spa pool of warm water in which the client sits. It is constructed from shaped, durable acrylic, or tiled concrete. Air is forced through small openings and jets of air pass through the water, creating bubbles. These bubbles massage the surface of the skin from all directions, which has a stimulating effect.

The spa pool may incorporate features such as jets placed to massage different body parts, for example the lower back, and water fountains which can massage the neck with the power of the water flow.

Hydro baths

An acrylic bath providing underwater massage through high-powered jets. A hose can also be used to manually direct water to stimulate circulation in specific areas.

Water may be applied at any temperature but is commonly heated to between 34–40°C (hot). Extreme temperature increases circulation and blood flow. The bath may be used to maintain well-being or as a rehabilitation treatment. Features include preset massage programmes to achieve different effects.

Additional effects of hydrotherapy treatment:

- Relaxation – the body weight is supported by the warm water and gently massaged.
- Skin cleansing – as the water massages the skin's surface, desquamation is increased.
- Muscle fatigue and joint pain can be relieved by the increased blood and lymph circulation and increased cellular metabolism.

> **TIP**
>
> Natural spas are swimming pools filled with mineral water. They are considered to have therapeutic effects.

> **TIP**
>
> Hydrotherapy pool
> **Weighing less**
> When in water the human body weighs 10 times less than normal.

Flotation, wet and dry

The body is suspended, floats, or is supported inducing physical and mental relaxation.

Flotation – wet

Bath or tank

Flotation baths or tanks are commonly capsule shaped, constructed from fibreglass, and the inside is lined with plastic resin.

Flotation pools are also available.

The treatment uses epsom salts diluted in water at high concentration, which enables the body to float and be suspended in the water.

In a pool approximately 280 kilogrammes of epsom salts are diluted in 500 litres of water which is maintained at body temperature. This is approximately 570g of epsom salts to 1 litre of water. Due to the high salt content, the skin does not lose body salts and does not wrinkle as would commonly occur when exposed to warm water for long periods of time.

The inside of the pool is lit and the lighting can be adjusted inside to suit the client. Gentle meditation music may be played during the treatment to enable the client to relax further. Again this can be adjusted to the client's preference.

As a safety feature there is a panic alarm system; an intercom system also enables the therapist to communicate with the client. This is an important feature to reassure a highly nervous/anxious client.

Flotation tank – wet

Floataway (www.floataway.co.uk)

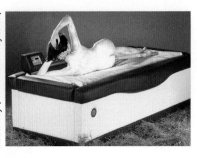

Flotation tank – dry

The door can be manually closed or motorised to close by a button once the client is inside the tank.

Flotation – dry

Here the client lies on a warmed tank of water, protected by a flexible polymer membrane covered with a paper roll. There is no direct client contact with the water.

The client lies on a bench which is lowered by the therapist, and is then suspended by the water.

The client may have specific therapeutic skin care products applied to the skin to nourish or purify and detoxify. The body is then wrapped to maintain heat and absorb the products. A head and scalp massage may be offered whilst the client relaxes.

Additional effects of flotation treatment:

- Stress is reduced as blood pressure is lowered.
- Skin conditioning occurs as circulation is increased, or in dry flotation the skin benefits from the therapeutic skin products applied.
- Beneficial to those with back injuries as the water supports the body, taking pressure off the back.
- Rheumatic conditions are relieved as there is improved blood circulation between the affected joints and relief of muscular tension.
- Slower brain wave patterns, known as theta waves, occur in wet flotation.

Body wrapping

This treatment does not apply electrical equipment. However, a small heater may be used to heat the towels before use.

Additional effects of body wrapping treatment:

- Cellular regeneration is increased.
- Waste products and toxins are eliminated.
- Temporary weight loss through increased sweating and therefore loss of body fluids.
- The therapeutic effect of each mineral balances the skin and body.

Reception

Heat treatments can be offered as individual treatments, but are also beneficial when given before other body treatments to increase their therapeutic effects. If you offer communal sauna, steam or other spa treatments, there will be a recommended number of clients who can use these facilities at once. Make sure you are aware of this to avoid overbooking. For the client's first heat treatment, treatment time is shorter to monitor response to treatment.

- **Sauna** – treatment may be received 2-3 times per week, treatment duration 15–20 minutes.
- **Relaxation room** – treatment may be received 2–3 times per week, treatment duration 30 minutes.
- **Steam room** – treatment may be received 2–3 times per week, treatment duration 10–15 minutes.
- **Steam bath** – treatment may be received 2–3 times per week, treatment duration 10–20 minutes.
- **Hydrotherapy spa pool** – treatment may be received daily, recommended treatment duration 10–15 minutes.
- **Hydrotherapy bath** – treatment may be received 2–3 times per week, treatment duration 15 minutes.
- **Flotation** – treatment may be received 1–2 times per week, wet flotation treatment duration 50–60 minutes; dry flotation treatment duration 40 minutes.
- **Body wrap** – treatment may be received 2–3 times per week, treatment time 45–60 minutes, dependant upon technique used.

Advise the client that a bathing costume may be worn if preferred for heat treatments. Inform the client beforehand that it is inadvisable for jewellery to be worn during heat treatments and may be required to be removed for body wrapping. She may prefer to not wear it for her appointment for reasons of security.

If the client is attending for a body wrap which contains iodine, check that the client does not have an allergy to it. If unsure the client may receive a patch test to assess skin reaction before treatment.

> **TIP**
>
> **Ice room**
> Chilled to a temperature of 10°C, some spas offer this room for clients to cool following heat treatments. Crushed ice may be available for application to the body.

HEALTH AND SAFETY

Patch test for allergies
If a client has allergies or hypersensitive skin, assess skin tolerance by applying a small amount of the treatment product to the skin behind the ear or at the inner elbow.
Skin allergy will be recognised by skin irritation – itching, redness and swelling.
Record this on the client's records and do not perform the treatment.

Heat and hydrotherapy treatments may be received 2–3 times per week. Body wraps should be recommended as a course if the client's aim is slimming, and these may be received twice a week; otherwise once a week would be appropriate. Advise the client that the slimming effect lasts 4–5 days. Complete personal details on the client's record card. Question the client to check for contra-indications.

TIP

Data Protection Act 1998
Remember client records should be stored securely and viewed only by those authorised to do so.

BEAUTY WORKS

Date	Beauty therapist name	
Client name		Date of birth
Address		Postcode
Evening phone number	Day phone number	
Name of doctor	Doctor's address and phone number	

Related medical history (conditions that may restrict or prohibit treatment application)

Are you taking any medication (this may affect the sensitivity of the skin and reaction to the treatment)

CONTRA-INDICATIONS REQUIRING MEDICAL REFERRAL
(Preventing spa treatment application)
(Temporary CI are listed*)

- ☐ bacterial infection, e.g. impetigo*
- ☐ viral infection, e.g. verruca*
- ☐ fungal infection, e.g. tinea corporis/pedis*
- ☐ skin disorders
- ☐ skin disease, e.g. malignant melanoma
- ☐ high or low blood pressure
- ☐ heart disease/disorder ☐ recent scar tissue
- ☐ medical conditions under supervision
- ☐ history of thrombosis/embolism
- ☐ dysfunction of the nervous system
- ☐ epilepsy ☐ respiratory conditions
- ☐ liver/kidney or pancreatic conditions
- ☐ lymphatic disorders ☐ recent wax depilation/epilation
- ☐ recent alcohol consumption*
- ☐ recent heavy meal – temporary*
- ☐ recent active exercise – temporary*
- ☐ recent UV exposure – temporary*

LIFESTYLE

- ☐ dietary and fluid intake ☐ exercise habits
- ☐ smoking habits ☐ sleep patterns
- ☐ hobbies, interests, means of relaxation

EQUIPMENT/MATERIALS

- ☐ sauna
- ☐ steam room ☐ steam cabinet
- ☐ flotation bath ☐ flotation pool dry/wet
- ☐ body wrapping ☐ hydrotherapy
- ☐ relaxation room ☐ wrapping materials
- ☐ treatment products

CONTRA-INDICATIONS WHICH RESTRICT TREATMENT
(Treatment may require adaptation)

- ☐ cuts and abrasions*
- ☐ bruising and swelling*
- ☐ recent scar tissue (avoid area)
- ☐ undiagnosed lumps, bumps, swellings
- ☐ recent injuries to the treatment area*
- ☐ mild psoriasis/eczema ☐ medication
- ☐ high/low blood pressure ☐ pregnancy*
- ☐ body piercings ☐ highly anxious client
- ☐ allergies ☐ claustrophobia
- ☐ menstruation* ☐ migraine*
- *temporary

TREATMENT OBJECTIVES

- ☐ improved skin and body condition
- ☐ slimming – improved contours
- ☐ lymphatic drainage ☐ relaxation

TREATMENT AREAS

- ☐ trunk – body wrap ☐ limbs – body wrap
- ☐ body – general

CLIENT PREPARATION

- ☐ exfoliation ☐ showering
- ☐ skin cleansing

PREPARATION FOR AND MONITORING OF TREATMENT ENVIRONMENT

- ☐ heat ☐ humidity
- ☐ water levels ☐ chemical concentrations
- ☐ treatment time ☐ ventilation
- ☐ consumables ☐ ambience of environment

Beauty therapist signature (for reference)

Client signature (confirmation of details)

TREATMENT ADVICE

This information includes
- advice on products that would be suitable for the client to use at home
- advice on how to gain maximum benefit from product use
- record samples provided, to evaluate effectiveness at next treatment with the client
- advice to enhance the effectiveness of the treatment including:
  - rest and relaxation advice
  - exercise advice
  - dietary advice
- advice to follow immediately after the treatment to include:
  - possible reactions to the treatment and recommended action to take
  - suitable rest period following treatment
  - general advice on food and fluid intake
  - avoidance of stimulants
- contra-action advice, action to be taken in the event of an unwanted reaction (e.g. skin reaction, nausea, dizziness)
- recommendations for further spa treatments and the benefits of continuous treatments
- the recommended time intervals between treatments.

Contra-indications

If whilst completing the record card or on visual inspection of the skin you find the client to have any of the following, heat treatment may not be carried out:

- severe skin conditions e.g. acute eczema
- systemic medical conditions
  - high/low blood pressure
  - thrombosis (a clot in the blood vessel or heart)/phlebitis (inflammation of the vein)
  - lymphatic disorders such as medical oedema
  - epilepsy (a disorder of the nervous system)

> ### HEALTH AND SAFETY
>
> **Flotation treatment and skin disorders**
> Some skin disorders can become aggravated by the salt used in wet flotation treatment. If unsure, refer your client to their GP for approval to treat.
> Alternatively, dry flotation treatment, if available, may be offered.

> ### HEALTH AND SAFETY
>
> **Increase in pulse**
> The heart works much faster during heat treatments. It needs to pump the blood to the surface of the skin to regulate body temperature and can increase from 72 beats per minutes to 150.
> Because there is an increase in pulse with body wrap it is necessary to gain the GP's permission to treat a client if they have high or low blood pressure.

- respiratory conditions e.g. asthma
- diabetes (decreased insulin secretion which causes excess glucose (sugar) to accumulate in the bloodstream. Increased urination occurs to excrete the excess glucose.)
- liver, kidney or pancreatic conditions
- viral, bacterial or fungal skin disorders such as verruca and athlete's foot (tinea pedis)
- disorders requiring medication, including vasoconstrictors and vasodilators
- allergy to iodine, found in seaweed-based skin preparations. This must be checked when performing body wraps

> ### HEALTH AND SAFETY
>
> **Preventing cross-infection**
> Disposable paper slippers may be worn to prevent cross-infection for spa therapy treatments such as body wrapping.
> Verrucae socks may be worn for hydrotherapy treatments.

EQUIPMENT LIST

sauna
client record card
appropriate ventilation
shower
body and hair shampoos
protective footwear
towels
wooden pail containing purified water to ladle over the coals
temperature gauge
electric stove
hygrometer

- varicose veins (heat treatment and body wrap to the lower limb)
- claustrophobia. Unsuitable treatments for clients with a fear of being in a confined area include flotation treatment and heat treatments such as the sauna and steam room.

Other contra-indications may be temporary and include:

- pregnancy
- menstruation, first days
- a recent heavy meal
- recent strenuous exercise (wait approximately 30 minutes)
- recent alcohol consumption
- recent drug use
- recent overexposure to UV light
- recent wax depilation, electrical epilation treatment (24–48 hours before a spa treatment) to avoid skin sensitivity and possible secondary infection
- migraine
- severe bruising
- high body temperature which infections such as influenza.

Spa equipment and materials

Sauna treatment

- Sauna (there must be adequate space for the air to circulate around the sauna).
- Client record card to assess client and record details of treatment.
- Appropriate ventilation.
- Shower to cleanse the skin and regulate body temperature; body and hair shampoos may be provided.
- Protective footwear to avoid cross-infection.
- Clean towels for each client: to drape the body after showering and to protect the hair.
- A wooden pail containing purified water to ladle over the coals. The water boils when poured onto the heated coals which increases the humidity (water vapour content of the air), cooling the air and making breathing more comfortable. This raising of humidity also makes the sauna feel hotter.

- Temperature gauge to record the heat of the sauna, 70°C for a mild sauna, 110°C for a hot sauna.
- An electric stove which heats the stones or coals, protected by a guard.
- Hygrometer, an instrument to measure relative humidity – generally the reading should be between 45–50 per cent.
- Water to rehydrate following treatment.
- Relaxation area to use following treatment.

Steam treatment

- Steam bath or steam room.
- Distilled water to fill the water tank.
- Essence to introduce into the steam room, e.g. pine.
- Appropriate ventilation.
- Client guidance instructions – clearly cited.
- Client record card to assess the client and record details of treatment.
- Shower to cleanse the skin and regulate body temperature.
- Body and hair shampoos may be provided.
- Protective footwear to avoid cross-infection i.e. disposable paper slippers.
- Clean towels for each client, to drape over the seat and over the floor to protect the back of the client's legs from scalding by the steam; to provide modesty, dry the body after showering and to protect the hair.
- Also a small towel may be draped around the opening of the cabinet during treatment to prevent moist heat escaping.
- Water to rehydrate following treatment.
- Relaxation area to use following treatment.

EQUIPMENT LIST

steam bath or steam room

distilled water

essence to introduce into the steam room (pine)

ventilation

record card

shower

hair and body shampoos

protective footwear

towels

Spa pool

- Spa pool with filtration system to maintain water quality; the floor area must be reinforced to withstand the weight of the water.
- Plant room within five metres of the pool with appropriate power supply and ventilation.
- A heavy duty control panel – all fittings should be strong, safe and reliable.
- Water testing equipment.
- Water temperature should be between 37–40°C.
- Client guidance instructions – clearly cited.
- Client record card to assess the client and record details of treatment.
- Shower to cleanse the skin and regulate body temperature.
- Body and hair shampoos may be provided.
- Protective footwear to avoid cross-infection i.e. disposable paper slippers.
- Clean towels for each client to dry the body after showering.
- Water to rehydrate following treatment.
- Relaxation area to use following treatment.

Hydro bath

- Water temperature should be between 37–40°C.
- Position duckboard (if used).
- Client record card to assess the client and record details of treatment.
- Shower to cleanse the skin and regulate body temperature.
- Body and hair shampoos may be provided.
- Protective footwear to avoid cross-infection i.e. disposable paper slippers.
- Clean towels for each client to dry the body after showering.
- Water to rehydrate following treatment.
- Relaxation area to use following treatment.

Flotation

Wet

- Flotation tank/pool.
- Epsom salts.
- Chemicals to maintain water cleanliness.
- Client record card to assess the client and record details of treatment.
- Client guidance instructions – clearly cited.
- Water temperature preheated to 33°C.

TIP

Body temperature
The temperature of the skin's surface is 33°C.
   Temperatures above 33°C heat the body – *a hyperthermal effect* – temperatures below 33°C reduce body temperature – *a hypothermal effect.*

- Shower to cleanse the skin the skin.
- Petroleum jelly to cover any small abrasions.
- Ear plugs to prevent water entering the ears.
- Neck support if required.
- Clean towels for each client to dry the body after showering.
- Treatment gown for client modesty.
- Protective footwear to avoid cross-infection i.e. disposable slippers.
- Relaxation area to use following treatment.
- Shower facility to use following treatment.
- Water to rehydrate following treatment.

Dry

- Flotation bed.
- Paper roll to cover the polymer membrane covering.
- Treatment product to apply to the skin during dry flotation if required.
- Clean towels for the client to dry the body after showering to cleanse the skin.
- Client record card to assess the client and record details of treatment.
- Client guidance instructions – clearly cited.
- Clean towels for each client to dry the body after showering.
- Treatment gown for client modesty.
- Protective footwear to avoid cross-infection i.e. disposable slippers.
- Shower facility to remove treatment product.
- Steamed towels should be used to cleanse the skin if there is no shower facility.
- Relaxation area to use following treatment.
- Water to rehydrate following treatment.

TIP	✓
Flotation treatment environment Depending on client choice the treatment may be received in silence or meditation/relaxation tapes may be played.	

Hydrotherapy materials

Different materials are used in conjunction with hydrotherapy. These include algae (seaweed), milk products, salt and aromatherapy oils for their therapeutic effect.

Algae

The therapeutic ingredients of algae contain minerals which stimulate the circulation, have a skin toning effect and help with detoxification.

EQUIPMENT LIST

flotation tank/pool

epsom salts

chemicals to maintain water cleanliness

record card

shower

petroleum jelly

ear plugs

neck support

towels

treatment gown

protective footwear

relaxation area

EQUIPMENT LIST

flotation bed

paper roll

treatment product to apply to the skin during dry flotation if required

towels

record cards

treatment gown

protective footwear

shower

relaxation area

Algae

Aromatherapy oils

HEALTH AND SAFETY ✚

Aromatherapy oils are not recommended for use during pregnancy.

Certain oils may cause allergies and make skin photosensitive (sensitive to sunlight).

Some oils are poisonous.

In spa treatments, only use aromatherapy oils as recommended by the supplier.

Milk

Whey powder, a derivative of milk, contains essential amino acids to nourish and soothe the skin. Useful for mature and sensitive skin types.

Salt

The therapeutic ingredients of mineral salts stimulate the circulation, have a skin-toning effect and help with detoxification.

Aromatherapy oils

Aromatherapy oils are extracted from roots, wood, flowers and fruits and are used for their aromatic properties. The sense of smell is controlled by the olfactory system and the sense of smell reacts in the brain in two seconds. The inhalation of aromatherapy oils therefore has an immediate effect on the senses, creating a psychological effect. The oils also have their own unique therapeutic effect on the systems of the body, creating a physiological effect.

Retail

Spa retail is important, as the client should want to continue the experience at home.

Many spa retail suppliers can provide expert specialist advice; they may support promotional activities and their products can be used within treatments offered. Treatment vouchers are an ideal opportunity to increase technical sales.

Again the retail supplier could advice you on appropriate treatment menus. If you have a web site, an explanation of the different services could be explained to encourage new clientele.

Image courtesy of Pevonia UK

Therapeutic body wrapping

Body wrapping

Various treatment techniques are used in body wrapping depending upon the effect to be achieved or treatment product used. Always refer to the manufacturer's instructions.

The skin may be prepared for treatment by applying an exfoliating treatment or body brushing which stimulates the circulation, both blood and lymphatic.

- The body may be wrapped in hot linen bandages which have been soaked in therapeutic ingredients.
- Alternatively treatment products using ingredients such as marine minerals or clay may be applied to the skin to achieve different skin conditioning results, including detoxification.
- The body can then be wrapped in a thermal blanket, foil, plastic or linen bandages to maintain and increase body heat which increases lymphatic circulation and fluid loss, achieving a slimming effect.

Therapeutic body wrap mediums include:

- algae
- mud
- clay
- peat
- milk products
- sand
- wine
- hay
- herbs.

The client often benefits from the aromatic effect of the ingredients as well as their physical effect.

Therapeutic spa skin conditioning treatment

> **TIP** ✔
>
> **Spa products**
> Seaweed is particularly high in minerals and is a key ingredient of many spa products. Sea water can be used on its own or mixed with seaweeds, muds and essential oils. Marine minerals include: sodium, copper, magnesium, zinc, potassium, iron, amino acids, protein.

- Treatment couch.
- Paper briefs for the client to wear.
- Treatment gown for client modesty.
- Headband to protect the hair.
- Clean bandages, plastic, metallic spa sheet (depending on the system used). There must be sufficient bandages available for demand.
- Bowls to mix products as applicable.
- Water used to mix with powder mask ingredients (as applicable).
- Treatment products, herbal, essential oils, sea clay, marine algae, seaweed.
- Spatulas/brushes to apply treatment products.
- Thermal blankets to maintain heat (if required).
- Tape measure to measure the client before and after treatment if performing a slimming body wrap.
- Client record card to assess the client and record details of treatment.
- Shower facility to cleanse the skin before treatment and remove products following treatment.
- Hot, steamed towels may be used to remove product if the workplace does not have a shower facility.

Relaxation room

- Neutral calm decor.
- Seating to allow the client to sit or lie down.
- Treatment gown for client modesty and to maintain warmth.
- Water facility to rehydrate.

EQUIPMENT LIST

| treatment couch |
| paper briefs |
| treatment gown |
| headband |
| clean bandages, plastic, metallic spa sheet |
| bowls |
| water to mix with powder mask ingredients |
| treatment products: herbal; essential oils; sea clay; marine algae; seaweed |
| spatulas |
| thermal blankets to maintain heat |
| tape measure |
| record card |
| shower |
| towels |

> **TIP** ✔
>
> **Headband**
> The headband may be removed following treatment product application, especially if a scalp massage is to be given whilst the treatment takes effect.

Sterilisation and sanitisation

Where the spa treatments are communal and involve heat and moisture they provide ideal breeding conditions for harmful micro-organisms. It is important that all furnishings are regularly cleaned and disinfected as recommended by the manufacturers. This will also avoid stale smells occurring.

Written instructions should be displayed in the treatment area and brought to the attention of the client of hygiene practice, e.g. showering thoroughly before using the spa pool etc.

Staff should make regular safety checks to ensure that the facilities are clean, safe and hygienic.

These checks may need to be made on a daily, weekly or monthly basis.

HEALTH AND SAFETY

- all chemical storage areas should be clearly identified and accessible to authorised persons
- keep all chemicals stored as directed
- handle the chemicals wearing protective clothing to avoid skin contact and potential injury. Protective eye goggles which conform to the relevant British Safety Standard may also be a requirement
- follow manufacturers' instructions when carrying out sanitisation procedures
- provide non-slip floor surfaces in the hydrotherapy areas
- a safety alarm is an important feature in the case of client/spa therapist emergency
- emergency first aid procedures must be operative and adequate
- first aid resources must be readily available in a designated place
- fire alarm systems may be available depending upon legal requirements and fire fighting equipment should be available. Regular training is important to ensure staff are familiar with evacuation procedures.

Safety checksheets

Sauna

- Clean the sauna furnishings and floor regularly with a disinfectant cleaner as recommended by the manufacturer.
- Check that the internal shelving is smooth to avoid splinters entering the skin and also harbouring germs.
- Empty the wooden bucket of water when not in use to avoid mould formation.
- When not in use, keep the sauna door open to allow fresh air to enter.

Steam

- Clean the steam cabinet/room internal walls and floor furnishings regularly with a disinfectant cleaner that removes surface grease as recommended by the manufacturer.
- This also prevents unpleasant smells created by stale body odours.

Shower

- Check after each client use, clean to remove residue body skin treatment products such as marine clay etc.

DAILY SAFETY CHECKS

CLUB: _____   DATE: Mon _____ to Sun _____ of _____ 20 _____

AREA	CONTROL MEASURES/ OBSERVATION POINTS	INITIALS AS CHECKED Please link to action required with an *							ACTION REQUIRED	URGENT YES/NO	DATE ACTIONED
		M	T	W	T	F	S	S			
Spa pool	No surround slip/trip hazards										
	No damaged surfaces										
	Access ladder/handrail secure										
	Air temperature and environment satisfactory										
	Water temperature set to appropriate level with temperature details on display										
	Emergency call button working/tested										
	Water test carried out every 2 hours										
Plant room	Doors kept locked										
	Hazardous substances stored in correct areas										
	Pool dosing controls working and set to correct levels										
	Pool pumps operating correctly										
	Chemical dosing tanks full										
	Chemical injectors not blocked										
	No leaks evident										
	Emergency call button working/tested										
	Evacuation routes/Fire exits clear and freely opening										

DATE	NUMBER OF WASTE BAGS TAKEN OUT DAILY	NAME OF STAFF MEMBER WHO TOOK OUT THE WASTE	DATE	NUMBER OF WASTE BAGS TAKEN OUT DAILY	NAME OF STAFF MEMBER WHO TOOK OUT THE WASTE
M			F		
T			S		
W			S		
T					

DAILY SAFETY CHECKS

CLUB: _____   DATE: Mon _____ to Sun _____ of _____ 20 _____

AREA	CONTROL MEASURES/ OBSERVATION POINTS	INITIALS AS CHECKED Please link to action required with an *							ACTION REQUIRED	URGENT YES/NO	DATE ACTIONED
		M	T	W	T	F	S	S			
Steam room	No slip/trip hazards										
	No damaged floors										
	Door in safe condition, including hinges										
	Light working and in safe condition										
	Wall thermostat in safe condition										
	Steam outlet cover secure, in place/properly guarded										
	Temperature set to appropriate level										
	Seating in safe condition										
	Guidance notes on display in the area										
	Emergency call button working/tested										
	Plant room door locked										
Office	No trip hazard from trailing cables										
	No damaged floor surfaces										
	Air temperature satisfactory										
	Equipment/files/stationery stored safely										
	Evacuation routes/Fire exits clear and freely opening										
	Waste bins emptied										

Daily safety checks charts

DAILY SAFETY CHECKS

CLUB: _____   DATE: Mon _____ to Sun _____ of _____ 20 _____

AREA	CONTROL MEASURES/ OBSERVATION POINTS	INITIALS AS CHECKED Please link to action required with an *							ACTION REQUIRED	URGENT YES/NO	DATE ACTIONED
		M	T	W	T	F	S	S			
Reception and foyer area	No slip/trip hazards										
	No damaged floor surfaces										
	Hazardous substances stored in secure locations										
	Furniture in safe condition										
	Electrical sockets covered										
	Glazing in safe condition										
	Air temperature satisfactory										
	Waste bins emptied										
	Emergency call button working/tested										
	Evacuation routes/Fire exits clear and opening freely										
Sauna	No slip/trip hazards										
	No damaged floor surfaces										
	Evacuation routes/Fire exits clear and freely opening										
	Walls and benches free from damage										
	Stove guarded and secure										
	Light working, in safe condition and properly guarded										
	Benches secure and stable										
	Door in safe condition, including hinges										
	Temperature set to appropriate level 80–100										
	Emergency call button working/tested										
	Guidance notes on display in area										

DAILY SAFETY CHECKS

CLUB: _____   DATE: Mon _____ to Sun _____ of _____ 20 _____

AREA	CONTROL MEASURES/ OBSERVATION POINTS	INITIALS AS CHECKED Please link to action required with an *							ACTION REQUIRED	URGENT YES/NO	DATE ACTIONED
		M	T	W	T	F	S	S			
Female changing rooms and toilets	Hairdryers in safe condition										
	Storerooms locked										
	No hazardous substances left out/unattended										
	No slip/trip hazards										
	No damaged floor surfaces										
	All mirrors in safe condition										
	No damaged lockers										
	No damaged benches										
	No damaged wash basins										
	No damaged toilets										
	No damaged showers/shower areas										
	Temperature of showers/hot water taps not scalding										
	Waste bins emptied										
	Evacuation routes/Fire exits clear and freely opening										
Male changing rooms and toilets	Hairdryers in safe condition										
	Storerooms locked										
	No hazardous substances left out/unattended										
	No slip/trip hazards										
	No damaged floor surfaces										
	All mirrors in safe condition										
	No damaged lockers										
	No damaged benches										
	No damaged wash basins										
	No damaged toilets										
	No damaged showers/shower areas										
	Temperature of showers/hot water taps not scalding										
	Waste bins emptied										
	Evacuation routes/Fire exits clear and freely opening										

Daily safety checks charts

NVQ2 SPA FACILITIES/PROVIDE SPECIALIST SPA TREATMENTS BT28/BT29
Spirit Health Club, Holiday Inn Hotel, Newton-le-Willows

DAILY SAFETY CHECKS

CLUB: _____   DATE: Mon ____ to Sun ____ of ____ 20 ____

AREA	CONTROL MEASURES/ OBSERVATION POINTS	INITIALS AS CHECKED Please link to action required with an *							ACTION REQUIRED	URGENT YES/NO	DATE ACTIONED
		M	T	W	T	F	S	S			
Children's playroom/ crèche	No slip/trip hazards										
	No damaged floor surfaces										
	No hazardous substances in the area										
	Furniture in safe condition and appropriate to children										
	Electrical items in safe condition/out of childs reach										
	Electrical sockets covered										
	Mirrors in safe condition										
	Air temperature satisfactory										
	Toilets clean, safe and undamaged										
	Wash basins clean, safe and undamaged										
	Temperature of hot water not scalding										
	Toys clean and in safe condition										
	Waste bins emptied										
	Emergency call button working/tested										
	Evacuation routes/Fire exits clear and freely opening										
Outside areas	Emergency access routes/Fire exits clear										
	Waste stored in containers										
	Chemical storage secure										
Other											

WEEKLY SAFETY CHECKS

CLUB: _____   DATE: _____

AREA	CONTROL MEASURES/ OBSERVATION POINTS	DATE CHECKED	INITIALS AS CHECKED	ACTION REQUIRED	URGENT YES/NO	DATE ACTIONED
Office	Wall surfaces in safe condition					
	Ceilings free from leaks or damage					
	Light fittings secure and working					
	Electrical sockets and wiring safe and undamaged					
	Electrical equipment safe and undamaged					
	All equipment used as intended and correctly stored					
Plant room	Wall surfaces in safe condition					
	Ceilings free from leaks or damage					
	Light fittings secure and working					
	Electrical sockets secure, not exposed to water					
	All glazing undamaged					
	All cables and wires not exposed					
	All electrical distribution boards locked					
	Area clean, tidy and secure					
	Day tanks sufficiently apart or partition separation is in place					
Reception and foyer area	Wall surfaces in safe condition					
	Ceilings free from leaks or damage					
	Light fittings secure and working					
	Electrical sockets secure					
	Reception/foyer furniture in safe condition					
	Sufficient supply of sunbed goggles or winkies					

Daily safety checks charts

WEEKLY SAFETY CHECKS

CLUB: _____   DATE: _____

AREA	CONTROL MEASURES/ OBSERVATION POINTS	DATE CHECKED	INITIALS AS CHECKED	ACTION REQUIRED	URGENT YES/NO	DATE ACTIONED
Outside areas	Walkways around Club are safe and free from potholes					
	Lighting sufficient, secure and working					
	Area around Club free from debris					
	External cables, wires or power sources safe, not dangerous					
Spa pool	Light fittings secure and working					
	All jets working properly					
Children's playroom/ crèche	Procedure in place to protect the children					
	All paper work in place for each child					
General	First Aid boxes checked and recorded					
	Check waste collection has been carried out					
	Fire alarm test carried out and recorded					
Circulation areas	Wall surfaces in safe condition					
	Ceilings free from leaks or damage					
	Light fittings secure and working					
	Glazing/mirrors secure and safe					
	Electrical sockets safe and covered					
	Notice boards secure and safe					
	Furniture safe and free from damage					

WEEKLY SAFETY CHECKS

CLUB: _____   DATE: _____

AREA	CONTROL MEASURES/ OBSERVATION POINTS	DATE CHECKED	INITIALS AS CHECKED	ACTION REQUIRED	URGENT YES/NO	DATE ACTIONED
Female changing rooms and toilets	Wall surfaces in safe condition					
	Ceilings free from leaks or damage					
	Light fittings secure and working					
	Lockers in working condition					
	Cubicles, benches and vanity units undamaged					
Male changing rooms and toilets	Wall surfaces in safe condition					
	Ceilings free from leaks or damage					
	Light fittings secure and working					
	Lockers in working condition					
	Cubicles, benches and vanity units undamaged					
Relaxation/ lounge areas	Wall surfaces in safe condition					
	Ceilings free from leaks or damage					
	Furniture in safe condition					
	Electrical sockets covered					
	Light fittings secure and working					
Sauna	Walls and benches free from damage					
	Light fitting secure and undamaged					
	Door in safe condition					
Steam room	Walls and benches undamaged, all areas sealed					
	Ceilings free from damage					
	Light fitting secure and undamaged					
	Essence tank full					

Daily safety checks charts

NVQ2 SPA FACILITIES/PROVIDE SPECIALIST SPA TREATMENTS BT28/BT29
Spirit Health Club, Holiday Inn Hotel, Newton-le-Willows

WEEKLY SAFETY CHECKS

CLUB: _____   DATE: _____

AREA	CONTROL MEASURES/ OBSERVATION POINTS	DATE CHECKED	INITIALS AS CHECKED	ACTION REQUIRED	URGENT YES/NO	DATE ACTIONED
Treatment/ beauty rooms	Wall surfaces in safe condition					
	Ceilings free from leaks or damage					
	Light fittings secure and working					
	Sharps disposal containers provided for the disposal of sharps (if applicable)					
Storage rooms	Wall surfaces in safe condition					
	Ceilings free from leaks or damage					
	No damaged floor surfaces					
	Light fittings secure and working					
	Electrical sockets safe and covered					
	Items in area stored in a safe location					
	Chemicals stored safely					
Others						

MONTHLY SAFETY CHECKS

CLUB: _____   DATE: _____

AREA	CONTROL MEASURES/ OBSERVATION POINTS	DATE CHECKED	INITIALS AS CHECKED	ACTION REQUIRED	URGENT YES/NO	DATE ACTIONED
General	Emergency lighting tested and recorded					
	Fire extinguishers checked and recorded					
	Personal Protective Equipment checked and recorded					
	Monthly eye wash station checked and recorded					
	Monthly ladder/stepladder checked and recorded					
	Monthly water analysis samples taken for pool/spa					
Female changing rooms and toilets	Monthly showerhead descale					
	Sanitary bins changed by contractor					
Male changing rooms and toilets	Monthly showerhead descale					
Plant room	Plant room safety signage in place					
	PPE available in area for use					
Sauna	Sauna guidance notices in place					
	Check temperature settings					
Steam room	Steam room guidance notices in place					
	Check temperature settings					
Outside areas	Check for damage/deterioration to perimeter walls/ fences					
Spa pool	Guidance notes on display					
	Handrails free from excessive movement					
	Check temperature settings					

Daily safety checks charts

- Tiled walls and floors should be cleaned regularly to using a disinfectant cleaner. Excess water should be removed to prevent slipping.
- Ensure there are adequate consumables, body shampoo etc.
- For therapeutic showers such as the affusion shower, the surface of the treatment couch should be cleaned as recommended by the manufacturer.

Hydrotherapy

Spa pool

- The spa is not drained and filled after every use, but relies on the water being continually filtered and chemically treated.
- The edge of the spa pool should be cleaned daily to remove body oils and dead skin cells, which would otherwise form a scum.

Water testing

It is essential in the spa to ensure that this damp and warm environment is as free from contamination as possible. Diseases such as legionella could prove fatal.

This is controlled by following stringent cleaning and water tests to check for water balance. Back washing is also important to filter out harmful organisms not killed by disinfectant. An integral strainer removes hair and other debris from the water and this should be routinely cleaned to maintain its efficiency.

Water is kept free from potential hazard by the use of chemical disinfectants such as sodium and calcium hypochlorite. The normal operating range of the chemical will depend upon the disinfectants used. The water is tested according to the chemical disinfectant selected to ensure it is safe, effective and balanced. This will also assess the water to prevent water corrosion, staining and scaling.

Water is regularly tested for the following:

- pH (acidity/alkalinity)
- hardness (calcium content)
- temperature
- regular testing of water and maintenance of records is an essential part of a spa operation.

These measurements are known as the **Langelier index** or **Palintest balanced water index**. Water samples are compared against acceptable operating levels. The quantity of disinfectant agents required will depend upon the hydrotherapy pool usage and the results of the water testing.

The amount of available free chlorine (that available to neutralise contaminants in the water) and the pH value need to be controlled and the amount and the effectiveness of the sterilising agent determined. Further chemicals may also need to be added to raise or lower alkalinity or calcium levels. Chemicals used to control the pH of water include sodium bicarbonate and carbon dioxide (CO_2).

A record of tests carried out by an authorised person should be kept for inspection by the Local Health Authority. Failure to carry out this legally required duty by a responsible staff member can result in disciplinary action being taken.

The Environmental Health Officer (EHO) will make regular checks to ensure that effective maintenance/hygiene is being enforced and will check standards.

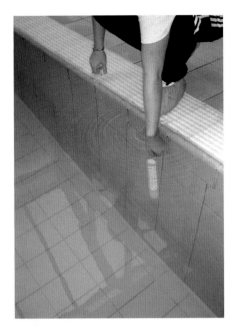

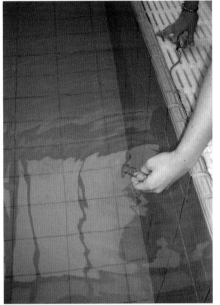

Using a thermometer to check the temperature of the water

A spa pool water sample is taken. A phenol red tablet is added to the water which develops in colour according to the chemical content. The resulting colour is compared against the colour metric system to identify the reading for pH. This indicates pH chemical level, which should read between 7.2–7.8.

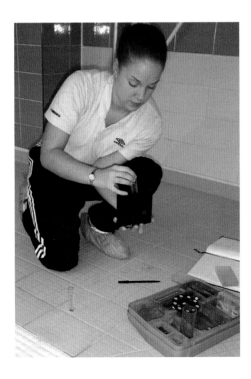

Calculate free chlorine level by adding DPD1 tablet to a pool sample.

Rotate disc until a colour match is found, then record the reading.

A total chlorine reading is taken by the addition of a DPD3 tablet to the coloured DPD1 sample. The tablet should be crushed and stirred into the water sample thoroughly.

Wait 2 minutes for the colour to develop.

Rotate disc until a colour match is found then record the reading.

When performing water testing ensure your hands are clean and always avoid touching the tablets.

Outdoor shoes must not be worn beside the pool, protective coverings must be worn.

To calculate the combined chlorine levels subtract the reading using the DPD1 tablet from the reading obtained from the DPD3 tablet.

Ideally, the free chlorine reading should be twice as much as combined chlorine.

HEALTH AND SAFETY ✚

pH levels in the water affect the power of disinfection. The pH should be at a level which renders the water safe. Risks to bathers from chemicals used in disinfection include sore eyes and skin irritation. All bathers must be instructed to have a thorough pre-pool shower to cleanse the skin and avoid water contamination, which will affect the pH level.

HEALTH AND SAFETY ✚

Heat treatments for use by the public are subject to inspection by the Environmental Health Authority. In spa treatment, the water is checked for safe bacterial levels and the presence of *E.coli* and coliform organisms.

HEALTH AND SAFETY ✚

When chlorine oxidises contaminants (chloramines) form. High levels of chloramines will produce an unpleasant smell and caused irritated eyes, making those using the bath think chlorine levels are high. In fact, there is sufficient free chlorine available.

Hydro baths

These should be drained and cleaned after each client use. Specialised cleaning agents should be used as directed by the manufacturer. The surrounding floor should be dry and dirty towels in the area should be removed.

All waste should be disposed into a covered lined waste bin.

Flotation

Wet

- The water should be checked to confirm that it looks clear. Hair etc. should be removed.

- The surface of the flotation tank should be cleaned regularly to remove body oils and dead skin cells which would otherwise form a scum. Use sodium hypochlorite solution mixed as per manufacturer's instructions.
- Chemicals are added to maintain water cleanliness.
- The pH of the water is tested daily, pH 7.2–7.4 is the normal reading.
- The water is filtered between each session.
- The level of bromine should remain at 2 ppm (parts per million).
- The water depth should be 25cm.
- Epsom salts need to be added regularly to maintain water density. Add these as guided by the manufacturer.
- All waste should be disposed into a covered lined waste bin.

Dry

- Wipe the vinyl surface of the flotation bed with a proprietary disinfectant cleaner following the manufacturer's instructions.
- All waste should be disposed into a covered lined waste bin.

Body wrapping

- Wipe the surface of the treatment couch with a proprietary disinfectant cleaner following the manufacturer's instructions.
- Boil wash the bandages using a detergent or as directed by the manufacturer's instructions.
- Thoroughly clean bowls used to mix treatment products.
- Brushes used to apply products should be washed in warm soapy water, rinsed, dried and sanitised i.e. placed in the ultraviolet cabinet.
- All waste should be disposed into a covered lined waste bin.

Relaxation room

- Seating should be cleaned regularly.
- Used towels should be collected.
- Ensure there are no spillages from drinks etc.
- Replenish drinking cups and maintain water facility to rehydrate.
- Empty waste bins.

Preparation of the treatment area

In many cases the spa treatments may be used on a continuous basis such as sauna, steam and hydrotherapy and relaxation room.

Ensure the area is hygienically maintained, any waste such as disposable paper drinking cups removed, floor areas cleaned regularly and any water spillage dealt with to prevent slippage and accidents.

There are checks to be made on a daily, weekly and monthly basis. These ensure that the condition of the spa meets legal and organisation requirements.

Everyday consumables should be checked and replenished daily. Shortages should be reported to the supervisor.

HEALTH AND SAFETY

All equipment should be serviced as recommended by the manufacturers.

A trained member of staff should regularly check all electrical equipment for safety usually on a weekly basis, although daily safety checks occur.

This will follow compliance with the **Electricity at Work Regulation 1989**.

PROVIDING SPA TREATMENT

Sauna

- Switch the sauna on at the mains.
- Heat the sauna adequately before use to allow the heat to evenly penetrate the timber surfaces. This will be between 1 hour and 30 minutes depending on the size of the sauna.
- Select the preferred temperature: 70–110°C for a Finnish sauna, 55°C for a Laconium sauna.
- Ensure air vents are open and clear from obstruction.
- Ensure that there is no metal exposed which would burn the client's skin on contact.
- Fill the wooden water bucket with water if used. Water heated on the sauna coals raises the humidity of the sauna atmosphere.
- Clean towels may be provided to the client to place over the seating.

Steam bath

- Drape clean towels over the seat of the bath and the floor.
- Fill the tank with water to cover the heating element. There should be at least 5cms of water above the heating element.
- Cover the opening of the bath with a clean towel to prevent heat loss.
- Switch the machine on at the mains.
- Set the temperature of the bath with the temperature dial and set the control for 15 minutes to preheat the cabinet.

Steam room

- The preheating time will depend on the size of the steam room.
- The recommended temperature is 40°C.
- Provide water in the room for the clients to pour over their skin in the hamman steam room.

Hydrotherapy

- The water in the spa pool should be regularly tested to ensure that it has a balanced pH of 7.2–7.8.
- The operating temperature is usually 36–40°C.
- Check the water levels at the beginning of each day and regularly throughout the day.

Hydrobath

- Fill the bath with warm water.
- Add water-soluble ingredients to the bath including salts, essentials oils and powdered or liquid algae for their therapeutic properties.
- The operating temperature is usually 36–40°C.
- Switch the compressor on to aerate the bath through the duck board.
- The therapist may use the hose feature to perform underwater massage, directing water over the muscle groups. This helps tone weak muscles; it also helps improve the appearance of soft fat.

Flotation

Wet

- The water should be filtered between each use and the level checked daily.
- The temperature should be checked and maintained at surface body temperature, 34.5–35.5°C.
- The condition of the water must be regularly monitored and should be clear at all times.
- The water should be regularly tested to ensure it has a balanced pH of 7.2–7.4.
- Ensure the lighting in the room is working.
- Gentle meditation music may be played.
- Check the panic alarm is working.
- Test the alkalinity and free chlorine as per manufacturer's guidelines for usage.

TIP

The steam bath is less claustrophobic for clients than a steam room, as the head remains exposed. It also offers a more private treatment and the temperature may be adjusted to suit the client.

HEALTH AND SAFETY

Underwater massage
The hose attachment when used should be kept under water at all times to prevent injury and unnecessary water spillage.

TIP

Fibre optic lighting
Colour influences the senses through the autonomic nervous system. This can affect the client's mental and physical state. Importantly it reinforces the effects of the spa treatment, inducing relaxation and a feeling of well-being.

TIP

Music
Music selection is important for inducing the relaxation atmosphere of the spa. Meditational or peaceful background music is an appropriate choice.

Dry

- Heat the water to the correct temperature as advised by the manufacturer.
- Atmospheric mood music may be played to relax the client.
- Raise the board to the top of the tank. Protect the polymer membrane covering with paper roll.
- Ensure the floor is protected adequately to avoid marking from the skin treatment product mask if used.

Body wrapping

- Ensure the room is warm, clean and aromatic to enhance the sensory senses.
- Atmospheric mood music may be played to relax the client.
- Prepare the bandages if used, as appropriate. This may include soaking the bandages in the treatment product.
- Ensure there are sufficient bandages to cover the body treatment area adequately.

Relaxation room

- Ensure the room is of an ambient temperature (close to body temperature) 30–40°C.
- Ensure that any waste is removed on a regular basis.

Preparation of the therapist

Ensure that all equipment and materials are regularly maintained. Prepare equipment and materials for specific treatments as required, i.e. foam baths, body wrapping. Ensure the operating temperatures of heat and flotation treatments are correct.

Hair, if long, should be secured for reasons of hygiene. For body wrapping a protective apron may be worn to prevent the treatment mask marking the protective work wear.

Protective clothing may need to be worn when performing tasks such as water testing.

Preparation of the client

Complete a consultation, explaining the treatment thoroughly. This will enable the client to gain maximum relaxation from the treatment.

- Complete the client record card and check for contra-indications.
- Explain the treatment procedure to the client, and the effects and use of equipment as applicable.
- Explain expected skin sensations, treatment effects and contra-actions that she must inform you of as necessary.

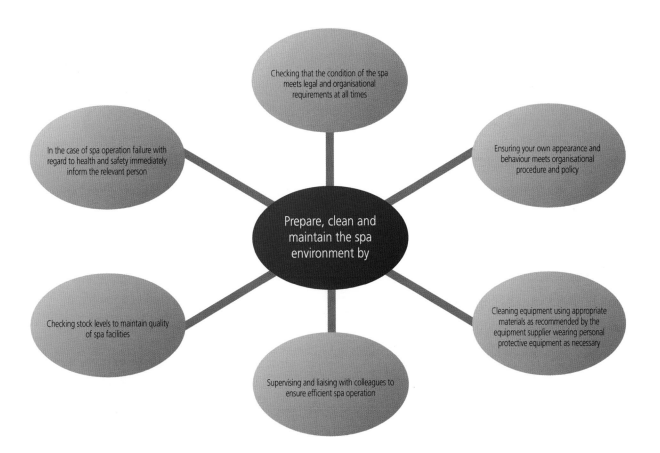

- Long hair should be secured and protected. If chemically treated it is advisable to protect the hair with a towel when receiving heat treatments or with a bathing cap for hydrotherapy.
- The client should remove all outside clothing in a private changing area.
- A secure area should be provided for the client to store clothing and personal possessions.
- Contact lenses, glasses and jewellery should be removed.
- Provide the client with clean towels and disposable slippers.
- Paper briefs may be provided to the client receiving body wrapping, dry flotation or body mask treatment.
- It is important to encourage the client to ask questions: allow time for this.
- Encourage the client to visit the toilet before treatment as spa treatments may cause a diuretic effect.
- Instruct the client to shower before treatment, to remove any cosmetics from the skin's surface. If there is not a shower available the skin can be cleansed before treatments such as body wraps with warm steamed towels and an exfoliating product.
- Ensure that the shower is at a comfortable temperature and instruct on shower operation. A non-slip mat must be placed in the shower to prevent the client slipping.
- Pre-treatment the client may receive an exfoliating treatment such as a salt, herb or enzyme scrub. This removes dead skin cells, increases blood and lymph circulation and increases cellular metabolism.

HEALTH AND SAFETY

Jewellery will become hot during a heat treatment such as sauna, as will any exposed metal. It is important that the client's skin is not in contact with any metal as this could cause burns.

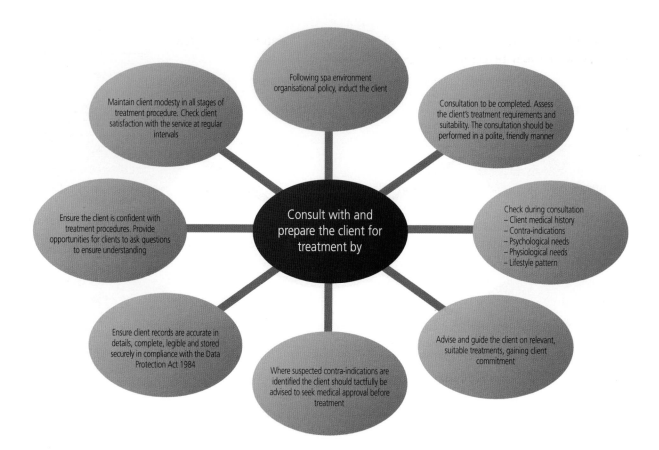

Maintain client modesty in all stages of treatment procedure. Check client satisfaction with the service at regular intervals

Following spa environment organisational policy, induct the client

Consultation to be completed. Assess the client's treatment requirements and suitability. The consultation should be performed in a polite, friendly manner

Ensure the client is confident with treatment procedures. Provide opportunities for clients to ask questions to ensure understanding

Consult with and prepare the client for treatment by

Check during consultation
– Client medical history
– Contra-indications
– Psychological needs
– Physiological needs
– Lifestyle pattern

Ensure client records are accurate in details, complete, legible and stored securely in compliance with the Data Protection Act 1984

Where suspected contra-indications are identified the client should tactfully be advised to seek medical approval before treatment

Advise and guide the client on relevant, suitable treatments, gaining client commitment

TIP	✔

Exfoliating treatments
To offer an exfoliating treatment to a client contra-indicated to a heat treatment, a spa ingredient such as mineral salt may be provided. Salt is dampened and massaged over the skin surface, exposing fresh new cells ideal before a massage treatment.

Showers

Shower facilities are essential in the spa to cleanse before, during and after spa therapy treatments.

Standard shower   Used to:

- Cleanse the skin of its natural oils and debris, body lotions etc.
- Warm the skin and muscles before any spa treatments such as hydrotherapy or sauna.
- To rinse the skin and regulate the body during spa heat treatment.
- To remove exfoliating products and body masks from the skin such as those with a mud, marine algae or seaweed base.

Affusion shower   This shower offers a hydrotherapy treatment. Water is applied from micro jets attached to a horizontal rail whilst the client lies on a treatment couch. Water pressure and temperature are adapted to suit the client.

The temperature is normally 37–40°C, controlled by a thermostatic tap and the pressure set at three bars, a feeling of gentle rain. Pressure is increased by turning the tap for this purpose.

Treatment time is normally a total of eight minutes, the anterior and posterior aspect of the body are normally treated.

Link selling is important and it would be beneficial to the client to receive another service such as a body wrap treatment following the afferent shower. The shower may then be used again to remove the body product.

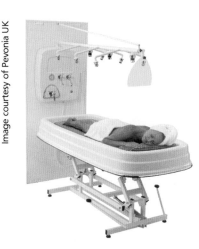

Image courtesy of Pevonia UK

Affusion shower

Power jet   A power jet massage provides a highly stimulating pressurised massage which may be directed at specific muscle groups.

Treatment application

Sauna

1 Before the client enters the sauna:
- check the temperature of the sauna by reading the thermometer
- check the relative humidity by reading the hygrometer.

2 The client then enters the sauna. New clients should be advised to sit on the lower benches where the air temperature is cooler. Existing clients may move to higher positions.

3 Check client comfort and close the sauna door.

4 After a 10–12 minute period the client should take a shower to cool the skin.

5 The client may return to the sauna for a further 10 minutes. During this time water may be poured onto the coals. The client then takes a final shower.

6 Treatment time is approximately 30 minutes.

7 Record details of the treatment on the client record card and provide aftercare advice.

8 The client should rest after the final shower to allow the blood pressure to return to normal.

Steam bath/room

1 Treatment time is normally 15–20 minutes.

2 Check the temperature in the steam/cabinet room.

3 In the steam bath, adjust the seating height for the height of the client. Close the hinged door. In the steam room the client sits in the steam atmosphere, in the hamman steam room the client must acclimatise to the heat in different chambers before entering the hottest room.

4 Drape a towel around the neck of the steam bath to avoid loss of steam.

5 The client should be supervised at all times in the steam bath.

6 A shower should be taken at the end of the treatment to cleanse and cool the skin.

7 Record details of the treatment on the client record card and provide aftercare advice.

Hydrotherapy

Spa pool

1 A bathing time of 15–20 minutes is recommended.

2 The client should be supervised.

3 A shower should be taken at the end of the treatment.

4 Provide the client with water for hydration and provide aftercare advice.

5 Allow the client to rest following treatment.

6 Record details of the treatment on the client record card.

TIP

Sea water therapy
Thalassotherapy is the therapeutic benefit of bathing in fresh sea water. The word is derived from the Greek *thalassa* meaning sea and *therpea* to treat. By the addition of marine salts and algae to a hydrotherapy bath a thalassotherapy effect can be achieved.

HEALTH AND SAFETY

Client safety
If at any time during a heat treatment the client feels light-headed, faint or nauseous, the therapist must be informed. Advise the client of this at consultation and monitor her reaction during the treatment. The client should never be left unattended, to avoid overexposure to the effects of heating which could lead to fainting etc.

Hydrobaths

1 The client may be advised to hold onto the handles for balance and support during the underwater massage.

2 The therapist may use the hose feature to direct water over the muscle groups. This helps improve muscle tone. It also helps improve the appearance of soft fat.

3 At conclusion of treatment – 15–20 minutes – switch the compressor off.

4 Assist the client from the bath if required.

5 Provide the client with water for rehydration.

6 Allow the client to rest following treatment.

7 Record details of the treatment on the client record card and provide aftercare advice.

Flotation

Wet

1 The client should take a cleansing shower, and make-up if used should have been removed. This would contaminate the water.

2 Advise the client on how long they will be in the flotation room.

3 Explain how to operate the door, demonstrate this and then observe them to confirm understanding.

4 Explain how to alter the lighting level, adjust the audio level and operate the panic alarm.

5 Show the client how to position themselves in the water. These procedures will facilitate relaxation.

6 The client may then apply the earplugs to prevent water entering the ears.

7 A neck cushion may be provided to support the client's neck.

8 Check on the client during treatment as necessary. If the client is enclosed in a room or capsule this may be through the intercom system. This is an important measure to reassure a highly nervous/anxious client.

9 Following treatment the client showers to remove excess salt and toxins from the skin's surface.

10 Provide the client with water for rehydration.

11 The client should take time to relax following treatment. A suitable area should be provided for this purpose.

12 Record details of the treatment on the client record card and provide aftercare advice.

Dry

1 The client should take a cleansing shower and make-up, if used, should have been removed.

2 A body spa treatment product may be applied before the treatment is received.

3 Advise the client on how long the flotation treatment will take.

4 The client lies on top of the board which is then lowered, controlled by the therapist.

5 A head and scalp massage may be offered whilst the client relaxes.

6 At the end of the treatment the board is raised.

7 The client may shower, specifically if a treatment product has been applied.

8 Provide the client with water for rehydration.

9 The client should take time to relax following treatment. A suitable area should be provided for this purpose.

10 Record details of the treatment on the client record card and provide aftercare advice.

HEALTH AND SAFETY

Client care
During treatment it is important to check the client at regular intervals. This reassures the client, and ensures that the client is not suffering from a contra-action. If the client has a disability it may be necessary to offer assistance following treatment.

Body wrapping

Ensure the room is warm, clean and aromatic to enhance the senses. Atmospheric mood music may be played to relax the client. Treatment will vary depending on the body wrapping system used. The client may receive a pre-treatment before the body wrap such as a heat treatment, shower and exfoliation or dry body brush.

Body wrapping using bandages to induce a slimming, detoxification effect

1 Measure the client in specific areas and record these measurements on the client record card.

2 Apply the treatment product to the skin and then unfold and wrap the bandages around the body part, **or** unfold and wrap the bandages around the body part that have already been soaked in active treatment ingredients. Always check that the temperature is tolerable when applying a heated bandage.

3 The client lies on the treatment couch, covered by a thermal blanket to maintain heat.

4 After the recommended treatment time, which varies with the treatment system (usually 60 minutes), remove the bandages and excess treatment product.

5 Re-measure the client and advice her of inch loss. Record the results on her record card. When the client redresses they will usually find their clothes much looser.

6 Provide the client with water for rehydration.

7 Provide aftercare advice and rebook the client if part of a slimming course.

Body wrapping to induce a skin conditioning/detoxification effect

1 Apply a specialist treatment product to body parts to intensify the effect.

2 Mix and apply the treatment product to the skin using a brush.

3 The body may then be wrapped in plastic film and foil or blanket to induce a heating effect depending on the system used.

4 After the recommended time, which varies with the treatment system (usually 20 minutes), remove any coverings and treatment product.

5 Further treatment may follow, such as massage to the area.

6 Provide the client with water for rehydration.

7 Provide aftercare advice.

TIP

Foot massage
With some body wrap systems a foot massage is given to the client whilst the body wrapping treatment takes effect.

HEALTH AND SAFETY

Ensure that the bandage application is not too tight or circulation will be poor in the area, resulting in loss of skin sensation and discomfort.

TIP

Body wraps may be applied to body parts only, such as the foot and lower limb.

HEALTH AND SAFETY

Spa cosmetic products
Always check to ensure that you are storing spa products correctly and that the use by date is clearly identified.

TIP

Body brushing
Body brushing may be provided before a body treatment mask. This will remove dead skin cells, stimulate lymphatic circulation and aid the absorption of the product. It is also an excellent treatment for the client to perform at home. The brush strokes are performed on each body part upwards towards the heart, starting with the soles of the feet. This should take five minutes until a mild erythema is achieved.

Relaxation room

1 Guide the client on facilities and use of the room.
2 Explain the importance of drinking water to rehydrate.
3 Check on the client's well-being at regular intervals.

Always ensure client satisfaction on treatment conclusion. All spa staff who come into contact with the client should be involved in this area of customer care to ensure the spa experience is a pleasurable one.

CONCLUSION

When you have been using the spa for treatments it is important that it is prepared for subsequent treatments.

Hygiene and cleaning of the spa areas should occur following legal and organisational procedures.

Treatment areas should be shut down in accordance with manufacturer's instructions and legal and organisational procedures.

Following treatments such as a hydrotherapy bath or foam bath, equipment, water supplies and electricity at the mains should be switched off.

Following flotation treatment and heat therapy treatments switch off the equipments at the mains.

The spa boosters that create the aeration of the spa pool are switched off at the end of the working day (the switch is located in the plant room). The pump which circulates the water is left on. A back wash, which reverses the flow of water through the filter removing waste particles and debris, may occur.

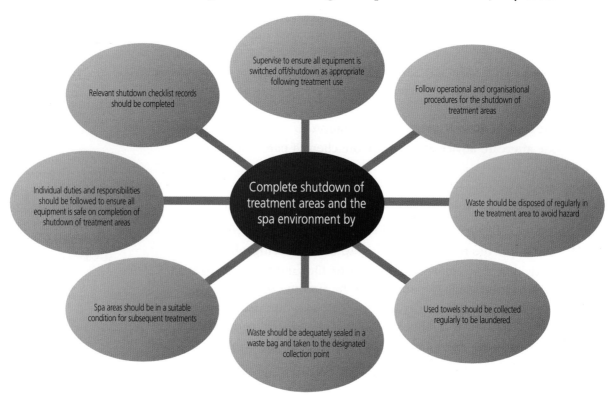

A final water test is recommended before pool shutdown in order that any problems with water quality can be rectified before the next working day. Regular testing and the maintenance of records is an essential part of spa plant operation and health and safety maintenance.

It is important to work within your responsibilities when operating shutdown of the spa area.

Aftercare

- Heat treatments and body wraps cause a loss of body fluids through perspiration, clients must be provided with still water or fruit juices to rehydrate following treatment. Water imbalances of only 1–2 per cent can lead to ill health. Increased water consumption aids toxin elimination.

- Following heat treatments, and those that induce relaxation such as flotation treatment, the client should rest for 20–30 minutes. In the case of heat treatments this is to allow body temperatures and blood pressure to return to normal. Sudden movements can cause dizziness and fainting.

- Avoid infra red or ultraviolet light treatments following heat treatments as the skin will be sensitised.

- Other treatments may follow the service, such as exfoliation and body massage depending on the service that has been received.

- If the client's aim is weight reduction give advice on healthy eating habits and increased regular exercise to raise metabolism, increase fitness and muscle tone. An aftercare leaflet may be given to your client suggesting healthy tips.

- Advise the client about other treatments that can be received.

- The client may be encouraged to recreate the benefits and of spa mineral treatments at home through the sale of retail products. These contain ingredients such as seaweed, sea salts, algae and mud.

Contra-actions

In the case of any contra-action to treatment it is important to discontinue treatment if it occurs while the client is being treated. Take the appropriate remedial action or contact the relevant member of staff trained to deal in this situation.

Aftercare advice should always be given to the client in the case of a contra-action occurring following the treatment.

Heat treatments

Treatment duration too long:

- Low blood pressure and loss of water from the body. Dehydration will occur, causing the cells to absorb fluid from other organs in the body. This may also cause the client to feel faint.

Sauna treatments

Relative humidity too low:

- Excessive water loss may occur, leading to dehydration. Also, breathing difficulties may be experienced due to lack moisture in the air. The temperature of the air will also be higher, causing discomfort when breathing.
- Nausea and dizziness caused by heat exhaustion. This can also be caused by the heat and motion in the spa pool.

Action:

- The client should rest and lie down. Raise the legs to avoid fainting.
- Apply a cool compress to the forehead.
- Water should be given to rehydrate.
- Seek medical attention if necessary.

Heat exhaustion

Caused by loss of fluids and sodium chloride (body salt). This results in symptoms such as dizziness, sickness, headaches and fainting.

Action:

- The client should rest and lie down, raise the legs to avoid fainting.
- Apply a cool compress to the forehead.
- Fruit juices or sports drinks may be taken.
- Seek medical attention if necessary.
- Salt tablets may be recommended by the GP to replace lost salts.

Cramp

Caused by excessive perspiration.

Action:

- Stretch the muscle and massage the area.
- Encourage the client to drink water. Salts may be added to replace lost body salts.

Burning/scalding the skin

This can be caused by not ladling the water over the coals in the sauna with an outstretched arm, the skin will then come into contact with the rising steam, checking the temperature of the standard shower before use or skin contact with the heated metal in the sauna.

Action:

- Cool the area with cold water immediately.
- Apply a dry dressing which will not stick to the skin injury. This will protect the skin against infection.

- Medical treatment may be advisable depending on the severity of the burn.

Nosebleed

Due to irritation of the mucous membranes and the effect of the high temperature upon the circulatory system.

Action:

- Bend the head forwards. The client should breathe through her mouth.
- The nose should be pinched for about 10 minutes.
- If the bleeding does not cease after 30 minutes seek medical attention.

Skin reaction

Skin irritation due to chemicals in the spa pool or high temperatures in the steam or sauna room and the irritant effect of the dry heat in the sauna room.

Action:

- The client should take a cool shower to remove the products/chemicals from the skin or lower skin temperature.
- Apply a soothing cream to reduce irritation.
- Medical treatment may be advisable if skin irritation continues.

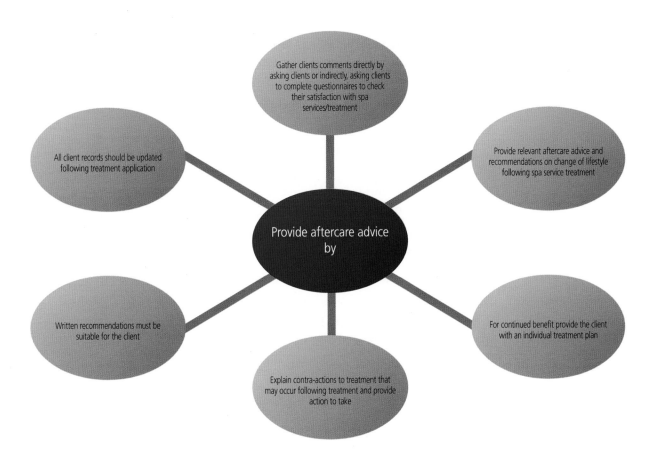

Respiratory disorders may be aggravated due to the heat of the sauna or steam room. Clients with respiratory disorders should avoid heat treatments where they have to breathe hot air.

Action:

● Sit the client down, and if she has medication with her, allow her to use it.

● Seek medical assistance if necessary.

Assessment of knowledge and understanding

You have now learnt about the different spa services and treatments that are available. To be effective in your work role in the spa it is necessary for you to be able to prepare, monitor, maintain and shutdown the different spa areas and to provide specialist spa treatments.

To test your level of knowledge and understanding in these areas, answer the following short questions. These will prepare you for your summative (final) assessment.

Organisational and legal requirements

1 How can you ensure that you comply with the requirements of the Data Protection Act 1998?

2 Who enforces and monitors local by-laws to ensure they are being followed with regard to water, temperature and quality for spa treatments?

3 How are water and chemical concentrations checked for the spa pool?

4 How can cross-infection be avoided in the spa area? State three examples.

5 What health and safety legislation should be complied with in the spa environment?

6 Where and why should written instructions on treatment usage be displayed?

7 What information should be recorded following a body wrap treatment?

8 What health and safety legislation states how chemicals required for spa should be stored and used?

9 For each of the following treatments explain how you would ensure the spa equipment was safe, clean and hygienic for each client
   a. wet flotation
   b. sauna
   c. foam bath
   d. steam cabinet.

10 What is the purpose of the client shower before entering the spa area? What is the effect of a shower received at intervals during heat application?

Client contact and consultation

1 Why should up-to-date records be kept for clients receiving spa treatments?

2 Which heat treatment would be most suitable for a client with a dry, sensitive skin? Discuss the reasons for your choice.

3 If a client was on a weight reduction programme, what benefits would heat therapy have? Discuss how you would design a treatment plan for such a client. Explain the spa treatments you could recommend and their benefits to the client.

4 Why must you check a client regularly when they are receiving spa treatments?

5 How would you ensure the client's understanding of the recommended spa treatment/service at the consultation?

6 Name six temporary contra-indications to spa therapy treatments/service.

Equipment and materials

1 Which treatments are referred to as dry heat?
   Which treatments are referred to as wet heat?

2 What is the recommended operating temperature of:
   a. spa pool
   b. hydrotherapy bath
   c. wet flotation
   d. mild sauna
   e. steam cabinet treatment.

3 What is the recommended pH level for the:
   a. spa pool
   b. wet flotation.

4 How is humidity measured in the sauna room?

5 What dangers could arise if the chemical pH concentrations in the spa pool were not checked regularly?

6 What should be checked on a daily basis in the spa environment? How is this check recorded?

7 How often should electrical equipment be serviced?

8 What health and safety legislation does this comply with?

Water, temperature and spa treatments

1 What is the water tested for when performing a spa pool test?

2 Why is adequate ventilation important in the spa?

3 How often may heat treatment be received per week?

4 State three physiological effect of cold, and three physiological effects of heat on the body.

5 Why is it important to shower, rest and rehydrate following spa treatments?

6 Why is it important for the client not to exceed the recommended treatment times?

7 How would you deal with the following contra-actions:
a. fainting
b. allergic reactions
c. headache?

8 Why is it important to follow organisational procedures for cleaning and maintaining the treatment areas?

Aftercare advice

1 Give three examples of aftercare advice that may be given following spa treatment.

2 Why is it important that the client is given post-treatment restrictions advice?

3 What opportunities can you take to promote additional services or products to a client ?

4 How is a body wrap treatment adapted to meet the treatment needs of the client?

chapter 17

Provide UV tanning treatments BT30

Provide self tanning treatments BT31

Learning objectives

This unit describes how to provide tanning treatment using ultraviolet tanning equipment and self tan cosmetic products.

It describes the competencies to enable you to:

- **consult with the client**
- **plan the treatment**
- **prepare for the treatment**
- **monitor UV tanning treatments**
- **apply self tan products**
- **complete the treatment**

When providing tanning treatment it is important to use the skills you have learnt in the following core mandatory units:

G1 ensure your own actions reduce risks to health and safety
G6 promote additional products or services to clients
G11 contribute to the financial effectiveness of the business

BT30 PROVIDE UV TANNING TREATMENTS

Tanning is where the skin darkens in response to ultraviolet light (UV) in order to protect itself from further sun exposure. UV light may be outdoor, natural sunlight or indoor, artificially created by tanning equipment or cosmetic products.

Sensible UV exposure minimises the associated risks and enables the associated benefits of tanning.

Beneficial effects of UV exposure:

- the treatment of seasonal affective disorder (SAD) – an emotional disorder that occurs between winter and spring and is related to a lack of sunshine
- induces a feeling of well-being and relaxation
- vitamin D is produced and released into the bloodstream – essential for healthy skin and bones; increases calcium absorption; important for blood clotting
- increased blood circulation increases skin healing
- the treatment of certain skin disorders. These include:
  – Acne vulgaris – through its healing and disinfecting effect
  – Psoraisis – through its healing effect.

Associated risks of UV over-exposure:

- thickening of the skin occurs, as the basal cells reproduce more quickly
- photo-ageing – sun damage occurs, causing loose skin and wrinkling
- skin cancer – commonly basal cell cancer, squamous cell cancer and the most harmful, melanoma
- damage to the eyes.

HEALTH AND SAFETY

If the client has moles (cellular naevi) ask her to keep a close check for any changes including irregular borders, darkening, colour change, bleeding and crusting. These may be an indication of cancer!

Always refer the client to her GP in this instance, and *never* name a specific contra-indication.

HEALTH AND SAFETY ✚

The skin disorder psoriasis appears to improve in the summer months in the presence of sunlight. UV as a treatment for the condition should only be provided by the medical profession.

Medical treating with UV is known as phototherapy.

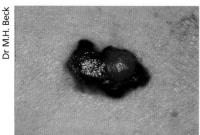

Dr M.H. Beck

Malignant melanoma

ANATOMY AND PHYSIOLOGY

A tan is the skin's method of protecting the body from exposure to the sun. The **melanocytes**, cells in the epidermis which create skin pigmentation, are stimulated to produce melanin. The melanocytes increase melanin production as a protective measure. Pigmentation changes can occur in the skin due to the changes in activity and numbers of melanocytes. This can result in increased ephilides (freckles), solar lentignes or chloasma (liver spots) and irregular pigmentation. Pigmentation changes are not uncommon in Asian skin and often result in large pigmentation marks. The skin also thickens as the cells in the epidermis multiply to absorb UV and reduce its penetration.

The sun's spectrum comprises different electromagnetic rays which travel in waves. The full range of radiations in the electromagnetic spectrum is:

Radio waves – radio, TV and radar
Infra-red rays – heat rays
Light
Ultraviolet rays
X-rays
Gamma rays – from radioactive substances
Cosmic rays – in outer space

The electromagnetic spectrum is an arrangement of these waves in order of wavelength. Wavelength is measured in nanometres (nm) – one nanometre is one millionth of a millimetre.

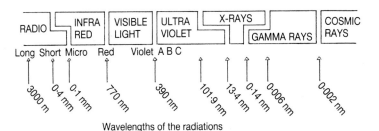

Wavelengths of the radiations

The electromagnetic spectrum

Natural UV

UV is part of this spectrum, which ranges from short rays including UV light (tanning) to visible white light (daylight) to infra-red rays (warmth) which are invisible.

UV wavelengths can be divided into three types according to their wavelengths – UVA, UVB and UVC.

- **UVA** rays are the longest (315–400 nm), providing 95 per cent of natural UV light.

- **UVB** rays are shorter rays (280–315 nm), providing 4–5 per cent of natural UV light. These are much stronger than UVA rays and the most active.

- **UVC** rays are the shortest (200–280 nm) and fail to reach the Earth as they are almost completely absorbed by the atmosphere.

HEALTH AND SAFETY

UV for medical and therapeutic use
UVB rays are mainly used for medical purposes and do not penetrate deep into the skin.

Artificial UV

Artificial UV is produced by high- or low-pressure tubes and lamps. The term pressure relates to the wattage of the lamps. Most sun tanning units emit both UVA and UVB rays. Tanning beds produce between 3–8 times the UVA the natural sun produces at noon in the summer.

Physiological effects

The shorter the wavelength, the higher the energy and possible damage. UVA rays have a longer wavelength. These stimulate melanin production, creating a rapid but short-lived tan. They also penetrate deeply into the dermis, damaging the elastin and collagen fibres which give the skin its

330–390 nm approximating to UV–A

290–330 nm approximating to UV–B

185–290 nm approximating to UV–C

Stratum corneum

Epidermis

Dermis

Penetration of UV rays into the skin

strength and elasticity. UVA exposure leads to premature skin ageing, seen as pigmentation disorders and wrinkling.

UVB rays have a shorter wavelength than UVA and penetrate only as far as the lower layers of the epidermis. They cause skin erythema, skin burning (sunburn) and stimulate the pigment cells, melanocytes, to increase melanin production, creating a longer lasting tan than UVA. UVB also stimulates vitamin D production. When UV hits the skin, a chemical in the skin changes it to vitamin D. This then aids the absorption of calcium.

When exposure to UV ceases, the tan eventually fades. This is because the pigmented cells are gradually lost and replaced through the process of desquamation.

ELECTRICAL SCIENCE

Starters send the high voltage required to get the tubes operating; a ballast device maintains and limits the electric current in a circuit. The ballast in the sunbed varies in size and weight, and it is important that the tube wattage is correct for the ballast of the sunbed.

Suntanning units may use tubes filled with mercury vapour at low pressure which is transformed to UV when the equipment is switched on, or quartz which are filled at a higher pressure. High powered compact lamps known as *burners* are featured in some tanning equipment; this intensifies the UV. They emit high levels of UVB and some UVC, which requires filtering.

Modern tanning units contain filter screens which control the intensity of the UV emitted. The short wavelengths which create skin burning are screened, but may still be sufficient to cause burning dependant upon application.

Modifications to the tubes can determine whether more UVA or UVB is emitted, through the different fluorescent linings.

Choice of tanning equipment

There is a variety of tanning equipment available. They are usually either **vertical**, where the client stands, or **horizontal**, where the client lies down. These units provide either total or partial tanning. They incorporate high-performance tanning tubes, closely packed together and protected with a safety layer of perspex. Additional equipment features include facial tanning tubes, shoulder tanning features, cooling body fans to prevent overheating, and stereo speakers for entertainment.

Helinova

A vertical tanning unit

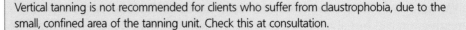

TIP	✔
Vertical tanning is not recommended for clients who suffer from claustrophobia, due to the small, confined area of the tanning unit. Check this at consultation.	

High-pressure tanning units

Helinova

High-pressure, horizontal tanning unit

These units achieve a tan very quickly as they emit a lot of UV rays. Application time is very short, commencing at 4–5 minutes with a maximum of 9–15 minutes dependant upon the unit. High-pressure units have an increased level of UVB and as such, over-exposure will result in burning of the skin.

Mercury vapour UV lamps

Mercury vapour UV lamps are used for the treatment of body parts. The tanning tube contains argon gas and a small amount of mercury. The mercury vaporises and ionises when in use to produce ultraviolet light. These lamps are of high or low pressure and produce UVA, UVB and some UVC rays, however the UVC rays are absorbed by the air. UV lamps require a skin patch test to be performed before treatment to assess the correct treatment distance and application time for the individual client.

Reception

Complete the client's personal details on the client record card. Question the client to check for suitability and for possible contra-indications.

Often, the tanning treatments are booked as part of a course and a discounted price is offered. Vouchers are usually provided for each session as proof of payment. Where the tanning unit is operated by coins or tokens it will be necessary to have a store of these which are issued at reception.

When using sunbeds, recommended UV session times should be given according to the manufacturers' recommendations, taking into consideration the sessions already received and skin type and, if carried out, the results of the skin test.

TIP

Data Protection Act 1998
It is necessary to ask the client questions before the treatment plan can be finalised; the details are recorded on the client record card.

Remember *this information is confidential* and should be stored in a secure area following treatment.

HEALTH AND SAFETY

The surface of a mercury vapour lamp becomes very hot and must not come into contact with the skin or burning will occur.

BEAUTY WORKS

[A sample client record card with fields for Date, Beauty therapist name, Client name, Date of birth, Address, Postcode, Evening phone number, Day phone number, Name of doctor, Doctor's address and phone number, Related medical history, medication, contra-indications, skin type, and various product checklists]

A sample record card

Skin patch test

In order to assess skin tolerance to UV and calculate the correct tanning dosage, a patch test may be performed.

When using a mercury vapour lamp on an area of skin not previously exposed to UV rays, the patch test is essential to calculate correct UV exposure. Protective eye shields must be worn to prevent damage to the eyes from the intense light.

The distance between the lamp and the client must be carefully measured with a tape measure. The area to be treated is cleansed to remove any barriers and to avoid sensitisation. A sheet of opaque paper with three differing shapes cut out of it is then placed over the area and held securely. Any surrounding skin parts are covered to avoid UV exposure.

The three shapes are then exposed to the UV light for one minute. Then the first shape is covered and the second and third shapes are exposed for one minute. Then the second shape is also covered and the third shape is exposed for another minute. A record of UV exposure is kept and the client should return 24 hours later for an assessment of skin reaction. If no skin reaction occurs then the patch test is repeated, increasing the exposure time.

A skin reaction resulting in a mild reddening (erythema) of the skin gives the correct treatment dosage to use for the initial treatment. If the therapist is satisfied that the client may receive UV tanning treatment, a course of tanning treatments is usually booked.

Calculating session times

When calculating the duration of exposure to tanning treatment and the frequency of sessions, the client's skin type must be taken into account:

- fair, sensitive – burns easily, never tans
- fair – burns easily but tans slightly
- medium colouring – burns moderately, tans slowly
- medium colouring – rarely burns, tans easily
- darkly pigmented – rarely burns and tans immediately
- dark, deeply pigmented – never burns and tans immediately.

Always start at the minimum recommended treatment exposure time to assess skin tolerance. Treatment time exposure should be increased as recommended by the equipment manufacturer. Ideally, no more than three sessions should be received per week. A time interval of at least one day should be taken between tanning treatments.

Once the tan has been achieved, treatment may be received once per month. Client leaflets may be made available to provide advice on sensible tanning and the risks of misuse.

GP approval must be sought before UV treatment if the client has a medical condition or is taking medication which contra-indicates treatment.

HEALTH AND SAFETY

Fair-skinned clients are more at risk than those with darker skins on exposure to UV light.

HEALTH AND SAFETY

Health and Safety Executive Copies of the HSE publication
Controlling health risks from the use of UV tanning equipment should be made available
to all sun-tan treatment clients.

The Sunbed Association (TSA)
This industry body sets the standards for safe tanning and provides supporting guidelines
and training for its members to promote good practice.

Contra-indications

During the client assessment, if you find any of the following, UV treatment
must not be recommended or carried out:

- the client is under 16 years of age
- vitiligo, hypersensitive skin or vascular skin disorders
- history of cancerous conditions
- recent x-ray treatment (within the last three months)
- infectious skin diseases – fungal, viral or bacterial
- medical conditions, such as liver, heart, lung and kidney disease
- medication which causes the skin to be UV sensitive – known as
  photosensitisers. These include antibiotics, medication for blood
  pressure and tranquillisers. This reaction can result in an itchy rash,
  sometimes followed by pigmentation

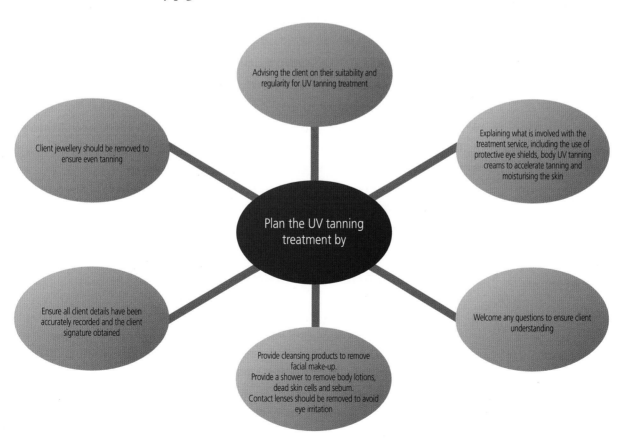

Tanning equipment

Sunbeds should be supplied by a reliable source and comply with relevant British Standards. They should be professionally installed and maintained.

A record of sunbed usage and maintenance should be kept.

When tubes are replaced treatment sessions should be reduced usually for the first 50 hours, as the UV output will be 50 per cent stronger than the old lamps.

- pregnancy – uneven pigmentation may occur
- immediately after other heat or sensitising treatments such as waxing hair removal, sauna or electrolysis
- fair skin unable to tan and sensitive skin
- excessive moles – more than 100
- alcohol consumption before treatment
- contact lenses, unless removed – to avoid eye damage caused by ray concentration.

TIP

For those fair-skinned clients for whom UV treatment would be unsuitable, a self tanning treatment could be offered as an alternative.

Perform a patch test if you feel the client has indications of sensitivity.

EQUIPMENT LIST

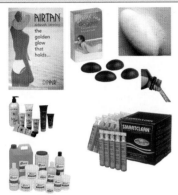

record card

tanning guidelines

protective eye shields

shower

unperfumed soap

towels

cleansers

cotton wool

tissues

tanning cosmetic preparations

hydrating body lotions

waste bin

water for client consumption

sunbed cleaning agent

Equipment and materials

- record card
- tanning equipment, sited in a fully screened area to avoid irradiation of other clients or therapists
- tanning guidelines, displayed in the treatment area
- protective eye shields to prevent eye disorders
- shower – to cleanse the skin before tanning
- unperfumed soap – to cleanse the skin
- clean towels – to dry the skin and protect the hair
- cosmetic cleansers – to remove make-up if worn
- cotton wool and tissues – to remove cleansing preparations
- tanning cosmetic preparations – to aid tanning and to care for the skin
- hydrating body lotions – to replace moisture lost from the skin following treatment
- waste bin in the area – to dispose of consumable items
- water for client consumption – to replace lost body fluids and cool following treatment
- sunbed cleaning agent.

Sterilisation and sanitisation

- The surface of horizontal tanning units must be cleaned after each client with an appropriate cleaning agent recommended by the equipment supplier. Vertical tanning units do not come into contact with the client's skin and do not require cleaning after each client.
- Flooring in the area must be cleaned to avoid contamination and cross-infection. Disposable floor covering may be made available where possible.

A film that covers the surface of the sunbed and is provided for each client maintains hygiene and may be used in conjunction with certain tanning equipment.

Wink-ease

- The shower must be cleaned after each client to avoid cross-infection.
- The tanning system should be wiped down daily with an appropriate cleaning agent.
- Waste bins in the area should be emptied after each client.

Preparation of the treatment area

- Ensure there is adequate ventilation in the tanning area. This is important for client comfort, to prevent the build up of ozone and to ensure that the equipment can operate efficiently.
- Check all general electrical safety precautions.

Actinotherapy goggles

HEALTH AND SAFETY ✚

Equipment maintenance
- Regularly check that the equipment is operating efficiently.
- A record should be kept to calculate equipment usage as the tubes/burners will become less efficient, emitting less UV, and require replacement after a specific time. Some equipment is able to store this information, which can be accessed as necessary. This is generally between 300 and 800 hours.
- Technical equipment must be serviced annually by a professional, and tested for efficiency and safety in line with European standards. Starters need to be replaced on average after 1000 hours of service.

Sunbed cleaners

- Ensure the tanning unit is cleaned with a recommended proprietary equipment cleaner between each client.
- Ensure that the distance between the overhead surface of the tanning unit and the client is fixed and stable.
- Refill consumable items as necessary in the shower, changing and tanning area.
- Provide a clean towel for use after showering.

Preparation of the client

Collect the client record card and carry out a consultation to assess the client's tanning requirements. Agree on an appropriate treatment plan and complete the record card.

If this is a repeat treatment, check the client's skin reaction to previous treatment and discuss treatment progression as necessary. It is important to

HEALTH AND SAFETY ✚

Ultraviolet treatment should not be received twice in one day. If the client has already been exposed to natural UV, artificial UV should not be received.

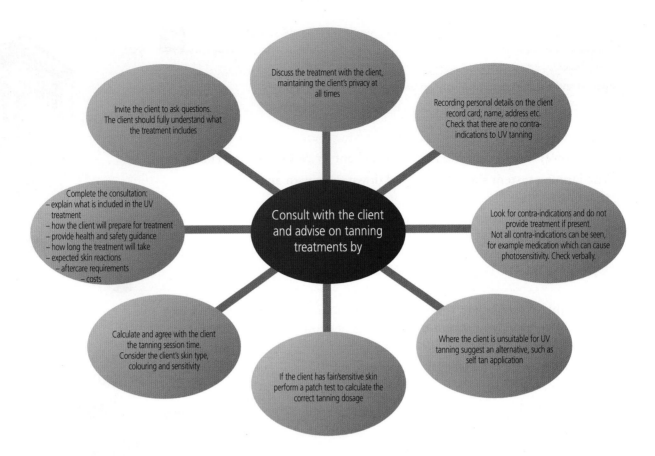

Invite the client to ask questions. The client should fully understand what the treatment includes

Discuss the treatment with the client, maintaining the client's privacy at all times

Recording personal details on the client record card; name, address etc. Check that there are no contra-indications to UV tanning

Complete the consultation:
– explain what is included in the UV treatment
– how the client will prepare for treatment
– provide health and safety guidance
– how long the treatment will take
– expected skin reactions
 – aftercare requirements
 – costs

Consult with the client and advise on tanning treatments by

Look for contra-indications and do not provide treatment if present. Not all contra-indications can be seen, for example medication which can cause photosensitivity. Check verbally.

Calculate and agree with the client the tanning session time. Consider the client's skin type, colouring and sensitivity

Where the client is unsuitable for UV tanning suggest an alternative, such as self tan application

If the client has fair/sensitive skin perform a patch test to calculate the correct tanning dosage

UV-Power UK

Specialised tanning preparations

assess the client's skin type in order to recommend the correct tanning dosage. Check if she has recently been exposed to natural or artificial UV.

Explain the treatment procedure to the client and the expected outcomes. Draw the client's attention to the safe tanning notice displayed in the treatment area. This information is sometimes also included on the record card.

If worn, the client should remove jewellery, contact lenses and make-up. A shower should be taken using unperfumed soap to remove skin creams and lotions which could cause skin sensitisation.

It is recommended that briefs be worn whilst tanning. Similar clothing should be worn for subsequent treatments to avoid exposure of new skin, which may result in burning. Advise the client to protect her hair if it has been chemically treated, to avoid colour change or drying.

HEALTH AND SAFETY

All jewellery should be removed as this could cause skin burning and uneven tanning.

HEALTH AND SAFETY

Eye protection
Traditional goggles must be disinfected before every used to prevent cross-infection. A reputable professional sanitising solution should be used, and the goggles should be thoroughly rinsed and dry before use to avoid skin/eye sensitisation.

Disposable eye protection is a good idea which is retailed to your client. These protect the eyes from UVA and UVB rays whilst allowing the client to see through them. They are disposed of after use.

Explain how the tanning equipment operates and the most suitable tanning position. Explain that a trained operator will be within calling distance at all times. Provide clean, sanitised goggles to protect the eyes.

A specialised tanning preparation may be recommended. This protects the skin, promotes tanning and keeps the skin hydrated as it contains moisturisers.

Exfoliation is not recommended directly before tanning as it may sensitise the skin. However, it is beneficial following tanning to remove dead skin cells and brighten the skin.

> ### HEALTH AND SAFETY
>
> Body parts respond differently to UV exposure. Areas not regularly exposed may burn and become sensitive more quickly. These areas include the neck, chest, shoulders and back.
> Pressure points on the body may not tan as efficiently. This is because the reduced blood supply to the area prevents the melanin being oxidised.

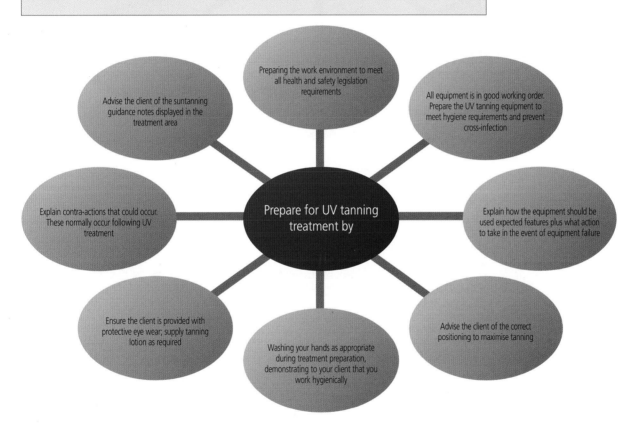

TREATMENT APPLICATION

All equipment must be operated according to manufacturers' instructions.

1 Switch the tanning unit on.

2 Set exposure time according to the client's skin type and stage of UV treatment exposure.

3 Allow the client to rest for a short period after the tanning treatment.

4 Record the date and duration of the treatment on the client's record card. The recommended treatment time and number should not be exceeded.

> ### HEALTH AND SAFETY
>
> Protective eye shields must be worn by the therapist if exposure to UV is likely.

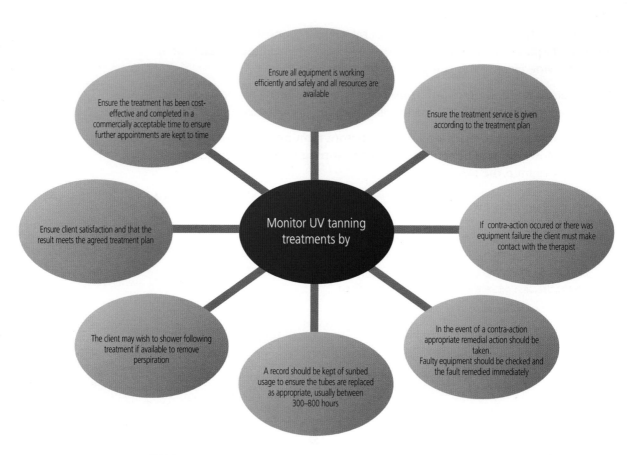

Monitor UV tanning treatments by

Ensure all equipment is working efficiently and safely and all resources are available

Ensure the treatment has been cost-effective and completed in a commercially acceptable time to ensure further appointments are kept to time

Ensure the treatment service is given according to the treatment plan

Ensure client satisfaction and that the result meets the agreed treatment plan

If contra-action occured or there was equipment failure the client must make contact with the therapist

The client may wish to shower following treatment if available to remove perspiration

In the event of a contra-action appropriate remedial action should be taken. Faulty equipment should be checked and the fault remedied immediately

A record should be kept of sunbed usage to ensure the tubes are replaced as appropriate, usually between 300–800 hours

---

HEALTH AND SAFETY

Tanning tips
When using horizontal tanning beds pressure points can sometimes occur, resulting in paler areas. Advise the client to change her position, i.e. sometimes lying on her front instead of her back.

To minimise white patches in unexposed areas, the client may be advise to place her hands behind her head to prevent white patches under her arms.

HEALTH AND SAFETY

During UV application, nobody should enter the treatment area as this would expose them to the UV rays.

HEALTH AND SAFETY

It is recommended by the Health and Safety Executive that 20 tanning sessions should not be exceeded per year. Many tanning operators have a policy to notify their users of this, formally notifying them when the level is exceeded.

Aftercare

- The client must not rise quickly or fainting may occur.
- Advise the client to shower after treatment – this removes perspiration which could cause a skin rash.
- Skin care preparations should be available and recommended to moisturise the skin and prevent skin dehydration.
- Drinks must be available for the client, to rehydrate to replace body moisture lost through sweat.
- Avoidance of heat treatments and further UV treatments must be recommended within the next 24 hours.
- Details of the treatment should be entered on the record card, to include date of session, period of session, any adverse reaction.
- Artificial tanning does not protect against burning in natural UV – a sunscreen should always be worn.

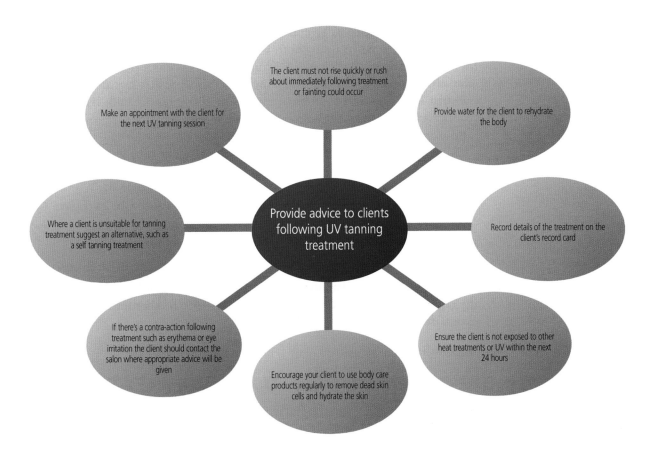

Artificial tanning is popular before 'sun' holidays and advice should be given on continued safe tanning. This provides an opportunity to increase retail sales of suncare cosmetics which protect against UVA and often also UVB damage. The correct SPF (sun protective factor) should be selected according to how long the client can safely stay in the sun without burning.

TIP

Sunscreens
Sunscreens are available in oil, foam, spray, mousse, lotion, stick, milk, gel and cream forms and may be **physical** or **chemical** in their preparation. Physical sunscreens act by reflecting UV rays. Chemical sunscreens absorb UV rays, releasing the energy as heat.

If a sunscreen is labelled SPF 12 it means that a person may stay in the sun 12 times longer than it would normally take for them to burn.

Contra-actions

- **Erythema** (reddening of the skin) – in severe cases this leads to blistering and peeling of the skin and free radical formation caused by UV over-exposure. Tanning should not be received until all skin reddening has gone. Medical advice should be sought with excessive UV overdose.

- **Prickly heat** – a skin rash caused by over-exposure to UV. Antihistamine tablets and a cooling, soothing lotion are usually prescribed, together with a period of absence from UV tanning. At the next session, tanning time should be reduced.

- **Eye disorders** – such as swelling and inflammation, resulting from failure to wear protective eye wear. Both UVA and UVB light can pass through the eyelids if protective eyewear is not worn. There is a possibility with excessive exposure that the following eye disorders may occur:
  - **Photo keratitis** a corneal burn caused by UVB rays. Cloudy vision can occur and they eyes become light sensitive and feel itchy.
  - **Photoconjunctivitis**.
  - **Cataracts** caused by the UV rays penetrating the cornea and lens of the eye. This causes the lens to thicken, becoming opaque resulting in blurred vision.
  - **Carcinomas** (cancer) of the delicate eye tissue a caused by excessive UV exposure.
- **Feeling faint** – due to sudden movement following heat treatment.
- **Nausea** – caused by increased body temperature and excessive exposure.
- If any abnormal skin reaction occurs either during or following treatment, the client must be advised to consult a GP before further tanning exposure.

Mystic tan

BT31 PROVIDE SELF TANNING TREATMENTS

The application of self tanning products creates a healthy, tanned appearance to the skin without any of the harmful effects of UV. The effect is temporary, as dead skin cells are shed – so too is the colour. This process of losing the tan usually takes 5–6 days.

There are many different self tan applications to choose from for professional or retail use including self tan tissue, spray, airbrush, spray booth, cream and gel.

Their formulations differ as they are often designed for different parts of the face or body, and for various skin tones – fair or dark – to achieve a realistic result. Maximum darkening takes between 8 to 24 hours depending upon the tanning product and the client's natural skin type/colour.

ANATOMY AND PHYSIOLOGY

The active ingredient in self tan products is *dihydroxyacetone* (DHA), a colourless sugar which reacts with the amino acids of the stratum corneum skin cells creating the pigmented tanned look.

Some contain UV protection and have a SPF, however, the skin still requires protection.

Reception

Depending on the system used time should be allowed for client preparation, self tan application and drying off.

Advise the client to wear an old bikini or underwear during self tan application. Some salons provide disposable briefs which are costed into the treatment service.

If you require the client to shower and exfoliate before the treatment explain this when she books. On arrival complete the client's personal details on the client record card. Question the client to check for suitability and for possible contra-indications.

If the client has hypersensitive skin or known allergies a patch test should be performed to assess skin suitability.

Contra-indications

During the client assessment, if you find any of the following listed below, self tan treatment must not be recommended or carried out.

- Pregnancy – due to the hormonal changes in the body, the colour result may change. There is also an insurance implication as no body treatments should be carried out in the first three months of pregnancy.
- Hypersensitive, allergenic skins – an allergic reaction can occur caused by the ingredients in the self tan product.
- Infectious skin conditions – fungal, viral or bacterial.
- Cuts and abrasions in the area – skin irritation and secondary infection could occur.
- Immediately after other heat or sensitising treatments such as waxing hair removal, electrolysis or sauna. Again, skin irritation and secondary infection can occur if the skin has been damaged.
- Contact lenses unless removed – to avoid eye irritation.
- Respiratory conditions – these may be aggravated by the chemical fumes.
- Skin conditions where the skin is broken such as psoriasis, eczema and dermatitis.
- Positive (allergic) reaction to a skin test.
- Skin erythema – the skin is already sensitised.

HEALTH AND SAFETY

Patch test
In order to assess skin tolerance to the self tan product, a patch test may be performed on a small area of skin to assess skin tolerance. This is usually done in the crook of the elbow or behind the ear.

HEALTH AND SAFETY

Storage
Ensure all products are clearly labelled and stored at room temperature away from heat and sunlight, ideally in a cupboard.

TIP

Vitiligo
Self tan application can help disguise the appearance of the skin condition vitiligo (lack of skin pigment), especially when the self tan can be applied specifically to one area e.g. using an airbrush technique.

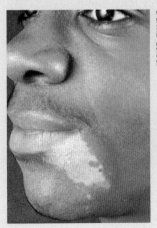

Derma Colour

Equipment and materials

- record card – to record client personal details and details of the treatment
- shower to cleanse the skin, if applicable to the self tan system
- unperfumed soap to cleanse the skin
- cosmetic cleansers to remove make-up if worn
- self tanning guidance instructions – if using the spray booth system
- barrier cream for the palms of the hands and soles of the feet – if using the spray booth system
- self tan product/s
- self tan equipment as appropriate i.e. booth, compressor and air brush etc.
- disposable briefs (if required)
- disposable gloves. These must be thin to enable even application and protect the therapist's hands from staining
- protective hair covering
- cotton wool and buds to remove self tan from parts not required and to remove cleansing preparations
- tissues to protect against staining and for removing cleansing preparations and self tan product
- protective disposable coverings, e.g. a paper bed roll for trolley surfaces and flooring
- mirror
- covered, lined waste bin in the area – to dispose of consumable items
- cleaning agents to clean equipment and work area.

Sterilisation and sanitisation

The shower if used must be cleaned after each client to avoid cross-infection. The treatment floor where the client stands during treatment application must be cleaned with a disinfectant cleaning agent and protected as appropriate using a disposable non-slip covering.

Airbrush and spray tanning have less opportunity for cross-infection in application as there is no direct contact.

Waste bins in the area should be emptied after each client.

The therapist's hands should be protected with disposable gloves during manual application, to prevent skin staining and for reasons of hygiene.

Preparation of the treatment area

Ensure that tanning equipment is serviced regularly as per the manufacturer's instructions.

For the spray tan application technique a cold water supply and waste pipe for drainage is required. It is essential that spray tan booths are sealed adequately to prevent chemical leakage into the atmosphere. Ventilation must also be adequate to ensure to avoid excessive chemical fumes.

There must be sufficient room in the working area to adequately perform the treatment.

Ensure there is adequate lighting when applying self tan manually to ensure an even application.

Trolley surfaces should be protected against accidental spillage of self tan product from manual and airbrush techniques.

Treatment couches required for the application of manual self tan applications must be adequately protected with disposable coverings to prevent staining and cross-infection.

Preparation of the client

Carry out a client consultation to assess the client's treatment requirements and expectations.

Choose the correct shade for the skin colour – light, medium or dark. Some manufacturers provide shade charts to enable the client to identify the colour.

Best results are achieved on clean skin which has been cleansed and exfoliated to remove skin lotions, sebum and dead skin cells, all of which will act as a barrier. This type of cleansing enables an even application, although not all tanning systems require this.

TIP

Self tan products
Some self tan products contain alpha hydroxy acids (AHA) which continue to gently remove dead skin cells, aiming to produce a more even colour as the product achieves the skin's colour change.

Some products contain ingredients to achieve a sparkly finished effect.

TIP

Link selling
It is a good idea for the client to receive an exfoliation treatment professionally applied before her treatment.

Ellisons

Exfoliating mitt

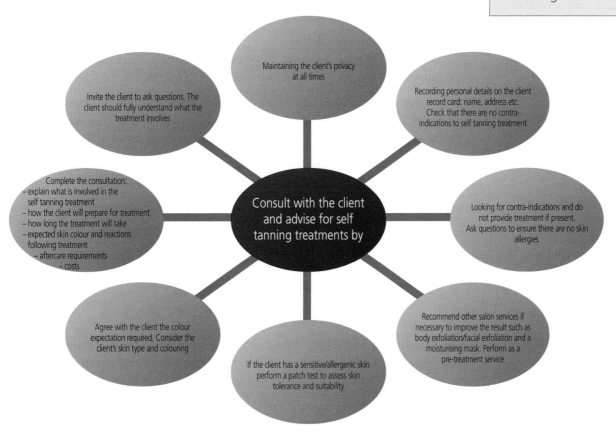

Maintaining the client's privacy at all times

Recording personal details on the client record card: name, address etc. Check that there are no contra-indications to self tanning treatment

Looking for contra-indications and do not provide treatment if present. Ask questions to ensure there are no skin allergies

Recommend other salon services if necessary to improve the result such as body exfoliation/facial exfoliation and a moisturising mask. Perform as a pre-treatment service

If the client has a sensitive/allergenic skin perform a patch test to assess skin tolerance and suitability

Agree with the client the colour expectation required. Consider the client's skin type and colouring

Complete the consultation:
– explain what is involved in the self tanning treatment
– how the client will prepare for treatment
– how long the treatment will take
– expected skin colour and reactions following treatment
– aftercare requirements
– costs

Invite the client to ask questions. The client should fully understand what the treatment involves

Consult with the client and advise for self tanning treatments by

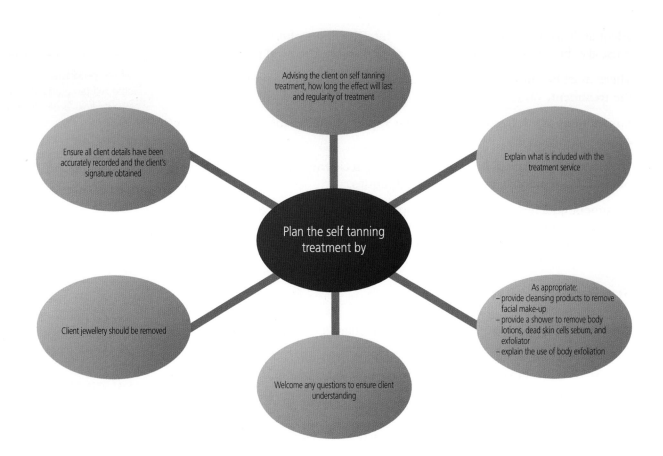

Exfoliation is important prior to application, and this maybe performed in the salon or by the client at home, depending on the self tan product. Areas requiring exfoliation attention are the elbows, knees, ankles where dead skin cells build up.

All jewellery should be removed from the treatment area to ensure an even application, and make-up should be removed from the face.

It is recommended to provide paper briefs to prevent staining the clients underwear. In the spray booth technique underwear is not necessary during application.

In the self tan spray techniques a barrier cream is applied to the palms of the hands, soles of the feet and nails of the client to prevent skin staining.

A protective cap is worn to cover the hair. Ensure this is not too low on the forehead or a demarcation line will occur.

TREATMENT APPLICATION

Gloves should be worn by the beauty therapist to prevent skin staining where there is contact with the self tan product. Always follow the manufacturer's instructions to ensure the optimum effect is achieved.

When applying self tan to the face, the eyes should be closed or protected as per the manufacturer's instructions. Hair should be covered.

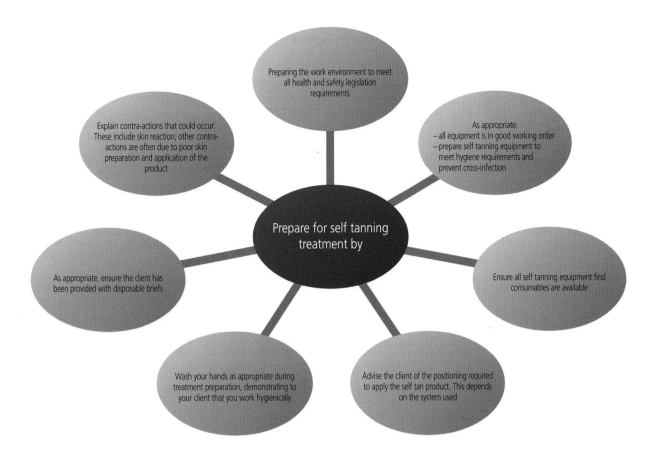

Prepare for self tanning treatment by

- Preparing the work environment to meet all health and safety legislation requirements
- Explain contra-actions that could occur. These include skin reaction; other contra-actions are often due to poor skin preparation and application of the product
- As appropriate:
  – all equipment is in good working order
  – prepare self tanning equipment to meet hygiene requirements and prevent cross-infection
- As appropriate, ensure the client has been provided with disposable briefs
- Ensure all self tanning equipment find consumables are available
- Wash your hands as appropriate during treatment preparation, demonstrating to your client that you work hygienically
- Advise the client of the positioning required to apply the self tan product. This depends on the system used

Self tan application techniques

Spray application technique

1 The client and her skin are prepared for application.

2 Liquid product is sprayed evenly all over the client's skin in a large booth which has filters to remove chemical particles from the air. Some systems also have inbuilt heaters so that the environment is temperature regulated to prevent the skin drying too quickly.

3 If required a second application may be given when the skin has dried. An immediate colour is achieved and then the tan continues to develop.

4 Ensure the client is satisfied with the finished result and understands how the finished result will appear. Application and drying time: 5–10 minutes.

5 Alternatively the tan can be applied mechanically in a cubicle, through nozzles which may be static or moving. The client stands in the cubicle where the front and then the back of the body is sprayed with self tan. Different positions are adopted by the client to ensure even application. The client then strokes the product over the skin until it has dried. Excess product should be removed from the palms of the hands and soles of the feet. This system offers additional privacy for the client. Application time: 1–10 minutes depending on the system.

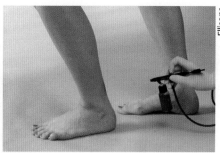
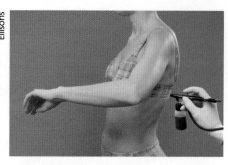

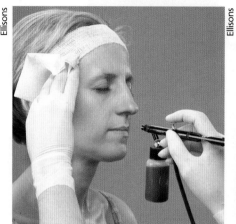
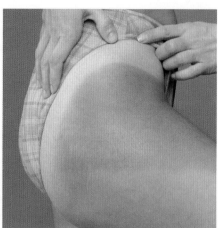

Spray application technique

Airbrush application technique

This technique uses a compressor, a pump producing a stream of compressed air, to power an airbrush that directs the self tan product onto the skin through a nozzle.

1 The client and her skin is prepared for application.

2 The client stands in a booth or working area protected from spray, whilst the beauty therapist applies self tan with an airbrush. It is important that the client does not move to avoid getting self tan on the soles of her feet.

3 Ensure the client is satisfied with the finished result and understands how the finished result will appear.

Application and drying time: 20–30 minutes.

> **TIP** ✔
>
> **Care of the airbrush**
> Temporarily between use store the airbrush in water to prevent clogging.
> When not in use, store the airbrush in an airbrush holder.

> **TIP** ✔
>
> **Air brush application**
> To ensure even application a small rotating platform which the client stands on can be used to facilitate application.
> To create a more natural, lighter result reduce pressure and increase the distance.
> Ensure no body parts are missed, e.g. under the chin!
> Wipe over fair brow hair to avoid staining.

Manual application technique

1 The client and her skin are prepared for application. This usually requires showering and the application of an exfoliant.

2 Moisturiser may be applied to the elbows, knees, ankles and feet. Adding moisturiser lightens the result but should only be used if recommended by the manufacturer.

3 The self tan product is applied over the body following the manufacturer's guidelines for application using the hands, which are usually protected with gloves to prevent staining.

4 Treatment must be methodical to ensure no body parts are missed and that an even coverage is obtained.

5 Product should be removed, using a clean tissue, from the palms of the hands, toe and fingernails to prevent staining.

6 Time should be allowed for the product to dry.

7 The skin is moisturised, which also seals the skin.

8 Ensure the client is satisfied and understands how the finished result will appear.

> **TIP**
>
> **Protecting the hands**
> The hands have more pores than other body areas and will soon tan. To prevent staining wear thin gloves during application.

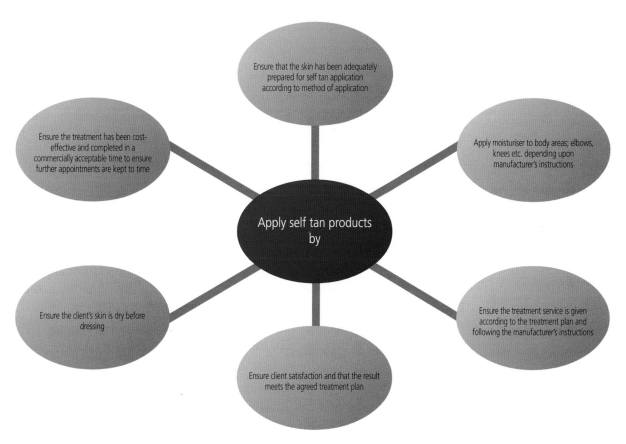

Aftercare advice

- Details of the treatment should be entered on the record card, to include date, colour, result, any adverse skin reaction. To ensure effective tan development, avoid streaking and to maintain the result:

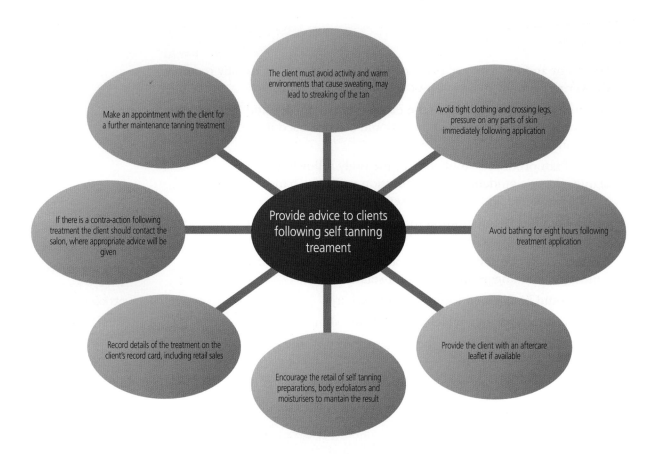

– Avoid anything that will make you sweat immediately following treatment as this will dilute the product, disturb application affecting the finished effect.
– Avoid tight clothing immediately following application to avoid product removal.
– Do not bath/shower for at least eight hours following treatment application.
– Avoid chlorinated pools, excessive bathing and heat treatments such as sauna as they encourage fading.

• Encourage the retail of self tanning preparations. Tinted products are useful as this assists in even application. They often contain ingredients to keep the skin moisturised, such as vitamins and plant extracts.

• Other relevant products are exfoliators, which can be used between treatments and prepare the skin for future self tan applications.

• Moisturiser should be applied daily to prevent the skin becoming dry and to keep the skin hydrated.

• If a contra-action occurs contact the salon for professional advice.

• Encourage a repeat appointment booking.

Assessment of knowledge and understanding

You have now learnt about how to provide tanning treatment using ultraviolet tanning equipment and self tanning cosmetic products. To test your level of knowledge and understanding, answer the following short questions. These will prepare you for your summative (final) assessment.

Client consultation

1 What should be checked to assess the client's suitability for UV treatment?

2 What considerations should be made when deciding the treatment time per UV session for a client?

3 How can the client's modesty and privacy be maintained during self tan application?

Preparation for treatment

1 Why is good lighting important when applying self tan?

2 How should the skin be prepared before UV tanning treatment?

3 How should the skin be prepared for self tan treatment?

4 Why is adequate ventilation important in the UV tanning treatment area?

Contra-indications

1 Name three contra-indications observed at consultation which would prevent self tan treatment being carried out.

2 Name three contra-indications which would require referral to a GP for medical advice.

3 Why is it important to not name specific contra-indications when encouraging clients to seek medical advice?

Equipment and materials

1 When should UV tubes be replaced?

2 How is the treatment area prepared for UV treatment?

3 How often should the client's receive a self tan service if they wish to maintain the effect?

Treatment-specific knowledge

1 What aftercare advice should be given to a client following UV tanning treatment?

2 What aftercare advice should be given to a client following self tan application?

3 a. What is a contra-action?
   b. State three contra-actions to UV tanning treatment.

4 What would be a contra-action to self tan application?

5 What retail products could be recommended to a client to care for the appearance of her skin following UV tanning treatment?

6 What are the risks of UV overexposure?

7 What are the beneficial effects of UV on the body?

8 How do UV rays create the tanned appearance of the skin?

9 How does self tan product create the tanned appearance of the skin?

10 What retail products could be recommended to a client to care for the appearance of her skin and maintain the result following self tan application?

chapter 18

Prepare to change the performer's appearance   BT32

Assist with the continuity of the performer's appearance   BT33

Apply make-up to change the performer's appearance   BT34

Apply special effects   BT35

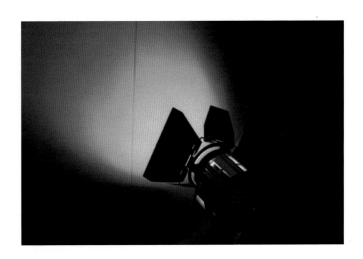

BT32 PREPARE TO CHANGE THE PERFORMER'S APPEARANCE

Learning objectives

This unit outlines the preparation methods undertaken to change the performer's appearance in a safe manner. To achieve this unit, you must show a satisfactory level of personal dress and hygiene. You must organise and arrange your workstations, materials and equipment for easy access by all users and keep workstations clean, hygienic and tidy.

You must ensure that you make full use of lighting and ventilation of the workstation and its environment, including using materials and equipment safely. You are required to recognise infectious and contagious skin and hair conditions, and deal with contamination of materials and equipment.

You must advise performers of any possible discomfort and encourage them to ask questions about make-up and/or hair work to minimise their concerns.

It describes the competencies to enable you to:

- **prepare to change the performer's appearance**

This unit was developed by Skillset, the Sector Skills Council for the Audio Visual Industries.

When preparing to change the performer's appearance it is important to use the skills you have learnt in the following core mandatory units:

G1 ensure your own actions reduce risks to health and safety
G6 promote additional products or services to clients
G11 contribute to the financial effectiveness of the business

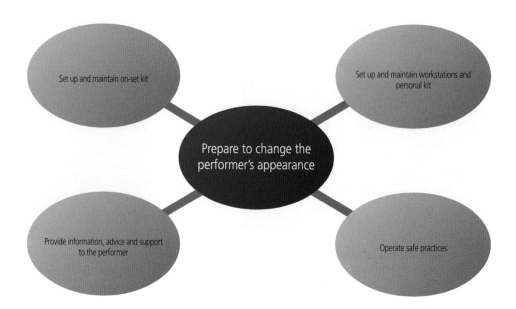

Set up and maintain on-set kit

Set up and maintain workstations and personal kit

Prepare to change the performer's appearance

Provide information, advice and support to the performer

Operate safe practices

INTRODUCTION

When preparing to change a performer's appearance, there are several things to take into consideration before you start. You must be very organised and set up your working area with the relevant kit for the day, and organise kit to take on set. You must operate safe and hygienic working practices and provide information, advice and support to your performer.

ORGANISING AND ARRANGING WORKSTATIONS, MATERIALS AND EQUIPMENT

Suitable work areas for make-up should incorporate:

- Good lighting, usually in a well-lit room, with natural daylight if possible.
- A make-up mirror with light bulbs or fluorescent tubes around it. This will illuminate the face, making it much easier to view your work as you progress.
- Seating for the performer should be comfortable and at the correct height for the artist to work. This is usually provided by means of a high director's chair or barber's chair, which can be adjusted for height.
- The work surface should be of an adequate size to lay out all your equipment. Trolleys are rarely used but do help when work surface space is limited.
- Electric points to plug in hairstyling equipment.
- A sink should be present to wash hands and backwash sinks to wash hair when required.
- A good source of ventilation is important when using hazardous or strong-smelling materials.

Your workstation should be wiped down with a disinfectant cleaner, your personal kit should be kept scrupulously clean at all times and should be set out on a towel when at your workstation.

ON-SET WORK

When going on set you will need a set bag, which ideally should be see-through so you can reach items quickly. It is useful if it has a lid to keep out the rain, dust, leaves etc. It should contain the make-up you have applied to your performer/s in case of touch-ups and all the other essentials such as brushes, sponges, tissues, cotton buds, compact powders, blotting papers, hair pins and grips, hair combs, hairsprays etc. Baby wipes are handy for cleaning any spillages and your own hands. Items will vary according to the type of production and images you have created.

EQUIPMENT LIST

good lighting

a make-up mirror with light bulbs or flourescent around it

seating – high 'director's chair/barber's chair

work surface (not typically a trolley)

electric plug-in points

a sink (and backwash sink?)

Make-up mirror

Make-up chair

OPERATING SAFE WORKING PRACTICES IN THE WORKING ENVIRONMENT

All major companies now require you to have Public Liability insurance and Health and Safety training.

Follow these guidelines:

1 Check that the working environment is safe and hygienic – electrics are in good working order and your workplace is clean. A qualified electrician should check your electrical equipment every 12 months.

2 Wash your hands.

3 Gown up your performer to protect their costume.

4 Use clips to pin hair back off the face.

5 Check for any contra-indications. As a make-up artist you may have to work with contra-indications such as herpes simplex or conjunctivitis. The reason behind this decision is that if a performer is sent home, the whole day/s scheduling has been disrupted and it is both costly and inconvenient to have to reorganise the day/s. Obviously if you consider the situation to be very serious, speak to the director. There are often hundreds of other people involved, therefore if the performer has something contagious it would be more cost-effective to use disposable tools or the performer's own brushes and even to throw products away after use. Do not touch the performer's skin with your hands, and wash them with an anti-bacterial cleanser afterwards.

6 Check if the performer has allergies to any common make-up items or a particular brand. A skin test should be performed when using materials such as adhesives, solvents, latex and other special effects make-up.

7 Work in a hygienic manner, removing products from their own containers as you progress. This can be done with a spatula or the end of your brush, and placed on a palette or the back of your hand.

8 Pay particular attention when working around the eyes, especially if the performer/s are wearing contact lenses.

9 Wash your hands and clean your brushes, sponges and powder puffs on completion of the make-up. These tools can be cleaned using washing up liquid or shampoo and warm water. Specialist brush cleaners are very useful when time is limited, or on set. Electrical equipment such as tongs, clippers and shavers should be wiped over with surgical spirit. Tidy away your make-up and re-stock your set bag ready to follow your performer onto set.

10 When working on set there are many hazards to watch out for – electrical leads and cables, props, other make-up artists set bags, light boxes etc. You constantly have to be aware not to trip over items lying on the floor. They need to be there! You often find yourself ducking and squeezing through places to reach your performers. You must wear flat shoes and nothing that is going to make a noise if you move around whilst filming. You should look clean and presentable at all times.

11 Follow COSHH guidelines. Store all chemicals safely – clearly labelled, upright, replacing lids immediately after use, and in a dark, cool place: a

HEALTH AND SAFETY

Contra-actions can be recognised by:
Redness, itching, rash, burning or stinging. In severe cases there may be blistering. Remove make-up immediately and seek medical advice if necessary.

Work area

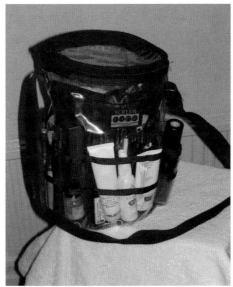

Set bag

lockable cupboard is ideal in a studio situation. Hazardous materials should be disposed of carefully whether you are working in an interior or exterior location. Check manufacturers' instructions for directions of use and disposal.

If the performer has observed all of the above, the will know that they are in safe hands.

Maintaining good working relationships

It is very important that as a student that you experience every type of make-up that you will apply to a performer. You need to explain to them exactly how a process is going to work, how it feels on the skin and how long the process is going to take. Good make-up will help a performer get into character more easily. If you have designs, show them. You also have to be aware that whilst some performers love being in make-up, being pampered and see it as a fascinating process, others positively hate being touched and have little patience when in the make-up chair. You have to be aware of body language and not take things too personally. You should try to build up a good, professional relationship with your artiste and they will often confide in you: therefore confidentiality is paramount. When performers are nervous about particular scenes or have other personal problems, try to be sympathetic and give reassurance. Finally let the performer know how the make-up will be removed.

The performer may be an experienced actor, adult or child or a member of the public. Everyone is an individual and people's moods can change from day to day, however you as a make-up artist should always be cheerful, helpful and reassuring.

Filming taking place (1920's set)

Working area on location

Additional safety

If equipment fails to work when at your workstation or on set, you should check the electrical supply, call one of the electricians to check it out. Do not be tempted to mess around with electricity yourself. It is also a good idea to carry non-electrical appliances such as portable heated curlers, straighteners and rollers just in case you may be shooting in a location where there is no electricity at all. You may also have no water supply, so make sure you have water sprays filled.

On set

Working environments

Before turning up at a job, check where you are likely to be filming. You can then choose your attire and kit accordingly, being prepared for every eventuality. You may be working inside on a small 'interior' fixed television studio set, or a huge film set where it can still be cold in the morning, but end up very hot with sweating performers by the end of the day. Alternatively, you could be on location inside or out, with extremes of temperature. With your own clothing it is best to wear layers so you can add and remove when necessary. When choosing kit, if on location, will you have access to electricity? Do you need everything in waterproof bags and will you even need waterproof make-up? These are some of the questions you need to ask yourself.

Assessment of knowledge and understanding

You have now learnt how to prepare to change the performer's appearance. To test your level of knowledge and understanding, answer the following short questions. These will prepare you for your summative (final) assessment.

1   State the basic make-up and hair kit that you will need for your workstation and on set.

2   What checks should you carry out on your performer before you commence make-up application?

3   What action would you take if service supplies were to be interrupted or fail?

4   Why should products be labelled clearly?

5   State eight contagious skin and hair conditions, and how you would recognise and deal with them.

6   How do you prevent cross-contamination?

7   How often should a qualified electrician check electrical appliances?

8   What does COSHH stand for and how does it affect you in your work?

9   How should you dispose of hazardous make-up and/or hair materials?

10 How and where should hazardous materials be stored?

11 How do you clean make-up/hair materials and equipment?

12 Why should there be easy access to your make-up workstation?

13 What considerations do you need to take when choosing your own footwear and clothing when working?

14 How do you keep your kit and workstation clean, tidy and hygienic in difficult working environments?

BT33 ASSIST WITH THE CONTINUITY OF THE PERFORMER'S APPEARANCE

Learning objectives

This unit measures your ability to assist with the continuity of the performer's appearance.

You must ensure that your performer's make-up and/or hair meet the design specification at the start of shooting and, where appropriate, at the end of the previous sequential take. You must be able to decipher the developing effects presented in the script.

You must also keep complete and accurate continuity records and make sure that your presence on set is not intrusive or disruptive.

The unit describes the competencies that enable you to:

- **assist with the continuity of the performer's appearance**

This unit was developed by Skillset, the Sector Skills Council for the Audio Visual Industries.

When assisting with continuity of the performer's appearance it is important to use the skills you have learnt in the following core mandatory units:

G1 ensure your own actions reduce risks to health and safety
G6 promote additional products or services to clients
G11 contribute to the financial effectiveness of the business

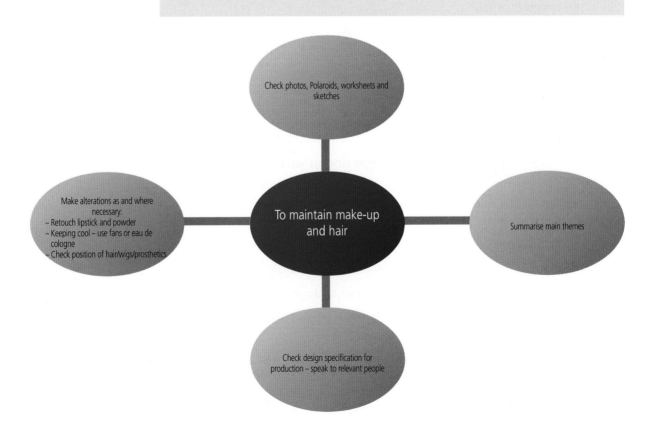

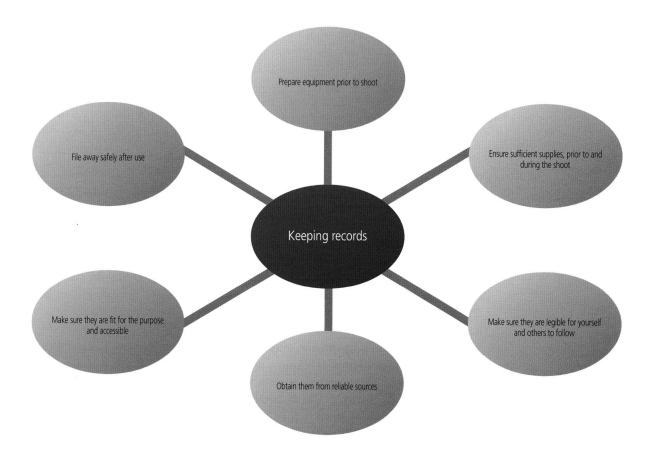

INTRODUCTION

Continuity is the maintenance of continuous action, and consistency of detail in the scenes of the film or programme. For example, you could be filming on one day and shoot several scenes which are not in the order in which they appear in the final film. For instance, you may shoot outdoor scenes one week then interior ones the next. In the final film you may see the performer in the street entering a house but they must look identical inside and out, even though they are shot at different times. You cannot rely on your memory when trying to recreate the look, so you refer to worksheets, make-up notes, Polaroids, digital camera photos and even videotapes as well as your own eyes. On worksheets you can add colour samples of the make-up and attach hair colour samples. Continuity is of the utmost importance when filming and if something is wrong it will be incredibly obvious.

You constantly refer to your reference material throughout the day to check the make-up and hair is as it should be and to check facial hair, wigs and prosthetics are still secure. Lipstick will need retouching and performers will need powdering. You may also have to add tears, dirt or sweat to the performer.

Your story may follow a character over a period of several years, and you would therefore need to consider the effects of ageing, change of hair colour, style and growth, healing of wounds, the progress of disease and the effect of the environment on hair and skin. Skin tones and colours of make-up can change depending on locations, time of day and the general environment that they are placed in. With experience you can anticipate these changes.

Pre-production

When a make-up designer is asked to work on a production, the first real piece of information they will receive is the script, which is then broken down, marking any areas which will affect make-up and hair. The designer will also receive a character list to include background artistes, and a shooting schedule. A meeting will initially take place with the producer, director and costume designer about the design specification for the production, and the budget required. Using this information, the make-up and hair are researched and designed onto the continuity character sheet, details filled in and photos added as the shoot progresses. Test shots can be carried out to check that the make-up and hair is going to work on screen. The director must approve the overall appearance, and the make-up artist takes *their* instructions from the make-up designer. Performers will need to be checked for any allergic reactions, and pre-production make-ups are carried out on the main performers, especially when the script calls for more complicated looks, including prosthetics, wigs, hairpieces, and casualty effects. Wigs etc. will need to be pre-ordered or even made from scratch, depending on the length of preparation time and budget.

Lighting effects

In a television studio, the lighting is already fixed before you arrive on set. If you have done the best make-up job you can with the performer, but they look pretty lousy on the monitor, you can speak nicely about your concerns with the director of photography or the lighting crew, and they may just be able to alter the lighting to make your performer look a bit better.

For exterior shots the lighting will vary depending on the weather and time of day. Often 'fill-in' lighting is used, and silver or gold reflector boards. Interior lighting on location is usually set up for a shorter period, and your make-ups can look different inside and out due to different colour temperatures.

On a film set the performers are lit, rather than the set, so you will find it much more flattering for the overall look of your performer. Much more time is allowed, and there will be lighting changes for close-up, middle and long distance shots.

The keeping and storage of continuity references

Continuity records for the scenes you are filming, and where appropriate, previous sequential ones should be kept on set whilst filming, then stored in the make-up room and indexed in scene order for easy reference when needed. Occasionally a scene may need to be re-shot at a later date. You may have to recreate again a make-up that you did six months previously.

Make sure you always keep a good stock of continuity reference materials and equipment.

Good working relationships and checking your performer

Good working relationships should be maintained at all times, with performers and colleagues. You should always be friendly, calm and professional. When filming you work long hours which can be both tiring and stressful. The make-up room should be a safe haven and always have a good atmosphere. One difficult performer or crew member can cause feelings of animosity and cause problems, which in turn can cause ill-feeling in many others. Teamwork and the support of colleagues are very important.

During filming, when you need to check a performer you need to be as quick, unobtrusive and efficient as possible, so as not to hold up filming. You must position yourself on set carefully. Ideally you should be able to see the monitor and not be standing in the performer's eye line or in the way of filming. Check which way the camera/s are pointing and make sure you are somewhere behind them. Do not stand in anyone else's way or cause an obstruction to colleagues or filming equipment.

Frequency and length of checks will depend on the performers needs and/or the director. Wait for 'checks' to be called before a take. Some performers will like to be fussed over and checked more than others – you will soon find out their needs; some directors will give you more time and opportunity to 'check' than others. Another make-up artist may have to check your performer at some time so make sure your records are accurate and legible.

Remember and realise time factors in the script, how make-up would wear naturally throughout the day, action and environmental conditions. Overall you must achieve realism and credibility on screen.

SIMPLIFIED SCENARIO FOR A TWO-DAY SHOOT

The following example is following one particular character – Julie – and her life over the course of one day and an evening. The lengths of the scenes vary and there are other characters in the film, including her friend Sally and people at the restaurant, on the street, and her attacker. Continuity sheets will be filled out for each main performer. It becomes especially important when the character has different make-up/hair changes and is in more than one scene. If a character is only seen once in one scene and never seen again, continuity sheets are not relevant unless they are going to be wearing particular make-up that is deemed important to the plot or story in some way.

On the first days filming, a substantial amount of time had to be allowed for make-up changes between scenes 2 and 8 and then 8 and 4. Changes had to be carried out as quickly and effectively as possible. A time of 30 minutes was requested by the make-up designer between scenes 2 and 8, and 40 minutes between scenes 8 and 4 as the removal of the previous make-up also had to be taken into account. Remember that between scenes most of the crew have work to do, such as changes of lighting, props and laying camera track, so you are not necessarily holding anyone else up.

SHOOTING SCHEDULE

Filming day one – Interior shots

EP/SC	SET/TIME	CHARACTERS	SYNOPSIS	STORY DAY
1 / 1	Julies house 8am	Julie	Julie getting up. Having breakfast	Day 1
1 / 2	Julies office (home) 12am	Julie	Julie working on computer. Phone conversations	Day 1
1 / 8	Julies house 6pm	Julie Sally	Sally visits Julie. Julie distressed and crying	Eve 2
1 / 4	Int. restaurant 830-1030pm	Julie Sally Waiter 20 x other diners	Meal scene. Discussing men and life in general. Having lovely time.	Eve 1

Filming day two – Exterior shots

EP/SC	SET/TIME	CHARACTERS	SYNOPSIS	STORY DAY
1 / 3	Ext. street outside Julies house 745pm	Julie Sally 2 x passers by	Julie leaving house with Sally to go for dinner.	Eve 1
1 / 5	Ext. restaurant 1045pm	Julie Sally Attacker 1 x passer by	Julie and Sally leave restaurant a bit tidily. Friends say goodnight.	Eve 1
1 / 6	Ext restaurant/street 1050pm	Julie Attacker	Julie gets attacked.	Eve 1
1 / 7	Ext. Street outside Julies house	Julie 2 x passers by	Julie stumbles home. Passers by offer to help. Julie refuses	Eve 1

Anna Bessent

Before make-up

Anna Bessent

Julie scene 1

Anna Bessent

Julie scene 2 – front

Anna Bessent

Julie scene 2 – side

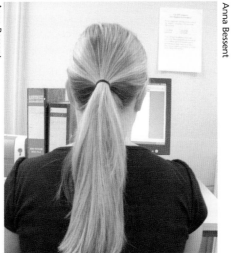

Anna Bessent

Julie scene 2 – back

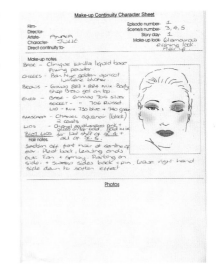

Anna Bessent

Julie scenes 3 and 4

Anna Bessent

Sally scenes 3 and 4 (make-up by S. Foy)

Anna Bessent

Julie scene 3 and 4 – left side

Julie scenes 3 and 4 – back view

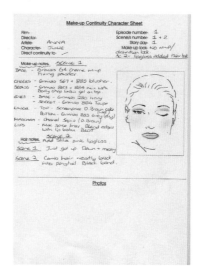

Julie scenes 3 and 4 – right side

Julie and Sally – after meal

Scene 6 – attacked

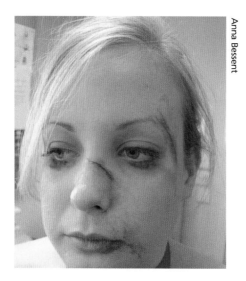

Julie – scene 7 – smudged eyes and blood

Julie scene 8 – next day at home, injuries starting to heal

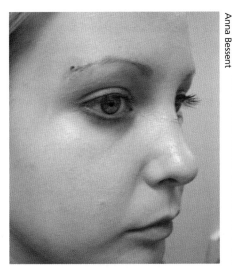

Anna Bessent

Scene 8 – right side

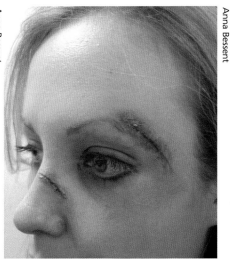

Anna Bessent

Scene 8 – left side

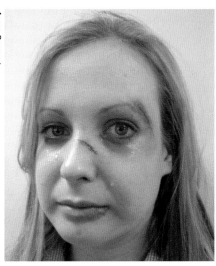

Anna Bessent

Scene 8 – crying

Assessment of knowledge and understanding

You have now learnt how continuity works in a filming environment. These skills will enable you to carry out your job efficiently without making mistakes that will be obvious to the viewer.

To test your knowledge and understanding, answer the following short questions. These will prepare you for your summative (final) assessment.

1 Why is it so important to maintain the continuity of the performer's appearance throughout the production?

2 How do you ensure that the performer's make-up and hair meets the design specification for the production?

3 Who are the decision-makers, and how do you check that they approve your changes?

4 How do you record continuity detail?

5 Why is it important to have a good supply of continuity materials and equipment?

6 How do you store continuity details, and how do you ensure that they are available and accessible to those that may need them?

7 Where should you stand on set?

8 How do you minimise disruption of the production when making continuity changes?

BT34 APPLY MAKE-UP TO CHANGE THE PERFORMER'S APPEARANCE

Learning objectives

This unit describes how to apply make-up to change the performer's appearance.

To achieve this unit you must show that you are able to ensure that your performer is comfortable and fully informed about the make-up process. You must check that the make-up is compatible with the performer's skin, taking action if there is an adverse skin reaction. You must apply the selected make-up to achieve the desired effect 'on camera'.

It describes the competencies to enable you to:

- **apply make-up to change the performer's appearance**

This unit was developed by Skillset, the Sector Skills Council for the Audio Visual Industries.

When applying make-up to change the performer's appearance it is important to use the skills you have learnt in the following core mandatory units:

G1 ensure your own actions reduce risks to health and safety
G6 promote additional products or services to clients
G11 contribute to the financial effectiveness of the business

INTRODUCTION

When applying make-up to a performer, first carry out all the health and safety checks mentioned in HM1, refer to your make-up and continuity notes, and make sure your performer is comfortable on the make-up chair.

1 If there is a headrest, make sure it is in a suitable position, height and angle wise to minimise any discomfort. Do not assume that they are comfortable, ask!

2 Inform your performer of the process you are going to carry out on them and encourage them to ask questions.

3 Check the performer's skin type so suitable skin care, make-up and removers can be chosen.

4 Ask them if they have allergies to any make-up products. It is useful to carry more than one brand just in case this occurs, and choose brands that are known to be good for use on sensitive skins.

5 If you are using any special effects products, carry out a skin compatibility test 24 hours before.

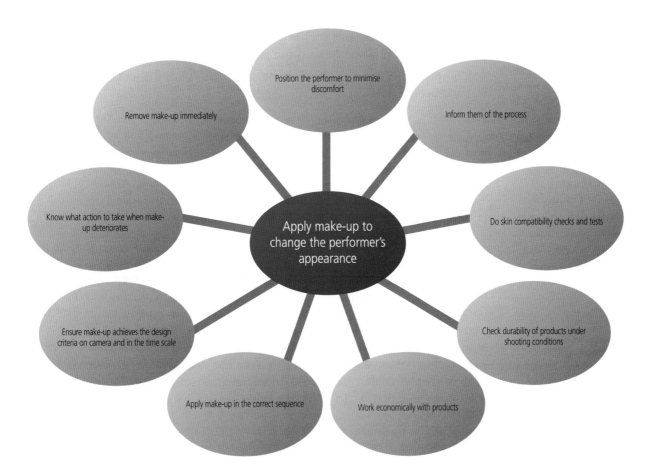

Position the performer to minimise discomfort

Inform them of the process

Remove make-up immediately

Do skin compatibility checks and tests

Know what action to take when make-up deteriorates

Apply make-up to change the performer's appearance

Check durability of products under shooting conditions

Ensure make-up achieves the design criteria on camera and in the time scale

Work economically with products

Apply make-up in the correct sequence

6   Choose products that are compatible with your performer's skin type so maximum durability can be obtained. For example, if they have an oily skin, do not use a heavily moisturising foundation for a dry skin as it will need powdering much more frequently and cause a build up, appearing 'cakey' by the end of the day.

7   Consider the durability of all products you use so you can limit the number of times you have to retouch your performer.

8   Some products work better in certain environmental conditions. For example, do not use a liquid foundation and other non-waterproof cosmetics for a scene shot outside in the rain where the make-up could run, unless it is deemed necessary to the plot.

9   If the above does happen you will have to take immediate action to rectify it, so make sure you have all the relevant products in your set bag, ready to retouch your performer.

10 If a performer does have a reaction to a particular make-up product, remove it immediately with an appropriate cleanser for a sensitive skin, splash the face with cold water and ask them to seek medical assistance if necessary.

11 Use your products in an economical way. Do not remove more than you are going to need from a container, as this causes wastage. Place lids back on containers to prevent evaporation and spillage.

12 Make sure you apply make-up in the required sequence, using appropriate techniques to get the best results.

13 Ensure that the image you have created matches the design brief, and make sure you have checked the result on camera.

14 Complete the make-up in the time stated on the call sheet, which will have been approved by the designer.

MAKE-UP EFFECTS

Corrective

This refers to the type of make-up that is almost invisible to the eye. It is very useful for 'no make-up looks', which the male performer will generally always have, unless there is special character make-up involved. The corrective make-up is applied to the female performer if she is the type of character who does not wear any make-up, or for that type of scene, but still needs to look her best, or for when she has just got up out of bed. Definition is needed for the camera, as the face can look flat without it. We need to cover blemishes, give definition to the eyes and lips and sometimes to strengthen cheekbones and jaw lines, and basically make the performer look more presentable. To apply the make-up, follow these basic steps.

Males

1 Apply a light wash of liquid foundation or concealer in the places where it is needed. It should look natural.

2 Apply powder to set.

3 Neaten up eyebrows.

4 Add some lip balm if the lips look dry.

It is very rare that you will need to apply any colour to the cheeks, eyes or lips. The performer may have a very good skin and you may just need powder. Use your judgement.

Females

1 Apply colour corrector under the foundation if necessary.

2 Apply foundation to even out the skin tone.

3 Apply concealer over any blemishes.

4 Apply powder to set the base.

5 Brush on a natural pink/peach colour to the apples of the cheeks.

6 Check eyebrows; add colour and/or a brow gel to set them in place.

7 Brush on a pale matt shade as a base over the whole eye area.

8 Using a sable brown shade, apply colour to the socket.

9 Brush on pale grey dry shadow under the lower lashes.

10 Apply a very thin line of dark brown to the upper lash line.

11 Apply dark brown mascara.

12 Use a neutral lip pencil to outline the lips.

13 Brush on a clear lip base or balm to the lips. Blend in the lip liner so there is no hard line.

Anna Bessent

Before

Anna Bessent

Base applied

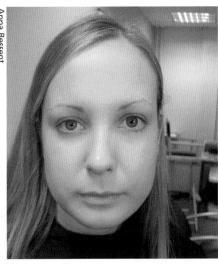

Anna Bessent

Subtle blusher added to the apples of the cheeks

Anna Bessent

Eye socket colour added

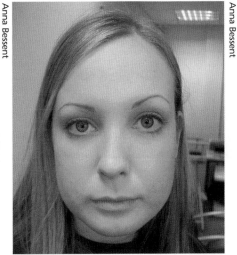

Anna Bessent

Finished corrective make-up – brow colour, mascara and lip liner added

Glamour

A glamorous make-up on a female performer could result in many different looks. Follow the same formula as above but add more product and colour so it is obvious the performer is wearing make-up. You may wish to colour co-ordinate to match the clothing.

Death

When simulating death, it is important to find out how the character died, what the cause was, and how long they have been dead. Do your research carefully. The natural colour will leave the skin tone and the character will

Glamorous 1920's make-up

appear paler and often more of a straw colour or greyed tone. Shading will need to be added to the frontal bone on the forehead, temples, under cheekbones, the eye area and naso-labial fold. For example, if someone died of heart failure, the skin tone will take on a purple hue, and the lips would look quite blue. If the problem were liver failure, then the skin tone would look yellowish. Make sure you take colour over the lips, to remove the natural redness.

Certain companies produce 'Death colours' and even special wheels. The pictures show how to help simulate the death and decaying process.

Base is applied

Shading added

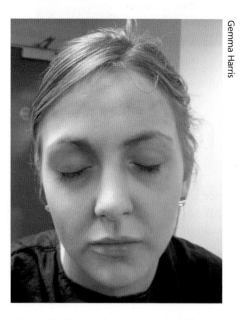

Extra shading colours and mottling

Finished result

Ageing

When ageing a performer, you need to find out how old they should look. It is possible that you may need to age them throughout the production, which is a real challenge along with continuity. For male performers, facial hair and spectacles can be a great help along with changes to their own hair and make-up. For the female performer, the emphasis will be on the make-up, hairstyle and possibly spectacles. Along with the make-up artist's work, costume will also play a big part, as will the acting.

As we age the skin tone will become greyer. We need to apply a shader or darker colour into all the wrinkles and natural indentations of the face, and then to give a three-dimensional effect, apply a highlighter or paler colour to all the protruding areas of the face and on the opposite side to the wrinkles and folds of the face. You can successfully age a performer by about 20 years with highlight and shading; after that you need to work with latex or old age stipple to visibly wrinkle the skin, or prosthetics which will create three-dimensional eye pouches, jowls and so on.

Facial ageing with highlight and shadow

1 Determine how old your performer needs to appear.

2 Mix an old age cream-based make-up and the performer's natural shade together with this. This also applies to black skins. Apply all over the face and hands. If more of the body area requires covering, use the same colours in a cake make-up. Cake make-up is a water-based make-up, which is used for body make-up. Apply using a damp sponge; once dry it can be buffed with a soft cloth or chamois leather to give a slight sheen, making it look very realistic.

3 Examine the natural folds and wrinkles in your performer's skin. Starting at the forehead, paint the shader colour, which will be a dark grey/brown, into any lines where wrinkles would appear.

4 Continue down the face, shade the inner eye sockets and draw the colour down the sides of the nose.

5 Sink in the temples at the sides of the face and under the cheekbones.

6 Going back to the eyes, paint in the lines in between the brows, then the eye pouches under the eyes, and any laughter lines at the outer corners.

7 Apply shader around the edges of the nose and into the naso-labial fold which runs from the lower side of the nose to the outer edge of the mouth. Feather the colour outwards.

8 Draw down the corners of the mouth.

9 Shade the indentation above the top lip.

10 Shade under the lower lip, bringing the colour outwards around the fleshy part of the chin.

11 Add some shading to the jowl area if the character needs it.

12 Continue down the neck, following lines and indentations.

13 Add highlighter to the opposite sides of the forehead wrinkles, laughter lines and the folds of the face. Also apply it to any protruding parts such as the centre of the nose, chin, apples of the cheeks and top of the cheekbones.

14 Finally, blend to soften the edges, taking care not to blend everything away or one line into another!

Before   Ageing – front view   Ageing – side view

Types of camera film

It is always better to check your make-ups on the monitor to see the final effect on film, but it is also a good idea to know what sort of camera film is involved in the production. You may come across:

Electronic

This is basically videotape. It is much cheaper than film and produces a hard clinical look in its natural form. Lighting, camera lenses and filters can alter the effect. It is widely used in television for soap operas, documentaries, sport, news, game shows, other studio-based work and many series/productions.

Also included are home video and the use of digital camcorders, which are used on home and garden make-over programmes.

8mm

This is now just about obsolete. It has been used in recent years for 'special effects' to produce an old home movie effect.

16mm

This has been superseded by super 16mm.

Super 16mm

This is fairly standard in the industry and widely used for better quality projects. It is more expensive than shooting on video, and used on the top end high-quality drama series and also for most commercials.

35mm

This is the best quality. It is used for all movies plus many American-produced series and better quality projects in general, especially those that are aiming to achieve worldwide sales. It produces a much more flattering effect on the performer, picking up more detail and being more forgiving on skin tones.

SPECIAL EFFECTS MAKE-UP

This is an area of make-up that covers injuries, diseases, three-dimensional work and some character effects. It can be especially challenging for the make-up artist and can involve extensive research.

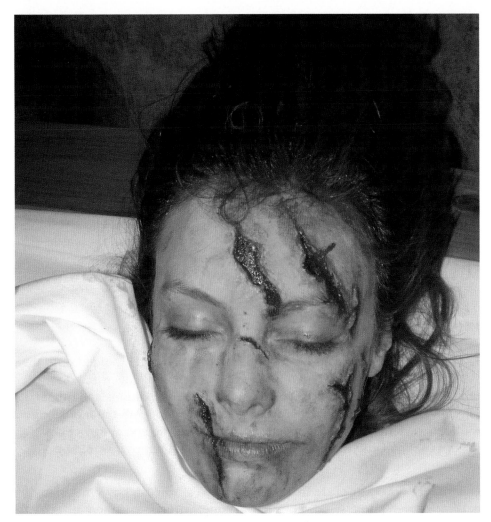

Dead victim – deep wounds created with wax

Slit throat – face missing ear lobes and blood efffects

Research

Research must be carried out thoroughly. Sources may include medical publications and forensic pathology books and subject-knowledgeable people, so you need to be able to switch off and have a strong stomach. Injuries may need to be created fresh then recreated at various stages of the healing process. Remember about continuity!

Products available

Derma wax is a fabulous product, which is softened and moulded onto the skin with a modelling tool, leaving very fine transparent edges that do not require colouring. It can be used for a large variety of wounds and other effects such as pimples. It is removed by scraping it off with the modelling tool. Any stickiness left can be removed with cleansing cream or alcohol. Do not use too close to the eyes, as application and removal would be uncomfortable for the performer.

Gelatine is a product made from horse's hooves. You can buy vegetarian gelatine as well as the standard variety at supermarkets. It is then mixed with

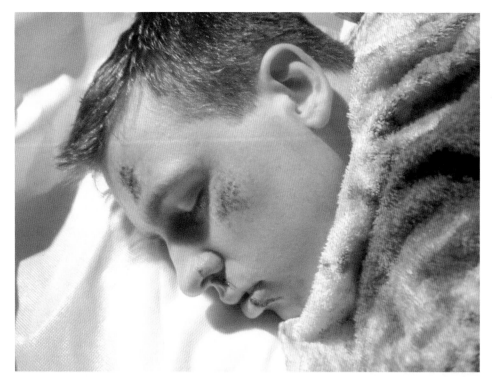

Grazes and split lip created with wax and latex

boiling water and glycerine. If you are limited for time it can be purchased ready made in a block and heated in a microwave or a bowl full of boiling water. It is useful in the creation of burns and 3-D appliances such as eye bags and split lips, as it is removed very easily with warm water.

Liquid latex has a variety of uses such as ageing and as a false skin. It can be painted on and left to dry, or use a hairdryer to accelerate the drying. It is useful in the production of burns, and skin diseases if combined with food ingredients. It is removed from the skin by peeling it off. Avoid hairy areas, as it would be very painful to remove.

Scar material is available in a tube such as tuplast, which is like semi-liquid glue and makes excellent blisters, pimples, chicken pox and other raised scars. Liquid scar material in a bottle, such as collodian, is painted on and leaves indented scars by contracting and drawing in the skin. It is removed by gently peeling it from the skin.

Food ingredients such as porridge oats, rice crispies, cornflakes and other cereals, treacle, food colourings, coffee granules and tea can be used in combination with adhesives and any of the above to create effects where texture is needed. For example, to create eczema, you could apply a red tint to the area first, then some latex with some porridge oats on top, then a final layer of latex to seal. Add more colour if necessary for the effect you require.

Colours for bruising and other effects are usually achieved by means of creme or oil-based make-up, as it is the most realistic. There are also gel bruise shades available, which have a transparent effect and palettes such as skin illustrator, which require alcohol to activate them, and are extremely waterproof and durable.

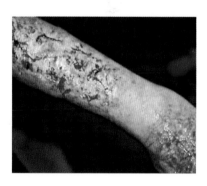

Gelatine burns (2 different effects)

Scar material and bruising

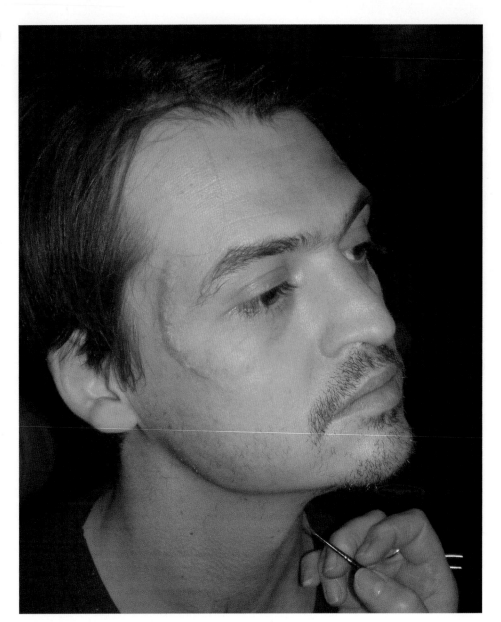

Blood depending on the brand it is also available in liquid for fresh wounds, gel and more solid forms, like wound fillers, to simulate older and dried-out blood effects and scabs. Be aware that some bloods can stain skin and clothing.

Other useful items

- Glycerine – for shine or to mix with gelatine for flexibility.
- Petroleum and KY jelly – for blisters and oozing or shiny effects.
- Tear stick – menthol stick to help produce tears.
- Spray bottles – for water and glycerine mix to simulate perspiration.
- Eye/ear dropper – for placing tears and blood.
- Sealer – hardens wax products and seals edges.
- Spirit gum/mastix adhesives and appropriate remover.

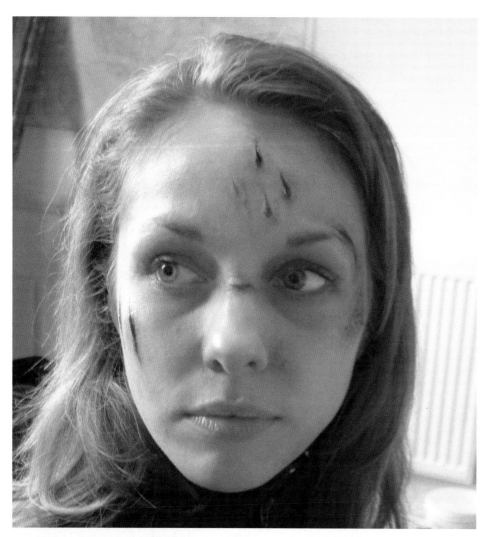

Waterproof injury make-up
(injuries occurred at different
times)

- Scissors.
- Hair pins – for adding colour by dotting and dragging.
- Black cotton – for simulating stitches.
- Modelling tools – for sculpting wounds, creating scratches and texture.
- Stipple sponges – for texturising and creating grazes.
- Tooth enamel – for creating missing, chipped and rotten teeth and bleeding gums. Available in black, nicotine, white, ivory, red and gold.
- Barrier cream – helps to protect the skin. Find one that is not greasy.

HEALTH AND SAFETY

1 Carry out skin compatibility tests on your performer.
2 Remove the products gently with the correct remover.
3 Make sure you have experienced the products on your own skin so you can advise your performer of what they feel like.
4 Check your performer is comfortable during application and retouching. You may be doing a leg or back injury and need them in a reclined or upright position. Make sure you keep them warm and protect their privacy. They may be required to lie down for long durations outside which could bring on hypothermia, so keep an eye on them.

Beaten up

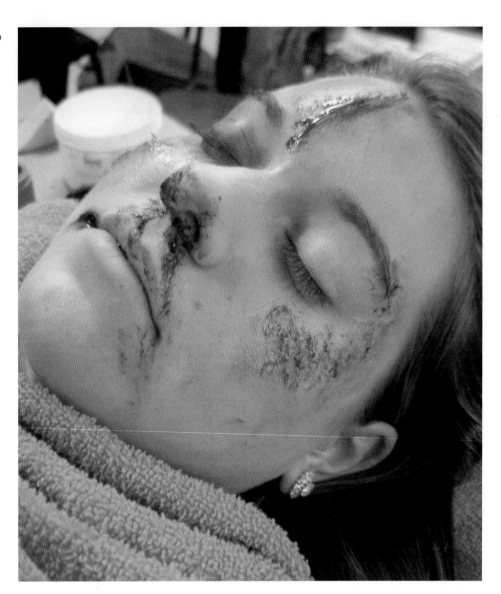

You should refer back to BT32 and BT33 for other health and safety aspects and care of your performer.

HEALTH AND SAFETY

Skin compatibility tests

These are of the utmost importance when carrying out special effects make-up, as performers are much more likely to react to the chemicals in these products and removers. Carry out the tests 24 hours before on an area of skin preferably close to the area where you are planning on using the product. The best place is behind the ear, so it is fairly hidden by the hair. Do not apply it on the face itself just in case there is a reaction.

If a contra-action occurs, you would recognise it by redness, rash, itching, burning, and stinging sensations. Remove the make-up immediately in a careful manner and ask them to seek medical assistance if it looks serious. It is important to note that a slight redness is quite normal after peeling off latex and collodian and even after scraping off wax. Please inform your performer that this is quite likely to happen to prevent any unnecessary panicking.

Suitability to skin, environment and durability

The products should have now been tested for use on the performer's skin, by means of the skin compatibility test. You also have to consider the durability of the product. You may have been asked to produce an old scar down a performer's cheek and be trying to decide whether to use collodian or latex. A performer may be slightly more likely to react to collodian, but if it has to be in place 12 hours a day, you may find latex would have peeled off by then. You may have to reapply the scar half way through the day. Also the product may deteriorate more quickly on a certain area such as near joints and creases, and need reapplying more often.

Assessment of knowledge and understanding

You have now learnt how to apply make-up to change the performer's appearance. To test your level of knowledge and understanding, answer the following short questions. These will prepare you for your summative (final) assessment.

1 State how you would carry out a skin compatibility test.
2 State how you would use make-up and special effects products economically.
3 What are skin types, and how would you recognise each one?
4 Which products are most likely to be incompatible with your performer's skin?
5 How are make-up and special effects products likely to deteriorate when subjected to different shooting conditions?
6 State the health and safety precautions you should carry out before and during application and removal of special effects products.
7 State what types of make-up and special effects products would be suited to different shooting conditions, e.g. windy and rainy.
8 How should you position your performer to alleviate discomfort when applying make-up?
9 How should you position your performer to alleviate discomfort when applying special effects make-up?

BT35 APPLY SPECIAL EFFECTS

Learning objectives

This unit describes how to apply, fix and dress facial hair to change the performer's appearance. You must ensure that your performer is comfortable and fully informed about the process and be able to select adhesives that are skin compatible, prepare the skin and take action if there is an adverse skin reaction. You must apply and fix the facial hair to achieve the desired effect 'on camera', and dress facial hair using styling and finishing techniques that achieve the required design. You will also need to select and attach loose hair to achieve the desired design effect.

It describes the competencies to enable you to:

● **apply special effects**

This unit was developed by Skillset, the Sector Skills Council for the Audio Visual Industries.

When applying, fixing and dressing facial hair it is important to use the skills you have learnt in the following core mandatory units:

G1 ensure your own actions reduce risks to health and safety
G6 promote additional products or services to clients
G11 contribute to the financial effectiveness of the business

INTRODUCTION

Facial hair is an important part of changing a performer's appearance. It is used widely in period productions, is useful in the ageing process of males, and great for the creation of certain characters. Facial hair includes beards, moustaches, sideburns, whiskers and eyebrows. Colours and pieces need to be chosen carefully to create a realist effect.

Lace-backed facial hair

Ready made lace-backed beards and moustaches can be ordered from specialist wigmakers and require a sample of the performer's own hair or the colour of the wig they may be wearing. They take a considerable amount of time, skill and patience to make, as each hair is hand knotted onto fine lace. The finest of lace is used for film work. Measurements of the area should be given if possible, as ill-fitting facial hair can cause great discomfort to the performer, affecting their performance and speech. Cheaper ready-made facial hair can be purchased from outlets such as professional make-up and fancy dress suppliers. All facial hair will generally require dressing before application to the performer's face.

Equipment

- Ready-made human hair lace-backed facial hair.
- Pin tail comb.
- Adhesive – may be called different names depending on brand: mastix, spirit gum, matte lace adhesive, medical adhesives for very sensitive skins, water based mastix for short durations etc.
- Remover – mastix/spirit gum remover or surgical spirit.
- Chin block and pins.
- Facial hair tongs and heater.
- Cotton wool, cotton buds and brushes.

Application

1 Your performer should have been allergy tested. See HM6 for details of the skin compatibility test.

2 Gown up your performer, make sure they are in a comfortable upright position, explain the process and check the skin is free from any grease.

EQUIPMENT LIST

ready made human hair lace backed facial hair

pin tail comb

adhesive

remover (mastix/spirit remover/surgical spirit)

chin block and pins

facial hair tongs and heater

cotton wool, cotton buds and brushes

Apply and fix facial hair to change performer's appearance

- Position performer for easy access and to minimise discomfort
- Inform performer of application process and any potential discomfort
- Carry out skin compatibility tests
- Prepare skin for adhesion
- Position facial hair correctly to meet design specification
- Check positioning for comfort and mobility
- Know what action to take in case of durability problems or adverse skin reaction
- Complete application to meet time schedules
- Ensure the desired effect is achieved on camera
- Use cleansing methods to keep hair in good condition
- Ensure hair is correctly and safely removed and stored

Before female to male conversion

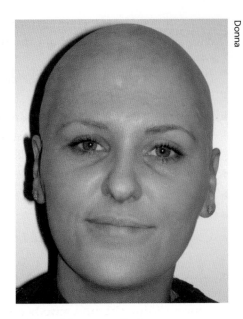

With bald cap applied

Completed make-up with lace backed facial hair

You will need to ask your performer to turn their head, and raise their chin as necessary throughout the process, so check that they are comfortable at all times.

3 Hold the piece up to the performers face to check size, overall look and position.

4 Apply adhesive to the actor's skin using a brush. Wait until tacky.

5 Press the piece in place. A tail comb or dampened powder puff is useful to do this. Take care not to get adhesive all over your fingers.

6 Check position again. Look at them in the make-up mirror.

7 Make sure all edges are secured down properly and that the performer can move their face comfortably.

8 Dress the facial hair further if necessary.

NB If you are working with a large piece, glue the middle first and work outwards to the edges. Explain to your performer that the area will feel a bit tight where the adhesive has been applied. If applying a full beard or sideburns, lift up the performer's own hair in front of the ears, and place the piece under their natural hair to hide the join.

Lace backed facial whiskers

DRESSING FACIAL HAIR TO THE DESIGN BRIEF

You may be working on a contemporary (present day), or a period production. Moustaches and beards may come as standard but you will need to adapt them to the performer's face and the era. Research well and get the

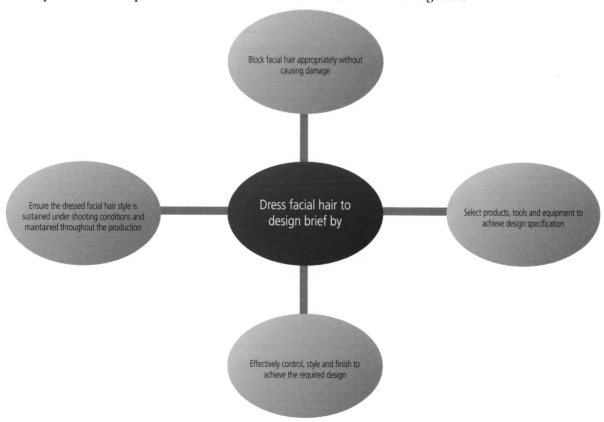

Block facial hair appropriately without causing damage

Ensure the dressed facial hair style is sustained under shooting conditions and maintained throughout the production

Dress facial hair to design brief by

Select products, tools and equipment to achieve design specification

Effectively control, style and finish to achieve the required design look right. Use reference pictures and check the image achieves the design criteria specified on camera. Facial hair may be trimmed with scissors or a beard trimmer, and styled using hot irons and styling products, just as you would on natural hair. Wherever possible style the facial hair on a block before applying it to the performer's face. It can be styled whilst on the performer's face but take great care to have your performer steady and comfortable, and do not touch the face with the tongs.

1 Pin the facial hair piece to the block.

2 Heat the tongs and test the temperature on a tissue.

3 Starting at the top of the hairpiece, take a section at a time, lifting and tonging the hair from the roots.

4 Comb into place.

5 Dressing aids such as moustache wax and hairsprays can be used to keep elaborate styles in place.

Removal and cleaning the facial hair

Make sure you place a towel around the shoulders of your performer in case of any drips. Using a clean brush, apply remover first to loosen the edges of the facial hair, then over the whole area until it is easily released from the skin. On no account should you pull at it. This can harm the performer's skin as well as the delicate lace edges. Clean any remaining adhesive from the skin using a little more remover on some cotton wool until the area no longer feels sticky.

To clean the facial hair, place it on a clean tissue or lint-free towel and using a firm stipple brush, or toothbrush, dab and stipple remover onto the lace which displaces it onto the towel, taking great care not to cause any damage to the lace. Remove and reposition as the towel or tissue gets loaded with adhesive. Be patient when cleaning as it can take quite a bit of time. More stubborn adhesive can be cleaned with acetone, but remember it is more harsh then other removers. Facial hair will not last forever, so it must be looked after. After cleaning, the hairpieces should be allowed to dry and stored pinned to a board or chin block.

ATTACHING LOOSE HAIR TO CHANGE A PERFORMER'S APPEARANCE

Loose hair can come from various sources – yak, acrylic, human hair – but more commonly crepe hair/wool is used. Crepe hair, the cheapest option, comes braided, and is most commonly used in theatre as it is not as realistic as human hair lace-backed pieces. However, it can be used for distance shots and for background characters. It also has the advantage of no observable edges like a lace-backed facial hairpiece, and is a great back up when you suddenly need to produce a beard and there is no time to order one. It can also be used to blend an obvious lace edge. The process from preparation to application can seem quite complicated at first, but is in fact easy when you have done it a couple of times.

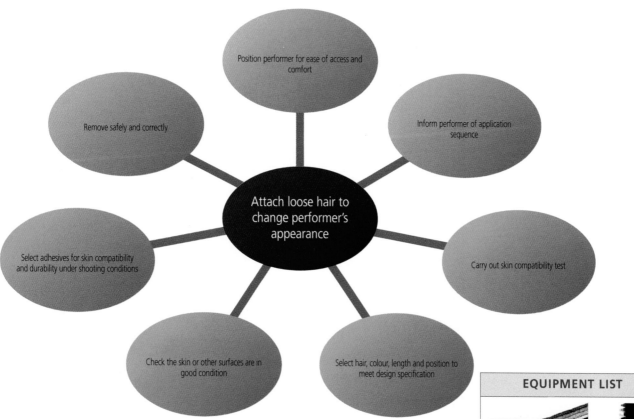

Position performer for ease of access and comfort

Inform performer of application sequence

Remove safely and correctly

Attach loose hair to change performer's appearance

Select adhesives for skin compatibility and durability under shooting conditions

Carry out skin compatibility test

Check the skin or other surfaces are in good condition

Select hair, colour, length and position to meet design specification

Equipment

- crepe wool
- scissors
- tweezers
- modelling tool or pin tail comb
- acetone and bowl
- eyebrow pencils
- fine tooth comb
- mastix/spirit gum
- mastix/spirit gum remover
- iron/straighteners/tongs.

Optional

- hackle
- latex thinned with distilled water
- curling irons.

EQUIPMENT LIST

crepe wool

scissors

modelling tool or pin tail comb

acetone and bowl

eyebrow pencils

fine tooth comb

mastix/spirit gum

mastix/spirit gum remover

iron/straighteners/tongs

hackle

latext thinned with distilled water

curling irons

Work area ready for application
of crepe hair

Preparation

1 Choose the colour/s you require – hair is available in over 20 shades including bright red, green, blue and yellow as well as more natural colours. It is possible to mix as many colours together as you wish to get a perfect match. You will also get a more realistic effect if you take the main colour which is closest to the performer's own hair colour, then also select one shade lighter and one shade darker.

2 Pull some hair out of the braid. You will need roughly 1/4 metre to end up with a full beard and moustache.

3 Straighten the hair with tongs, straighteners, or an iron until you are happy with the result. You can leave the hair un-straightened if you require African-Caribbean facial hair, and to the other end of the spectrum, you will need it poker straight for Oriental hair. For Caucasian hair leave it with a very slight wave.

4 Start to tease the hair out along its length. What you have to remember is that the hairs running through this length are approximately 15 cm long. Try not to pull it too much or the length will break, but remember it is not the end of the world if this does happen.

5 Always keeping your fingers that 15 cm apart, split the length of hair in two.

6 Continue to split into two until you end up with one piece which will be approximately 15 cm. Your hair is now prepared.

7 If you need to mix other colours in, now is the best time to do it.

8 Place one colour on top of the other length, and holding each length, pull, and then take the piece back to its original position. You can use a hackle (a board with pins on it), if you have access to one, which is useful for blending of colours, especially if you have lots of beards to create.

Before

Laying on hair – front view

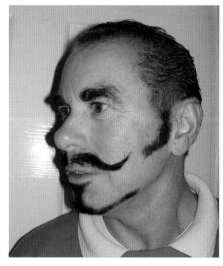
Laying on hair – side view

Method for laying on hair

1 Prepare the skin.

2 Apply adhesive to the area you are working on.

3 Start layering the hair with the first piece under the chin and continue as per the illustration. Fan the hair out and press in place with the end of your scissors or modelling tool.

4 Use the acetone after applying each section to clean the adhesive off your scissors or modelling tool.

5 Each section laid, overlaps the previous section so no joins can be perceived.

6 As you lay up the face change your colour slightly for the very top sections (7, 8, 9).

7 Use a towel over the whole beard to press the beard onto the skin. This will make sure the beard is fully secure and lasts all day.

8 Tweezers can be used to pull out any thick clumps of hair.

9 When the moustache is applied, trim it carefully. Use the towel to press it onto the skin. You do not want any bits falling out throughout the day and ending up in the performer's mouth.

10 Trim the whole beard to shape.

11 Comb through to remove any stray hairs that are not stuck down properly.

12 An eyebrow pencil can be used to fill in any gaps in the beard or moustache.

13 Use professional curling irons to lift and shape the beard.

14 If you do not have these, you can use a mixture of liquid latex and distilled water. Apply this to your hands and pat over the beard. It gives the beard a personality. You can also use hairspray or other hair preparations for this.

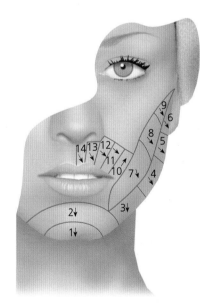
Sequence of application for laying on a full beard and moustache

- Make sure the skin is free from any grease before starting. Wait for the adhesive to go tacky before applying. If you do not, you run the risk of it falling off again.
- Apply the hair as if it is growing straight out from the skin. This adds realism and if applied well looks realistic close up. As stated previously this method is used mainly for theatre, but can also be used successfully for long distance shots or for background artistes in television.
- Practise on a ceramic head and pre-make facial hair in advance.
- Always have equipment laid out in an organised manner. Observe the direction of growth on real beards and moustache.
- Mastix or spirit gum will dry out quickly so do not over-glue an area.

Removal

Use the mastix or spirit gum remover rather than acetone, as it is very drying on the skin. There is a surgical spirit-based cream available for use on the skin, which is gentler than the liquid. You can 'float off' the whole beard to save it for use again by using remover carefully and ease it off as you would with a lace-backed beard. Spray the beard as you go with a liquid fixative or strong hairspray.

Stubble beards

Stubble may be created by different methods, either using a stipple sponge and crème-based colour alongside a slight natural beard growth, or with shadow and loose hair attached with stubble paste. It is not always possible for the performer to grow a beard in time, as filming schedules may require the performer to be clean-shaven in one scene and with three days' stubble in the next.

Application

If your performer has dark hair, it is useful to apply some shading underneath the cut hair first. You can do this with either a crème base and powder or a powder shadow along the beard area. Cut up your loose hair on a tissue, and trim to the length/number of days growth you require. Apply stubble paste evenly to the area. Using a blusher brush, 'pick up' the cut hair on the end, and brush it over the paste. It will stick well and give the appearance of short stubbly hairs sticking out of the skin.

Removal

The easiest way to remove a stubble beard is to apply a generous amount of cleansing cream, massage it into the beard and then remove using a modelling tool and a shaving movement down the face. Wipe the mixture onto a tissue. Repeat again over the area and your performer should then be clean and hair-free.

Assessment of knowledge and understanding

You have now learnt about applying, fixing and dressing facial hair. To test your knowledge and understanding, answer the following short questions. These will prepare you for your summative (final) assessment.

Facial hair on lace

1 What products and tools do you need to clean facial hair?

2 Which products would you use to
   a. Clean adhesive from the face, and
   b. Clean stubborn adhesive from the lace?

3 Where would you source facial hair and what details may the company need in order to carry out your requests?

4 Name the different types of adhesives available and when you are likely to use them?

5 How would you go about dressing facial hair?

6 What should you test the tongs on before applying to the hair?

Loose hair

1 When may you decide to lay on a beard with loose hair and what are its advantages?

2 What types of loose hair are available when laying a beard directly onto the face?

3 How do you prepare the hair before applying to the face?

4 How would you mix different colours of hair?

5 Where on the face would you start to lay a beard?

6 Describe how you would carry out a skin test.

7 What other safety precautions should you observe when laying facial hair?

chapter 19

G12 Check how successful your business idea will be

Learning objectives

This unit describes how to research and check on how successful your business idea will be. It discusses:

- **being able to explain your business idea**
- **identifying the market for your business**
- **using the information you have researched to make a sound decision that your business will be a success**

This unit has been developed by the Small Firms Enterprise Development Initiative (SFEDI) as part of the standards to start your own business.

INTRODUCTION

When deciding to set up your own beauty therapy business it is essential to look at all the options and make sure that your business idea will work. Planning properly for success will give you a much better chance of succeeding.

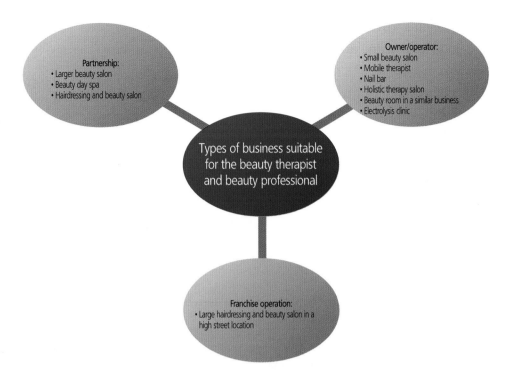

There are several types of business that you could be suitable for the beauty therapist:

- Setting up a new business, such as an independent room within an existing business, a salon, or a mobile therapist.

- An existing single business that you might buy.

- A franchise operation, which you could buy into.

EXPLAINING YOUR BUSINESS IDEA

Describing what your business will be is necessary if you are to have a clear idea of what you want to achieve. There are a number of options, including a beauty therapy salon offering a full range of treatments through to a more specialist service offering holistic treatments only or a nail technician service only. More specialist treatments will reduce the number of potential clients you have, so it is especially important to do your market research to make sure that this is viable.

Being able to explain why your business is going to be successful will take research into all areas of setting up and running your business, including how you are going to finance it, where the money will come from, where it will be situated and how profitable it will be when it is running.

The skills you will need to run your business successfully will include:

- managing finances
- managing people
- managing workflow and resources

- managing information
- a good knowledge of law and regulations that affect business
- marketing skills
- qualifications in the treatment areas you intend to provide if working yourself
- you will also need to be able to stay motivated – even when things are not easy – and to be a self-starter who wants to succeed.

FINANCING THE START-UP OF YOUR BUSINESS

You will need to have clear costings for how much money you will need to start your business. This will include:

- how much your equipment will cost
- how much your products will cost
- how much your consumables will cost
- the cost of the business building (leasehold or freehold), or room
- the price you will pay if you are buying an existing business
- how much you will need if you are doing building alterations or decoration

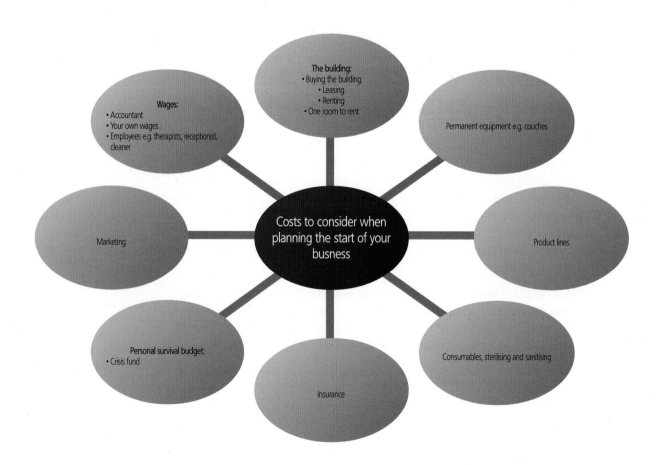

- marketing costs
- money you will need to run as you start up but are not making any profit: this includes your own and any employees' wages
- a personal survival budget so you can still afford your own living expenses
- a crisis fund or budget so you have extra money in case of an unforeseeable event.

How much should you charge your clients in order to be profitable?

This will vary depending upon your overheads, but it is important not to under charge. You must cover your running costs for each treatment and also meet the profit targets you have set your self in order to be successful.

Example

You have worked out that your overheads, that is the cost of everything from your heating and lighting through to your products, average out at £10.00 an hour if you are open for 40 hours a week.

This means you must take more than £10.00 an hour if you are to start to make a profit. You will not be able to have every single hour booked, so this must be taken into account. You may decide, therefore, that you need to be taking at least £20.00 an hour in order to meet your costs and make some profit. Treatments such as waxing where you would charge £12.00 for a half leg wax, which takes 20 minutes, would therefore be profitable if you could fit three into an hour. A full facial, which takes an hour but for which you only charge £15.00, would not be profitable.

Market research is essential in order to make sure you can charge enough to make your business work. Check local prices to see where you can position your own prices. It is possible to be easily affordable and work at getting a lot of clients through the door or go to the other end of the market and be expensive but have fewer clients. Either way can be successful.

The contingency fund

It is a good idea to have a fund of money that is for emergencies and unforeseen problems. This can be the difference between success or failure if you hit a problem. There are a number of things that may affect your business and are beyond your control.

For example:

- You may be unable to work due to ill health or an accident.
- Business rates may be increased beyond your budget.
- There may be a downturn in the economy, which results in fewer people coming into the salon.

Deciding on the kind of business that you want

This could be as simple as having a personal preference. It is necessary, however, to make sure that it is viable. If you dream of a nail bar but there are already a number in your local area it may be that you would not be able to find enough clients. It is also important that you decide on a type of business that really interests you and motivates you to do well. If holistic therapy is your real interest then it is unlikely that you will be happy doing a lot of leg waxing and eyelash tinting. Make sure that the treatments and services you offer are ones that your clients want but also that you enjoy.

ACTIVITY

Strengths, weaknesses, opportunities, threats (SWOT)
Do a SWOT analysis to help you plan for business success.
Strengths What are the strengths of your business idea? i.e. what are the unique selling points, how is it better than other local businesses? Are your people better?
Weaknesses What are the weaknesses? Are there areas that can be improved on, such as a better treatment selection or different products?
Opportunities What opportunities for improvement are there? Can you offer a new treatment that others don't have? Has a local competitor begun to lose business, which you could pick up?
Threats Is there a new competitor? Has a larger chain moved into the area or a new spa/gym opened up?

How will you run your business?

There are several ways you can run your business:

- **The owner/operator**. This is most usual, particularly in new a business. The owner also does all the treatments and often works on her own to build up the business to begin with.

- As a **manager/administrator** who either does not do any treatments or only a few of the more technical or expensive ones. This gives time to run the business side and is often the best way if a number of therapists are employed.

- By **employing a manager** to run the business from day to day so you are only involved in the ownership duties such as the finances. This is normally suitable when you have a well-established business and possibly several salons.

Deciding where to base your business

Location is important for the success of the salon or clinic. A High Street shop front location will give high visibility and walk in trade but will also be more expensive in business rates or rent (it is unlikely that you will be able to buy a high street building). It is sometimes possible to have a first floor High Street location, which is more affordable but still has the same advantages.

You could be situated within an associated business such as a gym/spa, hairdressing salon, chiropractor or physiotherapist. This way both businesses can gain clients from each other and share overheads.

You could be based in your own house and have a converted room for your business. It is also possible to have a mobile therapist business, which does not have a base at all. The location you decide upon will be as a result of what sort of business you want to run and how much you have in your start-up budget.

Parking for your clients should always be considered. Most will want the convenience of being able to park close by to come in and out for their treatments.

How to make sure there is a market for your business

A market for your business is the potential clientele that may be in the area that you want to set your business up in. There are a number of ways of trying to find out if that market actually exists.

It is necessary to make the decision as to where you are going to position your business in the market. Are you going to aim for the less expensive treatments or the more expensive ones? If there are a number of businesses locally that are all much the same, is that because that is the only sort of market or is it because no one has thought of being different?

Market research

You can do your own research with questionnaires and interviews: this is called primary research. You get the information first hand and it is specifically for what you want.

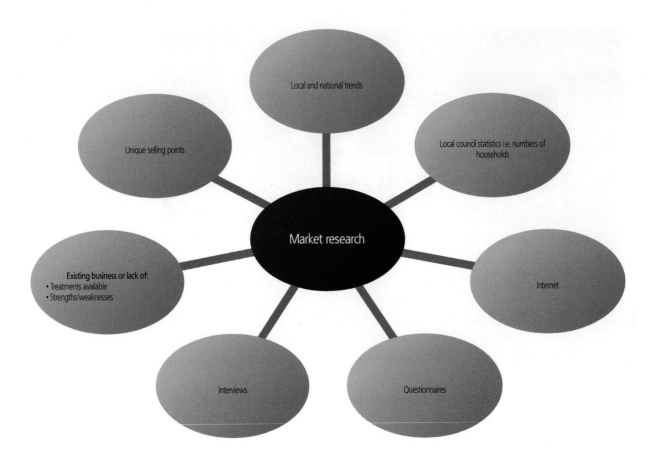

You can use existing information such as local government statistics on households, incomes, types of business and so on: this is secondary research.

You must look at the other businesses in the area that are competitors and carefully analyse what they are offering and how they are doing it. This could be from price lists or from going and having treatments done yourself. This will show you what their strengths and weaknesses are. This will help you to decide what sort of business will be needed and what variety of treatments will sell well.

Market and business trends also need to be taken into account. Beauty therapy and associated treatments are fashion-led, so things can come and go in popularity. It is not always a good idea to offer only the latest trend as it may be that it will soon be out of fashion.

It is always possible that other trends beyond your control might affect your business proposal. This is particularly so when the national economy rises and falls. It is necessary as a business person to be up-to-date with business trends; you should read good quality newspapers and watch current affairs television programmes.

Market review

This should include the following:

- Which market position is going to be best for your proposed business.
- A clear understanding of what your potential clients' likely needs are.
- What trends in fashion and the economy may affect your business.
- What possible factors beyond your control may affect your business.

ACTIVITY

Research past trends in treatments to see what is currently in fashion and what has now gone out of fashion. See if you can predict what will be the next really desirable treatment to be offered in salons. What factors help to make a treatment fashionable and desirable?

Deciding if your business idea will be a success

Once you have your business idea and your market research you can then make a decision as to whether it has the potential for success. There are business consultants who can also give you an objective and impartial view on whether or not your idea has potential. There are small business advisors in local banks who can help you and this service is usually provided free.

Your business *must* be profitable in order to succeed. Working out the likely profits from your business idea will also help you to make the decision.

Cash-flow forecast

You will need to do one of these to estimate the cash and profitability of the business. This is normally done for a period of 6 to 12 months. This can then be used when looking for finance, to plan your future business and as a way of checking that your business is going to plan.

Cash is normally the term used for money paid in and also paid out of the business. This includes:

- Receipts: money expected in from clients.
- Payments: money spent on various things to keep the business going, i.e. products, running costs, wages.

Always be careful in estimating how much money you could have coming in to the business. Predicting too much coming in too quickly will be unrealistic. If you are buying an existing business it is important to know the cash flow history of that concern.

ACTIVITY

Using the table work out the cash flow and decide whether or not this new business, owned and operated by one person will be a success.

The Beauty salon
Cash Flow Forecast/Cash Budget

	Jan	Feb	March	April	May	June
Income						
Sales	NIL	200	300	400	400	400
Treatments	300	500	2,000	2,500	3,000	3,000
Total Income	300	700	2,300	2,900	3,400	3,400
Expenditure						
Rent	300	300	300	300	300	300
Salary	800	800	800	1,000	1,000	1,000
Expenses	100	200	200	200	200	200
Purchases	NIL	100	200	200	300	300
Total Expenditure	1,200	1,400	1,400	1,700	1,800	1,800
Opening Balance						
Net Cash Flow						
Closing Balance						

ACTIVITY

Write down how much money you have coming in each month. Then work out what you have to pay out each month to maintain your lifestyle. This will give you a basic idea of your personal budget needs.

You must also have a budget for your own personal survival and living expenses. Work out what money you need in order to have somewhere to live, food, transport and so on. Everyone's needs will be different so it is necessary to put together your own personal cash flow plan to make sure you are meeting your needs and can pay yourself enough.

Profit and Loss Account

This is a trading statement which can be done for a period of time such as 1 month, 6 months or 1 year. It compares the cost of all the goods that have been bought with the total selling price of the goods and services. In this way it shows the gross profit (or loss) in a stated period of time. It can be used to see how the business is doing over the stated period in time, plan investment and compare profit levels with other periods in time and other similar businesses.

Beauty Works Beauty Salon
Profit and Loss account January – June
Figures taken from the Cash flow forecast/Cash budget

Sales	£	14,200
Cost of sales		
Opening stock	0	
Purchases	1,100	
Closing stock	450	
Total	650	
Gross profit		13,550
Indirect costs		
Expenses	1,100	
Rent	1,800	
Salary	5,400	
Total	8,300	
Net profit		5,250
(before tax)		

Funding your business

It is likely that you will need to borrow money from an outside source in order to get you business going. Money provided by you is considered to be capital and is an asset; money borrowed from other sources is called liabilities.

Borrowing money

A business can borrow money from:

- Banks
- Finance houses
- Building societies

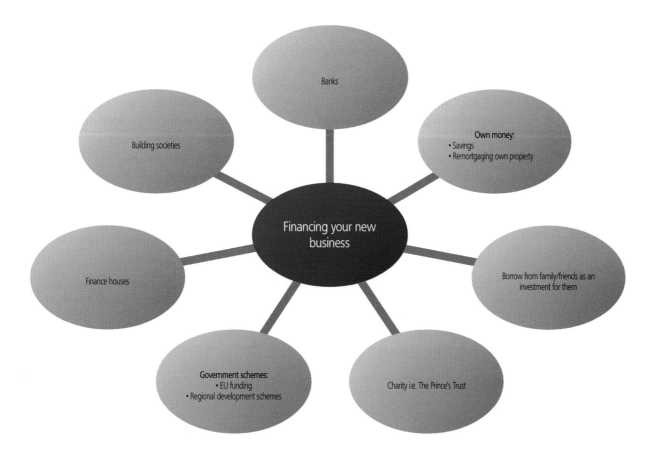

- Creditors
- Government-sponsored schemes
- The Prince's Trust.

Deciding on the business aims

Successful planning and start-up of the business should include a set of business aims. Ask yourself what you want the business to achieve. This could be simple or ambitious. There are several examples:

- To support yourself, meet your living costs and enable you to be your own boss.
- To make a good profit so that you can afford to have a comfortable lifestyle.
- To be the best beauty therapy salon in the city and to have a high profile with a celebrity clientele.
- To be a fully committed holistic clinic where clients are treated for general day-to-day problems.
- To offer a specialist electrolysis and laser clinic working alongside the medical profession.

Remember that whatever you decide upon as the aim of your business, it must always be profitable in order to survive.

Assessment of knowledge and understanding

You have now learnt about how to check how successful your business idea will be. To test your knowledge and understanding, answer the following short questions. These will prepare you for your summative (final) assessment.

Business attractiveness

1 What is a unique selling point? Why would this make a business competitive?

2 Give examples of how you could balance your own needs with that of your business.

3 In what ways can you make sure that your proposed business will be profitable and that your existing business is continuing to be profitable?

Financial aspects

1 Why is it important for you to have a personal survival budget?

2 How would you work out your personal survival budget?

3 Show how you can work out your planned profits.

4 What are cash-flow forecasts and how can you produce them?

5 What is a profit and loss account?

6 What information do you need to produce a profit and loss account?

7 What are marketing and sales forecasts and how would you use them?

Skills and abilities

1 How can you judge your own skills and abilities?

2 What skills and abilities do you think you need to successfully run your own business?

3 How do you then decide what skills and abilities your business needs?

Market research

1 What sources would you use to get hold of published market research?

2 How would you go about deciding what sort of research you need and how you can do it?

3 How do you think your clients' actions and choices might affect your business?

4 How can you decide if your local competitors could affect your business?

Market and business trends

1 What political changes could affect your business?

2 What sort of commercial changes could affect your business and how?

3 State how your business opportunities could be improved or limited by local, national and international events.

Business aims

1 How can you choose and explain the following:
   a. your business size
   b. your business profit
   c. your business market share
   d. your business position
   e. your own achievements.

2 Explain why it is important for you to research and decide on your business needs
   a. when you set up
   b. during the first year of trading
   c. during the first five years of trading.

More research and planning

1 What sort of information can you find out from published sources?

2 What sort of information can you find out from your own research?

3 What would make you decide to do more research into particular areas and give examples of how you would do this.

Your survival budget

1 How can you work out your personal budgetary needs?

2 Show how you can match this to your estimated cash flow and profit and loss.

chapter 20

G13 Check what law and other regulations will affect your business

Learning objectives

This unit describes how to check what law and other regulations will affect your business. It explains how to:

- **make sure your business will be set up legally**
- **make sure your business trades legally**
- **meet current regulations for health and safety**

This unit has been developed by the Small Firms Enterprise Development Initiative (SFEDI) as part of the standards to start your own business.

INTRODUCTION

There are a number of laws and regulations that affect the business owner whether they are alone or in partnership. When setting up a new business, buying an existing business or buying a franchise it is essential to be aware of these. This will ensure that your business is started as you mean to go on, with best practice in mind and not causing yourself unnecessary problems. Businesses that are properly set up within the law quickly build and maintain an honest and trustworthy reputation, which improves their chances of long-term success. No one starts a business with the intention of failing.

The laws and regulations that are important to you cover building regulations and planning permission, licence to trade, company law, health and safety, fire safety, employment law, taxes, the selling of goods, the supply of goods and services and insurance requirements. There are general laws that affect all businesses in the same way, such as health and safety and taxes, and there are local regulations like planning permission and licences, which may be different in various regions, cities and towns.

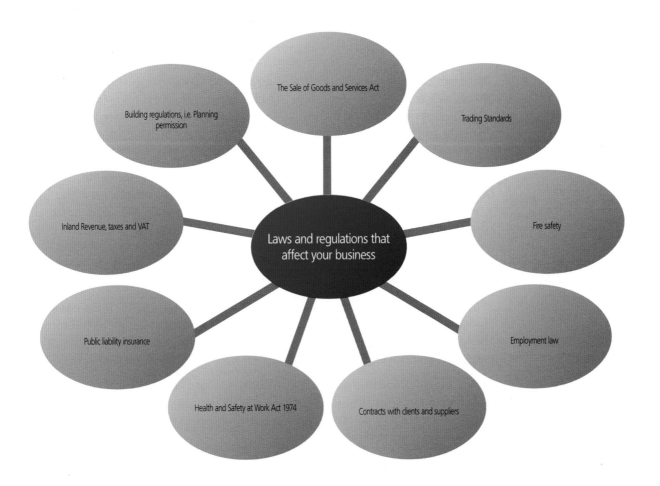

STARTING UP

To start a business you will need somewhere to work. Planning regulations, a licence to trade and planning permission if you are changing a building need to be sorted out. Do your research and ensure you can do what you want to do in the building you have chosen. Working from home is not an easy option, as you will need planning permission from the local council for the change of use of the building from wholly residential to partially business use. This may not be successful, particularly if you are living in an area that has no other businesses in it, such as a new housing estate. Your neighbours will have the opportunity to challenge the request for change of use and could stop you getting planning permission on the grounds that there will be increased traffic, noise and inconvenience to themselves. If you do not do your research properly and get the right permission, you may find that you are quickly made to close down.

If you are moving into existing premises it is still worth checking what you can do with them. Old buildings may be listed, which means that there are restrictions on what can be done to change them internally as well as externally. Always check with your local council planning officials and take independent advice before you start to spend money on your project.

Naming your business

There are rules and regulations that govern the name of a business. It is always worth spending some time on choosing the right name – it will say a lot about you and your business. The name will help or hinder your business and will attract different types of customers.

If you are trading as a Sole Trader or Partnership you can use your own name or a different business name. However, the name must not be offensive or use inappropriate words or expressions. You cannot use the words limited or plc. Always check first if someone else is using the name you want to use. It may cause you a real problem if a national company is already using it, as they tend to guard their names and you may be sued. You can easily do a search on the Companies House website to check this and save yourself problems in the future.

Setting up a Limited Company means you will need to register your name and other details with Companies House. Your name must end with limited, Ltd, plc (or Welsh equivalent) and must not, like the Sole Trader names, be inappropriate or offensive.

There are rules about displaying your business name as well including where you run your business and on all stationery such as orders, invoices, business letters and so on. Don't get anything printed before you are certain you can use your proposed name.

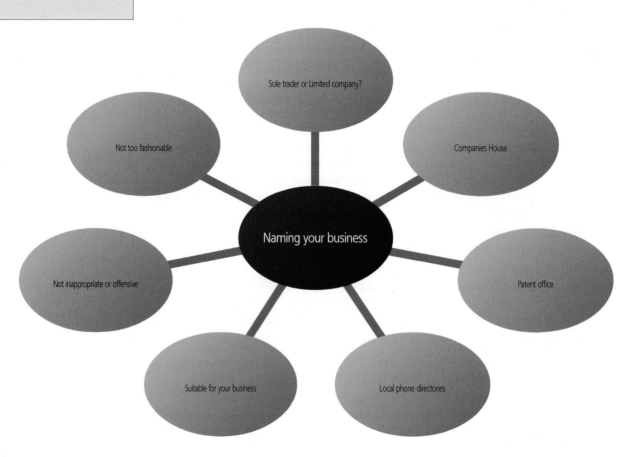

RUNNING YOUR BUSINESS

Once you have got through setting up your business to suit your requirements you must then be able to run it successfully and legally.

Areas that you need to know about are:

- Providing goods and services to your clients – The Sales of Goods and Services Act – Trading Standards.
- Terms and conditions you will offer your clients, i.e. guarantees, payment facilities.
- Terms and conditions that you will have from your suppliers and will offer to them.
- If you need to copyright or patent any new part of your business.
- Employment law if you are employing anyone, even if they are self-employed.
- Tax that will be payable on your income and VAT regulations.
- Preparing and keeping accounts records.
- Insurance that you must have by law and as a sensible precaution.

It is a legal requirement for every business, whether you are a mobile therapist or an owner of a chain of salons, to ensure that the products or services you sell meet minimum standards. All goods that you sell must correspond to any description given, be of satisfactory quality and be fit for their purpose. All services you supply (treatments) must be carried out with reasonable care and skill, within a reasonable time and for a reasonable charge. Customers have a range of rights if they are unhappy with goods or services and may be able to claim compensation or replacements.

Terms and conditions that you offer your clients and your suppliers should be agreed. These could be special offers such as pay for five treatments and have six, or could cover charges for missed appointments or late cancellations. Suppliers will have their terms and conditions written down and will include payment terms and delivery charges.

Payment of bills on time is not only professional and good practice but a legal requirement (Late Payment of Commercial Debts (Interest) Act 1998). It is possible to charge interest on debts over 30 days, but most businesses choose not to do this in the interest of good relations.

Always pay your bills on time and do not make the mistake of overtrading – this is when you are spending more than you have coming into the business. It is possible for your business to fail if you then cannot pay future bills and it is illegal to do this. It is best to have good, independent financial advice about cash flow. This is freely available from your High Street bank or you may chose to pay a financial advisor.

Employment law is very detailed and is regularly updated and changed. As an employer you will have a number of responsibilities to your employees, including those who are self-employed or temporary. These include recruitment and selection, data protection, pay, maternity and paternity rights and termination of contract. There is good free advice available from ACAS (Advisory, Conciliation and Arbitration Service). It is also possible to

ACTIVITY	

Find out about your local Trading Standards from the Trading Standards website, and the Sale of Goods Act and how it applies to you at the DTI website.

visit their website for details on contracts of employment and statutory holiday requirements, minimum wage levels and so on. As employment law is very detailed it will be worth using an employment law legal specialist if you have any problems. For general information the Citizens Advice Bureau can also be useful.

A contract of employment should be a written contract or statement which is given to the employee within two months of being employed. It should contain the following:

- Name of employer
- Name of employee
- Date employment began
- Remuneration (pay)
- How and when you will be paid
- Hours of work
- Holidays and public holidays
- Holiday pay
- Length of notice employer must give
- Length of notice employee must give
- Job title
- Disciplinary rules (can be in a separate handbook)
- Grievance procedure (can be in a separate handbook)
- Place of work
- The contract of employment is binding so it is unlawful for either party to change the terms and conditions without the agreement of the other
- Job description.

FINANCIAL REGULATIONS

ACTIVITY

Depending upon the type of business you are running you will be liable for different types of taxation. Using the Inland Revenue website, research which types of taxation will be relevant to your proposed business.

It is essential to get advice on financial regulations, including income tax, from a professional advisor. It is very difficult to do this yourself. There is free advice available from High Street banks and other similar sources and it is normal to have an accountant who will keep the business financial records and deal with income and business taxes. If you are employing people then you need to set yourself up as an employer with the Inland Revenue.

TIP

When do you need to register for VAT?
There is a threshold of sales over which you need to register. If your sales of taxable supplies is more than £58,000 in the last 12 months then you need to register. Taxable supplies are any goods and services that are subject to VAT at any rate including zero rated.

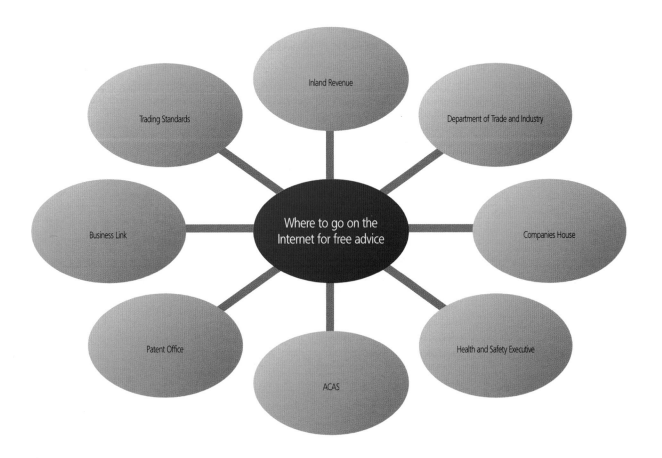

HEALTH AND SAFETY

The Health and Safety at Work Act 1974

Under this Act you have a duty of care towards your employees, your clients, yourself, and anyone else who may come into your business premises such as a contractor, maintenance person, or electrician. Employees also have a duty of care to work in such a way as to look after themselves and their colleagues and clients. Health and safety is therefore the responsibility of everyone not just one individual. You have to have a health and safety policy and if you employ five or more people it has to be written down. Your local Environmental Health Officer will want to inspect your premises from time to time and you must be able to show, with the correct documentation, that you are following the guidelines. Your local EHO can be contacted at the council offices and will also be able to advise you if you want to make sure you are doing things the right way. Failure to follow health and safety regulations can result in fines, closure of your business and even imprisonment for very serious offences that result in death.

Health, safety and security in the salon

When working in a service industry you are legally obliged to provide a safe and hygienic working environment. Careful attention must be paid to **health**, **safety** and **security**.

A health and safety checklist

HEALTH AND SAFETY CHECK LIST

Salon name: Date: Prepared by:

Tick the appropriate box for when each check should be done. Use a separate booklet to record and sign the check.	Daily	Monthly	3/6/12 Monthly	Monthly
1 **Registration of premises** – notifying authority				
2 **Written Health & Safety Policy Statement** Revision				
Attention of all employees				
3 **Health & Safety Law** – poster – displayed and conspicuous Addresses – displayed and conspicuous				
4 **First Aid Kit** – Contents – No personal medications Accident book				
5 **'Appointed Persons'**, who? Allow for shiftwork, holidays, illness, leaving, etc.				
6 **Fire fighting appliances**. Checking, sitting, suitability				
7 **Emergency procedures**, doors, routes (internal/external)				
8 **Thermometer**, displayed and condition. Heating systems, including portable				
9 **Welfare arrangements** Sanitary, maintenance, cleanliness, lighting				
Washing, maintenance, cleanliness, soap/towels. H/c, etc.				
Eating/drinking facilities				
Rest periods, facilities				
10 **Ventilation** Workroom(s), window openings, and/or mechanical extraction. Sanitary facility				
11 **Lighting**, artificial and natural, all areas (including stairs, passages, steps)				
12 **Handrails to stairs**, condition, adequacy				
13 **Handrails to steps**, condition, adequacy				
14 **Furniture**, chairs, tables – condition, suitability, support, back, legs, feet				
Cabinets (including filing cabinets, etc.) secure				
16 **Electrical**. V = Visual Check. AC = Approved Contractor *Apparatus Hair* El. Lead Plug Fuse Rating				
i.e. Large dryers				
i.e. Portable dryers				
i.e. Tongs				
Apparatus Beauty				
i.e. Facial electrical machines				
i.e. Body electrical machines				

BEAUTY WORKS

		Daily	Monthly	3/6/12 Monthly	Monthly
	Apparatus General				
	Water heaters				
	Vacuum cleaners				
	Lighting				
	Displays (inc. 'counters')				
	The Till				
	Fixed system wiring				
	Sockets				
	Fuse board Markings/Identification and accessibility Records kept – updated				
17	COSHH Assessment. Emergency procedures New substances to salon – assessment Training – new staff, casual staff (inc. holiday relief) Work placement/training				
18	**Consideration 'Out of Hours' staff,** e.g. cleaner(s) Training, first aid, reporting, COSHH, telephone contact, emergency line				
19	**Provision of protective clothing** and protective means				
20	**Public protection** Access and egress. Clothing. Personal possessions				
21	**Skin piercing work** – registration – byelaws, no smoking, records				
22	**Public Liability Certificate** (Health & Safety enforcement)				
23	**Refreshments**				
	Compliance with food hygiene regulations				
	Registration				
	Separate Bowls. 'Wash hands' sign				
	Storage of food. Handling				
24	**Telephone contacts** Emergency/reporting Listed, updated				
25	**Floor and surfaces**				
	Cleanliness				
	Trip hazards				
	Slip hazards, inc. 'wet' flooring				
	Changes of levels – conspicuous markings				
	Mat wells				
	Passageways, unobstructed, lighting				
	Head of stairways				
	Wear & tear – floor coverings				
26	**Employees** Clothing. Personal possessions. Access/egress				
27	**Schoolchildren** All under 16's i.e. juniors need to be registered with local Country Council				

BEAUTY WORKS

Staff for whom you have responsibility must be informed and kept aware of current health and safety legislation which they are required to adhere to. Staff training will ensure that employees understand the health, safety and hygiene requirements for the services provided, and standards of behaviour expected of them.

Employees must co-operate with their employer to provide a safe and healthy workplace. Any potential hazard must be reported to the designated authority so that the problem can be put right.

Salon health and safety policies and procedures

Writing a **health and safety policy** is the responsibility of any employer who has five or more employees working on the premises and is required by law. This is a written evaluation of potential health and safety risks that may occur in the workplace, and the measures taken to prevent their occurrence. The policy must be issued to each employee and outlines their safety responsibilities. It should include items such as:

- details of the storage of chemical substances
- details of the stock cupboard or dispensary
- details and records of the checks made by a qualified electrician on specialist/mechanical equipment
- names and addresses of the key-holders
- escape routes and emergency evacuation procedures.

Failure to provide a written health and safety policy contravenes the **Health and Safety at Work Act 1974**. Employers have a responsibility to implement the Act to ensure the workplace is safe for both employees and clients. Insurance companies may refuse to insure if the salon does not have a health and safety policy.

Regular and random checks should be made to ensure that safety is being satisfactorily maintained. If harm is caused to employees or clients through negligence caused by poor health and safety practice, you will be liable to prosecution, with the possibility of being fined.

There is a good deal of legislation relating to health and safety. The legislation is constantly reviewed and you must be aware of any changes. Such information can be obtained from the Health and Safety Executive (HSE).

Current health and safety legislation

The following legislation is that which applies to the management of health and safety within the beauty therapy salon.

Health and Safety at Work Act 1974

It is the employer's or supervisor's responsibility to implement the Act and to ensure that the workplace is safe. This Act lays down the minimum standards of health, safety and welfare required in each area of the workplace. It covers a variety of legislation and regulations which you have a responsibility to implement. Current regulations (at the time of writing) are listed and outlined below.

The Management of Health and Safety at Work Regulations 1992

These require salon owners to make formal arrangements for maintaining and improving safe working conditions and practices. This includes training for employees and the monitoring of risk in the workplace, known as risk assessment.

The Workplace (Health, Safety and Welfare) Regulations 1992

These provide the employer with an approved code of practice for maintaining a safe, secure working environment. The Regulations cover the legal requirements in relation to the following aspects of the working environment:

- maintenance of the workplace and equipment
- ventilation
- cleanliness and handling of waste materials
- safe salon layout
- falls and falling objects
- windows, doors, gates and walls
- safe floors and traffic routes
- escalators and moving walkways
- sanitary conveniences
- washing facilities
- drinking water
- facilities for changing clothing
- facilities for staff to rest and eat meals.

> **TIP** ✔
>
> The salon temperature should be 16°C within one hour of employees arriving for work.
> The salon should be well ventilated or carbon dioxide levels will increase which can cause nausea. Many substances in the salon can become hazardous without adequate ventilation.

The Manual Handling Operations Regulations 1992

The employer is required to carry out a risk assessment of all activities undertaken which involve manual lifting. The risk assessment should provide evidence that the following have been considered:

- risk of injury
- the manual movement involved in performing the activity
- the physical constraint the load incurs
- the environmental constraints imposed by the workplace
- workers' individual capabilities
- action in order to minimise potential risks.

The Personal Protective Equipment (PPE) at Work Regulations 1992

These require managers to identify through a risk assessment those activities or processes which require special protective clothing or equipment to be worn. The clothing and equipment must then be made available, in adequate supplies.

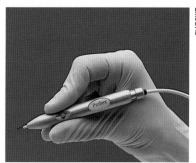

A therapist wearing gloves

Employees must wear protective clothing and use the protective equipment provided, and make employers aware of any shortage so that supplies can be ordered.

Provision and Use of Work Equipment Regulations (PUWER) 1998

These Regulations lay down important health and safety controls on the provision and use of equipment. They state the duties for employers and for users, including the self-employed. They affect both old and new equipment. They identify the requirements in selecting suitable equipment and in maintaining it. They also discuss the information provided by the equipment manufacturers, and include instruction and training in the safe use of equipment. Specific regulations address the dangers and potential risks of injury that could occur during the operation of equipment.

The Control of Substances Hazardous to Health Regulations (COSHH) 1992

These Regulations were designed to make employers consider the substances used in their workplace and assess possible risks to health. Many substances that seem quite harmless can prove to be hazardous if used or stored incorrectly.

Hazardous substances are usually identified through the use of known symbols, examples of which are illustrated. Any substance in the workplace that is hazardous to health must be identified on the packaging and stored and handled correctly.

Each beauty supplier is legally required to make available guidelines on how materials should be used and stored; these will be supplied on request.

HIGHLY FLAMMABLE

TOXIC

HARMFUL

CORROSIVE

EXPLOSIVE

OXIDIZING

The Electricity at Work Regulations 1989

These Regulations state that every piece of electrical equipment in the workplace should be tested every 12 months by a qualified electrician. It is the responsibility of the employer or supervisor to keep records of the equipment tested and the date.

Employees should report to the supervisor if any potential electrical hazards are seen. These include:

- exposed wires in flexes
- cracked plugs or broken sockets
- worn cables
- overloaded sockets.

Reporting of Injuries, Diseases and Dangerous Occurrences Regulations (RIDDOR) 1985

RIDDOR requires the employer to notify the local enforcement officer, in writing, in cases where employees or trainees suffer personal injury at work. When this occurrence results in death, major injury or more than 24 hours in hospital, it must be reported by telephone first, and followed by a written report within 7 days. In all cases where personal injury occurs, an entry must be made in the salon's accident book.

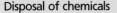

HEALTH AND SAFETY ✚

Disposal of chemicals
Certain chemicals, especially if flammable, must not be disposed of in sanitary systems as this will lead to pollution. For disposal of chemicals observe the manufacturer's instructions and consult the local environmental health department.

Accidents

Accidents in the workplace occur usually through negligence by employees or unsafe working conditions. Any accidents must be recorded on a report form, and entered into an accident book. The report form requires more details than the accident book – you must note down the following:

- date
- name of the person involved
- accident details
- injuries sustained
- action taken.

Accidents can damage stock, resulting in the breakage of containers. Such damage should be dealt with immediately to prevent further accidents such as slippages. Always consider your COSHH data and check to see how the product should be handled and disposed of.

ACCIDENT REPORT FORM

Date of accident: _____

Time of accident: _____

Location of accident: _____

Address: _____ Post code: _____

Telephone number: _____

Name of injured person: _____

Address: _____ Post code: _____

Telephone number: _____

Injuries

Part(s) of the body affected: _____

Nature of injuries: _____

How did the accident happen?
Provide as much information and detail as possible. _____

_____

First aid given, record details: _____

Name of first aider: _____

Witnesses

Name/s: _____

Address: _____ Post code: _____

Telephone number: _____

Details recorded in accident record book? _____

Signature of injured person _____

Signature of first aider _____

Signature of witnesses _____

Signature of supervisor _____

An accident report form

HEALTH AND SAFETY

First Aid

- It is useful to have a qualified first-aider amongst the staff who can deal with minor accidents.
- The **Health and Safety (First Aid) Regulations 1981** lay down the minimum requirements for the provision of first aid in the workplace. This varies dependant upon the number of employees.
- A basic first aid kit should be available, the contents of which must be monitored and replaced as necessary.
- The appointment of a person responsible for maintaining the first aid equipment and seeking assistance if required is useful if there is not a designated first-aider.

Emergency evacuation procedures

In the case of an emergency all staff should be trained in the appropriate action to take. Emergency situations include fire, gas leaks, flooding and bomb alerts.

Fire

The **Fire Precautions Act 1971** states that all staff must be aware of and trained in fire and emergency evacuation procedures for their workplace. The emergency route will be the easiest route by which staff and clients can leave the building safely. It should be clear of obstructions and clearly signed.

A smoke alarm should be fitted to forewarn you of a fire, and fire doors should be fitted within the premises to help control the spread of flames.

Firefighting equipment must be available, located in a specified area. This should only be used when the fire is small and the cause of the fire has been identified. Using the wrong extinguisher could make the fire worse.

Cause of fire and choice of fire extinguisher

Cause	Extinguisher and colour code	
Electrical fire	Carbon dioxide (CO2) extinguisher	Black
Solid material fire (paper, wood, etc.)	Water extinguisher	Red
Flammable liquids	Foam extinguisher	Cream
Vaporising liquids	BCF extinguisher	Green
	Dry-powder extinguisher	Blue

Note: Green and blue extinguishers can be used with all types of fire

Never put yourself at risk – fires can spread quickly. Leave the building at once if in danger, and raise the alarm by instructing other staff and clients to evacuate and telephoning the emergency services on the emergency telephone number **999**.

Gas leaks

If there is a smell of gas there may be a gas leak. Staff must be trained in how to turn off the gas stopcock.

To ensure the maintenance of safe gas use, an inspection is required by law, annually, by a qualified gas engineer. A gas maintenance record must be kept and be available for inspection.

Flooding

In the event of a flood emergency, staff must be trained in how to turn off the water stopcock which will cut off the water supply.

TIP ✓

Fire Procedures
It is essential that staff know the following:
- fire prevention
- raising the alarm
- evacuation during a fire
- assembly points following evacuation.

Chubb Fire Ltd

Fire extinguishers

HEALTH AND SAFETY ✚

Gas leaks
Never press any electrical switches in the event of a gas leak, as a spark in the circuit could ignite the gas causing an explosion.

Bomb alerts

The risk of a bomb will vary according to many factors, including where the premises are situated. In the event of a bomb alert staff must be trained in the appropriate emergency procedures. This will involve recognition of a suspect package, how to deal with a bomb threat, evacuation of staff and clients and contacting the emergency services. Your local Crime Prevention Officer will advise on bomb security.

Environmental impact

Everyone has an impact on the environment. It is important to save energy, recycle, and to keep the use of packaging and non-essential materials to a minimum. Check with the local council to see if there are any local regulations you need to be aware of. General good housekeeping practices such as switching off lights and having appliances such as wax pots on time switches are good for the environment and your bills and expenses.

Fire

The Fire Precautions Act 1971 amended recently by the Fire Precautions (Workplace) (Amendment) Regulations 1999.

You have to have an inspection and fire certificate for your work premises. The areas covered are:

- firefighting equipment and their maintenance
- fire detectors and alarms
- fire fighting measures
- emergency routes and evacuations including exits
- drills.

<table>
<tr><td>

ACTIVITY

Research what sort of fire extinguishers should be available in a beauty therapy salon.

</td></tr>
</table>

Checklist of legislation affecting employers and employees

1970 Equal Pay Act

1974 Health and Safety at Work Act

1975 Sex Discrimination Act

1976 Race Relations Act

1995 Disability Discrimination Act

1998 National Minimum Wage Act

1998 Working Time Regulations

1998 Data Protection Act

1998 Employment Rights Act

1998 Human Rights Act

1999 Employment Relations Act

2000 Part-time Workers Regulations

NB This is regularly changed and expanded, so make sure you do your up-to-date research.

Assessment of knowledge and understanding

You have now learnt about how to check what law and other regulations will affect your business. To test your knowledge and understanding, answer the following short questions. These will prepare you for your summative (final) assessment.

Ways for businesses to be set up

1 Describe the main business types which would be suitable for the beauty therapist.

2 Explain how the different business types are run and how this affects the legal liabilities.

Legal requirements

1 With your own business in mind, describe which part or national and local law would apply to the lawful running of the business.

2 Describe which parts of national and local regulations apply to all businesses.

How to decide the right way to set your business up

1 What will be the effect on your own tax position?

2 What sort of liabilities will you and your business have?

3 What sort of financial risks do you think are involved?

4 With your own proposed business in mind, what type of trading would best meet the needs?

5 List and explain the other areas that you need to take into consideration i.e. insurances, planning permission, and so on.

Finding and using advice and information

1 What information is available on law and regulations and from which organisations?

2 State why you think it is important to use proper technical and professional advice to find out about law and regulations.

3 What role do you think the professional advisor could have within your business?

4 How would you go about getting the best from both free and paid-for sources of advice?

Regulations and laws affecting the business

1 List all the requirements you will have to meet for your business to trade legally.

2 Describe how the law can protect you and your business.

3 What thresholds are there for some laws and regulations, i.e. VAT, health and safety?

4 Who has the power to inspect your business activities and to enforce the law and regulations?

Agreements and contracts

1 Is it important to agree terms and conditions with your clients, suppliers and backers, and if so why?

2 Why is it recommended to take professional advice about contracts and agreements?

Laws and regulations

1 What Health and Safety regulations apply to your business?

2 What environmental laws apply to your business and how can you make sure you are operating in an environmentally-friendly way?

glossary

Acid mantle the combination of sweat and sebum on the skin's surface, which creates an acid film. The acid mantle is protective and discourages the growth of bacteria and fungi

Acrylic sculptured nails the use of powder and liquid to make a strong acrylic from which to form artificial nail structures

Aftercare advice recommended advice given to the client following treatment to continue the benefits of the treatment

Airbrush used in the application of nail art airbrushing technique and self tan application. The brush is attached to a compressor by a hose and is held in the hand. In the airbrush, air is mixed with paint before being forced out under pressure to create a coloured spray

Allergen a substance that the skin is sensitive to and which causes an allergic reaction

Alternating current (AC) an interrupted electrical current which reverses the direction of flow of electrons

Anagen the active growth stage of the hair growth cycle

Anion a negative ion, an atom that has gained more electrons than protons

Anode a positive electrode or pole of a constant electrical current

Aromatherapy massage the use of essential oils combined with massage to bring about a feeling of well-being

Assessment (client) techniques used to assess the needs of the client to ascertain the treatment objectives, including questioning and natural observation

Audio sonic a hand-held electrical massage treatment applied to the face or body. The equipment produces sound waves, which vibrate through the skin's cells and tissues. The treatment is used for its physiological benefits on the skin and muscle tissues

Ayur-veda (art of life) a sacred Hindu text written around 1800BC. In Ayurveda life consists of body, mind and spirit – each person is different. By restoring balance and harmony of the body, mind and spirit, the health of the individual improves

Base note a measure of the evaporation rate of essential oils – base notes have the slowest evaporation rate of all essential oils and are absorbed slowly into the skin

Blend epilation the combined use of both high frequency and direct current to destroy the hair; both currents retain their individual effects in the hair follicle

Blood nutritive liquid circulating through the blood vessels; it transports essential nutrients to the cells, removes waste products and transports other important substances such as oxygen and hormones

Body language communication using the body rather than speech

Body mass index (BMI) a formula that uses weight and height to calculate an individual's body fat

Body wrapping a body treatment where the body is wrapped in bandages, plastic sheets or thermal blankets to achieve different therapeutic effects

Camera film it is good practice for the make-up artist to know what sort of camera film is involved in film production or at a photographic shoot when planning their make-up application

Camouflage make-up cosmetic make-up products used for remedial work to disguise blemishes or scars to the face or body

Catagen a brief, transitional stage in the cycle of hair growth – anagen, catagen and telogen – in which the hair moves up the hair follicle

Cathode a negative electrode or pole of constant electrical current

Cation a positive ion; an atom that has lost an electron and has more protons than electrons

Cell the smallest and simplest unit capable of life

Cellulite terminology used to describe fatty tissue that causes the overlying skin to appear dimpled

Chakras non-physical energy centres, located about an inch away from the physical body, which cannot be seen. In ancient Eastern belief the body is said to have seven major chakra centres each with a function, all of which work together in balance with each other

Circulatory system transports material around the body

Cold therapy spa treatments that use temperatures lower than the body temperature to improve circulation, e.g. cold water showers

Compressor a piece of equipment used to compress air, the air pressure is then regulated by the attachment of a regulator. Used in the application of nail art airbrushing and self tan application

Conductor a substance that conducts electricity and heat. Good conductors include metals and solutions which have conducting properties such as acids and alkalis

Consultation assessment of the client's needs using different techniques, including questioning and natural observation

Consumer Protection (Distance Selling) Regulations 2000 these regulations are derived from a European Directive and cover the supply of goods/services made between suppliers acting in a commercial capacity and consumers. They are concerned with purchases made by telephone, fax, Internet, digital television and mail order

Consumer Safety Act 1978 this Act aims to reduce risks to consumers from potentially dangerous products

Continuity is the maintenance of continuous action and consistency in detail in the scenes of films or television programmes

Contra-action an unwanted reaction occurring during or after treatment application

Contra-indication a problematic symptom which indicates that treatment may not proceed

Control of Substances Hazardous to Health (COSHH) 1999 these regulations require employers to identify hazardous substances used in the workplace and state how they should be stored and handled

Cross-infection the transfer of contagious micro-organisms

Cut-out designs a nail art technique where pieces are cut out of an artificial nail tip to create different shapes and effects

Data Protection Act 1998 legislation designed to protect client privacy and confidentiality

Dermal papilla an organ that provides the hair follicle with blood, necessary for hair growth

Dermis the inner portion of the skin, situated underneath the epidermis

Desincrustation ionisation of a solution forming alkalis during galvanic therapy which softens dead skin and the fatty acids of sebum. Used to achieve a cleansing action

Diathermy uses a high frequency alternating oscillating current, oscillating at millions of cycles per second. The current is introduced into the skin via a needle which produces heat as the water molecules in the cells are agitated by the high frequency energy

Digestive system breaks down food into nutrients that can be absorbed by the body

Dihydroxyacetone (DHA) the active ingredient in self tan products. A colourless sugar which reacts with amino acids in the skin creating the pigmented tanned look

Direct current (DC) an electrical current using the effects of polarity. The electrons flow constantly, uninterrupted, in one direction

Disability Discrimination Act (DDA)1995 this Act makes it unlawful to discriminate on the grounds of disability

Disinfectant a chemical agent that destroys most micro-organisms

Ectomorph a body figure type, usually with long limbs and a slender body

Effleurage a massage movement which has a sedating and relaxing effect; applied with the whole palm it can be made superficially or deeply

Electric current the flow of electrons along an electric circuit between the electrical supply and the appliance

Electricity at Work Regulations 1989 these regulations state that every piece of equipment in the workplace should be tested every 12 months by a qualified electrician. It is the responsibility of the employer to keep records of the equipment tested and the date it was checked

Electrolysis the chemical reactions that occur when ions arrive at their respective electrodes. Acids are formed at the anode and alkalis at the cathode

Electrolyte solution of electrically charged particles capable of conducting electricity

Electro-therapy the use of mechanical or electrical equipment to improve the condition and appearance of the face and/or body

Embedding also known as encasing. A nail art technique to create three-dimensional designs by embedding decorative items such as stones

Employers Liability (Compulsory Insurance) Act 1969 this provides financial compensation to an employee should they be injured as a result of an accident in the workplace

Endocrine system co-ordinates and regulates processes in the body by means of chemicals (hormones), released by endocrine glands into the bloodstream

Endomorph a body figure type, usually with short limbs and a plump, rounded body, often pear-shaped

Epidermis the outer layer of the skin

Equal opportunity non-discrimination as to sex, race, disability, age etc.

Equal Opportunity Policy the Equal Opportunity Commission (EOC) states it is best practice for the workplace to have a written Equal Opportunity Policy. This will include a statement of the commitment to equal opportunities by the employer and the structure for implementing the policy

Erythema reddening of the skin

Essential oils the aromatic substances used in aromatherapy. They have an infinite range of aromas, being extracted from flowers, seeds, roots, fruits and bark

Exfoliant a cosmetic treatment preparation of chemical or vegetable origin to accelerate the process of natural skin loss – called desquamation. It is normally applied to the face after facial cleansing and steaming. Exfoliants may also be applied to the skin of the hands and feet, which tend to be coarser in texture

Exfoliation a salon treatment used to remove excess dead skin cells from the surface of the skin, which has a skin cleansing action. This process can be achieved using a specialised cosmetic, or mechanically, using facial equipment applied over the skin surface

Facial a treatment to improve the appearance, condition and functioning of the skin and underlying structures

Faradic current an alternating current which is used to cause nerve and muscle stimulation

Faradic treatment also known as electro-muscle stimulation. This is an electrical treatment applied to both the face and body. An electrical current is used to exercise muscles by stimulation, which creates a tightening and toning effect

Fibres these are found in the dermis and give the skin its strength and elasticity. Yellow elastin gives the skin its elasticity, white collagen gives skin its strength.

Fire Precautions Act 1971 legislation that states that all staff must be familiar with and trained in fire and emergency evacuation procedures for their workplace

Fire Precautions (Workplace) Regulations 1997 this legislation requires that every employer must carry out a risk assessment for the premises in relation to fire evacuation practice and procedures, under the **Management of Health and Safety Regulations 1999**

Flotation a spa treatment where the body is suspended (wet flotation) or supported (dry flotation) to induce relaxation

Foam bath a shallow bath of water containing a foaming agent which surrounds the body, achieving a thermal effect. Increased perspiration caused by this effect aids elimination of waste and toxins

Frictions a massage manipulation which causes the skin and superficial structures to move together over the deeper, underlying structures. The movements help to break down fibrous thickening and fat deposits, and aid the removal of any non-medical oedemas (areas of fluid retention)

Fungus microscopic plants, which are parasites. Fungal diseases of the skin feed on the waste products of the skin. They are found on the skin's surface or they can attack deeper tissues

Galvanic current a constant direct current which creates chemical effects

Galvanic epilation hair removal using direct current. The needle from the electrical epilation machine is inserted into the follicle and direct current flows out over the length of the needle. Sodium hydroxide (lye) is formed in the moisture of the hair follicle. This chemically decomposes the follicle tissue and remains in the follicle to continue to destroy the cells

Galvanic therapy therapeutic substances are introduced into the skin using a direct current to achieve specific effects upon the skin's surface and underlying tissues

Gyratory vibratory treatment an electrical body massage treatment which produces frictions on the skin's surface, creating a heating, stimulating effect

Hair follicle a structure in the skin formed from epidermal tissue. Cells move up the hair follicle from the bottom (the hair bulb), changing in structure, to form the hair

Health and Safety at Work Act 1974 legislation which lays down the minimum standards of health, safety and welfare requirements in each area of the workplace

Health and Safety (Display Screen Equipment) Regulations 1992 these regulations cover the use of visual display units (VDUs) and computer screens. They specify acceptable levels of radiation emissions from the screen and identify correct posture, seating position, permitted working heights and rest periods

Health and Safety (First Aid) Regulations 1981 legislation which states that workplaces must have first aid provision

Health and Safety (Information for Employees) Regulations 1989 these regulations require the employer to make health and safety information via notices, posters and leaflets published by the Health and Safety Executive (HSE) available to all employees

High frequency current an electrical current which moves backwards and forwards at very high speed; referred to as an alternating or oscillating current

High frequency treatment a popular facial or body treatment, which may be applied directly or indirectly to stimulate, sanitise and heal the skin

Hirsutism hair growth pattern considered to be abnormal for the persons sex, i.e. female hair growth following a male hair growth pattern

Histamine a chemical released when the skin comes into contact with a substance to which it is allergic. Cells called mast cells burst, releasing histamine into the tissues. This causes the blood capillaries to dilate, which increases blood flow to limit skin damage and begin repair

Hydrotherapy spa treatments where water is used for its therapeutic effect

Hygiene the recommended standard of cleanliness necessary in the salon to prevent cross-infection and secondary infection

Hyperpigmentation increased pigment production

Hypertrichosis excessive hair growth. It is usually due to abnormal conditions in the body caused by disease or injury

Hypopigmentation loss of pigmentation

Indian head massage a massage treatment traditionally practised in India, applied to the upper body using the hands. The massage helps to relieve stress and tension and create a feeling of well-being. Oils may be applied to the scalp and hair to improve its condition

Insulators poor conductors of electricity often used to prevent the flow of electrons. Poor conductors include rubber, plastic and wood

Iontophoresis the introduction of water-soluble preparations into the skin during galvanic therapy to assist rehydration and cellular metabolism in the area

Job description written details of a persons specific job role, duties and responsibilities

Lanugo hair hair found on the unborn foetus; usually shed at the eighth month of pregnancy

Legislation laws affecting the operation of the business: treatments and how they are promoted and delivered, employees and systems and procedures in the work environment

Lighting effects in a television studio, the lighting is fixed before the make-up artist arrives on set. It may be necessary to discuss any concerns with the director of photography or lighting crew to alter the lighting to improve your performer's appearance

Local Government Miscellaneous Provisions Act 1982 legislation that requires that salons offering any form of skin piercing be registered with the local health authority. This registration includes both the operators who will be carrying out the treatment and the salon premises where the treatment will be carried out

Lymph a clear straw-coloured liquid circulating in the lymph vessels and lymphatic system of the body, filtered out of the blood plasma

Lymphatic system closely connected to the blood system. Its primary function is defensive: to remove bacteria and foreign materials in order to prevent infection

Make-up effects – corrective this refers to the type of make-up application that is almost invisible to the eye. Definition is needed for the camera, as the face can look flat without it. Corrective make-up includes the concealment of blemishes and giving definition to the facial features

Management of Health and Safety at Work Regulations 1999 this legislation provides the employer with an approved code of practice for maintaining a safe, secure working environment

Manual Handling Operations Regulations 1992 legislation which requires the employer to carry out a risk assessment of all activities undertaken which involve manual handling (lifting and moving objects)

Marma (pressure point) incorporated into Indian head massage, this is a technique of pressure point application, based upon the principles and practice of *Marma*. Pressure is applied to the nerve junctures which stimulates vital energy points on the head, face and ears to improve circulation, relieve tiredness and indice relaxation. Marma pressure points also balance the body

Mask a skin cleansing treatment preparation applied to the skin which may contain different ingredients to have a deep cleansing, toning, nourishing or refreshing effect. It may be applied to the hands, feet and face

Massage manipulation of the soft tissues of the body, producing heat and stimulating the muscular, circulatory and nervous systems

Massage manipulations movements which are selected and applied according to the desired effect to be created, which may be stimulating, relaxing or toning. Massage manipulations include effleurage, petrissage, percussion (also known as tapotement) and vibrations

Melanin a pigment in the skin that contributes to skin colour

Melanocytes the cells that produce the skin pigment melanin, which contributes to skin colour

Mesomorph a body figure type, usually a muscular build with well-developed shoulders and slim hips: an inverted triangle shape

Microcurrent based on a modified direct current and as such creates similar effects to galvanic current. It is a direct current interrupted at low frequencies of one to a few hundred times per second

Microcurrent therapy an electrical treatment used on the face and body, which achieves an immediate skin toning and firming effect

Micro-dermabrasion a mechanical exfoliating treatment for use on the body or face. Microcrystals are applied under pressure over the skin's surface: they gently break down the skin's cells to achieve a skin rejuvenating effect

Middle note a measure of the evaporation rate of certain essential oils. Middle notes have a moderate evaporation rate and are absorbed into the skin fairly quickly

Moisturiser a skin-care preparation whose formulation of oil and water helps maintain the skin's natural moisture by locking-in moisture, offering protection and hydration

Motor point a location on the muscles where the motor nerve can be most easily stimulated

Muscle contractile tissue responsible for movement of the body

Muscle tone the normal degree of tension in healthy muscle

Nail art nail decoration applied to the natural nail or artificial nail, using nail art materials including nail polish, transfers, gemstones, glitter and foils

Nail forms made of paper or metal, these are placed at the end of the nail. The natural nail is lengthened onto the nail using a nail extension product

Nail tips plastic nail tips used to artificially lengthen the length of the natural nail

Nail wrap a material such as silk or fibreglass is attached to the nail to repair or strengthen the natural nail

Nerve a collection of single neurones surrounded by a protective sheath through which impulses are transmitted between the brain or spinal cord and another part of the body

Nervous system co-ordinates the activities of the body by responding to stimuli received by the sense organs

Neurones nerve cell which makes up nervous tissue

Oedema the retention of fluid in the tissues, which causes swelling

Olfactory system located high inside the nose and responsible for the sense of smell. When we breathe in aromas, nerve endings in the olfactory system are stimulated and relay messages to the brain, which then cause the body to respond

Palintest-balanced water index the method of regular testing and maintenance of water quality in the spa whirlpool/swimming pool

Papillae projections near the surface of the dermis, which contain nerve endings and blood capillaries. The supply the upper epidermis with nutrition

Patch test method used to assess the skin's tolerance to products or treatments

Personal Protective Equipment (PPE) at Work Regulations 1992 this legislation requires employers to identify, through a risk assessment, those activities which require special protective equipment to be worn or used

Petrissage massage manipulations which apply intermittent pressure to the tissues of the skin, lifting them from the underlying structures. Often known as compression movements

pH the degree of acidity or alkalinity measured on the pH scale

Photosensitisers something that causes the skin to become UV-sensitive such as certain medication

Posture the position of the body which varies from person to person. Good posture is when the body is in alignment

Pre-heat treatments treatments that are beneficial when applied before other body treatments because they make the body's tissues and systems more receptive

Pre-production when a make-up designer works on a production, the first real piece of information they receive is the script. This is reviewed to check hair and make-up requirements

Pressure points the application of pressure on specific points of the head, face or body during massage treatment using the fingertips or thumbs. This helps to release blocked energy channels flowing through the body, improving the body's circulation, function and repair

Prices Act 1974 this states that the price of products has to be displayed in order that the buyer is not misled

Provision and Use of Work Equipment Regulations (PUWER) 1998 this regulation lays down important health and safety controls on the provision and use of equipment

Public Liability Insurance protects employers and employees against the consequences of death or injury to a third party whilst on the premises

Race Relations Act 1976 this Act makes it unlawful to discriminate on the grounds of colour, race, nationality, ethnic or national origin

Record cards confidential cards recording personal details of each client registered at the salon

Relaxation room a room of ambient temperature (close to the body's temperature) often referred to by the Latin name tepidarium

Reporting of Injuries, Diseases and Dangerous Occurrences Regulations (RIDDOR) 1995 RIDDOR requires the employer to notify the local enforcement officer in writing in cases where employees or clients suffer personal injury in the workplace

Resale Prices Act 1964 and 1976 this Act states that the manufacturer can supply a recommended price (MRRP), but the seller is not obliged to sell at the recommended price

Resources the equipment, products and time required to complete a service

Respiratory system brings air into close contact with the blood in the lungs and enables oxygen to enter the bloodstream and be transported to all cells in the body where it can be used to provide energy by cell respiration

Sale and Supply of Goods Act 1994, this Act replaced the **Sale of Goods Act 1982**. Goods must be as described, of merchantable quality, and fit for their intended purpose

Sanitisation the destruction of some, but not all living micro-organisms

Sauna a timber construction where the air inside is heated to produce theraputic effects

Sculptured nails artificial nails formed using a liquid and powder system or a gel. The mixture is sculpted and built over the natural nail plate and extends past the end of the nail onto a nail form

Sebaceous gland a minute sac-like organ usually associated with the hair follicle. The cells of the gland decompose and produce the skins natural oil sebum. Found all over the body except the soles of the feet and the palms of the hands

Sebum the skin's natural oil which keeps the skin supple

Secondary infection bacterial penetration into the skin causing infection

Self tan products cosmetic products containing an ingredient which gives a healthy, tanned appearance to the skin. Different methods can be used to apply self tan products including spray, manual and airbrush application

Set bag used to hold all necessary make-up, hair kit and tools for on set work

Skeletal system supports the softer tissues of the body and maintains the shape of the body

Skin allergy if the skin is sensitive to a particular substance an allergic skin reaction will occur. This is recognised by irritation, swelling and inflammation

Skin analysis assessment of the client's skin type and condition

Skin appendages structures within the skin including sweat glands (that excrete sweat), hair follicles (that produce hair), sebaceous glands (produce the skins natural oil sebum) and nails (a horny substance that protects the ends of the fingers)

Skin sensitivity test this is performed at consultation before the application of electro-therapy treatments to ensure that the client can differentiate skin sensations. A tactile skin sensitivity test and thermal skin sensitivity test are performed

Skin tone the strength and elasticity of the skin

Skin type the different physiological functioning of each person's skin provides their skin type. Skin types include dry (lacking in oil), oily (excessive oil) and combination (a mixture of two skin types, e.g. dry and oily)

Spa pool a pool of warm water with jets of air passing through to create bubbles which massage the skin

Steam treatment water is heated to create steam which is applied to the body for therapeutic purposes

Sterilisation the total destruction of all micro-organisms

Stock keeping maintenance of stock levels to anticipate needs. Stock records note how much stock has been used and when a new order is needed. This may be achieved using manual or computerised systems

Stress a condition which develops when a person becomes pressurised. This may result in undesirable side effects such as insomnia, muscular tension and skin disorders

Stretch marks (striations) scarring of the skin as a result of the skin breaking beneath the surface in the dermal layer

Subcutaneous tissue a layer of fatty tissue situated below the epidermis and dermis

Superfluous hair hair considered to be in excess of that of normal downy hair

Sweat glands small tubes in the skin of the dermis and epidermis which excrete sweat. Their function is to regulate body temperature through the evaporation of sweat from the skin's surface

Systemic medical condition a medical condition caused by a defect in one of the bodies organs e.g. the heart

Tapotement also known as percussion. A massage manipulation which is used for its general toning and stimulating effect

Target a goal or objective to achieve, usually set within a timescale

Telogen the resting stage of the hair growth cycle where the hair is finally shed

Terminal hair deep-rooted, thick, coarse, pigmented hair found on the scalp, underarms, pubic region, eyelash and brow areas

Tips and overlays a nail tip is applied, blended to remove the visible line, and is overlayed by acrylic, gel or fibreglass

Top note a measure of the highest evaporation rate of an essential oil. These commonly have a sharp aroma and a stimulating effect

Trades Description Act 1968 and 1972 legislation that states that information when selling products, both in written and verbal form, should be accurate

Treatment plan after the consultation suitable treatment objectives are established to treat the clients condition and needs

Ultraviolet light (UV) invisible rays of the light spectrum with a wavelength shorter than visible light rays

Urinary system filters waste products from the blood, maintaining its normal composition

UV tanning the skin is exposed to artificially produced UV and the skin darkens creating a tan. Artificial UV is produced by high or low pressure tubes and lamps. The term pressure relates to the wattage (power or energy) of the lamps

Vacuum suction treatment a mechanical treatment which can be applied to the face or body. External suction is applied to the surface tissues causing lift and stimulation of the underlying tissues. Locally blood and lymphatic circulation is improved which aids removal of tissue fluid accumulation. It also improves skin texture and appearance

Vellus hair hair which is fine, downy and soft; found on the face and body

Vibrations massage manipulation used to relieve pain and fatigue, stimulate the nerves and produce a sedative effect. The movements are firm and trembling, performed with one or both hands

Virilisation a condition where the female body becomes more masculine resulting in heavy, facial and body hair growth in a masculine pattern

Virus the smallest living bodies too small to see under an ordinary microscope. They are considered to be parasites, as they require living tissue to survive. Viruses invade healthy body cells and multiply within the cell. Eventually the cell walls break down and the virus particles are freed to attack further cells

Workplace (Health, Safety and Welfare) Regulations 1992 these provide the employer with an approved code of practice for maintaining a safe, secure working environment

index